Musical Im

Musical Imaginations

Multidisciplinary perspectives on creativity, performance, and perception

Edited by

David J. Hargreaves
Applied Music Research Centre
Roehampton University
Southlands College
London, UK

Dorothy E. Miell
College of Humanities and Social Science
University of Edinburgh
Edinburgh, UK

Raymond A.R. MacDonald
School of Life Sciences
Glasgow Caledonian University
Glasgow, UK

OXFORD
UNIVERSITY PRESS

OXFORD

UNIVERSITY PRESS

Great Clarendon Street, Oxford ox2 6DP

Oxford University Press is a department of the University of Oxford.
It furthers the University's objective of excellence in research, scholarship,
and education by publishing worldwide in

Oxford New York

Auckland Cape Town Dar es Salaam Hong Kong Karachi
Kuala Lumpur Madrid Melbourne Mexico City Nairobi
New Delhi Shanghai Taipei Toronto

With offices in

Argentina Austria Brazil Chile Czech Republic France Greece
Guatemala Hungary Italy Japan Poland Portugal Singapore
South Korea Switzerland Thailand Turkey Ukraine Vietnam

Oxford is a registered trade mark of Oxford University Press
in the UK and in certain other countries

Published in the United States
by Oxford University Press Inc., New York

British Library Cataloguing in Publication Data
Data available

Library of Congress Cataloging in Publication Data
Data available

Typeset in Minion by Cenveo, Bangalore, India
Printed and bound by CPI Group (UK) Ltd,
Croydon, CR0 4YY

ISBN 978–0–19–956808–6

10 9 8 7 6 5 4 3 2 1

Whilst every effort has been made to ensure that the contents of this book are as complete,
accurate and up-to-date as possible at the date of writing, Oxford University Press is not
able to give any guarantee or assurance that such is the case. Readers are urged to take
appropriately qualified medical advice in all cases. The information in this book is intended
to be useful to the general reader, but should not be used as a means of self-diagnosis or
for the prescription of medication.

Preface

The original idea for this book was developed at the 9th International Conference on Music Perception and Cognition in Bologna in 2006, when the three of us were considering how we should follow up our previous two edited books for Oxford University Press, *Musical Identities and Musical Communication*. We knew that we wanted to work in the general area of creativity, but also that we wanted to go beyond the usual bounds of the study of composition, improvisation, and performance: in particular, we wanted to consider listening, as this clearly seemed to be a central but under-researched area from the point of view of creative perception: and listening is also, of course, a fundamental part of composition, improvisation, and performance. Whilst trying to come up with a single noun that referred to creative processes, but which also represented this broader view, we were joined during a morning coffee break by Jon Hargreaves: his suggestion was the one that eventually stuck, and we soon began to see the advantages of pursuing imagination rather than creativity as such.

Looking back, the decision to avoid 'creativity' was a wise one. Although many readers will still regard this to be the main domain of this book's contents, we shall see in Chapter 1 that scholars from several different academic traditions and disciplines are beginning to express the view, for different reasons, that 'creativity' has become a hopelessly over-inclusive term: that it is time to lay it to rest, and to focus instead on the specific 'creativities' of particular people, processes, and products in particular musical domains and situations.

For both *Musical Identities and Musical Communication*, we worked out advance plans of the broad subject areas we wanted to cover, and invited experts in those areas to write on specific topics that we had in mind. For this book we abandoned that strategy, and decided instead to invite eminent authors to set their own agendas: to write about the issues which they personally felt to be the most significant or important to them, rather than to attempt any kind of comprehensive coverage, or to work to any predetermined agenda. This approach had the advantage of highlighting the most vital current issues, whatever their main focus of discipline or content. The contents list shows that the book is very wide-ranging in its scope—but it was nevertheless relatively easy for us to divide this range of topics into five broad areas, namely those with perspectives from musicology, sociology, and ethnomusicology; from cognitive, social, and developmental psychology; from sociocultural psychology; from neuroscience; and from the 'applied' areas of education, psychiatry, and therapy. We are also very fortunate that Nicholas Cook agreed to write a concluding chapter based on the contents of the book, 'Beyond creativity?', which takes an extremely wide-ranging and high-level perspective on the full sweep of these contents from a very sophisticated musical point of view, as well as making new connections and conceptual advances.

Looking at the wide range and advanced level of development of these chapters, we suggest that the status of music psychology in the 2010s resembles that of psycholinguistics in the 1960s and 1970s. Language is a complex symbol system which can not only map directly on to the real world, but which can also enable creative expression in the form of poetry and metaphor, for example. Chomsky's revolutionary view of the child as an active acquirer of language led to new developments which would not have been possible within the earlier view that language developed as a result of children being taught and reinforced. Music is an even more complex and abstract symbol system whose elements do not necessarily correspond in any meaningful way with the real world: yet recent advances in music psychology mean that it can now deal with musical issues previously regarded as intractably difficult to subject to empirical enquiry.

Topics such as music and emotion, composition and improvisation, performance and performance traditions, listening strategies, the nature of musical styles and genres, social collaboration, identity formation, and the development of psychologically-based strategies and interventions for the enhancement of performing musicians are now within our grasp because the sophistication of the discipline has reached a new level. The book deals directly with these issues, demonstrating how music psychology is now making a demonstrable contribution to their understanding and enhancement.

We would like to express our gratitude to the reviewers of the original drafts of all the chapters, whose invaluable (and unpaid) work has greatly improved the quality of the book, namely Anna-Rita Addessi, Aleksandar Aksentijevic, Leslie Bunt, Charles Byrne, John Finney, Tuomas Eerola, Alf Gabrielsson, Christian Gold, Allan Hewitt, Alexandra Lamont, Elaine King, Helen Minors, Laura Mitchell, Susan O'Neill, Katie Overy, Stephanie Pitts, Suvi Saarikallio, Keith Sawyer, Mari Tervaniemi, Jason Toynbee, Graham Welch, Tony Whyton, Susan Young, and Betty-Ann Younker.

We should like to thank all those authors and publishers who have given permission for copyright material to be reproduced: the details appear within the chapters concerned. We would like to thank Linda, Jon, and Tom Hargreaves, as ever, for their valuable discussions and different perspectives: Matthew, Thomas, and Anna Miell, Kim Lock, and Vicky Watters for their various forms of invaluable support throughout: and Tracy Ibbotson, Maria MacDonald, and Eva MacDonald for their support, encouragement and constant good humour. We are also indebted to Martin Baum and Charlotte Green of OUP for their constant helpfulness, efficiency, encouragement, and patience.

David Hargreaves, Dorothy Miell, and Raymond MacDonald
March 2011

Postscript, August 2011

Anthony Wigram, the author of Chapter 27, passed away in June 2011: we are very fortunate that he was able to complete the chapter for us, and would like to add our voices to the many tributes that have been paid to his outstanding contributions to music therapy and research.

Contents

Contributors

Aleksandar Aksentijevic
Department of Psychology
Whitelands College
Roehampton University
London, UK

Esa Ala-Ruona
Finnish Centre of Excellence in
Interdisciplinary Music Research
Department of Music
University of Jyväskylä
Finland

Vanya Green Assuied
UCLA Pediatric Pain Program and Chase
Child Life Program
Mattel Children's Hospital UCLA
Los Angeles, CA, USA

Margaret Barrett
School of Music,
The University of Queensland
St Lucia, Brisbane, QLD, Australia

David Castle
University of Melbourne and St Vincent's
Hospital
Melbourne, VIC, Australia

Terry Clark
Royal College of Music
London, UK

Eric Clarke
Faculty of Music
University of Oxford
Oxford, UK

Annabel Cohen
Department of Psychology,
University of Prince Edward Island
Charlottetown, PE, Canada

Nicholas Cook
Faculty of Music
University of Cambridge
Cambridge, UK

Lori Custodero
New York, NY, USA

Tia DeNora
Department of Sociology & Philosophy
University of Exeter, Exeter, UK

Jaakko Erkkilä
Finnish Centre of Excellence in
Interdisciplinary Music Research
Department of Music
University of Jyväskylä
Finland

Jörg Fachner
Finnish Centre of Excellence in
Interdisciplinary Music Research
Department of Music
University of Jyväskylä
Finland

Göran Folkestad
Malmö Academy of Music
Lund University
Malmö, Sweden

Simon Frith
Music, School of Arts, Culture &
Environment
University of Edinburgh
Edinburgh, UK

Howard Gardner
Harvard Graduate School of Education
Cambridge, MA, USA

Denise Grocke
Melbourne Conservatorium of Music
University of Melbourne
Melbourne, VIC, Australia

John Gruzelier
Goldsmiths
University of London
London, UK

David Hargreaves
Applied Music Research Centre
Roehampton University
Southlands College
London, UK

Jonathan James Hargreaves
Trinity Laban Conservatoire of
Music and Dance,
London, UK

Juniper Hill
Faculty of Music
University of Cambridge
Cambridge, UK
Department of Music
University College Cork
Cork, Ireland

Karin Johansson
Malmö Academy of Music
Lund University
Malmö, Sweden

Shira Lee Katz
Harvard Graduate School of Education
Cambridge, MA, USA

Vladimir Konečni
Department of Psychology
University of California, San Diego
La Jolla, CA, USA

Karen Littleton
Centre for Research in Education and
Educational Technology
Faculty of Education and Language Studies
The Open University
Milton Keynes, UK

Raymond MacDonald
Department of Psychology
Glasgow Caledonian University
Glasgow, UK

Neil Mercer
Faculty of Education
University of Cambridge
Cambridge, UK

Dorothy Miell
College of Humanities and Social Science
University of Edinburgh
Edinburgh, UK

Istvan Molnar-Szakacs
Tennenbaum Center for the Biology of Creativity
Semel Institute for Neuroscience and
Human Behavior
University of California
Los Angeles, CA, USA

Adrian North
School of Life Sciences
Heriot-Watt University
Edinburgh, UK

Adam Ockelford
Applied Music Research Centre
Roehampton University
Southlands College
London, UK

Katie Overy
Institute for Music in Human and
Social Development
School of Arts, Culture and Environment
University of Edinburgh
Edinburgh, UK

Marko Punkanen
Finnish Centre of Excellence in
Interdisciplinary Music Research
Department of Music
University of Jyväskylä
Finland

Emery Schubert
School of English, Media and
Performing Arts
University of New South Wales,
Sydney, NSW, Australia

Ian Sutherland
Faculty of Postgraduate Studies
IEDC-Bled School of Management
Bled, Slovenia

Mari Tervaniemi
Cognitive Brain Research Unit
Institute of Behavioural Sciences
University of Helsinki
Helsinki, Finland

Colwyn Trevarthen
School of Philosophy, Psychology &
Language Sciences
University of Edinburgh
Edinburgh, UK

Bradley Vines
Institute of Mental Health
Department of Psychiatry
University of British Columbia
Vancouver, BC, Canada

Graham Welch
Department of Arts and Humanities
Institute of Education
University of London
London, UK

Anthony Wigram
Anglia Ruskin University
Cambridge, UK

Aaron Williamon
Royal College of Music
London, UK

Graeme Wilson
Institute of Health & Society
Newcastle University
Newcastle-upon-Tyne, UK

Chapter 1

Explaining musical imaginations: Creativity, performance, and perception

David J. Hargreaves, Raymond MacDonald,
and Dorothy Miell

1.1 Introduction and definitions

Questions like 'How can music make us laugh and cry?'; 'What made Mozart a genius?'; 'How can music affect our spending in shops?'; 'Why did jazz innovators like Charlie Parker and Miles Davis have such a powerful effect on the way other musicians played?'; 'How does the conductor's leadership style interact with the mood of the musicians in the orchestra'?; or 'How can psychology help professional musicians to overcome stage fright?' are exceedingly complex and difficult to answer. Making music involves not only very high levels of technical skill and physical dexterity, but also the expression of emotions and feelings, which in the past have been notoriously difficult areas for psychological investigation.

The massive recent growth of music psychology has meant that things have changed: answers to questions like those above are now within our grasp because the sophistication of the discipline has reached a new level. The conceptual and methodological advances that have taken place in recent years mean that we can now deal with complex musical issues previously regarded as intractably abstract, complex, and difficult to subject to empirical enquiry. This book deals directly with some of these issues: the topics of musical imagination and creativity, from the points of view of both musical perception and musical production, involve fundamental concepts of core importance to all aspects of music-making, and psychologists are beginning to make a demonstrable contribution to their understanding and practical application.

Another important aspect of this is that the role of music in people's everyday lives has changed in the last decade or so as a result of rapid technological developments which continue to emerge at bewildering speed. The growth of the digital media and global communication has meant that people seek out and are exposed to much more music of different kinds than hitherto, and this seems to have an increasing impact on their behaviour. This is reflected in the growth of applied music psychology, which deals with applications in education, communication, health, medicine, therapy, broadcasting, the media, consumer behaviour, leisure, musicianship, social inclusion, and many other areas of contemporary life (see the review of this field by North & Hargreaves, 2008). At the same time, the study of creativity and imagination in various disciplines such as psychology, sociology, neuroscience, and education, is prominent in the UK as well as in many other countries. The rapid growth of the inter- and multidisciplinary study of music, and developments in music psychology in particular, mean that studies of real-life musical imagination and creativity are now distinctly possible, and this book undertakes a wide-ranging multidisciplinary review of these developments.

This multidisciplinary approach, drawing on the arts, sciences, and social sciences, is the same as that we adopted in our first two edited volumes for Oxford University Press—*Musical Identities*

(MacDonald, Hargreaves, & Miell, 2002), and *Musical Communication* (Miell, MacDonald, and Hargreaves, 2005), and our approach in this book has four main features. First, we started with an open theoretical and conceptual agenda rather than imposing any preconceived structure on the book's organization: we consider the cognitive, social, emotional, and musical aspects of musical imaginations, drawing on philosophical, developmental, neurological, musical, and sociological perspectives to do so. The second feature is our emphasis on imagination and invention rather than creativity, which enables us to move beyond the usual focus on composition, improvisation, and performance in this field. Third, our own foundations in social and developmental psychology and social cognition will once again be apparent: we feel that it is vital to take account of the social and cultural contexts of musical imagination; and fourth, we have a strong interest in the applications of music psychology to real-life settings, and the ways in which it can help those who produce and consume music.

The second point above means that we need to start with a careful consideration of the different definitions and concepts that have been employed. Although 'musical creativity' is probably the most widely-used term across different disciplines, we need to consider its relationship with concepts such as musical invention, improvisation, generation, composition, arranging, performance, and listening. We use the term 'musical imaginations' as the book's main title to indicate that all of these aspects are included, following Aaron Copland's (1952) view that 'it is the freely imaginative mind that is at the core of all vital music making and music listening' (p. 17). We use this term rather than referring specifically to 'creativity' or 'performance' in order to move beyond the traditional debates and ways of thinking which are associated with these terms.

The long-standing debates about the differences between composition and improvisation are now outdated in some respects by the advances and applications of digital technology, which mean that new forms of musical communication and creation render some old distinctions obsolete: musical *invention*, a term already used by one of us (MacDonald, Byrne, & Carlton, 2006), may be a more appropriate and all-embracing term which avoids these connotations. These technological advances have given rise to new forms of musical invention. The increasing importance of the arranger, the sound engineer, and the producer can overlap with and extend the contributions of the composer and the performer. To take the analogy further, we could argue that the audience can form an integral part of the performance, as in the ways in which contemporary club DJs can be seen to use audience reaction to shape their performances (see Brewster & Broughton, 1999). Our focus on musical invention and imagination involves a broader and more contemporary perspective on all of these roles, which depart from existing orthodoxies, and which are partly created by the nature of music-making in the digital age.

Musical invention involves the generation of new material, of course, and although the composer and the performer are traditionally at the heart of these, imagination is also a crucial aspect of listening, which therefore forms an integral part of its study. The arts of critical and imaginative listening are no less inventive than those of the performer and the composer, though they have been neglected to a much greater extent. Very little attention has been paid to the use and deployment of different listening strategies, which might relate to cognitive/analytic, emotional/affective, social/contextual/interpersonal, and other psychological functions. Similarly, the investigation of different *levels of engagement* within music listening has been almost non-existent, even though the psychological processes involved in 'peak experiences' on the one hand, and those in very low involvement experiences on the other—such as where music is played in shops or other commercial environments—are clearly very different. We tackle some of these issues in this book.

The chapter is divided into six main parts. Following this opening scene-setting section, we follow up the conceptual distinctions between creativity and imagination in more depth, and also cover the associated field of imagery. The third section deals with the social, cultural, and musical contexts of musical imagination, which draw on the disciplines of musicology, sociology, and ethnomusicology. The fourth section focuses on the neuroscientific approach, which is probably the most rapidly-growing branch of contemporary music psychology, and the fifth deals with the vitally important yet neglected topic of improvisation, and in particular its widespread use in music therapy. Finally, we take a brief and speculative look ahead at what the future might hold.

1.2 **Creativity, imagination, and imagery**

Following the line of argument above, it is very clear from the literature that 'creativity' has been the central focus of this field, and this has been used as a generic term for the phenomena of musical invention, improvisation, generation, composition, arranging, and performance. Sloboda's (1988) *Generative Processes in Music*, for example, an influential edited collection containing some chapters which are still widely cited today, is subtitled *The Psychology of Performance, Improvisation and Composition*: listening is not dealt with as such, although it is of course an integral part of all of these activities. As argued above, we conceive of musical *imagination* as a broader term which encapsulates perception—the active interpretation and transformation of sound input—alongside performance and invention. The notion of imagination and creativity in music listening—viewing perception as creative construction of knowledge—is pursued in much more depth in Chapter 10.

Defining creativity has always been problematic because creativity exists in an infinite variety of different forms, and in different domains: however, most current definitions involve the use of original thinking in tackling a problem, and using that original thinking to produce a practical solution. For example, Kaufman and Sternberg (2007: p. 55) suggest that 'A creative response to a problem is new, good, and relevant', and there are several other similar definitions. Kaufman and Sternberg's focus is therefore on the *products* of creativity: but others have defined it in terms of the characteristics of the *person* who is solving the problem; of the *processes* involved in reaching that solution; or of the *environment* in which the solution is reached. All of these approaches are equally valid, and any comprehensive definition would need to include all of them.

One important distinction which emerges from this analysis is that between creative thinking, which is presumably part of the process, and actual creativity, which requires some kind of product or outcome: this is directly related to our comments above about the distinction between imagination and creativity. Imagination is essentially *perceptual*: those mental representations which arise in music listening are internal, and not directly observable. Creativity, on the other hand, involves *production*: imagination is very likely to have been involved, but it is used in the creation of some kind of product. In this book we claim that a focus on imagination—on internal mental processes—is more useful than one on creativity because it encompasses a much broader range of concepts and behaviour. For the same reason, the Froebel Research Fellowship programme involving one of us, working with young children (see, e.g. Fumoto et al., in press), has focused explicitly on creative thinking rather than on creativity as such. Our work has involved observational studies of children's behaviour, and involves two implicit inferences: that certain types of behaviour indicate creative thinking in young children, and that creative thinking is a predictor of real-life creativity when linked with optimal environmental conditions, and appropriate levels of motivation and persistence.

There are several good and varied reasons why different writers have suggested that 'creativity' is a term which should be abandoned, and we will mention just three of these. First, Hudson (1966) pointed out long ago that the term had become over-used and abused, suggesting that 'In some circles "creative" does duty as a word of general approbation—meaning, approximately, "good". . . (it) covers everything from the answers to a particular kind of psychological test, to forming a good relationship with one's wife' (p. 119). The essential argument here is that creativity is mistakenly seen by many as a monolithic entity whose general features can be described, and possibly even explained, by one of the many theories that have been developed (see review by Kozbelt, Beghetto, & Runco, 2010). Since creativity actually exists in so many different forms, activities, and contexts, giving rise to an infinitely variable range of products, any attempt to formulate a unitary description or explanation is doomed to failure.

Instead, it makes much more sense to formulate more specific explanations of particular aspects of creativity. In Chapter 4 of this book, for example, Simon Frith contrasts the view that creativity results from 'special individual talent' with the sociological view that creativity is a social fact: it is 'a way of thinking about what people do such that certain kinds of activity give people a particular social status' (p. 62). This emphasis on the practice and social context of music-making leads him also to the conclusion that the concept of musical creativity is best abandoned: and a third line of argument with the same conclusion is advanced by Dietrich (2007). Dietrich is a cognitive neuropsychologist who has written a hard-hitting and polemical article which argues that the study of creativity has been stuck in a rut for decades. He identifies four central ideas which still hold sway in creativity research ('creativity is divergent thinking'; 'creativity is in the right brain'; 'creativity occurs in a state of defocused attention'; 'altered states of consciousness facilitate creativity') and demolishes each one in turn, arguing that it is important to discard these outmoded ideas and to focus instead on the specific cognitive mechanisms and neural substrates which are involved in particular types of creative activity, rather than to hold on to a monolithic view.

Another concept which needs to be distinguished from imagination, but which is equally relevant to music, is imagery: Terry Clark, Aaron Williamon, and Aleksandar Aksentijevic have reviewed the current state of play of work on musical imagery in Chapter 22 of this book. Musical imagery is the recreation of sounds in the mind when no audible sounds are present, and it differs from musical imagination in that the latter involves invention—whereas musical imagination involves the mental creation of new sounds, musical imagery involves the recreation of existing ones. Musicians often refer to imagery in such terms as mental rehearsal, mental practice, inner hearing, visualization, or finger practice.

Some of these terms make it clear that musical images are not necessarily auditory, but can also occur in other sensory modalities, and Lehmann (1997, p. 146) distinguished between three main forms of mental representation that might be used to recreate music in the mind. These are *visualization*, in which some form of visual image, such as a mental picture of the score, is used to represent the music; *audiation*, in which the musician is able to mentally 'hear' or 'play through' a given piece; and what Lehmann terms '*the photographic ear*', in which musicians are able to analyse the piece and to identify specific elements or aspects of it. One important and consistent finding from the neuroscience literature is that live and imagined performances of a given piece of music are functionally equivalent to the performer. Zatorre and Halpern's (2005) review, for example, concluded that 'Converging evidence now indicates that auditory cortical areas can be recruited even in the absence of sound and that this corresponds to the phenomenological experience of imagining music' (p. 9).

The widespread acceptance that musical performance and imagery function in a similar manner at the neurological level means that many of the advantages of physical practice can also be gained through imagery, and Clark, Williamon, and Aksentijevic discuss the various ways in which musicians are able to use imagery techniques in their practice regimes and performances. Holmes' (2005) interviews with two elite solo musicians suggested that they used three types of imagery in their activities, namely *mental rehearsal*, in which they could think through their performance and focus on or rethink certain aspects of it, such as interpretation; *auditory imagery*, an internal impression of the sound of the music; and *motor imagery*, the internal impression of what it feels like to play the music, and which is strongly linked with auditory imagery in the sense that an auditory representation of the music could also give rise to a sensation of what it would feel like to play the music. Clark, Williamon and Aksentijevic's chapter provides a very useful review of the practical details of the ways in which performers can utilize imagery in their work.

1.3 Social, cultural, and musical contexts

As we said earlier, our own foundations are in social and developmental psychology and social cognition, such that the social and cultural contexts of musical imagination are of central importance to us. We have taken a very wide-ranging view of these contexts in this book, which includes not only sociological and historical perspectives on musical imagination and creativity, but also those from what has become known as 'empirical musicology', which incorporates empirical approaches and methodologies from the social sciences into musicological analysis (see, e.g. Clarke & Cook, 2004). The discussion of this wide range of phenomena can be clarified by the use of Doise's (1986) distinction between four levels of analysis in social research. The first is the *intraindividual* level, which deals with the cognitive and perceptual mechanisms by which people appraise and organize their social environments, and the second is the *interindividual and situational* level, which deals with social effects in small groups and other specific situations involving others. The third, *social-positional* level deals with influences which exist beyond the immediate situation to differences in social position, such as people's membership of different social groups; and the fourth, *ideological* level is the most abstract, dealing with the systems of cultural beliefs and norms that people take with them into immediate situations.

In Chapter 4, Simon Frith is working at the ideological level in proposing a basic contrast between those accounts of musical creativity which see it as a property of particular creative individuals, and those sociological accounts which see it as a kind of 'business behaviour'; people are creative because it is their job to be so, and they need to be productive in order to earn a living. The emphasis in the first explanation is on individual originality and autonomy which, as Frith points out, form the basis of the copyright system and the notion of intellectual property, whereas the latter is more likely to involve ideas such as spotting gaps in the market, and being aware of the social and cultural context of one's creative work: 'Music is a social activity, made for an audience and to serve social purposes (whether for the church or the entertainment industry, for the academy or a private social function). Financial incentive certainly is relevant to many music-making activities but it is not thereby *necessary* for creativity' (p. 68). This distinction is also echoed by Margaret Barrett's *ecological* account of musical creativity and learning (Chapter 13), also working at the ideological level, which considers the social and cultural factors involved in particular domains such as music alongside individual artistic talent and ability. This leads her to the concepts of the 'knowledge economy' and the 'creative economy': the latter refers to those 'creative industries' in which creativity is either central to the enterprise (such as the film industry), or in which a number of creative workers are employed.

In Chapter 6, Juniper Hill also takes an ideological approach to the role of social influences in the sense of examining 'differing cultural belief systems, values, and attitudes that may restrict, inhibit, encourage, or liberate musical creativity' using ethnomusicological methods. She does so by comparing six very diverse music-cultures, which include pre-1970s Suya ceremonial music from Mato Grosso in Brazil as well as Finnish contemporary folk music, and investigating the beliefs and attitudes which underlie questions such as how new musical material is generated, who in the culture is allowed to do so, and with which priorities and goals. Hill insists that the ideologies which underlie musical creativity determine its direction.

Ian Sutherland and Tia deNora are concerned with the effects of some very powerful ideological influences upon the musical creativity of one particular German composer in Chapter 5: this is a detailed analysis of the specific socio-political contexts which shaped the music of Paul Hindemith, who was working in Germany at a time of intense political upheaval, in World War I, the Weimar Republic, and the Third Reich. Their emphasis is on 'musical creativity as social agency', i.e. on the role of music in connecting personal and social change (a concept which they draw from Giddens, 1991). Their analysis of letters written by Hindemith during his early professional years are used to show how he began to use his music as an agent of social change: this is particularly clear in his involvement in *Gebrauchsmusik* ('utility music') during the period of the Weimar Republic (*c.*1919–1933), which enabled him to come to terms, to some extent at least, with his incongruous political situation. In the following era of the Third Reich, Hindemith (along with Schoenberg and others) was regarded as 'musically degenerate' by the Nazi press and bureaucracy, and his response was to use his music as a means of rehabilitating his own public reputation.

Several chapters in the book take an explicitly socio-cultural and/or ecological approach to musical creativity and imagination. We have already touched on Barrett's account of the ecological approach, and the chapters by Karin Johansson (14), Göran Folkestad (12), and Karen Littleton and Neil Mercer (15) do the same, thereby adopting a combination of interindividual and situational, and social-positional levels of social explanation.

Johansson's chapter on organ improvisation explicitly adopts the approach of Russian cultural-historical psychology, which originated in the work of Vygotsky in the 1930s, and whose most recent manifestation is Engeström's cultural-historical activity theory (CHAT: Engeström, Miettinen, & Punamäki, 1999). This approach grounds creativity in the social context of the past, the present, and also the future, such that: 'musical fantasy and imagination are seen as dynamic, social processes and the interplay between receptivity, creativity and change might in Vygotsky's terms be expressed as a relationship between internalisation, externalisation and transformation: "Internalisation is related to reproduction of culture; externalisation as creation of new artefacts makes possible its transformation (Engeström, Miettinen & Punamäki, 1999: p. 10)"'. Once again, this approach implies that an 'individual talent' explanation of creativity is inadequate, because individual development does not occur in isolation, but builds and draws on the long tradition and history of organ improvisation.

This corresponds with Göran Folkestad's view that creative musical activity is part of *discourse in music*, which he sees as an ongoing socio-cultural and musical dialogue: he conceives it 'as *situated practice*', which 'constitutes a good example of the dialectic between theory and practice in research. Key analytical concepts . . . are *affordances* as described by Gibson (1986) and *tools*, *artefacts* and *mediation* as described and defined by Vygotsky (1934/1986) (p.195)'. Folkestad (1996) used this approach in his own doctoral research on young people's composition using the computer software packages available at that time. In Chapter 12, he develops it in formulating two interesting new concepts: the first is what he calls the 'double dimension of collectivity' in creative music-making. His suggestion is that there simultaneously exist two levels of collective communication: the interpersonal processes which exist between the members of the musical group (e.g. in small group improvisation), and the implicit dialogue which takes place with the collective experiences and knowledge of previous composers. Folkestad's second concept is that of the *personal inner musical library,* which refers to people's repertoires of musical experience which they have built up over their entire lives. These are dynamic and active rather than passive 'archives': any new musical experience is actively interpreted in the content of their inner library, which may change as a result of that experience. This means that people's personal inner musical libraries are in a constant state of change, and they almost certainly form an important part their musical identities (see MacDonald, Hargreaves & Miell, 2009).

Littleton and Mercer also adopt an explicitly sociocultural approach to the explanation of collaborative creativity processes observed in three groups of musicians: their emphasis on discourse analysis enables them to 'shed light on: 1) the processes by which musicians negotiate musical common knowledge; 2) the significance of disputes and conflicts in the pursuit of common goals; 3) how influences are fused and connected to produce a distinctive and unique "sound" and 4) how language is used in conjunction with other modes to produce a persuasive "discourse" in joint preparation for musical performance' (p. 233). They do this by analysing the recordings and field notes from their observations of rehearsals by the three different bands (a teenage rock group, a group of three adult musicians preparing to accompany a musical play, and a country/roots band).

One important general implication of their analysis is that different 'communities of practice' (Rogoff, 2003) have distinctive forms, and that the participants' shared historical knowledge of their own community is the foundation of collaborative creativity: this applies specifically to communities built up around musical genres, and the practices that go along with them. This particular issue is explored in more detail by Graham Welch in Chapter 24, who suggests that creativity is valued and nurtured to different degrees in different musical genres. His study of the informal learning practices of the communities of Western classical, Scottish traditional, jazz, and popular musicians revealed some important differences between these genres, and in particular between the Western classical musicians on the one hand, and what he calls the three 'other-than-classical' genres on the other. In comparison with the Western classical musicians, the other three genre groups tended to spend more time listening to their own music, and to play for fun; to see the ability to sight read as relatively less important; to rely more heavily on improvisational skill and 'playing by ear'; to place more value on group than on individual practice; and to gain more pleasure from performing in their own genre.

To conclude this section, the chapters by Emery Schubert (8) and David Hargreaves, Jonathan James Hargreaves, and Adrian North (10) adopt an intraindividual level of explanation in trying to explain the cognitive processes which people use to appraise their social environments. Schubert proposes a 'spreading activation' theory of creativity, which has its roots in the 'associationist' theories of Mednick (1962), Koestler (1964), and others. This suggests that information is created and stored in *nodes*, and that these are interconnected through associative *links*, such that creativity is defined as the creation of a new link to solve a particular problem. Schubert is keen to point out that this is a cognitive rather than a biological theory: 'nodes and links are analogous to biological neurons and synapses respectively, but are generally not intermingled to avoid an implied assertion that they are necessarily the same thing' (p. 127).

What Schubert adds to the earlier models is the principle of *dissociation*: this is defined as the activation of a large number of nodes by a stimulus whilst 'pain nodes' are inhibited. His argument (Schubert, 1996) is that people strive to maximize positive affect (pleasure) at the phenomenological level, and (following Martindale, 1984) that this occurs as a result of node activation, but that they simultaneously dissociate at the neurological level. The creative process is then defined as the spontaneous formation of a new link that leads to dissociation, such as in the composer's 'Eureka' moment at which the solution to a particular compositional problem becomes clear, or in the concept of 'flow' as described by Csikszentmihalyi (1996).

The idea of networks of cognitive association is pursued in Chapter 10 by Hargreaves, Hargreaves, and North, who propose three different varieties of them. The first are networks of *musical* association: these are the connections that people make between different musical materials, pieces, and styles, and they could be thought of as people's 'musical geographies', i.e. the mental maps which they use to interpret any new pieces of the music they might encounter. The second type are networks which are based on the *cultural* aspects of musical reference, and the concept of 'musical fit' is helpful in understanding this: it is simply that certain pieces and styles are seen by members of particular cultural groups as being more appropriate to some situations than to others. The music appropriate for a church funeral is unlikely to sound good in a fashion boutique on a busy Saturday morning, for example; and Martindale's (1984) theory of 'cognitive hedonics' explains musical preferences in terms of the degree to which different pieces or styles activate different parts of our individual networks of cultural association. Thirdly and finally, we suggest that people construct their own *personal* networks of association by linking their cultural networks—the key people, situations, and events they have experienced in their lives—with their musical geographies. These may well form the basis of our musical identities.

1.4 **Neuroscientific studies**

As we said in the introduction to this chapter, neuroscientific research is probably the most rapidly-growing branch of contemporary music psychology, and it has only been in existence for two decades or so. The field was mapped out by Peretz and Zatorre (2003), but has advanced considerably since then. The early emphasis on cognitive studies showed how the brain processes the basic elements of music, including rhythm, metre, pulse, timbre, pitch, interval, contour, and harmony, as well as complex sounds such as speech in relation to music. Since Blood and Zatorre (2001) first demonstrated that intense musical pleasure was associated with those brain regions implicated in reward and emotion, there has been more research on the neural correlates of the emotions aroused by music, as well as on aesthetic responses towards it. Some further new frontiers are represented by research such as that reported in Chapter 20 of this book, which is beginning to deal with the interpersonal, expressive, and social aspects of music from a neuroscientific perspective. Istvan Molnar-Szakacs, Vanya Green Assuied, and Katie Overy show how our new understanding of the mirror neuron system (MNS) is able to provide a neuroscientific explanation of the bases of empathetic understanding between people, and this seems to have both a cognitive perspective-taking component as well as an emotional one.

Clinical studies of those with brain disorders or damage, in particular those with amusia and/or aphasia (the inability to process music and/or language), represent an important part of this field in revealing how music processing is multimodal, as well as widely distributed across both cerebral hemispheres. Comparisons between the neural activites of musicians as compared with non-musicians, and also between musicians with different instrumental specialisms have been undertaken since Schlaug, Janck, and Huang's (1995) pioneering finding that the structure of the corpus callosum differed between musicians and non-musicians. Bangert and Schlaug (2006) also revealed differences between the cortical asymmetry of string as compared with keyboard players, and further investigations have subsequently been made of other instrumental specialisms (e.g. Tervaniemi, Just, & Koelsch, 2005). The general conclusion to emerge from these studies of different types of musical activity is that musicians' superior performances on their own specialist activities, and the neural differences underlying them, are the result of the long-term plasticity of the auditory cortex and of the effects of training rather than the effects of innate differences between individuals.

In the realm of creativity and imagination, our main focus here, Brattico and Tervaniemi (2010) have written an excellent short review of the current state of play of neuroscientific research on creativity in musicians, beginning with the suggestion that 'The generative ability of humans is common to everyday behaviors, including humming of novel tunes, spontaneous language, mathematics, drawing, and so on' (p. 233): in other words, creativity is not the special gift of a few especially talented individuals, but an 'everyday' ability possessed by all of us to varying degrees. They also suggest that this domain-general generative ability is based in Broca's area in the brain; we might also note that Molnar-Szakacs and Overy (2006; see also Chapter 20) suggest that a MNS for music production and perception might also exist in this region. Brattico and Tervaniemi review the (comparatively few) studies that have been carried out on differences between the neural activity of musicians who are skilled improvisers, and who thereby create new musical material (e.g. jazz musicians), and those who are non-improvisers (as in the case of many classical musicians).

Tervaniemi et al. (2001), for example, found that improvising musicians had faster and more accurate memory traces for the pitch contours of complex tonal patterns, suggesting that their brains were plastically modified by experience to facilitate the extraction and recognition of musical patterns, and thereby to be able to play these patterns more quickly. Limb and Braun's (2008) fMRI (functional magnetic resonance imaging) study of six jazz pianists incorporated reproduction and improvisation tasks based on scales as well as on a jazz composition that had been memorized several days earlier—the musicians were asked either to reproduce this piece from memory, or to improvise freely on its chord sequences. They found that these tasks evoked activation in far more subcortical, cortical, and cerebellar areas than had been found in previous studies, and Brattico and Tervaniemi provide a useful analysis of the ways in which these findings complement and further develop those of earlier studies in this literature. There is still a long way to go in this field since it is difficult to recruit large numbers of the specialist musicians who are needed, and also because of the difficulties of carrying out brain activity recordings in situations that possess some degree of ecological validity for those musicians—nevertheless, this is a very fruitful area for further investigation.

Finally, Hargreaves, Hargreaves, and North point out in Chapter 10 that there are functional equivalences between the main domains of musical activity: Zatorre and Halpern's (2005) research on mental imagery in music led them to the conclusion that 'auditory cortical areas can be recruited even in the absence of sound and . . . this corresponds to the phenomenological experience of imagining music' (p. 9), and we suggested in section 1.2 above that there is widespread acceptance that musical performance and imagery function in a similar manner at the neurological level. Chapter 10 also suggests that 'there is a clear consensus amongst all the research literature reviewed . . . that common mental structures underlie the three main activities of invention (composing and improvising), performance, and listening, and that these structures are constantly changing, revealing imagination and creativity', and that 'there is some limited but growing evidence that these mental processes have identifiable neural correlates' (p.162). The idea that 'musical imaginations' may have a neural basis is a powerful one, and it adds further weight to Copland's (1952) view, mentioned earlier, that 'it is the freely imaginative mind that is at the core of all vital music making and music listening'.

1.5 Improvisation and music therapy

Two important areas addressed within the book are music therapy and improvisation. While these fields are not entirely distinct, since improvisation is at the heart of many music therapy interventions, they do make unique and quite different contributions.

For example, contemporary music therapy is a profession with a history dating back to the early 20th century, and there is increasing interest in the effects of music listening and participation on health and well-being. This interest has prompted multidisciplinary research across a whole range of music related activities, including music listening and pain reduction (Mitchell, MacDonald, & Knussen, 2008); music and stroke rehabilitation (Magee, 2006); and community singing and enhanced self-esteem (Davidson & Faulkner, 2006). A forthcoming text titled *Music, Health and Well-being* is devoted to these research developments (MacDonald, Kreutz, and Mitchell, in press). A key point is that the potential of musical activities to produce positive effects hinges, to some extent, upon the creative aspects of both music listening and participation. For these reasons we include a number of chapters relating to music therapy in this book.

Improvisation is another topical area of music research that has constructions of creativity at its core. It appears in a number of places throughout the book and is the specific focus of two chapters (14 and 16). Interest in improvisation research continues to grow and comes from areas including jazz and experimental music (MacDonald & Wilson, 2006), music therapy (Wigram, 2004), and community music (Elliott and Silverman, in press). This increased interest is facilitated by one of the key assertions made by Raymond MacDonald, Graeme Wilson, and Dorothy Miell in Chapter 16, that improvisation is an accessible, social, collaborative, and uniquely creative process. Moreover, improvisation affords opportunities to challenge musical and cultural hegemonies and to develop new ways of collaborating and thinking in music. Improvisation is, by definition, an artistic practice that is temporal, subjective, and open to individual interpretation, and it has given rise to interdisciplinary research that challenges conventional notions of creativity. While Chapter 16 deals with improvisational practices in a broad sense, Karin Johansson's chapter (14) looks at a very specific type of improvisation with a long tradition; organ improvisation. Her interviews with improvising organists shed light not only upon improvisational practices within the organ tradition, but also but also upon improvisation more generally. One of her conclusions is that improvisational practices can challenge the hegemonic power relations between composers and performers.

Improvisation is also a central focus of Eric Clarke's chapter (2), which investigates creativity in performance. Clarke observes that the existing literature on improvisation tends to focus upon the cognitive aspects of real-time music creation and that there is still much to be learned about its social and contextual aspects, and how these influence the process and outcomes of improvisational practices. Annabel Cohen's chapter (11) focuses on singing—another area of music that has enjoyed increased interest in recent years. A key feature of this chapter is the observation that while certain features of musical development may be yoked to age-related neural plasticity (in other words that some musical skills are easier to acquire for the young), the capacity for singing, vocal creativity, and—most importantly—developments in competence continue across the lifespan. Using the example of scat singing in jazz improvisation, she highlights how the key elements of a seemingly mysterious and complex process can be learned by people of any age. This observation echoes Eric Clarke's suggestion that the basic elements of improvisational practice may not be as complex as the casual listener might think.

One group of music practitioners who require a particularly sensitive and nuanced conception of improvisation is music therapists, and a number of chapters in the book use a clinical and therapeutic context to develop new ideas about improvisation. Jaakko Erkkilä and his colleagues focus upon improvisational music therapy in Chapter 26. They assert that musical participation is universally accessible, and they present a new model of musical interaction within therapeutic contexts. This model combines psychodynamic theory, improvisational practices, and important features of the clinical environment. These key features of the model are utilized to suggest how improvisational music therapy can produce significant improvements in health and well-being.

In a chapter that resonates with Annabel Cohen's approach, Anthony Wigram signals the centrality of improvisational practices within music therapy in Chapter 27. This chapter also shows how improvisational skills can be learned and honed within a facilitative environment. Music therapists make a significant and important contribution to the book in several different areas; this is unsurprising since their work is predicated upon a sophisticated and nuanced understanding of the creative and expressive components of musical communication. These chapters shed new light upon musical creativity and its role within healing. In Chapter 25, Denise Grocke and David Castle discuss the use of song writing for people with schizophrenia. They demonstrate how one of the most archetypically creative processes within music, song writing, can have significant positive impacts upon health and well-being. Their qualitative research shows how socialization can be enhanced through creative and enjoyable group-based music-making that facilitates positive interactions and helps participants deal more effectively with psychotic symptoms.

Bradley Vines outlines a particular type of therapeutic intervention, Melodic Intonation Therapy, in Chapter 19, and in doing so demonstrates how the disciplines of neuroscience, speech therapy, and music therapy can be synthesized to aid recovery in stroke patients with non-fluent aphasia. In Chapter 20, Istvan Molnar-Szakacs and his colleagues also utilize neurological approaches within a music therapy context in their discussion of what they call the Shared Affective Motion Experience (SAME). This innovative approach employs recent advances in cognitive neuroscience to show how shared emotional experiences during creative interactive music therapy can have significant positive emotional outcomes for patients. Although not explicitly a music therapy contribution, John Gruzelier's chapter (21) highlights how uses of EEG (electroencephalography)-neurofeedback can have beneficial effects on health and well-being in terms of enhanced musical and wider educational developments, particularly for individuals with attention deficit hyperactivity disorder (ADHD).

1.6 **Future directions**

This chapter has given some idea of the scope of contemporary music psychology in relation to imagination and creativity, as well as of its various interdisciplinary links; we could identify many potential areas of future development, but will restrict ourselves to the four broad directions which seem to us to be the most significant. The first stems from the overlap between music psychology and music theory and analysis, which has given rise to the proposal of subdisciplines such as 'cognitive musicology', 'empirical musicology', 'systematic musicology', and 'applied musicology'. Ockelford (2009) has charted the history of this, describing how the protagonists of the two disciplines have had some heated disagreements in recent years, 'Perhaps because proponents from the two camps feel that they have an equal claim over a common territory: an understanding of how music "works"' (p. 542). Ockelford's feeling about the future of this relationship is that 'further developments may well mean having to accept that the initial research questions and the *evaluation* of data may well be guided by musical intuitions, but that the gathering and *analysis* of data should be rigorous and undertaken with a "scientific detachment"' (p. 550). Whether or not this turns out to be the case, it seems clear that research which crosses this interdisciplinary divide will grow and develop further.

The second direction, which is very healthy already, is that which builds on socio-cultural (sometimes described as 'ecological' or 'cultural') psychology, which is covered in the third part of this book. This is probably because this approach has a clear and widely-accepted set of theoretical foundations which stem from Vygotsky's original ideas, and also because it is widely applicable to the detailed analysis of musical behaviour in real-life situations. There is widespread acknowledgement of the importance of cooperation and collaboration; of social communication through verbal and other forms of dialogue; of 'communities of practice', and of the resulting development of individuals' self-concepts and identities. These ideas can be readily applied to many different aspects of musical behaviour, including listening, performance, and composition and improvisation, as well as in music teaching and learning.

The third direction of development, which we have suggested is the most rapid, is in neuroscientific research on music: this has come a long way in the 20 or so years of its existence, but is still a long way from getting to grips with real-life musical behaviour. In Chapter 18, Mari Tervaniemi summarizes the current state of the art in this area, pointing out that there are four distinct 'demands' that future work in this area will need to come to terms with. These are the ecological validity of the musical material used in these studies, and also of the listening (or performing) environment in which they take place; the importance of accurate assessment and control of participants' levels of previous musical training and experience, individual differences in which may swamp any experimentally-induced effects; and individual differences in ways we experience and process music, which also underlie the manifestation of any experimentally-induced effects.

Finally, it is already clear that the real-life applications of the theories and methods of music psychology will continue to advance as our knowledge and understanding increases. Their usefulness in promoting health and well-being, and in other fields of medical and dental practice, for example, have particular current prominence. As the importance and ubiquity of music in our lives continues to increase, we can anticipate further developments in fields such as education, broadcasting, consumer behaviour, the leisure industry, and social inclusion, as well as in musicianship itself. The scope of these potential developments is as wide as that of our musical imaginations themselves.

References

Bangert, M. & Schlaug, G. (2006). Specialization of the specialized in features of external human brain morphology. *European Journal of Neuroscience*, **24**, 1832–4.

Blood, A.J. & Zatorre, R.J. (2001). Intensely pleasurable responses to music correlate with activity in brain regions implicated in reward and emotion. *Proceedings of the National Academy of Sciences*, **98**, 11818–23.

Brattico, E. & Tervaniemi. M. (2010). Creativity in musicians: Evidence from cognitive neuroscience. In R. Bader, C. Neuhaus, & U. Morgenstern (Eds.) *Concepts, experiments and fieldwork: Studies in systematic musicology and ethnomusicology*. Frankfurt: Peter Lang, pp. 233–44.

Brewster, B. & Broughton, F. (1999). *Last night a DJ saved my life*. London: Headline.

Clarke, E. & Cook, N. (Eds.) (2004). *Empirical musicology: Aims, methods, prospects*. Oxford: Oxford University Press.

Copland, A. (1952). *Music and imagination*. New York: Mentor Books.

Csikszentmihalyi, M. (1996). *Creativity: Flow and the psychology of discovery and invention*. New York: HarperCollins.

Davidson, J.W. & Faulkner, R. (2006). Men in chorus: Collaboration and competition in homo-social vocal behaviour. *Psychology of Music*, **34**(2), 219–37.

Dietrich, A. (2007). Who's afraid of a cognitive neuroscience of creativity? *Methods*, **42**(1), 22–7.

Doise, W. (1986). *Levels of explanation in social psychology*. Cambridge: Cambridge University Press.

Elliott, D.J. & Silverman, M. (in press). Why music matters: Philosophical and cultural foundations. In R.A.R. MacDonald, G. Kreutz, & L. Mitchell (Eds.) *Music, health, and well-being*. Oxford: Oxford University Press.

Engeström, Y., Miettinen, R., & Punamäki, R.L. (Eds.) (1999). *Perspectives on activity theory*. Cambridge: Cambridge University Press.

Folkestad, G. (1996). *Computer based creative music making: Young people's music in the digital age*. Göteborg: Acta Universitatis Gothoburgensis.

Fumoto, H., Robson, S., Greenfield, S., & Hargreaves, D.J. (in press). *Creative thinking in young children*. London: Sage.

Gibson, J.J. (1986). *The ecological approach to visual perception*. Hillsdale, NJ: Erlbaum.

Giddens, A. (1991). *Modernity and self-identity: Self and society in the late modern age*. Cambridge: Polity Press.

Holmes, P. (2005). Imagination in practice: A study of the integrated roles of interpretation, imagery and technique in the learning and memorisation processes of two experienced solo performers. *British Journal of Music Education*, **22**, 217–35.

Hudson, L. (1966). *Contrary imaginations*. Harmondsworth: Penguin.

Kaufman, J.C. & Sternberg, R.J. (2007). Resource review: Creativity. *Change*, **39**, 55–8.

Koestler, A. (1964). *The act of creation*. New York: Macmillan.

Kozbelt, A., Beghetto, R.A., & Runco. M. (2010). Theories of creativity. In J.C. Kaufman & R.J. Sternberg (Eds.) *The Cambridge handbook of creativity*. New York: Cambridge University Press, pp. 20–47.

Lehmann, A.C. (1997). Acquired mental representations in music performance: Anecdotal and preliminary empirical evidence. In H. Jørgensen & A. Lehmann (Eds.) *Does practice make perfect?* Oslo: Norges musikkhøskole, pp. 141–64.

Limb, C.J. & Braun, A.R. (2008). Neural substrates of spontaneous musical performance: an FMRI study of jazz improvisation. *PLoS ONE*, **3**, e1679.

MacDonald, R.A.R., Byrne, C., & Carlton, L. (2006). Creativity and flow in musical composition: An empirical investigation. *Psychology of Music*, **34**(3), 292–307.

MacDonald, R.A.R., Hargreaves, D.J., & Miell, D.E. (Eds.) (2002). *Musical identities*. Oxford: Oxford University Press. pp. x, 213.

MacDonald, R.A.R., Hargreaves, D.J., & Miell, D.E. (2009). Musical identities. In S. Hallam, I. Cross, & M. Thaut (Eds.), *The Oxford handbook of music psychology*. Oxford: Oxford University Press, pp. 462–70.

MacDonald, R.A.R, Kreutz, G., & Mitchell, L.A. (Eds.) (in press). *Music, health, and well-being*. Oxford: Oxford University Press.

MacDonald, R.A.R &. Wilson, G.B. (2006). Constructions of jazz: How jazz musicians present their collaborative musical practice. *Musicae Scientiae*, **10**(1), 59–85.

Magee, W.L. (2006). Electronic technologies in clinical music therapy: A survey of practice and attitudes. *Technology and Disability*, **18**(3), 139–46.

Martindale, C. (1984). The pleasures of thought: A theory of cognitive hedonics. *Journal of Mind & Behavior*, **5**(1), 49–80.

Mednick, S.A. (1962). The associative basis of the creative process. *Psychological Review*, **69**, 220–32.

Miell, D.E., MacDonald, R.A.R., & Hargreaves, D.J. (Eds.) (2005). *Musical communication*. Oxford: Oxford University Press.

Mitchell, L.A., MacDonald, R.A.R., & Knussen, C. (2008). An investigation of the effects of music and art on pain perception. *Psychology of Aesthetics, Creativity and the Arts*, **2**(3), 162–70.

Molnar-Szakacs I. & Overy, K. (2006). Music and mirror neurons: from motion to 'e'motion. *Social and Cognitive Affective Neuroscience*, **1**, 235–41.

North, A.C. & Hargreaves, D.J. (2008). *The social and applied psychology of music*. Oxford: Oxford University Press.

Ockelford, A. (2009). Beyond music psychology. In S. Hallam, I. Cross, & M.Thaut (eds.), *The Oxford handbook of music psychology*. Oxford: Oxford University Press, pp. 539–51.

Peretz, I. & Zatorre, R.J (2003). *The cognitive neuroscience of music*. New York: Oxford University Press.

Rogoff, B. (2003). *The cultural nature of human development*. New York: Oxford University Press.

Schlaug, G., Jäncke, L., & Huang, Y. (1995). Increased corpus callosum size in musicians. *Neuropsychologia*, **33**, 1047–55.

Schubert, E. (1996). Enjoyment of negative emotions in music: An associative network explanation. *Psychology of Music*, **24**(1), 18–28.

Sloboda, J.A. (Ed.) (1988). *Generative processes in music: The psychology of performance, improvisation and composition*. Oxford: Oxford University Press.

Tervaniemi, M., Rytkönen, M., Schröger, E., Ilmoniemi, R.J., & Näätänen, R. (2001). Superior formation of cortical memory traces of melodic patterns in musicians. *Learning and Memory*, **8**, 295–300.

Tervaniemi, M., Just, V., & Koelsch, S. (2005). Pitch-discrimination accuracy in musicians vs. nonmusicians: an event-related potential and behavioral study. *Experimental Brain Research*, **161**, 1–10.

Wigram, T. (2004). *Improvisation: Methods and techniques for music therapy clinicians, educators and students.* London: Jessica Kingsley.

Vygotsky, L.S. (1934/1986). *Mind in society. The development of higher psychological processes.* Cambridge, MA: Harvard University Press.

Zatorre, R.J. & Halpern, A.R. (2005). Mental concerts: Musical imagery and auditory cortex. *Neuron,* **47**, 9–12.

Part 1

Perspectives from musicology, sociology, and ethnomusicology

Chapter 2

Creativity in performance

Eric F. Clarke

2.1 Introduction

'It is different each time I play', Emil Gilels is quoted as saying (Mach, 1991: p. 123) in a phrase that forms the title of a paper by Roger Chaffin, Anthony Lemieux, and Colleen Chen (2007). Every musical performance is unavoidably 'creative' in the sense that if the analysis is sufficiently fine-grained it is bound to differ from every other performance in some way, somewhere. But such a statement collapses together significantly different ways in which the term 'creative' can be used: residually, and perhaps unhelpfully, simply to indicate that there are features not found in any other performance; combinatorially, to indicate that while none of the elements of a perform-ance belong to a new category, they appear in an arrangement not previously encountered; or more radically, to identify the kind of striking innovation that seems to come from nowhere. Three decades ago, Henry Shaffer pointed towards similar distinctions when he wrote:

> Skilled performance is creative in two ways: first in the sense intended by Chomsky (1957) for language, that it is based on a generative grammar which enables the construction of an infinite variety of sentences (sequences, patterns) using a finite set of rules. And second, that over time the person may explore the consequences of extending or modifying parts of the grammar.
>
> (Shaffer, 1981: p. 1.)

In this chapter I examine the different ways in which performance can be said to be creative, discuss the significance of these different varieties of creativity, and explore some of the varied manifestations of creativity that can be found in performance.

First, it is important to recognize that not all musical performance takes creativity in any form as its aim. The contemporary preoccupation with creativity in the Western classical performing tradition is the consequence of a specific aesthetic outlook and particular commercial pressures, and at other times and in other musical traditions it is unchanging identity that performers are trying to preserve. This is easy to overlook because of the tendency to concentrate on music as art, rather than as an 'action craft' (Godlovitch, 1998), and as it is involved in a wide range of other social functions. When music is used in rituals, in coordinating physical work, or as a reassuring greeting song in music therapy the overwhelming imperative may be to avoid creativity or novelty, and to aim at unvarying replication so as to preserve the social or psychological function that the music accomplishes.[1]

---

[1] The songs of the Blackfoot Native American Indians are a documented case: Robert Witmer has shown how two recordings of the same song made nearly 60 years apart are '*virtually identical* down to the very smallest of details' (Witmer 1993: 243; original emphasis), despite being by different performers within an aurally transmitted tradition. The performances of tribute bands exemplify another context where the preservation of something close to literal identity is at a premium.

Why, then, does classical performance in the West place such a strong emphasis on creativity in performance, and to what extent is this a permanent and ubiquitous feature of the culture? Contemporary circumstances—and most obviously the recording industry and broadcast media—place a huge emphasis on the distinctiveness of performers for simple commercial reasons, and as part of an ideology of aesthetic and cultural 'authenticity'. Since the overwhelming majority of concerts, recordings, and broadcasts deal with a more or less static musical repertory, the primary way to attract an audience, or sell recordings, is to focus on the personal identity and creative attributes of the performer. The emphasis on creativity in performance is strongly bound up with the institution of the public concert, which emerged in Europe around the middle of the 18th century, and with Romantic and post-Romantic musical traditions that still play a central role in the dominant culture.

There is very little in the literature on the psychology of performance that directly addresses the question of innovation and aesthetic value from the perspective of production, but from the other side of the coin, Bruno Repp (1997) has investigated how listeners respond to more or less normative performances. Repp cites research on face recognition which shows that participants gave the highest aesthetic ratings to pictures of faces that were constructed (by digital image processing) as the average of a collection of faces—and that this preference increased with the size of the pool of individual faces from which the average was made. In other words, viewers preferred the most normative, or prototypical, face. The proposed explanation (termed the 'minimal-distance' hypothesis by Repp) is as follows: 1) an average face from a large collection of individual faces approximates to a prototype face; 2) the prototype serves as an aesthetic standard; 3) the *average* response from a collection of viewers is to judge this average face to be most aesthetically pleasing—even though some individual viewers may prefer one of the individual faces over both the average and by implication the prototype.

Applying this same idea to music, Repp explored how an arithmetically average performance was rated in relation to individual performances by both students and internationally recognized expert performers. In two experiments using piano music by Schumann and Chopin, Repp showed that an average performance is indeed given a very high—and for the Chopin piece, the highest—preference rating. Repp sees the result in terms of a conflict between the need to communicate on the one hand (which depends on adherence to generally shared conventions) and the need to assert a performing identity on the other (which depends on creative transformation or transgression of those conventions). In the context of a laboratory study, albeit presented to the participants as a mock piano competition, it may be that familiarity and 'acceptability' are favoured rather more than the projection of a specific performer identity—hence the overall preference for the average performance. By contrast, in a study using very simple musical materials (a highly conventional unaccompanied tonal melody), music students judged the *least* structurally communicative performances of the melody to be their most preferred (Clarke & Windsor, 2000). Simple music may require more idiosyncratic or structurally ambiguous performances to engage the interest, and hence the preference, of listeners.

2.2 Expression and creativity

The most intensively studied aspect of performance, and one that is closely related to a consideration of creativity, is expression. It seems uncontroversial to assert that playing music expressively is a kind of creativity, but there are significant difficulties in agreeing on a definition of expression in performance that will support such a claim. 'Deviations from the exact' or 'departures from the score', which were once regarded as defensible characterizations of performance expression (e.g. Seashore, 1938/1967), have been increasingly challenged, as different musical traditions have been considered, as less literal-minded attitudes to the nature of a score have been recognized (Clarke, 2002), and as studies of historical recordings have revealed changing conceptions of expression over time (Leech-Wilkinson, 2009). Nonetheless, the idea that expression is a transformation of, or a departure from, some kind of norm, still prevails as a background assumption (for a review, see Gabrielsson, 1999).

To what extent, then, can these transformations or departures be regarded as a manifestation of creativity? Creativity itself is notoriously hard to define, but most definitions resist the inclusion of phenomena that are either accidental, or completely determined. Johnson-Laird (1988), for example, makes use of a definition of creativity as 'mental processes that lead to solutions, ideas, conceptualizations, artistic forms, theories, or products that are unique and novel' (Reber, 1985, cited in Johnson-Laird, 1988: 203), while Boden writes that 'Creativity is the ability to come up with ideas or artefacts that are *new, surprising and valuable*' (Boden, 2004: p. 1; emphasis in original).

What light do these definitions shed on expression in performance? First, a distinction can be drawn between expressive features of performance that can be regarded as the unconscious symptoms of underlying cognitive processes, and those that are the result of deliberate interpretative choices. In a study that explored the relationship between metrical structure and expressive communication, Sloboda (1983) asked pianists to play two versions of a melody that differed only in their metrical notation (one was notated starting on the first downbeat, the other with an upbeat by virtue of a shift in the position of the bar lines). None of the pianists in his study noticed that the two sequences of pitches were identical, and that the only difference between them was a metrical shift. Nonetheless, all of the performers played the two melodies with expressive features that distinguished the two melodies metrically—in terms of measurable performance features, and as confirmed by the perceptual judgements of a group of listeners who subsequently heard the performances. It would be hard to argue that these expressive features are creative components of the performances, since they seem to be an unconscious and perhaps even involuntary consequence of the performers' parsing of the musical structure, though it is still defensible to regard them as *expressive* features of the performances: the timing, dynamic, and articulatory features of the performances express the performers' understanding of the metrical structure.

By contrast, consider the performances of the Prelude in E minor (Op. 28 no. 4) by Chopin discussed in Clarke (1995). The pianist in this study gave six performances of the Prelude in the course of about an hour, of which two are analysed in the chapter. The performer had not been asked to attempt deliberately different interpretations, nor had he been asked to adhere to a single view: these were freely given, and apparently spontaneously varying, performances. Analysis of the two performances demonstrated significant differences between them, amounting to distinct interpretations of the music that appear to prioritize different aspects of the music's structure. In this case it seems rather more persuasive that these distinctions do constitute a creative use of expression in performance, though it is worth noting that there was no evidence that the performer was conscious of trying to articulate these different interpretations.[2]

The research by Chaffin, Lemieux, and Chen (2007), to which the opening line of this chapter refers, similarly demonstrates systematic variability among a number of performances in the absence of any conscious awareness by the performer. The performer, a professional pianist, had spent a period of months preparing Bach's *Italian Concerto* for a commercial recording, and

----

[2] This is entirely consistent with other evidence for the fluid relationship between creativity and conscious awareness, which demonstrates that creative solutions may often be the result of an unconscious process. A well-known example is Kekulé's discovery of the structure of the benzene molecule when, after puzzling for days over the problem, he fell asleep and dreamed of a snake biting its own tail, and upon waking realized that the molecule's structure must be a ring (see Weisberg, 1988).

towards the end of that period made video recordings of seven complete performances of the last movement, alone in her own practice studio. Given the absence of an audience, and the aim of reaching a fixed and stable conception of work for the purposes of recording, these conditions would seem to be the least likely to give rise to performance variation, yet the paper demonstrates non-random and structurally-related changes from one performance to another. The performer herself judged all the performances to be very similar, differing only in tiny technical matters and how 'cautious' they sounded. Having demonstrated the systematic nature of the performance changes in the recordings, Chaffin et al. (2007: p. 467) conclude that 'musically meaningful differences between repeated performances are an unavoidable by-product of the psychological processes involved in playing musically', the striking implication being that this kind of creativity is unintended, inevitable, and yet meaningful. Jonathan Dunsby has proposed that the third performance of a piece is often the moment at which 'magically everything seems to come together' (Dunsby, 1995: p. 10)—the 'magic' being attributable to the intervening conscious and unconscious processes of assimilation, and the dialogical relationships between the component parts of what can be seen as a single temporally extended 'meta-performance'.[3]

Novelty and uniqueness, which Reber (above) takes as defining attributes of creativity, are central to that powerful Romantic notion of creativity which still dominates our culture—creativity portrayed as the mysterious appearance of the radically new, apparently from nowhere. Earlier, and perhaps also more recent, notions of creativity are far more ready to incorporate influence and recombination into such a definition, and this has an interesting bearing on creativity in performance. In a number of studies, Repp has examined sizeable collections of recorded performances of the same work, and has used these to explore the relationship between commonality and idiosyncrasy in interpretation. One such study (Repp, 1992) examining 28 performances of Schumann's *Träumerei*, demonstrates that the strong underlying similarities between manifestly diverse performances by some of the 20th century's most celebrated pianists tend to be found at more global levels of performance, with diversity increasing at lower hierarchical levels. This might be understood either as a reflection of deep-seated general cognitive constraints that necessarily regulate performance, or as the expression of very general (though arbitrary) cultural conventions of performance practice. The distinction between these two kinds of explanation is widespread but nonetheless questionable: how plausible is the idea that culture-free cognitive constraints might be directly expressed in expert performance, and conversely how likely is it that performance conventions could ever be entirely arbitrary? The norms of performance must necessarily—at least at the limit—be subject to the constraints of human biology as well as being a repository of common cultural practices, just as creativity itself arises out of the conjunction of novelty (whether accidental or deliberate) with more slowly evolving norms and traditions.[4]

The relationship between novelty and acceptability is a complex question that depends as much on the values and sensitivities of listeners as it does on any objective properties of performances, but there is very little research that has addressed either this or the related question of what leads to a performance being evaluated as strikingly original. A simple approach might suggest that the relationship between novelty and aesthetic preference shows the same kind of inverted-U function

---

[3] In this way, the sequence of performances forms its own 'micro history', mirroring the wider web of relationships and influences within which every performance is arguably entangled (see below).

[4] Krampe and Ericsson define an 'eminent' performer as one who 'irrevocably changes and expands the known possibilities for a given instrument or repertoire' (Krampe and Ericsson, 1995: 97), which they regard as something that cannot be taught, and that lies 'beyond the mere acquisition of skills and interpretative techniques' (ibid)–raising significant questions about how (or even whether) such achievements can be accounted for.

as that between complexity and arousal (as in the Yerkes–Dodson law), or between complexity and aesthetic preference—as in Berlyne's (1971) version of the principle, so that people's preferences for a performance peak at some optimal level of novelty. Berlyne and others (e.g. Dowling & Harwood, 1986) assert that the position of the peak in the inverted-U varies with expertise, such that more sophisticated listeners reach a peak of preference at a higher level of complexity than do their more naïve counterparts: more sophisticated listeners might therefore be expected to prefer more idiosyncratic (novel, or creative) performances.

Although the arousal theory is appealing in its simplicity and generality, there are problems when it is applied to a highly culturally embedded phenomenon like musical performance. The recorded performances of the pianist Glenn Gould, for example, provide a case: Gould was famously idiosyncratic and eccentric—and some of his recordings seem to bear out this reputation. His recording of the opening theme and variations movement of the Mozart piano sonata in A major (K.331) takes the theme at about half the speed (20 dotted crotchet beats per minute) of almost any other recording, and with a deliberateness of articulation that is very peculiar. On a variant of the Berlyne model, we might expect to find that only highly sophisticated or expert listeners show a preference for performances like these, but Taruskin (1995) has claimed that Gould's performances (by contrast with those of Vladimir Horowitz, for example) have become celebrated not so much for their brilliant innovation or idiosyncrasy but because they correspond to a particular cultural preoccupation—what Taruskin characterizes as 'modernist' performance, with its focus on a particular conception of structure and 'integrity'. Significantly, Bazzana (1997) suggests that Gould's apparently incomprehensible initial tempo in the first movement of K.331 is part of a deliberate strategy of integration and unification, in which the elements of the theme are progressively brought together across the succeeding variations, which become increasingly fast and loud. Contrary to the view of Gould as wayward, Taruskin's perspective would explain the critical endorsement of Gould's recordings as the consequence of his adherence to a culturally favoured aesthetic norm.

The example highlights the fluid boundaries between the normative, the creative, and the incomprehensible, their position and evaluative significance being a function of judgements made within a shifting cultural and historical context. Cognitive approaches have tended to tackle such questions by focusing on supposedly universal underlying principles (the Yerkes–Dodson law being one such), perpetuating a dubious division between 'natural' and 'cultural' processes. A more constructive approach, particularly for music, is to acknowledge the complex relationship between culture and cognition, and to try to tease apart and identify different components in this network of relationships. The GERM model proposed by Juslin, Friberg, and Bresin (2001–2) is one such attempt, that identifies four factors within performance expression, previously studied in a rather disparate fashion, related to one another in a manner that suggests how their interactions might be empirically investigated. Indeed, an indication of this increasing cultural sensitivity is Juslin's subsequent modification of what was a four-factor GERM model (G = generative; E = emotional; R = random; M = motion) into a five-factor GERMS model that explicitly incorporates the culturally-specific factor (S) of 'stylistic unexpectedness' (Juslin, 2003).

A rather different way to try to combine culture and cognition is represented by studies of historical recordings that have incorporated a psychological component (e.g. Cook, 2007, 2009; 2010; Leech-Wilkinson, 2006, 2009). Historical recordings demonstrate powerfully how attitudes and approaches to performance have changed over a century or more of recording history. What may at one time appear to be the 'timeless' norms of expressive performance turn out to be far more historically specific, raising challenging questions about the status of supposedly fundamental psychological principles. For example, in an analysis of a large number of recordings of Chopin's Mazurkas, Cook (2009) has shown that the principle of coordinated rubato and dynamics, proposed by Todd (1992) as a basic principle of performance expression, is only found to any great extent in recordings by Russian, or Russian-trained performers in recordings made after World War II, demonstrating the cultural and historical contingency of what might otherwise be all too easily portrayed as a 'universal' of classical piano performance. Similarly, Leech-Wilkinson (2006) has discussed the disappearance of *portamento* (expressive pitch glides up to, or away from a note) in recordings of classical singers after World War II, having previously been an extremely widespread feature of most singers' expressive styles. He argues that the relatively sudden disappearance of this conspicuous expressive feature can be understood as a complex interaction between the psychological impact of a developmentally fundamental and universal human vocal phenomenon ('motherese'—which Leech-Wilkinson argues is the basis for the expressive effect of *portamento*) with the profound cultural changes, and 'loss of faith', that were a consequence of World War II. An expressive approach that had previously seemed 'natural' and 'heartfelt' suddenly seemed embarrassingly naïve and uncritical in the wake of the Holocaust.

The study of recordings also throws into relief an issue that is all but absent from previous research into expression and creativity—the effects of 'influence' on the creativity or distinctiveness of performers. Other performances have always been a potential influence, but with the advent and now global reach of the recording and broadcast industries, performers potentially face overwhelming exposure to the sound of other people's interpretations. Harold Bloom's important study of he called 'the anxiety of influence' in poetry (Bloom, 1973), in which he argued that poems are not self-contained entities, and that poets are subject to the potentially paralysing influence of the past, is an approach that Straus (1991) has also adopted in relation to 20th-century composition. As a much more porous and provisional phenomenon, it seems likely that musical performance is even more subject to these intertextual processes, but the extent to which performance may be influenced by, or directly imitative of, other performances has so far been the object of only a small amount of systematic research. Studies of performers' abilities to deliberately imitate other performances (Clarke, 1993; Repp, 2000; Lisboa et al., 2005) have shown that imitation is more accurate and stable when the expressive profile of the target performance maintains a conventional relationship with the phrase structure of the music, and when the target performance is clearly distinct from the imitator's own spontaneous expressive profile for the music. These are only preliminary forays into a whole range of questions about whether and how performers try to develop their own distinctive 'voice', and how they work with, or resist, the influence of others.

It is certainly possible that an overwhelming body of influence might be crushing in its effects, but such dire warnings often seem to come from a perspective that clings to the model of performance as an uncompromisingly personal inspiration. The teacher/apprentice relationship, which was more or less the only model for instrumental learning prior to the development of the conservatoire system, and which persists in musical traditions all over the world, provides one way to see influence and creativity as by no means incompatible. Recordings, too, can be understood as a rich and heterogeneous resource, or a developing tradition, from which new interpretations can be shaped, provoked, or inspired.[5] Despite pronouncements about the destructive and homogenizing consequences of recording (e.g. Philip, 2004), there is very little systematic evidence on

---

[5] Peter Hill (2002) cautions performers against listening to the recordings of others too early in the learning process, when the performer's own ideas have not yet taken shape: 'The great value of studying recordings . . . should be kept to a later stage when one is better placed to make an independent critical assessment.' (Hill, 2002: 143 fn.4)

whether this is borne out in practice—and Cook's (2009) Mazurka study in fact seems to demonstrate the converse. With over 100 years of recordings now available, and with rapid changes in technology allowing for very different attitudes to both the permanence and authority of a recording, there is a fascinating opportunity to carry out a proper exploration of this contested question.

Hans Keller (1990) described performance as the 'improvisatory tail-end of composition', and the literature on expression in performance has demonstrated some of the ways in which that improvisatory flexibility in performance is organized and achieved. Nonetheless, improvisation proper allows for a degree of spontaneous innovation that is of a different order from present-day score-based performance, and it is therefore with the subject of improvisation—the most conspicuous illustration of creativity in performance—that the second half of this chapter is concerned.

2.3 **Improvisation**

A renowned exponent of so-called 'free improvisation', Derek Bailey starts his book on improvisation with the statement that 'Improvisation enjoys the curious distinction of being the most widely practised of all musical activities and the least acknowledged and understood'. He continues: 'Defined in any one of a series of catchphrases ranging from "making it up as he goes along" to "instant composition", improvisation is generally viewed as a musical conjuring trick, a doubtful expedient, or even a vulgar habit' (Bailey 1992: p. ix). Writing his introduction to the second edition of the book, 12 years later, Bailey observed that he had no reason to revise those views, and that despite what he saw as huge changes in the general musical climate, these 'seem to have made very little difference to improvisation' (p. xiii).

Psychological writing on improvisation has been largely concerned with proposing cognitive models for the ways in which this particular structured but unpredictable manifestation of creativity might be understood (e.g. Clarke, 1988; Johnson-Laird, 1988, 2002; Pressing, 1988, 1998). Johnson-Laird's computational approach presents three possible models for creativity, neo-Darwinian, neo-Larmarckian, and 'mixed', based on the metaphor of evolutionary mechanisms. In the neo-Darwinian model, random generation of musical material is followed by a selection process that discards 'competitors' until a single 'winner' remains. As Johnson-Laird points out, the advantage of such a model is its potential for unpredictable novelty (the generation of material is completely unconstrained), but its inefficiency makes it an extremely unlikely contender for the real-time creativity of improvisation. In the neo-Lamarckian model, the generation of material is itself governed by criteria derived from the previous history of the system (i.e. experience, or semantic memory), such that any one of the much smaller number[6] of outputs will satisfy the original constraints. When there is more than one output, a random process arbitrarily selects one.[7] In the mixed model, partial versions of both processes are combined, so that a reasonably small, and partially pre-selected collection of competitors is generated under inherited constraints, followed by a second stage of (non-random) selection. Because the neo-Lamarckian model requires no time-consuming selection process, it is well-suited to the rapid creativity of improvisation, while the mixed model, incorporating the potentially stimulating unpredictability of semi-random

---

[6] The size of the number depends on the restrictiveness of the constraints: the tighter they are, the smaller the number of outputs that will satisfy them.

[7] There is therefore a complementary relationship between the neo-Darwinian and neo-Lamarckian models: random generation in one, random selection in the other; constraint-based selection in the one, constraint-based generation in the other.

generation followed by selection with the greater continuity and stability of some inherited characteristics, seems more appropriate as a model of composition.

Johnson-Laird argues that the type of jazz improvisation that is characteristic of the period
from Louis Armstrong to Charlie Parker and his successors should be seen as a combination of
neo-Lamarckian and mixed model processes. The speed of jazz improvisation suggests that the
immediate melodic components (rhythms and pitches) must be generated by a neo-Lamarckian
process—in other words a tightly constrained generative process that makes minimal demands
on working memory. He describes simple finite-state grammars that are capable of generating
both of these components, and counters the objection that these grammars cannot generate
melodies with large-scale or complex structures, by proposing that larger-scale complexity arises
from a separate compositional component of jazz. The non-real-time activity of jazz composition
(the elaboration of large-scale structures—ballads or blues-based, for example, and defined primarily by harmony) creates a musical 'environment' to which the small-scale elements of melodic
improvisation adapt, giving the illusion that it is these local elements that are somehow cumula-
tively creating the larger structure. The argument is reminiscent of Herbert Simon's (1969) observation that the apparently complex path of an ant traversing the surface of a sand dune is not to
be explained in terms of some complex process internal to the ant, but as the consequence of a
very simple programme in the ant (move towards a fixed goal) interacting with a complex environment (the unpredictable slippage of the sand on the dune surface).

Johnson-Laird's model is firmly focused on pitch and rhythm, while Jeff Pressing (1988), also
adopting a computational approach, gives a rather broader account of the processes involved in
improvisation, which builds more complexity into the generative process itself.[8] His model brings
together a wide range of components including acoustical and structural features, physical movement, and the influence of previous events held in working memory, as well as the impact of the
improviser's aims, interactions with co-performers, and the cultural references of the material with
which he or she works. The model identifies a considerable number of rather abstract processes
and kinds of 'data' that may be involved in producing an improvised performance, but despite the
formalism of its diagrammatic representation, it is actually not formal enough to be implemented
as a testable working system. It is a laudable attempt to identify and coordinate as many as possible
of the components that might be involved in improvising (and it would be hard to disagree with
the rather generic collection that is given in Pressing's model), but with little sense of how these
rather abstract components really work in any particular instance.

Improvisation is a much more physical, embodied, and socially embedded kind of music-
making than Pressing's representation might suggest—as collections edited by Nettl and Russell
(1998), and Sawyer (1997, 2003), and a substantial paper by Iyer (2002), recognize. John Baily has
pointed out the significance of physical factors in musical performance and creativity (e.g. Baily,
1985, 1991; Baily & Driver, 1992), showing how an understanding of the physical properties of
stringed instruments can help to explain the transformation of a musical style as it passes from
one culture (and set of instruments) to another, and how the spatial layout of the guitar, for
instance, influences the harmonic sequences used in rock music. In a more idiosyncratic and
phenomenological vein, David Sudnow's book *Ways of the Hand* (2001) documents the physicality
of his own experience of learning improvised piano playing, with a strong emphasis on the developing sensorimotor awareness that is embodied in the hands' relationships with the keyboard.
Sudnow rejects the kind of top-down approach in which a central controller in the head 'tells' the

---

[8] See also Pressing (1998) for a discussion of many of the same elements of this approach, but couched in
terms of expertise theory.

body where to go and what to do, in favour of a much more distributed understanding of where, and in what form, improvised knowing resides. For an improvising pianist, the interactions of the hands with the keyboard (as well as a more extensive engagement of the whole body[9]) are as much the repository of this improvising knowledge as is the brain. 'I intend my descriptions as indications for how one might eventually speak methodically and rationally, if only crudely for now, when saying things like: the hand—in music, eating, weaving, carving, cooking, drawing, writing, surgery, dialing, typing, signing, wherever—this hand chooses where to go as much as "I" do' (Sudnow, 2001: p. 2).

The physical actions in performance—whether of the hands, or the whole body—might be thought of as lying on a continuum from ergonomics to choreography. At the ergonomic end, performers want to try to make sounds by means of movements that feel easy and comfortable. Fingering patterns in instrumental performance are one area where ergonomic factors are likely to be important, and Parncutt et al. (1997) present a model for pianists' fingering choices that is based entirely on ergonomic considerations (finger strength and span, hand position, the placement of black and white keys, thumb turning, etc.). Although in a highly rehearsed performance other factors (such as style and expression) undoubtedly influence final finger choice, the ergonomic model is surprisingly successful at predicting the essentially improvised finger choices that skilled pianists make when they sight read. If musical performance involves playing within, or perhaps playing *with*, the ergonomic constraints of the body/instrument relationship, it would not be surprising to find that the creativity of improvising performers goes with the grain of what comes easily or feels good. This is a more embodied version of the principle that Johnson-Laird (2002) presents in more abstract (computational) terms: the speed of improvisational creativity imposes demands that can only be met by player/environment interactions that require little or no decision-making and have negligible working memory implications.

At the other end of the spectrum, the choreography of performers' movements represents a potentially powerful and persuasive way to communicate with an audience. Jane Davidson has analysed such displays in video recordings of performances by the pop performers Annie Lennox (Davidson, 2001) and Robbie Williams (Davidson, 2006); Peter Elsdon has done the same in relation to jazz performances by Keith Jarrett (Elsdon, 2006); and Nicholas Cook (2010) offers a similar approach to video recordings of a number of pianists playing Chopin. How much of this kind of choreography is conscious and deliberate, and to what extent it is rehearsed, or created in the course of performance, are questions that remain to be investigated.

For methodological reasons as much as anything, the overwhelming majority of research on improvisation focuses on single performers, but while there is a significant tradition of solo improvisation (from church organists to free improvisers), the great majority of musical improvisation is an explicitly social activity involving sometimes complex interactions between performers, as well as between performers and audience. Because of the predominantly cognitive orientation of the psychology of music, this aspect of performance has only recently begun to be investigated, and only to the most limited extent in improvisation (Sawyer, 2003). Ethnomusicologists have been more keenly aware of the social dimension, as Ingrid Monson (1996) makes plain:

> Rather than being conceived as foundational or separable from context, structure is taken to have as one of its central functions the construction of social context. In other words, there is a mutually defining relationship between structure and context, rather than one of autonomy. . . . At issue is the capacity

---

[9] A seminal moment for Sudnow in learning to play jazz is when he goes to hear the pianist Jimmy Rowles play: it is the *sight* of Rowles's whole body at the instrument, as much as the sound of his playing, that has a decisive impact on Sudnow's whole approach.

> of aural signs to signify in multiple directions—their ability to simultaneously constitute structure and a broader field of human relationships through a communicative discourse . . .
>
> (Monson 1996: p. 186.)

Musical material is a far more social 'substance' than a cognitive view implies, which often seems to present improvisation as if it were a special case of musical problem solving, and it is in the social character of improvisation that psychological research still has much to explore.[10] Improvisation, and particularly so-called free improvisation, is as much concerned with the exploration and negotiation of interpersonal dynamics as it is concerned with musical materials and processes. Free improvisation provides opportunities for very unpredictable and extreme social dynamics to develop, and the music that is created in these circumstances often seems to be primarily a product of the particular social context. There is an interesting complementarity between composition and improvisation in this respect: composition can be viewed as a way of prescribing a musical structure which has as a consequence the construction of certain kinds of social context and (perhaps temporary) interpersonal relationships. A composition for string quartet requires the formation of certain kinds of social relationships and interactions between the players that are distinctly different from those required to perform a symphony, or a work for big band. In free improvisation, the converse often seems to be the case: a certain social context may be established or engineered (it is not uncommon for improvising groups to prescribe certain kinds of interaction without specifying the musical material) and the resulting music is then a consequence of the nature of these social relationships. There is a potential problem here—namely the danger that stereotyped musical consequences will result from these social relationships if there is no other factor to pull the musicians out of their own 'lines of least resistance', or familiar patterns of social (and hence musical) interaction. But at present, there is almost no psychological research that has attempted to explore this potentially fascinating domain.

How might a psychological approach to creativity in performance bring together the somewhat disparate material that currently exists? Creativity in any domain takes place within a complex physical and cultural environment, and this context not only provides the substrate within which creativity can grow, but is also the arbiter of whether what *does* grow is viewed as creative. Csikszentmihalyi and Rich (1997: pp. 45–6) argue that:

> whether an idea or product is judged creative depends on the effect it is able to produce in others who are exposed to it. Therefore it follows that what we call creativity is a phenomenon that is constructed through an interaction between producer and audience. Creativity is not the product of single individuals, but of social systems making judgments about individuals' products.

In a similar vein, Boden (2004) points out that in her definition of creativity as 'new, surprising and valuable' (see above), the 'newness' of something can be measured at one end of the scale in relation to an individual's life history, and at the other in relation to human history;[11] and the 'value' of something new and surprising can only be socially defined. 'Because creativity *by definition*

---

[10] An important part of this social component are the ways in which jazz and pop musicians learn their creativity, which tend to be more aural and informal than their classical counterparts, and in which a different relationship between re-creation and creation obtains (see Green, 2001).

[11] A teenager's first attempts at improvisation may be creative in the first sense, but are unlikely to be in the second. Equally, a young pianist's early attempts to play Schumann's 'Träumerei' may be expressively creative in the first sense, but perhaps not in the second—given the long history of expressive performances of that piece. All of which raises the question of whether we can ever be sure that something is creative in the second, global sense—particularly something as ephemeral and temporally distributed as a performance.

involves not only novelty but value, and because values are highly variable, it follows that many arguments about creativity are rooted in disagreements about value' (Boden, 2004: p. 10; emphasis in original).

Once again this emphasizes the social component in what can all too easily be seen in individualistic terms—and the tendency for psychological theories to place creativity firmly inside the heads of its creators is one of the primary problems. It would be manifestly wrong to dismiss the role of cognitive processes altogether, but it makes little sense to try to explain such a practical and concrete phenomenon as creativity in performance without reference to the physical apparatus (bodies and instruments) and cultural substance and context (stylistically constituted musical materials and performance circumstances) by means of which it is expressed. Difficult though it is to find practical ways to study a complex phenomenon in a manner that does full justice to that complexity, there are ways in which continually developing quantitative methods for performance analysis can be combined with the more culturally embedded insights of participant observation. The 'raw data' of performance can inevitably only tell a very partial story about what performers might have been trying to achieve, and in circumstances where direct access to performers and composers is possible it makes sense to take advantage of the very different kind of information that this can provide (e.g. Clarke et al., 2005; Fitch & Heyde, 2007; Bayley, 2010).

Creativity in performance takes place at the interface between socially constructed musical materials and performance practices, the possibilities and constraints of the human bodies and instruments with which they interact, and the perceptual, motor, and cognitive skills of individual performers. The psychology of music has made some progress in studying this complex phenomenon, particularly in understanding the cognitive processes that underlie this highly regarded behaviour. Nonetheless there is still a great deal more that is not well understood, partly because of the desocialized and rather disembodied way in which performance has often been studied. The engagement of cognitive processes with both social factors (performance traditions, socially constructed notions of 'innovation' and the limits of acceptable radicalism, the interactions between narrowly defined musical processes and the social context of performance) and physical factors represents a considerable challenge to the psychology of music—but a challenge which is already being tackled in various ways. In *Supersizing the Mind*, Andy Clark (2008) argues persuasively for an extended and distributed conception of the mind, in which tools, symbols, technologies, social structures, and the human body and its actions all play a crucial role in our thinking and creating—'a complex cognitive economy spanning brain, body, and world' (Clark, 2008: p. 217)—which just leaves the minor matter of turning this exciting conception into manageable programmes of research.

References

Bailey, D. (1992). *Improvisation. Its Nature and Practice in Music*. London: The British Library.

Baily, J. (1985). Music structure and human movement. In P. Howell, I. Cross, & R. West (Eds.) *Musical Structure and Cognition*. London: Academic Press, pp. 237–58.

Baily, J. (1991). Some cognitive aspects of motor planning in musical performance. *Psychologica Belgica*, **31**, 147–62.

Baily, J. & Driver, P. (1992). Spatio-motor thinking in playing folk blues guitar. *The World of Music*, **34**, 57–71.

Bayley, A. (2010). Multiple takes: Using recordings to document creative process. In A. Bayley (Ed.) *Recorded Music: Performance, Culture and Technology*. Cambridge: Cambridge University Press, pp. 206–24.

Bazzana, K. (1997). *Glenn Gould: The Performer in the Work. A Study in Performance Practice*. Oxford: Oxford University Press.

Berlyne, D. (1971). *Aesthetics and Psychobiology*. New York: Appleton-Century-Crofts.

Bloom, H. (1973). *The Anxiety of Influence: A Theory of Poetry*. New York: Oxford University Press.

Boden, M.A. (2004). *The Creative Mind: Myths and Mechanisms*. London: Routledge.

Chaffin, R., Lemieux, A.F., & Chen, C. (2007). "It's Different Each Time I Play": Why highly polished performances vary. *Music Perception*, **24**, 455–72.

Chomsky, N. (1957). *Syntactic Structures*. The Hague: Mouton.

Clark, A. (2008). *Supersizing the Mind. Embodiment, Action, and Cognitive Extension*. Oxford: Oxford University Press.

Clarke, E.F. (1988). Generative principles in music performance. In J.A. Sloboda (Ed.) *Generative Processes in Music*. Oxford: Clarendon Press, pp. 1–26.

Clarke, E.F. (1993). Imitating and evaluating real and transformed musical performances. *Music Perception*, **10**, 317–41.

Clarke, E.F. (1995). Expression in performance: generativity, perception and semiosis. In J. Rink (Ed.) *The Practice of Performance*. Cambridge: Cambridge University Press, pp. 21–54.

Clarke, E.F. (2002). Understanding the psychology of performance. In J. Rink (Ed.) *Musical Performance. A Guide to Understanding*. Cambridge: Cambridge University Press, pp. 59–72.

Clarke, E.F., Cook, N., Harrison, B., & Thomas, P. (2005). Interpretation and performance in Bryn Harrison's *être-temps*. *Musicae Scientiae*, **9**, 31–74.

Clarke, E.F., Parncutt, R., Sloboda, J.A., & Raekallio, M. (1997). Talking fingers: an interview study of pianists' views on fingering. *Musicae Scientiae*, **1**, 87–109.

Clarke, E.F. & Windsor, W.L. (2000). Real and simulated expression: A listening study. *Music Perception*, **17**, 277–313.

Cook, N. (2007). Performance analysis and Chopin's Mazurkas. *Musicae Scientiae*, **11**, 183–207.

Cook, N. (2009). Squaring the circle: phrase arching in recordings of Chopin's Mazurkas. *Musica Humana*, **1**, 5–28.

Cook, N. (2010). The ghost in the machine: towards a musicology of recordings. *Musicae Scientiae*, **14**, 3–21.

Csikszentmihalyi, M. & Rich, G.J. (1997). Musical improvisation: a systems approach. In K. Sawyer (Ed.) *Creativity in Performance*. Greenwich, CT: Ablex Publishing Corporation, pp. 43–66.

Davidson, J.W. (2001). The role of the body in the production and perception of solo vocal performance: a case study of Annie Lennox. *Musicae Scientiae*, **5**, 235–56.

Davidson, J.W. (2006). 'She's the One': Multiple functions of body movement in a stage performance by Robbie Williams. In A. Gritten & E. King (Eds.) *Music and Gesture*, Aldershot: Ashgate Press, pp. 208–25.

Dowling, W.J. & Harwood, D.L. (1986). *Music Cognition*. New York: Academic Press.

Dunsby, J. (1995). *Performing Music: Shared Concerns*. Oxford: Clarendon Press.

Elsdon, P. (2006). Listening in the gaze: the body in Keith Jarrett's solo piano improvisations. In A. Gritten & E. King (Eds.). *Music and Gesture*. Aldershot: Ashgate Press, pp. 192–207.

Fitch, F.J. & Heyde, N. (2007). 'Recercar'—the collaborative process as invention. *Twentieth-Century Music*, **4**, 71–95.

Gabrielsson, A. (1999). The performance of music. In D. Deutsch (Ed.) *The Psychology of Music*. Second Edition. New York: Academic Press, pp. 501–602.

Godlovitch, S. (1998). *Musical Performance: A Philosophical Study*. London: Routledge.

Green, L. (2001). *How Popular Musicians Learn: A Way Ahead For Music Education*. Aldershot: Ashgate Press.

Hill, P. (2002). From score to sound. In J. Rink (Ed.) *Musical Performance. A Guide to Understanding*. Cambridge: Cambridge University Press, pp. 129–43.

Iyer, V. (2002). Embodied mind, situated cognition, and expressive microtiming in African-American music. *Music Perception*, **19**, 387–414.

Johnson-Laird, P.N. (1988). Freedom and constraint in creativity. In R.J. Sternberg (Ed.) *The Nature of Creativity. Contemporary Psychological Perspectives.* Cambridge: Cambridge University Press, pp. 202–19.

Johnson-Laird, P.N. (2002). How jazz musicians improvise. *Music Perception,* **19**, 415–42.

Juslin, P.N. (2003). Five facets of musical expression: a psychologist's perspective on musical expression. *Psychology of Music,* **31**, 273–302.

Juslin, P.N., Friberg, A., & Bresin, R. (2001–2). Toward a computational model of expression in music performance: the GERM model. *Musicae Scientiae* (Special Issue on Current Trends in the Study of Music and Emotion), 63–122.

Keller, H. (1990). The gramophone record. In R. Matthew-Walker (Ed.) *The Keller Column. Essays by Hans Keller.* London: Alfred Lengnick & Co., pp. 22–5.

Krampe, R.T. & Ericsson, K.A. (1995). Deliberate practice and elite musical performance. In J. Rink (Ed.) *The Practice of Performance.* Cambridge: Cambridge University Press, pp. 84–102.

Leech-Wilkinson, D. (2006). Portamento and musical meaning. *Journal of Musicological Research,* **25**, 233–61.

Leech-Wilkinson, D. (2009). The Changing Sound of Music: Approaches to Studying Recorded Musical Performance. London: CHARM. Available at: http://www.charm.rhul.ac.uk/studies/chapters/intro.html.

Lisboa, T., Williamon, A., Zicari, M., & Eiholzer, H. (2005). Mastery through imitation: A preliminary study. *Musicae Scientiae,* **9**, 75–110.

Mach, E. (1991). *Great contemporary pianists speak for themselves.* New York: Dover. (Originally published in two volumes, 1980 and 1988.)

Monson, I.T. (1996). *Saying Something. Jazz Improvisation and Interaction* Chicago, IL: University of Chicago Press.

Nettl, B. & Russell, M. (Eds.) (1998). *In the Course of Performance. Studies in the World of Musical Improvisation.* Chicago, IL: University of Chicago Press.

Parncutt, R., Sloboda, J.A., Clarke, E.F., Raekallio, M., & Desain, P. (1997). An ergonomic model of keyboard fingering for melodic fragments. *Music Perception,* **14**, 341–82.

Philip, R. (2004). *Performing Music in the Age of Recording.* Hew Haven, CT: Yale University Press.

Pressing, J. (1988). Improvisation: methods and models. In J.A. Sloboda (Ed.) *Generative Processes in Music.* Oxford: Clarendon Press, pp. 129–78.

Pressing, J. (1998). Psychological constraints on improvisational expertise and communication. In B. Nettl & M. Russell (Eds) *In the Course of Performance. Studies in the World of Musical Improvisation.* Chicago, IL: University of Chicago Press, pp. 47–67.

Repp, B.H. (1992). Diversity and commonality in music performance: an analysis of timing microstructure in Schumann's "Träumerei". *Journal of the Acoustical Society of America,* **92**, 2546–68.

Repp, B.H. (1997). The aesthetic quality of a quantitatively average music performance: two preliminary experiments. *Music Perception,* **14**, 419–44.

Repp, B.H. (2000). Pattern typicality and dimensional interactions in pianists' imitation of expressive timing and dynamics. *Music Perception,* **18**, 173–211.

Sawyer, R.K. (Ed.) (1997). *Creativity in Performance.* Greenwich, CT: Ablex Publishing Corporation.

Sawyer, R.K. (2003). *Group Creativity: Music, Theater, Collaboration.* Mahwah, NJ: Lawrence Erlbaum.

Seashore, C.E. (1938). *Psychology of Music.* McGraw-Hill. (Reprinted 1967, New York: Dover Publications).

Shaffer, L.H. (1981). Creativity in Skilled Performance. Paper presented at NATO Conference on Adaptive Control of Ill-Defined Systems. Moretonhampstead, UK.

Simon, H.A. (1969). *The Sciences of the Artificial.* Cambridge, MA: MIT Press.

Sloboda, J.A. (1983). The communication of musical metre in piano performance. *Quarterly Journal of Experimental Psychology,* **35A**, 377–96.

Straus, J.N. (1991). The 'Anxiety of Influence' in twentieth-century music. *The Journal of Musicology*, **9**, 430–47.

Sudnow, D. (2001). *Ways of the Hand: The Organisation of Improvised Conduct. A Rewritten Account.* Cambridge, MA: MIT Press.

Taruskin, R. (1995). *Text and Act: Essays on Music and Performance.* New York: Oxford University Press.

Todd, N.P.M. (1992). The dynamics of dynamics: a model of musical expression. *Journal of the Acoustical Society of America*, **91**(6), 3540–50.

Weisberg, R.W. (1988). Problem solving and creativity. In R.J. Sternberg (Ed.) *The Nature of Creativity. Contemporary Psychological Perspectives.* Cambridge: Cambridge University Press, pp. 148–76.

Witmer, R. (1993). Stability in Blackfoot Songs, 1909–1968. In S. Blum, P.V. Bohlman, & D.M. Neuman (Eds.) *Ethnomusicology and Modern Music History.* Urbana and Chicago, IL: University of Illinois Press, pp. 242–53.

Chapter 3

Imagination feeds memory: Exploring evidence from a musical savant using zygonic theory

Adam Ockelford

This chapter explores the relationship between musical imagination, creativity, and memory through the lens of zygonic theory. Epistemologically, the study is founded on the belief that the performances of a prodigious musical savant, who has the ability to reproduce on the keyboard much of what he can enauralize, offer powerful evidence of his music-cognitive processing, and, arguably, a window onto the 'musical mind' more generally. Over a period of 4 years, the savant, working entirely by ear, made successive attempts to reproduce a specially-composed piece using a 'listen and play' protocol. The musical stimulus was intentionally created to lie beyond the capacity of the savant's working memory, to enable the research team to observe and analyse the strategies that he adopted when the limits of what could he could remember were reached. Informal observation had previously indicated that, when confronted with such situations, he would invariably produce music that 'made sense' and conform broadly to the content and structure of the piece in question, rather in the way that most people intuitively use techniques of 'creative reconstruction' when retelling a story. And, as is the case in oral narrative traditions, changes were made: some elements were dropped, some were added, and others were reconstituted. This chapter considers what processes were used in the creation of new musical material, and investigates the strategies that were adopted to enable what was created (or re-created from elsewhere) to be combined seamlessly with what was remembered from the stimulus. The results lend support to the existence of a previously postulated 'music processing module' ('MPM') in working memory. It is further proposed that, for all of us, the MPM is central to musical imagination and creativity, enabling material to be constructed using remembered fragments and features of pieces as starting points, and underpinning musical improvisation (at any level) within a given style system.

3.1 **Introduction**

The findings reported here are one outcome of the *Fragments of Genius* project, based at Roehampton University, which is investigating the abilities of musical savants: people who have exceptional skill in the context of learning difficulties (Rimland & Fein, 1988; Howe, 1989; Miller, 1989, 1998; Treffert, 2000; Ockelford, 2000, 2007a; Hermelin, 2001). The aim is to glean insights into savants' musical abilities, in particular learning, memory, musical reproduction, and creativity, and to use these findings to generate models of the cognitive processes involved, adopting a fusion of music-psychological and music-theoretical approaches. The underlying methodological assumption is that the music savants produce following exposure to musical input—specifically the manner in which their responses can be considered to derive from or be influenced by the stimuli with which they are presented—provides powerful evidence of the mental processing involved. Hence, while the work belongs to the venerable psychological tradition in which 'overt human behaviour is the central form of data, and explanatory frameworks are developed in primarily intentional and functional terms' (Sloboda, 2005, pp. vi, vii), it is also novel in using music theory to analyse the relationship between stimulus and response, and to use this analysis to formulate hypotheses about cognitive functioning.

One strand of the *Fragments of Genius* research involves Derek Paravicini, a 'prodigious' musical savant (Treffert, 2000; Ockelford, 2007a). Although Derek is blind and has severe learning difficulties, he is a highly accomplished pianist, with a dazzling (if idiosyncratic) pianistic technique. He specializes in early jazz, learning entirely by ear, and has a large repertoire of pieces that are available to him immediately in any key. Musically, he is deft and quick-witted, having the ability to improvise on familiar compositions or newly presented themes in a range of styles.

Derek's musical creativity was not the main focus of the work initially undertaken with him, which examined how he *learns* pieces, and the findings of one study in this area, termed 'listen and play', are reported extensively elsewhere (Ockelford & Pring, 2005; Ockelford, 2007b, 2008a). However, an aspect of the 'listen and play' research design, whereby the piece used as a stimulus was intentionally constructed to be too long and complex for Derek to learn immediately, taken in conjunction with his tendency, as a wholly intuitive performer, to produce material that invariably makes musical sense, meant that his responses had a creative element too. That is, whenever the limitations of Derek's memory were reached, his imagination took over—and it is the story of the intricate relationship between these two cognitive processes that is the principal concern of this chapter.

3.2 **The 'listen and play' study—materials and method**

A piece—*Chromatic Blues*—was especially composed for the 'listen and play' study according to the following criteria:

(a) The style should be broadly familiar to Derek;

(b) There should, in addition, be specific features that were unusual within the style, offering higher degrees of salience;

(c) The structure should be relatively easy to discern, including both the repetition and transformation of key materials, thereby enabling the researchers to gauge the impact of these relationships on the learning process;

(d) The piece should be of sufficient difficulty for Derek to find it challenging though possible to learn after a number of hearings, given its complexity, tempo and length; and

(e) It should be well within his capacity to play, so that technical considerations would not interfere with issues of music-processing.

Created within these constraints, *Chromatic Blues* took the following form (see Figure 3.1).

Statistically, *Chromatic Blues* comprises 312 events that occur within 49 seconds (an average rate of 6.4 events per second). The structure of the piece is as follows (see Figure 3.2).

The 'listen and play' study was conducted over 14 sessions, comprising 26 trials, which occurred over a period of approximately 4 years—see Figure 3.3.

Following the first session, every other followed the same protocol:

(a) Derek played *Chromatic Blues* as well as he could. The results were recorded in digital audio and in MIDI format.

(b) Derek listened to the original recording of *Chromatic Blues.*

Fig. 3.1 The stimulus for the 'listen and play' study—*Chromatic Blues*.

(c) Derek played *Chromatic Blues* again.

(d) Derek listened to the recording of *Chromatic Blues* once more.

In the first session, stage 'a' was omitted.

To give an idea of what Derek's renditions were like, here are transcriptions of four of them (Trials 1, 2, 5, and 7)—see Figures 3.4–3.7.

segment	$A_{1.1}$	$B_{1.1}$	$A_{2.1}$	$B_{2.2}$	C
function	**Theme A** exposition	**Theme B** exposition	**Theme A** reprise	**Theme B** transposed, extended	Coda
tonal regions	$I \rightarrow (V \text{ of } ii)$	$\flat VII \rightarrow V$	$I \rightarrow (V \text{ of } ii)$	$\flat III \rightarrow V$	I
range (beat.bar)	$0.4 - 4.3$	$4.4 - 8.3$	$8.4 - 12.3$	$12.4 - 18.3$	$18.4 - 20.4$
excerpts analysed	Excerpt 1 $0.4 - 2.3$	Excerpt 2 $4.4 - 6.4$	Excerpt 3 $8.4 - 10.3$	Excerpt 4 $12.4 - 14.3$	Excerpt 5 $18.4 - 20.4$

Fig. 3.2 The structure of *Chromatic Blues*.

Session number	Trials	Days since previous session	
1	1	–	
2	2 & 3	2	⎫
3	4 & 5	5	
4	6 & 7	2	≈ 2 weeks
5	8 & 9	7	⎭
6	10 & 11	25	≈ 1 month
7	12 & 13	2	⎫
8	14 & 15	5	
9	16 & 17	2	≈ 2 weeks
10	18	5	⎭
11	19 & 20	96	≈ 3 months, 1 week
12	21 & 22	198	≈ 6 months, 2 weeks
13	23 & 24	342	≈ 1 year
14	25 & 26	777	≈ 2 years
Total	**26**	**1,468**	**≈ 4 years**

Fig. 3.3 The schedule of the 'listen and play' study.

Trial 1

Fig. 3.4 Derek's first rendition of *Chromatic Blues*.

In order to limit the amount of quantitative data to be analysed, only excerpts were transcribed from most of Derek's responses: bars 0.4 to 2.3 ('Excerpt 1'), 4.4 to 6.4 ('Excerpt 2'), 8.4 to 10.3 ('Excerpt 3'), 12.4 to 14.4 ('Excerpt 4'), and 18.3 to 20.4 ('Excerpt 5'). These extracts were chosen since they are representative of *Chromatic Blues*, varying in salience according to their position within the piece (including the beginning and the end), their musical complexity and stylistic conformity. Also, Excerpt 1 was identical to Excerpt 3 in the original, while Excerpt 4 was a transposed and extended version of Excerpt 2, enabling comparisons to be drawn within each rendition.

Fig. 3.5 Derek's second rendition of *Chromatic Blues*.

3.3 **Musicological analysis (i)**

The first stage in analysing the excerpts was to evaluate their strength of derivation from:

(a) Their probable source in the original;

(b) Their probable source from elsewhere in the same rendition; and

Trial 5

Fig. 3.6 Derek's fifth rendition of *Chromatic Blues*.

(c) Their probable source in previous renditions.

The notion of 'strength of derivation' combines the concepts of 'salience' (Ockelford, 2004) and 'zygonicity', which was developed in the context of zygonic theory to give some measure of the perceived similarity of groups of musical events (Ockelford, 2005a). Zygonic theory (Ockelford, 2004, 2005b, 2006b, 2009, 2010) holds that musical coherence is based on a (typically non-conscious) sense of derivation, whereby a given *per*ceived a*spect* or 'perspect' of musical sound (such as a particular pitch, harmony, interonset interval or duration) is felt to imitate another. The cognition of derivation between perspects is predicated on the existence of 'interperspective relationships'—cognitive constructs through which, it is proposed, perspects may be compared. It is hypothesized that these are usually formulated unthinkingly, passing listeners by as a series of qualitative experiences. However, through the metacognition typical of Western music theory, interperspective relationships can be captured conceptually and assigned 'values', some of which are expressible as a difference (for example, melodic intervals such as a major second) or ratio (implicit in the notion that a crotchet is twice as long as a quaver, for instance).

Fig. 3.7 Derek's seventh rendition of *Chromatic Blues*.

Figure 3.8 shows interperspective relationships symbolized by an arrow with the letter 'I' superimposed. Superscripts indicate the perspects concerned, each represented by its initial letter—here 'O' for 'onset' and 'P' for 'pitch'. Relationships can exist on different levels, with 'primary' relationships linking perspects directly, 'secondary' relationships connecting primaries, and 'tertiary' relationships comparing secondaries (Ockelford, 2002). The level of a relationship is indicated by the appropriate subscript (here, 1). The values of relationships are shown near the arrowheads. Note that arrowheads may be open or filled—the former showing a link between *single* values, and the latter indicating a *compound* connection within or between 'constants' (typically, values extended in time)—implying a network of relationships the same.

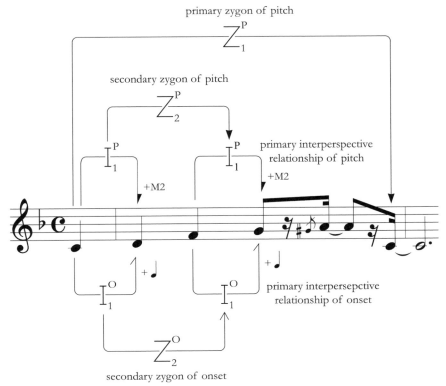

primary zygon of pitch

secondary zygon of pitch

primary interperspective
relationship of pitch

+M2

+M2

+M2

+ ♩

+ ♩

primary interpersepctive
relationship of onset

secondary zygon of onset

Fig. 3.8 Examples of interperspective and zygonic relationships.

Interperspective relationships through which imitation is cognized are deemed to be of a special type, termed 'zygonic' (from the Greek 'zygon' for 'yolk'—a relationship between two things the same; see Ockelford, 1991, pp. 140ff). Zygonic relationships, or 'zygons', are depicted using the letter 'Z'. In Figure 3.8, the primary zygonic relationship of pitch reflects the apparent derivation of the last note of the opening phrase from the first. The secondary zygons of pitch and onset (indicated through the subscripts '2') show imitation at a more abstract (intervallic) level.

Full arrowheads signify relationships between values that are the same. Half arrowheads are indicative of difference, and are used in zygonic contexts to show approximate imitation.

The perceived strength of derivation of one group of sounds from another cannot be gauged simply by comparing their values in a mechanistic way: zygonicity is a subjective measure, in which a number of musical and extra-musical factors are likely to play a part (see Ockelford, 2009). In the case of the 'listen and play' study, it was decided that 'strength of derivation' should be ascertained by considering pitch (as a combination of pitch-class and octave) and rhythm (taking into account durations and interonset intervals), because these were the variables regarded as having the greatest salience in the task that Derek was asked to undertake.

The algorithm used to determine the strength of derivation (known as the 'derivation index') of one excerpt from another is determined as follows:

(a) First, with regard to rhythm . . . align the two series of 'onset + duration' events to ensure maximal congruence. Events from one series that have no equivalent in the other may be discounted in the matching process that follows (stage b), though need to be included as spawning a 'potential rhythmic relationship' (in stage c). If an event is omitted, the following

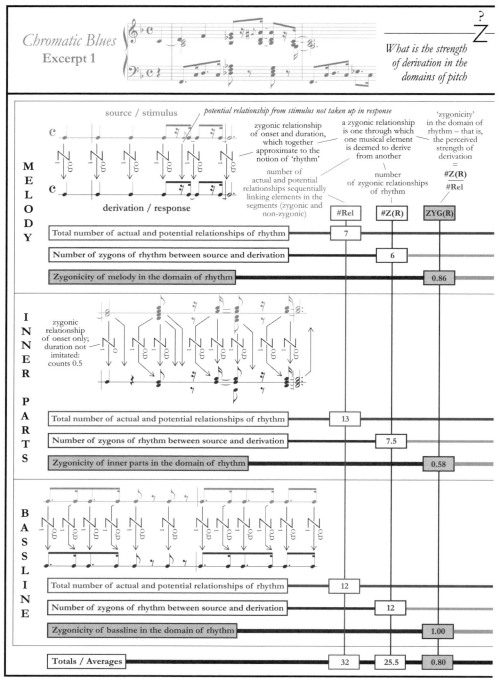

Fig. 3.9 (See also Plate 1) Protocol for calculating strength of derivation of one excerpt from another.

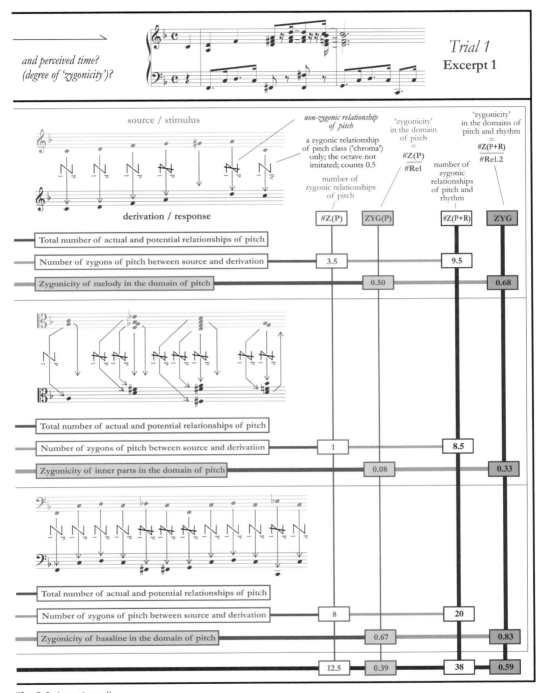

Fig. 3.9 (continued).

onset can be measured from the next most recent event to have occurred, or, in the case of two onsets of more, from a new 'data zero'.

(b) For each match count 1. For an incorrect duration but correct onset, count 0.5. Total score = #Z(R) (that is, the number of zygonic relationships of rhythm).

(c) Let the total number of sequential actual and potential rhythmic relationships between excerpts = #Rel.

(d) The derivation index for rhythm is ZYG(R) (zygonicity of rhythm), where ZYG(R) = #Z(R)/#Rel.

(e) The derivation index for pitch is similarly determined as follows. Align the two series of pitch events to ensure maximal congruence, if necessary omitting those from either series that have no equivalent in the other.

(f) For each match count 1. For an incorrect octave but correct pitch-class, count 0.5. Discounting exact or partial matches involving pitch-class, identify among any remaining pitch events *intervallic* matches. These must be between sequentially adjacent events; the minimum number of events involved in any intervallic match is two. For each event involved in an intervallic match, count 0.5. The total congruence score = #Z(P).

This considers each note of Derek's response separately in relation to pitch and rhythm and to what extent this can be deemed to derive from the corresponding note in the stimulus. This analysis is undertaken separately in relation to three textural strands—the melody (at the top), the inner parts (considered as a single item) and the bass line (at the bottom). This is in accordance with earlier research undertaken with savants into chordal disaggregation (Ockelford, 2008a), and with the findings of Huron and Fantini (1989) and Huron (2001), who give more general empirical evidence of our capacity to process a textural density of three auditory streams. While this method of calculating the derivation index is necessarily limited, the results appear to be intuitively satisfying, and a worked example for Excerpt 1 is shown in Figure 3.9.

The derivation indices for the five excerpts from *Trial 1* appear in Figure 3.10. They show a mean strength of derivation from *Chromatic Blues* of 0.31. But what of the other 69%? Elements that involved the alteration of material, or its addition, can be attributed to the working of Derek's imagination, and regarded as acts of musical creativity.

As the study progressed, Derek's level of creativity declined with the ascent of memory, particularly in the course of Trials 5–9. Indeed, the last eight trials, (which occurred over a period of three and a half years) show a consistently high fidelity to *Chromatic Blues*, with a mean derivation index of 0.84, and standard deviation of only 0.02 (see Figure 3.11). Here, the differences between Derek's renditions and the original are modest, frequently pertaining to matters of harmonic or rhythmic detail in the inner parts. But Trials 1–5, with an average derivation index of only 0.25 and a standard deviation of 0.10, offer a rich source of data relating to Derek's musical imagination, and it is to the outcomes of these early sessions (1–3) that we will devote our attention. Zygonic theory will be used to analyse what occurred in musicological terms. These findings will then be used to construct hypotheses as to the nature of the mental processing underlying Derek's output, focusing particularly on creativity.

3.4 **Musicological analysis (ii)**

Turning first to *Trial 1*, as the analysis in Figure 3.9 indicates, some aspects of bars 1 and 2 can be considered to be derived in a straightforward manner from the opening of *Chromatic Blues*, with events being imitated in sequence. Rhythmically, for example, the origin of 80% of Derek's material is attributable in this way, as opposed to 39% in the domain of pitch; an average of 59%.

	#Rel	#Z(R)	ZYG(R)	#Z(P)	ZYG(P)	#Z(R+P)	ZYG
Excerpt 1							
Melody	7	6	0.86	3.5	0.50	9.5	0.68
Middle Parts	12	12	1.00	8	0.67	20	0.83
Bassline	13	7.5	0.58	1	0.08	8.5	0.33
Total / Average	**32**	**25.5**	**0.80**	**12.5**	**0.39**	**38**	**0.59**
Excerpt 2							
Melody	7	6	0.86	3.5	0.50	9.5	0.68
Middle Parts	14	11	0.79	10	0.71	21	0.75
Bassline	14	6.5	0.46	2	0.14	8.5	0.30
Total / Average	**35**	**23.5**	**0.67**	**15.5**	**0.44**	**39**	**0.56**
Excerpt 3							
Melody	11	4.5	0.41	1	0.09	5.5	0.25
Middle Parts	9	2	0.22	1.5	0.17	3.5	0.19
Bassline	22	3.5	0.16	5	0.23	8.5	0.19
Total / Average	**42**	**10**	**0.24**	**7.5**	**0.18**	**17.5**	**0.21**
Excerpt 4							
Melody	11	4	0.36	1	0.09	5	0.23
Middle Parts	10	2.5	0.25	0	0.00	2.5	0.13
Bassline	20	5.5	0.28	0.5	0.03	6	0.15
Total / Average	**41**	**12**	**0.29**	**1.5**	**0.04**	**13.5**	**0.16**
Excerpt 5							
Melody	17	8	0.47	4	0.24	12	0.35
Middle Parts	7	1	0.14	1	0.14	2	0.14
Bassline	25	0	0.00	2	0.08	2	0.04
Total / Average	**49**	**9**	**0.18**	**7**	**0.14**	**16**	**0.16**
Averages / Totals							
Melody	53	28.5	0.54	13	0.25	41.5	0.39
Middle Parts	52	28.5	0.55	20.5	0.39	49	0.47
Bassline	94	23	0.24	10.5	0.11	33.5	0.18
Total / Average	**199**	**80**	**0.40**	**44**	**0.22**	**124**	**0.31**

Fig. 3.10 Derivation indices for *Trial 1*.

This means, though, that a good deal of what Derek produced (41%) is unaccounted for in direct derivational terms, a tendency that characterizes *Trial 1* as a whole to an even greater extent. Most likely provenances are:

(a) Elsewhere in *Chromatic Blues*;

(b) Other pieces (more or less specifically); or

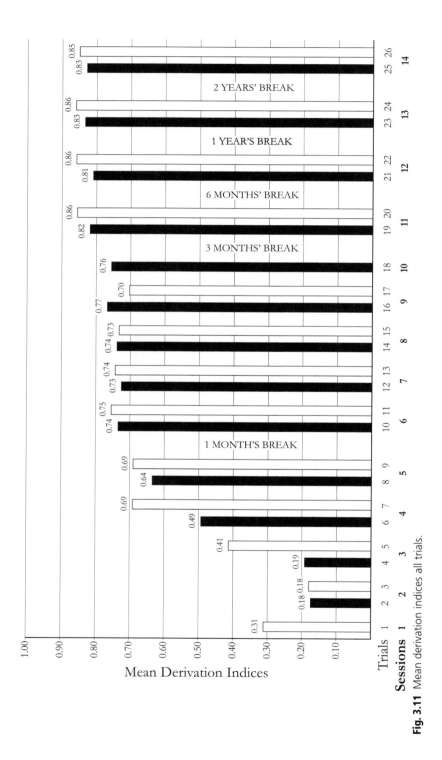

Fig. 3.11 Mean derivation indices all trials.

(c) Other pieces (more generally, as features of style);

(d) or a combination of these.

Moreover, since musical fragments and features can have a multiplicity of roots (see Ockelford, 2005a, p. 114), those features of *Trial 1* that had direct sequential equivalents in *Chromatic Blues* may additionally have been generated elsewhere.

These potential sources will now be explored in relation to the opening bars, by identifying relationships through which fragments of music can reasonably be deemed to have been derived from one another according to their similarity and salience. In undertaking this analysis, a crucial factor is the author's detailed knowledge of Derek's repertoire, which informed the accounts of the possible connections between pieces that follow. Clearly, this approach, which relies on the intuitive judgements of a musician who knows Derek well, potentially suffers from a lack of objectivity. However, it is important to acknowledge the ontological status of the analyses that follow: they are merely indicative of the *type* of musical relationships that are present (and therefore, as a further step to be taken in due course, of the *kind* of cognitive processes that created them). The principles that are illustrated are more important than the verifiability of any particular aspect of them. This is methodologically comparable with the approach adopted, for example, by John Livingston Lowes (1951) in his detailed investigation into the sources of Samuel Taylor Coleridge's imagery; as Margaret Boden points out (2004, p. 127), '"evidence" and "probably" are the best we can expect in investigations of this kind'.

With regard to material that Derek took from elsewhere in *Chromatic Blues*, the first four bars provided a rich vein of ideas for him to tap. He adopted a number of transformational techniques, including reordering material in the domain of pitch. For example, he used the contour of the second phrase at the beginning of his version, which emphasizes the D major harmony that was particularly salient in the original. At the same time, the rhythm of the opening phrase (without the acciaccatura) is used twice, producing a new symmetry. Hence, in creating his version of *Chromatic Blues*, Derek separated elements of pitch and rhythm and re-synthesized them to produce material that was closely related to the original, though distinct from it.

In parallel with these intraopus connections, Derek appears to have borrowed material from other pieces, both generally (through stylistic features) and specifically (from individual works; a technique that is characteristic of traditional jazz—see, for example, Berliner, 1994, pp. 103ff). For example, the first two bars of the bass line seem to derive from a standard bass riff, whose harmonic pattern also constitutes a widely-used Blues 'turnaround'. Moreover, the bass line and harmonies of the first four bars closely resemble those from the chorus of *It's Only a Paper Moon* by Harold Arlen (1933). It is impossible to say to what extent these pieces (with which Derek was very familiar) *actually* played a part in his rendition—though the probability of complex, integrated patterns of pitch and rhythm resembling others by chance is statistically remote.

So what is the status of *Trial 1* in musicological terms? While the analysis above suggests that its opening is made up of motivic shreds and patches taken from other pieces (particularly, of course, *Chromatic Blues*), it is evident from the first four bars alone that Derek had created what can reasonably be regarded as an original piece. The rising pitch contour of the opening gesture, comprising intervals that increase arithmetically by semitones (a major 2nd, minor 3rd, major 3rd and perfect 4th), appears to be shared by only one other piece in the 'standard' Western repertoire (*Indian Love Call* from *Rose Marie* by Rudolf Friml, 1924; see Ockelford, 1999, p. 517 and Narmour, 2000, p. 364), and here the rhythmic framework is quite different. That is, as many composers and improvisers do, Derek used his imagination to forge something new by borrowing, transforming and recombining materials with which he was familiar.

Clearly, the notion of just what constitutes creativity in a musical context is of primary importance here, and at the heart of the matter lies the fact that the degree of novelty required to create an original piece of music is surprisingly small. This is shown by the author's previous analysis of Mozart's piano sonata, K. 333 (Ockelford, 2005a, pp. 35ff), which indicates that the piece shares many common features with other of the composer's piano sonatas, including:

(a) 86% similarity in the distribution of relative durations;

(b) 92% similarity in the distribution of interonset ratios;

(c) 92% similarity in the distribution of pitches;

(d) 77% similarity in the distribution of melodic intervals; and

(e) 89% similarity in the use of harmonies.

Hence, in statistical terms, the sonatas are very closely related. Their originality lies in moment-to-moment features, though even here the differences between pieces need only be slight, as the presumed derivation of the opening of K. 333 from J.C. Bach's keyboard sonata, Op. 5, No. 3 testifies. One can argue that Mozart's creativity lay in his ability to craft something original within such tight stylistic constraints, and that his greatness as a composer lay in his ability to have created something of lasting musical worth within such a narrow bandwidth of freedom.

The claim of lasting musical value is not one that I am seeking to make in relation to Derek's attempt to reproduce *Chromatic Blues*. To assert that Derek is musically 'creative', it is sufficient, according to Boden, to demonstrate that he is capable of producing abstract sonic artefacts that are *'new, surprising and valuable'* (2004, pp. 256ff). This is an argument that at least seems worth making, although, of course, it was not Derek's intention to generate something new. But the fact that his creativity was a by-product of short-term memory limitations does not diminish the value of his musical output to psychomusicological understanding. Indeed, it will be argued that the material produced in *Trial 1* is evidence of an intimate, reciprocal relationship between musical memory and imagination.

3.5 From musicological analysis to psychological hypothesis

To make this case requires us to connect the findings of musicological analysis and hypotheses about cognitive processing. What can the former can tell us about the latter? We should acknowledge the methodological limitations inherent in this approach, in order to contextualize the potential validity of what follows. For example, while we can assume that the music Derek produced bore some relationship to his mental representations of *Chromatic Blues*, we should not presume that the mappings between model and product were exclusive or regular. For instance, it seems likely there were traces of *Chromatic Blues* in Derek's memory that were not realized in sound. Partly, as we have seen, this situation will have arisen due to Derek's (unwitting) aim of producing something that was musically coherent based on imperfect recall. Beyond this, however, it may be that the motor processes required for his reproduction influenced what he played (through the use of kinaesthetic schemata that may have been triggered) and, indeed, that these motor patterns may have been the source of musical material that bore no auditory relationship to anything found in *Chromatic Blues*. Nonetheless, it seems reasonable to assert that the music Derek produced provides sufficient evidence for a number of assumptions to be made about the cognitive processing that lay behind his efforts.

Let us begin by reaffirming the supposition, based on past experience of working with Derek, that, since he was requested to do so, he would have tried to reproduce *Chromatic Blues* as faithfully as he could. This leads to the conclusion that, because he did not reproduce the piece accurately, it must have lain beyond the limitations of his working memory. The transcription of *Trial 1* in Figure 3.4 shows us just what he did remember and, by implication, what was beyond his capacity to recall. Evidently, what Derek did *not* do was to recreate *Chromatic Blues* sequentially up to a certain point and then stop (as a computer buffer of limited size may have done). *Trial 1* was at once an act of creation and reconstruction, in which Derek utilized specific items from the beginning and end of *Chromatic Blues*, higher level structural characteristics of the piece as a whole, and attributes (such as tempo and meter) that were present throughout. That is, he appears to have assembled a 'bundle' of musical fragments and features from the original piece, of varying lengths, types and degrees of abstraction. With regard to the opening bars, for example (see Figure 3.4), a *fragment* that was preserved in terms of both pitch and rhythm was the opening motif in the bass-line. A *feature* that was stored was the F major tonality. Derek's *Chromatic Blues* memory bundle should not be regarded as a collection of auditory traces (and their abstractions) laid down like immovable rock strata. Rather, it seems likely (and the accounts below of further renditions support this) that the system evolved dynamically as *Chromatic Blues* unfolded, and continued to develop during *Trial 1* and in the period that followed.

These observations and hypotheses beg a number of questions. For example, why did some items find their way into Derek's *Chromatic Blues* bundle and others (apparently) not? Under what conditions were the memories of items from other pieces stimulated? How did the process of 'creative reconstruction' work?

First, we consider the selection and storage of items in the bundle and their durability. The fact that *Chromatic Blues* exceeded the capacity of Derek's working memory meant that there would have been competition among its elements, whereby some would be captured and retained while others were not. We may surmise that among the determining factors in this process were:

(a) *Salience*, including the immanent qualities of an item and how these related to the perceived attributes of surrounding stimuli (cf. Ockelford, 2005b, pp. 81ff);

(b) *Structure*, including the degree of internal regularity of an item, which may have permitted its parsimonious encoding (Ockelford, 1999, pp. 115ff);

(c) *Resilience*, the degree to which an item could retain its encoded identity among a welter of interference from rivals; and

(d) *Reinforcement*, brought about through the repetition of items (see Ockelford, 2004).

These factors frequently took effect in combination. Consider, for example, the opening RH rhythmic motif, which Derek reproduced accurately (though without the grace note). We can assume this motif had particular *salience*, being among the first things that Derek heard, and therefore suffering no pre-stimulus interference; *structurally*, it had moderate rhythmic regularity that proved to be *resilient* in the face of competing post-stimulus input; and it was heard twice in the course of *Chromatic Blues*—repetition that offered *reinforcement*.

Second, we consider the manner in which memories of elements from other pieces were stimulated. The indicative analysis shown in Figure 3.12 suggests that memory traces were activated through the perception of new items with which they were similar. These were often incomplete, and comprised either direct perceptual features or the relationships between them. Hence, we can conclude that the 'pattern matching system' used had a broad degree of tolerance—a fuzziness that arguably is a key feature of any act of creativity that operates within a probabilistic style-system. Elements pertained to one piece or more, being in nature either 'veridical' (relating to particular episodes) or 'schematic' (relating to probability matrices in the domains of pitch or perceived time that derived from many such episodes; see Ockelford, 2006a). One memory trace was able to stimulate another (in the case of the bass riff and *Paper Moon*, for example), resulting in only an indirect relationship between features of *Chromatic Blues* and *Trial 1*. For Derek, producing material at an average rate of 7 events per second, the process of stimulation was evidently rapid and unthinking.

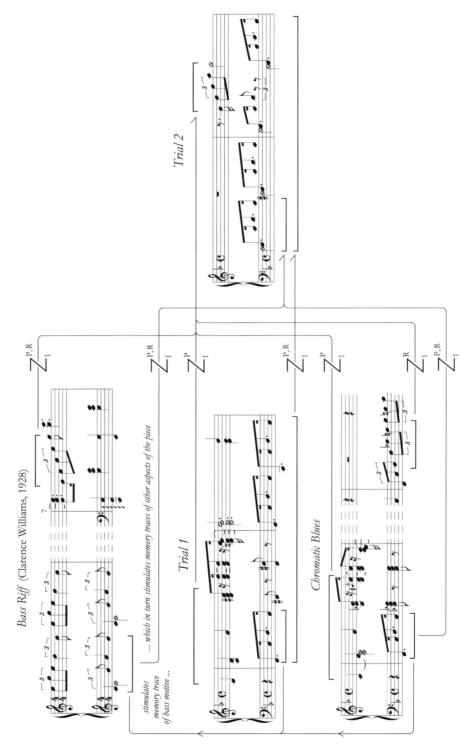

Fig. 3.12 The putative derivation of material in *Trial 2* from a motif in *Organ Grinder Blues*.

Third, how did the process of 'creative reconstruction' work? This can be understood using the analogy of a 'music processing module' ('MPM') in working memory (see Ockelford, 2007b) whose primary input on this occasion was the auditory information deriving from *Chromatic Blues* and whose secondary input comprised Derek's memories of fragments and features from other pieces. The two outputs were the imagined auditory trace of *Trial 1* and the necessary motor instructions to realize this on the keyboard. From *Trial 1*, we can surmise that the two guiding principles under which the MPM operated were to produce something that made 'musical sense', and that resembled, as far as possible, *Chromatic Blues*. In the case of potential incompatibility, the evidence of *Trial 1* indicates that former would take precedence over the latter.

These general principles can facilitate a more detailed understanding of the cognitive processes that we may hypothesize occurred. As we observed, zygonic theory holds that a necessary condition for music to make sense is that every feature of each perceived sonic event should be related to another or others, such that each is felt to derive from or generate at least one other through imitation. Even this is not sufficient to guarantee immediate musical comprehensibility, however. For that, the relationships between simultaneous and successive events in the domains of pitch and perceived time and, in some instances, the relationships between *these* have also to be derived from other pieces and be capable of anticipation according to the probability of their past occurrence (see Huron, 2006; Ockelford, 2008b; Thorpe, Ockelford, & Aksentijevic, in press). The analysis of K. 333 cited above illustrates this principle in action in what can be taken to be a broadly representative piece from the 'common practice' period of Western tonal classical music (Ockelford, 1999, pp. 704 ff): at any point around 40 forms of zygonic organization are likely to be in operation, variously involving pitches, harmonies, and melodic and harmonic intervals; durations and interonset intervals; transition probabilities; tonal and metrical frameworks *et cetera*. It is postulated that this supersaturation with repetition is both typical and necessary for pieces to be readily comprehensible, implying that a similarly high level of 'background' organization was a prerequisite for coherence in whatever music Derek improvised.

This suggests that the proposed MPM, which, it is hypothesized, is central to musical imagination and creativity, must be wired with neural correlates of the fundamental zygonic process of derivation through imitation. Indeed, the universal predisposition of very young infants to replicate and transform their mothers' vocal patterns through the principle of 'communicative musicality' (Malloch & Trevarthen, 2009) suggests that this aspect of brain architecture is fundamental to human musical design. For sure, the surface features (the musical 'content') of what children produce may become increasingly culturally coloured as they move through their early years (for example, the 'potpourri' songs, comprising familiar musical fragments, that children spontaneously create around the age of 3—see Moog (1976); Hargreaves (1985)—will inevitably vary according to their musical exposure), but the basic structural principles underlying the music they create appear to be universal (Sloboda, 1985, pp. 154, 259; Ockelford, under review).

In my view, what makes the *Chromatic Blues* study of more than idiosyncratic interest, is the likelihood that Derek's MPM is, in broad terms, the same as everyone else's. After all, what is *Trial 1*, if not a sophisticated 'potpourri' song for keyboard? And the capacity to take fragments and features from whatever music is in the air and modify them to fit within informal vocal improvisation seems to be commonplace. For example, Figure 3.13 shows a spontaneous attempt to sing *Happy Birthday* by Tom, aged 3 years and 9 months. He overshoots the initial leap, but then modifies the second phrase with the same degree of error in order to maintain the rising pattern of pitch that leads the ear to the highest note of the piece in the third phrase.

So, just as Derek's musical mind must have computed that, by starting the second phrase of his rendition with D5 and C5 (Figure 3.4), he was committing a surface 'error' in order to maintain

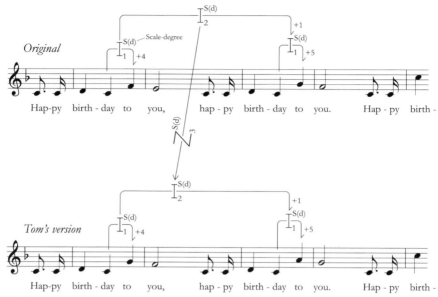

Fig. 3.13 Tom, aged 3 years and 9 months, manipulates familiar musical materials to maintain coherence in a vocal improvisation.

the deeper level connection between the opening phrases, so Tom's hypothesized MPM must similarly have preferred to adhere to structure rather than content in modifying the second phrase of *Happy Birthday* to follow logically from the first. That is, what apparently makes Derek's MPM 'different' is not the essence of what it enables him to do, but the fact that his exceptional perceptual abilities potentially afford him more complex, multidimensional musical material with which to work. Furthermore, his capacity to play the keyboard by ear means that he can realize ideas in sound that are more wide-ranging than the voice alone could manage (which is the only form of external melodic musical expression open to most people), including the production of harmonies. These things mean that Derek's paths of creativity may be more vivid than most of us could tread, but his perambulations in the musical landscape seem to be of a type that we can all make.

What, then, are the characteristics of an MPM? The evidence from the *Chromatic Blues* study suggests that among its key functions are the capacity to:

(a) Acquire and store musical fragments and features in readiness for use—both from immediate perceptual input and from the memory traces that are stimulated by what is heard;

(b) Establish (with varying degrees of sophistication) a multidimensional style system that is congruent with the features of new and remembered elements;

(c) Select fragments or features from the available 'bank' that would fit with each other—albeit with modification—within the evolving style system;

(d) Transform these fragments and features as necessary, through the addition, deletion or modification of material;

(e) Synthesize the selected elements, integrating them 'horizontally' (melodically) and, in the case of some instruments, 'vertically' (harmonically) within the unfolding matrix of pitch and perceived time;

(f) Potentially create new material within the style system, as required, to provide links between given material, to fill potential gaps and to ensure coherence; and

(g) (In the case of skilled improvisers) track and direct the musical narrative simultaneously at different levels to ensure both short- and longer-term coherence.

This synthesis of schematic and veridical forces must all occur in real time as an improvisation proceeds, and, in Derek's case, it appears to have taken place quite unwittingly; he was unable afterwards to reflect upon what he had done (just as most people, unthinkingly whistling or humming a half-remembered tune, could not).

A visual representation and summary of the MPM model operating in relation to *Trial 1* is presented in Figure 3.14. This also shows how the musicological analysis connects to assumptions in the psychological domain.

3.6 **The model in action: sessions 2, 3, and 4**

The second session occurred two days after the first and began with Derek attempting to play *Chromatic Blues*. What sources of material were potentially open to him? As Figure 3.14 shows, there were the two hearings of *Chromatic Blues* from the first session, Derek's own *Trial 1*, and traces of other pieces that either of these may have stimulated. What actually happened in *Trial 2* is shown in Figure 3.5. Derek's version is constructed over a two-bar bass pattern that appears 15 times, followed abruptly by a coda of three bars. Prominence is given to an ascending triplet figure in the RH that appears first in bar 2 and on eight further occasions. *Trial 2* has a derivation index from *Chromatic Blues* (based on the five excerpts shown in Figure 3.2) of only 0.18.

An indicative zygonic analysis of the first two bars illustrates the probable derivation of material from the opening of *Chromatic Blues* and *Trial 1*, as well as possible borrowing from *Organ Grinder Blues*—a piece with which Derek was known to be very familiar. Specifically, it is suggested that the initial bass motif in *Chromatic Blues* (and *Trial 1*) may have stimulated a memory trace of an almost identical figure that occurs at the beginning of *Organ Grinder Blues*, which in turn gave access to other features of the piece, notably an ascending triplet figure in the RH which first occurs in bar 7.

Session 2 continued with Derek hearing *Chromatic Blues* once more, and again being asked to play what he could remember. To the surprise of the research team, Derek came up with something that most closely resembled *Trial 1*, taking the first phrase as a starting point and using it to create a four-section musical structure of the form $A_{1.1} A_{1.2} A_{1.3} A_{1.4}$.

Tonally, this trial has a single substantive modulation, to the subdominant (B♭ major), that occurs in $A_{1.3}$, emulating the same transition found towards the end of the *Trial 1*. There is a hint too in bars 13–14 of the chromatic transition found in bar 8 of *Chromatic Blues*. These features notwithstanding, it is in the initial melodic gesture of each trial that the musical identity of Derek's renditions is principally vested, and the derivation indices between these and the opening of *Chromatic Blues* are captured in Figure 3.16.

These data show that the opening melody of Derek's *Trial 1* is quite closely based on that of *Chromatic Blues* (derivation index 0.68), while the equivalent connection with *Trial 2* is far weaker (0.11). The comparable links between *Trials 1* and *2*, and between *2* and *3* are also tenuous (0.17 and 0.14 respectively). However, the opening of *Trial 3* is, again, quite strongly derived from that of *Chromatic Blues* (0.63), but to an even greater extent from the initial melody of *Trial 1* (0.75). Hence it is reasonable to categorize these renditions as follows (see Figure 3.17), where 'D-V1' and 'D-V2' stand for 'Derek Version 1' and 'Derek Version 2' respectively.

Hence it appeared at this stage that Derek had two discrete bundles associated with *Chromatic Blues* in his long-term memory, either of which could input into his MPM. This impression was reinforced

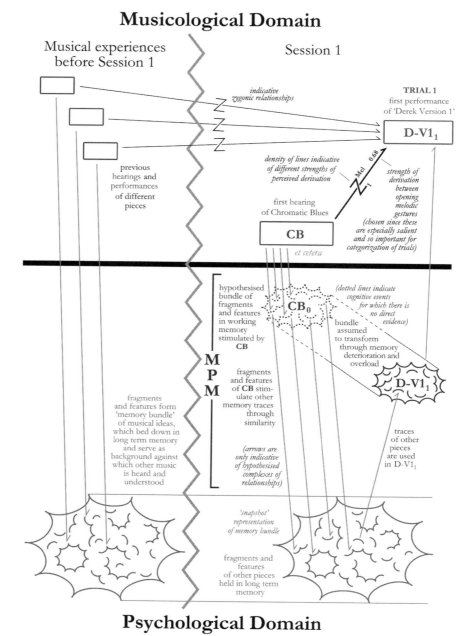

Fig. 3.14 (See also Plate 2) Musicological analysis of Derek's *Trial 1* leads to the psychological hypothesis of a 'music processing module' in working memory.

in Session 3 (5 days later), when Derek opened proceedings with a rendition (*Trial 4*), shown in Figure 3.18, whose opening bars derived from *Trial 2* with a strength of derivation of 0.95.

This derivation index and those shown in Figure 3.17 suggest that, in the first four trials, the two memory bundles D-V1 and D-V2 were more potent forces in Derek's reproductions than the

Trial 3

Fig. 3.15 Derek's third rendition of *Chromatic Blues*.

original *Chromatic Blues*. However, after hearing the piece for the fifth time, something remarkable happened (see Figure 3.6; *Trial 5*). Derek set off as if he were going to produce a further rendition of D-V1, with the melody rising up to D5, but after three beats, there was an audible hesitation in his playing as he switched to a different version of the tune that closely resembled the opening of *Chromatic Blues*, which sinks back to C4. For the first time in this study, it seems that Derek's desire for accurate recall overwhelmed his inclination to produce music that made sense, and we can hypothesize that, as, in his mind, he crossed the threshold between one memory bundle pertaining

Derivation indices	Trial 1	Trial 2	Trial 3
Chromatic Blues	0.68	0.11	0.63
Trial 1	–	0.17	0.75
Trial 2	–	–	0.14

Fig. 3.16 Derivation indices of the opening melody of *Trials 1, 2* and *3* from *Chromatic Blues*, *Trial 1* and *Trial 2*.

Categories	Version 1	Version 2
Trial 1	D-V1$_1$	–
Trial 2	–	D-V2$_1$
Trial 3	D-V1$_2$	–

Fig. 3.17 Derek's two versions of *Chromatic Blues* as they appeared in *Trials 1* and *2*.

to *Chromatic Blues* and another, his MPM was unable to paper over the fault line that opened up in the musical narrative as a result. Ironically, it is this very failure in musical syntax that sheds particular light on Derek's mental processing, enabling us to surmise two features of his cognitive activity in relation to the *Chromatic Blues* study.

First, it appears that that an 'authentic' version of *Chromatic Blues*, 'D-CB', was evolving in Derek's mind prior to *Trial 5*, in which it appeared for the first time, spontaneously, in more or less complete form (derivation index, 0.41). Second, we can surmise that D-V1 continued to exist for some time after *Trial 5* as a discrete memory bundle (though for how long we do not know, since Derek never chose to access it again). But what of D-V2? This next appeared in *Trial 7*, in the second part of Session 4. The preceding *Trial 6* had been straightforward enough: a further version of D-CB with a derivation index of 0.49. (See Figure 3.19.) But *Trial 7* was extraordinary.

Trial 4

Fig. 3.18 Derek's fourth rendition of *Chromatic Blues*.

The initial four bars are virtually identical to those that open *Trial 4*, and so constitute a third appearance of D–V2; yet the music breaks off prematurely and, in retrospect, is heard to function merely as an introduction to what is by far the most accurate rendition of D-CB to date (derivation index 0.69). The effect is of Derek enjoying himself, unable to resist playing with the materials at his disposal, turning them over in his mind, and reconfiguring them in a manner that at once

Fig. 3.19 Derek's sixth rendition of *Chromatic Blues*.

sheds new light on the relationship between D-V2 and *Chromatic Blues*, while creating a convincing new musical entity.

These examples illustrate just how complex learning music can be, and how creativity can serve as the metaphorical glue to bind the imperfect (and sometimes concealed) shards of memory together in ways that make sense. As one with advanced improvisational skills, Derek has evidently taken a further step, and is able to manipulate his 'creative glue' in order to assemble musical fragments in novel ways—purely for his own amusement.

Using these qualitative accounts, and the quantitative data set out in Figure 3.11, it is possible to extend the model shown in Figure 3.14 to illustrate how analyses undertaken in the musicological domain can underpin hypothesis-building in the psychological domain over the first six sessions of the *Chromatic Blues* study (Figure 3.20).

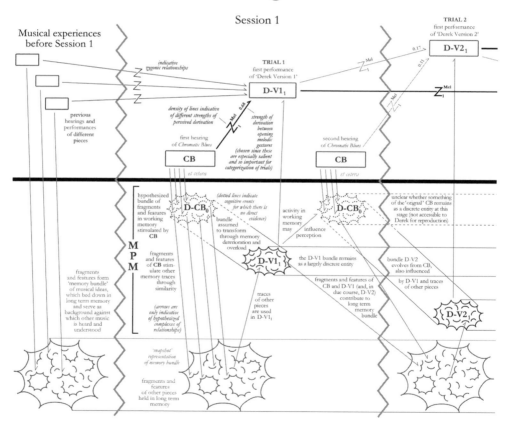

Musicological Domain

Psychological Domain

Fig. 3.20 (See also Plate 3) Sessions 1–6 modelled in the musicological and psychological domains.

Musicological Domain

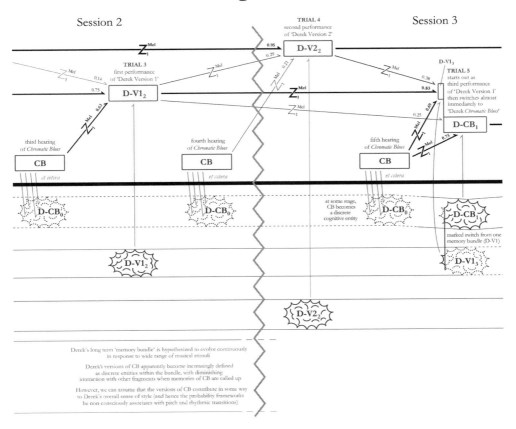

Psychological Domain

Fig. 3.20 (continued).

Musicological Domain

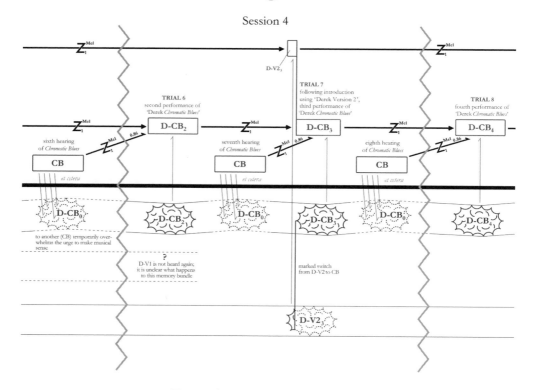

Psychological Domain

Fig. 3.20 (continued).

Musicological Domain

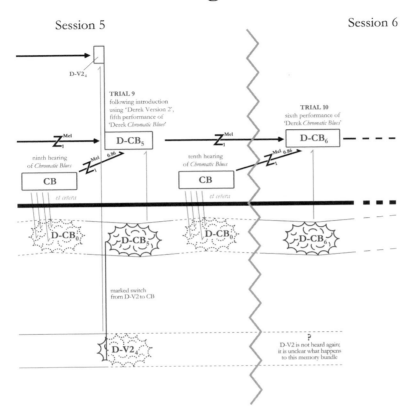

Fig. 3.20 (continued).

3.7 **Conclusion**

This chapter uses a memory study with a musical savant, Derek Paravicini, to show musical imagination in action, and it illustrates in some detail how the acts of musical creation and re-creation can interact. Although Derek has exceptional musical abilities, which, among other things (through his capacity to play by ear), offer researchers a window onto his musical mind, it is posited that the essence of what he does when improvising—taking fragments and features of familiar material and reconstituting them—is typical, as the universal 'pot pourri' songs of young children attest. It is hypothesized that the 'pot pourri' capacity arises from the operation of a 'music processing module' ('MPM') in working memory, with can draw on data from both current perception and long-term memory, and manipulate these to form more or less original combinations and permutations of musical elements within an evolving style system.

Acknowledgements

I would like to offer my sincere thanks to Derek Paravicini, without whose good-natured partici-pation the *Chromatic Blues* study would not have been possible—and to colleagues involved in the *Fragments of Genius* research, particularly Graham Welch, Evangelos Himonides, Linda Pring, and Sally Zimmermann.

References

Berliner, P.F. (1994). *Thinking in Jazz: The Infinite Art of Improvisation*. Chicago, IL: The University of Chicago Press.

Bernstein, L. (1976). *The Unanswered Question*. Cambridge, MA: Harvard University Press.

Boden, M. (2004). *The Creative Mind* (2nd Edition). London: Routledge.

Borthwick, A. (1995). *Music Theory and Analysis: The Limitations of Logic*. New York: Garland Publishing, Inc.

Bregman, A.S. (1990). *Auditory Scene Analysis: The Perceptual Organization of Sound*. Cambridge, MA: MIT Press.

Cone, E.T. (1987). On derivation: syntax and rhetoric. *Music Analysis*, **6**, 237–55.

DeWitt, L.A. & Samuel, A.G. (1990). The role of knowledge-based expectations in music perception: Evidence from musical restoration. *Journal of Experimental Psychology: General*, **119**(2), 123–44.

Fauconnier, G. (1985/94). *Mental Spaces: Aspects of Meaning Construction in Natural Language*. Cambridge: Cambridge University Press.

Hargreaves, D. (1985). *The Developmental Psychology of Music*. Cambridge: Cambridge University Press.

Hermelin, B. (2001). *Bright splinters of the mind: a personal story of research with autistic savants*. London: Jessica Kingsley.

Howe, M. (1989). *Fragments of genius: the strange feats of idiot savants*. London: Routledge.

Huron, D. (2001). Tone and voice: a derivation of the rules of voice-leading from perceptual principles. *Music Perception*, **19**(1), 1–64.

Huron, D. (2006). *Sweet Anticipation: Music and the Psychology of Expectation*. Cambridge, Massachusetts: MIT Press.

Huron, D. and Fantini, D. (1989). The avoidance of inner-voice entries: perceptual evidence and musical practice. *Music Perception*, **7**(1), 43–7.

Krumhansl. C.L. (1990). *Cognitive Foundations of Musical Pitch*, New York: Oxford University Press.

Lakoff, G. (1987). *Women, Fire, and Dangerous Things: What Categories Reveal about the Mind*, Chicago, IL: University of Chicago Press.

Livingstone Lowes, J. (1951). *The road to Xanadu: a study in the ways of the imagination* (2nd Edition). London: Constable.

Miller, L. (1989). *Musical Savants: Exceptional Skill in the Mentally Retarded*. Hillsdale, New Jersey: Lawrence Erlbaum Associates.

Miller, L. (1998). Defining the savant syndrome. *Journal of Developmental and Physical Disabilities*, **10**(1), 73–85.

Moog, H. (1976). *The Musical Experiences of the Pre-School Child* (C. Clarke, Trans.). London: Schott.

Narmour, E. (2000). Music expectations by cognitive rule-mapping. *Music Perception*, **17**(3), 329–98.

Ockelford, A. (1991). The role of repetition in perceived musical structures. In P. Howell, R. West, & I. Cross (Eds.) *Representing Musical Structure*, pp. 129–60. London: Academic Press.

Ockelford, A. (1999). *The Cognition of Order in Music: A Metacognitive Study*. London: Roehampton Institute.

Ockelford, A. (2000). Music in the education of children with severe or profound learning difficulties: Issues in current UK provision, a new conceptual framework, and proposals for research. *Psychology of Music*, **28**(2), 197–217.

Ockelford, A. (2002). The magical number two, plus or minus one: Some limits on our capacity for processing musical information. *Musicæ Scientiæ*, **6**(2), 177–215.

Ockelford, A. (2004). On similarity, derivation and the cognition of musical structure. *Psychology of Music*, **32**(1), 23–74.

Ockelford, A. (2005a). *Repetition in Music: Theoretical and Metatheoretical Perspectives*. Aldershot: Ashgate.

Ockelford, A. (2005b). Relating musical structure and content to aesthetic response: A model and analysis of Beethoven's Piano Sonata Op. 110. *Journal of the Royal Musical Association*, **130**(1), 74–118.

Ockelford, A. (2006a). Implication and expectation in music: a zygonic model. *Psychology of Music*, **34**(1), 81–142.

Ockelford, A. (2006b). Using a music-theoretical approach to interrogate musical development and social interaction. In N. Lerner & J. Straus (Eds.) *Sounding Off: Theorizing Disability in Music*. New York: Routledge, pp. 137–55.

Ockelford, A. (2007a). *In the Key of Genius: The Extraordinary Life of Derek Paravicini*. London: Hutchinson.

Ockelford, A. (2007b). A music module in working memory? Evidence from the performance of a prodigious musical savant. *Musicae Scientiae* [Special issue on performance], 5–36.

Ockelford, A. (2008a). *Music for Children and Young People with Complex Needs*. Oxford: Oxford University Press.

Ockelford, A. (2008b). Review article: D. Huron's Sweet Anticipation: Music and the Psychology of Expectation. *Psychology of Music*, **36**(3), 367–82.

Ockelford, A. (2009). Similarity relations between groups of notes: music-theoretical and music-psychology perspectives. *Musicae Scientiae* [Discussion Forum], **4B**, 47–98.

Ockelford, A. (2010). Zygonic theory: Introduction, scope, prospects. *Zeitschrift der Gesellschaft für Musiktheorie*, **6**(2).

Ockelford, A. (under review). Derivation through imitation: a universal of musical structure? *Musicae Scientiae*.

Ockelford, A. and Pring, L. (2005). Learning and creativity in a prodigious musical savant. *Proceedings of Vision 2005 Conference* (International Congress Series), **1282**, 903–7. London: Elsevier.

Rimland, B. & Fein, D.A. (1988). Special talents of autistic savants. In L.K. Obler and D. Fein (Eds.) *The Exceptional Brain: Neuropsychology of Talent and Special Abilities*. New York: The Guilford Press, pp. 474–92.

Sloboda, J.A. (1985). *The Musical Mind: The Cognitive Psychology of Music*. Oxford: Oxford University Press.

Sloboda, J.A. (2005). *Exploring the Musical Mind: Cognition, Emotion, Ability, Function*. Oxford: Oxford University Press.

Thorpe, M., Ockelford, A., & Aksentijevic, A. (in press). Empirical evidence for the zygonic model of expectation in music. *Psychology of Music*.

Treffert, D.A (2000). *Extraordinary People: understanding Savant syndrome* (2nd Edition), Lincoln, NE: iUniverse.com.

Chapter 4

Creativity as a social fact

Simon Frith

4.1 Introduction

For a sociologist the 'question of creativity' is not why are some people creative and others not, nor how can we develop and encourage creativity in everyone, nor even what sort of mental processes does creativity involve. Rather, sociologists are interested in creativity as a discourse—under what social and cultural circumstances are some human activities considered 'creative'—and an ideology. Why is human creativity considered to be such a good thing? This was certainly not always the case: when it was believed in Europe that only God could create, for humans to claim to be creative was a sign of hubris and self-delusion if not a pact with the devil.

In this essay I will argue that what's at issue in our understanding of creativity is not 'creativity as a special sort of human activity' nor creators as people with 'special powers' (see Nelson, 1999) but creativity as a social fact, a way of thinking about what people do such that certain kinds of activity give people a particular social status. Such a way of thinking is the effect of social institutions. I will illustrate this argument with reference to musical creativity, but the most useful starting point for this discussion is the recent history of 'creativity' as a more general term in political debate.

4.2 The policy of creativity

During the New Labour period in British politics (1997–2010) 'creativity' became a key policy concept. The new government began its regime with a map of Britain's 'creative industries' (DCMS, 1998) and by its demise had in place a 'creative economy programme'. Music-making was clearly a significant creative industry, a major contributor to the creative economy, and it became a task for both local and national policy-makers to ensure that British musical creativity was properly developed. I have discussed the problems of such music policy elsewhere (Frith, Cloonan, & Williamson, 2009); the point I'm making here is that if, from a sociological perspective, 'musical creativity' describes something that has to be understood as an effect of particular social institutions, then policy debates are significant for what they tell us about both discourse, how creativity is talked about, and practice, how some kinds of creativity are encouraged and others not.[1] And from an academic perspective there can be no doubt that the policy concerns and funding of the last decade have had a significant effect on how research questions about musical creativity have been posed and how it has been theorized.

In everyday language, 'creativity' is taken to describe both a particular kind of activity, something to be distinguished from routine rule following, and something done by a particular kind of person, someone who is creative. This approach to creativity is obviously derived from Romantic theory, from early 19th-century accounts of the individual genius/artist/inventor/scientist/author.

[1] This argument derives from my participation in the AHRC funded project, *Creativity: policy and practice. A study of the UK government, the BBC and UK Film Council*, ID No. 112152, directed by Philip Schlesinger.

Individuality is the key term here as it describes both who is creative (particular individuals) and how they are creative (in their very individuality). This is the account of creativity that underpins the copyright system (and the subsequent development of the idea of intellectual property). Creativity is equated with originality, innovation, and difference, but what is also implied here is that creativity is by its nature an autonomous, self-determined activity. Hence the familiar contrasts: art (creativity) vs. commerce; art (creativity) vs. craft; artistic production (creativity) vs. serial production.

I'll return to the way these contrasts are played out in musical institutions, but note here that even in this account of creativity as clearly a good thing there is an underlying drag of something negative: creativity is also associated with irrationality, unpredictability, difficulty (and, indeed, with madness, self-destruction, and, from the composer's own perspective, a necessary 'anxiety'— see Nelson (1999). This becomes a particular issue in the context of collective production (a 'creative' footballer is not 'a team player') and with regard to the commercial exploitation of creative activity (inventors and scientists, like artists and musicians, are seen as unworldly and impractical). And this, in turn, raises two sorts of policy problem. On the one hand, creativity becomes a management issue: how can businesses manage talent, promote, and harness it? These questions were a significant strand of creative industry analysis, focused on such issues as creative labour markets, career/reward structures, and so forth (see Cox, 2006; Pratt & Jeffcut, 2009). On the other hand, creativity became an education issue: how should the state work to produce talent, to uncover and nurture it (see Robinson, 1999; Roberts, 2006). These questions became a significant strand of pedagogical discussion. What is creative education in schools? Are we all creative (as human beings) or just some of us? Is education about drawing out a common human creativity from everyone or about recognizing and supporting a small number of special people? Is creativity in its very irrationality something that cannot be managed or taught?

In addressing these questions, policy-makers introduced a second definitional approach: creativity as a kind of business behaviour. The concern here was the ability of British companies to innovate, to produce and/or market a different sort of product, to spot market gaps and opportunities. In this context 'creativity' is the ability to react to market conditions in certain ways rather than to produce something *ab initio*. Creativity in business terms involves a pragmatic judgement about what works, and one of the peculiarities of the creative industries as they developed in the pre-digital age was that most of what they produced didn't work, that is to say did not produce a return on the investment. Publishing company profits (whether in the book or recording business) derived from the mass success of a small number of products, depended on economies of scale that absorbed the costs of all the products that flopped. This, again, hinted at a negative undertow to the celebration of creative businesses. How could one rationally invest in production processes that mostly involved failure? 'Creative' industries, to put this another way, are those that not only have to manage talent, to embed what's seen as irrational into a rational production process, but also have to manage taste, to embed equally 'irrational' consumer decisions into rational marketing procedures, and 'creativity' thus describes both the (disorganized) expressive practices articulated by Romanticism and the (organized) business practices that turn inventions into assets. (This is the double-sided definition of creativity materialized as 'intellectual property' by copyright law.)

I have begun this essay with a discussion of creative industries policy because policy discussion so clearly illustrates the sociological argument that musical creativity is a social fact, that 'creativity', as both a practice and an idea (a way of understanding that practice), is an effect of social activities and institutions. It may describe something that individuals do, but it is something they do in particular social arrangements of imagination, action, belief, and value. I will turn now to these social arrangements, to what musicians do.

4.3 **Musical practice**

Consider, then, the observations of a couple of music-makers. The first, guitarist Vic Flick, was one of Britain's most successful session musicians following his teenage debut in the 1950s as a member of the Bob Cort Skiffle Group. He worked on a remarkable variety of British pop hits and television theme tunes in the 1960s and 1970s, though I doubt if many of the readers of this article know his name. On the other hand, I'm certain that even fewer readers are unfamiliar with the most famous example of his craft, the guitar line in the James Bond film theme, which first appeared in 1962.

As Gordon Thompson records:

> Vic Flick remembers driving into town for a morning session and hearing a radio interview with George Martin; the host asked the producer, 'Mr Martin, what do you think of session musicians?' Martin responded with something like, 'Oh, session musicians are just robots. They've got no creative ideas. It's the artists, it's the producers, it's the musical directors that are the ones who have the ideas. These session musicians, they're far overrated.' The comments startled Flick and several other musicians who also heard the broadcast. Coincidentally, a few days later, these same musicians had a booking with Martin to record a backing track for singer Cilla Black. Martin arrived with 'the normal thing, like D7///from G///. And all this other business.' Martin turned to the musicians and began a quick routine of the material before recording it: 'OK, well let's run through this, fellows. You know, it's a sort of Harvey thing, so one, two, three, four . . .' Flick describes their musical interpretation of this notation as 'chunk, chunk, chunk, chunk,' which elicited a stunned response from the producer: 'What are you doing? What are you doing?' The musicians deadpanned their reply, 'Well, this is what you've written, George.' As the reality of the situation began to sink in, Martin, stepping back from his music, drew a breath and backpedalled: 'Oh, I see, I didn't really mean what I said, you know.'

(Thompson, 2008, p. 264.)[2]

The second musician is an anonymous player in an unnamed London orchestra, quoted in Stephen Cottrell's excellent ethnography of London's classical music concert life in the 1990s:

> There's always something that the individual can give, without sticking out like a sore thumb, without interfering. I think there is. There should be. Even if it's just somebody thinking 'right this is a nice tune, I'm glad we've got to play it, I'm going to make a really beautiful sound and I'm going to feel that it's all fitting'. You can get that sort of feeling, although you wouldn't ever put it into words particularly. It would just be a thought—'Right here we go'—and you'd do it. There is individuality, and there is room for each individual to have a feeling that he's creating something.

(Cottrell, 2004, p. 106.)

There are a number of assumptions about musical creativity here that I need to unpick. Note, first, that though these musicians occupy quite different music worlds, they both understand music-making as a collective process, involving the collaboration of a number of actors. For Flick, a pop record is created by performers, session musicians, record producers, and sound engineers working together on a song; for the orchestral player, a concert performance is created by the interaction of players, conductor, and composer, organized but not completely determined by the score.

What's also clear, though, is that in these collaborative processes 'creativity' is the term around which collective action is organized *hierarchically* and that it is, consequently, a matter for dispute. 'Creativity' doesn't simply describe a particular kind of individual action but the way in which

---

[2] Thompson's account is drawn from Flick's unpublished 2001 memoir. A full autobiography has since been published (Flick, 2008).

such action is recognized and acknowledged. Vic Flick's anecdote is reflective of a long-held view that what session musicians do is not creative, that they are simply in the studio to provide musical services under someone else's direction. This was my working assumption as a rock critic. In rock ideology a distinction was drawn between the real—creative—musicians, who wrote/interpreted the songs, gave a record its individual/band voice, made a difference, and the session players who were technically far more adept but were, by the same token, characterless. It was not simply that session musicians' contributions to a record were under instruction, but that even when they made their own music it was dully anonymous. When I was working on the record reviews section of *Let It Rock* in the early 1970s 'session musicians' music' was a routine term of abuse, applied to any music that lacked personality. We assumed a negative correlation between musical ability and musical creativity, one reason why progressive rock has always been a problematic form for rock critics.

From this perspective Flick's anecdote is doubly telling. In his story it is record producer, George Martin, who is claiming the creative role; in rock discourse the record producer was regarded with the same disdain that Martin shows here for studio musicians (see Frith, forthcoming). In his famous 1971 *Rolling Stone* interview, for example, John Lennon dismissed George Martin's contribution to the Beatles' work, mentioning him in passing alongside music publisher, Dick James, as just 'one of those people who think they made us. They didn't. I'd like to hear Dick James' music and I'd like to hear George Martin's music, please, just play me some' (Wenner & Levy, 2007: p. 43).

Lennon uses this interview, indeed, to explain himself as a genius ('Yes, if there is such a thing as one, I am one'), someone who, in the Romantic tradition of Beethoven and Van Gogh, was simply 'different':

> A couple of teachers would notice me, encourage me to be something or other, to draw or to paint—express myself. But most of the time they were trying to beat me into being a fuckin' dentist or a teacher. And then the fuckin' fans tried to beat me into being a fuckin' Beatle . . .

> (Wenner & Levy, 2007: p. 61)

The 1960s ideological shift from pop to rock involved a new understanding of musical creativity in the studio (which was why George Martin's role in the Beatles' recording was by 1971 a bone of contention for John Lennon). In the early to mid-1960s it was the performers who were regarded as uncreative, as malleable voices to which producers, writers, arrangers, and engineers gave shape and texture. In this setting, studio musicians could claim their own creative input (as Vic Flick does); they were recognized as innovative in the way they came up with new sounds and experimented with new technology such as guitar amplification (see Thompson, 2008: chapter 6). The emergence of rock reversed this hierarchy, re-sited the source of creativity—which was why session musicians like Jimmy Page and John Paul Jones emerged from the studio to form their own performing bands (Led Zeppelin in their case).

The point here is that this was a matter of changing institutional status rather than the development of a coherent new aesthetic understanding of the actual sources of new musical sounds and ideas. Take the case of an iconic rock track, Lou Reed's 1972 'Walk on the Wild Side' (produced by David Bowie). The most musically distinctive features of this recording are the introductory bass lines (played by Herbie Flowers) and the closing sax solo (played by Ronnie Ross). Flowers was a session musician who had some commercial success (but little critical acclaim) with his own performing groups (Blue Mink, CCS, Sky) but whose professionalism was not treated as the equivalent of Reed/Bowie's artistry; Ronnie Ross was a respected jazz musician whose presence here was quite anonymous. Neither musician was seen by fans or critics then (or by rock historians now) as having had a creative input into this 'Lou Reed song'; their names were not featured in the single's packaging.

'Creativity' here describes economic as well as musical relationships. The assigned authors of a recorded work get performance royalties, the hired-in session musicians get a fee, and in general terms one could say that legal contracts determine who is taken to have a creative input into a piece of music rather than vice versa—if producers and session musicians do share in the royalties as assigned 'authors' their status has been the effect of deals done before the recording process starts. The organization of reward is rarely a result of precisely who did what creatively in the studio. It is not surprising, then, that disputes over who really contributed to a record's sound or success tend to be disputes about money rather than aesthetics:

> The songwriter Stephen Morrissey treated the less well-known members of the pop band The Smiths as 'mere session musicians as readily replaceable as the parts of a lawnmower', the High Court was told yesterday. While he and Johnny Marr, lead guitarist, each took 40 per cent of the profits, Mike Joyce, the drummer, and Andy Rourke, the bass player, got 10 per cent. Joyce, 33, has launched a legal action claiming that his share of past profits could amount to as much as £1 million which he believes he is owed by Morrissey and Marr. He is also claiming a 25 per cent stake in royalties from any future sales instead of the 10 per cent he has been offered.

(*The Times* 3 December 1996.)

In the orchestral musical world the creative hierarchy is organized around the idea of the composer. Music authority is materialized in the score, which provides instructions to the musicians as to what to play. There is still room for interpretation, of course (a written note is not the same thing as produced sound), but for orchestral performances, at least, this is under the secondary authority of the conductor. As Stephen Cottrell suggests, for classical musicians whose training is individualized (they learn musical performance as a form of self-expression), playing in an orchestra is a somewhat contradictory experience. The classical musician I quoted from Cottrell earlier certainly seems slightly desperate in his/her attempt to find a creative role in the orchestral performing process, a recurring issue in Cottrell's chapter on 'orchestras, the self, and creativity' (Henry Kingsbury has described similar issues facing students at a US conservatory—see Kingsbury, 1988). And the relationship between individual musical creativity and institutional authority is clear in the internal organization of orchestras, in the distinction between 'principals' and 'the rank and file'. As Richard Morrison entertainingly describes in his history of the democratic, musician-run London Symphony Orchestra, this is a recurring issue of dispute (Morrison, 2004).

There are two issues here. To begin with, there is the classical world version of the rock distinction between musical creativity and technical facility, between playing the notes as written and somehow going beyond the notes to something more profoundly meaningful. This is certainly as common a distinction in classical as in rock criticism:

> Kissin has been appearing in Britain for 14 years, since he was 17. His platform appearance is now just as mechanical as it has ever been—one suspects the back of his tailcoat hides the hole for a giant wind-up key—and his fingers are as stunningly accurate as ever, but all traces of spontaneity have progressively obliterated . . . On Thursday he rampaged through his programme in a totally repellent and scarcely credible manner . . . the paeans of the final Great Gate of Kiev carried no weight or majesty because all the sound and fury that preceded them had generated no tension or excitement, except of a most primitive kind. . . . [Kissin] started out on his career as a musical talent of apparently limitless potential, and has turned into the biggest pianistic circus act since David Helfgott; there's nothing there but technique.

(Andrew Clements, quoted in Frith, 2004: p.17.)

What matters here, though, is that the meaning of classical music, its creative urgency so to speak, is still referred back to the composer. This is, of course, a legacy of the cult of the composer that developed at the beginning of the 19th century (see De Nora, 1995). But I am less interested here in the way in which the idea of the individual genius was originally constructed than in the resulting account of musical creativity in which one form of musical practice, writing music, is privileged over another form of musical practice, performing it. This argument is made most pithily by the French composer, Pierre Boulez:

> If the player were an inventor of forms or of primary musical material, he would be a composer. If he is not a composer, it is because he is by choice and capacity a performer; so that if you do not provide him with sufficient information to perform a work, what can he do? He can only turn to information that he has already been given on some earlier occasion, in fact to what he has already played. Since he cannot play C, D, E, F, G, A, B, C, he plays something 'modern' that he has played before and attaches precise schemas to the vaguer ones he has been given.

> (Boulez, 1986: p. 461.)

Boulez's concern here (as a conductor as well as a composer) was the ability of orchestral players to work with the 'open' instructions provided by certain sorts of avant-garde score; he believed that the result of such adventurous scoring (using diagrams, for instance) was inevitably musical cliché. These composers were misguided in expecting that classically trained musicians could be creative. On other occasions Boulez made the same point about improvisation more generally:

> Instrumentalists do not possess invention—otherwise they would be composers. There has been a lot of talk of 'improvisation', but even taken in the best sense of the word it cannot replace invention. True invention entails reflections on problems that in principle have never been posed, or at least not in a manner which is readily apparent, and reflection upon the act of creation implies an obstacle to be overcome. Instrumentalists are not superhuman, and their response to the problem of invention is normally to manipulate what is stored in the memory. They recall what has already been played, in order to manipulate and transform it.

> (Quoted in Durant, 1989: p. 277.)

The suggestion seems to be that whatever skills *any* musical performers may have, they can't invent; they can't produce something that is really new.

What can we take from these arguments about musical creativity? The most obvious point is that music-making is necessarily a collective process but within that process some actors have more creative roles than others. Music, to put this another way, is the result of institutional practices in which some musicians have authority over others; creativity is both an explanation and justification of that authority. Musical authority may also be invested in the person who initiates a project, whether writing the music or hiring the musicians. Music producers in a broad sense of the term—the people who put a performance together, record companies and music publishers, orchestral managers, and concert promoters—may also therefore claim creative status (as in recent record industry campaigns for copyright extension).

The paradox of this situation is that such institutionalized social status is explained in terms of innovation (producing sounds or patterns of sounds that have never been heard before, which are not formulaic or plagiarized) and individuality (the expression of a unique person or group). And the analytic problem is that the sources of such originality, whether they're being identified by Pierre Boulez or by a rock critic, are not as easy to read off a musical performance as Romantic ideology (and copyright law) suggest.

4.4 **Creative freedom/creative necessity**

So far I have been assuming that the idea of creativity articulated by Romanticism and the legal-economic account of creativity articulated by the concept of intellectual property are different aspects of the same underlying cultural forces: they mutually make sense of creative practice in a market economy (see Marshall, 2005). But it is also clear that they involve contradictory accounts of what one might call creative *motivation*. On the one hand, we have the suggestion that artists only create if they have a financial incentive to do so, a recurring theme in debates about copyright law and the effects of digital 'piracy': as record executive, John Kennedy, told the *Financial Times* in January 2003, 'Ultimately, if creators do not get paid, you will not get music' (Kawohl and Kretschmer, 2004: p.44).[3] On the other hand, we have the argument that true artistic creativity (as against craft skill) is autonomous, self-directed; it is not—and cannot be—the result of production for an employer or a market, of demands that restrict the free individual expression of the artistic imagination.

Sociologically speaking, both these positions seem wrong. It is not at all clear that musicians wouldn't create if they didn't have a financial incentive to do so. Music-making is something that happens in all societies, whether or not they have a market system and, indeed, in Western musical history before and after the development of market capitalism. There's an empirical question here: as Ronan Deazley has observed:

> The simple fact remains that there is a dearth of evidence as to the relationship between copyright and creativity, or as to the actual value of the copyright regime in contributing to the success of the creative economy. No definitive evidence exists, for example, to indicate that stronger intellectual property regimes result in greater levels of creativity or innovation.

(Deazley, 2010: p. 22.)

Andreas Rahmatian agrees, though also arguing that while,

> . . . there will probably never be incontrovertible evidence in one way or another on this issue . . . one may permit the author, as a musicologist originally from Vienna, to make the following slightly unkind observation: in the history of classical music, before the advent of copyright, England was one of the absolutely leading countries in music in the 16th and 17th centuries, and for that period it still is: it was the time of Taverner, Tallis, Byrd, Bull, Gibbons, Dowland, Campion, Lawes, Blow, Purcell and others. In the 18th century, English music already relied much on emigrants, especially Handel and J. Chr. Bach, J. S. Bach's youngest son. The latter's royal privilege was the basis for the case of *Bach v. Longman*, which established that musical compositions are also protected by the Statute of Anne. From then onwards, the United Kingdom certainly had the finest copyright protection of music in Europe in the late 18th and much of the 19th century, but the English contribution to the music of especially the 19th, but also the 20th century, is insignificant compared with the European continent: J. S. and C. P. E. Bach, Scarlatti, Gluck, Haydn, Mozart, Beethoven, and the later French, Italian, Austrian, German and Russian composers defined the centres of music in the last 250 years. One could presume that the impact of copyright on the promotion of creativity in music is very limited indeed.

(Rahmatian, 2007: p. 354.)

But there's a conceptual question here too: what is being defined as 'creativity'? Is folk music uncreative because it is unauthored? Can art really be distinguished from the craft on which it is based? From a sociological perspective it is not clear what 'autonomous' musical creativity actually describes. Music is a social activity, made for an audience and to serve social purposes (whether for the church or the entertainment industry, for the academy or a private social function). Financial incentive certainly is relevant to many music-making activities but it is not thereby *necessary* for creativity. One problem of the financial incentive argument is the distinction between

[3] Kennedy, now chairman of IFPI, the international record industry lobbying body, was then working for Universal.

'amateur' and 'professional' musicians in this context. Professionals are those who make their living from music and it is often assumed (at least by professional musicians!) that only they can be truly creative—amateurs, hobbyists, are simply 'playing at' creativity. On the other hand, one could argue that amateurs are more purely creative precisely because their work is entirely uncorrupted by financial concerns, though this is equally unconvincing (for a discussion of the issues here see Prior, 2010).

Rather than assume that musical artists are either rational investors in their own talent or irrationally oblivious to economic forces it would seem more fruitful to explore the idea that as a social fact musical creativity is defined by the tension *between* artistic freedom and material necessity (or, to use the terms in which the debate is usually expressed, between art and commerce). Consider the self-reflection of a third music-maker, Mike Jones, songwriter (for the band Latin Quarter) turned academic (at the Institute for Popular Music Studies, Liverpool University):

> As a songwriter, my immediate response to the representation of writing as tainted because a composer expects to make money from his or her compositions is to ask how else, by what other means, a composer is meant to live? Popular music, all music, is made at least in part for economic reward (in whatever form) so that the composer might continue to write, to *work*. There is no contingent reason why this reality should impact on what is composed and neither should the need for income be the primary, determining dimension of what work is done. Writers write for a range of reasons, my point is that all of these reasons need to be factored in to an explanation of why certain aesthetic choices are made. For example, a songwriter can be argued to write for her or himself (or, more accurately, for an idealised version of the self), to a set of internally established and internally audited criteria of what makes 'good' music. Further, the composer writes for an intended and imagined audience—to be assembled and affected, positively, at some point in the future– where this is not the same as anticipating success in the marketplace.
>
> Consider 'Model Son' in this light: the potential number of audiences for the song is not exhausted by the foregoing list. In writing it the meaning I encoded was intended for an audience of exactly one—my father. I did not write the song to make a profit, I wrote to express myself; but I wrote also in the hope that, by expressing myself, I would make a living. In undertaking this work I was neither cynically manipulative nor cynically manipulated; rather I wrote what I could out of my internalisation of the terms and conditions of my role as a songwriter as they were configured at the time of writing. Consequently, I was neither entirely an agent, but neither was I entirely without agency. I was free to choose to write about my father, to demolish him for public consumption, but I made sure that I did it in three verses, a chorus and a bridge—and all in four minutes and six seconds. Agency is what gives the cultural commodity its life—the need to encode meaning for a living audience—but audiences can only be reached (constituted and consolidated) through the marketplace. In this way, I expressed my agency through conceding it to a complex of constraining forces and by working hard, with and through them, in a consistent and self-regulated way, to deliver a combination of words and music that we all recognise as a song but which was effective because it was, also, and fundamentally, a musical product.[4]

I want to draw two arguments out of Jones's suggestions here: one simple, one more complex. The simple point is that musical creativity doesn't just happen. It describes a practice, a set of decisions and choices, with a purpose: to produce a work or event that also exists for a reason. To make music is to be both free—musicians choose what to play—and constrained. The musical work or performance has to be recognized as such both institutionally (by the various social actors who make it materially possible—players, publishers, promoters, audiences, etc.) and discursively

---

[4] Taken from a private email correspondence. For an extended discussion of song writing as 'creative work' and the example of 'Model Son' see Jones (2005).

(in these social actors' shared understanding of what music is for—entertainment, uplift, profit, comfort, or whatever). The most influential theorists for the contemporary sociology of music, Howard S. Becker and Pierre Bourdieu, who both drew on the sociological ideas of Emile Durkheim, are thus concerned to explain how cultural 'worlds' or 'fields' work as organizing social structures *within* which individual creativity becomes possible (see Becker, 1982; Bourdieu, 1993) and, for an overview of this approach to the sociology of music, Martin (2006). Musical creativity thus means different things in different musical settings. To return to an earlier argument, classical composers are not more inventive than improvising jazz performers; rather, the musicians in these different musical worlds 'create' according to different principles of collaboration, originality, expressiveness, and so on. That said, there are aspects of musical creativity that cross different musical worlds.

To begin with, most musicians understand creativity as a form of problem solving. What needs to be done is materially or institutionally determined (by this project, this commission, this group of musicians, this job); the individuality or originality of the work describes how the problem is solved. In the early days of rock, for example, bands were told by their managers that, for their artistic credibility (and profit) they should write their own songs. As John Lennon remembers:

> We [Lennon and McCartney] always wrote separately, but we wrote together because we enjoyed it a lot sometimes, and also because they would say, well, you're going to make an album, get together and knock off a few songs, just like a job. . . . In a rock band you have to make singles; you have to keep writing them . . .

(Wenner & Levy, 2007: pp. 41, 55.)

Lennon was obviously uneasy at describing his creative practice as a job; he wanted to distinguish between his 'professional songwriter's attitude to writing pop songs' (as in the Beatles) and his self-expressive post-Beatles' approach: 'It's me! And nobody else. That's why I like it. It's real, that's all.' (ibid pp. 33, 55). But this familiar distinction between music-making as art and craft does not stand up to close scrutiny: both before and after the Beatles Lennon was writing songs for audiences that had to reached in specific ways—on record, on the radio, through the star system. The distinction is equally problematic in the classical world. In what sense, for example, are the commissioned, collaborative film scores by Prokofiev and Philip Glass or ballet scores of Stravinsky and Aaron Copland less creative than their 'pure' music?

A second aspect of creativity that seems shared across musical worlds is the process of pragmatic experimentation, trying things out, whether on paper (in a score) or as sound (with musical instruments). Creativity here describes not something 'inside' the creator, being given expression in material form, but the working on material until it takes on its final conceptual shape (and following this process, grasping creativity as technique, is an important aspect of audience pleasure and appreciation). Such shaping of material is what we mean by expression: what is expressed is what exists at the end of the process not what was there at the beginning. And this leads me to my more complex point. I am not convinced by the suggestion that all humans are creative even if their creativity takes on different forms in different social circumstances. The argument should be, rather, that all humans are musical but only in certain social circumstances is their musical activity expected to be 'creative', to involve innovative individuality. Creativity, to put this another way, is only possible in societies in which there is a particular sense of selfhood and the valorization of the new. Creative freedom is not something that people naturally aspire to, as part of their humanity. It is, rather, a Durkheimian social fact: in capitalist societies musicians are *constrained* to be creative, both culturally and as a matter of political economy. Musical activity, which is by its nature social and collaborative, is thus redefined as something driven by individual expressive needs.

4.5 **Conclusion**

In 2008, newspapers began to report that the money made from live music in Britain was greater than the money made from the sale of all available kinds of recording, including downloads (see, for example, J. Prynn, 'Festival explosion turns live music into £1.9bn big business', *Evening Standard*, 10 September 2008). This was widely understood as an effect of digital technology on record sales and as therefore reflecting a music business 'crisis' (and another justification for the record industry's campaign for copyright reform). But even in the 50-year era of record company dominance (it seems likely that the income from record sales only began to exceed that from live performance in the 1950s) the vast majority of musicians made their living from providing a service rather than from owning an asset.[5] What interests me about this situation is that the dominant understandings of musical creativity, whether developed in the terms of political economy or Romantic ideology are clearly misleading. On the one hand, the copyright system and music policy initiatives combine to suggest that what most matters culturally is the production of new assets (individually authored works; intellectual property). On the other hand, Romantic accounts of the troubled genius and the mystery of individual talent continue to underpin critical judgement in both academic and popular music worlds. In these circumstances the concept of 'musical creativity' is more of a hindrance than a help in understanding music-making practice, hence my conclusion: we should cease to use the term altogether, even if it remains the sociologist's task to explain why the concept matters so much.

------

[5] I base these assertions on work in progress. See http://www.gla.ac.uk/departments/livemusicproject.

References

Becker, H.S. (1982). *Art Worlds.* Berkeley, CA: University of California Press.

Boulez, P. (1986). *Orientations. Collected Writings.* Cambridge, MA: Harvard University Press.

Bourdieu, P. (1993). *The Field of Cultural Production*, Cambridge: Polity Press.

Cottrell, S. (2004). *Professional Music-Making in London.* Aldershot: Ashgate.

Cox, G. (2006). *Review of Creativity in Business: Building on the UK's Strengths.* London: HM Treasury.

DCMS (1998). *Creative Industries Mapping Document.* London: Department of Culture, Media and Sport.

Deazley, R. (2010). Taking Forward the Gowers Review of Intellectual Property: Second Stage Consultation on Copyright Exceptions. *Intellectual Property Foresight Forum*, March, 14–15, 30–1.

De Nora, T. (1995). *Beethoven and the Construction of Genius. Musical Politics in Vienna 1792–1803.* Berkeley, CA: University of California Press.

Durant, A. (1989). Improvisation in the political economy of music. in C. Norris (Ed.) *Music and the Politics of Culture.* London: Lawrence and Wishart, pp. 252–82.

Flick, V. (2008). *Guitarman.* Duncan, OK: Bearmanor Media.

Frith, S. (2004). What is bad music? In C.J. Washburne & M. Derno (Eds.) *Bad Music.* New York and London: Routledge, pp. 15–36.

Frith, S. (forthcoming). The place of the producer in the discourse of rock. In S. Zagorski-Thomas & S. Frith (Eds.) *The Art of Record Production.* Aldershot: Ashgate.

Frith, S., Cloonan, M., & Williamson, J. (2009). On music as a creative industry. In A.C. Pratt & P. Jeffcut (Eds.) *Creativity, innovation and the cultural economy.* London: Routledge, pp. 74–89.

Frith, S. & Marshall, L. (Eds.) (2004). *Music and Copyright.* Edinburgh: Edinburgh University Press.

Jones, M. (2005). Writing for your supper—creative work and the contexts of popular songwriting. In J. Williamson (Ed.) *Words and Music.* Liverpool: Liverpool University Press, pp. 219–50.

Kingsbury, H. (1988). *Music, Talent and Performance: A Conservatory Cultural System.* Philadelphia, PA: Temple University Press.

Kretschmer, M. & Kawohl, F. (2004). The history and philosophy of copyright. In S. Frith & L. Marshall (Eds.) *Music and Copyright.* Edinburgh: Edinburgh University Press, pp. 21–53.

Marshall, L. (2005). *Bootlegging: Romanticism and Copyright in the Music Industry.* London: Sage.

Martin, P.J. (2006). *Music and the Sociological Gaze.* Manchester: Manchester University Press.

Morrison, R. (2004). *Orchestra: The LSO—a Century of Triumph and Turbulence.* London: Faber.

Nelson, P. (1999). *Creativity and Embodied Rationalisation.* Proceedings of the Society for the Study of Artificial Intelligence and Simulation of Behaviour Edinburgh: AISB, 1–5.

Pratt, A.C. & Jeffcut, P. (2009). *Creativity, Innovation and the Cultural Economy.* London: Routledge.

Prior, N. (2010). The rise of the new amateurs: popular music, digital technology and the fate of cultural production. In John R. Hall, Laura Grindstaff & Ming-cheng Lo (Eds.) *Handbook of Cultural Sociology.* London: Routledge.

Rahmatian, A. (2007). The Gowers Review on copyright term extension. *European Intellectual Property Review,* **29**(9), 353–6.

Roberts, P. (2006). *Nurturing Creativity in Young People. A Report to Government to Inform Future Policy.* London: Department of Culture Media and Sport.

Robinson, K. (1999). *All Our Futures. Creativity, Culture and Education.* London: Department of Education and Enterprise.

Thompson, G. (2008). *Please Please Me. Sixties British Pop, Inside Out.* Oxford: Oxford University Press.

Wenner, J.S. & Levy, J. (2007). *The Rolling Stone Interviews.* New York: Black Bay Books.

Chapter 5

Musical creativity as social agency: Composer Paul Hindemith

Ian Sutherland with Tia DeNora

5.1 Introduction

This chapter explores musical creativity as social agency. Using the activity of German composer Paul Hindemith (1895–1963) during periods of significant situational incongruity—World War I (WWI), Weimar Republic (*c.*1919–1933), early Third Reich—this research explores how music is mobilized for social agency in self situation and social action. Central to this is a consideration of how music is involved in 'connecting personal and social change' (Giddens, 1991: p. 33). Key concepts developed include: music as a resource for reflexive thinking to situate the self (particularly through counterfactual reasoning); music used to colonize the future; music as a resource and tool for managing and acting situational incongruity. Back-grounding this work is a survey of research on music (and arts/culture in general) during the Weimar Republic (Bullivant, 1977; Gilliam, 1994; Hinton, 1989; Peukert, 1991; Sachs, 1970) and the Third Reich (Etlin, 2002; Kater, 1997, 2000; Kater & Riethmüller, 2003; Levi, 1991, 1994; Meyer, 1993; Mosse, 2003; Petropoulos, 1999; Prieberg, 1982; Steinweis, 1993; Wulf, 1963), historical source documents from the period, and significantly Hindemith's own correspondence (as edited and translated by Geoffrey Skelton—see Hindemith, 1995) in which the composer thinks through his compositional processes and products to appropriate (and act within) wider social contexts.

Following a brief outline of Hindemith's professional activities relating to the sociopolitical contexts discussed in this chapter, letters from Hindemith's early professional years are considered to explicate how music is a resource for self-reflexivity. Here Hindemith's activities show how music is used to understand his own immediate art world and to appropriate wider social, cultural, and political conditions. Hindemith's engagement with *Gebrauchsmusik* (utility music) is then considered to argue that musical creativity is not just involved in self-reflexivity but is also mobilized as a change agent within incongruous situations. Having introduced these key concepts, the focus shifts to an exploration of Hindemith's social agency as constitutive of, and constituted by, musical creativity in the Third Reich.

Approaching the Third Reich, Nazi cultural ideologues continued a process of destroying modernist movements in the arts that had begun to mature during the Weimar Republic. In this onslaught Hindemith was identified, along with others such as Schoenberg, as an emblem of musical 'degeneracy' and became increasingly vilified by the press and members of the new Nazi cultural and political bureaucracy. Within Nazi Germany many historic and contemporary cultural producers and products were attacked, banned, destroyed, etc. on the grounds that they contravened the ideology of National Socialism and the 'true spirit' of German art and culture. These projects (which were often contradictory) involved denigrating cultural producers and products in attempts to frame Nazism's abhorrent political, racial and xenophobic ideologies. Eventually this climate led to Hindemith's emigration. However, for several years he attempted to remain active in the Third Reich. By exploring an operatic project he abandoned—*Etienne und Luise*—and one he completed—*Mathis der Maler* (1936)—consideration is given to how Hindemith used his creativity reflexively to appropriate the incongruence of the changing sociocultural-political climate and to act to re-align himself within this incongruity.

5.2 Paul Hindemith: career amid turbulent times

Paul Hindemith was a prodigious composer, noted violinist, violist, theorist (see Hindemith *The Craft of Musical Composition*, 1941, 1942), pedagogue, conductor, and musical thinker (see *A Composer's World*, 1952). Hindemith was a musical polymath with seemingly endless reserves of energy expended in an impressive array of musical activities throughout his career. Born in Hanau (near Frankfurt am Main), Germany, 16 November 1895, Hindemith lived through turbulent times experiencing WWI; the social, political, and economic complexities of Germany's failed Weimar Republic; and the ascension of Nazism. His early career (including studies at the Frankfurt Hochschule für Musik, founding member of the Amar Quartet, member of the programme committee of the *Donaueschingen* festival, professor of composition at the Berlin Hochschule für Musik, etc.) established him as one of Germany's foremost musicians, and a central actor in 1920s modernist circles. However, the social, cultural, and political upheavals which saw the establishment of Hitler's Reich (1933) challenged this status and eventually resulted in the composer's emigration. When Hindemith fled Nazi Germany (for Switzerland in 1938) and in 1940 joined the mass exodus of Germany's cultural producers to the USA (see Brinkmann and Wolff, 1999) he became professor of composition at Yale and Charles Eliot Norton Lecturer at Harvard. After World War II (WWII) Hindemith and his wife Gertrude retired to Switzerland. Though he never moved back to his native Germany, he died unexpectedly while visiting Frankfurt on 28 December, 1963 (Briner, 1971; Kemp, 1970a; Noss, 1989; Skelton, 1975/1977; Streller, 1985).

Throughout his career Hindemith used his musical activities to map and structure his social situation and inform his social agency. Within this chapter snapshots of this activity are taken from approximately 1917–1938. Beginning with early correspondence this work demonstrates how Hindemith developed an aesthetic agency to understand himself as an artist within wider social and political conditions at the end of WWI and to map those conditions for himself to plot future action. Considering Hindemith's later involvement with *Gebrauchsmusik*, the concept of music as a change agent is introduced to explore how Hindemith composed in the belief that musical products were tools for social action. Bringing these concepts together affords an investigation of how Hindemith dealt with the difficulties he faced in relation to Nazi cultural invective by social mapping activities through, somewhat ironically, an opera he never composed *Etienne und Luise* and one he did composer *Mathis der Maler*. Based on references to *Etienne und Luise* in Hindemith's letters it is argued that through its planning Hindemith developed understandings of what it meant to be a cultural producer in the early Third Reich and then used those understandings to compose *Mathis der Maler* as a tool for social action to rehabilitate his professional status.

5.3 Music as resource for self-reflexivity: situating the self

Hindemith's earliest career was coterminous with significant social, cultural and political change: WWI, birth of the Weimar Republic, and burgeoning forms of modernism. Coming to a head at the end of WWI and exploding throughout post-war Europe (especially in Germany's Weimar Republic) it was a time in which artists from various disciplines created and explored a vast array of new means and media for cultural expression; it was the 'classical era of modernity'

(Peukert, 1991, p. 164). Hindemith's correspondence from this period indicates an individual struggling to manage and act within sociocultural contexts brimming with unfamiliarity: liberalizing social attitudes, new political structures and movements, a wealth of new aesthetic considerations and artistic 'isms'. Part of Hindemith's struggle emanated from a desire to experiment musically, to join with others in challenging traditionally held aesthetic beliefs on form, tonality, timbre, etc. Through his musical creativity he experienced the changing times—the rapid growth of modernism—in which he felt stifled by his traditional conservatory education. In a letter to his friend Emmy Ronnefeldt from June 1917 he exclaimed with surprise the reaction of his teacher (Bernhard Sekles) to his new works in progress:

> I showed him my songs with orchestra (2 are finished) and do you know what worried him? That the songs are too free in form and bear no resemblance to 'usual' Lieder! And these are our modern musicians! Something written from the depths of one's soul, with not a thought in hell of Lieder forms or such-like rubbish, something a little bit unusual—this makes them nervous! I want to write music, not song and sonata forms!! [...] I am not bound to keep on thinking in these old patterns! And I have the feeling that it's precisely my new songs that, through their lack of restraint, are more genuine than Sekles's Temperamente, for instance. With all respect to my teacher! I'm coming more and more to the conclusion that it's high time I shook myself free of all this conservatory nonsense. What ties me to these people, after all? Tradition, and nothing else [...] And all I want to do is make music. I don't care a damn if people like it or not—as long as it's genuine and true.
>
> (Hindemith, 1995: pp. 11–12.)

This letter is a tempestuous outburst of a young composer situating himself, producing and re-producing his social situations, and not least his musical self as self within and through them. It opens up the idea of thinking through musical creativity—mobilizing music as a reflexive resource—to construct understandings of the individual agent within wider contexts. Here Hindemith reflects through his creative projects to understand the art world in which he is active. While Hindemith uses language to do this it is his musical creativity that serves as the catalyst for this reflexive thinking. By reflecting through compositional projects and their initial reception by his teacher, Hindemith develops understandings of his art world—what is old, what is new and how he situates himself within these concepts. Hindemith understands the old as 'tradition' emblematized by patterns of 'song and sonata forms'; musical forms serve as icons for old versus new. Hindemith is not interested in being tied to tradition; he wants to shake himself 'free of all this conservatory nonsense'. Here Hindemith is planning for the future plotting musically how he will act, what Giddens would call the 'colonisation of the future' (1991: p. 111).

In a later letter to the same Emmy Ronnefeldt (November 1917) Hindemith further indicates how music is used to understand the future as a 'counterfactual possibility' (Giddens, 1991: p. 111). Writing about a new 'degenerate' piano work he recounts:

> I have finished the third of the piano pieces. It sounds terribly degenerate, has neither time signature nor key, nor harmony in the accepted sense. If I go on working in this genre, I shall end up one day in a territory beyond good & evil.
>
> (Hindemith, 1995: p. 16.)

Hindemith uses music as a counterfactual conditional (see below in relation to *Etienne und Luise*), that *if* he continues creating in this way he will end up in some indefinable future territory which lies beyond the traditional definitions of good and bad (perhaps a territory in which musical production and consumption transcends concepts of good and bad). While Hindemith is ultimately vague about what this future landscape might be, thinking about music is used to imagine it in the present; creativity is mediating the future. Returning to the earlier June letter (above) it appears that Hindemith understands and plans his future through musical activity, a path of writing 'music not song and sonata forms!!' His development can be understood as unbounded by 'thinking in these old patterns'. This phrase is particularly important and shows how the composer *thinks* through musical parameters. Put another way, musical constructs (forms, meters, harmonies, etc.) are used to structure and elaborate thinking. Of course, there is a wider system at play here, it is not just the composer thinking about his creative processes and products in isolation. Hindemith also employs written language to express these sentiments and his friend Emmy Ronnefeldt as a sounding board. However, ultimately it is musical creativity that is catalyst and medium for this activity.

As Hindemith thinks through music, constructing his present situation within a musical art world he is engaging in activity 'usual' for a composer, reflexive work to understand the immediate conditions in which he is operative as an artist. As Becker would say the art world frames the composer's aesthetic choices (1982: p. 201). However, other parts of Hindemith's correspondence show that this reflexivity with and through musical creativity is not just mobilized to appropriate and understand the context of the immediate art world, it extends beyond to wider and more pervasive issues bringing into Hindemith's reflexive process elements of sociocultural and political change. In a letter from November 1918 he shows how musical creativity is mobilized for appropriating the political crisis in Germany at the end of WWI, most especially the tensions surrounding socialist political thought.

> Of course I know nothing at all about politics, and for that reason have in the past few days become a keen social democrat. When the war ends, I too shall be inscribing Liberté, Egalité, Fraternité on my banner. Infected by the democratic bacillus, I shall from now on compose only bright red pieces. I have now completed a sonatina (yet again), the first movement of which is so left-wing and radiates so much bolshevism that on listening to it the whole right-wing loudly cries 'shame' and rises from its seats, but that does not worry the composer Hindemith.

(Hindemith, 1995: p. 23.)

Written to his friends Fried and Emma Lübbecke while Hindemith was in active military service at the end of WWI, this letter documents the composer's thinking about the changing world around him. It is an artefact of appropriating contemporary, salient political concepts, particularly the rise of socialism (the Russian Bolshevik revolution occurred in 1917 and the socialist movement was becoming increasingly influential in German politics—see Fowkes, 1984; Hertzman, 1963; Hunt, 1969; Kolb, 2005). Though Hindemith claims he is unfamiliar with politics he goes on to show how he is coming to 'know' politics through something familiar— music. Claiming he has become a 'keen social democrat' Hindemith goes on to say he will compose 'bright red pieces'—socialist inspired music. While discerning what 'socialist' music might be proves tenuous at best, Hindemith is using music as an emblem of what socialism is for him; he understands socialism through music. Hindemith then comments on a sonatina he has completed claiming the first movement is 'left-wing' and bolshevistic. To know politics Hindemith appropriates key political concepts through musical creativity by mapping political concepts with his musical creations, mapping the unfamiliar with the familiar. Hindemith is mobilizing music to connect sociopolitical changes to his personal self by thinking through music, developing understandings about politics by relating salient political concepts to familiar musical concepts. This is done by reflecting on the conditions of reception of his music such as the anticipation of the political right decrying his sonatina. Hindemith comes to his own understandings of politics by anticipating political reactions to the artefacts of his musical creativity. For Hindemith, politics is not just getting into music, music is constitutive of and is constituting politics for him.

5.4 *Gebrauchsmusik*: from reflexive resource to music as change agent

Musical creativity is mobilized by Hindemith to construct his situation within his immediate art world and to develop understandings of wider more pervasive social, cultural, and political conditions. As Hindemith engaged in this activity he used music to draw the future into the present and to make plans for action; he planned the colonization of the future through future musical activity. In the following sections attention is focused on the use of music not just for reflexive thinking but for acting, how Hindemith followed a belief in engineering music as a change agent. Within the Weimar Republic (*c*.1919–1933) this type of musical agency came to be focused on *Gebrauchsmusik* (literally 'utility music' or 'useful music') while in the Third Reich Hindemith came to understand and design music as a more personal change agent, one to rehabilitate his own reputation—his public self.

During the Weimar Republic Hindemith maintained a reflexive stance regarding music and wider sociocultural trends and changes relating these conditions back to his musical creativity. An important development along these lines was his recognition of, and desire to remedy, a widening gap between contemporary art music (what in German was referred to as *Ernstmusik*—'serious' music—as opposed to *Unterhaltungsmusik*—'popular' music) and the general population. Hindemith sought to bridge this gap through musical agency, to compose new music (and support it through festivals, radio broadcasts, etc.) accessible to a wider population to draw them into contemporary musical trends. This type of music came to be known as *Gebrauchsmusik* referring to music created for specific social purposes (i.e. not 'art for art's sake') and often tailored for amateurs rather than professional musicians (Hinton, 1989). Perceiving a gap between contemporary music and the public Hindemith and others (e.g. Kurt Weill and Hans Eisler) engaged in 'an attempt to re-establish contact between the composer and his public' (Muser, 1944: p. 33).

As a concept, *Gebrauchsmusik* emphasizes music *for* everyday life; widely accessible music tailored for amateur performers and less experienced art music consumers. In the latter half of the Weimar Republic, Hindemith focused much of his creative energies on pedagogical and 'social' music for amateurs and children. These compositions included, among others, the children-oriented works *Tuttifänchten* (1922), *Wir bauen eine Stadt* (1930), and the series of instrumental and choral works encompassing *Plöner Musiktag* (1932). In these works his musical creativity was focused on a project of connecting himself and his music to broad social strata. Hindemith did this by writing music accessible to amateur musicians and the musically 'untrained'. Such works made minimal musicianship demands on the performers. Vocal music was based on uncompli-cated step-wise melodies with narrow ranges. Instrumental works required elementary technical skill employing, for example, only the open strings of a violin. This was not musical creativity understood as leading to immutable masterworks, but rather as musical creativity leading to par-ticipatory works for the social masses where 'quality' was a secondary consideration (Hinton, 1989). Though not explicitly described as such by Hindemith, this was a political project with social democratic overtones, that '. . . the Weimar avant garde sought to employ the major inno-vations of 20th century music to elicit forms of emancipatory consciousness and action in the broadest strata of the population' (Zabel, 1992: p. 621).

What is being developed here is a view of the mobilization of musical creativity for social agency. As illustrated above, musical creativity was a resource for reflexive thinking about self-situation in art world and political contexts. With *Gebrauchsmusik* one can see musical creativity mobilized not just to understand how 'elements of an art world come to bear' (Becker, 1982, p. 201) on cultural producers, but to make a critical turn in understanding how musical creativity is involved with social agency, that it comprises a tool for social action. Hindemith engaged in writing

Gebrauchsmusik to involve a wide putative other in contemporary music. He did not write works such as *Plöner Musiktag* as immutable masterworks for reverential consumption in sacralized concert halls, he wrote them to encourage the involvement of school children, amateur musicians, and so on, in contemporary music. Hindemith's activity in another period of sociopolitical change, the early years of the Third Reich warrants exploration to chart how these reflexive projects and music as social action are combined to manage and act the social world around him, particularly situational incongruities.

5.5 **Musical creativity in action:** *Etienne und Luise* **and** *Mathis der Maler*

As early as 1925 Hindemith was acutely aware of controversy surrounding modernist musical projects. In a letter to his publishers (Ludwig and Willy Strecker) at the Schott und Söhne firm he declared 'I am firmly convinced that a big battle over new music will start in the next few years— the signs are already there' (Hindemith, 1995: p. 38). Hindemith was referring to tensions between traditional musical values based in practices and patterns of the past (familiar forms, functional tonality, triadic harmony, etc.) and more experimental modernist trends (atonality, serialism, microtonal works, etc.). Though Hindemith could not have foreseen the future decimation of modernism in Germany with the rise of National Socialism and its abhorrent anti-Semitic, anti-modernist, xenophobic policies, what he was experiencing in 1925 was a stage of a right-wing, conservative backlash against various elements of liberalism, including musical modernism, within the Weimar Republic (for examples of right-wing attacks of musical modernism during the Weimar Republic see Sachs, 1970).

  As Hindemith approached the Third Reich he found himself in a climate of increasing hostility from the Nazi ideological press; he was particularly vilified by the Nazi cultural ideologue Alfred Rosenberg and his *Kampfbund für deutsche Kultur*[1] and conservative music critic Fritz Stege[2] (Kater, 1997, 2000; Levi, 1994). Within the conservative musical press of the Third Reich Hindemith was declared, along with others, a member of the degenerate, Bolshevistic Weimar Republic, a period understood as anathema to the National Socialist desire to 'rehabilitate' German cultural life. This propaganda emanated from the highest levels of Nazi bureaucracy notably touted by Joseph Goebbels: 'During the last fourteen years art has lived behind the times.'[3] (Bullerian, 1933: p. 656 quoting Joseph Goebbels). Article's such as Herzog's '*Was ist deutsche Musik?: Erkenntnisse und Folgerungen*' (What is a German music?: Thoughts and Conclusions) attempted to define 'German' music and frame the history of European music in accordance with Nazi racial and xenophobic ideology claiming that which is undesirable in music '*ist nicht Musik aus unserer Zeit*' ('is not music of our time') (Bullerian, 1933: p. 805).

---

[1] The KfdK was founded in February of 1929 by Alfred Rosenberg, a committed National Socialist party member and editor of the party organ *Völkische Beobachter*, to combat modernism and secure 'proper' German artistic values, based as much upon anti-modernist aesthetics as Nazi racial thought (Levi, 1994; Kater, 1997).

[2] As early as August 1930 Fritz Stege wrote the following regarding Hindemith's children's opera *Wir bauen eine Stadt*: 'This experimentation with the hearts of children is the more reprehensible as the trouble of rehearsing is not compensated by the musical substance... Can one imagine a cruder artistic swindle than these children's choruses, which cannot be performed by children?' (quoted from Strobel, 1961: p. 44).

[3] 'In den letzten vierzehn Jahren hat die Kunst hinter der Zeit gelebt.' (Bullerian, *Die Musik* **25**(9), 1933, p. 656).

Hindemith's reception within this climate was becoming increasingly tenuous eventually leading to *der Fall Hindemith* (the Hindemith affair). On 25 November 1934 the celebrated conductor Wilhelm Furtwängler published an article in support of Hindemith that incensed Nazi cultural ideologues already unsympathetic to his cause (Kater, 1997, 2000). In December 1934 an article in *Die Musik* again derided Hindemith's Weimar connections, specifically his association with the *Donaueschingen* festival of contemporary music which was described as a forum for raving experimenters, creators of music devoid of *Volk* connections (Majewski, 1934). On 6 December Goebbels verbally attacked Hindemith himself when addressing an assembly of the *Reichsmusikkammer* (the National Socialist bureaucratic entity designed to oversee the music profession). In a widely reported address Goebbels referred to Hindemith's opera *Neues vom Tage* (1929) as indecent, common and kitschy, 'surrounded with the discordant dissonances of a musical nonsense'[4] (Goebbels, 1935, p. 247). 'Finding the deck stacked against him' Hindemith took leave of his position at the Berlin *Hochschule für Musik* and over the next years, during which he witnessed the 'gradual eclipse of his music' in Germany, he spent increasing amounts of time outside the Reich (Kater, 1997: p. 181) before emigrating to the USA in 1940.

Before, during and after the scandal surrounding *der Fall Hindemith* the composer believed in his creative efforts as change agents for his reception within Germany, that they would rehabilitate his reputation. Throughout this period musical creativity served as primary resource for this agency and tool for his actions. The following exploration of this activity begins with Hindemith's counterfactual reasoning round an opera he never completed *Etienne und Luise* before considering an opera he did complete *Mathis der Maler*, an opera intended to act for him to re-align his public reputation.

5.5.1 *Etienne und Luise*

As the Weimar Republic was falling and the Third Reich rising Hindemith was thinking about a new operatic project. In letters to his publishers between November 1932 and March 1933 Hindemith was discussing an opera based on a novel by Ernst Penzoldt, *Etienne und Luise*, a love affair between a French prisoner of war and a German girl during WWI.[5] 'Penzoldt is the new favourite, having already sent me a detailed outline of a theme we had previously discussed [*Etienne und Luise*]... Something will certainly come of it.' (Hindemith, 1995: p. 64). In a subsequent letter dated 20 January, 1933 (10 days before Hitler became Chancellor) Hindemith is still enthusiastic, planning to complete the majority of work on the opera during the following summer with a planned completion and premiere date sometime in winter 1933/1934 (Hindemith, 1995: p. 65). Then, in March, after the establishment of the Third Reich, Hindemith re-evaluates the project and his previous assertions in a letter to his publishers:

> Esteemed brothers [Ludwig and Willy Strecker], you haven't heard from me for some time. Here there was such chaos that writing was unthinkable... The prospects for the next few weeks are of course bad, and I also have no idea to what extent it might be possible to bring out new operas in the autumn. To judge by what I now see happening in musical and theatrical affairs, I believe all the key jobs will shortly be occupied by rigidly national types. Next spring, by which time the first difficulties should have been got over, the prospects for an opera by Penzoldt and myself should be very good. Maybe not

---

4 '...sich dagegen aufzulehnen, mit den misstönenden Dissonanzen einer musikalischen Nichtskönnerei umgeben.' (Goebbels, 1935, p.247)

5 For full discussion on the development of this incomplete opera see: Nickel, G. & Schaal, S. (1999). 'Die Dokumente zu einem gescheiterten opernplan von Paul Hindemith und Ernst Penzoldt'. *Hindemith Jahrbuch*, **28**, 88–253.

this particular text, though one cannot really know. Anyway, caution is called for, and I am in favour of shelving this particular subject for a while and seeking another. I have been looking around and have come on something that is innocuous and interesting and will this year and next be particularly topical.[6]

(Hindemith, 1995: pp. 66–7.)

There are several key points in this correspondence that indicate the centrality of musical creativity to Hindemith's agency during the Third Reich. He is readily aware of the chaos and uncertainty for himself caused by the sociopolitical developments in Germany at that time. Hindemith is engaging reflexively by surveying the wider sociocultural context of early Nazi Germany recognizing shifts in the musical field that 'all the key jobs' are going to 'national types'. Hindemith appropriates these changes by how they will affect his own creative projects. He is all but certain the time is not right for an opera about a French prisoner of war and a German girl. Though not abandoning the idea of working with Penzoldt, Hindemith decides this project needs to be shelved and replaced by something 'innocuous' and 'interesting' something that will connect with the nationalist topics and social conservativism salient at the time. Hindemith comes to connect social changes to himself by considering how they affect his musical creativity. This is done by making the creative project, in this case a nascent *Etienne und Luise*, a counterfactual conditional asking himself 'If I compose this what will happen?'. His answer to this question was that should he and Penzoldt continue to work on *Etienne und Luise* their creative actions would prove problematic within the cultural climate of National Socialist Germany. He comes to understand this avenue of creativity—as if he can see the opera in completion—as dangerous, that when premiered in the public domain its reception would lead to negative consequences. This counterfactual reasoning indicates even an incomplete musical project affords social reflexivity. By using a formed concept of *Etienne und Luise* Hindemith constructs and interprets his social situation through anticipating conditions of reception. This directly informed his agency—do not proceed with this musical project, it is too professionally dangerous.

Though Hindemith abandoned *Etienne und Luise* he soon took up another operatic project, one that he did see to completion—*Mathis der Maler* (Mathis the Painter). The subject matter of *Etienne und Luise* was deemed too controversial by Hindemith in the context of the Third Reich but *Mathis der Maler*, based in the historic years of the Peasant's Revolt during the Lutheran Reformation, was deemed 'particularly topical'. By June 1933, barely three months after he decided to abandon *Etienne und Luise*, he wrote to his publishers saying 'I am very busily occupied with Grünewald' (Hindemith, 1995: p. 70) referring to the painter Mathis Grünewald the central character of this opera for which Hindemith not only composed the music but also researched and wrote the libretto. Hindemith's correspondence regarding this opera shows how musical creativity and its resulting products are imbued with agential power by a composer who believes in his work as a change agent, as an actant in its own right.

5.5.2 *Mathis der Maler* (1936)

With *Etienne und Luise* Hindemith used a creative project as a counterfactual conditional to understand sociocultural conditions of reception to inform his agency. Surrounding *Mathis der Maler* he mobilized his creativity to influence those conditions positively. While he did so with the opera itself he first prepared the waters of reception with other works. In a letter dated 23 November, 1933 (a year before *der Fall*) Hindemith wrote to his publisher: 'I have been thinking whether it might not be advisable to put down a little bait beforehand [before *Mathis der Maler*] . . . Might it not be

---

6 Hindemith was planning a comic opera on the construction of the railroad. These plans never came to fruition either. The operatic work he did begin in 1933 was *Mathis der Maler*, discussed in depth below.

to our advantage to put a volume of cadenzas to all the (7 or 8) Mozart concertos on the violinists' Christmas table?' (Hindemith, 1995: p. 73). Hindemith, who had already composed these cadenzas, goes on to argue such works are easy to market, are cheap and quick to produce. Mozart's works are central to the canon of Western art music; Hindemith is keen to appropriate this to bring his name in association with Mozart's directly into the homes of Germany's musicians during the Christmas season. Hindemith's idea is to prepare the ground for *Mathis der Maler* by combining his compositional output with Mozart's, by writing for a widely consumed and appreciated genre, to put into the public domain accessible, useful musical material. At the request of the conductor Furtwängler Hindemith also composed a symphony based on the themes for the incomplete opera. Premiered by the Berlin Philharmonic in March 1934 the work was a success acclaimed by public and critics alike (Paulding, 1976), laying the groundwork for the opera. Though the symphony was successful it did not deter attacks from right-wing critics like Paul Zschorlich who within a week of the *Mathis* symphony's premiere again berated Hindemith's 'degenerate' connections particularly his association with the International Society for Contemporary Music (ISCM) an organization Zschorlich considered 'dominated by Jews, musical Bolshevism, dilettantishness and atonality . . .' (Strobel, 1961: p. 50). Though Hindemith was somewhat successful in mobilizing music, through the *Mathis* symphony, to positively present himself it was not enough to overcome the negative views of him amongst Nazi cultural ideologues.

It was not only the press or even Goebbels with whom Hindemith had to contend. As described by Hindemith one of the central sources of his problems was Hitler himself who in 1929 was offended by Hindemith's opera *Neues vom Tage* (Hindemith, 1995, p. 85). To overcome this significant obstacle the composer again indicates his belief in music as a change agent. To resolve this incongruity Hindemith reasons that exposure to another work will reverse the damage believing if Hitler could attend a performance of his *Plöner Musiktag* all will be set right:

> I shall write him [Hitler] a letter in which I shall ask him to convince himself to the contrary and perhaps visit us some time here in the school, where I would have the cantata from Plöner Musiktag performed for him—no one has ever been able to resist that.
>
> (Letter to Willy Strecker 18 November, 1934; Hindemith, 1995: p. 85.)

Though no such letter was ever sent, nor is there evidence Hitler attended a performance of the work, the centrality of music to Hindemith's thinking and acting is evident. Hindemith believes his creative work has agential power that framed positively it can be a resource for changing his social situation.

During this period of considerable unrest and incongruity Hindemith maintains a focus on his musical creativity as constitutive of and constituting his agency. Hindemith structures and believes his musical works as forces in their own right that they will achieve his public rehabilitation. With the Mozart cadenzas and the *Mathis* symphony he attempted to influence the reception of the forthcoming *Mathis der Maler*. Likewise Hindemith felt the controversy with Hitler could be overcome with a letter and the *Führer's* exposure to his *Plöner Musiktag*. Throughout Hindemith's correspondence during this time it is the composition of the opera *Mathis der Maler* that garners consistent attention becoming for Hindemith a salvationary activity. Before *der Fall* Hindemith's letters to Willy Strecker at the Schott publishing firm highlight Hindemith's investment of agency in the developing opera:

> 'Mathis' will do a lot to put things right.
>
> (Letter to Willy Strecker 29 July 1934; Hindemith, 1995: p. 80.)

> Once the opera [*Mathis der Maler*] is firmly on its feet, all the better armed will we be to set out.
>
> (Letter to Willy Strecker 28 October, 1934; Hindemith, 1995: p. 82.)

Hindemith refers to the work anthropomorphically as 'Mathis' and giving it 'feet'. He believes, perhaps naively, that the work *itself* will help 'put things right' and will be an armament for their cause when it is completed. Hindemith felt the opera itself would save his reputation and put him back in good standing. The work is more than a future theatrical production; it is for Hindemith a central agent, understood personally, in a struggle between artist and totalitarian state.

Hindemith's letters following *der Fall*, though descriptive of the very negative position of the composer within Nazi Germany, still maintain a hopeful focus on *Mathis*. To his colleague Johannes Schüler he wrote: 'In place of lengthy thanks, I am sending you herewith a provisional print of the Mathis text. But please keep it strictly to yourself, nothing may be said about it in public for the present' (Hindemith, 1995: pp. 86–7). Hindemith is still occupied with the opera but cautious about discussing it publicly. In a letter to his colleague Darius Milhaud (March 1935) Hindemith promised to send the score of the *Mathis* symphony and the text for the progressing opera (Hindemith, 1995: pp. 87–8). While the composer senses it unwise to disseminate the work publicly he is still promoting *Mathis der Maler* amongst trusted colleagues. In March 1935 to Willy Strecker he wrote: 'The fifth scene is finished . . . Reading through the score and playing the piano arrangement I have assured myself that "Mathis" is a respectable piece' (Hindemith, 1995: p. 87). Even into 1936 Hindemith is still hopeful about the opera. Writing again to Willy Strecker (8 July, 1936) Hindemith refers to a possible commission for the *Luftwaffe* but orients this commission to *Mathis der Maler*: 'The Luftwaffe is standing firm on its decision. I want to give them something really good—I am certain that this piece, if reasonably successful, will mean "Mathis" in the State Opera' (Hindemith, 1995: pp. 93–4). As with the Mozart cadenzas and the *Mathis* symphony Hindemith is harnessing his musical creativity for specific purposes, he plans his compositional activity as social action that if he writes 'something really good' for the *Luftwaffe* it will garner permission for the premiere of *Mathis der Maler* in Germany.

While Hindemith is keen to influence the conditions of reception for *Mathis der Maler* with other works, his work on the opera was designed to score a critical success by drawing upon 'safe' musical and dramatic material. Hindemith abandoned *Etienne und Luise* because he felt the thematic content too risqué in light of National Socialism. *Mathis der Maler* however draws upon 'historic halcyon years for the Nazis' (Kater, 2000: p. 33) the period of the Lutheran Reformation. The opera revolves around the struggles of the painter Mathis Grünewald (creator of the famous Isenheim altarpiece) during the Lutheran reformation era Peasant Revolt of 1524–1525 (see appendix for plot synopsis). While a number of scholars (Briner, 1971: p. 140; Kemp 1970a: pp. 30–1, 1970b: p. 271; Skelton 1975: p. 112) have concluded the plot and libretto (which Hindemith researched and authored himself) are reflections of the composer's own experiences during a time of social, political, and cultural upheaval, Hindemith never made such connections. Given that Hindemith believed so strongly in this opera's ability to work for him, to revive his professional situation in Nazi Germany, it would seem unlikely that he would create a work that foregrounds his own feelings of struggle. Rather, the assertion here is that Hindemith was writing an opera he anticipated, through the same counterfactual reasoning that led to the abandonment of *Etienne und Luise*, would be received positively. It has an interesting German nationalist oriented plot with recognizable historic references (Mathis Grünewald, Cardinal Albrecht, Martin Luther), includes singable melodies, uses a tonal language and is of course in the vernacular. What is crucial is not so much what is contained in the opera as the process and purpose through which Hindemith came to create it.

It is evident from his early Third Reich correspondence that he wanted to avoid material he felt inappropriate for the time (*Etienne und Luise*) and that he was searching for something 'innocuous' but 'interesting', something 'particularly topical'. Hindemith himself considered the opera 'a respectable piece' and through his aesthetic reflexivity assured himself of a positive reception for this work, if only he could get it performed. Hindemith firmly believed that if the opera was premiered in Germany it would be received positively and would 'put things right', that the opera would work for him because he had written something right for the times. He engineered *Mathis der Maler* to act for him on the public stage. *Mathis der Maler* was intended to colonize the future for him, to re-align himself as a respectable composer in Nazi Germany, to act as a change agent to his negative association with a now reified degenerate past, and to construct his future in the National Socialist state.

For Hindemith this activity ultimately failed. *Mathis der Maler* was not premiered in Germany (the premiere took place in Zürich in 1938) and Hindemith eventually found it impossible to remain in his own country. Despite his harnessing of music as a reflexive resource and tool for action he could not sufficiently change his situation and eventually, like so many others, fled the tyranny of National Socialism.

5.6 **Concluding thoughts**

This chapter has brought to attention the relationship of musical creativity—in the guise of western art music composition—and social agency. This research has explored how creativity is used in reflexive processes, in the Giddens (1991) sense, of aligning personal and social change. Key concepts developed have included how musical creativity is part of reflexive projects of self—that creativity is a resource for reflexive thinking (such as through counterfactual reasoning) engaged in situating the self; how musical creativity is used to colonize the future—that creativity is a resource for drawing the future into the present and as a means for planning future activity; and how musical creativity is a resource and tool for managing and acting within situational incongruity. With reference to Hindemith's musical activity, largely as described by the composer in his correspondence, this study has considered how creativity can be part of social agency, both informing processes of social self situation and as a tool for social action. The key conceptual innovation of this study is the critical turn to identifying links between creativity and social agency. The assertion is 'creating' involves a reflexive engagement with the world around us—that it is a resource for constructing our social situations—and a means of acting within those situations to produce, re-produce and potentially change those situations.

The links between creativity and social agency are found in how creativity and resultant products afford spaces for reflexive thinking. In this case study on Hindemith we see how a composer uses music to situate himself within the contexts of changing art worlds and wider sociopolitical conditions. Hindemith uses music to map unfamiliar territory with familiar musical concepts. As a young composer he mobilizes aspirations about his musical creativity by thinking through musical patterns to colonize the future to draw the future into the present and plan future action. Moreover, Hindemith not only mobilizes musical creativity to situate himself within musical art worlds but to create personal understandings regarding salient sociopolitical concepts. For example, while declaring he knows nothing about contemporary politics his letters show how he uses musical concepts to develop understandings of politics and situate himself within these understandings. Here Hindemith maps concepts of right versus left-wing politics with music, again using music as an emblem for largely extra-musical things. Hindemith accomplishes this through anticipating conditions of reception politically. Implicit in this process is the use of music as a space for counterfactual reasoning.

This chapter explicates how music is constitutive of social agency in the sense of appropriating wider social, cultural and political conditions to the individual—the process of connecting personal and social change. With Hindemith's involvement in *Gebrauchsmusik* in the Weimar

Republic we see how musical creativity is not just part of a reflexive project but is mobilized for action. When Hindemith and others recognize the growing incongruity between contemporary music and the general public they turn to musical creativity as a change agent to remedy this gap. Hindemith engineers musical works (such as *Plöner Musiktag*) for specific social purposes—to encourage the participation of broad social strata in contemporary music. Hindemith focuses not on more elitist forms of concert music but on creating 'social' and pedagogical works for children, amateurs, and the musical laity. By creating works with basic vocal or instrumental demands Hindemith creates works that afford participation by others regardless of their musical training or skills. Understanding this concept is central to seeing how creativity connects to social agency. It is not just that creativity affords a space for thinking about the world around us, but that creativity is a resource for acting within the world around us.

This final point is clearest when Hindemith faces the significant difficulties in reception which arose with the conservativism of the Third Reich and its racial, xenophobic, and anti-modernist ideologies. As he finds himself increasingly attacked by Nazi officials and supporters and becoming an emblem of 'degenerate' music he continuously relies upon his musical creativity as the source for his agency. Through work in *Etienne und Luise* and *Mathis der Maler* Hindemith both reflexively appropriates the conditions of the changing sociocultural-political climate and attempts to manage the incongruence emanating from these changes.

In *Etienne und Luise* Hindemith uses music as a counterfactual conditional to both appropriate the changing cultural climate and find a way to act, in fact, a way not to act, within it. Abandoning *Etienne und Luise* Hindemith moves to *Mathis der Maler*, creating both the libretto and the music. Drawing upon musical and thematic content he felt assured was respectable Hindemith seeks to put things right believing that *Mathis der Maler*, properly designed, would be a change agent for him. Not willing to rely only upon the opera Hindemith attempts to influence the conditions of reception by producing Mozart cadenzas and a successful *Mathis* symphony. Even in the fallout of *der Fall Hindemith*, which eventually led to his emigration, Hindemith maintains his devotion to musical agency through *Mathis der Maler* disseminating it to his colleagues and even planning a commission for the *Luftwaffe* in the hopes of having the opera premiered in Germany.

With *Etienne und Luise*, and his early career discussion of compositional projects, Hindemith's activity shows how musical creativity can be harnessed, such as through counterfactual reasoning, to reflexive projects of situating the self in wider sociocultural and political conditions. Through his *Gebrauchsmusik* work and the activities surrounding and including *Mathis der Maler* Hindemith shows how composers believe in music, and use this belief, as a change agent in their lives.

Musical creativity is not just a process of developing musical products. Musical creativity is linked to a reflexive engagement with the world around us and can be mobilized as part of reflexive projects of the self. However, creativity is not just a tool or resource to situate the self, creativity is a resource and tool for action. Thus understood, creativity is a means of social situation and a resource for action to produce, reproduce and potentially change one's social reality.

Appendix: plot synopsis for *Mathis der Maler*

The town of Mainz is embroiled in conflict from the reformation to the 1524–1525 peasant revolt. Additionally Cardinal Archbishop Albrecht is dealing with financial difficulties and seeking a way to maintain his authority. The painter Mathis, who is under the patronage of the Cardinal, has fallen in love with the daughter (Ursula) of a rich Lutheran supporter (Riedinger). The Cardinal himself has an interest in the wealthy Riedinger for he needs his financial help. However, the Protestant Riedinger is furious over the papal plan to oppress the reformation through the burning of Lutheran books. The Cardinal at first promises Riedinger that Lutheran books will not be burned if Riedinger will give the Cardinal financial backing. In the end the Cardinal follows the papal order and allows the book burning. Meanwhile Martin Luther has sent a letter to the Cardinal Archbishop suggesting he marry a Protestant to heal the division in his prelature resulting from the reformation. Ursula, with whom Mathis is enamoured, is the best candidate as marriage to her is another means of getting to her father's money. When Ursula learns of the marriage plans she begs Mathis to take her away. Despite the advice from his counsel (Capito) the Cardinal refuses to betray his religious vows and decides against the marriage. In the ensuing violence Mathis flees but has a vision of himself as St Anthony tempted by various vices. Eventually St. Anthony (Mathis) meets St. Paul (the Cardinal Archbishop) who urges him to return to his art and finish painting the Isenheim altarpiece. Following the vision Mathis returns to his studio where he is once again amidst his work. At the end his work on the famous Isenheim altarpiece is complete. Following a visit from the Cardinal Mathis leaves, prepared for death.

References

Becker, H. (1982). *Art worlds*. Berkeley, CA: University of California Press.

Briner, A. (1971). *Paul Hindemith: Leben und Werke*. Mainz: Schott.

Brinkmann, R. & Wolff, C. (1999). *Driven into paradise: The musical migration from Nazi Germany to the United States*. Berkeley, CA: University of California Press.

Bullivant, K. (Ed.) (1977). *Culture and society in the Weimar Republic*. Manchester: Manchester University Press.

Bullerian, H. (1933). 'Das Deutsche Konzertleben und Seine Erneuerung'. *Die Musik*, **XXV**(9), 652–7.

Etlin, R.A. (Ed.) (2002). *Art, culture, and media under the Third Reich*. Chicago, IL: University of Chicago Press.

Fowkes, B. (1984). *Communism in Germany under the Weimar Republic*. London: Macmillan.

Giddens, A. (1991). *Modernity and self-Identity: Self and society in the late modern age*. Cambridge: Polity Press.

Gilliam, B. (Ed.) (1994). *Music and performance during the Weimar Republic*. Cambridge: Cambridge University Press.

Goebbels, J. (1935). 'Reichsminister Dr. Goebbels: Aus der Kulturkammerrede vom 6. Dezember 1934'. *Die Musik*, **27**(4), 246–7.

Hertzman, L. (1963). *DNVP: right-wing opposition in the Weimar republic, 1918–1924*. Lincoln, NE: University of Nebraska Press.

Herzog, W.H. (1934). Was ist deutsche Musik?: Erkenntnisse und Folgerungen (What is German music?: Thoughts and conclusions). *Die Musik*, **26**(11), 801–6.

Hindemith, P. (1941). *The craft of musical composition, Book II: Exercises in two-part writing*. O. Ortmann (Trans). London: Schott.

Hindemith, P. (1942). *The craft of musical composition, Book I: Theoretical part*. A. Mendel (Trans). London: Schott.

Hindemith, P. (1952). *A composer's world*. Cambridge, MA: Harvard University Press.

Hindemith, P. (1995). *Selected letters of Paul Hindemith*. G. Skelton (Ed and Trans). New Haven, CT: Yale University Press.

Hinton, S. (1989). *The idea of Gebrauchsmusik: A study of musical aesthetics in the Weimar Republic (1919–1933), with particular reference to the Works of Paul Hindemith*. New York: Garland Publishing.

Hunt, R.H. (Ed) (1969). *The creation of the Weimar Republic, stillborn democracy*. Lexington, MA: Heath.

Kater, M. (1997). *The twisted muse: Musicians and their music in the Third Reich*. Oxford: Oxford University Press.

Kater, M. (2000). *Composers of the Nazi Era: Eight portraits.* New York: Oxford University Press.

Kater, M. and Riethmüller, A., Eds. (2003). *Music and Nazism: Art under tyranny, 1933–1945.* Laaber: Laaber.

Kemp, I. (1970a). *Hindemith.* London: Oxford University Press.

Kemp, I. (1970b). Hindemith's 'Cardillac'. *The Musical Times,* **111**(1525), 268–71.

Kolb, E. (2005). *The Weimar Republic.* P.S. Falla and R.J. Park (Trans). London: Routledge.

Levi, E. (1991). Atonality, 12-tone music and the Third Reich. *Tempo, New Series,* **178**, 17–21.

Levi, E. (1994). *Music in the 3rd Reich.* London: Macmillan Press.

Majewski, H. (1934). 'Neue Deutsche volksmusik—Donaueschingen'. *Die Musik,* **XXVII**(3), 200–2.

Meyer, M. (1993). *The politics of music in the Third Reich.* New York: Peter Lang.

Mosse, G.L. (2003). *Nazi culture: Intellectual, cultural and social life in the Third Reich.* Madison, WI: University of Wisconsin Press.

Muser, F.B. (1944). The recent work of Paul Hindemith. *The Musical Quarterly,* **30**(1), 29–36.

Noss, L. (1989). *Paul Hindemith in the United States.* Urbana, IL: University of Illinois Press.

Paulding, J. (1976). Mathis der Maler—The politics of music. In *Hindemith Jahrbuch 5* (Hindemith-Institut, Ed). Frankfurt am Main: Paul Hindemith Gesellschaft, pp. 102–22.

Petropoulos, J. (1999). *Art as politics in the Third Reich.* Chapel Hill, NC: University of North Carolina Press.

Peukert, D.J.K. (1991). *The Weimar Republic: The crisis of classical modernity.* R. Deveson and A. Lane (Trans). London: Penguin Press.

Prieberg, F.K. (1982). *Musik im NS-Staat.* Frankfurt am Main: Fischer Taschenbuch Verlag.

Sachs, J. (1970). Some aspects of musical politics in pre-Nazi Germany. *Perspectives of New Music,* **9**(1), 74–95.

Skelton, G. (1975/1977). *Paul Hindemith: The man behind the music.* London: Gollancz.

Steinweis, A.E. (1993). *Art, ideology, & economics in Nazi Germany: The Reich chambers of music, theatre, and the visual arts.* Chapel Hill, NC: University of North Carolina Press.

Strobel, H. (1961). *Paul Hindemith: Zeugnis in Bildern (Testimony in pictures).* Mainz: B. Schott's Söhne.

Streller, F. (1985). *Paul Hindemith.* Leipzig: VEB Deutscher Verlag für Musik.

Wulf, J. (1963). *Musik im Dritten Reich: Eine Dokumentation.* Gütersoh: Siegber Mohn Verlag.

Zabel, G. (1992). Escaping the dark time. Are modernism and politics irreconcilable? Hindemith, Weill and Eisler didn't think so. *The Musical Times,* **133**(1798), 621–3.

Chapter 6

Imagining creativity: An ethnomusicological perspective on how belief systems encourage or inhibit creative activities in music

Juniper Hill

> It may well be that the social and cultural inhibitions that prevent the flowering of musical genius are more significant than any individual ability that may seem to promote it . . . Men [and women] are more remarkable and capable creatures than most societies ever allow them to be.
> *How musical is man?* John Blacking (1973: p. 7)

Why do some music scenes seem more conducive towards creativity while others seem to stifle it? What is it about some subcultures that gives individual artists freedom for personal expression and encourages them to experiment and explore, and what is it about other music-cultures that seems to inhibit or discourage artists from engaging in creative activities? Several extramusical, environmental, and sociocultural factors contribute to the enabling and restricting of musical creativity, including cultural conventions, pedagogy, institutional and state infrastructures, market demands, and copyright legislation, among others. In this essay, I focus on one of the most fundamental sociocultural determinants of creative activities: ideology. Drawing from ethnomusicological ethnographic research,[1] I examine differing cultural belief systems, values, and attitudes that may restrict, inhibit, encourage, or liberate musical creativity.

---

[1] This essay is based upon research that I conducted in Finland on amateur and professional folk music and on art music education (30 months' fieldwork between 2002 and 2011); on research that I conducted on American singer-songwriters and their fans (1999–2002); and on my personal experiences growing up with Western art music training in Los Angeles and participating as an adult in old-time and other music communities. I also draw upon the work of several colleagues for my comparative studies: John Blacking (1967, 1973, 1980, 1982, 1986, 1987, 1989) on the South African Venda; Anthony Seeger (2004/1987, 1979; personal communications, 2009) on the Brazilian Suyá; Thomas Turino (1993; personal communications, 2009) on the Peruvian Conimeños; Henry Kingsbury (1988), Nicholas Cook (2006), and Robin Moore (1992) on Western art music; and Benjamin Filene (2000), Stephen Groce (1991), Bruce Molsky (personal interview, 2009), Neil Rosenberg (1993), Amy Wooley (2003) and the liner notes from *The Best of Broadside* (2000) and *Fast Folk* (2002) on American revival and post-revival folk musics.

I define musical creativity as the process of using divergent thinking and exercising volition in the creation of a sound product that does not conform to an entirely predetermined model (building upon Guilford, 1950; Webster, 1992; Deliège and Wiggins, 2006). (I use the descriptor 'not entirely predetermined' instead of 'novel' or 'original' in order to include creative variations and oral composition that are emically considered to be traditional.) Creative musical activities— such as composing, improvising, arranging, varying, embellishing, and interpreting—may fall along a spectrum, engaging greater or lesser degrees of creativity. Conversely, performing a piece of music using convergent thinking to conform entirely to a pre-existing model would not be a creative activity.

The ideology influencing the type and degree of creative activities in a given music-culture includes culturally-specific beliefs regarding inspiration, talent, authority, and values. In this essay, I compare how six diverse music-cultures answer the following questions: Where does new musical material come from? Who has the ability and the permission to create, innovate, or alter music? What are the priorities and goals of music-making? The answers to these questions are often based on deeply held beliefs, which may be taken for granted or legitimized by powerful arguments based on science or religion (for example, the predeterminist views that creative ability is inherited through genes or bestowed by God or spirits). It is important to examine these ideologies related to musical creativity, because these beliefs and attitudes shape the possibilities (or lack thereof) for creativity in practice.

6.1 Case studies: an overview of creative practices in six music-cultures

I have chosen six case studies that demonstrate widely varying beliefs and conventions concerning musical creativity. They are: 1) Venda traditional music from South Africa; 2) pre-1970s Suya ceremonial music from Mato Grosso, Brazil; 3) Western Classical and Romantic art music as studied and performed in Western Europe and North America in the late 20th century; 4) American post-revival folk music; 5) Finnish contemporary folk music; and 6) festival music of the Aymara-speaking indigenous people from Conima, Peru. Note that I am not examining musical styles (which, I would argue, all have creative potential). Rather I focus on the specific cultural conventions, performance practices, and ideas about music shared by particular communities of people involved in making and consuming music.

6.1.1 Venda traditional music, South Africa

The Venda are a Bantu-speaking people from the Northern Transvaal of the Republic of South Africa. They provide a model example of a communal, participatory music-culture in which everyone is expected and encouraged to participate in music-making. Music and dancing permeate every social activity from youth to old age. Most Venda children are competent musicians and no one, not even disabled persons, is excluded from music-making in Venda society (except by virtue of membership in the wrong social group, e.g. boys and married women do not sing in young girls' initiation ceremonies). Venda traditional society, while more egalitarian than many other societies in the world, is not free of hierarchies. Some individuals are recognized as having exceptional musical skill, some have greater access to musical training (if they are born into certain families), and some pursue solo instrumental traditions. Nevertheless, there are multiple genres in which every member of society performs, such as the *tshikona* national music-dances, and ceremonies in which everyone of a given social status performs, such as the *domba* girls' initiation rituals (Blacking 1967, 1973).

Based on John Blacking's ethnographic descriptions, creative activities seem to be widespread in collective performance. For example, singers often improvise harmonies and 'fill out a song with counter melodies' (Blacking, 1973: p. 85, 1980: p. 208). Xylophone and *mbira* (lamellophone) players create accompaniment by varying song melodies (1980: p. 211). Children often improvise new words to existing melodies (Blacking, 1973: p. 98, 1967: p. 25), and compose their own children's songs (Blacking 1973: p. 115). Blacking (1982: p. 298) uses the metaphor of a waterfall to depict Venda ensembles:

> At a distance, a waterfall is frozen, apparently static and monumental, but in reality it is always changing, always moving . . . At a distance, the hocket music sounds like a shimmering block of sound; but as one approaches the players or singers, who are usually dancing in a circle as they perform, the sounds become more and more varied and a variety of melodies can be extracted from the total pattern . . . these extractable patterns generate a variety of compositions.

Thus, every member of Venda society has the opportunity, encouragement, and expectation to engage in both performance and creative musical activities such as variation, improvisation, and composition. (For musical examples, listen to the cassette accompanying Blacking's *How musical is man?* and the CD *Ancient Civilisations of Southern Africa 2*.)

6.1.2 Suya ceremonial music, Brazil

The Suya indigenous people from the Amazon basin in Brazil are similar to the Venda in that music performance is a communal participatory activity. Everyone sings and dances—though who performs what, when, and how is determined by social group, such as gender, age, marital status, name group, and various moieties (or sometimes individuals may choose to perform certain genres or styles in order to assert a new social status). However, Suya beliefs about the creation/acquisition of new songs are distinct. Suya appreciate new songs, and there is a mechanism in their traditional rituals for new music and innovations, but all new songs are believed to originate from outside the Suya, either from foreigners or spirits. Suya 'composers' are individuals whose spirits reside in villages of particular animal spirits, which gives them the ability to acquire songs from spirits. The songs are then transmitted to individual singers who own and perform the songs, but do not alter them. Songs are used in ceremonies, and are considered to be extremely powerful, transformative, and potentially dangerous (Seeger, 2004/1987, 1979, personal communication, 2009). Thus, while participation in musical performance is open to all, creative activities in music are restricted by religious beliefs to individuals in particular spiritual states. (For musical examples, listen to the cassette tape accompanying Seeger (1987) and Judith and Anthony Seeger's LP *Música Indígena a arte vocal dos Suyá*.)

6.1.3 Western Classical and Romantic art music in the late 20th century

The music-culture surrounding and perpetuating Western Classical and Romantic art music in Western Europe and North America in the late 20th and early 21st centuries is selective and hierarchical, with distinct divisions of labour between listeners, performers, and composers. Many musicians, educators, and audience members believe that musical talent, for both performance and composition, must be either genetically inherited or divinely bestowed. A canon of great composers and great works of the past is highly revered, and considerable value is placed on the faithful execution of their scores. Creative activities by performers are restricted to a very small degree of interpretation. Improvisation is strongly discouraged, and variation of existing works is restricted by heavy community censorship (though improvisation and variation were widely practised in earlier eras; cf. Moore, 1992, Sancho-Velazquez, 2001). Only a small and select group of specialists is given the opportunity to compose, and they often must achieve institutional, academic, or other social recognition and legitimization in order for their creative work to be accepted.

6.1.4 American post-revival folk music

After the American folk revival of the 1950s and 1960s, several post-revival folk music communities developed in the USA. Here I focus on old-time and singer-songwriter subcultures, which each developed distinct ideals and performance practices. The contemporary old-time scene, comprised primarily of dedicated amateur instrumentalists, aims to be relatively participatory and egalitarian in its performance contexts (especially in jam sessions), and values the development of individual style expressed through subtle and stylistically appropriate variations of traditional pieces. However, in striving for historically authentic reproductions of traditional repertoire, traditional styles, and traditional sounds—which are often enforced through community censorship—there is little encouragement of new compositions, and little room for extensive improvisation. In contrast, the folk song revival, spearheaded by figures such as Pete Seeger and Bob Dylan, led to a post-revival contemporary singer-songwriter scene that strives for a different type of authenticity: instead of aiming to be faithful to a historical repertoire and historical sound, singer-songwriters strive to be authentic to the personal experiences and emotions from the lives of themselves and/or their contemporaries. Every singer-songwriter is expected to be, by default, both a performer and composer, and the constant composition of new songs is highly valued. (For an example of contemporary old-time music, listen to the CD *Bruce Molsky and Big Hoedown*. For singer-songwriter folk music, listen to the CD box sets *Fast Folk* and *The Best of Broadside*.)

6.1.5 Finnish contemporary folk music

In Helsinki, a professional urban contemporary folk music scene has grown out of a conservatory folk music programme led by the charismatic pedagogue, Heikki Laitinen. Laitinen was rebelling against a perceived lack of creative freedom in Western classical music, in conventional music education, and in the nationalistic uses of folk music in Finland. Through his teaching, writing, and artistic work, he propagated the belief that every person has the right to be creative, and that every musician of every age and skill level is capable of improvising and composing—including complete beginners, unskilled amateurs, and small children. The ideal of authenticity to which contemporary folk musicians strive is not to replicate a traditional sound, but rather to embody a folk creative process—a process in which one learns the tradition and then expresses it in one's own personal way, incorporating whatever influences may have touched the artist's life.

  This process is believed to capture the historical creative spirit of the folk while simultaneously keeping folk music innovative and relevant to contemporary society (cf. Hill, 2009b). The resulting contemporary folk music scene, centred at the Folk Music Department of the Sibelius Academy, is characterized by extensive individuality, innovation, and stylistic eclecticism. The majority of musicians exercise high degrees of creative activities. Though small and underground, the institutional power and prestige of these Academy-trained musicians has amplified the dissemination of their ideology and methods, resulting in increased composition and improvisation in professional and amateur folk music circles across Finland (cf. Hill, 2009a). (For musical examples, listen to the recordings available online at http://etno.net, or to the *Arctic Paradise* compilation CDs.)

6.1.6 Conimeña festival music, Peru

Amongst the indigenous Aymara-speaking people of Conima, Peru (or 'Conimeños'), festival music is very competitive. Innovation is highly valued for it gives community groups a unique identity and a competitive edge. Before each large festival, members of each community's ensemble work together to compose new repertoire to represent their communities. The compositional process is collective: ensemble members sit in a circle brainstorming musical motifs on their instruments. If others in the ensemble like someone's musical ideas, they start playing along. Once new motifs are adopted by the ensemble, they become communal property and the group works together to brainstorm variations and alterations until the new piece is completed to the consensual satisfaction of the entire group (Turino, 1993, personal communication, 2009). Creativity is not linked to individual expression or owned by individuals (as in many Western music-cultures), but rather is a collective experience enhancing group solidarity. All interested male adults in the community have an open invitation to participate in both musical performance and the composition process. (For musical examples, listen to Cohen and Turino's CD *Mountain music of Peru. Vol. 2*.)

These six music cultures present greatly varying models of what types and degrees of creative activities are accepted and encouraged, as well as which types of people are allowed to be creative. The following sections illuminate how these distinct creative practices correspond to ideas about the origins of music, beliefs about the nature of musical abilities, and the functions and values ascribed to music in specific cultures.

6.2 Inspiration: where does music come from?

Many different cultures have greatly varying beliefs about how inspiration works and whence new musical ideas are acquired. Some notions make the creative process seem relatively inaccessible to most people and may inhibit some musicians from even trying to compose or improvise, while other cultures' beliefs may encourage extensive creative activities by the majority of musicians or members of society.

In contemporary Western cultures, popular myths, perpetuated and legitimized even in dictionaries, may make creative acts appear to be an enigma. In *The Creative Mind: Myths and Mechanisms*, Margaret Boden identifies two popular Western beliefs about creativity: the inspirational approach, which views creativity as 'essentially mysterious, even superhuman or divine,' and the romantic view, which claims that creativity is an innate talent or gift that only exceptional people have and that others cannot acquire or be taught (2004: pp. 14–15). She critiques these popular Western myths, arguing:

> If we take seriously the dictionary-definition of creativity, 'to bring into being or form out of nothing', creativity seems to be not only unintelligible but strictly impossible.
>
> (Boden, 2004: p. 11.)

Such common Western notions about general creativity can be found in today's Western Classical and Romantic music circles. For example, Nicholas Cook (2006) demonstrates how 18th- and 19th-century Romantic views of great composers as geniuses channelling the divine are still pervasive in 20th-century Western music theory scholarship. In the Romantic conception of creative inspiration, a genius is someone through whom God speaks. Schenker provides a florid description of this process:

> The lightning flash of a thought suddenly crashed down, at once illuminating and creating the entire work in the most dazzling light. Such works were conceived and received in one stroke.
>
> (Schenker (1894) cited in Cook 2006: p. 11.)

The late 19th- and early 20th-century concept of musical inspiration welling up from the unconscious is also linked to divine inspiration, or, in Schoenberg's words, 'a subconsciously received gift from the Supreme Commander' (Schoenberg, 1906 cited in Cook, 2006: pp. 10–11).

Similar Western concepts of musical creation are rampant in many listeners' and musicians' understanding of jazz improvisation, obfuscating the many years of learning and preparation that jazz musicians undergo before becoming accomplished improvisers. Paul Berliner (1994) observed that both popular and music dictionary definitions perpetuated the myth of improvisation as a mythical mysterious act:

> To improvise is to compose, or simultaneously compose and perform, on the spur of the moment and without any preparation.
>
> (*Webster's New World Dictionary,* 1988 cited in Berliner, 1994: p. 1.)

> Improvisation is the art of performing music spontaneously, without the aid of manuscript, sketches or memory
>
> (*Harvard Dictionary of Music,* 1969 cited in Berliner 1994: p. 1).

To beginning jazz musicians, 'the "cats" seemed to be "standing up and making something out of nothing" . . . "When you're just learning jazz, everything is mystical"' (Berliner 1994: p. 2, quoting Arthur Rhames and Wynton Marsalis, respectively).

Concepts about new musical ideas coming from thin air, from the divine, or from the subconscious of a genius make the ability to compose and improvise appear to be something that cannot be taught, learned, or acquired by individuals who are not deemed to be exceptionally talented or who do not regularly receive divine communications. Such notions may serve as self-inhibitors or self-censorship, in which individuals impose artificial limits on themselves. These beliefs also serve to inhibit others, such as parents and teachers, from teaching or encouraging students and young musicians to be creative.

The Suya have perhaps more extreme views about the supernatural and divine origin of music. They believe that all music originates from outside of their village; it is either introduced by foreigners, or acquired from spirits. The only way in which people 'compose' or, more appropriately, acquire and transmit, new musical material is by having their spirit sent to a village of animal spirits, where they are able to listen to and learn songs belonging to spirits and then transmit them to their human colleagues (Seeger, 2004/1987, personal communication, 2009). These beliefs about the origins of songs place many restrictions against possible compositional processes. The nature of the new song that one can acquire from animal spirits is further limited by the type of spirit village in which an individual's spirit dwells (e.g. one person might be able to hear only fish songs, another person only deer songs, etc.). However, since anyone who has lost his or her spirit may acquire new songs, Suya beliefs allow for a larger percentage of the population to participate in the acquisition and introduction of new musical material than Western classical music culture allows. Seeger observed that, 'in the previous generation, approximately 30% of Suya men and women had spirits living with bees, birds, fish, and trees' (Seeger, 2004/1987: p. 55).

In some cases beliefs about spiritual origins of music primarily encourage rather than restrict more members of society to compose. According to Bruno Nettl (1990/1954), Native Americans of the Great Plains of Montana, Colorado, and Wyoming believe that music can be acquired through visions or dreams. Nettl observed that:

> The acquisition of songs in visions is associated with prestige and is a part of the experience of most men . . . Each man, among most of the Plains tribes, is supposed to have at least one vision during his life, and many have several. Thus we may say that at least most men in these tribes are composers.
>
> (Nettl, 1990/1954: p. 85.)

Thus, depending on the cultural context, ideology of divine musical origins may greatly restrict or encourage individuals to compose.

In contrast to the notions about spiritual, subconscious, or visionary origins of music, Conimeños believe in more practical and unmystical means of inspiration. New musical ideas in

Conima are derived from brainstorming on one's instrument, and from borrowing and altering pre-existing phrases and motifs (Turino, 1993: pp. 78–9, 206, personal communication, 2009). (Similarly, some scholars, such as Brailoiu (1984), Lord (2000/1960), and Merker (2006), maintain that traditional music systems can be generative, in that they provide formulas and structures which traditional musicians manipulate to create new variations.) Thus in Conima, composing is neither enigmatic nor inaccessible, but rather achievable by any interested individual.

Another belief, perpetuated in both the American singer-songwriter and Finnish contemporary folk music subcultures, is that new musical material comes from one's inner self—from one's own emotions, personal life experiences, or interpretation of contemporary events. Finnish contemporary folk musicians adhere to a folk creative process in which musicians learn from the traditions and then express them in their own individual, personal ways. Through this process of personal expression, they naturally incorporate musical and extra-musical elements from their own life experiences. Some Finnish contemporary folk musicians also define folk music as anything that is played *omasta päästä*, or from one's own head (cf. Hill, 2005: pp. 190–6). In the American folk song revival, Pete Seeger advocated a similar creative process, encouraging everyone to create their own personalized interpretations of folk songs, and especially to write new songs as a response to current events (Filene, 2000: p. 194). The composition of new songs arising through a critique of contemporary politics and world events was fostered in burgeoning singer-songwriter communities in New York and elsewhere (cf. *The Best of Broadside 1962–1988*, 2000). In recent decades, numerous post-revival singer-songwriters have emphasized emotion and life experience as primary sources of inspiration, as exemplified in the following opening statements to articles in the magazine *American Songwriter*:

> Living life to its fullest, experiencing a myriad of emotions and then putting those feelings into words and music others can relate to is what makes a songwriter successful.
>
> (Price, 1989a.)

> No one will argue that the best songs come from the heart. Combining pure emotion with finely honed craft results in great tunes. The ability to take a feeling, develop and mold it into a poignant song is a talent that has made . . . [the] most successful songwriters.
>
> (Price, 1989b.)

Thus, the primary prerequisites for being a songwriter are relatively widely accessible: having sensitivity and emotional depth; having rich life experiences and/or engagement with contemporary world events; and having the desire and ability to express them. These widely varying beliefs about where music comes from shape perceptions of who has the ability to create music.

6.3 Talent and authority: who can be creative in music?

Different cultures have vastly different beliefs concerning which types of people have the ability to be musically creative. Such beliefs result in and are reinforced by different practices concerning who is expected and who has permission to engage in creative musical activities. Sometimes these notions about who can be creative are so internalized into cultural conventions and formalized in institutions that they are completely taken for granted—yet they still serve to grant the authority to be creative to some individuals and deny it to others. In a few music-cultures, participation in creative musical activities is accessible to all people. However, in most societies there is a division of labour, either between musicians and non-musicians, or between listeners, performers, and composers/creators. Such divisions delimiting who can be creative with music and who cannot may be determined by socially constructed notions of talent, one's spiritual condition, one's social status (such as class, age, or sex), or one's status as insider or outsider to a tradition.

In Venda society, every person is believed to have musical ability. Though some people are recognized as having more exceptional skill than others, everyone is expected to be able to sing and dance, and to participate in various communal ceremonies and events. Such participatory ceremonial performances normally allow for improvisation and variation within traditional conventions, as in this girls' *tshigombela* dance song:

> If performers substitute for words various combinations of phonemes such as *ee, ahee, huwelele wee, yowee,* and so forth, they give themselves greater freedom of musical expression. This is important, because it is the part of the shared experience of musical activity which may become transcendental . . . In the development of a *tshigombela* song during a performance that may last from ten to more than thirty minutes, the straightforward call and response is elaborated into a quasi-contrapuntal sequence, and words are abandoned. During the course of freer musical expression, a variety of melodies come out.

(Blacking, 1973: pp. 70–1.)

It seems that everyone participating in this ceremony has a free license to improvise on traditional material, but, as a girls' dance, musical participation in this particular event is limited by sex and marital status. Blacking does not mention any Venda beliefs restricting who has the talent or ability to compose, improvise, or vary. He provides accounts of children improvising and composing (cf. Blacking, 1967: p. 29, 1973: p. 98, 115, 1987: p. 37) and of composing by young working-class women (cf. Blacking, 1989).

Blacking's extensive fieldwork amongst the Venda led him to the conclusions that 'human creativity and musicality are as innate as the ability to speak' and that 'divisions between composer and performer and between performer and listener are products of the division of labor in society rather than consequences of a fundamentally different musical ability' (Blacking, 1986: p. 127). This led him to question Western beliefs regarding musical ability in European art music:

> If, for example, all members of an African society are able to perform and listen intelligently to their own indigenous music, and if this unwritten music . . . can be shown to have a similar range of effects on people and to be based on intellectual and musical processes that are found in the so-called 'art' music of Europe, we must ask why apparently general musical ability should be restricted to a chosen few in societies supposed to be culturally more advanced. . . . Must the majority be made 'unmusical' so that a few may become more 'musical'?

(Blacking, 1973: p. 4.)

In Finland, leading pedagogues of contemporary folk music also critique the limiting of creative musical activities—which they feel occurs in Western art music institutions—and actively encourage people of all skills and age levels to create their own music in their own way. Kristiina Ilmonen, former Head of the Folk Music Department at the Sibelius Academy, asserts:

> The philosophy behind all of the [folk music] teaching is that there should be personalities that create new things. And we have also pedagogically the view point that already a student can be an artist. I think this is what differs from classical music quite a lot, because many of the people there believe that you are only an artist after you have graduated, or if you are world famous and you are giving solo concerts. But we believe that already children can be artists.

(Personal interview, 2004.)

Heikki Laitinen, an activist pedagogue who was influential in shaping the Finnish contemporary folk music scene, has critiqued Finland's music school system for 'the eradication of the creativity on the part of some 50,000 children' with its emphasis on 'repetition, obedience, subjugation, and conformity' (Laitinen, 1989: pp. 9–10, my translation). He and his colleagues have devised alternative teaching methods, 'for the salvation of musical creativity' (ibid.), that emphasize personal variation of traditional melodies, improvisation, arranging, and composition. Believing that everyone has the ability to be creative, they teach improvisation, variation, and composition to professional musicians, children, and adult beginners; they require folk music students at the Sibelius Academy to give recitals of their own music; and they encourage amateurs to 'defend their right to be creative' (cf. Hill, 2009b). Furthermore, they use experimental techniques that combat attitudes and conventions limiting creative activities, which students have internalized from their exposure to Western classical music superculture (cf. Hill, 2009c).

Western notions of talent and giftedness may serve to effectively restrict the opportunities, encouragement, and self-motivation for individuals who are not labelled as talented to engage in creative activities. Davidson, Howe, and Sloboda found that:

> Because the experience of being a performer is unfamiliar, most people are unaware of how performance skills are developed. The tendency has been to label these achievements as being the consequence of special 'gifts' or 'talents' that are believed to involve some form of special biological endowment, possessed by only a minority of people. The 'gifts' and 'talents' explanation of musical achievement is consistent with the determinist belief that abilities are largely hereditary . . . explaining musical achievement only or mainly in terms of 'gifts' and 'talents' denies the many varied and potentially vital environmental influences which affect development.

> (Davidson, Howe, and Sloboda, 1997: p. 189.)

Although Davidson, Howe, and Sloboda's research focuses on musical aptitude in performance, the same belief system applies to notions of talent and giftedness for musical aptitude in composing–in Western culture the talent or gift for composing is believed to be even more rare and specialized than the talent deemed necessary for performing music. The fatalistic belief that exceptional talent is necessary for musical composing is compounded by the canonization of a select number of great genius composers, providing a lack of accessible composing role models with which young musicians can personally identify or strive to emulate. As I was growing up in Los Angeles, receiving conventional classical training on the clarinet, I had already internalized by a young age the notion that one had to be an exceptionally gifted child prodigy genius in order to compose. My best friend was composing symphonies by the age of 13, but all of our music teachers considered her to be a child prodigy genius, and thus she fit the model. However, when the 12-year-old girl sitting next to me in the clarinet section of my youth symphony orchestra told me that she was entering a junior composer competition, I was shocked and flabbergasted. I thought to myself at the time, how could a normal person like her, not a genius or prodigy at all, possibly be able to compose? It was completely against the classical music belief system with which I had been brought up, and inhibited me from attempting to compose until I was exposed to other belief systems later in life. Conversely, Finnish composer Jarmo Saari grew up singing in a prominent boys' choir that performed the work of contemporary Finnish composers who would often make guest appearances to lead rehearsals of their new pieces. Saari reflects that being able to see and work with living composers with whom he could identify was instrumental in inspiring him to compose himself, and in instilling in him the belief that a person like him had the ability to compose (personal interview, 2008).

In addition to its effect on self-inhibition or motivation, the Western notion of talent as a rare innate musical ability may also be used to restrict who has the social authority to be creative. In his ethnography of an American music conservatory, Henry Kingsbury observed that 'both the manifesting and the assessing of musical talent are to a great extent matters of social power and authority' (1988: p. 77). Furthermore, 'the validity of a given person's musical talent is a direct function of the relative esteem of the persons who have attributed the talent' (ibid.: p. 68). Authority figures within the conservatory confer talent upon certain individuals. These few musicians socially recognized as talented are then the only ones whose creative activities—such as editing scores or creating their own interpretations of canonical works—are considered acceptable. Authority figures also identify certain students as 'less talented' and 'less musical', thereby delegitimizing the students' creative work and, in some cases, denying them further access to musical training and careers (ibid.: pp. 64–7, 105).

Western belief systems and practices concerning the selective authorization and specialized training of musicians have spread to other music-cultures, especially as the Western-style conservatory training system has been adopted. In his book *The Western Impact on World Music* (1985), Bruno Nettl found that Westernization often resulted in increased specialization and division of labour, canonization of great composers, and significant decline in creative activities such as improvisation.

While today's Western classical music-culture is perhaps one of the more extreme examples of divisions between listeners, performers, and composers, it is not the only society to enforce social restrictions on who can engage in which musical behaviours. The Suya have no divisions between listeners and performers; every member of society performs (though what they perform when is regulated by social status, such as sex and moiety membership). There is a very clear division between performers and those with the ability to produce new songs; however, this division is not based on talent, but rather on one's spiritual condition. Since the Suya receive most of their songs from the spirit realm, one must be able to hear and understand the spirits in order to produce/transmit new songs to the community. Based on his ethnographic research, Anthony Seeger believes that the Suya would consider any adult man or woman capable of producing new songs, provided that his or her spirit had been lost and resided in one of the villages of animal spirits. Spirit loss may be temporary or permanent; thus, the ability to transmit songs from spirits may be temporary or ongoing. If a person's lost spirit is found and returns to the person's body (for example, with the help of a curer) that person loses the ability to hear and understand the language and songs of the spirits (Seeger, personal communication, 2009). In order to lose one's spirit, one must become ill or injured, and that illness or injury is frequently caused by a witch. The ability to introduce new music is not determined by genetics, giftedness, or talent as in Western classical music, but rather by an individual's spiritual state, and by witches (Seeger, 2004/1987).

In contrast, the American singer-songwriter community has clear divisions between listeners (fans) and musicians, but no division between performer and composer. As decreed by the very label of the idiom, each singer creates his or her own musical material. No musical training or legitimization by academies or institutions is required; in his study of 15 US singer-songwriters, Groce found that none of them had majored in music in college but rather English, history, sociology, and anthropology (1991: p. 34). During the folksong revival, Pete Seeger encouraged amateurs to personalize and write their own songs. Since the revival, singer-songwriters have continued to downplay elitism and star status and to emphasize proletarian identities and connections with the common person (Filene, 2000: pp. 202, 207; see also Palmer, 1997).

Insider or outsider status is another social boundary that may limit who is allowed to be creative in certain traditions. During the American old-time revival, there was a notion that one must be a traditional musician in order to have permission to innovate, and revivalists were often dismissed as inauthentic. Contemporary old-time fiddler Bruce Molsky, who grew up in the Bronx and passionately adopted old-time music in the 1970s along with other revivalists, only began composing his own tunes many years later under the encouragement of a musician (Tony Trischka) from outside of the old-time community. Molsky reflects:

> I never thought I was allowed to do that [compose my own tunes]. I didn't think anyone was allowed to do that. There was the barbed wire fence between me and the traditionalists. So if I'm a revivalist maybe that was where I didn't allow myself to be a traditionalist. I could never be Ed Haley [a traditional fiddler from West Virginia] and write a second part to 'Man of Constant Sorrow' because I don't qualify, because I'm not a traditional musician.

> (Personal interview, 2009.)

Molsky also related with some dismay that he has been criticized by some for appropriating musical traditions that do not belong to him. In the young generation of post-revival musicians who have grown up listening to old-time music at home, the rigid perceptions of insiders and outsiders to tradition are dissolving somewhat, but composing is still relatively uncommon in the old-time community (Molsky, personal interview, 2009; Thomas Turino, personal communication, 2009). Similarly, several ethnomusicologists who are cultural and ethnic outsiders to the traditions they study and teach feel that it would be inappropriate for them to take creative liberties with the music of other cultures. British ethnomusicologist David Hughes (2004: p. 264) expresses a deep uncertainty in performing creative, albeit traditional, variations in Japanese music: 'it seemed incredibly daring to tamper with another culture's music' (see also Averill, 2004: p. 100 and Hill, 2007: pp. 73–7).

Conimeña culture allows perhaps the most freedom of choice for participating in performing and composing. Any adolescent or adult male in the community may participate in festival performances, rehearsals, and/or group composing sessions if he so wishes. Oftentimes, many will pick up an instrument and join in during the festivals (extra beer and coca for performers serve as additional motivation), but only those with a particular interest in music will join in the rehearsal-composing sessions (which can be a fair amount of work). They have no notion of musical talent in the European/American sense; some people are recognized as being better performers and composers, but their skills are attributed to their interest in music and the greater amount of time and effort they devote to it. However, other social restrictions apply; women do not play instruments in Conima, and thus these performance and composition opportunities are not open to them (Turino, personal communication, 2009).

Thus, beliefs regarding who has the ability and the permission to create music vary drastically amongst different music-cultures. Some maintain that every human being has creative musical abilities; others believe that every performer can be a composer, others believe that only those in direct communication with the spirit world can produce new songs, and others feel that only a select few have inherited the talent to be creative. In many cases, only those who are socially perceived as having the ability to create are encouraged or permitted to, and in some cases social status further restricts who is allowed to create.

6.4 Values: why is music created?

> The functions of music in society may be the decisive factors promoting or inhibiting latent musical ability.

> (Blacking, 1973: p. 35.)

Why a community makes music, and what a community values in music making, play a huge role in determining what types of creative activities are acceptable and which aspects of music are allowed to be altered or innovated. Some of the goals and values of music-making that influence creativity in our case studies include: spiritual or divine communion, authenticity to historical traditions, novelty (for entertainment, commercial potential, or competitive edge), individual expression and identity, and group solidarity and communal bonding.

Permission to creatively alter music is often most restricted when music serves a religious purpose, especially in ceremonies meant to invoke divine beings or spiritual power. For example, the Suya believe that songs contain transformative power and that to change them would be too dangerous. As Seeger explains:

> The incorrect performance of an invocation . . . or the improper performance of a ritual could transform a patient, an individual or an entire society in undesirable ways.

(Seeger, 2004/1987: p. 61.)

Amongst the Suya, once a spiritless intermediary teaches a song, singers are expected to keep the song the same, and will be corrected if they diverge too much. There is no idea that they should improvise or vary on the basis of what they have been taught (Seeger, personal communication, 2009).[2] Similarly, Bruno Nettl found that some Native American cultures restrict any changes to music because they would invalidate religious ceremonies (Nettl 1990/1954: p. 89).

Music-cultures that highly value preservation and authenticity to historical traditions may also limit individuals' permission to creatively alter or innovate. In striving for authenticity, musicians pursue certain ideals, which vary according to community. In the American old-time revival and post-revival subcultures, musicians aim to maintain historical repertoire, play with historical techniques that produce sound according to a specific aesthetic, and create a relatively egalitarian interpersonal music-making environment (cf. Rosenberg, 1993; Wooley, 2003). While contemporary old-time communities often encourage communal participatory performance by people of all skill levels, and value a certain amount of stylistically appropriate creative variation, individuals who try to introduce musical material from outside of the community's historical ideal will often be reprimanded or censored.

Contemporary performance conventions in Western Classical and Romantic music are even stricter in upholding authenticity ideals, which, in this case, are to the composer's intentions and the score. The perfect execution and replication of existing great works are extremely highly valued, to the extent that scores may take on an almost sacred aura. When musicians deviate from the score, they may receive severe community criticism. For example, in Finland a very well respected concert pianist recorded a piece by Jean Sibelius, and decided to play the final chord three times, instead of twice as was written. The record was withdrawn because the Sibelius estate did not approve (whereas at the time that the piece was written, such variations would have been common practice in classical piano music; Pekka Gronow, personal interview, 2008).

Alternatively, when the authenticity ideal to which musicians strive is a historical process instead of a text or sound product, there may be greater opportunities for musicians to be creative while remaining authentic. In the Finnish contemporary folk music scene, many musicians strive to re-create and immerse themselves in historical creative processes. Some take inspiration from

---

2 Though these beliefs seem relatively restrictive of individual agency and volition in processes of musical creation, Seeger reflects that Suya engage in divergent thinking in deciding what ceremonies to perform. They also exercise individual agency when 'transmitters go for walks in the woods, or put their heads under the water, or go to sleep (respectively for songs of trees, fish, and spirits) in order to hear the songs of the spirits they will transmit. They did this intentionally, with the object of coming back with songs they could teach' (personal communication, 2009). Singers may also choose to alter their vocal timbre or pitch to assert their age or masculinity, or make a social statement by choosing not to sing (Seeger, 1979).

historical accounts of traditional musicians improvising alone for hours to pass the long winter nights or improvising new repertoire for multi-day wedding festivities, and most follow the creed that folk musicians should learn the tradition and then express it in their own way (cf. Hill, 2005: pp. 39–55, 245–51; Bithell & Hill, forthcoming).

Although keeping music the same may be more important than providing creative opportunities for current musicians in many of the above cases, there are several other music-cultures that prioritize musical change and novelty. In Conima, Peru, ensembles highly value originality as a means of capturing the attention of the spectators and thereby providing a competitive advantage in large festivals (Turino, 1993: p. 67). American ethnomusicologist Thomas Turino found that his own composition in the local style was successful amongst Conimeño musicians precisely because they found it to be unusual and 'weird'. However, Turino's novel piece would not have been successful if it had not been easy enough to be learned quickly by the majority of the community—Conimeño composers must strike a balance between novelty, which is valued for competitiveness, and familiarity, which is valued for accessibility (Turino, personal communication, 2009). Many music-cultures similarly value novel variations and interpretations of familiar traditional materials. In both Korean and Yugoslavian epic singing, audiences appreciate bards who are able to creatively adapt well-known epics to the immediate performance contexts (Lord, 2000/1960; Pihl, 2003).

Novelty may also be valued as a way of ensuring individual ownership and thus securing royalties, as reflected in Western copyright laws which offer monetary incentive to contemporary composers for creativity and originality. Thus, the valuation of novelty can provide significant motivation for individuals to compose their own material. At the same time, over emphasis on novelty may limit the materials that composers can use as source materials (cf. Demers, 2006). In music-cultures with a large body of material in the public domain (as in Finnish folk music), and attitudes that permit the recycling of existing material (as in Conima, Peru; Turino, 1993: p. 79), musicians may have greater freedom in the range of materials available for creative uses.

Western copyright laws' rewarding of individual creativity through individual ownership rights may be viewed as a manifestation of Western society's more general valuation of individualism, which can be seen in Western art, popular, and folk music-cultures. The emphasis on the individual affects creativity in several ideological domains: concepts of ownership (mentioned above), notions of progress, and valuation of self-expression.

Many Westerners believe that music (like other cultural and scientific domains) has progressed, and will continue to progress, through the contributions and innovations of individuals. In Western art music, selected historical genius-composers are honoured for their individual contributions that led to the development and refinement of Western classical music. Hence an elite group of contemporary composers is given the freedom to innovate and develop their own unique styles with the hope that they will progress the musical arts. Finnish contemporary folk music, which has undergone a process of artification and institutionalization into a conservatory environment (cf. Hill, 2009a), exhibits the same inherent belief in and ambition for artistic progress and development through individual creativity. However, because they believe that all musicians have creative potential and the ability to fill all musical roles, and that folk music should be created anew during the moment of performance, all musicians are expected to develop their own creative contribution.

In several Western folk music communities, and in some other traditional music-cultures, an emphasis on individuality is manifested not through a prioritization of progress, but instead through the valuation of personal expression. In American post-revival folk singer-songwriter communities, important musical goals for musicians are often their own personal expression and catharsis and the communication of their emotions, opinions, and life experiences to their peers and fans. Finnish contemporary folk musicians frequently value the process and experience of expressing oneself through music more than they value the final sound product, which allows more freedom for creative risk-taking and exploration (since there is less emphasis on critical judgement of the resulting sounds; cf. Hill, 2009c). Amongst the Suya, adult men sing the *akia* song genre in order to express their individual feelings to their sisters and mothers (Seeger, 1979), thus contributing to the need for individualistic interpretation in performance and unique songs for different individuals.

On one hand, emphasis on individuality, whether for progress or expression, encourages individual creative acts. On the other hand, over-emphasis on individuality, especially on individual ownership of music, obfuscates the collective nature of musical creativity. In order to create new ideas, people often combine existing material in new ways or explore the limits of existing conceptual systems—two of the most common forms of creativity (Boden, 2004: pp. 3–6). At times, certain copyright and social inhibitions against borrowing musical material may serve to restrict creative freedom. (In practice, Western copyright laws often restrict musicians from recycling melodic and textual material, but generally consider harmonic and rhythmic material to be tools or conventions for all to use.) The fear of being accused of plagiarism or stealing prevents musicians from drawing upon large bodies of existing music for ideas and source material (see Demers, 2006 for how this affects contemporary Western popular music). In music-cultures with beliefs that emphasize communal ownership, such as Conima, Peru (Turino, 1993: p. 79), musicians have more freedom to work together and build upon one another's ideas, drawing upon the collective creativity of their community and of humanity.[3] However, an overemphasis on collective composition by earlier generations of folk music scholars ran the danger of mystifying creative processes into myth and making invisible the creative contributions of individuals (cf. Ballantine, 1997; Blacking, 1989; Brailoiu, 1984).

Both Conimeña and Venda music-cultures deemphasize the individual and value music-making as a means for group solidarity and communal social cohesion. In Conima, collective solidarity is far more important than individual recognition. Any man who wishes to participate in musical performance during the festivals is allowed to do so, regardless of musical skill, and Conimeños value the louder volume and greater show of communal solidarity that come from having more performers. Any man may also participate in the collective creative process, and new compositions are valued as the property of the group and a marker of group identity regardless of who contributed their ideas (Turino, 1993; personal communication, 2009). For the Venda, when singers improvise and vary together as a group, their collective musical expression becomes a means for a shared experience of transcendence (Blacking, 1973: p. 71). Both the Conimeños and the Venda provide examples of emphasis on group solidarity in music-making as encouraging collective creativity. However, sometimes emphasis on collective performance can deprioritize creativity. When I was conducting field research in Finland, I noticed a respected folk musician, Mauno Järvelä, leading ensembles with up to 100 fiddlers playing the same tune together in unison, with no improvisation, and only a small amount of variation by elderly fiddlers. Järvelä is not a member of the contemporary folk scene in Finland described earlier, which often showcases extensive improvisation by solo artists, and I was struck by his vastly different approach to performance practice. When I interviewed him, I found that his main goal in music-making was not the personal artistic expression that so many contemporary folk musicians espouse, but rather

---

[3] Conimeños believe that it is acceptable to borrow musical phrases and motives from pre-existing pieces of any genre, if they are owned by the group or come from outside, nonlocal sources (such as the radio). However, it is taboo to borrow musical materials from one's local competitors, and ensembles sometimes accuse other groups of 'stealing' their music (Turino, 1993:pp. 78–9; personal communication, 2009).

social harmony and the creation of a musical community in which young and old, beginners and advanced come together (Järvelä, personal interview, 2007).

6.5 Conclusions

Musicians from Venda, Suya, Conimeño, Finnish contemporary folk, American post-revival folk, and Western classical music-cultures maintain widely varying beliefs about the 'how', 'who', and 'why' of musical creativity. Creative musical ideas are believed to originate in flashes of inspiration from God, from the subconscious, from animal spirits' villages, from visions, from the heart, from personal emotions, from life experiences, by brainstorming on instruments, or by borrowing from others. These beliefs may make musical creativity appear to be mystical, difficult, and inaccessible to many, or to be straightforward and accessible to all. Perceptions of who is able to be musically creative range from prodigies and geniuses, to shamans and people without spirits, to any emotionally sensitive and expressive person, to interested persons who apply themselves, to every human being. Attitudes towards who has the authority to be creative vary from conservatory legitimized masters, to a handful labelled as gifted and talented, to cultural insiders, to all adult men—and these attitudes may serve to deny creative opportunities to those who do not fit into these social categories. A complex spectrum of why music is created and what is valued in musical performance also shapes the nature and range of creative opportunities that are desirable in different music-cultures.

Despite the diversity of attitudes towards musical creativity across different cultures, most of these beliefs are deeply held, naturalized, and rarely questioned. They can have far-reaching ramifications, influencing the nature of music pedagogy; informal and formal music education; parental, peer, and self-expectations; the way music is created and performed; copyright legislation; the way music and musicians are judged; and perhaps most of all self-censorship and self-set limitations. If we want to enable a greater range of creative activities amongst a larger population, we need to begin by challenging many of the notions that we may take for granted about musical creativity.

Acknowledgements

Many thanks to my colleagues and informants who took the time to share their thoughts and expertise, especially Heikki Laitinen, Kristiina Ilmonen, Anthony Seeger, Thomas Turino, Bruce Molsky, Liana, Pekka Gronow, Jarmo Saari, and many other musicians and scholars in Finland and elsewhere. I am also grateful to the Alexander von Humboldt Foundation for generously supporting my research on creativity.

References

Averill, G. (2004). Where's 'One'?: Musical encounters of the ensemble kind. In T. Solís (Ed.) *Performing ethnomusicology: Teaching and representation and world music ensembles.* Berkeley, CA: University of California Press, pp. 93–111.

Ballantine, C. (1997). Making visible the invisible: Creative processes and the music of Joseph Shabalala. *Papers presented at the Symposium on Ethnomusicology, no. 13, University of Zululand, 1995; and at the Symposium on Ethnomusicology, no. 14, Rhodes University, 1996.* Grahamstown, South Africa: International Library of African Music, pp. 56–59.

Berliner, P. (1994). *Thinking in jazz: The infinite art of improvisation.* Chicago, IL: University of Chicago Press.

Bithell, C. & Hill, J. (Eds.) (forthcoming). *The Oxford handbook of music revivals.* Oxford: Oxford University Press.

Blacking, J. (1967). *Venda Children's songs: A study in ethnomusicological analysis.* Johannesburg: Witwatersrand University Press.

Blacking, J. (1973). *How musical is man?* Seattle, WA: University of Washington Press.

Blacking, J. (1980). Trends in the Black music of South Africa, 1959-1969. In E. May (Ed.) *Musics of many cultures: An introduction.* Berkeley, CA: University of California press, pp. 195–215.

Blacking, J. (1982). Some principles of composition of the indigenous musics of Southern Africa. In J. Malan (Ed.) *South African music encyclopedia, Volume 2.* Capetown: University of Oxford Press, pp. 294–301.

Blacking, J. (1986). Ethnomusicological fieldwork, performance theory and problems of historical evidence. In M.L. Philipp (Ed.) *Ethnomusicology and the historical dimension: Papers presented at the European Seminar in Ethnomusicology, London, May 20–23, 1986.* Ludwigsburg: Philipp, pp. 127–8.

Blacking, J. (1987). *A commonsense view of all music: Reflections on Percy Grainger's contribution to ethnomusicology and music education.* Cambridge: Cambridge University Press.

Blacking, J. (1989). Challenging the myth of 'ethnic' music: First performances of a new song in African oral tradition. *Yearbook for traditional music,* **21,** 17–24.

Boden, M. (2004). *The creative mind: Myths and mechanisms, second edition.* London and New York: Routledge.

Brailoiu, C. (1984). Reflections on creative musical creation. In A.L. Lloyd (Ed. & Trans.) *Problems of ethnomusicology.* Cambridge: Cambridge University Press, pp. 102–9.

Cook, N. (2006). Playing God: Creativity, analysis, and aesthetic inclusion. In I. Deliège & G. Wiggins (Eds.) *Musical creativity: Multidisciplinary research in theory and practice.* East Sussex and New York: Psychology Press, pp. 9–24.

Davidson, J.W., Howe, M.J.A., & Sloboda, J.A. (1997). Environmental factors in the development of musical performance skill over the lifespan. In D. Hargreaves & A. North (Eds.) *The social psychology of music.* Oxford: Oxford University Press, pp. 188–206.

Deliège, I. & Wiggins, G.A. (Eds.)(2006). *Musical creativity: Multidisciplinary research in theory and practice.* East Sussex and New York: Psychology Press.

Demers, J. (2006). *Steal this music: How intellectual property law affects musical creativity.* Athens, GA: University of Georgia Press.

Filene, B. (2000). *Romancing the folk: Public memory and American roots music.* Chapel Hill, NC: University Of North Carolina Press.

Groce, S.B. (1991). On the outside looking in: Professional socialization and the process of becoming a songwriter. *Popular Music and Society,* **15**(1), 33–44.

Guilford, J.P. (1950). Creativity. *American Psychologist,* **5,** 444–54.

Hill, J. (2005). From ancient to avant-garde to global: Creative processes and institutionalization in Finnish contemporary folk music. PhD dissertation, University of California, Los Angeles.

Hill, J. (2007). 'Global folk music' fusions: The reification of transnational relationships and the ethics of cross-cultural appropriations in Finnish contemporary folk music. *Yearbook for traditional music,* **39,** 50–83.

Hill, J. (2009a). The influence of conservatory folk music programs: The Sibelius Academy in comparative context. *Ethnomusicology Forum,* **18**(2), 205–39.

Hill, J. (2009b). Rebellious pedagogy, ideological transformation, and creative freedom in Finnish contemporary folk music. *Ethnomusicology,* **53**(1), 86–114.

Hill, J. (2009c). Transformative teaching methods in Finnish folk music and wilderness education. In K. Oehme & N. Çiftçi (Eds.) *Musik im interkulturellen Dialog: Festschrift für Max Peter Baumann.* Bamberg: Forschungsstelle für fränkische Volksmusik, pp. 91–102.

Hughes, D. (2004). 'When can we improvise': The place of creativity in academic world music performance. In T Solís (Ed.) *Performing ethnomusicology: Teaching and representation and world music ensembles.* Berkeley, CA: University of California Press, pp. 261–81.

Kingsbury, H. (1988). *Music, talent, and performance: A conservatory cultural system*. Philadelphia, PA: Temple University Press.

Laitinen, H. (1989). Miksi kansanmusiikkia opetetaan? *Musiikin suunta*, **11**(4), 2–11.

Lord, A. (2000/1960). *The singer of tales*. Cambridge, MA: Harvard University Press.

Merker, B. (2006). Layered constraints on the multiple creativities of music. In I. Deliège & G. Wiggins (Eds.) *Musical creativity: Multidisciplinary research in theory and practice*. East Sussex and New York: Psychology Press, pp. 25–41.

Moore, R. (1992). The decline of improvisation in Western art music: An interpretation of change. *International Review of the Aesthetics and Sociology of Music*, **23**(1), 61–84.

Nettl, B. (1985). *The Western impact on world music: Change, adaptation, and survival*. New York: Schirmer Books.

Nettl, B. (1990/1954). Notes on musical composition in primitive culture. In K. KaufmaM Shelemay (Ed.) *Musical processes, resources, and technologies*. London: Garland, pp. 81–96.

Palmer, G. (1997). Bruce Springsteen and masculinity. *Sexing the groove: Popular music and gender,* edited by Sheila Whiteley. London: Routledge, pp. 100–117.

Pihl, M. (2003). *The Korean singer of tales*. Cambridge: Harvard University Press.

Price, D.E. (1989a). Eddy Raven: Bring me hit songs. *American songwriter*, 1 January. Available at: http://www.americansongwriter.com/1989/01/eddy-raven-bring-me-hit-songs/ (accessed 13 September 2009).

Price, D.E. (1989b). Jeff Gibson: Heavenbound's Gibson pens heart songs. *American songwriter* 1 November. Available at: http://www.americansongwriter.com/1989/11/jeff-gibson-heavenbound%E2%80%99s-gibson-pens-heart-songs/ (accessed 13 September 2009).

Rosenberg, N. (Ed.) (1993). *Transforming traditions: Folk music revivals examined*. Urbana, IL: University of Illinois Press.

Sancho-Velazquez, A. (2001). The legacy of genius: Improvisation, romantic imagination, and the Western musical canon. PhD dissertation, University of California, Los Angeles.

Seeger, A. (1979). What can we learn when they sing? Vocal genres of the Suya Indians of Central Brazil. *Ethnomusicology*, **23**(3), 373–94.

Seeger, A. (2004/1987). *Why Suya sing: A musical anthropology of an Amazonian people*. Urbana, IL: University of Illinois Press.

Turino, T. (1993). *Moving away from silence: Music of the Peruvian Altiplano and the experience of urban migration*. Chicago, IL: University of Chicago Press.

Webster, P. (1992). Research on creative thinking in music: The assessment literature. In R. Colwell (Ed.) *Handbook of research on music learning and teaching, a project of the Music Educators National Conference*. New York: Schirmer Books, pp. 266–80.

Wooley, A. (2003). Conjuring utopia: The Appalachian string band revival. PhD Dissertation, University Of California, Los Angeles.

Discography

Ancient civilizations of Southern Africa 2: Tribal drums of the Venda people (2005). CD. ARC Music. EUCD2026.

Arctic Paradise: Contemporary folk music from Finland (1997–2010). CD Series. Helsinki, Finland: Finnish Music Information Centre.

The Best of Broadside 1962–1988 (2000). Five-CD Box Set. Washington, DC: Smithsonian Folkways Recordings. SFWCD 40130.

Blacking, J. (1977). *How musical is man?* Cassette tape. Seattle, WA: University of Washington Press.

Cohen, J. & Turino, T. (1994). *Mountain music of Peru. Vol. 2.* CD. Washington, DC: Smithsonian Folkways Recordings. SFW40406.

Fast Folk: A community of singers and songwriters (2002). Two CD box set. Washington, DC: Smithsonian Folkways Recordings. SFW CD 40135.

Molsky, B., Smith, B., & Stefanini, R. (1997). *Bruce Molsky and Big Hoedown*. CD. Rounder Records 011661042124.

Seeger, A. (1987). *Why Suyá sing: A musical anthropology of an Amazonian people*. Cassette tape. Cambridge: Cambridge University Press.

Seeger, J. & Seeger, A. (1982). *Música Indígena a arte vocal dos Suya* . Série etnomusicologia, T007. LP. São João Del Rei, Brasil. Tacape.

Sibelius Academy Folk Music Department. Folk Music Finnovations. http://etno.net (accessed 1 February 2010).

Part 2

Perspectives from cognitive, social, and developmental psychology

Chapter 7

Musical materials or metaphorical models? A psychological investigation of what inspires composers

Shira Lee Katz and Howard Gardner

You know, my pieces are much more like being made as they go, and changing and transforming . . . there's an improvisatory flair about them. They're very handmade, very at-the-moment-made. I want the next note to sound fresh.

> -Reflection of the Within-Domain process; composer Augusta Read Thomas (2006 interview)

There's this opening chord that's very ethereal . . . and represents this kind of mystery. And then from it come these episodes that represent the stages of walking through the cloakroom.

> -Reflection of the Beyond-Domain process; composer Michael Gandolfi (2006 interview), inspired by a physical structure in a garden by Scottish architect Charles Jencks

Abstract

Of the studies of musical composition that exist, most are accounts of individual composers or analyses of scores divorced from the writing process. We lack information on the prototypical ways that pieces take shape and the core ideas and impulses that catalyse the process. In this chapter, which draws on in-depth interviews with 24 'creative' New Music composers, we examine the ways that these composers write and relate our findings to broader theories of the creative process. The creative process in this group of composers can be characterized in part by a single Stage Theory (i.e. distinct stages through which all of these creators pass). But extending beyond traditional stage theories, we also identify and detail two basic prototypical compositional strategies: Within-Domain and Beyond-Domain. Within-Domain processes are inspired predominantly by musical materials themselves. Beyond-Domain processes are influenced mostly by conceptual frameworks such as metaphors and associations from outside of the discipline of music. A small subset of processes called Hybrids more evenly reflect both Within-Domain and Beyond-Domain processes.

7.1 **Establishing composition as a process**

Perhaps as a legacy of the Romantic era, many commentators a century ago believed that an all-powerful being (e.g. God, a muse) was literally 'breathing' into the ear of the music composer. For example, some people believed that the act of composing music was similar to a lightning-bolt flash of inspiration involving little to no process and that it could not be studied systematically from a scientific perspective (Duchesneau, 1986). A handful of researchers, however, sought to learn more about what spurred creativity. Among them were psychologists like Carl Jung who studied the unconscious motivations behind creativity and Julius Bahle, who believed instead that the creation of a musical work was based on a series of conscious decisions (Duchesneau, 1986).

However, in recent decades, many researchers have sought to unravel the 'mysteries of creativity'. Gruber and Davis (1988) conducted literature-based studies of creative work documented in doctoral dissertations from 1962 to 1985. The researchers found that apparent epiphanies could be traced to similar ideas that had cropped up repeatedly earlier in creators' lives. In the case of one widely quoted example, Benjamin Franklin actually drew on scientific and cognitive frameworks that he had employed before and applied them to the new problem of his work relating to electricity. There is now general consensus that the creation of a substantial new work or idea involves problem-solving and reworking over time as opposed to one 'Aha!' moment during which the entire piece is suddenly formulated (Simonton, 2007).

7.1.1 **Stage Theory may unduly simplify**

Some of the most enduring theories of the creative process point to a single pathway that encapsulates all creative processes. These theories are generally referred to as 'Stage Theories' (Wallas, 1926). The stages are: preparation, incubation, illumination, and verification. Preparation is the period when a creator becomes acquainted with and evaluates a problem. Incubation is when the creator is distanced from the problem—when conscious work is put on the back burner. Illumination is sometimes referred to as the 'flash of insight' when there are signs that the solution is soon to come. Verification is the stage of refinement and development.

Some researchers have sought to modify Stage Theory (Wallas, 1926) or even question its central thrust. For instance, Ghiselin (1980) argued for a more integrated conceptualization of the process in which stages are not demarcated so sharply. Other researchers also argue that rigid stage models are over-simplistic. Calwelti, Rappaport, and Wood (1992), for instance, argue that many of the processes that are outlined in each stage actually take place to some degree during all stages.

Even though Katz's (2009) study identifies a similar Stage Theory (Wallas, 1926) trajectory among composers, we argue that Stage Theory may unduly simplify the creative process because it does not address the core ideas and impulses that influence composers as they write. Guilford (1950) argued that many researchers of the creative process document its steps without addressing what is happening in creators' minds from a cognitive perspective and this chapter seeks to examine these cognitive psychological factors.

7.1.2 **Dearth of research on composers' creative process**

Few studies investigate the factors that inspire music composers when they write and, to our knowledge, no studies explore how composers' initial ideas and impulses are then synthesized within their musical scores. Do composers begin with musical or non-musical ideas? Are composers aware of the factors that influence their work? If so, do they believe that these elements take root consciously or subconsciously? How are these ideas or subconscious impulses manifested in the scores themselves as musical representations? Are there patterns in this evolution? The scant material that has been written about the creative process (as opposed to product) in the domain of composition has been almost exclusively in the form of personal accounts by individual composers as opposed to findings synthesized across a group of composers.

One area for which existing studies of the composition process hold value, though, is in understanding more about the Preparation and Incubation stages of the creative process. These studies show composers who stay true to the basic parameters that they establish during the Preparation and Incubation stages even while reworking and 'riffing' as the piece progresses.

For example, Collins (2003) conducted a 3-year case study of one composer, collecting computerized versions of his scores and interviewing him repeatedly during the writing process to learn how his ideas evolved over time. He found that the composer was reluctant to abandon or alter the main ideas that cropped up virtually on the first day of creating. Collins's finding that the initial premises or impulses for pieces endure to the end jibe with our findings as well.

McAdams (2004) and John-Steiner (1997) conducted studies that show the large role of revision and problem-solving that helps evolve a piece to its final form. McAdams (2004) conducted an in-depth case study of Pulitzer Prize-Winning winning composer, Roger Reynolds. From this study in which McAdams collected data from Reynolds's piece, *The Angel of Death*, over a several month period of several months, McAdams casts Reynolds's composition process as a series of problems and solutions that reflects a guiding problem-solving mindset.

A similar problem-solving mindset is identified by John-Steiner (1997), who found that the method of many of the historically great composers (e.g. Beethoven) was to expand their initial impulses or ideas about a piece by reworking them repeatedly. Her findings emerge from a study of one hundred creators in a variety of content domains, including music. Composer Roger Sessions (Ghiselin, 1980) writes about how sketches made by Beethoven in the "*Hammerklavier Sonata*" were a methodical plotting of different versions of the theme and fugue. This example of Beethoven's work habits exemplifies that the creative process—at least for some composers—is a matter of constant modification over time.

Studies by Collins (2003), McAdams (2004), and John-Steiner (1997) confirm that many composers engage in experimentation and problem-solving as they write—particularly during the initial stages of creation—but that the defining elements of their piece identified at the outset are maintained well in tact throughout. These finding helped us distinguish between the macro and micro decisions involved during different stages of the writing process.

7.1.3 Filling a research gap

Overall, Stage Theory (Wallas, 1926) illuminates a progression of the creative process that is reflected in the processes of the composers that we discuss in this chapter, but does not take into account composers' cognitive psychological orientation towards their pieces. Katz's (2009) study upon which this chapter is premised therefore adds a dimension to the study of the creative process because it explores: 1) the mindset of composers during the writing process; 2) the factors that inspire them; and 3) the large- and small-scale choice points that buoy the process forward.

One of the purposes of this chapter is to show how the process prototypes that we discuss relate to these established theories. In this chapter then, we: 1) explicate the Within-Domain and Beyond-Domain process prototypes identified in Katz's (2009) study, describing the themes that dominate both processes; 2) place these two prototypes in the context of the aforementioned models of the creative process; and 3) speculate on subsequent studies that could test whether these processes are more composition specific or an enduring process that is reflected in most works that the composer creates.

7.2 **Methodology**

To answer questions about whether there are prototypical ways that composers write, Katz (2009) interviewed 24 creative New Music composers about the source, nature, and manifestation of inspirational influences on two of their own pieces that they believe to be particularly successful. She defined 'creative' as having made a new contribution in a particular domain through continued exploration from a variety of vantage points (synthesis of definitions from Csikszentmihalyi, 1996; Gardner, 1993; Perkins, 1981). By 'New Music' she was referring to current day classical music (i.e. programmatic and abstract, though no film music).

Her study focuses specifically on composers who are living. This genre is often associated with dissonance, atonal pieces, and extended techniques, breaking with many of the established music forms and norms dating back to the Classical Period.

Participants were a diverse group (e.g. genre, level of professional development) of 24 New Music composers from two levels of professional development. Katz (2009) arrived at her sample through a mixture of peer nomination and snowball sampling. Interviews focused on two pieces pre-selected by composers because they 'particularly liked' them. Interviews were conducted in person and were videotaped as the composers discussed their works with scores in hand. Interviews were transcribed partially verbatim and analysed using two forms of analysis: 1) Grounded Theory (Strauss & Corbin, 1990) to identify Emergent Theme, and 2) Theoretical frameworks that centered on factors that influenced composers, the direction from which inspiration manifested, and the symbolic realization of these influences in the final score.

Themes were considered 'emergent' if they were identified by anywhere from three to 23 of the composers (though the majority were identified by seven or more composers). In the development of thematic codes, Katz (2009) drew on Boyatzis's (1998) recommendations for assigning labels, definitions, and descriptions. Inter-rater reliability agreement was more than 70%, which means it satisfied 'reliability' for a study of this type (Boyatzis, 1998: p. 156).

Katz (2009) then reconstructed the chronology of composers' writing by again reading through composers' accounts of: 1) their normative composition processes, and 2) the specific writing processes that they described relating to the two pieces. In total, Katz (2009) found that approximately one-third of the composers were focused more on small musical elements and fragments. We refer to this process as the 'Within-Domain' process in this chapter. Overarching conceptual frameworks from outside of the domain of music drove approximately another third of the composers. We label this process 'Beyond-Domain' in this chapter. The remaining composers we classify as hybrids—engaging in both Within-Domain and Beyond-Domain processes because both processes are reflected in their work in seemingly equal weight (approximately the same number of Emergent Themes that were in opposite categories), either simultaneously or at different times.

7.3 **Process prototypes**

We provide an overview of prototypical Within-Domain and Beyond-Domain processes and then explicate them in greater depth. From hereon, we will use the terms 'Within-Domain' and 'Beyond-Domain' composers as shorthand to describe the processes in which composers engage. We are not asserting that these composers always write in this way, but that for the pieces for which they were interviewed this process was the more prominent driving force. During the Preparation/Incubation stages, the Within-Domain composer concentrates on the musical materials themselves (e.g. pitch, rhythm, instrumentation, and phrasing) by focusing on small snippets of music in a hands-on fashion. These composers allow these materials to sink in for long periods of time until the Illumination stage; at that point they rely heavily on kinesthetic memory or instinct vis-à-vis their instruments as a means of launching the initial bits of sound into a more coherent work. Finally, Within-Domain composers develop the musical materials more extensively and realize them in notated form during the Verification stage.

Beyond-Domain composers develop a conceptual framework that is rooted in a content domain outside of music during the Preparation/Incubation stage (Box 7.1). This is often a domain with which they have been intimately familiar for a great length of time. Once they have determined the conceptual basis for their piece, Beyond-Domain composers then 'translate' salient features of this extra-musical content onto the piece itself in musical terms. As the basic extra-musical framework is translated into musical aspects of the piece, the Beyond-Domain composer fills in this basic conceptually driven structure with more specific elements related to the broader framework during the Verification stage. Table 7.1 shows how Within-Domain and Beyond-Domain composer prototypes map onto Stage Theory (Wallas, 1926).

Box 7.1 Within-Domain stages 1 and 2

Preparation/incubation

Dominant themes: imagination, improvisation, hands-on.

7.3.1 Imagination

The theme of 'imagination' that is prevalent in Within-Domain composers' process refers to the musical possibilities that they envision before penning actual notes. Imagining is often one of the first steps of the Preparation/Incubation stage. Within-Domain composers literally try to imagine the sound they intend to create or the way parts or instruments will blend. Not surprisingly, Within-Domain composers describe having well-developed musical 'ears' so that they are able to hear the mix of multiple instruments in their head without feeling the necessity to physically test them.

When asked what instrument(s) he uses when composing, Within-Domain composer Peter Gilbert says, 'I often use a coupling of my imagination and something else' to help launch the piece 'before the actual pitches, before the singing'. The act of conjuring up different musical scenarios for Within-Domain composers—especially ones that are ridiculous—can be mentally freeing.

Table 7.1 Within-Domain and Beyond-Domain processes mapped onto Stage Theory

	Stage 1 Preparation	Stage 2 Incubation	Stage 3 Illumination	Stage 4 Verification
Stage Theory	Creator becomes acquainted with and evaluates a problem	Creator is distanced from the problem; conscious work is put on the back burner	Creator has a 'flash of insight' when there are signs that the solution is imminent	Composer refines and develops the basic model
Within-Domain	Experimentation with musical materials (e.g. sound, instrument) in a hands-on fashion		Bits of music gel into a more cohesive work	Details of piece are worked out and notated
Beyond-Domain	Attachment to a conceptual model from outside of the music domain		Major characteristics of the conceptual model defined and mapped onto piece	Fleshes out models with smaller ideas and associations connected to the larger framework

Hearing sounds in their heads can be useful for Within-Domain composers because it allows them to set the foundation for the musical themes that have yet to unfold. Within-Domain composer Howie Frazin compares the organic emergence of this frame to his experience with drawing classes at the Art Institute in Chicago when he was young. Frazin recalls that he only had to place a few marks on the page to imagine what the completed image would look like. In essence, Within-Domain composers run through a variety of scenarios during the Preparation/Incubation stage as a means of seeing what sticks—what will be the musical impetus for the piece.

7.3.2 Improvisation, hands-on

After running through a host of imagined musical scenarios, Within-Domain composers compare them by playing or singing them. Now able to hear how sound translates from their mind's ear to their actual ear, they begin to test, shape, and reshape material. This period of experimentation is intense, and can be both rewarding and frustrating. Says Within-Domain composer Dominique Schafer, he initially 'run[s] through [musical] scenarios that might be really absurd', which he says gives him licence to play with a wide variety of stimuli and sounds. For Schafer, experimenting with different possibilities engenders a mentality of non-constraint. For others, this period of experimentation can be daunting because it is bounded by no formal parameters.

This gradually strengthening relationship with the musical materials seems to correspond with a heightened physicality for Within-Domain composers. Integral to the process of Within-Domain composers is improvisation, which we define as: in-the-moment creation that has a strong physical basis (Nachmanovitch, 2001). Because Within-Domain composers rely on kinesthetic feedback to a large degree during this initial stage, their music may appear to have little structure or obvious direction. There appears to be no clear musical or extra-musical framework guiding their pieces.

Physical spontaneity and vigor drive the composition process for Within-Domain composers during this stage. Within-Domain composer Peter Gilbert talks about dancing around his studio as if limbering up for a sporting event. Hybrid composer Jeff Roberts talks about how the energy that he feels during this stage is not unlike the 'flow' that he experienced playing high school sports. Within-Domain composer Augusta Read Thomas refers to her pieces as 'live emergencies', by which she means that she feels an urgency to attend to them.

> I like all of my music to sound like it was just being made . . . right there. You're never quite sure what's coming next. Like there's a surprise. Like you go bee-da-da-deeyah; vo-but-do-but-do. It's like, what is that second thing? You know, that shouldn't be there. But it kind of keeps you on your toes. And then it comes back: Jum! You're like, ok, we're back. And then you think you're gonna go digadiga, but you don't. You go bu-yuh jee-yah! It's another third thing. And yet they all make logic together. There's a certain motion involved.

(Thomas interview, 2006.)

Feeling non-constraint does not mean that this period of experimentation is a cakewalk. In fact, Within-Domain composers during this period may reconfigure material repeatedly. They may conjure up several different beginnings, a variety of rhythmic variations on one theme, and test material using different tone colors. John-Steiner (1997) studied the creative processes of 100 preeminent creators and found that a healthy portion of them revise and rework their pieces repeatedly.

In conclusion, Within-Domain composers will likely have little idea of the direction a piece will take during the Preparation/Incubation stages. They may run through myriad musical scenarios in their head; they may test them on their instruments or with their voice in a fashion that underscores their physical connection with the materials; they may then experiment with different permutations of these improvisations until ones prove promising. The seeds of the musical materials are planted during these first two stages.

The work pace of Within-Domain composers generally quickens during the Illumination stage (Box 7.2). Ideas that were fragmented during the initial stages of the creative process now cohere. In contrast to Beyond-Domain composers who employ a conceptual framework from outside of music to provide structure for their pieces, the focus of Within-Domain composers in this stage remains on the musical materials themselves. Within-Domain composer Bert Van Herck says that he never intends to translate non-musical concepts into music with his pieces. He instead maintains an ethic of music for music sake.

Box 7.2 Within-Domain stage 3

Illumination

Dominant themes: sound impressions, sound worlds, positive physicality.

7.3.3 Sound impressions, sound worlds

Within-Domain composers in this stage of creation gravitate toward sounds that can yield a more coherent sound impression. According to Within-Domain composer Bert Van Herck, sound impressions—or 'sound images,' as he calls them, are impressions of sound that are too nebulous to be notated but suggest elements that will eventually be fundamental to the piece. Hybrid composer John Howell Morrison refers to these amorphous sounds as 'timbral magic' that allow him to access an 'expressive power of sound' that is more unified.

While Within-Domain composers generally do not rely on frameworks from outside of the music domain, they do begin to explicitly recognize the music theory that underlies their gelling work. Within-Domain composer Augusta Read Thomas says that she slowly clues in to the music theory that underlies her improvisations. For instance, she says that she comes to realize that she is favoring certain intervals or harmonies over others. These preferences become increasingly clear for Within-Domain composers as their pieces unfold and they can then further build parts of their pieces based on this knowledge. Within-Domain composers seem to recognize the music theory underpinning their work gradually as opposed to setting up a conceptual model at the outset.

7.3.4 Positive physicality

The physicality that was evident in the earlier stages seems to be elevated during the Illumination stage for Within-Domain composers. Within-Domain composer Michael Miller's (2005) description of the sound world for 'Blood Spattered Haze' from *Flesh of My Flesh* emphasizes his increased physical connection with the instruments. He flutter-picks his guitar and uses the 'infinite reverb' setting that allows sound to resonate violently. He creates syncopation between the guitar and marimba lines in the piece, which adds to the harsh underlying sound world.

The sound world that Hybrid composer Eric Roth (2005) strives for in *Together Is the New Forward* is similar to that 'in free jazz'. To reach this heightened state of 'positive physicality' as he puts it, Roth believes that music should be an extension of the body. He writes in pitch bending for the guitar, which causes him to 'push the guitar around' as a way to be more physically connected to the process. In general, Roth believes that instruments should be pushed to their limits.

His 'manhandling' of these instruments highlights a link between physicality and musical materials during the Illumination stage.

We have argued that Within-Domain composers cohere disparate scraps of sound into enduring musical elements during the Illumination stage. These 'sound impressions' reflect particular sequences and phrases that prove more central to pieces as they progress. As they grow more attached to certain sound elements, Within-Domain composers' energy heightens. They engage more closely with their instruments; they play more aggressively with sound; they throw their bodies into the process.

During the Verification stage (Box 7.3), Within-Domain composers fill out the piece's sound world with details—scales, arpeggios, and other extensions of the basic sound landscape. For example, a chord that has been prominent during the earlier stages may now be voiced differently and expanded so that it becomes the lynchpin for other material. In addition, Within-Domain composers eliminate superfluous material during this stage of the process.

Box 7.3 Within-Domain stage 4

Verification

Dominant themes: sketches, good ears, drawing on existing language.

7.3.5 Sketches

One of the prime ways that Within-Domain composers may augment the existing material from the Illumination stage is by filling in the shells of notation sketched earlier in greater detail. These outlines might consist of the piece's basic harmony and simple melody overlaying it or basic chords without written-out embellishments, such as trills or turns.

Within-Domain composer Easley Blackwood describes filling out a bare bones version of the first movement of his third string quartet (Blackwood, 1998) by first filling in the version of the piece that fit on two staffs with two hands playing the parts, then expanding the piece to four staffs and four hands. After this stage, Blackwood was able to write out the rest of the piece, complete with details such as dynamics, phrase markings, and articulations.

7.3.6 Musical ear

Within-Domain composers are generally characterized as having well-developed musical ears. This means that they describe having relative or perfect pitch and the ability to notate complex passages without playing them first. They essentially hear these figures in their mind's ear and are able to translate them expeditiously to written form. Since their work is centered so squarely on sound and the musical materials, they rely heavily on their ears to compose. Within-Domain composer Easley Blackwood describes the phenomenon as follows:

> I cannot only hear all of the individual parts . . . I went to the rehearsals of the Chicago Symphony Orchestra every week when I was working on my 5th symphony . . . and so when I construct an orchestral sound, what I hear is the Chicago Symphony Orchestra playing in Orchestra Hall. . . . I hear the reverberation and the echo. I hear the basses on this side [pointing to his right].

(Blackwood interview, 2006.)

Within-Domain composer Michael Miller also describes being able to hear notes in his head. He describes composing whole passages as he walks around aimlessly in nature and then rushes home to write them down so that they are not forgotten. The ear of Hybrid composer Shulamit

Ran seemed to be exceptional from a very young age. Ran would compose tunes to go along with the storybooks that her mother read her. When her mother asked Ran where the melodies had come from, Ran would respond that they were in the text—in the book. Explains Ran, 'I did not realize I was making that melody up. As far as I was concerned, it was there'.

Within-Domain composers expand their work during the Verification stage, focusing on the minutiae of the process, the piece's last details. They do this by filling in and expanding their musical scores and also by cutting out materials that are not core. We speculate that Within-Domain composers are able to fill in these elements of the piece because their musical 'ears' have been primed.

7.4 Prototype B: Beyond-Domain

Beyond-Domain composers differ from Within-Domain composers in that the majority of the material on which Beyond-Domain composers draw emanates from outside of the music domain. This content is often that which they have been exposed to previously—an interest, hobby, or belief system that they have held long before applying it to a piece of music.

Box 7.4 Beyond-Domain stage 1

Preparation/incubation

Emergent theme: ideas 'marinate', familiar material.

7.4.1 Ideas 'marinate'

Beyond-Domain composers seem to take a long time to determine what extra-musical ideas or theoretical constructs will influence their pieces (Box 7.4). The process of identifying a worthy framework can be a major challenge for Beyond-Domain composers, stymieing them for days, weeks, years, even decades. Perhaps it takes Beyond-Domain composers so long to write because they are devising frames that will serve as structures for entire pieces.

An example of how ideas 'steep' for these composers in particular comes from the reflections of Beyond-Domain composer Joshua Fineberg. Fineberg describes a lengthy period of waiting while his ideas for his opera *Lolita* (Fineberg, 2006) took hold. The piece was based on the well-known book by Nabokov. The story takes place in the head of Humbert, the book's narrator who is in jail as he tells his tale. Though he did not concentrate on this story continuously during this time period, Fineberg says it took him 20 years to solidify the idea for an opera based on this story. Fineberg's timeline is extreme, but not an exception by any means. Gruber and Davis (1988) discuss the idea that so-called epiphanies often result not from one episode of extreme insight but from ideas that reoccur repeatedly over time and that eventually come to the forefront.

7.4.2 Familiar material

The matter that influences Beyond-Domain composers is often quite personal. For instance, since his teenage years, Beyond-Domain composer Michael Gandolfi has made theoretical physics one of his major hobbies. He in fact vowed to understand as much as possible about Einstein's theory of relativity by the 100th anniversary of the theory in 2005. This physics framework manifested in Gandolfi's (2004) work, *Impressions from the Garden of Cosmic Speculation*. Gandolfi based the work on the famous garden by renowned Scottish critic and architect Charles Jencks. The aesthetics of the garden were dictated in large part by quantum mechanics, super-string theory, and other physics principles. The extent to which Gandolfi felt emotionally connected to this garden and its underlying principles of physics runs deep—so much so that Gandolfi says he feels a closeness with Jencks himself.

Similar to Gandolfi, Hybrid composer Shulamit Ran based her piece *O the Chimneys* (Ran, 1969) on subject matter that was intensely personal to her: the Holocaust. Ran was first inspired to write the piece after stumbling upon the Holocaust poetry of Nelly Sachs (1969) at a bookstore.

> I remember very, very clearly the sensation of reading that poem and having to read it as fast as I could. It's not the kind of poem where you could read a sentence and then stop to reflect . . . There was an urgency to it . . . I absolutely had to go through to the end knowing very well what the end would be.
>
> (Ran interview, 2006.)

The intensity with which Ran read through Sachs's poems seems indicative of what she describes as her personal dedication to writing music about the Holocaust. Ran further explains:

> It was absolutely not a piece where I could have said, well it could have been written and on the other hand it could have been not written . . . It was my personal way, really, of saying, 'do not forget'.
>
> (Ran interview, 2006.)

One of the greatest interests of Beyond-Domain composer Ken Ueno is architecture. He says he might even have become a professional architect had he not become a composer. It is not surprising then that architecture was a major influence on Ueno's (2005) piece *Kaze-no-Oka*.

A set of three burial structures by Japanese architect Fumihiko Maki inspired Ueno. Says Ueno:

> Embodied in the structures [too] was an irresolvable tension between multiplicities . . . the buildings can be seen as separate as well as belonging to the same complex; they are individual and together at the same time.
>
> (Ueno interview, 2006.)

Ueno drew on the dichotomies represented in the buildings (i.e. uniqueness of design but cohesion across the buildings) to launch his piece.

Rabbi Moshe Cotel based two of his major works on stories of intolerance against the Jews. This subject was so meaningful to him, in fact, that in 2000 he left his professorship at the Peabody Conservatory to be a Rabbi. As if a foreshadowing of his career switch, Cotel (1983) wrote a Zionist opera called *Dreyfus* based on the 19th-century Dreyfus Affair in which an assimilated Jewish journalist in Europe was wrongly accused of treason. With another piece called *Deronda* (after George Eliot's final novel, *Daniel Deronda*), Cotel's strong connection with Judaism is evident once again. The opera is about a Jew who is adopted by a Protestant woman and then ends up falling in love with a Jew much to the horror of the community.

As a final example, Hybrid composer Peter Child uses his political views as the basis for several of his pieces. For instance, Child writes *Estrella: The Assassination of Augusto César Sandino* (Child, 1988) based on his 'sense of frustration about the abuses in Central America—particularly United States foreign policy in this area of the world'.

> There was a fantastically beneficent socialist government in Nicaragua that was doing fantastic things with education and health care, and what upset me the most was the hypocrisy. The U.S. was sending in liberators to liberate a country from its own best interests.
>
> (Child interview, 2006.)

The creative process is usually launched much more gingerly for Beyond-Domain composers than for Within-Domain composers. Whereas Within-Domain composers rely very much on intuition and getting their hands dirty with the physicality of composing, Beyond-Domain composers are much more conventionally cerebral about the process. They allow ideas to bubble up naturally and over time. They also gravitate toward conceptual frameworks and material outside of the music domain. This is material with which they have been familiar with previously and which becomes the impetus for the music.

During the Illumination stage, Beyond-Domain composers develop the conceptual ideas from the Preparation/Incubation stages into something that is cohesive during Illumination (Box 7.5). It becomes clear during this stage not just what extra-musical model they will use but *how* these models will be employed.

Box 7.5 Beyond-Domain stage 3

Illumination

Dominant themes: parameters/constraints, metaphors, and images.

7.4.3 Parameters and constraints

Beyond-Domain composers often develop a set of guidelines or 'parameters' by which they work. This might be a handful of guidelines that they will work with while composing. By the same token, they might impose a set of constraints or things that they will avoid. These parameters may or may not be at the discretion of the composer depending on the specific commissioning guidelines.

Beyond-Domain composers often welcome parameters because they speed up their process and make it more efficient. For instance, Hybrid composer Shulamit Ran admires a composer like György Ligeti because she says that he is able to employ a scarcity of source materials (e.g. limited pitches, rhythms, a textural idea) in some of his most captivating works. Beyond-Domain composer Michael Gandolfi says that he aims for clear communication with his pieces in order to achieve simple elegance. Hybrid composer Peter Child welcomes the idea of constraining his process as well:

> The fact is that having the parameters laid down is actually incredibly helpful. It takes away that *tabula rasa*—that anxiety that is actually part of my process. I don't really like that feeling. I think some composers like that feeling of 'anything's possible,' and I don't. I don't feel comfortable until the possibilities start to narrow and I feel some point of orientation. I think I don't like the disorientation.

> (Child interview, 2006.)

The pursuit of economy may carry over to teaching for Beyond-Domain composers. At the University of Chicago Ran requires her students to write pieces with limits on pitches and other prescribed constraints. She says that the products students fashion with these limitations can be better than ones created without them. Beyond-Domain composer David Kechley of Williams College devises exercises similar to those of Ran. To illustrate his point, Kechley tells a story of a character in Robert Pirsig's book *Zen and the Art of Motorcycle Maintenance* who is discussing a student who wanted to write a short story about the history of Montana. The teacher in the book instead convinces the student to pare down her idea. The student ends up writing about a brick in one building in one city in Montana and the story is judged a success.

The benefits of setting parameters is summed up eloquently in a well-known remark by Stravinsky:

> My freedom will be so much the greater and more meaningful the more narrowly I limit my field of action and the more I surround myself with obstacles. Whatever diminishes constraint diminishes strength. The more constraints one imposes, the more one frees one's self of the chains that shackle the spirit.

> (Stravinsky, 1982: p. 68.)

7.4.4 **Metaphors**

During the latter part of the Illumination stage, extra-musical models used by Beyond-Domain composers are often solidified. By 'solidify,' we mean that the Beyond-Domain composers develop their ideas about the musical matter through formal devices such as metaphors and images. In this instance, metaphor refers to the conceptual schemas that express the relationship between extra-musical domains and music and do not carry with them a literal or linguistic meaning (Ortony, 1979); images refer to the visual matter (e.g. real images, imagined images, sculpture) that influences a composition.

We have discussed how Beyond-Domain composer Michael Gandolfi (2005) draws on the principles of theoretical physics encapsulated in Jencks's garden as a basis for his piece, *Impressions from the Garden of Cosmic Speculation*. During the Illumination stage he develops this metaphor even further by equating each movement with a different place in the garden and then imbuing that movement with characteristics from the physical area. For instance, 'The Zeroroom' is the name of the garden's entryway. Of 'The Zeroroom's' structure, Gandolfi writes:

> It is a fanciful, surreal cloakroom flanked by an orderly procession of tennis racquets that appear to be traveling through the wall in a 'quantum dance,' and large photographs that progress from our place in the universe, galaxy, solar system, planet, to the precise position of the garden in the north of Scotland.

> (Gandolfi, 2004.)

The music of the movement with the same name reflects the progression from the broad view of outer space to that of a tree. This change in perspective is represented with a beginning in which an 'ethereal' chord is played 'con sordino' or with mutes and gets increasingly more insistent as the percussion and brass enter with more distinctive, syncopated lines.

The metaphor that drives Beyond-Domain composer Ken Ueno (2005) with his piece *Kaze-no-Oka is* that of duality, encapsulated by the crematorium discussed previously. Ueno says he recognized a unified structure across the buildings, but individuality within each one as well. He saw a sharp contrast between the ancient ground on which the buildings sat and the contemporary architecture of the buildings themselves. This juxtaposition played out in part in the piece's instrumentation. Ueno scored the piece for the airy Japanese woodwind called the Japanese shakuhachi and for a Japanese lute called a biwa, which has a more 'earthy' sound. Also, the piece is separated in a way that distinguishes the body of the work from the cadenza. Ueno made this decision in part to represent the compartmentalization of the buildings.

Another type of metaphor that Beyond-Domain composers may use connects story character with musical character. Beyond-Domain composer Michael McLaughlin describes reading a Sherlock Holmes story that begins with a murder scene that is followed by flashbacks about how the murder may have occurred. This story inspired McLaughlin's (2005) work *Murder,* which begins with an intense, climactic murder scene scored for multiple horns and insistent percussion. The musical characters are the 'pious,' represented with church-like sounds; the 'trickster' is delightfully devious and so McLaughlin represents his presence with campy material from Hitchcock's *Psycho, Vertigo,* and *North by Northwest;* the 'morose' is represented by slides up and down the string from the cello as if to convey a 'woe is me' attitude. The victim is represented differently depending on with whom he or she is tussling.

Another example: Beyond-Domain composer Melissa Carubia bases many of her pieces on storybook or real life characters. Carubia's (2005) *Overture to the Lost Histories* is based on a real life role-playing game that resembles Dungeons and Dragons. In the mix are a pirate with a heart of gold who is represented by a beautiful, clear theme, a Spanish conman, and a respected, church member, all of whom have their own themes. Carubia invited the friends involved in the role playing game to the piece's premiere. However, she did not tell them which themes were associated with which characters. Carubia recounts with glee that her friends were able to tell the themes apart based solely on what they heard at the performance.

7.4.5 Images

Images—real life ones such as photographs, paintings and sculpture or imagined ones—can dictate some of the most salient features of a piece. Beyond-Domain composer Lei Liang reminisces about a series of pieces he wrote when he was small. This series of pieces called *Mice Celebrating the New Year—Short Piano Works of Lei Liang* (Liang, 1996), were composed in large part based on images. Liang describes receiving a stamp from his parents for each piece that he wrote. A beautiful swan stamp was the impetus for his piece with the same name. He says that he composed the piece by placing the stamp in front of him at the piano and using it as inspiration while he composed. The piece has a dreamy quality to it that is carried out when performers lay their whole hand over the black keys. The effect is like ripping water. Over this dreamy sequence is laid an elegant melody, which is supposed to represent the swan on the stamp floating over the rippling water.

Other pieces that Liang composes were influenced strongly by images. When Liang's Chinese grandmother visited the United States, he visualized her plane making an arc over the Sea of Japan. The piece that resulted was called *The Sea of Japan* (Liang, 1996 later edition) and is based the rising and falling trajectory of his grandmother's plane. He represented this movement with ascending and descending scales accompanied by crescendos and decrescendos respectively.

The visual arts seem to be a major influence on the work of Beyond-Domain composers. Composers of this ilk often refer to the parallels of the art and music domains or talk about the influences of artists or art on their work. Beyond-Domain composer Karola Obermüller describes her music as having distinct edges and being a patchwork of color. Beyond-Domain composer Lei Liang feels that he *is* painting when composing. Beyond-Domain composer Ken Ueno discusses the strong influences on his music of contemporary artists such as George Baselitz, Anselm Kiefer, and Gerhard Richter.

During the Illumination stage, Beyond-Domain composers essentially concretize the influential frameworks from outside of the music domain. They do this by limiting the variables they can work with—setting parameters and imposing constraints on the process themselves or as a product of being commissioned. They then develop these ideas by drawing on metaphors, associations, or images as a means of binding pieces into cohesive frameworks. Generally, Beyond-Domain composers identify the salient features of these extra-musical frameworks and translate them in some way to the major musical elements of their work.

Box 7.6 Beyond-Domain stage 4

Verification

Dominant theme: spin-offs.

In the final Verification stage Beyond-Domain composers develop and perfect the smaller elements—the conceptual spin-offs—of the overall organizing framework (Box 7.6). For instance, composers who decide to base their pieces on Niagara Falls themes might represent rushing water in a variety of ways. Beyond-Domain composer Joshua Fineberg refers to this more targeted process as 'biopsies'. By biopsies, Fineberg means doing 'tests' to figure out which approaches are most promising.

In a sense, this is a stage of re-testing and refining the material that Beyond-Domain composers have already determined to be viable.

Beyond-Domain composers demonstrate tenacity during the often-tedious Verification stage. Schoenberg (1975) said it was important to help students persevere with their pieces after the initial stages of excitement had worn off. He said that the creation of transitions and codas in particular were difficult for composers. Singer/songwriter Roseanne Cash (2008) believes that the more drawn-out processes can ultimately be more rewarding and more successful:

> Twenty-five years ago, I would have said that the bursts of inspiration, and the transcendent quality that came with them, were an emotionally superior experience, preferable to the watchmaker concentration required for the detail work of refining, editing and polishing. But the reverse is proving to be true.
>
> (Cash, 2008.)

Ultimately, the Verification stage is a time when Beyond-Domain composers develop conceptual frameworks to their fullest by testing ideas that spin-off from the broader conceptual framework. These ideas usually translate into music at the note level, phrase level, and into other smaller parts of music during this final stage.

7.5 **Finale**

While we recognize the utility of the stage conception of composition and use it in our own work, its deficiencies demand attention. In particular, Stage Theory does not address what is happening in composers' minds from a cognitive psychological perspective nor does it provide in-depth information about the nature and sources of their inspiration. These factors have proven to be illuminative in identifying two basic process prototypes that we have detailed in this chapter: Within-Domain and Beyond-Domain.

While the argument that we make in this paper hinges on the identification of two distinct processes, there are emergent themes that reflect similarities between Within-Domain and Beyond-Domain processes that we do not deny. Composers engaging in both processes begin with experimentation, become closer to the materials (musical or conceptual) they are working with, and finally develop and fill in these concepts or materials. Further, there are clearly themes that crosscut these two processes. For instance, composers whose work reflects both processes seem to employ some type of constraints or parameters in their work. With the Beyond-Domain process, composers whittle down or concretely define their ideas over time; composers reflecting the Within-Domain process narrow their palette of sounds through experimentation.

In an indeterminate number of cases there may be more overlap between Within-Domain and Beyond-Domain processes than is suggested in this chapter. After all, Katz's (2009) study was based on just two-dozen composers' descriptions of only two works. These were often composers' most recent pieces. Given the limited numbers of pieces, it is fair to speculate that the array of influences and methods used by composers could not be fully captured. Maybe composers oscillate in their approach throughout their lifetime or perhaps there is a hierarchy of the creative process and the pinnacle is to be a Hybrid. We were recently struck by the wide variance of activity described by acclaimed composer John Adams in his autobiography (2008). In college he describes writing a conceptually driven piece called *Electric Wake*.

> *The Electric Wake* was a 'wake' because the music was a setting of poetry about a psychedelic nymphet/goddess named Talley who consumes herself in a burning drug-induced ecstasy somewhere in a London park.
>
> (Adams, 2008: p. 49.)

Based on this description, a cursory analysis might suggest that Adams is a Beyond-Domain composer. But he describes times later in life when his process seems more Within-Domain because it is influenced by and rooted in sound.

> I made a piece called Triggering, in which I followed improvising dancers around the floor of a converted warehouse on Mission Street with a long-distance shotgun microphone. Each time a dancer hit the floor or slapped a hand or even grunted from exertion the microphone picked up the sound and caused circuits on my synthesizer to fire, emitting a loud sound. These I mixed with audio 'found objects' I kept on cassette tapes—everything from the sound of insect and animal noises to passing ocean vessels, cable cars, and the jostling of a crowded street.
>
> (Adams, 2008, p. 80.)

While some might argue that it could have been more beneficial to gather data over time as composers' compositions progressed, collecting data over a finite period of time was relatively unobtrusive. This method was also monetarily viable and captured an important element of reflection that may not have been possible while composers were in the midst of writing.

Given that a narrow portion of composers' work was investigated in Katz's (2009) study, we suggest a follow-up study that systematically documents composers' reflections about their work over several years or even decades. Still, the main implication of this chapter is that there is more variation within Stage Theory (Wallas, 1926) than is typically portrayed. The distinction in this paper between Within-Domain and Beyond-Domain processes brings more specificity to our understanding of inspirational factors on the creative process and sheds light on a spectrum of work habits.

7.6 How to improve composition pedagogy?

While we are not arguing that a given person engages only in the Within-Domain or Beyond-Domain process, the distinction between the two prototypes should not be overlooked either. Imagine teaching any course or individual lessons without having a clue what motivates students to work or without learning what is personally meaningful to them. Composer Bob Hasegawa (2006), classified in Katz's (2009) study as carrying out a Hybrid process, noted: 'The best composition teachers are very flexible and can quickly figure out what you're doing'. We speculate that compositions teachers are essentially in the dark about what and how their students are inspired. And it is hard to accept the argument that traditional theory, harmony, and counterpoint courses have the same motivating effect. Famed composer John Adams (2008) refers to the 'tedious written exercises' (p. 30) from the harmony classes in his college days that he fervently rebelled against.

In essence, understanding what inspires composers equates to understanding their personal motivation for doing what they do and how they do it. More specific knowledge would no doubt go a long way to help teachers tailor courses to different students' needs. Even for more seasoned composers, knowing about the range of influences on the work of their colleagues could bring added insight to the process.

Within the music domain, many researchers speculate about how composition pedagogy could be modified in the future. Webster (2003) makes a case for music teachers helping their students to engage in more critical thinking as they are writing music. Webster says, 'Such requests on the part of teachers need to be done in a spirit of genuine respect for a child's original thinking, but not eschewed because it is seen to interfere or be immediately critical'.

Hickey and Webster (2001) believe that music teachers would be well served if they drew on children's natural creative inclinations. As it stands, they argue, many of the behaviours that are associated with creativity, such as 'risk-taking' and 'silly behaviour', are ones those that are disparaged in classroom settings. Children exhibiting these behaviours are often viewed as rebellious and hardheaded. Hickey believes that it could be good for teachers to harness this energy in children and re-route it into more productive and creative activities. By giving children license to do things that are normally considered atypical, teachers might better foster their creativity more effectively.

References

Adams, J. (2008). *Hallelujah Junction: Composing an American Life*. New York: Faber and Faber.

Calvino, I. (1988). *Six memos for the next millennium*. Cambridge, MA: Harvard University Press.

Cash, R. (2008). Don't fact-check the soul. New York Times Online (Opinion section), 29 April. Available at: http://measureformeasure.blogs.nytimes.com/2008/04/29/dont-fact-check-the-soul/.

Collins, D. (2003). A synthesis model of thinking in music composition. *Psychology of Music*, **32**, 193–216.

Csikszentmihalyi, M. (1996). *Creativity: Flow and the psychology of discovery and invention*. New York: Harper Perennial.

Csikszentmihalyi, M., & Getzels, J.W. (1971). Discovery-oriented behavior and the originality of creative products: A study with artists. *Journal of Personality and Social Psychology*, **19(1)**, 47–52.

Duchesneau, L. (1986). *The voice of the muse: A study of the role of* inspiration in musical composition. New York: Peter Lang.

Galenson, D. (2003). The life cycles of modern artists: Theory, measurement, and implications (National Bureau of Economic Research Reporter Paper No. 9539. JEL. No. J4). Retrieved April 15, 2008, from http://www.nber.org/papers/w9539.

Gardner, H. (1993). *Creating minds*. New York: Basic Books.

Gruber, H.E., & Davis, S.N. (1988). Inching our way up Mount Olympus: The evolving-systems approach to creative thinking. In R.J. Sternberg (Ed.) *The nature of creativity: Contemporary psychological perspectives*. New York: Cambridge University Press, pp. 243–69.

Jencks, C. (2003). *The garden of cosmic speculation*. London: Frances Lincoln.

John-Steiner, V. (1997). *Notebooks of the mind*. Oxford: Oxford University Press.

Katz, S.L. (2009). Dichotomous forces of inspiration in the creative process: A Study of Within-Domain versus Beyond-Domain Music Composers. Doctoral Dissertation, Harvard Graduate School of Education. Retrieved from http://discovery.lib.harvard.edu/?itemid=|library/m/aleph|011903122.

Nachmanovitch, S. (2001). Freedom: Commentary on a paper by Philip A. Ringstrom. *Psychoanalytic Dialogues*, **11**, 771–84.

Ortony, A. (1979). *Metaphor and thought*. New York: Cambridge University Press.

Perkins, D.N. (1981). *The mind's best work*. Cambridge, MA: Harvard University Press.

Sachs, N. (1969). *O the chimneys: Selected poems, including the verse play, Eli* (M. Hamburger, Trans). New York: Farrar, Straus and Giroux.

Schoenberg, A. (1975). Tonality and form: 1925. In L. Stein (Ed.), *Style and idea*. Berkeley, CA: University of California Press, pp. 255–7.

Simonton, D.K. (2007). Creative life cycles in literature: Poets versus novelists or conceptualists versus experimentalists? *Psychology of Aesthetics, Creativity, and the Arts*, **1**, 133–9.

Wallas, G. (1926). *The art of thought*. London: Watts.

Webster, P.R. (2003). Asking music students to reflect on their creative work: Encouraging the revision process. *Music education research*, **5**(3), 243–47.

Interviews

Blackwood, E. 2 June, 2006. Chicago, IL.

Carubia, M. 25 April, 2006. Cambridge, MA.

Child, P. 12 June, 2006. Cambridge, MA.

Cotel, M. 23 July, 2006. New York, NY.

Fineberg, J. 24 May, 2006. Cambridge, MA.

Frazin, H. 7 June and 23 June, 2006. Cambridge, MA.

Gandolfi, M. 31 May, 2006. Cambridge, MA.

Gilbert, P. 14 April, 2006. Cambridge, MA.

Hasegawa, B. 30 May, 2006. Cambridge, MA.

Kechley, D. 21 July, 2006. Williamstown, MA.

Liang, L. 6 June, 2006. Cambridge, MA.

McLaughlin, M. 18 July, 2006. Cambridge, MA.

Miller, M. 25 May, 2006. Jamaica Plain, MA.

Morrison, J. H. 23 May, 2006. Cambridge, MA.

Obermüller, K. 19 April, 2006. Cambridge, MA.

Ueno, K. 26 June, 2006. Cambridge, MA.

Ran, S. 5 June, 2006. Chicago, IL.

Roberts, J. 17 July, 2006. Cambridge, MA.

Roth, E. 23 July, 2006. New York, NY.

Read Thomas, A. 22 June, 2006. Lee, MA.

Schafer, D. 29 June, 2006. Cambridge, MA.

Van Herck, B. 1 May, 2006. Cambridge, MA.

Chapter 8

Spreading activation and dissociation: A cognitive mechanism for creative processing in music

Emery Schubert

Abstract

A cognitive mechanism for musical creativity is described, founded upon spreading activation theory. Spreading activation theory explains how information is created stored and interconnected via nodes (representing information) and links (interconnecting information through association). The information represented can be objects, parts-of or entire-pieces of music, emotions, and so forth. Creativity is then defined, in part, as the spontaneous creation of a new pathway (link) to solve a (in this case musical) problem. A key ingredient of the present mechanism is the inclusion of the principle of dissociation that is defined as the activation of a large number of nodes, while inhibiting pain nodes. This dissociation (unrelated to association) is then defined as the outcome of the solution or moments of inspiration when solving a problem (such as 'compose a symphony') commonly found in music. The creative process, then, is defined cognitively as the spontaneous formation of a new pathway that leads to dissociation. Person-based propensity to be creative is also explained using spreading activation theory.

8.1 Introduction

From its evolutionary origins, our culture has organized and shaped the role of creativity in music (Miller, 2000; Burnard & Younker, 2004; Haselton & Miller, 2006; Sawyer, 2006). For example, many people in Western culture will agree that Beethoven was a creative genius, and that his third symphony was a creative work, if not a hallmark of creativity in that era. Cultural momentum has perpetuated and reinforced, and at various times re-invigorated, these kinds of beliefs about creativity (Sawyer, 2006). The same is true of the child composing a piece in primary school, or a soloist improvising (Hargreaves, 1986; Kaufman & Beghetto, 2009); our culture has established some more or less unwritten rules about which versions of these products (the composition and improvisation) are creative, or creative to some degree.

The evolutionary pressure to be creative was associated with some concomitant use or development of brain function associated with creativity. In this chapter, I will explore a cognitive model that can be used to explain the mental functions of creative processing, and particularly for music. I will draw on principles of spreading activation in associative networks. One restriction made in this chapter is that creativity from a Western perspective is explored (see Burnard & Younker, 2004; Batey & Furnham, 2006; Zha et al., 2006 for approaches to creativity in other cultures).

8.2 **Locus of creativity**

Before creativity is defined, we need to understand its source, or locus. In the introduction we already see that there are three possible answers to this. In the case of Beethoven and the child it is the individual person who is the one we think of as being creative (the first locus). Assessing the creativity of the person may range from eminence ratings, such as the amount of space allocated to the composer in an encyclopaedia (Farnsworth, 1969/1958; North & Hargreaves, 2002; Barrett, 2006; Simonton & Song, 2009) to personality measures that predict the capacity of the individual to be creative (Hargreaves, 1986; Martindale, 1989; Carson et al., 2005; Vartanian et al., 2007; Prabhu et al., 2008). In the case of the symphony and the improvisation (the second locus), it is the product that is likely to be of interest. Assessing this output can be done by marking it according to various criteria, but Amabile provides a succinct approach: 'A product or response is creative to the extent that appropriate observers independently agree it is creative. Appropriate observers are those familiar with the domain in which the product was created or the response articulated' (Amabile, 1996: p. 33). As an example in music assessment, McPherson (1995, 2005) used a global scale of improvisation to assess children given the task of playing a piece so that it had a beginning, middle, and end, and so that the piece ended in a way that sounded finished. As another example, Eisenberg and Thompson (2003) explicitly requested that creativity be rated as part of another improvisation assessment task.

The *process* involved in generating a product is the third locus of creativity. In some respects this is an intermediate locus, falling between the person and the product. Some measures may be viewed as identifying the capacity of an individual to process in a creative way. In the non-musical field this can be done with divergent thinking tasks (such as a divergent thinking test—see Hargreaves & Bolton, 1972; Hocevar, 1981; Feldhusen & Goh, 1995; Eysenck, 1996, 1998; Martindale, 1999; Kim, 2006; Runco et al., 2006). An example of such a task is to follow the instruction 'Write down as many possibilities as you can of things that can be done with a brick'. Generally, the first items written will be closely linked to the priming stimulus (in this case, the brick). But after several items are listed, some people will stop, others will continue and produce more obscure responses. These responses, more distantly related to the priming stimulus, are viewed as one index of the individual's divergent thinking capacity, and therefore creative potential. These three loci—person-based, output (including product), and process—have been proposed by several researchers (e.g. Hargreaves, 1986; Feldhusen & Goh, 1995; Eysenck, 1998; Simonton, 1999).

Regarding the 'output' locus terminology, for the purposes of music at least, it is more informative to refer to an output rather than 'a product'. A product has an inference of a physical item, yet musical creativity can vary from a musical score (indeed a product) through improvisation and even expressive nuances and interpretation in performance. These are, typically, auditory outputs (produced by a performer or composer), rather than a product.

8.3 **Traditional definitions of creativity**

Creativity can be understood in terms of the concepts with which it is commonly associated and assessed. As Hargreaves (1986) suggests '[t]he term "creativity" is perhaps best regarded as a convenient shorthand term in psychology—as an "umbrella" encompassing different aspects of ability, personality, affect, and motivation' (p. 143). These include terms such as innovation, discovery, curiosity, imagination, and inspiration.

The conventional definition of the creative output (or product) in general research focuses on novelty and usefulness (Batey & Furnham, 2006). So, for a popular music composer a piece of music that 'feels right' or has a great 'hook' is a kind of solution to a problem, and it is novel if the composer, and eventually any listener, does not find that the tune has already been used by someone else. A Western art music composer writing a symphony that represents climate change finds a way of using percussion, brass and strings to represent the searing heat of the landscape that no other composer thought of. The resulting score may be the solution that has not been applied before (but possibly having sources of inspiration elsewhere). In these instances the novelty/usefulness definition of creativity works well for music. But can a piece of music really be useful? Weisberg (2006) discusses the view that 'value' might be more appropriate an aspect of creativity than usefulness, because this can be applied to any output, without eliminating artistic stimuli.

8.4 **Temporal path**

The process of creating is seen by some as following a general time-dependent template or set of discrete stages (hence sometimes referred to as 'stage-theories'). Most of these models are based on that proposed by Wallas (1926). In the first stage the problem is stated and processed. If a solution is not found, then the next stage commonly consists of a period of time spent without consciously attending to the problem, a period of 'incubation'. It is a period of time in which the person doing the creating is not consciously attending to the problem (by doing activities not related to the problem or sleeping: Lubart, 2001; Sio & Rudowicz, 2007; Cai et al., 2009). At some point in time after this stage a flash of inspiration occurs which leads to a possible solution. The solution is then further processed, tested, and refined.

However, there is some controversy over this sequence, for example, when no incubation period occurs and a 'creative' solution is found almost instantaneously, and in those cases where time restrictions will not allow periods of incubation, such as a tight time deadline, or improvisation between two or more players. Therefore, the time stages of the creative process that follow the preparation-incubation-inspiration-verification/refinement sequence is appropriate to certain kinds of creative tasks, but recent literature suggests that stage-theory models are in need of some enhancement (Gruber, 1992; Collins, 2005; Barrett, 2006; McIntyre, 2008) or replacement (Dietrich, 2007; Dietrich & Kanso, 2010).

Consider the case of the commissioned composer. The composer may start thinking about the brief for the composition (if there was one), and allow musical thoughts to float around in her mind. Perhaps the composer will keep a diary of thoughts and musical ideas, or pay no particular attention. Musical ideas may come and go, and some may be developed, discarded, rekindled, and so forth. At some point, the composer may experience a flash of inspiration and commence a verification stage and a period of vigorous work that may last an hour or a few days. Indeed it is possible that several iterations of trial and error, incubation, insight and verification will occur during the process. It may occur over several, small matter-of-fact steps, or there may be periods of repeated flashes of insight that are each quite powerful. Gruber (1992) refers to these iterations as an evolving systems approach to creativity. Gruber's approach therefore provides an important enhancement to Wallis's original stage model to the temporal unfolding of the creative output (for an application to music composition, see Collins, 2005).

8.5 **Spreading activation theory**

The cognitive *mechanism* (Bunge, 2004) underlying creativity is not well understood (see Batey & Furnham, 2006; Bengtsson et al., 2007; Welling, 2007). Of the theories expounding a cognitive mechanism of creativity, I focus here on spreading activation approaches (sometimes coming under the broader banner of associative networks), proposed and applied by several researchers (for a review, see Hargreaves, 1986; Cai et al., 2009). The model is based on the view that information is stored as a collection of small, discrete units called nodes, and that these units are acted upon by other nodes through channels called links. Activation spreads from node to node (or nodes) via the links. These nodes and links are analogous to biological neurons and synapses respectively, but are generally not intermingled to avoid an implied assertion that they are necessarily the same thing (a cognitive model versus biological system respectively: see Smolensky, 1986).

A node, then, can represent an edge of a table, an emotion, a musical note or an entire symphony (Gilligan & Bower, 1984; Schubert, 1996). A node represents progressively more information when it activates, or is activated by, the nodes representing those components. For example, a series of pitches in a tune may activate a tonal system, such as a major key (Bharucha & Stoeckig, 1987), and the major key may then activate a happy emotion node (Bower, 1987; Schubert, 1996). At the same time, the first few notes of this tune activate the phrase that represents the corresponding phrase node of the tune, which then in turn may activate the node representing the entire piece of music (Schmuckler, 1989). A rich fabric of interconnected nodes form as a person is exposed to their environment and culture. Nodes are formed as a result of exposure to stimuli, whether by rote learning or mere, unconscious exposure to stimuli in the external world (Zajonc, 2001). But when a familiar stimulus is seen, heard, touched, smelt or even imagined, a series of nodes representing and associated with that stimulus are triggered through the spreading of activation.

Spreading activation theory (SAT) immediately ties in with creativity research because evidence supporting it comes from divergent thinking tasks (an important 'person-based' creativity assessment tool, discussed above). It is worth noting that a divergent thinking task requires memory recall (rather than the easier task of recognition, discussed later in this chapter). A *recall* task can be defined in SAT as the search for solutions made by scanning the network, and that this search is performed by spreading activation from nodes representing the task instructions (the prime) and other current and recently activated nodes (whether related to the task or not). Mednick (1962) proposed that when participants are given a divergent thinking task such as 'list all the things you can do with a brick', most people begin the list by mentioning conventional applications (e.g. build a wall, build a house, place between cement, stop an object from rolling . . .) and only then might they start to make less conventional responses (e.g. use it as weapon; place in a cocktail; compose an ode to it). This supports SAT because nodes representing items more regularly paired (e.g. a brick and building a house) are more activated than those nodes representing semantically or associatively distant relationships (such as a brick and a beverage). As Mednick proposes 'The more mutually remote the elements of the new combination, the more creative the process or solution' (p. 221). This associative network explanation is supported in research on memory models (Collins & Loftus, 1975; Anderson, 1988; Goldrick, 2007). Mednick's studies help us to understand how a person might have a propensity to think divergently and therefore, perhaps, be more creative (person-based locus of creativity), but it does not explain the mechanism of a creative *process*.

The explicit concept of spreading activation comes largely from Collins & Loftus (1975), where a node, representing an object or thought, becomes activated after the perception of the object or having of the thought, and that the activation spreads to the nodes to which that node is linked. Those nodes, in turn, spread activation to the next node. In the example shown in Figure 8.1 we see a special class of the associative network, the semantic network. Here nodes represent concepts in the form of nouns and adjectives. The important aspect of the layout is that items that appear closer together are more likely to activate one another. So, the word 'truck' is more likely to spread activation to the word 'car' and 'bus' than it is to 'flowers' or to 'sunset'. Of course such a two-dimensional diagram does not do justice to the complex non-linearities of associative networks—for example, environment context and the mood of the participant affect how information from

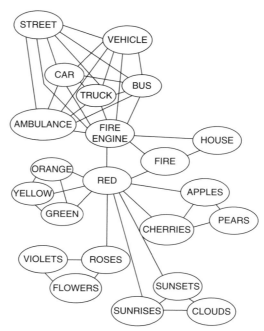

Fig. 8.1 A schematic representation of concept relatedness in a stereotypical fragment of human memory (where a shorter line represents greater relatedness).

Reproduced from Collins, A.M. & Loftus, E.F. (1975). A spreading-activation theory of semantic processing. *Psychological Review*, **82**(6), 407–28 with permission from the American Psychological Association.

the network is retrieved and how activation spreads (Gilligan & Bower, 1984; de l'Etoile, 2002; Barrett, 2006)—but it provides an introduction to the principle of spreading activation.

As a more recent example, Kokinov (2007) provides a computational model based on SAT where networks can alter through experience, exposure, and subconscious processing (such as a period of incubation):

> Spontaneous free recall is a result of simple spreading activation. Activation starts from agents representing the immediately perceived aspects of the environment (connected to the INPUT node) and the goals of the system (connected to the GOAL node). The result of the spreading activation entirely depends on the initial activation (residual from some priming task and perceptual) and the pattern of connectivity.

> (Kokinov, 2007: pp. 320–1.)

Further, spreading activation occurs with or without conscious attention, providing a system that can operate during the (subconscious) incubation period of the creative process. For example, Topolinski and Strack (2008), in their lexical memory studies, made conclusions about how the creative process may be working subconsciously, in particular during the incubation parts of the process, by defining intuition using a spreading activation model:

> We assume this intuition to be a cognitive feeling emerging from associative processing when activation spreads efficiently and independently from intentions from active representations to related concepts.

> (Topolinski & Strack, 2008: p. 1033.)

8.6 **Creativity as a subset of problem solving**

To understand how SAT could be used to explain a creative process, we turn to the family from which creativity comes: problem solving. Problem solving requires that a problem be stated and that a solution be found. There are different kinds of problem types, such as ill-defined and well-defined (Brown, 1989; Feldhusen & Goh, 1995; Pretz et al., 2003; Kozbelt, 2008). The well-defined problem is one where a correct solution can be found. Pretz, Naples, and Sternberg (2003) refer to these as problems whose solutions can be 'solved using a set of recursive operations or algorithms' (p. 4). Ill-defined problems, on the other hand, 'are characterized by their lack of a clear path to [the] solution. Such problems often lack a clear problem statement as well, making the task of problem definition and problem representation quite challenging' (p. 4). Several researchers since Mednick (e.g. Feldhusen & Goh, 1995; Sloman, 1996; Lubart, 2001) have argued that these kinds of problems are dealt with by associative processes.

There are some musical problems that could be classified as well-defined. Consider, for example, the musical problem, 'name the tune produced by the series of pitches shown in Figure 8.2'. It is likely that musically literate people (in Western notation) will respond with an answer such as 'a descending scale' or ringing rounds in bell ringing (Camp, 2006: p. 11). These solutions can be explained as an activation of the visual pattern representation that is linked to (among other things) the learnt semantic node (conceptually representing a one-octave descending major scale starting at C5), and therefore spreads activation to that node (the reader may have heard an imagined version of the scale in his/her mind, and possibly even the timbre of the bells (Halpern et al., 2004)). The problem is well-defined and relatively easy to answer in a manner that might be acceptable to many people. The problem required only *recognition* which can be defined by SAT as follows: no new paths are formed as activation spreads from the node representing the problem (in this case, the descending scale notation) to the target solution node (the verbal answer representation) through an *existing*, well-established path. No creativity is required, at least for those with appropriate musical literacy.

However, if asked whether there were any other possible answers, one might say 'no', but another might say it is an ascending scale reversed, or 'if you altered the rhythm slightly it could be the beginning of the Christmas carol "Joy to The World"'. Is this a creative answer? If the individual in question came up with this answer *spontaneously*, without assistance and without having heard this answer before, they may indeed be thought of as providing a creative solution to the, otherwise well-defined, problem. But it necessarily assumes that this listener will have a mental representation (a node) of the carol in question, acquired through previous experience. If they did not, the connection could not have been made. But, if the answer was discovered spontaneously after thinking about the question or incubating, then, according to SAT, a new pathway must have been formed to produce the solution. The response would then have been creative.

The 'Joy to the World' connection is one that I read about, and not one I discovered for myself, so it was not a creative experience for me. My spreading activation did not spontaneously stumble upon that solution—the new pathway was generated as a learning experience. According to SAT, I had a node (previously acquired knowledge representation) of a descending scale and of 'Joy to the World', and the connection between the two was not made till I read about it. It was an interesting revelation, but not a creative act on my part. As unlikely as it seems, I may, however, marvel

Fig. 8.2 Example of a prime stimulus for a well-defined problem-solving task (see text).

at the people who made this discovery—those who spontaneously provided a creative solution, a new set of connections, to this problem. And, I presume the reader who first makes this discovery while reading the chapter may well see that there was an element of revelation or creativity in making the connection. But for those who are aware of the connection, perhaps a less well-known example may be more convincing: By altering only the rhythm in a different way, the descending scale can be made to sound like the beginning of the main theme of the 'Pas de Deux', number 14 in Act II in the *Nutcracker Ballet Op. 71* by Tchaikovsky (albeit transposed). This discovery, like 'Joy to the World', may come about from activation spreading into musical memory, trying to find a connection that solves the problem. But SAT tells us that a mental representation of the music of 'Joy to the World' or the 'Pas de Deux' must exist in that listener. Such 'well-defined' problems in music may not be seen as requiring significant creative energies. The point was to demonstrate how SAT could be applied to the creative solution of well-defined problems.

However, musical creativity tasks are typically ill-defined problems, such as 'compose a symphony' or 'improvise on the jazz standard "Ain't Misbehavin'". Here there is no clear set of target nodes from which the question/prime is to be linked, in contrast to the well-defined problem or goal (to use Kokinov's term).

To summarize, activation of an existing pathway is the SAT explanation of recognition, and the development of new nodes is a SAT explanation for exposure to new stimuli. Neither of these mechanisms model creative acts. On the other hand a *new pathway* of activation between nodes that comes into existence from the individual's own (spontaneous) volition provides a mechanistic explanation of the novelty aspect of creativity. But the above discussion has not covered two issues: 1) how the second aspect of the definition of creativity, that a creative output must be *valued*, is explained and 2) what it is that must be solved for the ill-defined problem found in music. To explain how this works we need to consider another aspect of spreading activation: *dissociation* (a term, incidentally, unrelated to association: see Butler, 2006).

8.7 **Dissociated states**

In a recent paper (Schubert, 2009–2010), I have argued that the fundamental function of music depends on the level of explanation sought. At a phenomenological level, I argued, pleasure (and powerful positive affects in general) is the fundamental function, and at a biological or neuro-logical level it is to dissociate—defined in the present cognitive model as the activation of nodes but at the same time the inhibition of displeasure or pain nodes (Schubert, 1996). This state of dissociation applies the theory that activation of the cognitive units (what I call nodes here) in and of itself is pleasurable, an idea inspired by Colin Martindale as part of his activation theory (Martindale, 1984; Martindale & Moore, 1988: p. 662). Node activation, provided it does not acti-vate pain nodes, is pleasurable. There is no need for an explicit pleasure centre. As Martindale and Moore put it '[p]erception or recognition has to do with exactly which cognitive units are acti-vated, whereas aesthetic pleasure has to do with the net amount of activation of these units' (Martindale & Moore, 1988: p. 662).

Accordingly, music lovers learn to experience music in a safe, positive environment, and there-fore can learn to dissociate when listening to music. It relies on the same principles that game playing does—where behaviours are practised in a safe environment, for the purpose of pleasure and problem solving development through simulation. The principle of 'pleasure through activation' therefore has its origin in an evolutionary, adaptive function (Vygotsky, 1967/1933). Music can, therefore, be defined as any auditory signal that causes this dissociation, and that this dissociation manifests itself phenomenologically as a (for example) pleasure experience, but also the less trivial, more profound experiences that might be captured by words such as awe-inspiring, moving, spiritual and so forth (Krippner, 1999; Gabrielsson & Wik, 2003; Schubert, 2009–2010), sometimes collectively referred to as higher-order or aesthetic pleasures. Based on this view—that the fundamental function of music is to produce activation (while pain is inhibited), and that subsequently music can be defined as auditory signal that causes such activation—one goal of the creative musical act is to maximize activation, and dissociation; in other words, it is something that leads phenomenologically to profound and/or enjoyable affects in the mind of the listener.

8.8 **Biological evidence**

Martindale's theory, that activation of cognitive units is pleasurable, can be solely justified as a psychological theory, without need to provide neurobiological evidence. It is, nevertheless, interesting to examine if there exists any neurological evidence to support the theory. It is particularly interesting because conventional wisdom suggests that pleasure can be explained by a pleasure centre alone, somewhat in contrast to activation theory. However, the notion of a pleasure centre in contemporary literature is considered dated or simplistic, with the view of pleasure 'systems' holding favour (Bozarth, 1994; Knapp & Kornetsky, 2009). For example, Knapp & Kornetsky (2009) state that what had been thought of as the pleasure region (the septal areas) 'have now been identified as regions linked to the functioning of mesocortico-limbic systems' (p. 781). They go on to suggest that:

> The actual response of the brain to rewarding stimuli most likely involves extensively distributed networks of neurons that consist of, at least, thousands of cells. It is not clear, then, that studies in which the activity of only a few cells is monitored can provide a comprehensive picture of the changes in neuronal activity that occur following exposure to rewarding stimuli.

> (Knapp & Kornetsky, 2009: p. 783.)

Regardless of the state of the functional localization debate, the neurological literature has not produced any clear evidence against pleasure being related to activation, whether localized or not (e.g. see Dietrich & Kanso, 2010).

Another issue that is interesting to pursue for possible neurobiological evidence is the inhibition of pain; the second central element of spreading activation and dissociation theory (SAD). Here it is possible to draw on sensory interaction theory (Noordenbos, 1959) and gate theory (Melzack & Wall, 1994), which are still influential today (Koestler & Doleys, 2002), where impulse activity in narrow nerve fibres transmits pain, and impulse activity in wide fibres inhibits the transmission of the narrow ones. While no direct evidence is available, physiological mechanisms such as gate theory may have links with the neurobiological process of dissociation. Until such links are more explicitly demonstrated, activation and dissociation theory remain cognitive models that have neurological counterparts which may emerge through further research.

8.9 **Dissociation and musical creativity**

What does the principle of dissociation have to do with creativity? In creativity literature we frequently see reference to a problem and/or a goal of some sort that must be solved/reached. In the case of the ill-defined problems frequently found in music (such as composition and improvisation), the goal can be defined at the mechanistic level which I proposed here—dissociation. That is, the goal of the typical musically creative task is to produce dissociation through the auditory channel. The only additional requirement is that the dissociation be obtained along a new link pathway. So, reproducing a Sibelius symphony may well leave the familiar listener in a dissociated state, but it is only creative if the interpretation of the symphony takes the listener to this state of dissociation through a different 'neural' pathway, for example, by introducing interesting/ unusual changes in tempo, extending a fermata, bringing the timpani part further to the fore and so forth.

For the composer, the periods of thought and incubation are focused on creating a piece that leads to an experience stemming from the mechanism of dissociation. The 'Eureka moment' of the composer, which after further processing leads to the final work, is a moment of dissociation. Byrne, MacDonald and Carlton (Byrne et al., 2003; MacDonald et al., 2006) applied the concept of flow to the assessment of compositions. They defined flow, after Csikszentmihalyi (1988), as 'the effortless involvement with everyday life and may occur when a person is engaged in absorbing and enjoyable activities' (Byrne et al., 2003: p. 279). That is, applied here, flow is another conscious manifestation of dissociation that took place during the period in which the pieces were played but quite possibly during the composition process. They found that creativity scores for the compositions correlated significantly with flow (quantified using the *experience sampling form*).

The implications for creativity research are important because a neglected aspect of creativity is highlighted: the affect that results from dissociation, which Weisberg (2006) refers to as 'value'. While affect and emotion are frequently reported, the cognitive *mechanism* is rarely speculated. Consider the hypothetical pop music composer described earlier in section 8.3 ('Traditional definitions of creativity'). There also exist numerous historic anecdotal reports of intensely positive experience during and after a period of great creativity that could be explained by a spreading activation and dissociation (SAD) mechanism. For example, when Mozart was asked by an acquaintance (whom he addressed as Baron V) to explain his way of composing, he wrote:

> When I am, as it were, completely myself, entirely alone, and of good cheer—say travelling in a carriage, or walking after a good meal, or during the night when I cannot sleep—it is on such occasions that my ideas flow best and most abundantly. *Whence* and *how* they come, I know not, nor can I force them. Those ideas that please me I retain in memory, and am accustomed, as I have been told, to hum them to myself. If I continue in this way, it soon occurs to me how I may turn this or that morsel to account, so as to make a good dish of it, that is to say, agreeably to the rules of counterpoint, to the peculiarities of the various instruments, &c.
>
> All this fires my soul, and, provided I am not disturbed, my subject enlarges itself, becomes methodised and defined, and the whole, though it be long, stands almost complete and finished in my mind, so that I can survey it, like a fine picture or a beautiful statue, at a glance. Nor do I hear in my imagination the parts *successively,* but I hear them, as it were, all at once (*gleich allez zusammen*). What a delight this is I cannot tell! All this inventing, this producing, takes place in a pleasing, lively dream.

> (Cited by Holmes, 1854: p. 329.)

The principle of dissociation suggests that the positive feeling—whether it be delight, pleasure, ecstasy, immersion, flow—is an essential part of the creative experience in the artistic domain at least. A further implication is that this positive affect is a part of any successful creative process. Literature in the non-aesthetic domains also frequently report the presence and importance of positive affect appearing in conjunction with creative output (Amabile et al., 2005; Nelson & Rawlings, 2009).

The reasons for the effects of dissociation *not* being part of our understanding of creativity are twofold. First, the research community may not feel there is enough evidence to support the essential connection between creativity and intense positive affect. Second, creativity research has some roots in theories that stem from the behaviourist era of the early to mid 1900s (Sawyer, 2006). It could be that creativity research is, in some parts, restricted to views that were dominant in this era where Western psychological research shunned nearly anything that considered the supposedly hard-to-measure feelings of the individual, not unlike emotion in music which suffered a similar fate until scholars such as Leonard Meyer came to the fore (Atkins & Schubert, 2009).

8.10 **Person-based creativity**

While this chapter focuses on the *process* locus of creativity, I will briefly consider aspects of person-based creativity, the propensity or potential an individual has to be creative from an SAT perspective. The discussion will be viewed through the lens of SAT (for more general discussion of person-based creativity, see Hargreaves, 1986; Simonton, 1994; Eysenck, 1996).

It is taken as given that some individuals are more creative than others. There are two likely sources of creative potential that can explain these individual differences, one environmental and the other genetic. As far as environmental factors are concerned, it seems that the more experiences that the individual has, the greater the number of mental representations present, and therefore available for recombination (discussed below). For Vygotsky, imagination and experience are an integral part of creativity:

> Now we can induce the first and most important law governing the operation of the imagination. This law may be formulated as follows: the creative activity of the imagination depends directly on the richness and variety of a person's previous experience because this experience provides the material from which the products of fantasy are constructed. The richer a person's experience, the richer is the material his imagination has access to.

> (Vygotsky 2004/1967/1930: pp. 14–15.)

However, in addition to environmental factors, and in particular, the richness and variety of a person's previous experience, many researchers have also been interested in personality correlates of creativity (for a review, see Eysenck, 1998). SAT can explain this biological predisposition by refer-ence to the speed of activation of nodes. In the Collins and Loftus (1975) example shown in Figure 8.1, discussed above, this speed of activation is represented (inversely) by the length of the links between nodes. An activated node spreads its activation to nodes that are closer in the diagram more quickly than those that are located further away. Mednick (1962) formulated this as the 'flatness' of the network hierarchy. So, if a node is activated, and associated nodes are flat (or close together, using the Collins and Loftus visual analogy), activation spreads between nodes more easily, eventually making associations with more remotely connected concepts (as is required in some creative, and specifically divergent thinking tasks). People who have a steep associative network hierarchy will only be able to activate the nodes most closely associated with the primed object. Thus, if asking them to think of their favourite pieces of music—a *recall* task—these individuals are likely to begin with the last piece they have thought about (a node that most recently became active in connection with the task, and therefore has some residual activation, but enough to become activated) and name a few pieces that are similar to that one, before running out of ideas, or at least requiring a longer time to access the many other favourite pieces they may know but are not be able to recall sooner. This difference in network structure explains some individual differences in creativity.

Person-based creativity locus can then be explained by spreading activation theory as being based on the quantity of nodes representing various concepts (environmental aspect) and the general speed or strength of activation spreading and connectivity propensity between the nodes (presumably, or at least in part a genetic aspect).

8.11 **Is creativity a result of recombination or accident?**

If a problem is presented to a person's conscious attention, and mental representations of the components of the problem exist (for example, being asked to write a fugue presupposes the existence of nodes representing the rules of counterpoint, exemplars of fugues, or their emergent properties exist), SAT asserts that the path to the creative solution will commence through a series of spreading activations to other associations. Adjacent associations will be activated (topologically but, most probably semantically as well), and subsequently wind their way through different paths, return back, restart and so forth until the new path to the solution (in the case of the creative act) is discovered.

This process suggests that creativity is nothing more than recombination: an attempt to find a path to a solution by spreading activation through pre-existing representations of information, formed and parsed through earlier experiences. It is the path taken to the solution, in this case, that must be new and spontaneous. Several researchers agree with this view, including Vygotsky, who argued that 'to combine the old in new ways that is the basis of creativity' (2004/1967/1930: p. 12). The 18th-century painter, Sir Joshua Reynolds, proposed that '[i]nvention, strictly speaking, is little more than a new combination of those images which have been previously gathered and deposited in the memory: nothing can come of nothing: he who has laid up no materials, can produce no combinations' (from Reynolds, Discourse II, lines 83–7, cited by Martin, 1987: p. 6). But, assuming the network explanation is supported, what decides the direction in which the activation and subsequent associations will spread? Is it random and at best statistically measurable, or is it deterministic? Can we say that, given the experience, current state and genetic predisposition of an individual, he or she will follow a particular thought path as a consequence of a predictable spreading of activation?

The stimulation for the pathway of activation that would lead to the solution may have come about through an apparent accident—the pattern of undulating hills in the country side may provide the connection that leads a composer to start sketching out melodies based on the height of the hills, providing a partially solved problem that the complex web of neural interconnections can somehow 'see' a near-possible solution in a manner that Weisenberg (2006: p. 20) describes as the point of a jigsaw puzzle when you can start to see how the puzzle might end up—still a lot of work to go, but a flash in insight has occurred, and motivation is rekindled because a sense of having a solution is felt, a 'feeling of knowing' (Carroll & Nelson, 1993; Litman et al., 2005). Is seeing the undulating hills an accidental intrusion that allowed the pathway to the solution to be found, or found more quickly? Dennett, interpreting Sims's 'Evolved Virtual Creatures', suggests 'that when you're modelling creativity, there should be junk lying around that your creative processes can bump into, noises that your creative processes can't help overhearing' (Dennett, 2001: p. 287). Or is it that the network of associations are working through various combinations until the 'correct' new pathway is found, with the intrusion simply pulling the pattern of spreading activations in a different direction?

A solution to this conundrum is that both winding, snaking associations and an external intrusion ('inspiration') can each facilitate the formation of new pathways. The spreading activation account of creativity suggests that two unrelated concepts (represented in memory as nodes) can have a new pathway spontaneously found between them, and that this is the mechanism of the creative process. If an existing pathway is activated then the problem-solving task is nothing more than memory recall or recognition. The facilitation of a new path may have been catalysed by an external image (the activation of the rolling hills for our composer), or some other 'junk' lying around. Neuroscientists would refer to this kind of stimulus as a prime which produces 'pre-activation' (Kiesel et al., 2007). But it may also have been a result of the activation of adjacent nodes winding through various combinations of associations: As activation spreads, meanders, retreats, spreads again, takes different directions, eventually the new path reaches its target, in the case of musical creativity, the burst of activation that occurs with dissociation, and the newly discovered path to this target becomes reinforced. In other words, both the spontaneous winding through the associative network and the 'spontaneous intrusions' (Hofstadter, 1998; Dennett, 2001) can lead to the formation of a new path of spreading activation.

8.12 **Conclusions**

To understand my speculations on how SAT explains creativity, it is instructive to summarize how it explains the various memory processing tasks discussed in this chapter. Table 8.1 lists these and highlights the critical differences between creative and non-creative acts. Spontaneous, new *path* formation is essential for any creative process. In addition, for the typical musical or aesthetic problem, the goal is to produce dissociation—the 'pleasure' produced through spreading activation and the simultaneous inhibition of pain nodes. The spreading activation account in combination with the principle of dissociation (SA + D) are considered the two essential cognitive components that provide a mechanistic explanation of the musically creative process.

The spreading activation account of creativity suggests that the flash of inspiration, the stroke of genius, are unlikely to be any more than incremental changes in knowledge recombination. In the case of much of musical creativity this flash is the point when the spread of activation explodes to produce a great wealth of activation, concurrently with the spontaneous emergence of a new pathway, in a dissociated state (pain nodes 'switched off'). SAT tells us that the cusp of that event is not likely to be a major, new initiative that no one else could ever have thought of. This applies to creativity of young children through to the outputs of the most eminent scientist, musician, and those esteemed in one's society. For example, in his examination of the way some works of art come about, Weisberg (2006) concluded that '[c]reative ideas even those that are radically new, are firmly planted on ideas that came before. There are always antecedents to any creative idea. The reason that it sometimes looks like an idea comes out of nothing is because we observers are ignorant of the knowledge base of the individual producing the new idea' (pp. 52–3). Denial of this conclusion is one of the major obstacles in allowing acceptance of a spreading activation explanation for creativity, and its implications.

Simonton describes the effectiveness of such an explanation of creativity:

> Especially striking is the empirical demonstration of intuitive information processing as a regular manifestation of the *cognitive unconscious* [. . .]. The magic behind the sudden, unexpected, and seemingly unprepared inspiration has now been replaced by the lawful operation of subliminal stimulation and spreading activation.
>
> (Simonton, 2000: p. 152.)

The spreading activation and dissociation (SAD) theory provides a mechanistic explanation for some of the 'separation from reality' experiences that occur in listening to and producing music.

Table 8.1 Spreading activation theory (SAT) mechanism explanation of selected cognitive processing tasks

Process	SAT mechanism
Exposure (rote)	Deliberate (high level of conscious attention) formation of new nodes
Exposure (mere)	Spontaneous (low level of conscious attention) formation of new *nodes*
Instructed, associative learning	Deliberate formation of new paths (links)
Typical recall task	Search for existing paths
Typical recognition task	Matching of existing path
Creativity (general, for well-defined problem)	New path formed spontaneously
Creativity (musical/aesthetic)	New path formed spontaneously, with target being dissociation (producing large burst of activation while inhibiting pain)

Under this circumstance, any activation is reported as 'pleasant' (whether 'pleasure circuits', should they exist, are activated or not). It is the spreading itself in combination with the inhibition of pain that leads to the intense, positive affects. Sometimes this phenomenon is reported as a 'suspension of disbelief', and in music experiences is correlated with profound sensations such as awe, absorption, immersion, flow and trance. The evolutionary origins of such a cognitive activity is that it allows the individual to engage in imaginative play (Burghardt, 2004; Pellegrini et al., 2007), allowing the development and practice of skills in a realistic situation, without the danger associated with the 'real thing' (e.g. practice for hunting and gathering, or learning to operate within given real-life constraints: see, for example, Burghardt, 2004; Pellegrini et al., 2007).

The theoretical framework I am proposing has its roots in associative theories, which are commonly reported in the creativity literature (Mednick, 1962; Hargreaves, 1986; Gabora, 2000; Yarkoni et al., 2005; Cai et al., 2009). While some contemporary theories argue that other processes may be utilized in creative activities (e.g. Gabora, 2002; Strack & Deutsch, 2004; Welling, 2007), I have proposed that associative linking may be able to explain these other processes as well. This is not to deny that other processes may occur, or that they may provide better explanations of the creative mechanism. However, the associative network model and the spreading of activation through these networks in response to thinking and external input, and incubation, provides a unified cognitive, mechanistic explanation of the creative process: that a creative process involves a new, spontaneously formed pathway (from the perspective of the creator) that solves a problem.

The intention of this chapter was to present a cognitive model of the creative process, and in particular of the musically creative process from a mechanistic perceptive. The ideas here transfer comfortably to other artistic arenas such as theatre, film, and dance, and anywhere that dissociation (and its related phenomenological effects) can occur. A criticism of the SAT approach is that it utilizes a non-linear model (interacting webs of nodes and links), meaning that it can be expanded to explain highly complex phenomena but loses the advantages of simplicity and comprehensibility that is required of a predictive, reductionist model.

References

Amabile, T.M. (1996). *Creativity in context: Update to The social psychology of creativity*. Boulder, CO: Westview Press.

Amabile, T.M., Barsade, S.G., Mueller, J.S., & Staw, B.M. (2005). Affect and creativity at work. *Administrative Science Quarterly*, **50**(3), 367–403.

Anderson, J.R. (1988). A spreading activation theory of memory. In A.M. Collins & E.E. Smith (Eds.) *Readings in cognitive science: A perspective from psychology and artificial intelligence*. San Mateo, CA: Morgan Kaufmann, Inc., pp. 137–54.

Atkins, P. & Schubert, E. (2009). Music and the experience of spirituality: A study of religious people. *Musica Humana*, **1**(2), 307–29.

Barrett, M. (2006). 'Creative collaboration': An 'eminence' study of teaching and learning in music composition. *Psychology of Music*, **34**(2), 195–218.

Barrett, M.S. (2006). Inventing songs, inventing worlds: The 'genesis' of creative thought and activity in young children's lives. *International Journal of Early Years Education*, **14**(3), 201–20.

Batey, M. & Furnham, A. (2006). Creativity, intelligence, and personality: A critical review of the scattered literature. *Genetic Social and General Psychology Monographs*, **132**(4), 355–429.

Bengtsson, S.L., M. Csikszentmihalyi, & Ullen, F. (2007). Cortical regions involved in the generation of musical structures during improvisation in pianists. *Journal of Cognitive Neuroscience*, **19**(5), 830–42.

Bharucha, J.J. & K. Stoeckig (1987). Priming of chords: Spreading activation or overlapping frequency spectra? *Perception & Psychophysics*, **41**(6), 519–24.

Bower, G.H. (1987). Commentary on mood and memory. *Behaviour Research & Therapy*, **25**(6), 443–55.

Bozarth, M.A. (1994). Pleasure systems in the brain. In D.M. Warburton (Ed.) *Pleasure: The politics and the reality*. New York: John Wiley & Sons, pp. 5–14.

Brown, R.T. (1989). Creativity: What are we to measure? In J.A. Glover, R.R. Ronning, & C.R. Reynolds (Eds.) *Handbook of creativity*. New York: Plenum Press, pp. 3–32.

Bunge, M. (2004). How does it work? The search for explanatory mechanisms. *Philosophy of the Social Sciences*, **34**(2), 182–210.

Burghardt, G.M. (2004). Play: How evolution can explain the most mysterious behavior of all. In A. Moya & E. Font (Eds.) *Evolution: From molecules to ecosystems*. Oxford: Oxford University Press, pp. 231–46.

Burnard, P. & Younker, B.A. (2004). Problem-solving and creativity: Insights from students' individual composing pathways. *International Journal of Music Education*, **22**(1), 59–76.

Butler, L.D. (2006). Normative dissociation. *Psychiatric Clinics of North America*, **29**(1), 45–62.

Byrne, C., R. MacDonald, & Carlton, L. (2003). Assessing creativity in musical compositions: Flow as an assessment tool. *British Journal of Music Education*, **20**(3), 277–90.

Cai, D.J., Mednick, S.A., Harrison, EM., Kanady, J.C., & Mednick, S.C. (2009). REM, not incubation, improves creativity by priming associative networks. *Proceedings of the National Academy of Sciences of the United States of America*, **106**(25), 10130–4.

Camp, J. (2006). *Discovering bells and bellringing*. Buckinghamshire: Shire Publications Ltd.

Carroll, M. & Nelson, T.O. (1993). Effect of overlearning on the feeling of knowing is more detectable in within-subject than in between-subject designs. *American Journal of Psychology*, **106**(2), 227–35.

Carson, S.H., Peterson, J.B., & Higgins, D.M. (2005). Reliability, validity, and factor structure of the Creative Achievement Questionnaire. *Creativity Research Journal*, **17**(1), 37–50.

Collins, A.M. & Loftus, E.F. (1975). Spreading activation theory of semantic processing. *Psychological Review*, **82**(6), 407–28.

Collins, D. (2005). A synthesis process model of creative thinking in music composition. *Psychology of Music*, **33**(2), 193–216.

Csikszentmihalyi, M. (1988). The flow experience and its significance for human psychology. In M. Csikszentmihalyi & I.S. Csikszentmihalyi (Eds.) *Optimal experience: Psychological studies of flow in consciousness*. Cambridge: Cambridge University Press, pp. 3–35.

de l'Etoile, S.K. (2002). The effect of musical mood induction procedure on mood state-dependent word retrieval. *Journal of Music Therapy*, **39**(2), 145–60.

Dennett, D. (2001). Collision, detection, muselot, and scribble: Some reflections on creativity, in D. Cope (ed.), *Virtual music: Computer synthesis of musical style*. Cambridge, MA: MIT Press, pp. 283–91.

Dietrich, A. (2007). Who's afraid of a cognitive neuroscience of creativity? *Methods*, **42**(1), 22–27.

Dietrich, A., & Kanso, R. (2010). A review of EEG, ERP, and neuroimaging studies of creativity and insight. *Psychological Bulletin*, **136**(5), 822.

Eisenberg, J. & W.F. Thompson (2003). A matter of taste: Evaluating improvised music. *Creativity Research Journal*, **15**(2–3), 287–96.

Eysenck, H.J. (1996). The measurement of creativity. In M.A. Boden (Ed.) *Dimensions of creativity*. Cambridge, MA: MIT Press, pp. 199–242.

Eysenck, H.J. (1998). *Genius: The natural history of creativity*. Cambridge: Cambridge University Press.

Farnsworth, P.R. (1969/1958). *The social psychology of music*. Ames, IO: Iowa State University Press.

Feldhusen, J.F. & Goh, B.E. (1995). Assessing and accessing creativity: An integrative review of theory, research, and development. *Creativity Research Journal*, **8**(3), 231–47.

Gabora, L. (2000). Toward a theory of creative inklings. In R. Ascott (Ed.) *Art, technology, and consciousness*. Intellect Press, pp. 159–64.

Gabora, L. (2002). Amplifying phenomenal information—Toward a fundamental theory of consciousness. *Journal of Consciousness Studies*, **9**(8), 3–29.

Gabrielsson, A. & Wik, S.L. (2003). Strong experiences related to music: A descriptive system. *Musicae Scientiae*, **7**(2), 157–217.

Gilligan, S.G. & G.H. Bower (1984). Cognitive consequences of emotional arousal. In C. Izard, J. Kagen & R. Zajonc (Eds.) *Emotions, cognition,and behaviour*. New York: Cambridge University Press, pp. 547–88.

Goldrick, M. (2007). Connectionist principles in theories of speech production. In M.G. Gaskell & G. Altmann (Eds.) *The Oxford handbook of psycholinguistics*. Oxford: Oxford University Press, pp. 515–30.

Gardner, H. (1993). *Creating minds: An anatomy of creativity seen through the lives of Freud, Einstein, Picasso, Stravinsky, Eliot, Graham, and Gandhi*. New York: Basic Books.

Gruber, H.E. (1992). The evolving systems approach to creative work. In D.B. Wallace & H.E. Gruber (Eds.) *Creative people at work: Twelve cognitive case studies*. New York: Oxford University Press, pp. 3–24.

Halpern, A.R., Zatorre, R.J., Bouffard, M., & Johnson, J. (2004). Behavioral and neural correlates of perceived and imagined timbre. *Neuropsychologia*, **42**, 1281–92.

Hargreaves, D. & Bolton, N. (1972). Selecting creativity tests for use in research. *British Journal of Psychology*, **63**(3), 451–62.

Hargreaves, D.J. (1986). *The developmental psychology of music*. Cambridge: Cambridge University Press.

Haselton, M.G. & Miller, G.F. (2006). Women's fertility across the cycle increases the short-term attractiveness of creative intelligence. *Human Nature*, **17**(2), 50–73.

Hocevar, D. (1981). Measurement of creativity: Review and critique. *Journal of Personality Assessment*, **45**(5), 450–64.

Hofstadter, D.R. (1998). *Le ton beau de Marot: In praise of the music of language*. New York: Basic Books.

Holmes, E. (1854). *The life of Mozart: Including his correspondence*. New York: Harper and Brothers.

Kaufman, J.C. & Beghetto, R.A. (2009). Beyond big and little: The four C model of creativity. *Review of General Psychology*, **13**(1), 1–12.

Kiesel, A., Kunde, W., & Hoffman, J. (2007). Mechanisms of subliminal response priming. *Advances in Cognitive Psychology*, **3**(1–2), 307–15.

Kim, K.H. (2006). Can we trust creativity tests? A review of the Torrance Tests of Creative Thinking (TTCT). *Creativity Research Journal*, **18**(1), 3–14.

Knapp, C.M. & Kornetsky, C. (2009). Neural basis of pleasure and reward. In G.G. Berntson & J.T. Cacioppo (Eds.) *Handbook of Neuroscience for the Behavioral Sciences*. Hoboken, NJ: John Wiley & Sons, pp. 781–806.

Koestler, A.J. & Doleys, D.M. (2002). The psychology of pain. In C.D. Tollison, J.R. Satterthwaite & J.W. Tollison (Eds.) *Practical pain management*. Philadelphia, PA: Lippincott, Williams & Wilkins, pp. 26–39.

Kokinov, B., Petkov, G., & Petrova, N. (2007). Context-sensitivity of human memory: Episode connectivity and its influence on memory reconstruction. In B. Kokinov, D. Richardson, T. Roth-Berghofer & L. Vieu (Eds.) *Modeling and using context: Lecture notes in computer science*. Berlin: Springer Verlag, pp. 317–29.

Kozbelt, A. (2008). Longitudinal hit ratios of classical composers: Reconciling 'Darwinian' and expertise acquisition perspectives on lifespan creativity. *Psychology of Aesthetics, Creativity, and the Arts*, **2**(4), 221–35.

Krippner, S. (1999). *Altered and transitional states*. In M.A. Runco & S.R. Pritzker (Eds.) *Encyclopedia of creativity*. San Diego, CA: Academic Press, pp. 59–70.

Litman, J.A., Hutchins, T.L., & Russon, R. (2005). Epistemic curiosity, feeling-of-knowing, and exploratory behaviour. *Cognition & Emotion*, **19**(4), 559–82.

Lubart, T.I. (2001). Models of the creative process: Past, present and future. *Creativity Research Journal*, **13**(3), 295–308.

MacDonald, R., Byrne, C., & Carlton, L. (2006). Creativity and flow in musical composition: An empirical investigation. *Psychology of Music*, **34**(3), 292–306.

Martin, F.W. (1987). Sir Joshua Reynolds's 'invention': Intellectual activity as a foundation of art. *Art Education*, **40**(6), 6–15.

Martindale, C. (1984). The pleasures of thought: A theory of cognitive hedonics. *Journal of Mind & Behavior*, **5**(1), 49–80.

Martindale, C. (1989). Personality, situation, and creativity. In J.A. Glover, R.R. Ronning & C.R. Reynolds (Eds.) *Handbook of creativity: Perspectives on individual differences*. New York: Plenum Press, pp. 211–32.

Martindale, C. (1999). Biological bases of creativity. In R.J. Sternberg (Ed.) *Handbook of creativity*. Cambridge: Cambridge University Press, pp. 137–52.

Martindale, C. & Moore, K. (1988). Priming, prototypicality, and preference. *Journal of Experimental Psychology: Human Perception & Performance*, **14**(4), 661–70.

McIntyre, P. (2008). Creativity and cultural production: A study of contemporary Western popular music songwriting. *Creativity Research Journal*, **20**(1), 40–52.

McPherson, G.E. (1995). The assessment of musical performance: Development and validation of five new measures. *Psychology of Music*, **23**, 142–61.

McPherson, G.E. (2005). From child to musician: Skill development during the beginning stages of learning an instrument. *Psychology of Music*, **33**(1), 5–35.

Mednick, S.A. (1962). The associative basis of the creative process. *Psychological Review*, **69**(3), 220–32.

Melzack, R. & P.D. Wall (1994). Pain mechanisms: a new theory. In A. Steptoe & J. Wardle (Eds.) *Psychosocial processes and health: A reader*. Cambridge: Cambridge University Press, pp. 112–31.

Miller, G. (2000). Evolution of human music through sexual selection. In N.L. Wallin, B. Merker, & S. Brown (Eds.) *The origins of music*. Cambridge, MA: MIT Press, 329–60.

Nelson, B. & Rawlings, D. (2009). How does it feel? The development of the Experience of Creativity Questionnaire. *Creativity Research Journal*, **21**(1), 43–53.

Noordenbos, W. (1959). *Pain*. Amsterdam: Elsevier.

North, A.C. & Hargreaves, D.J. (2002). Age variations in judgments of 'great' art works. *British Journal of Psychology*, **93**(3), 397–405.

Pellegrini, A.D., Dupuis, D., & Smith, P.K. (2007). Play in evolution and development. *Developmental Review*, **27**(2), 261–76.

Prabhu, V., Sutton, C, & Sauser, W. (2008). Creativity and certain personality traits: Understanding the mediating effect of intrinsic motivation. *Creativity Research Journal*, **20**(1), 53–66.

Pretz, J.E., Naples, A.J., & Sternberg, R.J. (2003). Recognizing, defining, and representing problems. In J.E. Davidson & R.J. Sternberg (Eds.) *The psychology of problem solving*. New York: Cambridge University Press, pp. 3–30.

Runco, M.A., Dow, G., & Smith, W. (2006). Information, experience, and divergent thinking: An empirical test. *Creativity Research Journal*, **18**(3), 269–77.

Sawyer, R.K. (2006). *Explaining creativity: The science of human innovation*. Oxford: Oxford University Press.

Schmuckler, M.A. (1989). Expectation in music: Investigation of melodic and harmonic processes. *Music Perception*, **7**(2), 109–49.

Schubert, E. (1996). Enjoyment of negative emotions in music: An associative network explanation. *Psychology of Music*, **24**(1), 18–28.

Schubert, E. (2009–2010). The fundamental function of music. *Musicae Scientiae, Special Issue*, 63–81.

Simonton, D.K. (1994). *Greatness: Who makes history and why*. New York: Guilford Press.

Simonton, D.K. (1999). *Origins of genius: Darwinian perspectives on creativity*. New York: Oxford University Press.

Simonton, D.K. (2000). Creativity—Cognitive, personal, developmental, and social aspects. *American Psychologist*, **55**(1), 151–8.

Simonton, D.K. & Song, A.V. (2009). Eminence, IQ, physical and mental health, and achievement domain: Cox's 282 geniuses revisited. *Psychological Science*, **20**(4), 429–34.

Sio, U.N. & Rudowicz, E. (2007). The role of an incubation period in creative problem solving. *Creativity Research Journal*, **19**(2–3), 307–18.

Sloman, S.A. (1996). The empirical case for two systems of reasoning. *Psychological Bulletin*, **119**(1), 3–22.

Smolensky, P. (1986). Neural and conceptual interpretations of parallel distributed processing models. In J.L. McClelland, D.E. Rumelhart, & P.R. Group (Eds.) *Parallel distributed processing: Explorations in the microstructure of cognition. Volume 2: Psychological and biological models,*. Cambridge, MA: MIT Press/Bradford Books, pp. 390–431.

Strack, F. & Deutsch, R. (2004). Reflective and impulsive determinants of social behavior. *Personality and Social Psychology Review*, **8**(3), 220–47.

Topolinski, S. & Strack, F. (2008). Where there's a will—there's no intuition. The unintentional basis of semantic coherence judgments. *Journal of Memory and Language*, **58**(4), 1032–48.

Vartanian, O., Martindale, C., & Kwiatkowski, J. (2007). Creative potential, attention, and speed of information processing. *Personality and Individual Differences*, **43**(6), 1470–80.

Vygotsky, L.S. (1967/1933). Play and its role in the mental development of the child. *Soviet Psychology*, **5**(3), 6–18.

Vygotsky, L.S. (2004/1967/1930). Imagination and creativity in childhood. *Journal of Russian and East European Psychology*, **42**(1), 4–84.

Wallas, G. (1926). *The art of thought*. New York: Harcourt, Brace and Company.

Weisberg, R.W. (2006). *Creativity: Understanding innovation in problem solving, science, invention, and the arts*. Hoboken, NJ: John Wiley.

Welling, H. (2007). Four mental operations in creative cognition: The importance of abstraction. *Creativity Research Journal*, **19**(2–3), 163–77.

Yarkoni, T., Gray, J.R., Chrastil, E.R., Barch, D.M., Green, L., & Braver, T.S. (2005). Sustained neural activity associated with cognitive control during temporally extended decision making. *Cognitive Brain Research*, **23**(1), 71–84.

Zajonc, R. (2001). Mere exposure: A gateway to the subliminal. *Current Directions in Psychological Science*, **10**(6), 224–8.

Zha, P., Walczyk, J.J., Griffith-Ross, D.A., Tobacyk, J.J., & Walczyk, D.F. (2006). The impact of culture and individualism-collectivism on the creative potential and achievement of American and Chinese adults. *Creativity Research Journal*, **18**(3), 355–66.

Chapter 9

Composers' creative process: The role of life-events, emotion and reason

Vladimir J. Konečni

9.1 **Introduction**

This chapter presents reflections about an important and much-discussed aspect of art-music composers' creative *process*, namely, the role—if any—that emotions, and specifically acute emotional states induced by life-events, play in that process. By the proviso 'if any', I mean to suggest that in writing the chapter, I have adopted a sceptical attitude toward what I regard as the currently prevalent position in the study of, and talk about, music (but not only music)—'emotivism', which I define as the propensity for excessive insertion of emotion and 'feeling' into both lay and scientific theories of mental life, motives, needs, and daily behaviour, in matters artistic (perhaps especially music; cf. Bottum, 2000; Konečni, 2009) and non-artistic.[1] Whether emotion as a facet of the creative process should be considered all-important or negligible depends in part on one's reading of the empirical evidence concerning the relationship between music and emotion (and especially concerning the applicability of that evidence to composers' work), but also on one's worldview regarding emotivism. The latter point is especially pertinent in the present context—with regard to the presence, use of, and responses to music (cf. Konečni, 2009; North & Hargreaves, 2008). In contrast to the emotivist attitude, I shall argue for the paramount importance of contemplation, analytical and technical skills, problem-solving, and planning—in short, *reason*—as the key features of art-music composers' (including contemporary ones) daily work, especially when developing large-scale pieces (but not limited to those). I will also propose that when emotions are experienced by composers in response to others' and their own music of very high quality (including the piece on which they are working at the time), these are likely to be the states of *being moved* and *aesthetic awe* (Konečni, 2005b, 2008a, b)—which are very rare and have different phenomenological characteristics and evolutionary origin than the emotions with which psychologists and biologists are usually concerned (cf. Grewe et al., 2007; Zentner et al., 2008).

By 'creative process', I am referring to all phases of the work in which art-music composers engage as they develop a score—in other words, their habitual day-to-day 'toil'. The chapter shall explicitly not address creativity, which can be defined as a long-term personality trait, ability, or disposition that is measurable by various tests (in general, and in various art media and other domains). I shall also not write about performance, even though performance may include (even in art music, and prominently so in the 18th century) improvisation—and it is defensible to regard improvisation as a special case of the process of composing.

---

[1] My use of the term 'emotivism' is not related to the 'emotivist'–'cognitivist' dichotomy that has been described in the philosophy of music, notably by Kivy (1980, 1989, 1990). 'Emotivism'—mostly vacuous and well-nigh universal in contemporary life—is used here in a much broader and less technical sense.

Whereas creativity can be measured—with variable success, depending on the criterion and domain of prediction—the creative process is often justifiably seen as enveloped by mystery and privacy. This is especially true for the work of very successful art-music composers—and this chapter is limited to such, by definition rather singular, individuals. One can bring many dozens of talented conservatoire students of composition and even practicing second-echelon composers into the music-psychological laboratory, assign them the task of composing a piece (only very brief ones are, in fact, feasible), and obtain a record, including verbal commentary, of their behaviour and music output. The results might be interesting and publishable, but one would not be much closer to the subtleties of the creative process of the rare composing geniuses—even with the research realistically limited to the activities of composers not encumbered by brain-scanners, that is, to the externally observable behavioural and documentary manifestations of the creative process. Much more than the often insurmountable difficulties of recruitment of the desired top-echelon research participants is in question here: There is the crucial problem of the researcher's very presence.[2] When the creative process is closely observed, measured, and recorded, there is—in most art media, but perhaps especially in music and literature—an interference with the authenticity of the process, which in turn affects both the essential nature and the quality of the resulting work (Konečni, 1991).[3] In other words, an analogy to the 'Heisenberg principle' may be operative and therefore one might often be better off using 'unobtrusive measures' (Webb et al., 1966).

In the case of music composition, the use of 'unobtrusive measures' refers primarily to musicological, historiometric, and music-psychological work on sketches, studies made for didactic purposes (e.g. J.S. Bach's *Clavierbuchlein* that led to Book I of *The Well-Tempered Clavier*), and successive versions of scores—and the analysis of their relation to composers' diaries, autobiographies, interviews, and letters to relatives, friends, patrons, and publishers. In this task, one must keep in mind that some of these documents may contain deliberately misleading elements and therefore do not qualify as 'non-reactive' research sources.

9.2 Phases of the creative process

In comparison to some very elaborate models that have been proposed (a large number has been described, for example, by Arieti, 1976), what follows is a straightforward, but, for the present purpose, a sufficiently detailed account. The creative process can be usefully divided into two

----

[2] P.I. Chaikovsky wrote the following in letters in 1878 and 1877: 'During the actual time of creative activity, complete quiet is absolutely necessary to the artist' (Morgenstern, 1956: p. 254; Fisk, 1997: p. 157); 'When I am composing an opera . . . I must not see a soul during certain hours . . . and know that no one can see or hear me; I have a habit, when composing, of singing very loud, and the thought that someone could hear me disturbs me very much' (Fisk, 1997: p. 156). To the extent that insight is one of the key aspects of the creative process, relevant experimental research in non-auditory modalities has indirectly confirmed the necessity of Chaikovsky's composing habits. Results for electroencephalographic topography show that during verbal problem-solving leading to insight, there is a decrease in occipital activity that is consistent with a decrease in externally directed visual attention (Kounios et al., 2006). And the psychological work on 'verbal overshadowing' (Schooler & Engstler-Schooler, 1990) shows how, in problem-solving, one's verbal description of a present nonverbal stimulus diminishes the probability of insight.

[3] There is at least one well-documented exception to this generalization, but in the domain of painting—as any connoisseur of Picasso would testify after watching the 75-min film *Le Mystère Picasso* (1956), directed by H.-G. Clouzot, with cinematography by Claude Renoir. In this film (declared a national treasure by the French government in 1984), Picasso, at 75, created some 20 black-and-white sketches and color paintings in real-time, with his visual output filmed throughout.

major phases, the preparatory and the executive (Konečni, 1991). For a thoroughly schooled mature composer, the *preparatory phase* (cf. Wallas, 1926) consists of reviewing one's past work, an intense study of new (conceptual and technical) developments and other composers' accomplishments, and an active, multifaceted search for small- and large-scale musical and structural ideas. (A commission that the composer has received may give an additional impetus and direction to the search.) At some point the decision is made to begin concrete work on a specific piece.[4] Such a decision may be regarded as the beginning of the *executive phase* of the creative process; the decision may or may not be directly prompted by *inspiration*, which may take dramatically different forms in terms of suddenness of onset, sheer scale, musical purpose, the amount of detail, and therefore the amount of work that is necessary to flesh it out.

There is a voluminous anecdotal literature on inspiration in music and other arts. One of the most articulate accounts was provided by the writer V.V. Nabokov (1973), but his description is likely to be valid for composers also: 'A prefatory glow, not unlike some benign variety of the aura before an epileptic attack, is something the artist learns to perceive early in life . . . The beauty of it is that, while completely intelligible[,] . . . it has neither source nor object. It expands, glows, and subsides . . . [but] a window has opened . . . A few days elapse. (Wallas's, 1926, 'incubation' phase.) The next stage . . . is something ardently anticipated—and no longer anonymous' (p. 309). From this account of inspiration, and many others, two points seem clear: 1) 'the right background' and preparation are necessary—current emotions are rarely mentioned; and 2) inspiration is only the beginning of the executive phase. Moreover, instances of inspiration are relatively broad and somewhat vague, and should therefore not be regarded as solutions to specific problems (be they musical, mathematical, or poetic) that have been previously posed: that role is played by *insight* (Wallas's, 1926, moment of 'illumination'), with a long tradition as philosophers' *eureka* and psychologists' *aha!*, but, more recently, intensively studied by cognitive neuroscientists. One can think of inspiration as influencing the broader parameters of a work (regardless of its size), which, however, leaves a host of specific musical questions unanswered, and many of these require, or profit from, insight.

Prior to insight, having been fully immersed in a problem, a composer may, like other creative problem-solvers, experience a 'mental block'—and the mathematician Poincaré (1908), as part of his notable statement about the creative process, suggested that one should, upon reaching an impasse, relax or distract oneself by a walk or short trip: insight is not the result of incremental steps toward a solution, but requires a transformative act that is best accomplished by 'de-focus' and relaxation (cf. Bindeman, 1998; Ghiselin, 1952).[5] In the past decade, cognitive neuroscientists have, in a series of related studies (e.g. Jung-Beeman et al., 2004; Kounios et al., 2006, 2008; Miller & Cohen, 2001; Sandkühler & Bhattacharya, 2008; Sheth, et al., 2009; see also footnote 2, this chapter), discovered some of the neural correlates of events leading to, and just after, the moment

---

[4] It is noteworthy that among the traditional attempts to account for creativity by a single factor (which abound in that field), there is a recent one (Sternberg, 2002) that explicitly considers 'the decision to be creative' as the key attribute of creativity—even though it seems self-evident that the decision in question itself requires a multi-factor explanation (Konečni, 2005a).

[5] Work on the problem often continues 'in the background': 'Sometimes I observe with curiosity that an uninterrupted [musical] activity—independent of the subject of the conversation I may be carrying on— continues its course in that department of my brain which is devoted to music' (Chaikovsky in an 1878 letter, cited by Morgenstern, 1956: p. 255; see also A. Mahler, 1946/1969: pp. 46–7). Chaikovsky also mentions that his musical ideas, when they emerge, do so concretely, fully orchestrated: 'The musical thought never appears otherwise than in a suitable external form . . . I invent the musical idea and the orchestration simultaneously' (Morgenstern, 1956: p. 257).

of insight. The initial focus involves the prefrontal cortex, which also tries to decide which other areas need to be engaged in order to solve the problem, including parts of the right hemisphere (which, as it happens, is the insight route, as opposed to the methodical-incremental one). Once an impasse is reached, relaxation and letting the mind wander are helpful (as Poincaré suggested), presumably so that the more remote right-hemisphere associations can be sought. Up to 8 sec beforehand, insight can be predicted by the degree of steadiness of EEG (electroencephalogram) alpha rhythm (indicative of relaxation), in comparison to controls. During the second before insight, however, the anterior superior temporal gyrus (in the right hemisphere) becomes very active; some 300 millisec before a research participant gives the answer, the EEG registers a spike of gamma waves. (Note that the insight process is essentially emotion-free.)

Once the executive phase is underway on a given musical piece, there are bound to be multiple instances of both broad inspiration and specific insight (except perhaps for the shortest pieces); these can be examined by musicologists and music historians, but it is likely that the variability in frequency of these important creative and problem-solving events across both composers and works would prevent sound generalizations from being drawn.

9.3 The relationship between life-events and composers' work

Before turning to the question of whether or not it is reasonable to think that the executive phase of composers' creative process, and their decisions regarding the structure and contents of a piece, are influenced by their current emotional state, it is of interest to examine the evidence for the relationship between life-events and composers' output (A in Figure 9.1). To the extent

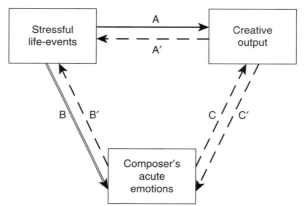

Fig. 9.1 Life-events, composer's emotions, and creative output. *Note.* 'Life-events' refers mostly to adverse, but also to some joyous events ('beginning of a reciprocated love affair', 'marriage'; Simonton, 1977: p. 796). Double solid lines (B) indicate that the relationship is self-evident. Single solid line (A) indicates that a relationship has been established on one measure (i.e. melodic originality: Simonton, 1980, 1987), though not on five other measures (see text regarding Simonton, 1977, 1987). Dashed lines indicate either a made but unsubstantiated theoretical claim (C: Simonton, 1980: p. 216; 2001, pp. 218–19) or hypothesized instances of reverse causation: e.g. high productivity may lead to neglect of family thus causing additional stress (A'); stressful life-events and acute emotions often amplify each other (B'; cf. the Prototypical Emotion-Episode Model, Konečni, 2008b); and C', high productivity may lead to a greater frequency of success, failure, and corresponding emotions (Simonton's five other measures cannot be readily related to composers' acute emotions).

that: 1) such evidence is solid and 2) at least some life-events can be safely assumed to have a major effect on acute emotions (B in Figure 9.1), the role of current emotion as a *mediator* of the effects of life-events on compositional output (B and C jointly in Figure 9.1) would become somewhat more plausible—in contrast to the vagueness of the appeals to composers' emotional states, which some musicologists and critics routinely indulge in when describing art music. (Some excesses in that vein are described by Kivy, 1980: pp. 13–14.)

In examining the relationship of composers' life-events and creative-output measures, the 'historiometric' work of Simonton (1998) is notable; he defines it as 'a multiple-case, quantitative, and hypothesis-testing approach' (p. 103). For present purposes, the most relevant aspect of Simonton's work is the relationship between major life-events and output. When studying this relationship for 10 composers—found on Farnsworth's list (1969, appendix A, p. 228), which includes Bach, Beethoven, Mozart, Haydn, Brahms, Handel, Debussy, Schubert, Wagner, and Chopin (in the order of 'eminence')—Simonton (1977), despite a sophisticated quantitative analysis, did not find a significant relationship between the 10 composers' 'biographical stress' and either their *total productivity* or, perhaps more significantly, their *thematic productivity* (using data from the Barlow & Morgenstern dictionaries of instrumental and vocal themes). The broadly inclusive biographical stress index (with multicollinearity statistically controlled) was based on numerous weighted factors, among which (weights in parentheses) were: lawsuits (30), beginning and/or end of a reciprocated love affair (30), marriage (50), death of a close family member (63), detention in jail or exile (63), divorce (73), and death of spouse (100). In contrast, 'physical illness' had the expected significant relationship with both productivity measures. Simonton (1977) summarizes as follows: 'Creative productivity appears remarkably immune from a wide range of external forces. Such impersonal social factors as warfare and civil turmoil have no noticeable impact, *nor do . . . tribulations of private life* '(p. 802, italics added); in short, A in Figure 9.1 is nil. As just one example, Bach composed some of his most respected and beloved compositions, the *Sonatas and Partitas for solo violin* (BWV 1001-1006) and the *Six Suites for unaccompanied cello* (BWV 1007-1012) between 1717 and 1723, with much of the work done after 1720, the year in which his first wife, Maria Barbara, suddenly passed away, in Bach's absence.

In a later study (Simonton, 1980), the basic data were all 5046 themes composed by the same 10 pre-eminent musicians (as in Simonton, 1977)—and controlling, for example, for Mozart accounting for 17% of the themes. It was found, among other things, that the melodic originality of the themes was greater during periods of 'biographic stress' (using data from Simonton, 1977, for the stress index). Finally, in a subsequent study (Simonton, 1987) that focused on Beethoven alone (105 pieces, 593 themes), the finding of greater melodic originality during times of life stress was replicated (A in Figure 9.1).

It is important to remember that Simonton's work examined correlations among conceptually distal 'macro'-variables and that there was no attempt to study proximal causes of psychological nature that might be involved in the generation of composers' acute emotions due to life-events, let alone any alleged effects of emotions thus induced on important musical creative decisions. As to the findings, there was no relationship between life-events and either the total or thematic productivity; there was, however, a positive correlation between the adversity of life-events and melodic originality.

The melodic originality of themes is a reasonable indicator of musical output, but it is only one of several possible candidates and should by no means be equated with compositional greatness in music. Composers as different as Mahler, Bernstein, Boulez, and many others have insisted, for example, that *development* is paramount. Moreover, as Simonton himself (1980: p. 211) has written, a 'simplified' operationalization of melodic originality was used, notably omitting rhythm. In addition, a minuscule amount of the explained variance in melodic originality was accounted by 'biographical stress' (Simonton, 1980: pp. 214–15; 1987, p. 99; 2001, p. 219). In short, this is a weak effect. And finally, in the Beethoven study (Simonton, 1987: table 2, p. 99), there was no relationship between 'biographical stress' and three other measures of output: melodic variation, metric originality, and metric variation (A in Figure 9.1 was nil).

In summary, at least in terms of the reviewed research, one can conclude that there is at present a very limited amount of solid evidence for the relationship between life-events and creative musical output.

9.4 **Composers' emotions and their music**

There is no doubt that many of the life-events comprising Simonton's 'biographical stress' index—all of them involving other human beings, including the composers' closest intimates— were able to cause emotions (B in Figure 9.1) that are important from an evolutionary standpoint, such as anger, fear, sadness, and joy (e.g. marriage was included in the index: Simonton, 1977: p. 796). In contemporary experimental psychology, emotions are generally defined as highly pro- nounced, subjectively identifiable and reportable, transient, *acute* states (as opposed to personality dispositions or low-intensity, long-lasting states like moods; e.g. Konečni, 2010; Parkinson et al., 1996). Longer duration and frequent reappearance of a particular emotion can be comfortably handled by reiterative models with a feedback loop linking the episode-initiating event, the inter- pretation/appraisal stage(s), the physiological, facial, and postural components, and the behavioural and mental consequences of the subjective emotional state (e.g. the Prototypical Emotion-Episode Model, or PEEM; see Konečni, 2008b, 2010; B′ in Figure 9.1 alludes to the mentioned feedback). Even treatments (e.g. cognitive/emotional-modification) of a chronic emotional malfunction, such as clinical depression, can be pursued on the basis of the reiterative component of PEEM.

However, the question is: given the view of emotion espoused above—which, I would main- tain, is more reasonable than any alternative, especially when one is dealing with the effects of life-events and not, for example, with the effects of music itself—is it truly plausible, for composers, listeners, and researchers to think of emotion as having an influence on important compositional decisions (C in Figure 9.1)? My answer is negative, in part because the following points should be kept in mind: 1) at issue are not vague moods or other ambiguous quasi-emotional states; 2) one must think of far-reaching decisions a composer must make, some of which will apply to large- scale works that take many months if not years to complete—during which new life-events will take place and the composer will experience emotional episodes on a daily basis, hundreds of them altogether, and of different kinds, in the course of working on a single composition; 3) myriad complex technical decisions will be involved that require careful study and a 'sober', analytical approach; 4) even very short works are likely to undergo revisions, at least some of which may remove the effects, if any, of some acute emotional state that was experienced previ- ously while composing the piece; 5) many composers keep sketchbooks and use these ideas when working on a score, but even if such sketches are closer in time and sentiment to an acute emo- tional state, they are likely later to be revised, combined with others, and thus lose whatever acute emotional identity they originally had.

In the view of Gabrielsson and Lindström (2001: p. 223), '[w]hile it is a popular conception . . . that composers express their present feelings in their compositions, a more plausible view is that [they] try to use various structural factors in order to achieve certain intended expressions, differ- ent in different works, with little or no direct connection to their present feelings.' The 'popular conception' referred to above—the emotivist concept of a musical piece as the composer's vehicle for self-expression—can be traced to the views of C.Ph.E. Bach (in an essay written in 1775), which were quoted and cogently criticized by Langer (1957: pp. 214–15). After showing how

Bach's view had been uncritically accepted by many musicians ('Beethoven, Schumann, Liszt, to mention only the great', p. 215), philosophers, average music-lovers, and 'even our leading [music] psychologists [like] Carl Seashore' (p. 216)—Langer argued persuasively for the alternative view that music 'expresses primarily the composer's *knowledge of human feeling*' (p. 221, italics in the original) and that a composer 'knows the forms of emotion and can handle them, "compose" them' (p. 222). Before Langer, Schenker expressed a complementary view: 'One must not seek in [C.Ph.E.] Bach's word "passions" [*Leidenschaften*] what certain aestheticians of the doctrine of affections bring to it . . . [Bach] means by it simply the consequences of a change in diminution: *pure musical effects*' (cited in Cook & Dibben, 2001: p. 47; italics added).

Indeed, many composers have insisted, in various ways, that music should be only about itself, most famously Stravinsky (1936) who incurred many music lovers', critics', and teachers' wrath by writing that 'music is, by its very nature, essentially powerless to *express* anything at all' (p. 53)—although, if they read on, they would have perhaps been impressed by Stravinsky stating that '[t]he phenomenon of music is given to us with the sole purpose of establishing an order in things . . . the coordination between *man* and *time*' (p. 54).[6] Boulez, also perceived as overly 'cerebral' by the emotivists, often echoed such opinions (see pp. 419–22 in Fisk, 1997). And consider Hans Werner Henze's statement, in a 1975 programme note on Mahler's *Second Symphony*, that in Mahler (and Berg), '[F]or the first time in musical history, music is interrogating itself about the reasons for its existence and about its nature' (Fisk, 1997: pp. 448–49). Henze's view of Mahler's music as self-critical and primarily *analysing itself*—and see Alma Mahler's analogous description (1946/1969: pp. 213–14) of the intent of Mahler's 'programme' of the *Second Symphony* that he prepared for the performance in Dresden on 20 December 1901—can be usefully contrasted with that of Schönberg, who, in 1904, wrote as follows to Mahler about his *Fifth Symphony*: 'I saw your very soul, naked, stark naked. It was revealed to me as a stretch of wild and secret country, with eerie chasms and abysses neighbored by sunlit, smiling meadows'. What is interesting is that the staunch emotivist in Schönberg (at least at the age of 30, long before developing the 'cold' 12-tone technique) refuses to be swayed by contrary 'evidence', for he continues the letter thus: 'What does it matter that what I was told afterward of your "program" did not seem to correspond altogether with what I had felt?' (Fisk, 1997: p. 245). A reader relying solely on Schönberg's account would be unlikely to surmise that Mahler, in fact, used and rationally combined numerous sketches for the *Fifth Symphony* and worked on the 'fair copy' for many months (A. Mahler, 1946/1969: pp. 42, 48).

How a composer's music is generally perceived is indeed a poor predictor of their views on composition as self-expression; for example, the alleged emotivist Chaikovsky thoughtfully wrote in a letter in 1878: 'Those who imagine that a creative artist can—through the medium of his art—express his feelings at the moment when he is *moved*, make the greatest mistake. Emotions—sad or joyful—can only be expressed *retrospectively* . . . a work composed in the happiest surroundings may be touched with dark and gloomy colors' (Morgenstern, 1956: p. 254; original italics). In other words, the score contains only the memories of past emotions; and even the current

---

6 An example of a begrudging, emotivist view of Stravinsky is provided by the music critic Alex Ross (2000: p. 86): 'Of the great composers, Stravinsky may have possessed the finest, subtlest mind. But in certain ways his intellect was a limitation, and he left the public with an image of the classical composer as a cerebral rather than a sensuous being.' Some 20th-century composers (just one example is Copland), even when defending the music of their time from accusations of being without expressions of 'feeling' (see, e.g. Fisk, 1997: p. 343), feel the obligation to stress that contemporary music, while not Romantic, is not without sentiment.

life circumstances do not affect the emotional tone of the piece.[7] Also, the reliance on old sketches ensures there is substantial distance between any past, however acutely felt, emotion and the score: 'A little notebook with over two hundred different renderings of the dominant theme in the finale [of *Ninth Symphony*] shows how persistently Beethoven pursued his search and *how entirely musical his guiding motive was*' (Debussy, in 1921, from *Monsieur Croche, The Dilettante Hater*, quoted in Fisk, 1997: p. 201; italics added). Moreover, even for an idea to get into a sketchbook required, in the case of Langer's alleged emotivist Beethoven, a lot of mulling over: 'I carry my thoughts about with me for a long time, often for a very long time, before writing them down' (Beethoven in an 1822 or 1823 letter, quoted in Fisk, 1997: p. 56).[8] Finally, the score itself often takes a long time to complete and 'it would be wrong to suppose that the musician remains absorbed in the contemplation . . . [of some emotion] during the whole course of composition of a long work' (Albert Roussel in a letter in 1928, quoted by Norman and Lubell Shrifte, 1946: p. 331). All this is understandable logistically and psychologically; it certainly does not support the view that current emotional states have an effect on the music being composed.

In fact, when some composers sincerely claim that their music expresses their 'emotions' (including 'innermost'), they are likely not to be referring to the current, acute emotions, but their memories and knowledge of them, thus using the term imprecisely—or as Stravinsky (1936: p. 54) would say, by 'force of [linguistic] habit'—as shorthand for their whole human and musical person, and their entire (presumably humanist, and perhaps emotivist) worldview (cf. Konečni et al., 2008). Such a reading is made even more plausible when one considers that some of the self-expressing composers (notably C.Ph.E. Bach) felt that *the only way* to 'move people' (Bach's words; see Langer, 1957: p. 214; Konečni, 1986b: p. 13) was by expressing their own emotions in their compositions, and that therefore it would be rather odd for a composer to assume that the listener would be moved by music that reflected, say, the composer's quarrel with his creditor or spouse.

In the philosophy of music, the idea that music sounds 'expressive' to listeners because composers express their personal current emotions in the process of composing is labelled 'expression theory' and it has received numerous criticisms (e.g. Goldman, 1995; Kivy, 1980; Tormey, 1971). Davies (2001: p. 32) has summarized one of the core problems as follows: 'we experience music's expressiveness not as a residue of feelings discharged in the compositional process but as resident in its nature'. There must be some hard-core emotivist listeners who would refuse to be counted in the philosophers' nonchalant 'we' and insist that in listening to music their goal is to commune with the soul of the composer, à la young Schönberg; others may be less adamant, but also likely to suffer from the forces of emotivist linguistic habits in musical matters. As Roussel put it in 1928: In 'a symphonic work . . . the composer is concerned only with the interplay of sound-combinations . . . It is possible that such music may suggest to certain hearers feelings that the

---

[7] Such is the pervasiveness of emotivism, that this dissociation is sometimes difficult even for composers' intimates to accept. For instance, Alma Mahler (1946/1969: p. 70) 'found [it] incomprehensible' that Mahler 'added three more to the two *Kindertotenlieder* already composed' while he, at that time in 1904, fully enjoyed their two children: 'What I cannot understand is bewailing the deaths of children, who were in the best of health and spirits, hardly an hour after having kissed and fondled them. I exclaimed at the time: "For heaven's sake, don't tempt Providence!" ' Alma Schindler Mahler has had academic detractors (the so-called 'Alma Problem'), but not regarding this matter.

[8] There are many articles and a number of books devoted solely to Beethoven's sketches, most of them based on the research by Gustav Nottebohm (1865/1880/1979); see also Lockwood (1992) and Mies (1929).

composer himself did not experience in the least, but this is one of the inevitable consequences of the undefined character of the musical language' (Norman & Lubell Shrifte, 1946: pp. 330–1).[9]

It is interesting to note some subtleties in the possibility of the composer's emotion finding its way into the score, with one of the most famous circumstances in the history of music (and emotion) as the background. Kivy (1980, p. 15) writes: 'It seems fairly clear . . . that parts of Mozart's *Requiem* (K. 626) express the composer's terror of death, and are not merely expressive of terror.' Note that in Kivy's usage, 'not merely expressive of' means 'not in reference to an emotion (here 'terror of death') in the abstract'; for Kivy means more—that specifically the 'Dies irae' (p. 15) expresses Mozart's own terror of death. And if it does, the composer must have inserted the terror into the score himself, by conscious intention or unconsciously; Kivy does not specify—and neither does Simonton when stating his own self-expression views (1980: p. 216).

The claim is dubious and an example of emotivist (in the sense the term is used in this chapter, not Kivy's) self-expression being read into Mozart's *Requiem* because of a biographical coincidence—and by Kivy, the unlikeliest of the philosophers of music to do it. First, there is the obvious question of the extent of Franz Xaver Süssmayr's contribution to the *Requiem* (cf. Cormican, 1991; Konečni, 1997).[10] Second, the best documentary evidence suggests that Mozart passed away quite suddenly and so would not have been aware of anything medically serious impending at the time of composing *Dies irae* (Cormican, 1991: pp.174–7). Third, there is the admittedly somewhat moot question of the 'Dies irae' proper, with a duration of only 1 min 52 sec (for a poem that has at least 17 musically exploitable stanzas), being too short for either 'expressing' or being 'expressive of' the terror of death. Fourth, and most significantly, the 'Dies irae' is *supposed* to sound terror-inducing: It brings up the Day of Judgment. So, on firm *a priori* grounds one needs to favour an 'expressive of terror', as opposed to an 'expresses Mozart's terror' interpretation. After all, the Second Vatican Council removed the 'Dies irae' from *missa ordinarium* precisely because it 'overemphasizes fear and despair' (Archbishop Annibale Bugnini, 1990: p. 773). And fifth, one could legitimately claim that listeners perceive Mozart's 'Dies irae' as sounding not terror-inducing but 'triumphant' or 'victorious', just as the successive bass, tenor, alto, and soprano parts in the subsequent 'Tuba mirum' sound respectively 'calm and dignified', 'beseeching, plaintive', 'anxious', and 'tender'—rather than fear-inducing (due to the trumpet announcing the Day of Judgment).[11]

---

[9] As to the possibility of listeners' own emotions being induced by instrumental music (*without the necessity of mediating involvement of* non*musical factors*), that is another and even more complex story (cf. Juslin & Västfjäll, 2008; Kivy, 1980, 1989; Konečni, 2003, 2008a, 2008b; Konečni, et al., 2008). As Hindemith wisely wrote in 1952: 'Real feelings need a certain interval of time to develop, reach their climax, and fade again; reactions to music, however, may change as fast as musical phrases do. Thus these reactions may, within a few instants, skip . . . without causing any discomfort to the mind experiencing them, as would be the case with a rapid succession of real feelings. In fact, if it happened with real feelings, we could be sure that it could be only in the event of slight insanity. The reactions music evokes are not feelings; they are the images, the memories of feelings' (Fisk, 1997: p. 314). This is perceptive and sound common sense—a feature that is, I would suggest, missing in some music-emotion experimental designs in the psychology of music, in which numerous different 'emotions' are said to be 'induced' in the same research participant by numerous brief music excerpts—all in a matter of minutes.

[10] On the basis of exceptionally careful archival research, Cormican (1991: pp. 272–6; 280) has concluded that five of the six parts of Mozart's *Requiem*'s 'Sequentia', including the 'Dies irae', were composed 'mainly' by Mozart, with 'additions' by F.X. Süssmayr; 'Lacrimosa' was 'mainly attributable to Mozart' (p. 275).

[11] Beethoven's letters (e.g. to Karl Amenda in 1801, Norman & Lubell Shrifte, 1946, p. 82-83) describe a broad range of emotions, including anger at deafness and fate. Volumes have been written that read emotions caused by deafness into different works; Kivy's (1989: p. 156) mention of 'the angry contortions of the *Grosse fuge*' is quite typical. However, one needs to consider technical, as opposed to emotional, issues

The conclusion in section 9.3 was that convincing evidence is lacking of a strong association between life-events and creative musical output (A in Figure 9.1). That statement should be viewed in conjunction with the conclusion from the material that has been presented in this section, to the effect that there is no unambiguous evidence for the popular notion—held by some composers, critics, and music lovers—that composers' current, acute emotions influence major compositional decisions (C in Figure 9.1).

In section 9.3, I also expressed some reservations about the construction of the melodic-originality measure and the weakness of the relationship between 'biographical stress' and melodic originality (Simonton, 1980, 1987). I would especially take issue with Simonton's—I believe unwarranted—strongly-worded claim (1980: p. 216) that 'we nonetheless have strong evidence that music expresses emotional states being experienced by the composer'—a claim made purely on the basis of the finding that composers who scored higher on the stress index composed melodies 'over the same period [which tended to] employ more chromatic notes and more dissonant or extreme intervals between consecutive notes' (Simonton's definition of 'melodic originality'). After all, Simonton himself (2001: p. 218) wrote that neither of the studies was 'specifically dedicated to scrutinizing the relation between music and emotion'. And, in this vein, it would be interesting to know why the obtained correlation was predicted to begin with, when the research on coping with stress would predict the opposite of novelty-seeking. More importantly, there are several families of plausible alternative explanations that *do not involve composers' acute emotions* while creating music—one of which is that changed life circumstances may be an optimal time to explore new musical paths. At the time of 'biographical stress' one may be especially prone to seek the approbation and respect of colleagues and critics, and this usually requires *innovation*—and an increase in various forms of chromaticism was an important novelty feature from before J.S. Bach and Haydn, for example, in Frescobaldi's *Fiori musicali* (1635), known to Bach (Ledbetter, 2002: p. 86).

In summary, Simonton's valuable work notwithstanding, my sceptical position on the relationship between life-events and creative output—and especially on the mediation of that relationship by composers' acute, current emotions—can remain in place.

9.5 **Contemplation, technical skills, problem-solving, planning**

It is to be expected that the technical (as opposed to romanticized) music literature would generally be immune to excessive emotivism, but one is nevertheless repeatedly struck by various authors' insistence—literally regardless of which well-known composer is their subject—on these musicians' thorough preparation, extensive study, and hard work on revisions of scores. As Carl Nielsen wrote, 'it is music that of all the arts requires the strictest discipline . . . the most exacting study there must be' (Fisk, 1997: pp. 214–15). In addition, in serious biographies, one often finds that authors of compositions perceived as 'cerebral' (e.g. Webern) were often quite emotional men, but little evidence that their private lives entered their compositions (e.g. Bailey, 1998: p. 79; Moldenhauer & Moldenhauer, 1979: pp. 340, 492–4; Polnauer, 1959/1967: p. 21).

A few examples of the paramount importance of *reason* in composition should suffice. Many authors (e.g. Geck, 2000/2006; Williams, 2004) comment on Bach's devotion to preparation, self-improvement, and study—for instance, of the Italian and French idioms for application in free organ works (not based on chorales) and solo violin pieces mentioned earlier—as well as

---

and the tendencies of innovation in conceptualization and technique that would have been operative with advancing years in any case; nor have all the necessary facts relative to Beethoven's *acute* emotions obtaining a place in the various *final scores—without considerable revision—*been established.

extensive contemplation, for instance, of the ways to advance music 'in the divine service' (Konečni, 1986a: p. 20).[12] Regarding Mozart's continuous striving for improvement, Kozbelt (2005, study 2) has documented that both the quality of Mozart's pieces judged as masterpieces and the proportion of masterpiece-level pieces per year grew over time, even during Mozart's maturity, with improvement occurring mostly in large-scale compositions; and this, one should note, despite the growing number of adverse life-events and tribulations. Beethoven's hard work, innumerable sketches (see footnote 8, this chapter), and multiple detailed revisions are legendary—with regard to the evolution of his mastery in the domain of the sonata as much as in any other. The 32 piano sonatas pushed the limits of the piano and are one long treatise on its developing technology. Careful study proceeds to this day of the thought and attention to detail that Beethoven displayed in the successive revisions of the *Sonata for violoncello and pianoforte* (Op. 69; Lockwood, 1992) and his 10 violin sonatas (Lockwood & Kroll, 2005), of which the last, in G-Major (Op. 96) was completed in 1812 but not published until 1816, due in large part to the process of revision. Schubert's letters testify to his careful cuts and revisions (e.g. see an 1828 letter in Weiss, 1967: pp. 211–12). Niecks (1902: pp. 113–14) documents the slow evolution, from 1828 to 1833, of Chopin's *Trio for piano, violin, and violoncello* (Op. 8) and generally Chopin's—that Romantic *par excellence*—continuous hard work from a young age. Protopopov (1990), on the other hand, analyses Chopin's studious approach to some classical forms (sonata-form, ternary form with trio, variations, and rondo) and ingenious modification to suit his unique creative agenda. Shostakovich strongly felt that a composer had to think, study, and 'write constantly . . . If you can't write a major work, write minor trifles. If you can't write at all, orchestrate something' (Fisk, 1997: p. 362). And he attributed the same habits to Chaikovsky, Rimsky-Korsakov, and Stravinsky. Finally, with regard to a contemporary composer with pronounced religious inclinations, Arvo Pärt, there is ample evidence of formal compositional behaviour, unemotional planning, and intellect. Pärt's notes (1998) regarding his *Kanon Pokajanen* are telling; it is worth remembering in the context of this formal canon that Langer (1957: p. 216) pointed to the following contradiction: composers' emotional self-expression should be hindered by musical form and yet forms have continued to be used and developed.

Emotivists would, of course, not entirely deny the importance of planning and reason, but the question is one of balance and emphasis. Simonton (1980, 1987, 2001), for example, emphasizes melodic originality, which is not unreasonable. What seems unwarranted is his conjecture that composers' current, acute and transient, emotions (caused by 'biographical stress') are chiefly responsible for the increase in chromaticism (C in Figure 9.1), thus ignoring the constraints inherent in his methodology with regard to causal inference, as well as several plausible alternative explanations (especially great composers' planned search for innovation)—in short, Simonton minimized the significance of reason. In the process, he ignored his own (negative) results, that is, no effect of 'biographical stress' on either total productivity or thematic productivity (Simonton, 1977).

9.6 Conclusions: emotivism and reason in art-music composition

With regard to contemporary composers, I have had the opportunity to discuss privately the issue of emotion in composition with about 20 mature, 'full-time', non-academic composers in Estonia,

---

12 This is not to say that Bach has escaped Romantic effusions entirely; rather, they are usually in the descriptions of Bach's music, rather than of the alleged effects of his emotions on it (see Konečni, 1986a: p. 20, regarding Blume, 1950). There are occasional attempts of the latter kind, though, such as the hypothesis that the (13'30") *Ciaccona* within the *Partita for solo violin No. 2* (BWV 1004) was composed as a requiem for Bach's wife Maria Barbara, even though the work is likely to have been completed before she passed away in 1720 (and there are other reasons for doubting this idea).

France, Germany, the Netherlands, Russia, Serbia, and the United States, some of them very well known, and with quite different musical affinities. The gist of these people's opinions that I heard over the years has largely contributed to how this chapter was framed and it can be described as follows: my informal research participants have experienced many private tribulations; they realize that they live in an emotivist world in which the words 'emotion' and 'feeling' are carelessly tossed into every discussion; they admit to over-using emotivist terms themselves in order to talk about their work in lay terms, but almost exclusively when dealing with non-musicians; and above all, that composing is a painstaking and drawn-out process—one in which there is little or no place for their current, transient emotions. And, as a broad generalization: positive emotional events generally energize composing work, whereas negative ones commonly lead to a withdrawal from composing.

But emotivist exaggeration, as I see it, is not present only in assertions that composers' acute emotions influence major aspects of their creative output, but also elsewhere in the music-emotion domain, notably in the notion (see footnote 9, this chapter), so convincingly criticized by Kivy (1980, 1989), that instrumental music may by itself cause the occurrence, in listeners, of biologically important, fundamental emotions (which Kivy unfortunately calls 'garden variety'): Compare the views on this issue espoused by Juslin and Västfjäll (2008) to Konečni's (2008a, b). Often it seems that music' effects are perceived by some music psychologists and many members of the general public as having the inevitability of gravity. 'Music and emotion' is an odd scientific field with regard to causation, for the word *and* to many practitioners apparently means *causes*. (And there indeed seems to be a lot of articles that begin with something like 'even the birds know that music causes emotions'.) Part of emotivism's origin is in Romanticism, of which the least desirable aspects have been put to use in Hollywood products and music industry's tearjerkers. The broader context is the contemporary anti-narrative and anti-intellectual social relativism (e.g. Bottum, 2000; Konečni, 2009), coupled with a pervasive insistence on 'emotional sensitivity'.

But of course music produces very important reactions in art-music listeners, be they ordinary music lovers or composers. My contention is that unlike life-events (especially those involving intimates), music is very unlikely to induce fundamental emotions in listeners (cf. Grewe et al., 2007; Kivy, 1989: p. 217; Konečni et al., 2008), but it most certainly can *move* them (cf. Grewe et al., 2007; Kivy, 1989: p. 229; Konečni, 2005b, 2008b; Zentner et al., 2008). In composers, this may happen when listening to others' music or their own, including at certain moments *while* composing.[13] But one would not consider the state of being moved—even induced by one's own just-written music—as *originally causal* in making important creative decisions in composition. This issue is not a part of the main thrust of the chapter, but it is closely related to it; for this reason, some concluding comments seem in order.

C.Ph.E. Bach used the term 'moved' when speaking of both himself and the public (Langer, 1957: pp. 214–15) and so has the 'cognitivist' Kivy to describe his own reaction to Beethoven's *Grosse fuge* (1989: p. 156) and *String Quartet in C#-Minor* Op. 131 (1989: p. 230), and the *Ave Maria* by Josquin (des Prez, or Josken van de Velde; Kivy, 1990: p. 158). Kivy's reasons for being moved are on the surface uncomplicated—beauty of the music and performers' skill—but each, of course, contains numerous ingredients (Kivy, 1989: pp. 231–32; 1990: pp. 159–60). An attempt has recently been made—in 'aesthetic trinity theory' (ATT, Konečni, 2005)—to place the state of *being moved* formally into a broader aesthetic hierarchically-structured framework together with,

---

[13] The crying-while-writing phenomenon is anecdotally known among poets, writers, and musicians, and I have personally heard about it from some of my composer-informants and have had intimations of it in other domains and personal situations.

as the most common component, the transient, but phenomenologically interesting physiological response of *thrills* (or *chills*; Konečni et al., 2007) and the rarest, *aesthetic awe* (defined as the prototypical response to independently defined *sublime* stimuli in music and other art forms). ATT deals with reactions that are comparatively rare and have different phenomenological attributes and evolutionary origin than the emotions with which psychologists and biologists are usually concerned.

With regard to the central theme of the chapter, however, the final observation would be this: To the view that treats the creative process as an emotivist enterprise, one ought to contrast the aesthetic position that great music, like all great art, exists at a *necessary distance from its creator* and that therefore a calm, analytical mastery is crucial.

References

Arieti, S. (1976). *Creativity: The magical synthesis*. New York: Basic Books.

Bailey, K. (1998). *The life of Webern*. Cambridge: Cambridge University Press.

Bindeman, S. (1998). Echoes of silence: A phenomenological study of the creative process. *Creativity Research Journal*, **11**, 69–77.

Blume, F. (1950). *Two centuries of Bach*. Oxford: Oxford University Press.

Bottum, J. (2000). The soundtracking of America. *The Atlantic Magazine*, **285**, 56–70.

Bugnini, A. (1990). *The reform of the liturgy: 1948–1975*. Collegeville, MN: Liturgical Press.

Cook, N. & Dibben, N. (2001). Musicological approaches to emotion. In P.N. Juslin & J.A. Sloboda (Eds.) *Music and emotion: Theory and research*. Oxford: Oxford University Press, pp. 45–70.

Cormican, B. (1991). *Mozart's death—Mozart's* Requiem. Belfast: The Amadeus Press.

Davies, S. (2001). Philosophical perspectives on music's expressiveness. In P.N. Juslin & J.A. Sloboda (Eds.) *Music and emotion: Theory and research*. Oxford: Oxford University Press, pp. 23–44.

Farnsworth, P.R. (1969). *The social psychology of music*, (2nd Edition). Ames, Iowa: Iowa State University Press.

Fisk, J. (Ed.) (1997). *Composers on music: Eight centuries of writings*, (2nd Edition). Boston, MA: Northeastern University Press.

Gabrielsson, A. & Lindström, E. (2001). The influence of musical structure on emotional expression. In P.N. Juslin & J.A. Sloboda (Eds.) *Music and emotion: Theory and research*. Oxford: Oxford University Press, pp. 223–48.

Geck, M. (2006). *Johann Sebastian Bach: Life and work*. (J. Hargraves, Trans.). New York: Harcourt. [Original work published in 2000.]

Ghiselin, B. (1952). *The creative process*. New York: Mentor.

Goldman, A. (1995). Emotions in music (a postscript). *Journal of Aesthetics and Art Criticism*, **53**, 59–69.

Grewe, O., Nagel, F., Kopiez, R., & Altenmüller, E. (2007). Emotions over time: Synchronicity and development of subjective, physiological, and facial affective reactions to music. *Emotion*, **7**, 774–88.

Jung-Beeman, M., Bowden, E.M., Haberman, J., Frymiare, J.L., Arambel-Liu, S., & Greenblatt, R. (2004). Neural activity when people solve verbal problems with insight. *PLoS Biology*, **2**, E97.

Juslin, P.N. & Västfjäll, D. (2008). Emotional responses to music: The need to consider underlying mechanisms. *Behavioral and Brain Sciences*, **31**, 559–621. [Target article with commentaries.]

Kivy, P. (1980). *The corded shell: Reflections on musical expression*. Princeton, NJ: Princeton University Press.

Kivy, P. (1989). *Sound sentiment: An essay on the musical emotions*. Philadelphia, PA: Temple University Press.

Kivy, P. (1990). *Music alone: Philosophical reflections on the purely musical experience*. Ithaca, NY: Cornell University Press.

Konečni, V.J. (1986a). Bach's *St Matthew Passion*: A rudimentary psychological analysis, Part I. *Bach*, **17**(3), 10–21.

Konečni, V.J. (1986b). Bach's *St Matthew Passion*: A rudimentary psychological analysis, Part II. *Bach*, **17**(4), 3–16.

Konečni, V.J. (1991). Portraiture: An experimental study of the creative process. *Leonardo*, **24**, 325–8.

Konečni, V.J. (1997). Vyacheslav Artyomov's *Requiem*: A humanist's chef-d'oeuvre. Moscow: Fond duhovnogo tvorchestva.

Konečni, V.J. (2003). Review of Music and emotion: Theory and research by P.N. Juslin and J.A. Sloboda (2001). *Music Perception*, **20**, 332–41.

Konečni, V.J. (2005a). On the 'golden section'. *Visual Arts Research*, **31**, 76–87.

Konečni, V.J. (2005b). The aesthetic trinity: Awe, being moved, thrills. *Bulletin of Psychology and the Arts*, **5**, 27–44.

Konečni, V.J. (2008a). A skeptical position on 'musical emotions' and an alternative proposal. *Behavioral and Brain Sciences*, **31**, 582–4.

Konečni, V.J. (2008b). Does music induce emotion? A theoretical and methodological analysis. *Psychology of Aesthetics, Creativity, and the Arts*, **2**, 115–29.

Konečni, V.J. (2009). Review of The social and applied psychology of music by A.C. North and D.J. Hargreaves (2008). *Psychology of Music*, **37**, 235–45.

Konečni, V.J. (2010). The influence of affect on music choice. In P.N. Juslin & J.A. Sloboda (Eds.) *Handbook of music and emotion: Theory, research, applications*. Oxford: Oxford University Press, pp. 697–723.

Konečni, V.J., Wanic, R.A., & Brown, A. (2007). Emotional and aesthetic antecedents and consequences of music-induced thrills. *American Journal of Psychology*, **120**, 619–43.

Konečni, V.J., Brown, A., & Wanic, R.A. (2008). Comparative effects of music and recalled life-events on emotional state. *Psychology of Music*, **36**, 289–308.

Kounios, J., Frymiare, J.L., Bowden, E.M., Fleck, J.I., Subramaniam, K., Parrish, T.B., *et al.* (2006). The prepared mind: Neural activity prior to problem presentation predicts subsequent solution by sudden insight. *Psychological Science*, **17**, 882–90.

Kounios, J., Fleck, J.L., Green, D.L., Payne, L., Stevenson, J.L., & Bowden, E.M. (2008). The origins of insight in resting-state brain activity. *Neuropsychologia*, **46**, 281–91.

Kozbelt, A. (2005). Factors affecting aesthetic success and improvement in creativity: A case study of the musical genres of Mozart. *Psychology of Music*, **33**, 235–55.

Langer, S.K. (1957). *Philosophy in a new key* (3rd Edition). Cambridge, MA: Harvard University Press.

Ledbetter, D. (2002). *Bach's well-tempered clavier—The 48 preludes and fugues*. New Haven, CT: Yale University Press.

Lockwood, L. (1992). *Beethoven: Studies in the creative process*. Cambridge, MA: Harvard University Press.

Lockwood, L. & Kroll, M. (Eds.) (2005). *The Beethoven violin sonatas: history, criticism, performance*. Urbana, IL: University of Illinois Press.

Mahler, A. (1969). *Gustav Mahler: Memories and letters*. (B. Creighton, Trans.). New York: Viking. [Original work published 1946.]

Mies, P. (1929). *Beethoven's sketches*. (D.L. Mackinnon, Trans.). London: Oxford University Press.

Miller, E.K. & Cohen, J.D. (2001). An integrative theory of prefrontal cortex function. *Annual Review of Neuroscience*, **24**, 167–202.

Moldenhauer, H. & Moldenhauer, R. (1979). *Anton von Webern: A chronicle of his life and work*. New York: Knopf.

Morgenstern, S. (Ed.) (1956). *Composers on music: An anthology of composers' writings from Palestrina to Copland*. New York: Pantheon.

Nabokov, V.V. (1973). Inspiration. In *Strong opinions* (V.V. Nabokov, Ed.). New York: McGraw-Hill. [Written on 20 November 1972 for *Saturday Review*.]

Niecks, F. (1902). *Frederick Chopin as a man and musician* (Vol. 1). London: Novello.

Norman, G. & Lubell Shrifte, M. (Eds.) (1946). *Letters of composers: An anthology 1603–1945*. New York: Knopf.

North, A.C. & Hargreaves, D.J. (2008). *The social and applied psychology of music.* Oxford: Oxford University Press.

Nottebohm, G. (1979). *Two Beethoven sketchbooks.* (J. Katz, Trans.). London: Gollancz. [Original work published 1865 and 1880].

Parkinson, B., Totterdell, P., Briner, R.B., & Reynolds, S. (1996). *Changing moods: The psychology of mood and mood regulation.* London: Longman.

Pärt, A. (1998). *Kanon Pokajanen* [Liner notes]. (C. Schelbert, Trans.) Germany: ECM Records GmbH.

Poincaré, H. (1908). *Science et méthode.* Paris: Flammarion.

Polnauer, J. (Ed.) (1967). *Anton Webern: Letters.* (C. Cardew, Trans.). Bryn Mawr, PA: Presser. [Original work published 1959.]

Protopopov, V. (1990). A new treatment of classical music forms in Chopin's compositions. *Chopin Studies,* **3**, 21–26.

Ross, A. (2000). Prince Igor: Reëxamining Stravinsky's reign. *The New Yorker,* 6 November, 84–93.

Sandkühler, S. & Bhattacharya, J. (2008). Deconstructing insight: EEG correlates of insightful problem solving. *PLoS ONE,* **3**(1), e1459.

Schooler, J.W. & Engstler-Schooler, T.Y. (1990). Verbal overshadowing of visual memories: Some things are better left unsaid. *Cognitive Psychology,* **22**, 36–71.

Sheth, B.R., Sandkühler, S., & Bhattacharya, J. (2009). Posterior beta and anterior gamma oscillations predict cognitive insight. *Journal of Cognitive Neuroscience,* **21**, 1269–79.

Simonton, D.K. (1977). Creative productivity, age, and stress: A biographical time-series analysis of 10 classical composers. *Journal of Personality and Social Psychology,* **35**, 791–804.

Simonton, D.K. (1980). Thematic fame and melodic originality in classical music: A multivariate computer-content analysis. *Journal of Personality,* **48**, 206–19.

Simonton, D.K. (1987). Musical aesthetics and creativity in Beethoven: A computer analysis of 105 compositions. *Empirical Studies of the Arts,* **5**, 87–104.

Simonton, D.K. (1998). Masterpieces in music and literature: Historiometric inquiries. *Creativity Research Journal,* **11**, 103–10.

Simonton, D.K. (2001). Emotion and composition in classical music: historiometric perspectives. In P.N. Juslin & J.A. Sloboda (Eds.). *Music and Emotion: Theory and Research.* Oxford: Oxford University Press, pp. 205–22.

Sternberg, R.J. (2002). Creativity as a decision. *American Psychologist,* **57**, 376.

Stravinsky, I. (1936). *An autobiography.* New York: Norton.

Tormey, A. (1971). *The concept of expression: A study in philosophical psychology and aesthetics.* Princeton, NJ: Princeton University Press.

Wallas, G. (1926). *The art of thought.* New York: Harcourt Brace.

Webb, E.J., Campbell, D.T., Schwartz, R.D., & Sechrest, L. (1966). *Unobtrusive measures: Nonreactive research in the social sciences.* Chicago, IL: Rand McNally.

Weiss, P. (Ed.) (1967). *Letters of composers through six centuries.* Philadelphia, PA: Chilton.

Williams, P. (2004). *The life of Bach.* Cambridge: Cambridge University Press.

Zentner, M., Grandjean, D., & Scherer, K.R. (2008). Emotions evoked by the sound of music: Characterization, classification, and measurement. *Emotion,* **8**, 494–521.

Chapter 10

Imagination and creativity in music listening

David J. Hargreaves, Jonathan James Hargreaves, and Adrian C. North

10.1 Introduction: the nature and ecology of music listening

The ways and situations in which we listen to music have changed significantly over the last two centuries, and this change has accelerated over the last few decades along with the pace of technological development. Back in the 1800s, the only way to listen to a piece of music was to go to a live performance, which meant that most people heard particular pieces only a few times in their lifetimes: listening to music occurred much less often, and was more focused when it did occur. The course of music listening was changed for ever by the invention of recorded sound, which was pioneered by Thomas Edison, and paralleled by the invention of the telephone (which is usually attributed to Alexander Graham Bell in the UK, but whose claim to this has been disputed). The subsequent advances of the phonograph, the Graphophone, the Gram-O-Phone, through to vinyl Long Playing records, cassette tapes, and eventually into the digital age are followed in Howard Goodall's *Big Bangs* (2001): there is no doubt these developments had a profound influence on the nature of music listening, and further developments in portable digital equipment are having the same effect today.

Studies by Sloboda, O'Neill, and Ivaldi (2000) and ourselves (North, Hargreaves, & Hargreaves, 2004) have established that today's adults typically experience music in one way or another for something like 40% of their waking lives, and Lamont (2006) reported a study of 3–4-year-olds which suggested that the equivalent figure for these children was about 80%. Young children in the Western world are exposed to music via multimedia devices in their toys, and in many other aspects of the world around them, and have little choice about the content of this massive exposure. As advances in music psychology continue to explore the ways in which this exposure influences many aspects of our behaviour, it follows that music exerts a powerful effect on human development. In Simon Frith's words, music has become a 'soundtrack to life': the effects of current developments such as the iPod, with its playlists and shuffle listening modes, the ease of music downloads from the Internet, and the increasing connectivity of digital devices have yet to be explored in any detail. Our soundscapes will continue to change and expand.

Many musicians are anxious to differentiate between 'listening' and 'hearing': the 'exposure' of young children referred to above clearly falls into the latter category, for example, whereas musicians and music teachers are concerned to educate the ear to discern, appraise, and evaluate. The eminent pianist and conductor Daniel Barenboim made this point very forcefully in one of his Reith lectures for the BBC in 2006:

> In the hotel where I stay they think that it is very culturally minded to play classical music in the elevator, or in the foyers of concert halls before the concert. And I have been on more than one occasion subject to having to hear, because I cannot shut my ears, the Brahms violin concerto in the lift, having

to conduct it in the evening. . . . And I ask myself, why? This is not going to bring one more person into the concert hall, and it is not only counter-productive but I think if we are allowed an old term to speak of musical ethics, it is absolutely offensive.

This is notable in that the piece itself was the same—the typical content and orchestration of 'background music' is not at issue here, but rather the context in which Brahms's music was played, and the particular uses that were being made of it.

The sheer quantity of music that people experience, voluntarily or involuntarily, in their every-day lives—in shops, lifts, restaurants, on-hold telephones, and so on, mean that music is experienced at varying *levels of engagement*. These vary from 'peak experiences' (e.g. Whaley, Sloboda, & Gabrielsson, 2009), or from the detailed analytical work of the music theorist, for example, which represent 'listening' at its highest levels of engagement, to the experience of music in shops or restaurants, which represent 'hearing' at the lowest levels of engagement, to the extent that some customers or diners may not even be aware that music is playing at all. To the psychologist, the experience of a concert performance of a great orchestral work and that of the music played in a supermarket are two poles of the same scale, and there are many other types and levels of listening in between: identifying these is an important task for music psychology, and one to which little attention has been directed so far. In between the ear's physical response to any sound, its physiological effects, its interpretation by the brain, and the listener's experience are numerous cultural, social, and psychological factors which are little understood.

Hargreaves, MacDonald, and Miell (2005) and Hargreaves, North, and Tarrant (2006) proposed a 'reciprocal feedback model' of responses to music which suggests that the three main determinants of any listening response are the characteristics of the music, of the listener, and of the listening situation. This is a 'reciprocal feedback' model because it shows how any one of these three main determinants can exert a simultaneous influence on each of the other two, and because these influences are bi-directional. The 2005 version of the model included some detailed content which was drawn from empirical research on the effects of these three main factors. It also included a parallel model of musical performance alongside that of response, suggesting that musical communication could be conceptualized as a complex interaction between the two models.

It is the response model (see Figure 10.1) that concerns us most here. 'Music' incorporates factors that have been studied in the psychological literature, and could easily be extended further to cover structural factors such as might be developed by music theorists. 'Situations and contexts' includes particular situations which have been investigated empirically, though this is almost infinitely extendable. The 'Listener' box contains some of the main factors on which individuals differ, such as their social class, age, sex, personality, and musical training. Perhaps the most interesting feature of the model is the reciprocal relationship between these three 'boxes', which are discussed in more detail in Hargreaves, MacDonald, and Miell (2005): we suggest how the music, the listener and the situation all interact to give rise to a particular response. In the case of aesthetic responses, for example, this means that the idea that 'beauty is in the eye of the beholder' (i.e. the ear of listener) is an oversimplification, as is the 'interactionist' view that the perception of beauty is part of the person's processing of the object (see Reber, Schwarz, & Winkielman, 2004): rather, we see it as the product of a three-way interaction, since a particular piece of music may be perceived by the same listener as beautiful in one context but not another.

Most relevant to our concerns here are the contents of the 'response' box itself, and the model identifies three main types of response. At the *physiological* level, Berlyne (1971) suggested that aesthetic responses are determined by the level of arousal of the autonomic nervous system, and that this is moderated by the characteristics of stimulus objects such as art works. This proposal is the foundation of Berlyne's 'new experimental aesthetics' (see North & Hargreaves, 2008). Two other important aspects of responses to music are the listener's *level of engagement* with it

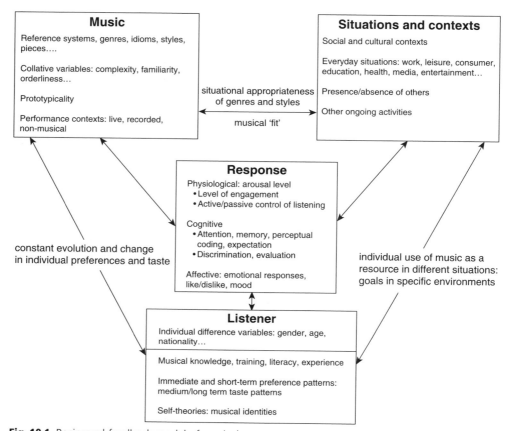

Fig. 10.1 Reciprocal feedback model of musical response.

(see above), and whether they are in active control of their listening (e.g. playing a CD whilst driving), or merely passive recipients (e.g. hearing music in a supermarket). Research in the clinical psychology of music shows that its therapeutic effects in reducing the experience of pain, for example, are much greater if the music is self-selected by the listener (e.g. Mitchell, MacDonald, & Brodie, 2006).

We can also identify the *cognitive* components of responses to music: listeners compare what they hear with their stored mental representations of the music they have previously heard, and code new pieces accordingly. Research in cognitive psychology has looked at phenomena including attention, memory, perceptual coding and musical expectation or expectancy: the high-level judgements which are made by music theorists and critics, which involve discernment, appreciation and evaluation, as we mentioned above, fall clearly within the cognitive domain. It is the emotional or *affective* components of responses to music which characterize its powerful effects most clearly, however, and this is manifested in people's likes, dislikes, preferences, and tastes, as well as representing the mood-inducing properties of music.

It is not only the determinants of response within this model—the listener, the music, and the situation—that are interdependent, as the model proposes, but also the different response components. The physiological, cognitive, and affective components are also in continual interaction with one another, and all take place within a social and cultural milieu which itself affects the nature of the response. In the case of aesthetic preferences, for example, we suggest that short-term preference responses as well as longer-term patterns of taste depend on both the cognitive and the emotional aspects of responses: and at a more deep-seated level, we can argue that our *musical identities* are ultimately built up from the ever-changing responses and preferences that constitute each individual's listening history (see MacDonald, Hargreaves, & Miell, 2002). In summary, 'responses to music' involve the mutual causal relationships between the music, the listener, and the listening situation, as well as those between the physiological, cognitive, and affective components of the response: and all these occur within an interactive social and cultural domain.

Various authors and researchers have attempted to identify individual *listening styles*, though this term has been used in different ways. In terms of our previous analysis, we could say that different listeners place more or less emphasis on the cognitive, emotional and social or referential components of their own responses, and that this balance constitutes the basis of different learning styles. This is reflected in Hargreaves and Colman's (1981) study, which made the distinction between 'objective-analytic' (factually descriptive), 'affective' (emotional), and 'associative' (linked with extra-musical objects or phenomena) responses to music, amongst others: listeners varied in the proportions of their responses falling into these categories, and these proportions varied predictably with other individual difference factors: for example, listeners with higher levels of musical training were more likely to give objective-analytic responses than non-musicians, and less likely to give affective or associative responses.

Behne (1997) produced a more elaborate description of different listening styles in trying to identify the German notion of *Musikerleben*, which has no precise equivalent in English, but which refers to 'the sum of psychic processes which accompany the experience of music in situations in which music is the focus of interest: When a person is not only hearing, but listening to and appreciating music' (p. 143). Behne (1986) developed a questionnaire which was given to 1224 young people aged 11–20 years, and carried out multivariate analyses which led him to propose nine different listening styles, namely *compensating* ('it changes my mood'), *concentrated* ('I like to close my eyes'), *emotional* ('I pay attention to what types of feelings are expressed through the music'), *distancing* ('I try to understand the words of the vocal part'), *vegetative* ('I assume a different body position',) *sentimental* ('I sometimes want to cry'), *associative* ('I have pictural images'), *stimulative* ('I like to play it very loud'), and *diffuse* ('my attention is divided'). His 1986 study found that the adoption of these different styles was dependent on the social and temporal context in which they listened to music, including features such as the physical location, and the presence of others. In other words, the participants responded to music in different ways in different listening situations according to its function in that situation.

We were able to demonstrate this latter point in some detail in our own study of 346 people who owned a mobile phone, who were sent one text message per day over a period of 14 days, which asked them to complete a questionnaire about various aspects of their music listening (North, Hargreaves, & Hargreaves, 2004). We collected a substantial body of normative data on 'the 5 Ws': on whom people listen with, what they listen to, when and where they listen, and why. We found very clearly that the functions of music ('why you listen') vary considerably according to the situation ('where you listen'), and were able to specify this relationship in terms of each of the other three Ws. We undertook separate analyses of the listening which occurs when the participants had chosen to listen to the music in question, and those in which they had no control over it, and found (perhaps unsurprisingly) that there were strong associations between control/no control, and the reported reasons for listening. We concluded that 'our results show very clearly that people do indeed consciously and actively use music in different interpersonal and social contexts in order to produce different psychological states, that the resulting musical experiences occur on a variety of different levels of engagement, and that the value placed upon the music is dependent on these contexts' (p. 75).

In this introduction we have outlined the ways in which music listening has changed over time, emphasized its present-day ubiquity, identified some of its different components, introduced a model of music listening which shows how responses are dependent on characteristics of the music, the listener, and the situation, and touched on the notion of individual listening styles. In the rest of the chapter we look more specifically at the notion of imaginative listening as a creative activity, and one which interacts with the social and cultural environment. We consider different approaches to listening as a process of creative cognitive construction, and look more specifically at how the listening styles of expert listeners such as critics and music theoreticians differ from those of non-expert listeners. We then consider the roles of the social, cultural, and intramusical contexts in shaping the listener's responses, considering sociocultural approaches to music listening, as well as the notion of reference and styles in musical composition.

One common idea that emerges from studies of these three broad areas—the music, the listening situation, and the listener—is that people use 'networks of association' which act as reference points for their mental representations of the world, and we conclude the chapter by expanding on the nature of these networks. We first consider the networks of association that exist within musical pieces themselves at the structural level, and secondly at the networks of cultural association that involving the music that people listen to, which form the basis of the 'neural networks' that are proposed by Martindale and Moore (1988) in their 'preference for prototypes' model of musical likes and dislikes (see, e.g. North & Hargreaves, 2008). Thirdly and finally, individuals combine their own personal networks of musical and cultural associations to include their corresponding associations with the people, situations and events that they have experienced in their lives: these are effectively personal networks of association, which are subject to constant change as new pieces or styles are experienced in different sociocultural situations. They form the basis of individuals' musical imagination and creativity: in other words, of their *musical identities*.

10.2 Cognitive aspects

10.2.1 Listening as active construction

Aaron Copland proposed that 'it is the freely imaginative mind that is at the core of all vital music making and music listening', and this view underlies our own view of musical listening. Psychology has long since viewed perception as an active process of cognitive construction in which new sensory input is interpreted in the light of the perceiver's accumulated schemata, or mental representations, and this includes music listening. It seems likely that listening draws on precisely the same internal representations as those involved in composition and performance, which both involve listening, of course, so that 'musical imagination' is a useful central construct which links all three. Merker (2006) points out that the internal networks against which we actively assess new input are not just the product of musical acculturation, but also of the inherent properties of our sense of hearing: that musical creativity 'takes place in a complex landscape whose contours are significantly shaped *in musically relevant ways* by the inherent properties of our sense of hearing' (p. 35).

The notion of listening as an active cognitive process has been taken up and demonstrated in different ways by a number of researchers and theorists. Bamberger (1991, 2006), writing from the musician's point of view, suggests that many musicians talk to one another about their 'hearings' of a piece: each person has his or her own particular way of hearing and playing certain aspects of the music, and these may well be different from one another, and subject to change over time as the piece becomes more familiar. Furthermore, it is because 'sound/time phenomena do not come already structured, but rather hold the potential for being structured, that different hearings are possible' (1991: p. 9). Bamberger takes this idea further, suggesting that the development of a 'hearing' of a composition, as it unfolds in time, can be thought of as a *performance*: and that 'listening performances' such as this, and actual performances (on instruments or voices) involve the same internal processes of active cognitive construction and reconstruction.

Addessi and Pachet (2005) were able to demonstrate this process in the performances of 3–5-year-old children who worked with an interactive musical system, the Continuator. This device is an electronic piano keyboard linked with a computer running interactive music software, programmed such that it responds in generative ways to sound input from the child on the keyboard. The child is then allowed a further response, which generates a new computer response, and so on. They were able to demonstrate the characteristics and 'life styles' of different patterns of interaction, showing how children actively construct developing 'hearings' of the output from the machine, and respond accordingly. Addessi and Pachet refer to these developing auditory constructions as 'listening conducts' in the sense of the French term 'conduite' as it was used by Janet, Piaget, and others. A conduct refers not only to the children's musical constructions (the 'acts' or actions which take place in the sequences of interaction), but also the mental origins of these actions—i.e. in effect, the processes of imagination. There is no doubt from their case studies of children's work with the Continuator that the listening conducts were expressive and creative, since the children could be seen to elaborate or dramatize the sounds they heard to produce a coherent overall narrative.

Baroni (2006, 2009) has worked for some time on different aspects of the recognition of musical styles as a creative act. He proposes a theory which involves the perception of similarities between musical elements and features which are organized according to hierarchy of rules (Baroni, 2009), and which builds on some of the seminal views of Meyer (1956, 1973, 1989): he has investigated those aspects of style recognition which could be regarded as creative (Baroni, 2006: see also Hargreaves & North, 1999). He feels that creativity in style recognition implies an objective, analytic approach to listening: and that categorization plays a fundamental part in this.

Baroni (2006) describes a small, informal interview study of musicians and non-musicians to whom he played an almost unknown fragment of a quartet by Gaetano Donizetti. Half of the participants were simply asked to guess the composer and to verbalize their thought processes in doing so, and the other half were given the same instructions but also told that the composer was not Haydn, Mozart, or Beethoven. All of them were then told the true identity of the composer, and asked to comment on this new information. Baroni found that the interview responses revealed two distinct stages of thinking, which he called 'looking for orientation' and 'looking for confirmation', and he gives examples from the interviews of the manifestation of creative thinking in his participants' attempts to solve the problem. His conclusion is that music listening can only truly be regarded as creative if it involves some sort of problem-solving, in the sense that the listeners mentally re-create the piece as they listen.

Bamberger, Addessi and Pachet, and Baroni were all able to demonstrate the existence of active, constructive processes in different listening situations at various levels: but there are also three more formal theoretical approaches to the same phenomenon, each of which we will summarize very briefly. First, Serafine's (1988) radical view of 'music as cognition' is based on the idea that a set of core cognitive processes exists which is common to composing, performing and listening: this prefigures our own remarks at the start of this section. She also proposes that there are two basic, general types of these, namely *temporal* and *non-temporal* processes, and specifies two varieties of the former, and four of the latter. Hargreaves and Zimmerman (1992) wrote a critical review of this theory, as it provides an alternative to traditional music theory as well as to many conventional approaches in music psychology: this is not the place to elaborate on it in any detail. For now, we will simply note that one of the fundamental theoretical foundations of Serafine's theory is that the processes of cognitive construction are more fundamental to the listener's perception of the piece than are musical relationships between its elements: 'tones and chords cannot in any meaningful and especially psychological way be considered the elements of music' (p. 7). Although some aspects of her theory (and the broader implications of it) need further elaboration and refinement, the thrust of Serafine's approach nevertheless clearly supports the view of listening as an active, creative activity.

Second, Finke, Ward, and Smith (1992) proposed a 'geneplore' model of creative functioning: although this does not deal with music listening as such, it nevertheless has some features in common

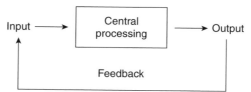

Fig. 10.2 Reybrouck's (2006) epistemic control system. Reproduced from Reybrouck, M. (2006). Musical creativity between symbolic modelling and perceptual constraints: The role of adaptive behaviour and epistemic autonomy, in I. Deliège and G.A. Wiggins (eds.), *Musical creativity: Multidisciplinary research in theory and practice*, with permission from Psychology Press.

with the other ideas we have reviewed in this section. This is a broadly descriptive, heuristic model which suggests that many creative ideas originate from the initial *gene*ration of a range of possible ways of dealing with a problem, or field of study, which is followed by extensive *explo*ration of the best of those ideas. The 'problem' could be that of style recognition of a piece, for example, as discussed by Baroni above. The model suggests that creative solutions involve the recognition of family resemblances, or category membership, with 'conceptual extension to new sounds or inputs', and also the use of creative imagery. The essence of the model is that creativity originates from internal, *pre-inventive* mental structures which are actively elaborated: and this could easily be said to characterize creative music listening.

Third, Reybrouck's (2006) 'systems approach' is based on ideas which come from cybernetics and systems theory, the most fundamental of which is the 'epistemic control system'. The essence of this is the *control system*, which is shown in Figure 10.2. This 'closed loop system' shows that (sound) input to the human listener is centrally processed, and that this gives rise to an output: the output then feeds back and becomes new input, such that the listener is in constant interaction with the sonic environment. Included in 'central processing' are the continuously-evolving mental representations of musical elements, styles, etc., which have been of concern throughout this chapter. The composer, for example, works by performing internal symbolic operations on these internal structures, such that new structures gradually emerge.

One novel and attractive feature of Reybrouck's approach is that it specifies a mechanism for the continual interaction between the listener and the environment, which is akin to the Piagetian concepts of adaptation, assimilation and accommodation (see, e.g. Hargreaves, 1986). Listeners *adapt* to the sound environment by *assimilating* new sounds or musical objects to their existing mental structures: this gives rise to the *accommodation* of those structures, which change as a result, and this gives rise to a state of balance, or equilibrium, between the listener's internal model and the external sound world. However, new sounds are continually being heard, and as soon as this happens the system once again reaches a state of imbalance, or what Piaget called 'disequilibration'. The system is therefore always trying to reach a state of equilibrium (though it can never do so, as there are always more sounds 'out there' in the world than the listener can experience), so that equilibration functions as a kind of 'cognitive drive' for people to seek out and explore new sounds and ideas.

In summary, there is a clear consensus amongst all the research literature reviewed in this section that common mental structures underlie the three main activities of invention (composing and improvising), performance, and listening, and that these structures are constantly changing, revealing imagination and creativity. Furthermore, there is some limited but growing evidence that these mental processes have identifiable neural correlates. Halpern and Zatorre (1999), for example, used positron emission tomography (PET) to examine the neural correlates of auditory imagery for familiar tunes. Their participants either imagined the continuation of tunes whose first few notes only were played, then listened to a short sequence of notes as a control task, *or* they listened and then imagined the short sequences. Subtraction of the brain activation in the control task from that in the real-tune imagery task showed primarily right-sided activation in particular areas of the cortex (the frontal and superior temporal regions, and the supplementary motor area). This conclusion was supported by Zatorre and Halpern's (2005) review of the literature, which concluded that 'Converging evidence now indicates that auditory cortical areas can be recruited even in the absence of sound and that this corresponds to the phenomenological experience of imagining music' (p. 9): they referred to these experiences as 'mental concerts'.

In Chapter 22 of this book, Clark, Williamon, and Aksentijevic discuss research showing that imagery can enhance musical performance, and suggest that at the neurological level, musical performance and imagery function in a similar manner. Mental imagery of familiar musical material is not the same as creative musical imagination, however, and evidence of the neural correlates of active creation is as yet very scanty. An early study by Beisteiner et al. (1994) compared the EEG activity of music students who completed one of three tasks: recall from memory of a well-known melody (memory task); mental reversal of a four-note sequence (analytic task); and imagining a completed version of this sequence (creative composition task). Of these three, the analytic task elicited the highest level of EEG activity, and the creative composition task produced the lowest. Petsche (1996) compared the EEG recordings of participants who mentally constructed a short story (verbal), did a painting (visual), and composed a short musical piece (musical). The data showed an increase in the functional coherence of different brain regions in all three tasks, and that the composition task required functional cooperation 'between distant parts of the brain (between left frontal, temporal, parietal, and occipital regions, and right frontal, paramedian, parietal and occipital regions)' (p. 301). This suggests that musical composition is a very complex task resulting in the activation and co-ordination of many parts of the brain: further evidence is needed to pinpoint this more precisely.

Olivetti Belardinelli (2006) proposes a systematic cognitive perspective on the neurological basis of creative music processing in which 'cognitive processing occurring during the composition, performance and enjoyment of music is a mental process in which the discrepancies created by incoming stimuli or information are reduced', and that 'In the frame of this dynamic model, all three modalities of music processing are considered to be equivalent' (p. 322). The idea of the continual adjustment to the discrepancy between incoming information and current representations has a lot in common with Reybrouck's systems approach described above, and Olivetti Belardinelli's research group's fMRI studies of the multimodality of the central representations implied by this model (see, e.g. Olivetti Belardinelli et al., 2004) show a great deal of overlap between mental imagination shown in the different modalities, as well as overlap between all of them and visual representation. 'The results indicate either the involvement of amodal functional circuits of mental imagination or the presence of a visual imagination component in different types of mental images' (2006: p. 330).

The idea that the same mental structures underlie composing, improvising, performing, and listening, and that these structures have identifiable neural correlates is a powerful one, implying that 'musical imaginations' may have a neural basis: this also implies that 'imagination' is a more fundamental construct than 'creativity', as the latter refers mainly to aspects of musical performance. There is a long way to go before research evidence is able to establish this clearly, but some early signs are beginning to appear. The research to date deals only with the reciprocal influences between the listener and the music, of course, and it may well be that situations and contexts can eventually be shown to have a direct influence on neural development: we just don't know whether a sociocultural neuropsychology of music might eventually emerge!

10.2.2 Critical listening and discrimination

In the opening section, we looked at different individual 'listening styles', and at examples of the typologies of those styles that have been proposed in the literature: but there is another, perhaps more fundamental bipolar distinction which is worth considering here. In the introduction we suggested that musicians like to differentiate between 'listening' and 'hearing'; and that truly critical, evaluative listening is the province of the music theorist and music critic, who have much greater immersion in and knowledge of a wide range of musical styles than the non-expert. The distinction is mirrored in that between 'musical' and 'everyday' listening, which was proposed by Gaver (1993a, b): the former refers to the musical-acoustic characteristics of sounds (pitch, loudness, timbre, etc.), and the latter to the characteristics of the *source* of the sound: thus the 'everyday' description of 'the sound of an approaching car' would be 'musically' described as a sound with rising volume, and perhaps also a rising level of pitch, and certain changes in timbre.

This can be related to a parallel distinction which has frequently been made in the musicological and philosophical literature: Dibben (2001), for example, considers its equation with that between 'autonomous' musical meaning, which is wholly intramusical, and 'referential' musical meaning, which refers to the external referents of the sound being described. Similar distinctions, which have been discussed at length in the semiology of music, have been made by other theorists: Meyer (1956), for example, refers to 'absolute' and 'referential' meaning, and Coker (1972) to 'congeneric' and 'extrageneric' musical meaning: we might also apply the more neutral terms 'intrinsic' and 'extrinsic'. Dibben rejects the argument that 'musical' and 'everyday' listening are equivalent to these other distinctions, proposing instead that they can coexist in a particular listener's perception; that they 'may be two kinds of listening which operate simultaneously but which the listener privileges in different ways according to his or her needs and preoccupations' (p. 162). This leads her to the suggestion that 'musical' listening is itself based on the social and cultural context of the sounds themselves rather than purely on their acoustic characteristics: the listener prioritizes one or other of these according to the demand characteristics of the particular listening situation.

This leads us on to the approach of ecological psychology to music listening (see, e.g. Clarke, 2005), which derives from the work of Gibson (1966, 1979). One central feature of this approach is the idea that the characteristics of sounds have different 'affordances', or ranges of possible interpretation, and that these affordances are taken up in different ways according to the interests and preoccupations of the listener, as well as to the nature of the listening context. In this way musical meaning can be seen as a product of the attributes of the sound object, of the listener, and also of the listening situation: sounds with different affordances are interpreted by listeners who have different individual needs and attributes, and this negotiation occurs in a variety of ways in different listening situations. This means that intrinsic and extrinsic musical meanings could be said to be negotiated and socioculturally mediated. (We might note that this approach to the explanation of musical meaning has fundamental similarities with our own explanation of the origins of different responses to music in the reciprocal-feedback model (see section 10.1 of this chapter)).

Merker (2006) has pointed out that true musical appreciation (e.g. 'critical listening' by expert musicians) is reliant on a listening history which 'must be informed by the contents of a genre or tradition' (p. 26), i.e. which is backed up by a historical and cultural understanding of the particular musical tradition in question, and Lehmann, Sloboda, and Woody (2007) concur that the extent to which analytic listening takes place is dependent on the perceiver's listening history. Furthermore, there is some clear neuropsychological evidence that musicians and non-musicians show different evoked brain potentials when processing musical input (e.g. Koelsch, Schroger, & Tervaniemi, 1999): musicians generally show superior levels of performance in memory and recognition tasks.

However, this is only true for music in those genres with which they are familiar: they perform no better, and sometimes even worse than non-musicians with unfamiliar material, as was strikingly demonstrated by Mito (2004, 2007) in his studies of musicians' and non-musicians' recall of traditional Japanese pop music and the more rhythmically complex and recent genre of 'J-pop'. Mito's 'non-musicians' (who were all 'pop-immersed') performed significantly better than 'pop-immersed musicians', and the lowest levels of performance were shown by 'non-immersed musicians', whose musical training and experience actually seemed to depress their level of performance on the task.

Mito's findings show that the notions of expert and novice listening are context-specific, and do not necessarily correlate with the experiences of musicians and non-musicians respectively: in the case of the specific style of J-pop, non-musicians outperformed expert musicians who were unfamiliar with it. Nevertheless, people with greater general knowledge of a wide range of musical structures and styles—musicians, music theorists and critics, for example—can still generally be considered as expert listeners. In other words, novice and expert listening can be discerned across contexts (musical styles), and this raises the issue of the nature of the difference between these two 'levels' of perception.

Leaving aside the musician–non-musician issue, it is clear that as an act of cognitive construction, listening is a skill in itself. On the face of it, the distinction between expert and novice listening is quantitative (if perhaps unquantifiable); experts are simply more skilled in perceiving than are novices. At the same time, however, the knowledge and sensitivities acquired by experts transforms their listening experiences, such that a qualitative difference develops alongside the quantitative one. Novice listeners, as we saw earlier, are more likely to adopt less sophisticated listening styles, making more judgements based on affective or associative criteria, for example, whereas expert listeners have access to these as well as to more sophisticated analytic criteria (e.g. Hargreaves and Colman, 1981).

The skill in question is the mental ability to assimilate and accommodate events within the remembered contexts (musical styles, structures, and pieces, as well as physical and interpersonal situations) in which they are perceived to occur. This implies a process of comparison between the music heard in the present, and previous listening experiences. Thus, consciously or unconsciously, listeners might generate a number of problems and explore a number of solutions as to how best to compare the present percept with their memory. Theoretically, the extra knowledge acquired by highly trained listeners enables them to generate and solve more (and more specific) problems and solutions, to prioritize the most salient, to understand the implications of that prioritization for assimilating further information from the same piece, and so on. Notionally, expert listeners' greater knowledge and awareness means that their mental maps of styles and pieces are more detailed than those of novices. Therefore, for an expert, the range of perceptual options is far broader than for a novice; 'highly trained' listeners construct and situate their experience within a *field* of remembered information, where (as an extreme example) 'less qualified' listeners might only appreciate the significance of a single pattern. This implies that experts perform a different kind of cognitive construction—choosing from a range—where novices identify a follow a particular path through the music. This means that greater contextual knowledge not only denotes a more *fine-grained* musical understanding, but also a more *flexible* one. Experts are also more likely to appreciate the broader subculture surrounding a particular musical style, whatever it may be; their superior flexibility goes beyond the music itself.

A classic illustration of how hearings of the same piece can differ appears in Nicholas Cook's (1987) discussion of Schenkerian analysis. He explains the implications for perception of different voice-leading graphs of the same music, and in doing so, shows how the same sequence of notes and chords can be mentally grouped and connected in various ways so as to form a whole. Clearly, this is representative of expert listening, as it discusses ambiguities of which novice listeners are most likely unaware. A central tenet of Schenkerian analysis is that the relationship between what is musically 'fundamental' and 'ornamental' exists at, and defines each level within a hierarchical structure. This suggests that the difference between expert and novice hearings of music lies in the listener's ability to engage with the implications of perceiving the interaction between elaboration and structure within a given style. In turn, this might have implications for theorizing different levels of engagement.

It is clear that a listener's perceptions are dependent upon how well qualified he or she is to respond to the music in question. The next section begins with a discussion of how this might work the other way around; often composers address this issue directly, such that their music might be considered as a response to the notion of 'expert and novice' in their listeners.

10.3 Musical, cultural, and personal reference networks in listening

Because of its flexibility, the term 'network' is very useful in considering the many forms of listening which take place in modern day life. As Merker (2006) suggests, the perception of musical meaning is dependent upon memory; individuals' listening *histories* influence their responses to music, although the crucial element which sparks that perception is their ability to 'make'—to imagine and appreciate—connections between musical materials, pieces and styles, and extra-musical associations. Thus, a given listening experience offers listeners a number of potential networks, and although listening itself happens in time, there is an important non-temporal character to the way these sets of connections might be formed; inevitably, those networks exist within what might be called the each individual's 'musical *geography*', i.e the mediums or contexts within which individuals construct or 'map' their own meaningful networks.

There are many advantages to thinking about perceiving musical meaning as an act of mapping musical geography. It allows for the subjective nature of musical perception, since networks are formed by and within individual listeners: and in particular, it allows for the context-specific notion of expert and novice hearings of the same music. Depending upon their listening tastes and habits, some listeners might have a more detailed map of certain regions (perhaps, although not necessarily, defined by styles) than other regions within their musical geography. In turn, the notion of relative precision in musical perception is clearly important, given the various social contexts in which modern-day listening occurs, and the different levels of engagement which they seem to invite. Indeed, even within a single piece, musical meaning can be considered to be dependent upon the interplay between the levels of a listener's understandings of previous musical experiences, and previous experiences of the listening situation.

Since time eternal, composers have played upon the extent to which listeners are familiar with different areas of their own musical geography by referring to and borrowing from other pieces and styles. This means of communication is of particular import in the 21st century, given the ubiquity of music from so many different traditions. A particularly clear example of this can be found in hip hop, in which sampling is common practice. Theoretically, to use a sample is to invite listeners to situate it within their musical geography relative to the 'home style' (hip hop). It might be that the borrowed material contributes to the overall hip-hop ambiance; alternatively, the sample might be remarkably distinct, and the perception of that 'stylistic distance' might evoke a variety of responses from the listener. A good example of this is the use of two bars of Prokofiev's music in A Tribe Called Quest's *Can I Kick It?*; this is invariably perceived as humorous. In the Western Art music tradition, arguably, musical reference is often used in a more considered and sophisticated manner, however; George Crumb's 'electric string quartet' *Black Angels* (1970), for example, is structured almost entirely on the basis of connotations of referential associations. (For a fuller discussion of the hip-hop and Crumb examples, and of musical geography in general, see Hargreaves, 2008).

We move now from musical networks of association to those which are based on the *cultural* aspects of musical reference. We suggested in the opening section that extremely low levels of engagement are represented by people's experience of music in shops, lifts, or restaurants, in which they may not even be aware that it is playing at all. If most people were not aware of it, the question would arise as to why supermarkets and other retail outlets spend the money that they do in 'piping' music into their stores: and this takes us into the field of consumer psychology. We have carried out research on the effects of music in various real-life listening situations including banks, restaurants, supermarkets, exercise classes and on-hold phones (see review by North & Hargreaves, 2008): this leaves no doubt that 'environmental music' does indeed affect people's behaviour, even when they are not deliberately attending to it.

Our review of our own research led us to conclude that 'music can influence the place that customers go to, customers' ability to achieve a desired level of arousal, the atmosphere of commercial premises, the amount that customers are prepared to spend, the amount they actually spend, the products they buy, their memory for advertising, and the amount of time they wait on-hold' (North & Hargreaves, 2008: pp. 488–9): we also pointed out that other researchers have investigated time perception, and shown that musical tempo and volume can influence the speed of customer behaviour. We proposed that these effects work via three main psychological mechanisms: the effects of music on physiological arousal (to which we referred in the opening section); the priming of particular thoughts by music; and the effect of music on emotional responses.

It is the second of these processes that concerns us here. In our 'reciprocal-feedback' model (see p. 158), the link between the music and the situation is represented by the concept of 'musical fit': the idea that certain pieces and styles are more appropriate to some situations than others. Sibelius' *Karelia Suite* is perfectly appropriate when heard in a concert hall, or at a patriotic gathering of Finns, for example, whereas it would be out of place in an Indian restaurant (as one of us confirmed empirically when visiting an Indian restaurant in Durham, UK about 30 years ago!).

Musical fit can be used to predict which products customers will actually buy. One of our own widely-reported studies (North, Hargreaves, & McKendrick, 1997) was carried out in a large suburban supermarket. We were able show that playing either stereotypically French or German music on alternate days from a small tape recorder placed on top of an aisle end display of French and German wines (chosen to be equivalent in price and in degree of sweetness/dryness) had a dramatic influence on customers' selections and purchases of the two wine varieties. On the days when French music was playing, approximately three times as many of them of them bought the French rather than the German wine, and vice versa for the German music, even though the majority of them said that the music had not influenced their decision. We have suggested (North & Hargreaves, 2008) that this powerful effect occurred because the music was priming certain thoughts: hearing an accordion-based band playing romantic French ballads, for example, might trigger thoughts of the Eiffel Tower, lovers strolling by the banks of the Seine, and so on. This is because the music activates a network of France-related associations in the shoppers' thoughts, and so they are more likely to purchase the French wine if they otherwise would have no particular preference for French rather than German wine. This would not happen if they simply disliked French wine, for example, or if it was much more expensive than the German choice: this was confirmed empirically by Yeoh and North (2010).

Other research has produced similar findings: playing 'upmarket' classical music can prime customers' cognitions such that they spend more on certain products (e.g. in an antique shop), and Areni and Kim (1993) showed that playing classical music in a wine store influenced shoppers to buy more expensive wine than did 'Top 40' pop music, though the number of bottles sold was no different in the two conditions. To summarize this more generally, our own review of the literature, as well as those of others (e.g. Bruner, 1990) suggests that musical fit is the process by which the cognitions primed by background music can bias choice towards one of several competing products, and/or influence their perception of the environment as a whole—which can also determine whether they visit one particular store rather than another in the first place.

This research illustrates the phenomenon of cognitive *priming* or *cueing*; another phenomenon which operates in everyday choice situations in which no single choice is preferred *a priori* from a set of alternatives is people's use of *heuristics,* and in particular the *recognition heuristic.* Research on this phenomenon (e.g. Goldstein & Gigerenzer, 1999, 2002) has shown that if only one of several alternatives is recognized, then that recognized alternative will be chosen (see, e.g. Newell & Shanks, 2003; Ritcher & Späth, 2006; Yeoh & North, 2010). When choosing between multiple items in supermarkets, this means that when more than one of the alternative items is recognized, recognition alone cannot be used as a cue, and people search for another cue that does discriminate one alternative from the others. When faced with a choice between one familiar and another less familiar option, people will select the familiar option, and musical fit should have no influence: but when two competing products are both familiar, cues such as musical fit should influence choice between them.

Colin Martindale has used the idea of what we have called networks of cultural association to explain people's likes and dislikes in his *preference for prototypes* theory (e.g. Martindale & Moore, 1988). Cognitive psychologists suggest that people classify objects in the world around them by matching them with an abstract schema, or 'prototype', which represents a particular *category* of objects (e.g. Posner & Keele, 1968), and that these prototypes develop in our minds by our experiences within the culture in which we grow up. Martindale suggests that people's mental representations of different domains (such as furniture, cars, or musical pieces) are composed of inter-connected cognitive units, and each unit holds the representation of a different object: units coding more prototypical stimuli are activated more frequently, because these objects are experienced most frequently. Units coding prototypical stimuli are activated more strongly than are those coding atypical stimuli, and Martindale and Moore propose that that 'aesthetic preference is hypothetically a positive function of the degree to which the mental representation of a stimulus is activated. Because more typical stimuli are coded by mental representations capable of greater activation, preference should be positively related to prototypicality' (p. 661).

Martindale's theory implies that our individual preference responses to particular pieces of music are based on the degree to which they activate different parts of our individual networks of cultural associations: and we can conclude this section by suggesting that people construct their own *personal* networks of musical and cultural association by linking the key people, situations, events and subcultures that they have experienced in their lives within their personal musical geographies. We suggested in the Introduction that these form the basis of individuals' musical imagination and creativity: which means that personal musical geographies form the context within which people construct their *musical identities.* Further insight into how this works is provided by sociocultural approaches to musical behaviour, which are the subject of Part 3 of this book: a brief consideration of three key sociocultural concepts can throw more light on our current concerns.

The first is that of *situated cognition*: the idea 'that cognition is *typically* situated in a social and physical context and is rarely, if ever, decontextualized' (Butterworth 1992: p. 1). This means that the acquisition of knowledge can *only* be explained in terms of its physical and social context, so that it is impossible to conceive of particular pieces or musical styles without them evoking associations with the social and cultural world. Musical imagination, in other words, is also socially situated. Second, we saw earlier that a key concept in ecological psychology is that objects have *affordances*, or ranges of possible interpretation: the ways in which these interpretations are made by individuals is also mediated by their particular social and cultural networks.

Third, we also mentioned Folkestad's notion of the *personal inner musical library* in the Introduction: in Chapter 12, he proposes that we each have a unique set of experiences of different pieces and styles which are built up over many years and stored and coded as internal mental representations: these inner representations may correspond to a greater or a lesser degree with the characteristics of the original. Folkestad suggests that the work of the composer involves a constant dialogue with his/her personal inner musical library, and that its two main features are a 'subjective-intuitive' phase in which new musical material is produced, and the composer's evaluation of that material by reference to the personal inner musical library, which has a collective cultural and historical dimension. This is precisely equivalent to the view of creative listening which we have developed in this chapter: people actively process and evaluate new pieces or styles on the basis of their personal, musical and cultural networks of association, which also have an historical dimension.

10.4 **Conclusion**

We have ranged fairly widely over various aspects of music listening in this chapter, and considered it from several different disciplinary points of view. We will conclude by advancing ten propositions that ought to be helpful in guiding further studies of this vitally important aspect of music psychology:

1 Our responses to music are determined by different properties of the music itself, the listener, and the listening situation: these three determinants have reciprocal-feedback relationships with one another, and together influence all types of response (including physiological, cognitive, social, and emotional responses).

2 Listening to music is an active, creative process which exists at different levels of engagement: people display characteristically different listening styles, and they consciously use music in different situations in order to produce different psychological states in themselves.

3 All music processing involves centrally-stored personal networks of association: our minds contain internal networks of mental representations, or schemata, which mediate all musical activities, and not just the act of listening itself: these include composition, improvisation, and performance.

4 These personal associative networks (which have also been called 'inner personal music libraries') are built up from inter- and intra-musical networks (i.e. the relationships which exist within musical pieces, and those relationships which listeners perceive between different pieces and styles), as well as from their social and cultural networks of association, which are linked with those pieces and styles.

5 Composers often communicate with their listeners by referring to and borrowing from other musical pieces and styles.

6 Different elements of these networks can be triggered in choice situations by cognitive mechanisms including cueing, biasing and the use of other heuristics.

7 These internal networks are subject to constant revision as we encounter new pieces and styles: the active processes of revision which our minds perform are most usefully described as 'musical imagination'. Imagination is a more fundamental process than 'creativity' as the latter involves the translation of internal cognitions into external sounds via the composer and the performer.

8 There is growing evidence from cognitive neuroscience that musical imagination may have identifiable neural correlates.

9 There are likely to be qualitative as well as quantitative differences between the associative networks of expert listeners (e.g. musicians, music theorists, and critics who are immersed in

and knowledgeable about a wide range of styles) and those of novices (non-musicians), and these are associated with characteristically different patterns of neural activity when processing music.

10 People's musical identities are determined by their personal associative networks and 'musical geographies', which are based on their accumulated lifetime experience of different pieces and styles, all of which are further associated with social and culturally-situated experiences.

Although music listening is central to all research in music psychology, as we have made clear in this chapter, it has received relatively little systematic attention in its own right. These ten propositions may help to suggest some, at least, of the ways in which that might be done.

References

Addessi, A.R. & Pachet, F. (2005). Experiments with a musical machine: Musical style replication in 3 to 5 year old children. *British Journal of Music Education*, **22**, 21–46.

Areni, C.S. & Kim, D. (1993). The influence of background music on shopping behavior: Classical versus top-forty music in a wine store. *Advances in Consumer Research*, **20**, 336–40.

Bamberger, J. (1991). *The mind behind the musical ear*. Cambridge, MA: Harvard University Press.

Bamberger, J. (2006). What develops in musical development? In G.E. McPherson (Ed.) *The child as musician*. Oxford: Oxford University Press, pp. 69–92.

Baroni, M. (2006). Hearing musical style: Cognitive and creative problems. In I. Deliège and G.A. Wiggins (Eds.) *Musical creativity: Multidisciplinary research in theory and practice*. Hove: Psychology Press, pp. 78–94.

Baroni, M. (2009).A different kind of similarity: the recognition of style in listening. *Musicae Scientiae, Discussion Forum* **4B**, 119–38.

Behne, K.-E. (1986). *Hörertypologien*. Regensburg: G. Bosse.

Behne, K.-E. (1997). The development of "Musikerleben" in adolescence: How and why young people listen to music. In I. DeLiège and J.A. Sloboda (Eds.) (1997). *Perception and cognition of music*. Hove: Psychology Press, pp. 143–59.

Beisteiner, R., Alternmuller, E., Lang, W., Lindinger, G., & Deecke, L. (1994). Watching the musician's brain. *European Journal of Cognitive Psychology*, **6**, 311–27.

Berlyne, D.E. (1971). *Aesthetics and psychobiology*. New York: Appleton-Century-Crofts.

Bruner, G.C. (1990). Music, mood, and marketing. *Journal of Marketing*, **54**, 94–104.

Butterworth, G. (1992). Context and cognition in models of cognitive growth. In P. Light & G. Butterworth (Eds.) *Context and cognition: Ways of learning and knowing*. Hillsdale, NJ: Lawrence Erlbaum, pp. 1–13.

Clarke, E. (2005). *Ways of listening: An ecological approach to the perception of musical meaning*. Oxford: Oxford University Press.

Coker, W. (1972). *Music and meaning*. New York: Free Press.

Cook, N. (1987). *A guide to musical analysis*. London: J. M. Dent & Sons Ltd.

Dibben, N. (2001). What do we hear, when we hear music? Music perception and musical material. *Musicae Scientiae*, **5**(2), 161–89.

Finke, R.A., Ward, T.B., & Smith, S.M. (1992). *Creative cognition: Theory, research, and applications*. Cambridge, MA: MIT Press.

Gaver, W.W. (1993a). What in the world do we hear? An ecological approach to auditory event perception. *Ecological Psychology*, **5**(1), 1–29.

Gaver, W.W. (1993b). How do we hear in the world? Explorations of ecological acoustics. *Ecological Psychology*, **5**(4), 285–313.

Gibson, J.J. (1966). *The senses considered as perceptual systems*. Boston, MA: Houghton Mifflin.

Gibson, J.J. (1979). *The ecological approach to visual perception*. Hillsdale, NJ: Lawrence Erlbaum.

Goldstein, D.G. & Gigerenzer, G. (1999). The recognition heuristic: How ignorance makes us smart. In G. Gigerenzer, P.M. Todd, & the ABC Research Group (Eds.) *Simple heuristics that make us smart.* New York: Oxford University Press, pp. 37–58.

Goldstein, D.G. & Gigerenzer, G. (2002). Models of ecological rationality: The recognition heuristic. *Psychological Review,* **109**, 75–90.

Goodall, H. (2001). *Big bangs: The story of five discoveries that changed musical history.* London: Vintage Books.

Halpern, A.R. & Zatorre, R.J. (1999). When that tune runs through your head: A PET investigation of auditory imagery for familiar memories. *Cerebral Cortex,* **9**, 697–704.

Hargreaves, D.J. (1986). *The developmental psychology of music.* Cambridge: Cambridge University Press.

Hargreaves, D.J. & Colman, A.M. (1981). The dimensions of aesthetic reactions to music. *Psychology of Music,* **9**, 15–20.

Hargreaves, D.J. and North, A.C. (1999). Developing concepts of musical style. *Musicae Scientiae,* **3**, 193–216.

Hargreaves, D.J. & Zimmerman, M. (1992). *Developmental theories of music learning.* In R. Colwell (ed.), *Handbook for research in music teaching and learning.* New York: Schirmer/Macmillan, pp. 377–91.

Hargreaves, D.J., MacDonald, R.A.R., & Miell, D.E. (2005). How do people communicate using music? In D.E. Miell, R.A.R. MacDonald, & D.J. Hargreaves (Eds.) *Musical communication.* Oxford: Oxford University Press, pp. 1–25.

Hargreaves, D.J., North, A.C., and Tarrant, M. (2006). The development of musical preference and taste in childhood and adolescence. In G. McPherson (Ed.) *The child as musician: a handbook of musical development.* Oxford: Oxford University Press, pp. 135–54.

Hargreaves, J.J. (2008). Music as communication: Networks of com*position.* Unpublished PhD thesis, University of York.

Koelsch, S., Schroger, E., & Tervaniemi, M. (1999). Superior pre-attentive auditory processing in musicians. *NeuroReport,* **10**, 1309–13.

Lamont, A.M. (2006). Toddlers' musical worlds: Musical engagement in 3.5 year olds. In M. Baroni, A.R. Addessi, R. Caterina, & M. Costa (Eds.) *Abstracts of the 9th International Conference on Music Perception and Cognition.* Bologna: Bononis University Press, pp. 946–50.

Lehmann, A.C., Sloboda, J.A. & Woody, R.H. (2007). *Psychology for musicians: Understanding and acquiring the skills.* Oxford University Press: New York.

MacDonald, R.A.R., Hargreaves, D.J. & Miell, D.E. (Eds.) (2002). *Musical identities.* Oxford: Oxford University Press.

Martindale, C. & Moore, K. (1988). Priming, prototypicality, and preference. *Journal of Experimental Psychology: Human Perception and Performance,* **14**, 661–70.

Merker, B.H. (2006). Layered constraints upon the multiple creativities of music. In I. Deliège and G.A. Wiggins (Eds.) *Musical creativity: Multidisciplinary research in theory and practice.* Hove: Psychology Press, pp. 25–41.

Meyer, L.B. (1956). *Emotion and meaning in music.* Chicago, IL: University of Chicago Press.

Meyer, L.B. (1973). *Explaining music.* Berkeley, CA: University of California Press.

Meyer, L.B. (1989). *Style and music: Theory, history and ideology.* Philadelphia, PA: University of Philadelphia Press.

Mitchell, L.A., MacDonald, R.A.R., & Brodie, E.E. (2006). A comparison of the effects of preferred music, arithmetic and humour on cold pressor pain. *European Journal of Pain,* **10**, 343–51.

Mito, H. (2004). Role of daily musical activity in acquisition of musical skill: comparisons between young musicians and nonmusicians. *Bulletin of the Council for Research in Music Education,* **161/2**, 1–8.

Mito, H. (2007). Learning musical skills through everyday listening. Unpublished PhD thesis, Roehampton University, London.

Newell, B.R. & Shanks, D.R. (2003). Take the best or look at the rest? Factors influencing 'one reason' decision making. *Journal of Experimental Psychology: Learning, Memory, and Cognition,* **29**, 53–65.

North, A.C. & Hargreaves, D.J. (2008). *The social and applied psychology of music.* Oxford: Oxford University Press.

North, A.C., Hargreaves, D.J., & Hargreaves, J.J. (2004). The uses of music in everyday life. *Music Perception,* **22**, 63–99.

North, A.C., Hargreaves, D.J., & McKendrick, J. (1997). In-store music affects product choice. *Nature,* **390**, 132.

Olivetti Belardinelli, M., Di Matteo, R., Del Gratta, G., De Nicola, A., Ferreti, A., Tartaro, A., *et al.* (2004). Intermodal sensory image generation: An fMRI analysis. *European Journal of Cognitive Psychology,* **16**, 729–52.

Olivetti Belardinelli, M. (2006). Beyond global and local theories of musical creativity: Looking for specific indicators of mental activity during music processing. In I. Deliège & G.A. Wiggins (Eds.) *Musical creativity: Multidisciplinary research in theory and practice.* Hove: Psychology Press, pp. 322–44.

Petsche, H. (1996). Approaches to verbal, visual and musical creativity by EEG coherence analysis. *International Journal of Psychophysiology,* **24**, 145–59.

Posner, M.I. & Keele, S.W. (1968). On the genesis of abstract ideas. *Journal of Experimental Psychology,* **77**, 353–63.

Reber, R., Schwarz, N., & Winkielman, P. (2004). Processing fluency and aesthetic pleasure: is beauty in the perceiver's processing experience? *Personality and Social Psychology Review,* **8**, 364–82.

Reybrouck, M. (2006). Musical creativity between symbolic modelling and perceptual constraints: The role of adaptive behaviour and epistemic autonomy. In I. Deliège and G.A. Wiggins (Eds.) *Musical creativity: Multidisciplinary research in theory and practice.* Hove: Psychology Press, pp. 42–58.

Richter, T. & Späth, P. (2006). Recognition is used as one cue among others in judgment and decision making. *Journal of Experimental Psychology: Learning, Memory, and Cognition,* **3**, 150–62.

Serafine, M.L. (1988). *Music as cognition: The development of thought in sound.* New York: Columbia University Press.

Sloboda, J.A., O'Neill, S.A., & Ivaldi, A. (2001). Functions of music in everyday life: an exploratory study using the experience sampling method. *Musicae Scientiae,* **5**, 9–32.

Whaley, J., Sloboda, J.A. & Gabrielsson, A. (2009). Peak experiences in music. In S. Hallam, I. Cross, & M. Thaut (Eds.) *The Oxford Handbook of Music Psychology.* Oxford: Oxford University Press, pp. 452–61.

Yeoh, P.S. & North, A.C. (2010). The effects of musical fit on choice between two competing foods. *Musicae Scientiae,* **14**, 127–38.

Zatorre, R.J. & Halpern, A.R. (2005). Mental concerts: Musical imagery and auditory cortex. *Neuron,* **47**, 9–12.

Recordings

A Tribe Called Quest. *Can I Kick It? (Boilerhouse Mix). On Can I Kick It?.* 7" Vinyl, Jive JIVE 265, 1990.

Crumb, George. *Black Angels.* Kronos Quartet. CD, Elektra Nonesuch, 79242-2, 1990.

Score

Crumb, George. *Black Angels.* New York, Frankfurt, London: Edition Peters, 1971.

Chapter 11

Creativity in singing: Universality and sensitive developmental periods?

Annabel J. Cohen

11.1 Introduction

The creation of song is a natural activity in early childhood. As every child learns to speak so does every child learn to sing. Whether singing or speaking comes first is a matter of definition, but it is safe to say that the child's speaking or singing relies on exposure to cultural models of speech and song respectively. This period of exposure to 'two distinct sound systems' (Patel, 2008: p. 9), enables internalization of the elements of the specific language or musical style, and this, in turn, eventually enables spontaneous production of linguistic and musical phrases.

From a linguistics perspective, the child's consequent production of song can be regarded as creative to the extent that its generative and novel, rather than merely imitative. The notion of generativity of language has been promoted since Chomsky's (1959) famous review of Skinner's (1957) book *Verbal Learning*. In his attack on Skinner's behaviourist and reductionist account of language acquisition as arising from the reinforcement and concatenation of verbal elements, Chomsky claimed that Skinner overlooked the speed with which language learning took place in the absence of appropriate verbal models or rewards for correct verbalizations. Chomsky instead emphasized the combinatorial productivity of language based on the notion of a universal grammar possessed by every child, particularized for a specific linguistic culture through a pre-adolescent critical period. A similar argument could be made for the infinite creativity of singing: children can understand songs they have never heard before; they rapidly learn to sing and to compose new songs. Perhaps there is equally a critical or sensitive period during which a universal grammar of music becomes particularized (cf. Cohen, 2000; Hauser & McDermott, 2003).

Accepting that language and singing are creative in a generative respect, singing is further aligned to creativity through its link to the arts. Creativity—in a non-linguistic sense—is intrinsic to aesthetics and the making of the art of music. The fundamentality of singing to music is underlined by the fact that unlike other aspects of musical behaviour, involving human-made musical instruments, in singing, the human body provides the instrument—there is no unnatural or artificial intermediary between performer and listener. In addition to its ties to music and the arts, singing is a behaviour that emerges early in life (de Vries, 2005; Dowling, 1984; Moog, 1976; Sloboda, 1985), and, it can continue throughout life to the most senior years, as a leisure, aesthetic, or professional activity (Cohen & Kleinerman, 2010). Within music, singing is a discipline unto itself and can offer a unique perspective on creativity in music. Thus, in a multidisciplinary exploration of musical imaginations, such as that of the present book, there are many reasons for focusing attention on singing.

In the present article, following a brief discussion of the definition of creativity in singing, the uniqueness of this human ability will be highlighted by contrasting it with the often assumed absence of creativity in birdsong. However, consistent with the notions of critical periods for the acquisition of birdsong, the potential for creativity in singing at different stages in the lifespan will be discussed. Examples of creativity in singing in Western culture, as revealed in research, are reviewed, and examples found in music performance are discussed, specifically skat singing in jazz improvisation. A new initiative which is developing a test battery of singing skills is then described as a means to obtain answers to questions of universality and sensitive period in the emergence and maintenance of creative singing across the lifespan trajectory. The aims of the article are first to show that singing provides one of the most important contexts for future studies of musical creativity and second to encourage increased opportunities for young and old to develop their abilities for song making.

11.2 Creativity in singing: definitions

Singing is one of two natural forms of human vocal communication, the other being speech. Because singing is the act of producing musical tones, in Western culture it is strongly linked to the arts, specifically to music.[1] Within Western culture, singing is heard in many contexts in playgrounds, classrooms, formal choirs, professional choirs, solo 'in the shower', and performances of popular or classical music. Singing usually involves both lyrics and music; in this sense it differs from music performance on instruments which cannot simultaneously control both a musical and verbal stream. In Western culture, singing is often associated with special occasions (e.g. the 'Happy Birthday' song, New Years, the singing of national anthems) whereas in other non-Western cultures, singing may routinely accompany everyday events with a song for particular activities (e.g. in the Xhosa songs of Africa, for beer, work, hunting, etc., cf. Heunis, 1998). In Western culture, for the majority of adults, singing entails listening to the voices of a talented minority of professionals—song-writers and performers who are endowed with or who have developed through hard practise special creative and artistic talents which the remaining public majority are able to enjoy in live concerts and through recordings.

For the present chapter, the term *creativity* refers to behaviours that are novel and judged worthy by the creator (small 'c' creativity) or by a larger audience or conventional gatekeeper (big 'C' Creativity), using Csikszentmihalyi's (1996) small 'c'/big 'C' distinction. The small 'c' category is broad and admits new compositions or improvisations that would not meet public standards of novelty or worth but do represent those characteristics within say a child's own limited experience. Yet, we want to distinguish this from the creativity of language where the purpose of language is simply to denote meaning in a non-artistic sense. If, however, a linguistic utterance were to please the utterer or audience for its poetry, then that production could also be regarded as creative. The point here is that when song creation produces an aesthetic response in the singer or listener, this would qualify the singing as creative, in accordance with the defining characteristics of novelty and value, whereas simply repeating a known song would lack the characteristics of novelty. Of course every human rendition of a song will contain variation, and the balance between meeting a standard of performance and adding an aspect of originality reflects the mysterious and ineffable aspect of aesthetic experience. The present discussion does not focus on this more subtle aspect of creativity in singing but instead focuses on the ability to vocally create new compositions, though again this too may be a matter of degree, viz., utterances which might not be regarded as aesthetic but merely novel also provide data of interest for many inquiries.

While the ability to produce new vocal melodies is evidence of creativity and is worthy of admiration, still everyday small 'c' creativity must be contrasted with large 'C' Creative performance

---

[1] Whereas the art of drama uses speech, the everyday function of speech is pragmatic and not artistic. Singing is also found in drama from the time of Ancient Greece, through to songs in Shakespeare and early opera, to which music theatre has been added in contemporary times.

feats of professional interpreters of standard songs, jazz improvisers and skat singers, vocal cadenzas, and da capo arias which can imaginatively incorporate conventions of elaboration particularly on the return to the original exposition. The question arises as to what allows for the unique performance of both small and large 'c (C)' creativity (Creativity)? A two-point thesis will be advanced here. First, the potential for learning musical rules for generating new outcomes may be partially constrained by age-based neural plasticity influenced in part by early opportunities, formal or informal, for music learning, training, and practice. Second, the capacity for vocal creativity remains throughout life, and may even increase in older years of reduced inhibition, high motivation, and high attentional control. Evidence from research and observation supporting this proposal will be reviewed, and the ongoing AIRS (Advancing Interdisciplinary Research in Singing) project for acquiring more evidence will be described.

11.3 **Beyond birdsong**

Over the last two decades, much behavioural and neuroscientific research has been conducted on birdsong (Zeigler & Marler, 2004). Songbirds are one of only a few species to engage in vocal learning, the others being humans, whales and dolphins. Over 5000 different avian species learn song; this number is not much below around 6500 different spoken world languages. Hundreds of studies on the acquisition of birdsong have served to reveal four stages of acquisition. The first is referred to as the *sensory learning period*, an exposure phase, during which the young bird hears songs to be acquired that establish a corresponding mental template. The second (which can overlap with the first and third) is the *subsong* stage, which is like a babbling stage of human infants, when the infant tests out and callibrates his vocal apparatus. The third stage is referred to as *plastic song*, during which the juvenile bird begins to approximate the template song. The final stage is the *adult stage* of *crystallized song* in which the adult song is more or less fixed. This 'crystallized' song of adulthood may vary but seldom does (Slater, 2001; Williams 2004); however, see Taylor (2010) for a contrasting view, as well as Beecher (2010), Berwick, Okanoya, Beckers & Bolhuis (2011), and Nottebohm (2005) with evidence of malleable adult song. The human analogy to birdsong is typically speech (Williams, 2004: p. 5) not song. When analogies to the musical realm are made it is to the acquisition of musical grammar and musical knowledge, not singing (cf. Slater, 2001; Whaling, 2001). Yet, the four stages of acquisition of birdsong serve as a preliminary model for the acquisition of human song development: 1) exposure to the culturally-specific songs; 2) a babbling stage during which experiments of vocal production are carried out; 3) a song production phase in which elements of the culturally-specific songs are accommodated by babbling which ultimately comes to reflect the singing style of the culture, and finally; 4) production of recognizable songs of the culture. However, this model captures imitative vocalization but not creative possibilities during adulthood. It is also the case that for songbirds, typically males acquire the ability to produce song, for the purpose of defining territoriality and for attracting mates. For humans, song acquisition occurs naturally for both genders and can be developed throughout adulthood by males and females. Who actually develops singing capabilities is the result of a combination of idiosyncratic and social situational factors. The comparison with a classic prototype of birdsong highlights the conclusion that creativity in human singing, which can be demonstrated in children younger than 3 years of age (de Vries, 2005), is quite an extraordinary, human phenomenon, well deserving of attention. It should be emphasized that the notion of reduced flexibility during the adult crystallized stage for birdsong is of current research interest, and the study of more species may be revealing (e.g., Beecher, 2010).

In contrast to the large numbers of studies of the acquisition of birdsong, there are embarrassingly few studies of the acquisition of human singing, and very few that focus on creativity in singing. This paucity of studies can also be contrasted to the much larger number of studies that focus on music perception in general, or performance on musical instruments. The topic of singing in creativity is rightly mentioned in an earlier book on musical creativity (Deliège & Wiggins, 2006). It is timely for the present volume on creativity to focus on this topic of singing.

In what follows, articles and studies that discuss research in singing and creativity will be reviewed followed by a description of a new short battery of singing tests which includes tests of creativity in singing.

11.4 Research on creativity in singing

11.4.1 Peter de Vries' parental scaffolding of a 2-year-old

In a unique case study,[2] Peter de Vries reports the stages of vocal improvisation and song acquisition of his son Jack, between the ages of 24 and 36 months. Until the age of 24 months, Jack engaged in babbling songs without tonal centre or similarity to heard songs. The father who was knowledgeable in Vygotsky's (1987) learning theory, chose to encourage the development of Jack's improvisations through imitation, variation, setting small new challenges, directing attention by describing what he did and modelling, and providing rewards for successes small or large. He reports how this 'scaffolding' led to Jack's repetition of phrases at 26 months, mirroring models provided by Dad (e.g. in dynamics, and tempo) at 28 months, expanding his interval repertoire and mirroring his own improvisations at 31 months, incorporating fragments of known songs such as 'Baa Baa Black Sheep' into his improvisations at 33 months, and aligning new lyrics to familiar tunes by the age of 35 months. There is certainly a need for more parent–child case studies of this type extending for an even longer time period. Clearly by the age of 3 years, in this particular child, the tools for vocal creativity are in place for representing sets of pitches (i.e. diatonic scale), rhythms, dynamics, tempo, integration of words, and rules of repetition.

11.4.2 Johannella Tafuri's study of children's musical creativity

Noting that improvisation is usually associated with performance on musical instruments, Johannella Tafuri (2006, p. 139) remarked that research on spontaneous singing 'provides interesting information about creative processes and assimilation of musical structures'. She briefly reviewed research on musical creativity that examined improvisation in singing in children, noting the melodic and rhythmic analysis carried out by Moorhead and Pond (1941/1978). Moorhead and Pond distinguished two kinds of singing—chant, which was carried out by groups and was structured around a central note, and plainsong, carried out by individuals with much freer melodic form and little dependence on words. Sundin's (1960) somewhat later study of children's invented songs concluded that musical creativity was influenced by the 'atmosphere of the school, social class, and gender' (Tafuri, 2006: p. 139).

Responding to the absence of research on teaching strategies that encourage the development of musical creativity, Tafuri and her colleague Gabriella Baldi conducted a study based on the assumption that teacher's strategies can influence the 'activation and maturation of the creative process' (p. 141). Although the study did not focus on singing, it provides a background for such studies. Tafuri and Baldi first reviewed research that encouraged musical improvisation and from this distinguished three kinds of prompts for creativity: 1) semantic, or expression of meaning; 2) musical rules; and 3) materials (musical instrument constraints). Hypothesizing (p. 141) that: 1) chosen structures would reflect semantic prompts; 2) rule prompts would lead to the most structured organizations;

---

[2] See Cohen (2010) on the value of the case study approach in creativity research.

3) absence of semantic or rule prompts and provision of musical instruments would favour exploration; and 4) evidence of organization procedures would increase with age, even in the absence of formal music training, they tested 132 children between the ages of 7 and 10 years, distributed across grades 2–5 in primary school. The children were of medium–low socioeconomic status and had no prior experience with music composition or improvisation. They were asked individually by the experimenter to improvise two examples for each of three types of prompts: semantic, rule, and materials. The semantic prompts were 'old man and a child' and 'waking up'. The rule prompts were alternation and repetition. The materials prompt were a glockenspiel with a range C^3–F^4 and a tambourine, having three sounds. Following the improvisation, the experimenter asked the child to introspect about the process. The entire session was audio recorded.

Transcriptions of the compositions and the dialogue were carefully analysed by both researchers, and the few discrepancies were resolved. The three types of prompts led to differences in the productions. The semantic prompt of 'waking' was not sufficiently explicit in comparison to the prompt of 'old man and a child'. Similarly the repetition rule led to more systematic organization than did alteration, and the tambourine, with its small tone alphabet, led to greater structure than did the more complex glockenspiel. The evidence that structure of the compositions increased with age led to the inference that 'patterns can be learnt through exposure and use of musical products . . . when the cognitive mechanisms are ready . . . [and] . . . underlines the important role of mechanisms such as memory, comparison, judgment, logic thinking, and reversible mind, and the role of an environment that is more or less culturally or musically stimulating, etc.' (p. 151). The general conclusion was that musical creativity was shown by all of the children, and the analysis of the improvisations gave access to the underlying cognitive musical processes. The value of longitudinal studies was proposed, along with the guidelines for teachers in the encouragement of musical creativity in their students, with the idealistic view that the early development of musical creativity may provide a resource for creative approaches to other problem solving throughout life.

Tafuri's study provides overwhelming evidence of musical creativity in children. It also shows increasing creativity with age. It is important, however, to consider the Italian cultural context of this study. We may be reminded that classical music has been broadcast in public areas of large cities in Canada and the USA as a deterrent to loitering. It is unlikely that such music would have the same effect in Italy, where opera arias may be as familiar to children as nursery rhymes are in America. So there remains a question of the generality of Tafuri's results to children in other cultures. There is also the question of generality to singing and a comparable study using voice rather than percussion and glockenspiel would be welcome.

11.4.3 Margaret Barrett's case study of Charli's invented song

Indeed, a review of invented songs elicited in a study by Barrett (2006) has suggested growth of this ability to make up songs from ages 18 months to 7 years with a subsequent decline, just at the age at which Tafuri has suggested musical creativity, in Italian children, began to increase. Barrett further suggests that the 'gradual disappearance (or submergence?) of invented song from children's music making as they enter formal schooling' may arise from the reification of 'vocal models, styles of vocal presentation, and song materials' and an emphasis on attaining correct adult renditions of particular repertoire that dismisses the 'playful and generative qualities of invented song-making' (Barrett, 2006: pp. 202–3). She says that 'Given the near ubiquitous nature of invented song in young children's activity, the careful examination of this phenomenon holds potential as a site for the exploration of creative thought and activity in young children'.

Consistent with Tafuri's plea for longitudinal research on creativity, Barrett reports a longitudinal case study of one child's invented melodies over a period of 2 years, beginning in kindergarten. Barrett's study focused on singing improvisation in two different schools, one more rural and the other more urban. The children in the first year had daily music training and in the second year had access just once a week to a music teacher in which formal instruction about music theory and elementary solfège took place. In the study, the experimenter (the author) was given a music corner of the class in the first year and a separate room nearby in the second year. The children were allowed to initiate a visit to the music corner. The activities at the music corner were video-taped for later analysis. The activities included the request by the experimenter to sing known songs, make up songs, and explore musical instruments. A detailed analysis of the responses of one child Charli were provided, focusing on three visits to the music corner during the first year.

The spontaneous song lyrics were presented as well as several transcriptions. Whenever the experimenter requests Charli to repeat her made-up song, she agrees but always changes it, wanting to sing something new each time. The content analysis of the lyrics reveals themes of significance to Charli, such as hidden motives of others and a visit from her father (as her parents are separated). The songs provide a means of communication with the experimenter.

In addition to this rich communication experience, there is communication with a group of children who learn and participate in her song. One child continues to sing one of Charli's songs, which is evidence of how children acquire songs from each other (Campbell, 1998). The musical notation reveals tonal centers, and phrases, but fails to reveal the strophic repetitions that adults might value, and as appear more with increasing age in the study of Tafuri (2006) previously described. Barrett makes the point that musical improvisation for children does not necessarily aim to create musical forms that imitate adult models but rather offers the opportunity to explore different ways of expressing the same thing. An interpretation of this free form that I would like to offer is that children blend the pragmatic rules of music and speech. In speech, every sentence communicates new information, and words are not repeated for their own sake. In music, repetition of note and phrase is common. Perhaps the child is caught between these speech and music rule systems when dealing with both lyrics and melody.

11.4.4 Sági and Vitány's (1988) study of vocal invention in Hungary

Sági and Vitányi (1988) examined vocal invention in over 200 persons representing students of junior and senior high school, younger and older industrial workers, and university age students some of whom were conservatory students. Participants were asked: 1) to compose melodies for four sets of lyrics representing 19th-century folk style, 20th-century serious poetry, and a lyric of a contemporary hit song; 2) to compose improvisations to seven different harmonic progressions that varied in complexity beginning with the simplest as I-IV-V-I; and 3) to improvise comple-tions to three short melodies by Bartók and Mozart . The data consisted of over 3700 tunes that were tape-recorded and subsequently transcribed by 10 professional musicians and checked by two independent judges. The first conclusion was that although the participants were not experi-enced at improvisation they were able to carry out the improvisation task to some degree. Improvisations typically mirrored the strophic character of the lyrics and suggested ideal forms that differed across the 11 different samples in the study, suggesting that compositional tenden-cies are influenced by one's listening environment which is cohort and situation specific. Given the enormous corpus of material analysed over an 8-year period, it is particularly unfortunate that the results of the Hungarian study are not accessible to the English speaking world.

11.4.5 The AIRS test battery

To partially address the lacuna in research on creativity in singing, a major collaborative research initiative called AIRS (Advancing Interdisciplinary Research in Singing, generously funded by the Social Science and Humanities Research Council of Canada), directed by the present author, is planning a large longitudinal study that focuses on measuring various singing skills across different ages and cultures.

The AIRS project in general responds to the relative lack of scholarly attention to the natural human communication ability of singing as compared to that directed to language acquisition. One technological development that accelerated progress in studies of child language was the establishment of a shared database of transcriptions of child discourse. The initiative known as CHILDES—the Child Language Data Exchange System—the inspiration of Brian MacWhinney and Catherine Snow (MacWhinney, 2000; MacWhinney & Snow, 1985) led to over 3000 publications in this field. A similar shared database of song, envisioned by Cohen (2000) and at the time referred to as CHIMES—Children's Music Exchange System—awaited further developments in computer technology which allowed for the storage of and fast access to acoustic data. The CHILDES system managed well with less resource-intensive symbolic transcription of utterances, however, part of the problem of understanding the acquisition of singing is to determine or develop consensus on what the vocal or musical elements are. In comparison, the international phonetic alphabet provides a basis for a fairly comprehensive coding system for speech discourse with additional elements developed by MacWhinney and his team to accommodate other sounds and their durations and inflections. Michael Forrester (personal communication) of Kent University who used CHILDES for research in developmental psycholinguistics confirmed the need for something additional for addressing the data of singing.[3]

A short AIRS test battery has been in development since 2008 to acquire data on a variety of aspects of singing ability including musical creativity (Cohen et al., 2009). The battery consists of 11 components, the first and last of which obtain data on language skills through conversation and through administration of short speech tasks such as repeating a sentence representing a large proportion of the phonemes of a language (a pangram) and making up a story. The remaining components acquire data on such aspects as vocal range, and the ability to sing back a familiar song.[4] The battery also includes learning an unfamiliar song, as well as singing back several scale patterns to the syllable 'la' (e.g. *doh re mi re doh, doh re mi fa mi re doh, doh mi sol*, and the entire diatonic scale, *doh re mi fa sol la ti doh*).

---

[3] A Digital Library acquired at the University of Prince Edward Island for a project (led by Annabel Cohen) focuses on the use of multimedia in education in a cultural context. The Digital Library Technology was exploited by the University Library Digital Library staff under the direction of University Librarian Mark Leggott as the server to support interactive web-sites through Drupal and an underlying architecture for a digital repository known as Fedora (or Flexible Extensible Digital Object Repository Architecture). The latter is an open-source product and project spear-headed over a decade ago by Cornell University through DARPA and NSF grants and currently used in major digital library projects such as the National Science Digital Library, having the tools and capacity to accommodate audio and video storage and indexing. The CHILDES system was an early example of a specialized digital library. The AIRS Digital Library will provide access to singing data, for example; in principle all of the data from the Hungarian study previously mentioned could be placed and indexed in such a digital library (although it would be a time-consuming process to do so).

[4] The song chosen, *Brother John* (*Frère Jacques*) has a simple repeating structure a a a₁ a₁ b b c c (Are you sleeping, Are you sleeping, Brother John, Brother John, Morning bells are ringing, Morning bells are ringing, Ding dang dong, Ding dang dong). The repetitions test whether the singer grasps the notion of higher order structure (i.e. the rule of repetition). If the singer produces the same incorrect pattern twice, for each of the four phrases, it is clear that the higher order rule has been grasped but the lower order ability to represent particular intervals has not. Translations of the lyrics in over 55 languages provide for cross-cultural investigation although familiarity with the song may not be equal for the various cultures.

Creativity in singing is directly tested with two tasks. In the first, the beginning portion of a simple song with lyrics was presented (*doh re re me re doh re me . . . I have a dog, and he goes bark . . .*) and the participant was asked to continue the song. This task has elements of both a rule task and a semantic task of Tafuri (2006). In our first studies using the test battery, the experimenter provided a sample ending. This appeared to restrict original completions, and future studies that used the battery have omitted the lyrics of the initial prompt and have provided no examples of continuations.

A second creativity task is more reminiscent of Tafuri's (2006) semantic task. Encouraged by Stefanie Stadler Elmer (2000) who has conducted research on children's singing for over 20 years, four picture prompts were provided, and the singer was asked to choose one and to make up a song about it. This task provided no musical ideas, although the prior musical content of the singing test may have had an influence as was shown in subsequent analysis.

The battery was initially administered by two students, Marsha Lannan and Jenna Coady, to participants representing an age range from 3 years to university students. There were two boys and two girls tested at each of the ages of 3, 5, and 7 years (i.e. 12 participants in total). There were two males and two females of university age tested who had musical training and a similar number of male and female university students who had no musical training (i.e. 8 participants in total). The aim was to test all participants monthly for 5 months; however, one university student and one of the children did not complete testing. The data are very rich and only several aspects have been submitted to detailed analysis. For the composition from the picture prompts, the lyrics and contour were transcribed and a preliminary analysis has been conducted by Lauren Mitchell.[5] Examples of lyrics for participants of different ages are provided in the Appendix. In particular she focused on the influence of prior exposure to the lyrics and melodic structure (particularly contour) of *Brother John* and *I have a Dog and he goes bark,* the prompt used in the song completion task.

Evidence of influence of prior exposure was seen and a negative correlation between the evidence of influence (e.g. use of the word bark) and age of the participant was significant. In other words the younger the child, the greater was the influence of prior words and melodic structure (i.e. contour) seen on the produced song. This greater influence for younger children suggests to me reverberating auditory imagery of recent information, poising the child for mimicry and rehearsal. Such a process, with emphasis on detailed acoustic information, would enable the acquisition of the phonology of the language as well as elements of the music. This is consistent with the ability of children to pick up a native accent as compared to those past adolescence.

The lyrics produced by the children also reflected their appreciation of the concept of composition and of song, and generally of a distinction between literal and poetic language. One half of the materials (those obtained by student Marsha Lannan) were passed on to a member of the Faculty of Education who specialized in the teaching of creative writing. He was asked if he could determine the age of the author from the lyrics. It was not easy for him to do so. This anecdotal finding does concur with the view expressed by Barrett (2006) that the ability to create songs does not improve after the age of 7 years, in that there was no marked distinction between the lyrics created by the six children and the four adults when their five sessions were considered.

The lyrics of the 3-year-old male are particularly striking with the repeated theme in sessions 2 to 5 (a period of 4 months) of the baby eating all the hearts, flowers, and sunshine—different visual images, eliciting lyrics about an interfering baby! This is reminiscent of the repeated theme of mischievous fairies of the 4-year-old Charli in the case study of Margaret Barrett. Song is serving a purpose for children as it does for adults of expressing what may be difficult to say in words.

---

[5] Lauren Mitchell was a visiting summer student in the AIRS/CMTC-E Research Laboratory at UPEI who worked on her senior thesis under a student Internship program from Kalamazoo College.

One can see from these lyrics a knowledge of phrasing and poetic language; in adulthood this entails a greater use of rhyme as part of the canonical song form.

A second administration of the battery was conducted by Emily Gallant with a senior population of four healthy elderly persons and six persons with suspected Alzheimer's disease (four of whom were institutionalized). The test was administered on two or three occasions at approximately monthly intervals, with the exception of one individual due to a family crisis. In contrast to the healthy elderly participants, persons with Alzheimer's disease (with one exception) were unable to create songs, although they were able to carry out other aspects of the test battery. This is of interest in that the resilience of song memory is often cited as an exception to the otherwise drastic deleterious cognitive impairment associated with the disease. Our preliminary results suggest a dissociation between the ability to recognize songs and the ability to use musical rules to create a new song.

The test battery, slightly revised, was administered a third time to eight native-born Canadian university students and eight native-born Chinese students enrolled at the same Canadian university. The melodic prompts were sung, and for the melodic completion task only the prompt was presented, not a sample completion. The data were collected by Lexy McIver and the melodic completion data were analysed by visiting undergraduate student Ruth Reveal.[6] This analysis entailed pitch extraction for each completion for two sessions, a contour analysis, and a rhythm analysis. Rules of the original melodic prompt were observed in the completions (e.g. in the first session, 50% of the completions preserved the rhythmic motive), both completions for an individual were often similar but differed across individuals, and completions were on average seven notes for both sessions. However, the main conclusion was that the richness of the data warranted additional investigation, for example, with respect to tonality, and that future studies should assure greater duration between sessions so as to reduce the role of memory of a prior session on the original composition in a subsequent session.

The relatively short completions of songs by the young adults contrasts with an extreme case of childhood singing of the vocal prodigy Bejun Mehta who reports that

> . . . as a small child I was always singing. When there was music in the house, which was all the time, I would imitate what I heard. If I heard a record, I would sing that. . . . I would go into my room and put on an opera recording . . . I would sing every part, every word, every thing—I would stay in my room and sing the entire opera. Nuvi [his older brother by 5 years] remembers listening to this . . . Even without an external stimulus, I would sing. . . . sing whatever came to mind. I would sing for hours upon hours, sing until I was hoarse . . . Singing was spontaneous with me. On car trips, I'd sit back and make up songs about whatever I felt like . . . When I was seven, my teacher sent home a report card which commented in part . . . 'he frequently sings or hums during independent work time . . . disturbing to those who are working near him. . . .' a tune bubbled in my throat twenty-four hours a day. Something just made it so.

> (In Kenneson, 1998: p. 337.)

While this is the introspective report of a someone who rose rapidly to acclaim as a professional vocalist (first boy soprano, later adult counter-tenor), it is well to think of the extent to which such proclivities for creative song are part of every child's make-up but are extinguished in the absence of appropriate scaffolding, such as exposure to song, singing and parental encouragement in the home (e.g. de Vries, 2005).

---

6 Ruth Reveal, a senior undergraduate student at Agnes Scott College in Atlanta Georgia, was a visiting summer student in the AIRS/CMTC-E Research Laboratory at UPEI.

Through continued application of the AIRS test battery, in age- and cultural-cross-sectional and longitudinal designs, and sharing audiovisual recordings of the sessions via the AIRS digital library, we expect to answer many of the questions about the natural creative ability of children to sing, whether this ability is influenced by cultural factors, and whether it declines during a critical period or is robust at least for some people throughout the lifespan. Data has been collected in Estonia by Marju Raju under supervision of Professors Jaan Ross and Stefanie Stadler Elmer and plans are underway to extend the collection of data of singing, including creativity in singing, in Asia, Africa, China, and South America. The aim here is to acquire and share longitudinal and cross-sectional data gathered in a short period of time from many participants. The methodology at the outset is very different from the case study approach of Barrett, and yet audiovisual records of singing are so rich in information that we believe a complete picture of the creativity in singing can emerge. Case studies of course can continue to provide additional important information. The two approaches go hand in hand.

11.5 Role of training and song improvisation

The skill of musical improvisation has been valued at various times in music history and by various cultures. Reference to improvisation in westernized society today raises associations of jazz, and if one thinks further, of creation of the continuo in early chamber music, the convention of embellishment in the ABA da capo aria, and perhaps the creation of the concerto cadenza, although in most of the latter cases, performers may resort to either using examples that have been passed down, or mapping out the variation prior to public performance. In music having an oral as opposed to notated tradition, improvisation may play more of a role, due to the training and reliance on memory. Indeed, improvisation places an enormous demand on memory, as one must know the rules and be able to apply them quickly, whereas, the availability of a score frees cognitive capacity for other needs, for example, that required by the instrument.

In early jazz, improvisation was associated with an instrumentalist playing within the field of liberty defined harmonically by the chord progression of the piece and thematically by the melodic motifs. The blues had a simple standard progression, and similarly, standard progressions characterized the jazz standards; even those which sounded complex often had a very logical progress based on the cycle of fifths (e.g. from Gershwin's *I Got Rhythm* to Jerome Kern's *All the things you are*, to Thelonius Monk, *Round Midnight*): however, improvisation was the territory of the instrumentalist. The vocalist sang the lead, when there was a vocalist at all. Louis Armstrong, however, popularized the potential of the voice for improvisation. The story goes that in 1926 during a recording session for the tune 'The Heebie Jeebies Dance', as Armstrong himself tells it . . . 'when I dropped the paper [with the lyrics], I immediately turned back into the horn and started to Scatting . . . to my surprise they all came running out of the controlling booth and said—"Leave That In".' (As quoted in Edwards, 2002: p. 619; square brackets inserted for explanation).

There were other examples of scat singing prior to this, but this recording drew attention to the phenomenon. The scat technique was developed by great jazz vocalists such as Ella Fitzgerald. In the 21st century, the technique has been to some extent demystified. Educator Bob Stoloff (1996, 2003) has written scat singing exercises with accompanying CDs (see also Fredrickson, 2003; Weir, 2000). These are a testament to real-time vocal creativity that can be taught through a rigorous and systematic curriculum and demanding practice. The concept is similar to teaching improvisation for any instrument, as can be acquired at many specialized schools and increasing numbers of university music programmes, the first, however, being the Berklee School of Music in Boston (formerly Schillenger House, and since 1970, the Berklee College of Music).

11.6 **Sensitive periods and over-riding constraints**

It is well-known that native active accent can be readily acquired by non-natives prior to adolescence, but afterwards it is more challenging to do so (Oyama, 1976; Pinker, 1994; Uylings, 2006). Accent entails fine articulatory motor coordination and the ability both to shape the vocal apparatus suited to vowel resonances characteristic of the particular language, and to move the articulators in appropriate timing and order to block the air stream in the manner characteristic of the phonemes of that language. The learning of the grammatical rules of the language however are not subject to the same articulatory-motor constraints, and whether they are also subject to a critical period for acquisition is more controversial. Similar questions arise for the acquisition of music grammar (Cohen, 2000 ; Trainor, 2005), and there is evidence of modest increase in the corpus callosum of the brain of children of 5–7 years of age who have been learning an instrument for 15 months as compared to age-matched controls who are not learning or practising an instrument (cf. Schlaug, 2009: p. 202). However, the questions have seldom been raised in the context of singing. Singing, in involving articulation and the vocal apparatus, parallels speech. If there is a critical period for the acquisition of native accent, there could similarly be one for acquisition of fine motor coordination required for singing. Yet, surprisingly voice lessons are among the few in the realm of music performance training that are typically postponed until well into adolescence. This is true for both genders, although it is the male voice that undergoes dramatic physiological change at puberty (a situation strikingly described by Mehta (Kenneson, 1998) in terms of the trauma experience over the metaphorical death of his boy-soprano voice).

The known facts of creativity in singing pose enormous questions for research. On the one hand there is evidence to suggest a universal natural vocal creativity between the ages of 18 months to 7 years. And on the other hand there is the evidence that training as in scat singing can lead to impressive real-time vocal creativity during adult years. Between these two poles are the examples of the minority of persons, young and old, in Western culture who can make up songs easily. The question of the extent to which everyone is a composer of songs invites the participation and insight of vocal educators, early child educators, vocal performers and jazz musicians at both amateur and professional levels and from countries throughout the world to join the behavioural scientists and researchers in music psychology who are addressing this problem.

11.7 **Concluding theoretical perspective**

In concluding with a theoretical perspective on creativity in singing, first consider a previous proposal of Cohen (2000) to account for the acquisition of music grammar. The proposal was that there existed an early critical or sensitive period during which exposure to music of particular styles established the grammar or vernacular which would serve as the native musical grammar for the rest of life. This theory was consistent with evidence that the music of one's youth was preferred throughout life, and that music that violated that style was more difficult to recognize or appreciate than music from that style. However, evidence from training of jazz improvisation and scat singing suggests that the constraints of a critical period for music grammar acquisition can be overridden through motivation and practice, such that the ability for real-time spontaneous vocal melodic composition can be acquired through dedicated years of practice at any time of life. The research of Sági and Vitányi (1988) and Tafuri (2006) has suggested that the ability to create songs is dormant within most adults. It is consistent with the passive but deep appreciation that most people have for songs, improving the quality of their life through concerts and recordings. The proposed framework suggests that favourable conditions of musical exposure and encouragement to create songs in early life may do much to set the stage for future creativity in singing. Further, passive appreciation of singing as an adult listener could instead become appreciation of one's own active creativity in singing given appropriate training, motivation, and practice in later years.

Acknowledgements

The support of the Social Sciences and Humanities Research Council for the AIRS (Advancing Interdisciplinary Research in Singing) Major Collaborative Research Initiative is gratefully appreciated. The technical support of Robert Drew and Jonathan Lane, the consultation and analysis of Anick Lamarche, the administrative support of Kristen MacDonald, the data collection and analysis of Marsha Lannan, Jenna Coady, Emily Gallant, and Lexy McIver for the UPEI Honours Theses, and the data analysis and reports of Lauren Mitchell and Ruth Reveal are gratefully appreciated. The Canada Foundation for Innovation is acknowledged for the provision of the laboratory facilities.

Appendix

The following are some examples of lyrics for participants of ages 3, 5, and 7 years and University-age students. The participants had received the AIRS test battery monthly for 5 months. The 8th component of the battery requests creation of a song based on one of four pictures: an apple, a sun, a flower, and heart. Prior to this component, the participants are asked to listen to the first phrase of a song and to produce an ending for it. The phrase begins 'I know a dog, and he goes bark'. Some elements of this appear occasionally in the lyrics that follow. The participants have also heard the song *Brother John* (Frère Jacques). The lyrics were transcribed by Marsha Lannan and verified or amended by Lauren Mitchell. Marsha had administered the tests.

Female child age 3

Session 3 (apple as choice of picture prompt):

> This apple has a worm in it
> And someone was going to eat it
> And saw a little hole
> And they were going to eat the worm

Session 5 (sun):

> I love the sun
> He plays bark
> Bark, bark, bark
> What a little Sunday bark
> Because he's a sun
> And while he maked up a ending
> He followed asleep

Session 5 (heart):

> A heart is in the afternoon
> In the afternoon
> I love you in the evening
> And underneath the moon

Male child age 3

Session 1 (sun):

> Ah sun come up
> And melt the snow away
> Sun come snow
> Snow (unintelligible)
> Sun will come out oh melt the snow
> Yes melt the snow all away

Session 2 (heart) (Marsha gave an extra example before he sang—she sings something like 'I love red hearts, they are beautiful' and the influence is seen):

> I love red hearts I love red
> They are beautiful
> But a baby named Sarah
> Walked up and ate them

Session 3 (heart):

> A baby a a lady brang all hearts
> But a baby ate them all

Session 4 (flower):

A baby a girl brang a um um a um all of em
Gave a baby all their flow
All her hearts
And the baby chewed em all up

Session 5 (sun):

I know a (unintelligible)
Gave all her hearts to a baby and ate them all up
And I know a baby gave
Who gave them all for baby (unintelligible)
And the sunshine
And the lady gave a bunch of sunshine
And she ate them all up
And she gave a bunch of flowers
And she ate them all up

Female child age 5

Session 5 (apple):

I know a apple it's bright and red
Bright, bright, bright red
[note, this shows similarities to the prior prompt to complete the ending to
'I know a dog and he goes bark, bark bark bark . . .']

Male child age 5

Session 3 (apple):

Once upon a time there was a apple
And in the apple there was a worm
As the worm was frustrated
Because it was too dark in there
So he went off to find a new one

Session 5:

Apples are great
They are red and shiny
And people eat them
Because they are healthy
And it also keeps the doctor away

Male child age 7

Session 3 (apple):

I like the apples
They are very sweet
But look out for the things
That worms eat

Session 5 (apple) (This session was rushed because his mom was waiting for him to finish):

I like the apples
They are yum
Um um um
Um um um um

Female age 7
Session 1 (flower):

> I have a flower, it's re-
> It's really nice
> I have a flower
> It's a -
> It's really nice
> My mom has a flower
> It's really nice
> My mom has a flower
> It's really nice
> When I gave my mom my flower
> Now she has two
> Really nice
> Flow-ow-ers

Male adult, non-musical
Session 1 (apple):

> My mother had an apple
> She crushed it into a pie
> We had a slice for dinner
> And I liked it

Session 4 (flower):

> As I start out small
> And get some water in me
> I grow up tall
> With petals all around
> Bright and shiny
> Are all my colours
> And I smell pretty good too

Session 5 (heart):

> I got this thing in my chest
> It kinda looks like a circle
> With a dent in the side
> It's called my heart
> It's big and it's full of love

Female adult non-musical
Session 5 (sun):

> In the month of August
> Two thousand and eight
> We've had so many days of rain
> So now that the sun is here
> For a few days
> I'm gonna go to the beach

Female adult musically trained
Session 1 (flower):

> *What shows up in Spring time*
> *Flowers, flowers*
> *Bringing in the morning sun*
> *What shows up in spring time*
> *Flowers, flowers*
> *To blow away the winter fun*

References

Barrett, M. (2006). Inventing songs, inventing worlds: the genesis' of creative thought and activity in young children's lives. *International Journal of Early Years Education,* **14**, 201–20.

Beecher, M.D. (2010). Birdsong and vocal learning during development. In Koob, G.F., Le Moal, M., & Thompson, R.F. (Eds.). *Encyclopedia of Neuroscience, Volume 1,* 164–168.

Berwick, R.C., Okanoya, K., Beckers, G.J.L., & Bolhuis, J.J. (2011). Songs to syntax: the linguistics of birdsong. *Trends in Cognitive Sciences,* **15**, 113–121.

Campbell, P.S. (1998). *Songs in their heads.* Oxford: Oxford University Press.

Chomsky, N. (1959). A review of B. F. Skinner's 'Verbal Behavior'. *Language,* **35**, 25–58.

Cohen, A.J. (2000). Development of tonality induction: Plasticity, exposure and training. *Music Perception,* **17**, 437–59.

Cohen, A.J. (2005). Music cognition: Defining constraints on musical communication. In D. Miell, R. MacDonald, & D.J. Hargreaves (Eds.). *Musical Communication.* Oxford: Oxford University Press, pp. 61–84.

Cohen, A.J. (2009). A protocol for cross-cultural research on acquisition of singing. Neurosciences and Music III-Disorders and Plasticity: *Annals of the New York Academy of Science,* **1169**, 112–15.

Cohen, A.J. (2010). Case study and creativity research. In A. Mills, E. Wiebe, & G. Durepos (Eds.), *Encyclopedia of case study research.* Thousand Oaks, CA: Sage.

Cohen, A.J. & Kleinerman, K. (2010). Transformative experience through voice lessons in later life. 11th International Conference on Music Perception and Cognition, Seattle. In S. M. Demorest, S.J. Morrison & P.S. Campbell (Eds.) *ICMPC11 Abstracts.* Seattle, WA: University of Washington, p. 115.

Csikszentmihalyi, M. (1996). Creativity: Flow and the psychology of discovery and invention. New York: HarperCollins.

Deliège, I. & Wiggins, G.A. (Eds.) (2006). *Musical creativity: Multidisciplinary research in theory and practice.* Hove: Psychology Press.

de Vries, P. (2005). Lessons from home: Scaffolding vocal improvisation and song acquisition with a 2-Year-Old. *Early Childhood Education Journal,* **32**, 307–12.

Dowling, W.J. (1984). Development of musical schemata in children's spontaneous singing. In W.R. Crozier & A.J. Chapman (Eds.). *Cognitive processes in the perception of arts.* Amsterdam: Elsevier, pp. 145–63.

Edwards, B.H. (2002). Louis Armstrong and the syntax of scat. *Critical Inquiry,* **28**, 618–49.

Fredrickson, S. (2003). *Scat singing method.* New Orleans, LA: Scott Music Publications.

Hauser, M.D. & McDermott, J. (2003). The evolution of the music faculty: a comparative perspective. *Nature Neuroscience,* **6**, 663–668.

Heunis, D. (1998). The vocal traditions of two indigenous cultures of South Africa. In B. Roberts (Ed.). *Sharing the voices: the phenomenon of singing.* St. John's, NF: Memorial University of Newfoundland, pp. 122–28.

Kenneson, C. (1998). *Musical prodigies: Perilous journeys, remarkable lives.* Portland, OR: Amadeus Press.

MacWhinney, B. & Snow, C.E. (1985). The child language data exchange system. *Journal of Child Language,* **12**, 271–96.

MacWhinney, B. (2000). *The CHILDES Project: Tools for Analyzing Talk*. Mahwah, NJ: Lawrence Erlbaum.

Moog, H. (1976). The musical experience of the pre-school child (C. Clarke Trans.). London: Schott.

Moorhead, G.E. & Pond, D. (1978) *Music of young children*. Santa Barbara, CA, Pillsbury Foundation for Advancement of Music Education. (Reprinted from works published in 1941, 1942, 1944, and 1951.)

Nottebohm, F. (2005). The Neural Basis of Birdsong. *PLoS Biol* **3**(5): e164.doi:10.1371/journal.pbio.0030164

Oyama, S. (1976). A sensitive period for the acquisition of a nonnative phonological system. *Journal of Psycholinguistic Research*, **5**, 261–85.

Patel, A.D. (2008). *Music, language, and the brain*. New York: Oxford University Press.

Pinker, S. (1994). *The language instinct*. Cambridge, MA: Harvard University Press.

Robinson, J.B. (1995). Scat singing. In Grove Music Online. Oxford Music Online, http://www.oxfordmusiconline.com.rlproxy.upei.ca/subscriber/article/grove/music/24717 (accessed 23 November, 2009).

Sági, M. & Vitányi, I., (1988). Experimental research into musical generative ability. In J.A. Sloboda (Ed.). *Generative processes in music* Oxford: Oxford University Press, pp. 179–94.

Schlaug, G. (2009). Music, musicians, and brain plasticity. In S. Hallam, I. Cross, and M. Thaut (Eds.). *The Oxford Handbook of Music Psychology*. New York: Oxford University Press, pp. 197–216.

Skinner, B.F. (1957). *Verbal behavior*. Acton, MA: Copley Publishing Group.

Slater, P.J.B. (2001). Birdsong repertoires: Their origins and use. In N.L. Wallin, B. Merker, & S. Brown (Eds.). *The origins of music*. Cambridge, MA: MIT Press, pp. 49–64.

Sloboda, J.A. (1985). *The musical mind: The cognitive psychology of music*. New York: Oxford University Press.

Stadler Elmer, S. (2000). A new method for analyzing and representing singing. *Psychology of Music*, **28**, 23–42.

Stoloff, B. (1996). *Scat! Vocal improvisation techniques*. Brooklyn, NY: Gerard and Sarzin.

Stoloff, B. (2003). *Blues Scatitudes*. Brooklyn, NY: Gerard and Sarzin.

Tafuri, J. (2006). Processes and teaching strategies in musical improvisation in children. In I. Deliège & G.A. Wiggins (Eds.). *Musical creativity: Multidisciplinary research in theory and practice. Hove*: Psychology Press, pp. 135–57.

Taylor, H. (2010). Blowin' in Birdland: Improvisation and the Australian Pied Butcherbird. *Leonardo Music Journal*, **20**, 79–83.

Trainor, L. (2005). Are there critical periods for musical development? *Developmental Psychology*, **46**, 262–78.

Uylings, H.B.M. (2006). Development of the human cortex and the concept of 'critical' or 'sensitive' period. *Language Learning*, **56**, 59–90.

Vygotsky, L.S. (1978). *Mind in society: The development of higher mental processes*. (M. Cole V., John-Steiner, S. Scribner & E. Souberman, Eds. & Trans.), Cambridge, MA: Harvard University Press.

Welch, G. (2005). Singing as communication. In D. Miell, R. MacDonald, & D.J. Hargreaves (Eds.). *Musical communication*. Oxford: Oxford University Press, pp. 239–259.

Weir, M. (2000). *Vocal improvisation*. Van Nuys, CA: Alfred.

Whaling, C. (2001). What's behind a song? The neural basis of song learning in birds. In N.L. Wallin, B. Merker, & S. Brown (Eds.). *The origins of music*. Cambridge, MA: MIT Press, pp. 65–76.

Williams, H. (2004). Birdsong and singing behavior. *Annals of the New York Academy of Science*, **1016**, 1–30.

Zeigler, H. & Marler, P. (Eds.) (2004). Behavioral neurobiology of birdsong. *Annals of the New York Academy of Science* [Special Issue], **1016**.

Part 3

Perspectives from socio-cultural psychology

Chapter 12

Digital tools and discourse in music: The ecology of composition

Göran Folkestad

12.1 Prelude

Even as a child when I started playing the piano, I found it much more fun to try out melodies and small musical pieces of my own, than to play the sheet music of my piano homework.

Throughout, it has been the creation of music that has fascinated me most, experimenting in notes and sounds and forming a musical unity out of small embryos of musical ideas. As a 14-year-old I got my first tape recorder. I used it to record one melody line and play or sing another line in harmony, and with the sound-on-sound technique the options were expanded to what I experienced as unlimited, recording the kick of a bass drum with a slipper, the snare drum with a box of matches, the hi-hat with two sheets of sandpaper, to give a few examples.

The starting point of my research was the meeting between my two musical practices: on the one hand in school, as a music teacher in secondary school (senior high school) and a senior lecturer at the University School of Music and Music Education, and on the other hand, outside school, as a musician, composer, and recording artist.

After having worked full time as a music teacher for 10 years (1974–1984), and playing in different rock, pop, and jazz bands in the evenings and on weekends, I took a break as a teacher, and during the years 1984–1987 I worked full time as a composer and as a recording and performing artist. This coincided with an intensive period in the development of music technology and the implementation of this equipment in the music production of recording studios, and in the practice of composition. All this I observed and experienced at close range. Almost every studio session involved the introduction of new kit or gear, and new ways of working: sequencers and drum machines steered by sync tracks; synthesizers connected via MIDI (musical instrument digital interface) to create full and rich sounds, and, eventually, computers with compositional software.

Returning to my music teacher practice in 1987, the question was obvious and clear: how could this equipment which had radically changed, not to say revolutionized, the music production in the studios and in the work of composers, be utilized to fulfil my teaching ambitions and the intentions of the National Curriculum to let the students create music of their own? Or phrased from the perspective of the 'academic world', and as a starting point of my research: what are the effects of the new technology, and what are its options in various educational situations?

This prelude serves two purposes: besides giving a short introduction to the personal background and the understanding of the author of this chapter, it also introduces, from my own individual perspective, some of the key issues of this chapter: the context-dependence of musical creativity, and the impact of the cultural tools and artefacts in the composition process.

The aim of the present chapter is twofold: 1) to summarize and reflect the experiences and results of the past two decades of research on musical creativity in a mirror of 'sociocultural theories', a field 'unified in its focus on the development of an understanding of the social formation of mind'

(Daniels, 2008, p. 51), and, in doing this, 2) to present a methodology for further research on composition and collaborative musical creativity. By 'methodology' the original definition of this term is intended: the theoretical foundations for the choice of methods of data collection and analysis.

12.2 **Creative music-making as situated cultural practice**

To the best of my knowledge, my PhD thesis on computer-based creative music-making, which was published as a book (Folkestad, 1996), is one of the first studies, internationally, within music and music education to adopt a *sociocultural* theoretical framework. By the beginning of the 1990s, the idea of implementing the literature on *situated cognition* and *situated learning* within the musical and educational fields was still undeveloped. However, there was an increasing interest in these theories, mainly emanating from the US West Coast, as a point of departure for analysing, understanding and discussing the educational phenomena under investigation—in my case, musical creativity and computer-based creative music-making.

Initially, three main aspects of this theoretical perspective and its methodological implications caught my attention, making it seem very applicable to the study of musical creativity: 1) it provided a framework for putting *the focus on the creator/the learner*—how various phenomena and types of learning content are experienced by the individuals in the actual processes of creation/learning; 2) it enabled an analysis which could provide categories of description of the variation on a collective level of *qualitatively different ways of experiencing the activity* under study; and 3) it emphasized a focus on the *context* of the activity.

This view of the importance of taking the full context into consideration when analysing an activity, of the inextricable link between contextual constraints and the acquisition of knowledge, in which the physical context is reunited with the social, asserts 'that cognition is *typically* situated in a social and physical context and is rarely, if ever, decontextualized' (Butterworth, 1993, p. 1). Or, as North and Hargreaves (2008) suggest, this perspective 'rests on the view that the acquisition of knowledge can *only* be explained in terms of its physical and social context—that we must think in terms of *situated cognition*' (p. 314).

The theoretical foundation of situated approaches such as *situated cognition* or *situated practice* is basically grounded in three traditions: 1) Vygotsky and the activity theory of his Russian followers (e.g., Leont'ev), 2) Mead and symbolic interactionism, and 3) Dewey, 'a tradition of educational theorizing about the relationship between knowing and doing' (Wineburg, 1989, p. 8).

Given the fact that I studied the actual process of composition, the activity itself—i.e. discourse *in* music—and not only how the participants talked about their experiences of that musical activity—i.e. discourse *on* music—my approach, right from the start, was to use various forms of data collection. Computer MIDI files were systematically collected which covered the sequence of the creation processes step by step, using the 'Save-as-method' developed in Folkestad (1996); interviews were carried out at the workstations with each of the participants; and observations were made of their work in order to capture the process of the activity (see Folkestad, 1996: pp. 117–25; Folkestad, Lindström, & Hargreaves, 1997: pp. 2–4; Folkestad, Hargreaves, & Lindström, 1998: pp. 85–6).

Having conducted the data collection and started the analysis, it became increasingly evident that a sociocultural theoretical perspective was needed in order to describe and understand the activity under investigation. In particular, the importance of the situational context became crucial, and the fact that the context did not only primarily seem to be the physical environment—in this case the workstation with the synthesizer and computer—but rather the musical situation in which the participants placed their music creation—'creating this song I was in the brass band, marching and playing' or 'in this song I was alone on stage, singing and playing the piano'. In order to understand and explain this, a theoretical perspective was needed which emphasized the *situatedness* and the *cultural-historical dimension* brought into the situation by the participants themselves and by the tools they used for composition.

Accordingly, the theoretical framework for viewing composition and creative music-making as *situated practice*, firstly presented in Folkestad (1996) and further elaborated in the view of musical learning as *cultural practice* (Folkestad, 1998), is just as much a result of the empirical studies as it is a foundation for the analysis of the data—in fact it constitutes a good example of the dialectic between theory and practice in research. Key analytical concepts in the 1996 analysis and onwards are *affordances* as described by Gibson (1986) and *tools*, *artefacts*, and *mediation* as described and defined by Vygotsky (1934/1986).

When studying a practice or activity (Wertsch, 1985), the holistic view described above leads to the perspective that learning is involved in any activity, and also that any activity involves some degree of learning. The corresponding mutual relation holds between learning and cognition, activity and cognition, and so forth. Consequently, to study one of these concepts or aspects of a situation is to study them all.

In music-making, activity, knowledge and learning can be considered as integrated. In previous literature, learning and the application of knowledge were often viewed as separate processes. For example, a piece of music or a method of composition is first learned, and the achieved knowledge is then used to perform the rehearsed music, or to produce compositions. In the present perspective however, learning, practice and execution are not seen as separable entities, but as inseparable facets of a unified whole, since practice involves performance and vice versa.

This paradigm implies that while a researcher might study how music is created, s/he also simultaneously studies how the participants learn to create music. In former studies, this was seen as problematic, and in need of clarification as to whether the study investigates: 1) how composing is done (i.e. the process of moving from no tune to a completed tune), or 2) if the study attempts to answer the question of how composition is learned (i.e. the process of moving from not being able to create music, to being able to create music). Although our studies have focused mainly on the former, the latter is seen as complementary, as in all other practices: *to create music also involves learning how to create music*.

It is evident from the presentation so far that a fundamental feature of a situated or sociocultural research approach is the emphasis on what has been generally called *context*, how context is defined, and the importance of this dimension when analysing a situation.

According to Wertsch (1985), context might be understood as the expectations of rules, objectives and possibilities present and used in a practice. Cole and Cole have proposed a 'cultural-context' view of development. They define context as involving 'the interconnected whole that gives meaning to the parts' (quoted in Butterworth, 1993: p. 6). From a phenomenological perspective, the situation is seen as the context itself (Husserl, 1989), and in musical activities the music itself might be seen as the context. The description made by Gurwitsch (1964) of *the theme, the thematic field*, and *the margin* as present in all human awareness can be applied in the musical context. When a piece of music is played or heard it is not only the music itself that is presented (i.e. the theme), but also the characteristic features of the musical style and the tradition of the genre the piece of music belongs to (i.e. the thematic field), as well as the situation in which this musical event takes place and the musicians (i.e. the margin).

In our studies, context has been defined as the total situation including not only the external conditions, such as the physical environment, but also the persons involved in the practice, and the cultural and historical background of these individuals. It also includes the music that is performed and created in that situation. In short, the context is defined in the activity itself. This definition is in accord with Engeström's (1993) view that 'contexts are neither containers nor situationally created experimental spaces. Contexts are activity systems. An activity system integrates the subject, the object, and the instruments (material tools as well as signs and symbols) into a unified whole' (p. 67). This view implies that production and communication are inseparable. Context is not seen as a fixed environment (a container) in which persons are located, but rather as changeable, defined not only by the environment, but also by the persons acting in that environment. In the former the context and subjects are seen as separate, whereas in the latter they are integrated and mutually defining.

12.3 **Affordances and creativity**

In his book *The Ecological Approach to Visual Perception* Gibson (1986) connects to this view on context from the perspective of perception and cognition. He formulates his approach by suggesting that the observer and the surroundings are inseparable and complementary, mutually defining each other. Gibson emphasizes the ability of the living organism to move and thereby to take new perspectives. 'Perception has two poles, the subjective and the objective, and information is available to specify both. One perceives the environment and coperceives oneself' (p. 126).

A central concept in Gibson's (1986) theory is *affordances*, explained as follows:

> The *affordances* of the environment are what it *offers* the animal, what it *provides* or *furnishes* for good or ill. The verb *afford* is found in a dictionary; but the noun *affordance* is not. I have made it up. I mean by it something that refers to both the environment and the animal in a way that no existing term does. It implies the complementarity of the animal and the environment.
>
> (Gibson, 1986: p. 127.)

In Gibson's theory—in which 'man', in these respects, is included in the category 'animal'—the surroundings and the organism together define the affordances, which can be positive as well as negative, and be understood as *being-in-the-time*. Moreover, everything is fundamentally situated; learning means to perceive new affordances, and in doing so perception and cognition cannot be separated.

The concept of affordances—a core concept in our studies since the mid 1990s (Folkestad, 1996)—has been found to be very useful in the analysis of musical creativity, not the least in understanding the different ways in which the digital tools are utilized by different individuals. Moreover, there is, as I see it, a connection between Gibson's *affordances* and *mediation* as described by Vygotsky: that which is culturally and historically mediated by the tools in a situated activity also becomes the possible affordances offered to the creator (agent) as means of his/her agency.

This view on discerning—or imagining—the affordances of the situational context implies a definition of *creativity*, or rather of *creative action*, as the ability to perceive new affordances, or old affordances anew, and to elaborate these affordances in each situation. Thus, the meaning of *creativity* involves a relation to the surrounding context in which the human being continuously seeks new angles of approach, and practises the ability to perceive new affordances. 'To expect, anticipate, plan, or imagine creatively is to be aware of surfaces that do not exist or events that do not occur but that could arise or be fabricated within what we call the limits of possibility' (Gibson, 1986, p. 255). Hence, the unique contextual conditions for each situation, together with the ability to perceive and elaborate new affordances, form the process as well as the result of creativity within each situation. This implies that the noun *creativity* is replaced with the verb *to create*, and our studies have investigated how people *act creatively* in certain situations and contexts.

This emphasis on the relation to the surrounding context of creative actions is in line with Greeno's (1989) discussion of creativity, which assumes that all our cognitive activity is connected to situations: 'Creativity, in this view, involves reorganizing the connection the person has with a situation, rather than a reorganization that occurs within the person's mind' (p. 140).

This is exemplified in the results of Folkestad's (2004) meta-analysis of studies on composition, which included studies of children, adolescents and adults, as well as beginners and experts:

> The creative music making takes place in a process of interaction between the participants' musical experience and competence, their cultural practice, the tools, the instruments, and the instructions—altogether forming the *affordances* in the creative situation.

> (Folkestad, 2004: pp. 87–8.)

The emphasis on the issue of the activity context also has implications for the research context. This definition of context implies that a situation can never be context-free, that is, de-contextualized, but rather, as is most often the case in research designs, that it is *re*-contextualized. This is particularly important in the discussion of research designs: the design of our empirical studies might be described as experimental in the sense that they involve creating a situation as similar as possible to an out-of-school situation: that is, they re-contextualize out-of school activity into the research context. However, once the situation has been created and the activity has started, a *naturalistic* approach has been used in which the settings were not changed. Hence, no interventions are made, and no variables are manipulated in the research situation, as no control groups have been used with which the work and statements of the participants in the study have been compared. The naturalistic ethnographical approach also implies that the activity is analysed as a genuine 'out-of research' situation in which the activities are seen as naturally occurring, including the verbal discourse, which is treated as *naturally occurring talk* (Potter, 2004).

Moreover, in line with the distinction made by Vygotsky (1934/1986), this is not a one-way naturalism, studying how nature effects man, but rather a *dialectical approach* in which the interaction between nature and man—between the context with its digital tools and the creating individuals—is in focus. In this process, nature and man interact and co-interact, mutually affecting, changing and developing each other as in an ecological system.

One concept that addresses the issue of experiments as contexts is *ecological validity*, 'normally thought of as the extent to which the conclusions drawn from experimental and test methods are applicable outside of the procedure itself and the extent to which they are representative of psychological functioning in everyday life' (Cole, Engeström, & Vasques, 1997, pp. 6–7).

12.4 **The double dimension of collectivity**

One consequence of the definition of context as involving the cultural-historical dimension is that *all* activities, in that sense, are seen as collective. Clancey (1995) points out that human activities always must be regarded as social and in that respect collective:

> Saying that activities are social has nothing to do per se with whether the activity is done alone or with other people present. Again, the superficial view that social means 'in the presence of other people' (compared to the superficial view that situated means 'in some location'), fully distorts the psychological claim. Action is situated because it is constrained by a person's understanding of his or her 'place' in a social process.

> (Clancey, 1995: p. 50.)

In common everyday and scholarly discourse, 'collective' often refers to the fact that two or more people are involved. This typically means that when speaking of 'collective memory', the concern is with how groups function as integrated memory systems (Wertsch, 1997). However, discussing collective memory, Wertsch (1997: p. 226) states:

> I have recently become increasingly concerned with another sense in which mental functions such as memory can be collective or social. This sense of collectivity has to do with the fact that these mental functions are mediated by sociohistorically evolved (i.e. collective) tools or instruments.

This is a good description of how traditional ways of composing are mediated by the computer software packages utilized in contemporary musical composition. This means that there are two levels of collective communication in the process of collective creative music-making: 1) one inter-personal, or '"interpsychological" functioning' (Wertsch, 1997, p. 226), between the individuals of the working group of the collective activity, and also 2) one intrapersonal, or 'intrapsychological' (p. 228), a dialogue with the collective experiences and knowledge of previous composers, medi-ated by the tools in use. The latter also constitutes the collective dimension in 'individual' activities. I refer to the existence of these two levels as the 'double dimension of collectivity'.

The studies conducted over the last two decades have focused mainly on 'individual' composi-tion, that is, one individual creating music in interaction with digital tools (e.g., Folkestad, 1996; Folkestad, Hargreaves, & Lindström, 1998; Nilsson, 2002; Nilsson & Folkestad, 2005). In the ongoing and planned studies, the focus is on the collective process of composition, in school set-tings and in professional music studio settings. As we now take this step within a new project on *Collaborative Musical Creativity* (Folkestad, in preparation, a) the notion of the double dimension of collectivity will be at the core of the analysis, as the explicit adaptation of Cultural Historical Activity Theory (CHAT), firstly described by Engeström (1987), becomes essential. His model might be seen as a way of explicitly pointing out and visualizing the cultural-historical dimen-sions of Vygotsky's triangle, thereby further emphasizing the relationship between the collective level of *activity*, as described in a cultural-historical activity system, and the *action* of an individual in a situated practice.

12.5 **The personal inner musical library**

As a tool for understanding and illustrating the relationship between previous musical experiences and the compositional process, I suggest the coining of a new concept: *the personal inner musical library*. In short, *personal* refers to Polanyi's (1958) thesis that all knowledge is personally acquired and unique. *Inner* indicates that the musical library is not an ordinary collection of recordings and musical scores—which by tradition is understood as a musical library—but comprises all the musical experiences of a person's mind and body.[1] The word *library* points to how all musical experiences, just like all recordings, scores and books in an ordinary musical library, are present and accessible even when they are not explicitly in focus. They may be brought to the forefront and referred to on demand, when the need or wish arises. The metaphor of *the personal inner musical library* thus illustrates that, while individual musical compositions and performances might draw on specific musical experiences, the full musical library still forms and functions as a backdrop of implicit references to the totality of musical experiences in the process of musical creation. Phrased in Gurwitsch's (1964) terms of intentionality: at the same time as the piece of music under creation and some specific musical experiences are in explicit intentional focus—the theme—so are implicitly all the other musical experiences of the full personal inner musical library—the thematic field. This refers to all the musical creation and performance of that individual, as a *tacit dimension* (Polanyi, 1967) of the musical and compositional process.

Accordingly, in the process of musical creativity, the composer establishes a constant dialogue with his/her *personal inner musical library*, that is, as described above, all previous musical experiences of that individual, all the music ever heard, collected and stored in the mind and body of that person.

In that respect, in this interactive process of composition, the first receiver of the musical mes-sage, and the first to assess the composition, is the composer herself/himself. The composition

---

[1] NB Inner does not indicate a dualistic view—on the contrary, the ontological and epistemological foundations of this chapter rest on a non-dualistic view of learning and knowledge formation.

process incorporates two basic phases: 1) the creative, subjective-intuitive phase, or state of flow (Csikszentmihalyi, 1990), in which new musical material is produced, and 2) the evaluation of that material on the basis of knowledge and previous experiences, the context of the composition, the parts always simultaneously related to the whole, and with the *personal inner musical library*, with its collective cultural and historical dimension, as the reference.

This also implies, in line with Vygotsky's (1930/2004) view that creativity increases with experience, that the more musical experiences that exist in the personal inner musical library, the more references and resources are available for creative musical actions: 'the creative activity of the imagination depends directly on the richness and variety of a person's previous experience because this experience provides the material from which products of fantasy are constructed. The richer a person's experience, the richer is the material his imagination has access to' (pp. 14–15).

12.6 **Digital tools and artefacts**

As music is and has always been a cultural artefact, so have the tools by which it has been created and performed—from the first 'musical instruments' to today's digital tools.

Two key concepts in Vygotsky's (1978) theory of the development of higher mental psychological processes that are of special interest when studying contemporary creative music-making are *tools* and *artefacts*, and how different human artefacts, such as musical instruments, sheet music, computers and digital devices, are used as tools in achieving musical ends.

> The tool's function is to serve as the conductor of human influence on the object of activity; it is *externally* oriented; it must lead to changes in objects. It is a means by which human external activity is aimed at mastering, and triumphing over, nature. (p. 55.)

Another key concept in Vygotsky's theory (1978) is that of *signs*: he distinguishes between two interrelated types of mediating instruments in human activity; tools and signs. The sign, which 'changes nothing in the object of a psychological operation' (p. 55) belongs to the broader category of 'psychological tools' (Engeström, 1987). Both the technical tools and psychological tools, including signs, mediate activity. Or as described by John-Steiner and Souberman (1978): 'the use of tools and signs share some important properties; both involve mediated activity' (p. 127). However, technological and psychological tools have different characters: the latter (e. g., language, mnemonic techniques, algebraic symbol systems) including signs, are *internally* oriented, 'a means of internal activity aimed at mastering oneself' (Vygotsky, 1934/1978, p. 55), that is, they are directed toward the mastery or control of someone else's or one's own behavioural processes. Technical tools (cultural artefacts, e.g. musical instruments and computers), on the other hand, are *externally* oriented: they are directed toward the control of processes of nature.

The connection between Vygotsky and Mead is further emphasized by Engeström (1987), who argues that this formation of psychological tools through the combination of previously separate gestures and technical tools is actually the essence of what Mead called the emergence of 'significant gestures' or 'significant symbols'.

All musical instruments are human artefacts, and in that sense all instruments are just as 'authentic' or 'real' as others. In their desire and need to express themselves in music, people have, besides their voices, always made use of their everyday tools and the technical conquests of each period. The bow of the caveman and agricultural tools, the lure of the Bronze Age and the clog fiddle, are all results of man's ingenuity regarding wider means of musical expression. And in that respect, the computer—one of today's everyday tools—is no exception or turn in the evolution of music-making, but rather a continuation of a well established line of development, and has become an everyday contemporary tool for music creation.

Forty years ago, McLuhan and Fiore (1967) coined the often cited expression 'the medium is the message'. McLuhan (1964) established that the influence of the medium on which the message is produced is so vital that it in fact forms the message itself. In some of our studies, we have described the role of the computer equipment in the different ways of creating music (Folkestad, 1996, 1998; Nilsson, 2002; Nilsson & Folkestad, 2005). The differences in how the different options available from the tool for composition (the computer) were utilized are interesting, as are the respective roles of the tool and the medium as a whole. Adopting Gibson's (1986) concept of *affordance*, this leads to a question about the role of the computer in music creation: what are the affordances of the technology, the digital tools, and how are they perceived by the participants?

In order to get a general view of the state of the art in Sweden, Folkestad (1989) investigated how digital music equipment was used in classroom teaching, and upon what ideas the teachers based their usage and testing. The result shows that the activities carried out could be divided into two main parts or categories: 1) *established activities*, with content that the teacher had carried out previously with other equipment, other instruments, or other methods, and in which music technology was used as a tool to achieve those ends, and 2) *new activities*, in which the music technology was intrinsic to achieving the goals and purpose formulated. In these activities the music teachers found it possible to illustrate, practise, create and accomplish musical aims, which had hitherto been seen as impossible in music teaching.

This might be a good description of the effects of the introduction of new tools in general: at first the references to the earlier and well-established tools dominate, resulting in the established ways of working being transferred to the new tool. Over time, however, the new tool gets 'a life of its own', and new ways of working are developed which are unique for this tool. Thus, the usage of a new tool refers both backwards—to the already established ways of working and thinking—and forwards: towards the future, and to new ways of working.

Further research focused on one of the activities in the second category: the possibility of letting classroom students create and perform music of their own with the help of synthesizers and music technology (Folkestad, 1991a, b). The results confirmed that in spite of the musical, motor, and conceptual limitations of their previous knowledge, pupils were now much more easily able to create music of their own and to instantly hear the sounding result. These results and the other findings regarding the impact of computer-based technology on music teaching and learning are supported by Webster (2002) in his review and analysis of the research conducted internationally in this area.

Analysing the portfolios of Folkestad (1996), the participants with experience of playing an instrument obviously had different prerequisites for music-making than the others. This fact seems to be important in explaining why these participants did not use the options of the equipment to the same extent as the others: they simply did not perceive a need to! Moreover, the experience of musical training seems to result in more fixed ideas about creating music, which indicates that while formal instrumental training may be an asset in realizing musical ideas, it might also become an obstacle in the exploration of the options of the equipment. On the other hand, for those who did not possess a tool in terms of instrumental performing skills, and thus needed all the help that the equipment could provide, exploration of its possibilities became a necessity.

In our studies, the awareness of the participants while performing has mainly been directed towards the creation of music itself, more rarely towards the computer. Although the digital tools to some extent mediate ideas of how to create music, as seen in Nilsson (2002), the computer seems to have had the function of a tool for realizing musical ideas, and thus was more or less transparent in the creative process. Previous experience of computers did not seem to be important as to how the participants in Folkestad (1996) succeeded in general, or for their strategies in creating music. This notion has been further confirmed in our subsequent studies. The activity seems not to be perceived as a computer activity, but as a musical activity; the intentional focus seem to have been on the music, the sonic outcome of the creative action, and not on the tool by which this is achieved.

The tools of creating, transmitting, storing, and remembering music have always affected the ways in which different musical practices have been developed in different times, cultures, and contexts. Lilliestam (1995) states that the basic difference between how music is made in oral/aural traditions vis-à-vis written traditions is 'the way the music is stored, how it is remembered—with or without the help of notation' (p. 169).

The introduction of new tools always results in established views on music and musical concepts being challenged, changed, and redefined. One example of this is the definition of and distinction between *composition* and *improvisation*. One method of creating music practised by music makers within genres of oral tradition, for example jazz musicians, has been to record several improvisations and versions of the same tune, and afterwards decide which of the takes is to be released on a record. By listening to the various takes, one of the improvisations is thus defined as the composition (Jones, 1992). By using digital technology and MIDI-based equipment, this way of working has been considerably refined, and new ways of creating music have consequently been developed (Moorefield, 2005).

In our studies, the collected data covers musical material from the first utterances and improvisations to the completed compositions. The definition of what is regarded as a composition is related to the second definition, though this becomes self-evident, as the elements which 'survive repetition' (Folkestad, 1996: p. 172) are those saved in the computer during work. Some of my current research (Folkestad, in preparation, b) establishes that today computers and new technologies are well established in professional composition in all kinds and genres of music, and regardless of whether the work is based on avant-gardist or traditional artistic approaches to composition.

One result of this development is that the two branches of musical creativity, improvisation and composition, may no longer be treated as distinctive and separate concepts. On the contrary, these concepts appear to merge more and more in contemporary improvisational and compositional practices—composition is a key aspect of improvisation and improvisation is, as a result of the digital tools, increasingly used as a method in composition.

12.7 Discourse in music

In Folkestad (1996) the concept *discourse in music* was introduced. Its essence is the assumption that music itself might be regarded as a discourse—musical actions and activities are seen as discursive practices or discursive activities.

The point of departure is *discourse*, defined in its most general linguistic definition as 'language in use', and quite often used in everyday speech as a synonym for conversation (Webster, 1977). This definition implicitly implies that for a conversation between two persons, an agreed meaning of the words is required. The agreed meaning of words, the discourse, differs from situation to situation, and from practice to practice. Wittgenstein (1967/1978) says in one of his theses that one cannot understand human speech unless one participates in and understands the context in which it is uttered. The same applies to music, which like language is connected to practice: literal as well as musical expressions which are adequate and make sense in one practice might be incomprehensible in others, and discourse in music has developed differently within various musical practices. Thus, *discourse* marks a view of language and other forms of human utterances and ways of communicating as something used during an ongoing process, rather than as a static code that can be analysed separately from its social practice.

Although *discourse* is mainly associated with talk, and in music research hitherto has mostly been used to describe how people talk about music and make distinctions about music in words (i.e. discourse *on* music), the concept of discourse also includes non-verbal forms of dialogue such as 'music, weeping/crying, the "non-said" in earlier utterances or the present unarticulated experiences when we are considering how we as humans create meaning' (Ruud, 1992: p. 100). Thus, wider definitions of *discourse* emerge, which include all forms of human communication and negotiation in situations of practice; 'the universe of discourse within which musical meaning arises' (Meyer, 1967, quoted in Ruud, 1992: p. 77) and 'a discourse becomes in practice the same as a settled situated social practice of humans talking, singing, telling, or writing to and about each other (Ruud, 1992: p. 100).

Discourse *in* music and the discourse *on* music are both cultural tools and as such resources in, for example, answering questions on musical creativity and performance, as demonstrated by Johansson (2008), who adopts and develops *discourse in music* as a methodological tool in her investigations of expert organists' improvisations (see Johansson, Chapter 14, this volume).

Taking into consideration the interactive attitude of young people when approaching music, the results of, for example, Folkestad's (1996) study might indicate that by listening to music, and in some cases by playing and trying things out on an instrument, an implicit and unreflected image of the discourse in music is formed; not only of how the music sounds and its meaning and message, but also of how it is created. Thus, the experience of music, that is, acquiring the discourse in music, also mediates insight into how to create the music. One conclusion of this study is that on the basis of their personal musical experience, their personal inner musical library, the participants implicitly or explicitly defined a musical context, and the musical features and discourse of that musical practice became the prerequisites for the creation of that particular tune.

When Dermott—who plays the saxophone in the brass band, the piano by ear at home, and who listens to music like techno—is about to write a tune, he determines, on the basis of his experience of various musical practices and discourses in music, what is in focus: where am I, who am I, what is my musical function, and what kind of music am I about to write? Writing a brass band tune, he situates himself in the brass band playing the saxophone, and uses his knowledge of the contextual conditions, including the discourse in music, in that kind of musical practice to create a tune on the basis of these prerequisites. Consequently, he situates himself by focusing on a previous experience. His experience affords him possibilities in the present, and thus the music which is produced is an expression based on his acquired musical experience.

Another example that demonstrates the role of the music comes from David, and the first time he used a horizontal strategy.[2] He explains it in the interview as 'this time I tried to start by making the music', which meant starting with the piano. In his previous tunes he had started by recording drums, which he found natural, as he had gained most of his musical experience from playing the drums at the start of the project. Subsequently, he completed the tunes in a vertical manner. As long as he identified himself as a drummer, and created music on the basis of that musical experience, his work turned out to be vertical. As in playing the drums, which is done together with other instruments, the music is experienced as a 'vertical unity', in the same way as it is when listening to recorded music.

However, during the project he became so good at playing the piano that he wanted to realize his idea of starting by 'making the music'. Doing so he 'became' a pianist making a piano tune, and started by playing and recording the piano from the beginning to the end, without any additional instrument, without even using the metronome, which later caused him problems when he wanted

---

[2] For a thorough presentation of the HORIZONTAL and VERTICAL categories, devised in Folkestad (1996), see Folkestad (1998), Folkestad, Lindström, & Hargreaves, (1997), and Folkestad, Hargreaves, & Lindström, (1998).

to copy and paste, a technique he had previously used frequently. The drums were recorded 'live' while listening to the completed piano track. Thus, changing from music based on drums to music based on melody and chords on the piano, from one discourse in music to another, David also changed his way of working—from vertical to horizontal.

In conclusion, people can understand, speak, and write a language, and master various linguistic dialects within that language, while other languages are not comprehensible to them. Literary creation takes place in a language and within a linguistic discourse that has been mastered, and the same is true of music and music-making. Young people of today, by listening, and sometimes by playing, have built up a knowledge and a familiarity with different forms of musical expression, usually called styles or genres, and may thus be able to express themselves within these musical languages in various musical practices. As music is always a historically and collectively defined object, every composer, whether professional or novice, has a dialogue with all the music heard before in which the music also carries the societal, traditional, and historical features of the *discourse in music*, the musical language in use.

12.8 **The ecology of composition: a summary**

In understanding and explaining the situated cultural practice of creative music-making—the ecology of composition—the concept of *context* refers not only to the people, features, and characteristics present when it is conceived. It also involves a historical dimension—cultural and personal—which includes the experience of previous situations. The experience of a previous situation thus becomes an ingredient of the context in the new situation. This dynamic aspect of context might explain how it is possible to switch between currently non-present situations and practices in such a familiar way, as demonstrated by some of the participants in Folkestad's (1996) study. For example, when creating music in front of the computer, the experience of playing the saxophone in a brass band situates the creator, and thus the discourse in music. The context of the situation—creating music by digital tools—thus expands to include not only present entities, but also the experience of musical situations in the past and in the future. It follows that in this situation the participant is not primarily making computer music, but, for example, brass band music within the discourse of brass band music, using the computer as a tool in achieving this.

Evidently, the music being created exerts an influence on the course of events, and thus the music itself becomes an important part of the context of the activity, a subject that is, at one and the same time, the basis for and the result of the *discourse in music*. Moreover, as the creation of music (and performance) never takes place in a 'vacuum' with nothing or no-one to relate to, and since it always involves communication in one way or another, music-making is consequently always a collective activity, regardless of whether it is done individually or in a group. The activity as such involves a dialogue, not only with the present, but also with the tradition and history of the music *and* of its creator. As language is the mediator of history and culture (Vygotsky 1934/1986), so are music and the musical instruments employed in the creation of new music.

What governs the way in which music is created seems to be the musical experience of the participants/composers—and not the *tools* of composition, in this case the digital tools as such. On the contrary, in the process of musical creation the computer rather becomes 'transparent', and adopts a mediating function in the musical discourse between the composers and their musical experiences when creating music. The music is the context, and the music situates the creator, thus defining the referential framework, and the *discourse in music* may provide not only the stylistic features and aesthetic values for the tune, but also the means of creating it.

In this chapter I have tried to bring together the theoretical points of departure and key concepts of a methodology of research on composition. Why is this approach, which was special when I started, nowadays a well-established methodology of investigating composition? The answer might be that it has been found to provide researchers with tools which enable them to explore the full range, complexity, and depth of the *ecology of composition.*

References

Butterworth, G. (1993). Context and cognition in models of cognitive growth. In P. Light & G. Butterworth (Eds.) *Context and Cognition. Ways of learning and knowing.* Hillsdale, NJ: Lawrence Erlbaum Associates, pp. 1–13.

Cole, M., Engeström, Y., & Vasquez, O. (1997). Introduction. In M. Cole, Y. Engeström & O. Vasquez (Eds.) *Mind, culture and activity.* Cambridge: Cambridge University Press, pp. 1–21.

Clancey, W.J. (1995). *A Tutorial on Situated Learning.* In J. Self (Ed.) *Proceedings of the International Conference on Computers and Education* (Taiwan). Charlottesville, VA: AACE, pp. 49–70.

Csikszentmihalyi, M. (1990). *Flow. The psychology of optimal experience.* New York: Harper & Row.

Daniels, H. (2008). *Vygotsky and research.* London: Routledge.

Engeström, Y. (1987). *Learning by expanding. An activity-theoretical approach to developmental research.* Helsinki: Orienta-Konsultit Oy.

Engeström, Y. (1993). Developmental studies of work as a testbench of activity theory: The case of primary care medical practice. In S. Chaiklin & J. Lave (Eds.) *Understanding practice—Perspectives on activity and context.* Cambridge, MA: Cambridge University Press, pp. 64–103.

Folkestad, G. (1989). *Elektrotekniska hjälpmedel i musikundervisningen* [Electro-technical means of assistance in music teaching]. Göteborg: Göteborg University, Department of Musicology.

Folkestad, G. (1991a). Datorn och den nya musikelektroniken i ett didaktiskt perspektiv [The computer and the new music technology in a didactic perspective]. *Datorer i musikundervisningen* [Computers in music education] (Vol. 12: 1991). Stockholm: Center for research in Music education (MPC).

Folkestad, G. (1991b). *Musikkomponerande på mellanstadiet med hjälp av synt-sequenser* [Music composition in the upper primary school with the help of synthesisers-sequensers] (Report No. 19: 1991): Stockholm: Center for Research in Music Education.

Folkestad, G. (1996). *Computer based creative music making: Young people's music in the digital age.* Göteborg: Acta Universitatis Gothoburgensis.

Folkestad, G. (1998). Musical learning as cultural practice. As exemplified in computer-based creative music making. In B. Sundin, G. McPherson, & G. Folkestad (Eds.) *Children composing.* Malmö: Lund University, Malmö Academy of Music, pp. 97–134.

Folkestad, G. (2004). A meta-analytic approach to qualitative studies in music education: A new model applied to creativity and composition. *Bulletin of the Council for Research in Music Education,* **161/162**, 83–90.

Folkestad, G. (in preparation, a). *Collaborative musical creativity: Towards a research methodology of composition.*

Folkestad, G. (in preparation, b). *Improvisation and composition: Two merging practices.*

Folkestad, G., Hargreaves, D.J., & Lindström, B. (1998). Compositional strategies in computer-based music-making. *British Journal of Music Education,* **15**(1), 83–98.

Folkestad, G., Lindström, B., & Hargreaves, D.J. (1997). Young people's music in the digital age. *Research Studies in Music Education,* **9**, 1–12.

Gibson, J.J. (1986). *The ecological approach to visual perception.* Hillsdal, NJ: Erlbaum.

Greeno, J.G. (1989). A perspective on thinking. *American Psychologist,* **44**(2), 134–41.

Gurwitsch, A. (1964). *The field of consciousness.* Pittsburgh, PA: Duquesne University Press.

Husserl, E. (1989). *Fenomenologins idé* [The idea of phenomenology]. Göteborg: Daidalos.

Johansson, K. (2008). *Organ improvisation—activity, action and rhetorical practice.* Malmö: Malmö Academy of Music.

John-Steiner, V. & Souberman, E. (1978). Afterword. In M. Cole, V. John-Steiner, S. Scribner, & E. Souberman (Eds.) *Mind in Society. The development of higher psychological processes.* Cambridge, MA: Harvard University Press, pp. 121–33.

Jones, S. (1992). *Rock formation: Music, technology, and mass communication.* London: Sage Publications, Inc.

Lilliestam, L. (1995). *Gehörsmusik. Blues, rock och muntlig tradering* [Playing by ear. Blues, rock and oral tradition]. Göteborg: Akademiförlaget.

McLuhan, M. (1964). *Understanding media.* Stockholm: Bokförlaget PAN/Norstedts.

McLuhan, M. & Fiore, Q. (1967). *The medium is the message. An inventory of effects.* New York: Bantam Books.

Moorefield, V. (2005). *The producer as composer. Shaping the sounds of popular music.* Cambridge, MA: MIT Press.

Nilsson, B. (2002). *"Jag kan göra hundra låtar". Barns musikskapande med digitala verktyg.* ["I can make a hundred songs". Children's creative music making with digital tools]. Malmö: Malmö Academy of Music.

Nilsson, B. & Folkestad, G. (2005). Children's practice of computer-based composition. *Music Education Research,* **7**(1), 21–37.

North, A.C. & Hargreaves, D. J. (2008). *The social and applied psychology of music.* Oxford: Oxford University Press.

Polanyi, M. (1958). *Personal knowledge: Towards a post-critical philosophy.* Chicago, IL: University of Chicago Press.

Polanyi, M. (1967). *The tacit dimension.* London: Routledge & Kegan Paul Ltd.

Potter, J. (2004). Discourse analysis as a way of analysing naturally occurring talk. In D. Silverman (Ed.) *Qualitative analysis: Issues of theory and method.* London: Sage Publications, pp. 200–21.

Ruud, E. (1992). Musikalisk stil som emosjonell diskurs. In O.A. Berkaak & E. Ruud (Eds.) *Den påbegynte virkelighet.* Oslo: Universitetsförlaget.

Vygotsky, L. (1934/1986). *Thought and language.* Cambridge, MA: MIT Press.

Vygotsky, L.S. (1934/1978). *Mind in society. The development of higher psychological processes.* Cambridge, MA: Harvard University Press.

Vygotsky, L.S. (1930/2004). Imagination and creativity in childhood. *Journal of Russian and East European Psychology,* **42**(1), 7–97.

Webster, N. (1977). *Webster's new twentieth century dictionary of the English language.* New York: William Collins and World Publishing Co., Inc.

Webster, P.R. (2002). Computer-based technology and music teaching and learning. In R. Colwell & C. Richardson (Eds.) *The new handbook of research on music teaching and learning.* Oxford: Oxford University Press, pp. 416–39.

Wertsch, J.V. (1985). *Vygotsky and the social formation of mind.* Cambridge, MA: Harvard University Press.

Wertsch, J. (1997). Collective memory: Issues from a sociohistorical perspective. In M. Cole, Y. Engeström, & O. Vasquez (Eds.), *Mind, culture and activity.* Cambridge: Cambridge University Press, pp. 226–32.

Wineburg, S.S. (1989). Remembrance of theories past. *Educational researcher,* **18**(4), 7–10.

Wittgenstein, L. (1967/1978). *Filosofiska undersökningar* [Philosophische Untersuchungen/Philosphical investigations]. Stockholm: Bonniers.

Chapter 13

Troubling the *creative imaginary*: Some possibilities of ecological thinking for music and learning

Margaret S. Barrett

13.1 Introduction

Creativity research has a rich and varied history and has sought to explore the phenomenon through the study of creative people, processes, products, and more recently, places. This focus on creative places has provided an opportunity to draw on the theory and practice of ecology as a means to understanding creativity. Ecology as a field of study is concerned with the investigation of living forms and systems, specifically, the relationships and interactions that hold between organisms and their physical and biological environments. Socioecological studies have expanded the lens of ecological investigations to consider the ways in which broad social and cultural factors shape the physical and biological environment, and, the human relationships and interactions that occur within these. Studies in developmental psychology (Bronfenbrenner, 1979; Bronfenbrenner & Morris, 1998) and ecological psychology (Reed, 1996) have sought to understand the ways in which individual thought and action both acts upon and is acted upon by the ecological systems in which it is situated. And, in the field of creativity, theorists are seeking to explain creativity as a 'rich mix of ecological factors, primarily learning, change, diversity and adaptation' rather than as a matter of 'exceptional artistic talent or cultural riches' (Howkins, 2009: p. 4). Human thought and activity both act on and are acted upon by a complex web of individual (biological and neurocognitive), social, cultural, and physical factors. In drawing on the concept of ecologies, scholars across an increasing range of disciplines are recognizing that human thought and activity are not isolated phenomena; rather, they occur in social, cultural, and physical contexts that are mutually constitutive.

The emergence of ecological thinking in the social sciences might be attributed in part to the work of Gregory Bateson (1972) and his conception of an 'ecology of mind'. Bateson introduced this concept in his seminal collection of essays *Steps to an ecology of mind: Collected essays in anthropology, psychiatry, evolution and epistemology*. For Bateson, the study of all living forms and systems (biological, social, cultural) involves the study of pattern, context, and meaning, and, the interrogation of the relationships that hold between these. Importantly such study is recursive and reflexive: it is shaped by the theoretical frames that are brought to bear on phenomena (the epistemological frame of the investigation) and the reflexive shifts of the investigator as s/he engages in the investigation and the generation of theory (meaning and interpretation). Crucially, in pointing to the recursive and reflexive nature of investigations, Bateson seeks to remind us that the mind is constituted in and through the systems with which it engages, it is not 'in the head' alone.

The emergence of an 'ecological paradigm' is well captured by Capra (1996) who comments:

> During the (20th century) the change from the mechanistic to the ecological paradigm has proceeded in different forms and at different speeds in various scientific fields. It is not a steady change. It involves

scientific revolutions, backlashes, and pendulum swings. A chaotic pendulum in the sense of chaos theory—oscillations that almost repeat themselves but not quite, seemingly random and yet forming a complex and highly organized pattern—would perhaps be the most appropriate contemporary metaphor. The basic tension is between the parts and the whole. The emphasis on the parts has been called mechanistic, reductionist or atomistic; the emphasis on the whole holistic, organismic or ecological.

(Capra, 1996: p. 17.)

Capra's characterization of the move toward an ecological paradigm as a 'chaotic pendulum' can be seen in the ways that concepts such as 'ecologies of mind' and 'ecological thinking' are taken up in various forms across a range of disciplines. For example, studies in the philosophy of place (Malpas, 1999) have begun to recognize that environments (physical, cultural, social, emotional) shape our epistemological and ontological understandings and practices, which in turn shape the ways in which we act on and in our environments. Music education scholars (e.g. Stauffer, 2009) have begun to draw on philosophy of place as a means to investigate and interpret music education theories and practices, in order to shape a more 'place-conscious' or 'ecologically valid' music education. Whilst such a move seeks to embrace the holistic nature of music learning and teaching in a particular setting, there are inevitable tensions in the ways in which the needs of the local can be addressed and accommodated within the structures and policies of national curriculum policies and practices, and the needs of the larger intersecting cultures of musical practice.

Whilst the field of cultural psychology (Cole, 1996) does not overtly locate its concerns in notions of ecological thinking, recognition of the mutually constitutive nature of thought, activity, and context and setting (viewed as a system) reflects concerns similar to those investigated through an ecological lens. Recent studies in music education that draw on the conceptual framework of cultural psychology suggest that ecological perspectives have much to contribute to our understanding of music development, engagement, and learning (Barrett, 2010).

A form of ecological thinking is also evident in the emergence of the concept of musical ecologies within the field of musicology. This use of the term and concept refers to the relational and mutually constitutive nature of music and person/s in culture, place, and time. Similar work is evident in the development of ecological thinking as a framework for knowledge that is conscious of local thought and practice (understood in terms of time, place, and sociality) and the ethical issues that arise from such consciousness. An emphasis on the inter-connectedness of person/s and their surrounding world/s holds implications for our understandings of creative thought, identity, and activity, and the ways in which these might be developed and supported.

The concept of creative ecologies has been taken up variously including as a phenomenon linked to commercial interests and the emerging creative economy (Florida, 2003, 2005, 2008) and, as a socially just and sustainable phenomenon that provides opportunity for the participation of all in creative work (Howkins, 2009). In this essay I shall explore contemporary understandings and applications of ecological thinking in order to interrogate current conceptions of creativity, and consider the implications for music and music learning.

13.2 **Ecological thinking**

The application of ecological perspectives to a range of disciplines may be attributed in part to a desire to move beyond Western individualist explanations of human thought and activity to recognition of more diverse and pluralist accounts. Such a move implies also the desire to move beyond the 'mechanistic, reductionist, and atomistic' (Capra, 1996) forms of investigation that have tended to dominate scientific investigation to embrace more holistic and divergent forms of investigation. As part of this movement, ecological thinking as a concept has been taken up in a range of fields including feminist philosophy and post-colonial and multicultural studies (Code, 2006).

Lorraine Code, for example, draws on ecological theory to interrogate the ways in which modernist Western epistemologies of individualism and mastery legitimate the subjugation and exploitation of peoples. She proposes an alternative epistemology that recognizes place and location as shaping forces, and celebrates and supports diversity and particularization as a means to understanding human thought and activity. Code describes her use of ecological thinking thus:

> The working definition of *ecology* that informs my conception of ecological thinking is something of an amalgam, pieced together from diverse sources. Broadly speaking, it is a study of habitats both physical and social where people endeavor to live well together; of ways of knowing that foster or thwart such living; and thus of the ethos and habitus enacted in the knowledge and actions, customs, social structures, and creative-regulative principles by which people strive or fail to achieve this multiply realizable end.
>
> (Code, 2006: p.25.)

Code suggests that the aim of ecological thinking is to propose:

> . . . ways of developing a conceptual framework for a theory of knowledge—an epistemology—sensitive to human and historical-geographical diversity and well equipped to interrogate and unsettle the instrumental rationality, abstract individualism, reductionism, and exploitation of people and places that the epistemologies of mastery have helped to legitimate.
>
> (Code, 2006: p. 21.)

Code's wish to embrace and account for historical and geographical diversity resonates with the theory and practice of cultural-historical psychology in which context and setting are viewed as more than a 'backdrop' for human thought and activity. As Code comments:

> Ecological thinking . . . redirects theoretical analyses toward situated knowledges, situated ethico-politics, where situation is *constitutive of*, not just the context for, the backdrop to, enactments of subjectivity.
>
> (Code, 2006: p. 19.)

Code's intent is to trouble the 'social imaginary', a project that echoes with Tom Barone's (2001, 2003) work in educational inquiry. She maintains that

> . . . entrenched *social imaginaries* work to hold certain conceptual frames in place, thereby maintaining the legitimacy of hegemonic interpretations of experience and the world, while discrediting others. . . .
>
> (Code, 2006: p. 22.)

Code does not necessarily seek to overthrow one model of thinking and acting with another, rather her intention is to '. . . uncover the social imaginary that has claimed ascendancy, to show how it can be challenged and enriched to make different ways of thinking possible' (2006; p. 284). In a similar vein Tom Barone suggests that educational researchers are compelled to 'challenge the prevailing educational imaginary' (2003) through recognition of the political, social, and cultural contexts in which the educational enterprise operates (2001, 2003). Similarly, I suggest that a task for researchers in the field of creativity is to 'trouble' the prevailing *creative imaginary* in order to understand the epistemological frames through which we approach the phenomenon of creativity (Bateson's notion of recursive investigation) and, our reflexive stance in and through our conceptions and investigations. I shall address this issue in greater depth in a later section of this chapter.

13.3 Ecological thinking in music and music education

Clarke's (2005) proposal of an ecological approach to music perception and meaning-making moves beyond a singular focus on the perception and cognitive processing of discrete tones and sounds (as evidenced in the early traditions of experimental and applied aesthetics) to consider the role of nature and culture in our musical meaning-making. He identifies three factors that underpin an ecological view of music listening, those of: the relationship between perception and action; adaptation; and perceptual learning (2005: p. 19). Clarke's account acknowledges that listeners draw on a range of information sources including the attributes of the environment in which the listening event occurs (including 'spatial location and physical source of musical sounds'), and the cultural and ideological understandings and values that listeners bring to the listening event (2005: p. 46), in order to construct new meanings. Importantly engagement in these processes is mutually constitutive as the perceiving organism and environment interact and change each other.

Clarke's model of ecological listening reflects Bateson's concerns with pattern, context, meaning, the need to admit and consider the interpretive frames through which we approach a listening experience (the recursive nature of the experience) and, the reflexive nature of the enterprise. The aim of Clarke's model (as I interpret this) is not to arrive at 'the' definitive understanding and interpretation of the musical work; rather, it is to bring to bear on the listening experience a range of 'ecological' factors in order to arrive at a 'new' understanding for the individual, and potentially, for others. This model of music listening and meaning-making works from a valuing of the individual's experience and the understandings that the individual brings to the listening experience; an approach that is less evident in 'mastery' models of music appreciation in which the listener is presented with an expert reading of the musical work (although these two approaches might be viewed as complementary rather than mutually excusive). The democratic and locally-contingent nature of the model reflects a number of characteristics of creative ecologies (Howkins, 2009) and shall be taken up further in a later section of this chapter.

The interplay between ecological thinking and philosophy of place has been taken up in recent work in music education (Stauffer, 2009). Stauffer returns to the argument that design processes in music curriculum have been driven by questions of 'what', 'how', and 'why', proposing that asking questions about 'who' and 'where' might more usefully focus curriculum design to contemporary and local concerns. Drawing on philosophy of place (Cresswell, 2002; Flay, 1989; Malpas, 1999; Pickles, 1985) and some of its educational applications (Gruenewald, 2003; Sobel, 1996) Stauffer argues that music curriculum developers should look to the *sociomusical* practices of the locale in order to develop a 'place-conscious music education' that seeks 'to reconnect schools and communities and lived experience' (2009: p. 178). In this view, music educators might become 'community music educators' who view music practices as 'fluid, dynamic, and contextual and who recognize the need for continual examination of the intersections of people, place, and practice' (2009: p. 183). Again, we see a concern with democratic approaches and the locally-contingent. One of the tensions for place-based approaches in education is the potential for conflict with the 'social imaginaries' of public education. Where educational reform is 'deeply committed to a standards and testing culture that tends to ignore the peculiarities of place in order to standardize the experiences of students' (Graham, 2007: p. 375), such ecological approaches to education are often ignored, if not actively discouraged.

Ecological thinking might be viewed as a striving for connectedness, for the establishment of a relationship of the self to the inter-connecting systems in which we live and work: cognitive, emotional, social, cultural, physical. Such a concern relates profoundly to notions of place and identity, to who we are, in what settings; to what we do and why. What might we take from the uses of ecological thinking outlined above in relation to creativity? In what follows I shall endeavour to trouble some of the prevailing *creative imaginary* in order to consider other ways of thinking about creative thought and practice, and the implications these may hold for music and music learning.

13.4 **Ecological thinking and creativity**

The scientific investigation of creativity is a relatively recent phenomenon, its birth being attributed to J.P. Guilford's (1950) landmark Presidential Address to the American Psychological Association. The last 60 years have witnessed exponential growth in the investigation of creativity. Researchers have investigated creative phenomena through the lenses of the person, process, product, and, environment. Creativity research has sought to identify the unique characteristics and features of: eminent creators (e.g. Csikszentmihalyi, 1996; Gardner, 1993a, 1995, 1997), and, their creative collaborations and/or partnerships (e.g. Farrell, 2003; John-Steiner, 2000; Moran & John-Steiner, 2003, 2004; Sawyer, 2003a, b, 2008). In other approaches the focus has been on creative processes (Bindeman, 1998; Sternberg, 1999), creative products (Runco, 2007a) and, more recently, creative environments (Florida, 2003, 2005, 2008), and creative ecologies (Howkins, 2009).

For some, creativity is domain-specific (Csikszentmihalyi, 1996, 2003; Gardner, 1993a, b, 1997; Sternberg & Lubart, 1995) and depends upon individuals acquiring advanced skills, knowledge and techniques in a particular domain of human endeavour. The most resilient model of the domain-specific view is perhaps the 'systems' or 'confluence' model of creativity, where creativity is defined as '. . . a process by which a symbolic domain in a culture is changed' (Csikszentmihalyi, 1996: p. 8). For such change to occur, the creative *product,* produced by a creative *person* (Csikszentmihalyi (1996) outlines ten characteristics of such individuals), must arise from a *domain* of thought and practice and be judged by experts in the *field* (for example, critics, fellow creators, gallery owners, marketers) to have made an original contribution to the domain. The characteristic features of the systems models are the emphasis on novelty, usefulness (in that the innovation or creative product is recognized by the field as contributing something new to the field), and, effecting social change. Clearly such a 'strong' reading of creative thought and action is achievable by few.

For others, creativity is viewed as a general capacity that applies across domains (Finke, 1995; Guilford, 1968; Richards, 2007). When viewed as a general capacity creativity is often defined in terms of thinking styles and processes, specifically problem-finding and problem-solving. A criticism of such a view is that creativity is thereby reduced to a cognitive process in which the discipline and history of particular domains of endeavour are rendered secondary, the emotions marginalized (Deliege & Richelle, 2006), and, the unique attributes of the creative individual ignored. In identifying creativity as a general capacity the notion of 'everyday' (Richards, 2007) or 'personal' creativity (Boden, 2004; Runco, 2007b) is admitted, including the view that everyone is capable of creative thought and activity.

13.5 **Troubling the *creative imaginary***

The *creative imaginary*, the sets of propositions, beliefs, and values that structure our views of what and who is creative as outlined above, bears some troubling. Whilst domain-specific and general views of creativity are often cast as oppositional, they may also be viewed as complementary. As Margaret Boden reminds us: 'Creativity draws crucially on our ordinary abilities. Noticing, remembering, seeing, speaking, hearing, understanding language and recognizing analogies: all of these talents of Everyman are important' (Boden, 2004: p. 245). These ordinary abilities, including the capacity to notice, or 'to pay attention' are also identified by Csikszentmihalyi (1996) as characteristic of the creative individual. To these he adds curiosity and drive, the capacity to tolerate ambiguity, to persevere, and to take risks (1996: p. 346). In drawing together domain-specific and general views of creativity Boden proposes two distinct forms of creativity; 'psychological' creativity' and 'historical creativity'. Psychological or 'P-creativity involves coming up with a surprising, valuable idea that's *new to the person who comes up with it*. It doesn't matter how many people have had that idea before. But if a new idea is H-creative, that means that (so far as we know) no one

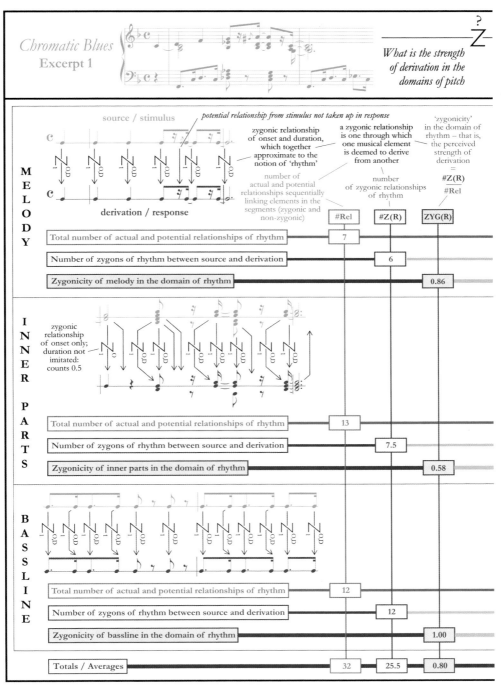

Plate 1 (See also Figure 3.9) Protocol for calculating strength of derivation of one excerpt from another.

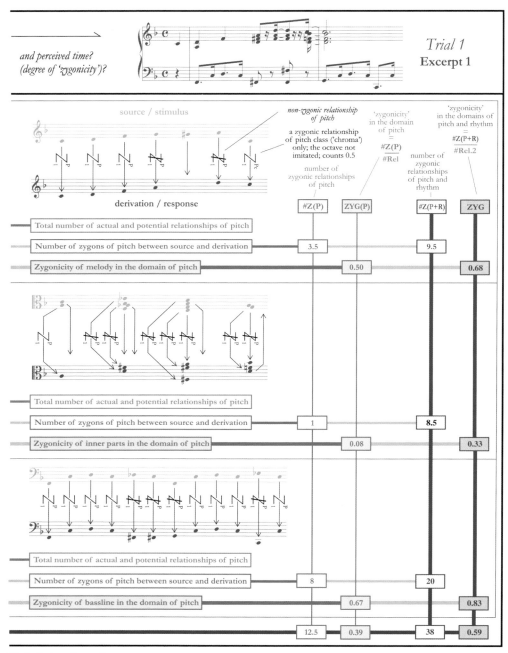

Plate 1 (continued).

Musicological Domain

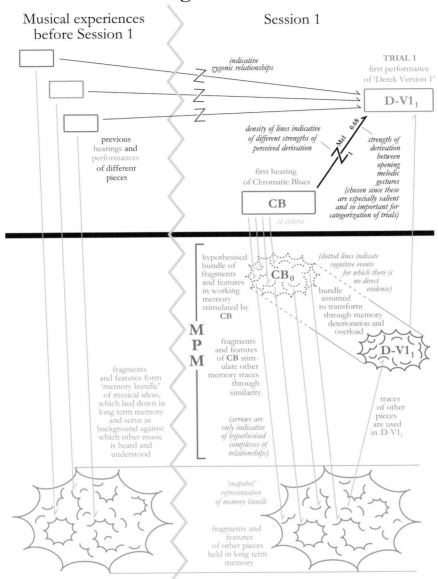

Psychological Domain

Plate 2 (See also Figure 3.14) Musicological analysis of Derek's *Trial 1* leads to the psychological hypothesis of a 'music processing module' in working memory.

Musicological Domain

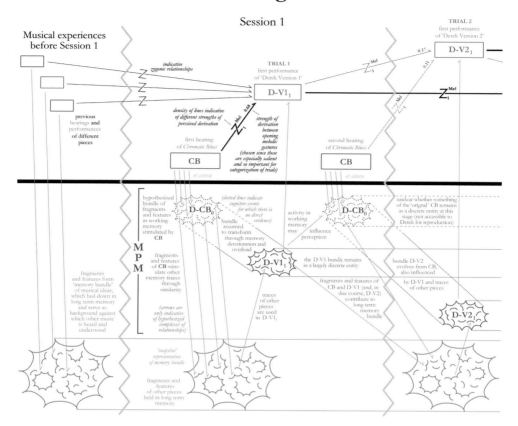

Psychological Domain

Plate 3 (See also Figure 3.20) Sessions 1–6 modelled in the musicological and psychological domains.

Musicological Domain

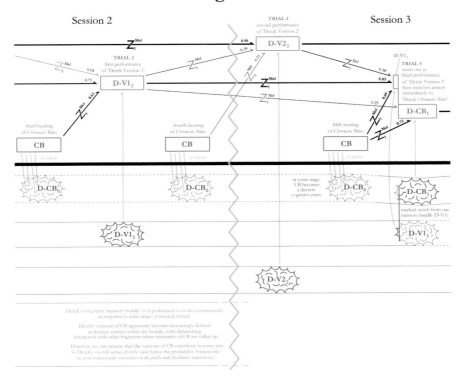

Psychological Domain

Plate 3 (continued).

Musicological Domain

Session 4

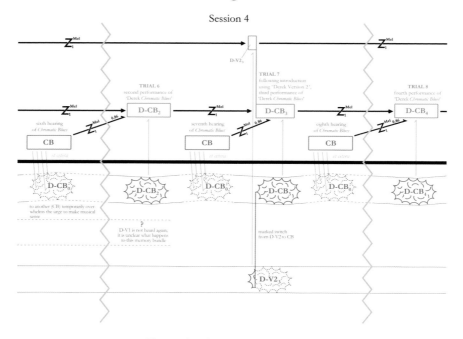

Psychological Domain

Plate 3 (continued).

Musicological Domain

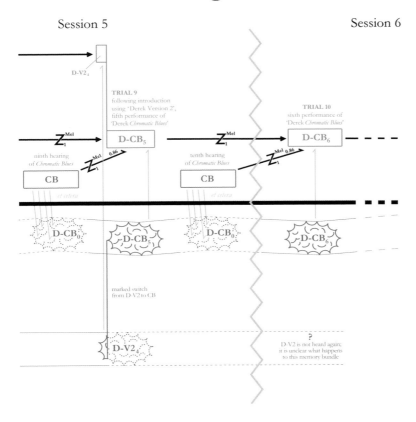

Plate 3 (continued).

Psychological Domain

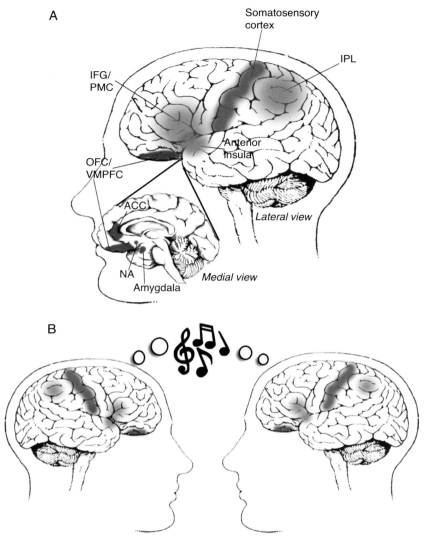

Plate 4 (See also Figure 20.1) A) Schematic representation of the core neural systems implicated by the Shared Affective Motion Experience (SAME) model of emotional music perception. Regions of the limbic system (in blue) include both cortical regions like the orbito-frontal cortex (OFC), the anterior cingulate cortex (ACC), the ventromedial prefrontal cortex (VMPFC), and the anterior insula, and subcortical structures including the amygdala and the nucleus accumbens (NA). The main neuroanatomical nodes of the human mirror neuron system (MNS) are shown in red, including, the inferior frontal gyrus (IFG) and premotor cortex (PMC) anteriorly and inferior parietal lobule (IPL) posteriorly. The anterior insula (in green), is connected with posterior parietal, inferior frontal, and superior temporal cortices, linking the limbic system and the mirror neuron system. B) The fact that the same neural networks are activated within the brains of individuals who participate in an interaction—the observer *and* the agent—allows for shared representations to be established among individuals, giving rise to a mutual understanding of the interaction. From this basic understanding, a shared sense of experience between a performer and listener can be achieved, such that even simply listening alone to pre-recorded music will have the capacity to create a sense of shared experience.

else has had it before: it has arisen for the first time in human history' (2004: p. 2). Others have seized upon a similar approach, proposing a distinction between Big 'C' and little 'c' creativity (Gardner, 1993a; Sawyer, 2006) where Big 'C' creativity is described as that creativity that leads to ideas and products that are culturally significant whilst little 'c' creativity pertains to those ideas and products that are individually significant. Similarly, Feldman and colleagues (Morelock & Feldman, 1999; Feldman 2003) propose that creativity be considered along a continuum of 'High C', 'medium c', and 'low c' creativity. These distinctions between different levels of creativity in terms of novelty, and social significance and impact recognize that creativity may be novel for the individual, rather than society, useful at the local level, and valued within the context in which the individual works, rather than more broadly.

Runco (2007) draws on constructivist epistemology (Piagetian) to propose that creativity is part of human nature, arises from our desire to understand and make meaning, and, is evident in our day-to-day constructions of understanding. He proposes that 'personal creativity' rests in our capacity to make *interpretations*, to exercise *discretion* in our decisions to make public either an original or conforming interpretation, and, to be aware of our *intentions* and values (2007b: p. 92). For Runco, all creativity is personal, with some manifestations of creativity becoming 'social' in terms of their originality and usefulness. He asserts: 'Creativity drives innovation and evolution, providing original ideas and options, but it is also a reaction to the challenges of life. It sometimes helps when solving problems, but also sometimes allows problems to be avoided. It is both reactive and proactive' (Runco, 2004: p. 679).

These various proposals for 'personal' and 'social creativity' (that is creative processes and products that are judged to be socially significant) provide a means by which domain-specific 'eminent' views and general views of creativity might be reconciled. Locating creativity in our 'ordinary abilities', these theories admit creative thought and action as a component of 'everyday' life, indeed, an essential survival skill if we are to construct understandings of our day-to-day experience that assist us in identifying, avoiding, and solving problems. Importantly, these approaches suggest that socially significant creativity is underpinned by ordinary abilities (writ large or profiled differently from individual to individual), whilst simultaneously drawing on the individual's developed knowledge and skills in a particular domain of practice. In short, thought and activity, creative or not, does not operate in the absence of a domain of practice, be that a function of daily life or, a recognized domain of socially significant creative practice, such as music.

There are three issues that remain unquestioned in the conceptualizations outlined above. First, in each, the creative enterprise is cast as an essentially individual enterprise in which the individual acts on his or her world in relative isolation rather than as part of an ecological system. Second, in each the notion that creativity is defined by the novel and useful remains unquestioned. Third, the view that creativity is always a positive end in itself, a positive social value, tends to be untroubled.

Is creativity individual or social? Systems theories of creativity such as that provided by Csikszentmihalyi (1996), propose that creativity occurs when an individual's original idea is judged by a field of experts to be sufficiently unique and useful to further a domain of practice in some way. Whilst recognizing the interdependence of a number of varying factors including those of the individual, the group, the field and, to some extent place, this view of creativity is still at foundation intensely individualistic. In a further conundrum, originality and usefulness are considered to be the defining characteristics of creative thought and activity and are twin features of most (Western) accounts of creativity (Csikszentmihalyi, 1996; Gardner, 1993a, b; Runco, 2007b). Creativity may be a social construction in the ways in which it is *recognized and judged* (for example, in domain-specific views), however, it is understood and made meaning of by the individual, and originality is judged as an attribute of the individual creator and/or the works s/he produces.

This latter is reinforced by copyright law that seeks to establish beyond question the 'ownership' of ideas and products by an individual or group of individuals. Whilst theories of group creativity (Sawyer, 2008) strive to demonstrate the ways in which individuals work collaboratively to effect a creative outcome (be it process or product), these theories are founded in a systems views that links the individual to the domain and field, a model that is fundamentally individualistic. This leads to another tension in the *creative imaginary*, the role of the novel and the useful in our conceptions of creativity.

In a deconstruction of creativity, Alf Rehn and Christian De Cock (2009) draw on Osborne's 'philistine rant' *Against creativity* to ask if the emphasis on novelty and usefulness in conceptions of creativity creates a form of 'compulsory individualism, compulsory "innovation", compulsory performativity and productiveness, (and) the compulsory valorization of the putatively new' (Osborne, 2007: p. 507)? They suggest that contemporary Western conceptions of creativity lock us into modernist teleological views of creativity, where progress is always predicated on the new. They argue further that uniqueness as a quality is over-rated in accounts of creativity and provide a range of examples in which repetition and (re)creation through 'copying, imitation, and mimicry' sometimes interpreted as an *homage*, may also be the hallmark of creative work. This questioning of the novel and the 'new' is taken up by others. As Marginson remarks, 'although the creative leap forward appears as a blaze of novelty, a sudden intuition, it rests also on an accumulated refusal of what has gone before. Even the sharpest break from the past draws on material from the past. Here the element of novelty in radical creativity can be over-stated' (2009: p. 93).

In a further deconstructive move, Rehn and De Cock question the ways in which creativity as an economic or market phenomenon is cast as morally neutral and 'necessarily beneficial' (2009: p. 227). As Florida notes:

> Creativity is not an unmitigated good but a human capacity that can be applied toward many different ends. The scientific and technical creativity of the last century gave us wonderful new inventions, but also terrible new weapons. Massive, centralized experiments in new forms of economic and social life led to fiascos like the Soviet Union, while here in the United States, free-market creativity has turned out a great deal that is trivial, vulgar, and wasteful.
>
> (Florida, 2003: p. 325.)

Rehn and De Cock describe their work as a form of 'necessary ethics for the field of creativity studies' (2009: p. 229). It is also I suggest a powerful example of ecological thinking in which the 'entrenched social imaginary' (Code, 2006) of creativity is uncovered and questioned.

As outlined above, the *creative imaginary* contains a number of inherent tensions including those that hold between domain-specific and general conceptions of creativity, individual and social notions of creativity, the role of novelty and originality in our conceptions of creativity, and the social and moral benefits of creativity. These latter draw our attention to the ways in which creativity has been taken up as a component of social, economic, and political theory, specifically, in conceptions of creative environments, their characteristic features, and their impact on social and economic change.

13.6 **Creative economies and ecologies**

The notion of a 'creative ecology' has emerged from economic and political theory that seeks to harness the benefits of creative thought and activity to effect broad economic, social, and cultural change (Cunningham, 2006; Florida, 2003; Howkins, 2001; Peters, Marginson, & Murphy, 2009). In a post-industrial age, governments seek to build economic power on the development of knowledge and ideas, rather than raw materials and resources in what has been variously described as the 'knowledge economy' and more recently the 'creative economy'. The creative economy is comprised in part of 'creative industries', that is industries in which creativity is either: core to the enterprise (for example, the film industry) with a high density of 'specialized' creative workers; or embedded in the enterprise where a number of creative workers are employed (for example, a public relations firm) (Cunningham, 2006). In defining creative industries Cunningham refers to the 'British' definition developed in the late 1990s of 'activities which have their origin in individual creativity, skill and talent and which have the potential for wealth and job creation through the generation and exploitation of intellectual property' (in Cunningham, 2006: p. 5).

In developing the notion of a creative ecology Howkins suggests (2009: p. 4) that:

> Creativity is not a matter of exceptional artistic talent or cultural riches but a rich mix of ecological factors, primarily diversity, change, learning, and adaptation. It exists only where the ecology permits, and it flourishes through adaptive efficiency.

For Howkins creativity is universal, operates most effectively in democratic structures, and requires functioning markets to prosper and evolve. He continues: 'a *creative ecology* is a niche where diverse individuals express themselves in a systemic and adaptive way, using ideas to produce new ideas; and where others support this endeavour even if they don't understand it' (Howkins, 2009: p. 11).

One manifestation of a creative ecology may be found in Richard Florida's accounts of the creative class (2003, 2005) and the creative city (2008). Florida describes the rise of the creative class as occasioned by profound changes in the socio-politico fabric of life and work:

> Both at work and in other spheres of our lives, we value creativity more highly than ever, and cultivate it more intensely. The creative impulse-that attribute that distinguishes us, as humans, from other species-is now being let loose on an unprecedented scale.
>
> (Florida, 2003: p. 4.)

Florida highlights the interplay between forms of creativity and the rich economic and social possibilities that arise from these pointing to the ways in which 'artistic and cultural creativity' blend with technology to give rise to 'whole new industries from computer graphics to digital music and animation' (2003: p. 5).

In Florida's account, the creative class is distinguished by the values held (creativity, individuality, difference and merit), the skills required for work ('complex problem-solving that involves a great deal of independent judgment and requires high levels of education or human capital' 2003: p. 8), and the nature of the work undertaken (to create and operate autonomously and flexibly). He also identifies a number of environmental factors that attract and sustain the creative class, those of 'talent', 'tolerance', 'technology' (Florida, 2003), and, more recently 'territorial assets' (Florida, 2008). For Florida, those communities that actively seek to provide social and economic structures that support talent, tolerance, technology, and territorial assets, will become more creative, and, strengthen their economic, social, and cultural base.

Creative ecologies and economies in these presentations are founded in 'personal' views of creativity, in which 'exceptional artistic talent or cultural riches' (Howkins, 2009: p. 4) are not pre-requisite, where diversity, individuality, flexibility, and autonomy are highly valued, as is the capacity for learning, positive change and adaptation. Florida's emphasis on this latter suggests that high levels of education are a requisite for the 'creative class', and, by implication, some access to 'cultural riches'. Florida recognizes the tendency toward individualism in his description of the creative class and exhorts members of the creative class to engage with their communities, in order to promote social cohesion and realize the benefits of creativity for all in the community, not just for those who are members of the creative class (Florida, 2003: pp. 320–4).

Recent accounts of the 'creative economy' have begun to express some reservations in relation to the unalloyed good that might emerge from creative economies with some suggesting that the emphasis on creativity and innovation is a form of 'snake oil' (Pratt & Jeffcutt, 2009). An inherent tension exists between the identification of some industries in the creative economy as 'creative' and theories of creativity that recognize and embrace notions of everyday, small 'c', or psychological creativity (see above). As Meusberger remarks, 'The attempt to label certain industries or professions as creative and the rest, by omission, as noncreative without evaluating their ideas and products contradicts any definition of creativity accepted in the core disciplines of creativity research' (2009: p. 142).

Others have been perhaps more reserved in their criticism:

> At the close of the twentieth century, many advanced economies had become enraptured with the idea that they were creative economies run increasingly by creative classes of technologists, artists, and the wielders of signs and symbols. As in the case of all dominant social self-conceptions, there is more than an element of truth in that assertion. Yet it is also an exaggerated truth.
>
> (Murphy in Murphy, Peters, & Marginson, 2010: p. 8.)

These authors suggest that scientific advances have allowed us to re-imagine ourselves and our relationship to the world, for example, the notion of the earth as a sphere floating in space, and part of a much larger and complex system, has brought greater awareness of place, space, and the ecological significances of our interactions with self, others, and our worlds. And, in that process, much as Florida fore-shadowed, the divides between 'class', and consequently, access and opportunity have increased rather than decreased. In a paradoxical manner, a model of creativity that has sought to effect social and economic change, and extend the reach, experience, and effects of democratic ideals may serve instead to reinforce the circumstances that de-bar some from active participation. Conceptions of creative ecologies have become harnessed to notions of competition, progress, consumption, and environmental 'control'.

In a recent conceptualization of economic creativity, Murphy et al (2010) suggest that creativity rests in three aspects:

> (a) the capacity of a society to manage a deep cultural ambidexterity even to the point of systemic paradox, (b) the ability of a society to avoid scientific or cultural path dependence, and thus be able to make the kinds of genuine intellectual leaps that create knowledge rather than just transmit, reproduce, or distribute it, and finally (c) the capability of a society to create ways, styles, and kinds of thinking. The latter may be described as the aesthetics of thought.
>
> (Murphy, Peters, & Marginson, 2010: p. ix.)

Drawing on historical examples such as the European renaissance, they propose the phenomenon of 'collective creativity', a conception that rests in a '. . . deep background of persistent aesthetic forms and enduring cognitive and metaphysical patterns that shape nature, society, and selves' (Murphy in Murphy, Peters & Marginson, 2010, p.7). These elements constitute a 'creative commons' that is 'recast' endlessly in 'adaptive, inventive and innovative ways'. Murphy proposes that we live in an era of 'imagineering' (Murphy in Murphy, Peters, & Marginson, 2010: p. 2) where '. . . a mix of feeling, sensing, and thinking' allows humans as a species to '"act" in the pursuit of meaning rather than "react" out of instinct as other species do' (Murphy in Murphy, Peters & Marginson, 2010: pp. 2–3).

13.7 Creativity, education, and learning

The emergence of notions of creative economies, ecologies, and industries, has had significant impact on education. As creativity has been identified as a means to effect substantial social and economic change, governments and educational policy makers have sought to shape an education that prepares students for work in the creative economy and the creative industries. Where education is viewed solely as preparation for the work force, an emerging emphasis on a creative economy demands that education prepares students for engagement in this economy. Creativity must now be taught and students must demonstrate creativity as a 'competence' or 'capability'. As Peters (2009: p. 132) notes:

> The focus on creativity has exercised strong appeal to policymakers who want to link education more firmly to new forms of capitalism, emphasizing how creativity must be taught; how educational theory and research can be used to improve student learning in mathematics, reading and science; and how different models of intelligence and creativity can inform educational practice.

Over the last decade we have witnessed models of the creative curriculum, of creative learning and, of creative pedagogies, thinking, and teaching (see Craft 2005; Craft et al., 2008; Jeffrey & Craft, 2004; Robinson, 2001). We have also witnessed the embedding of creativity in national curriculum policies and practices in an increasing range of countries where creativity is identified as an essential 'competency' or 'capability' to be developed in all children. Creativity has been identified in successive versions of the English National Curriculum over the last decade as a cross-curriculum learning area with documents providing teachers with guidance in how to spot and promote creativity in subjects (TES Connect, 2011). In Australia, the most recent manifestation of this may be found in the curriculum guidelines for the national curriculum where creativity was identified initially as one of eight general capabilities to be developed through engagement in all curriculum areas (ACARA, 2009). In subsequent work the eight capabilities have been reduced to seven by combining critical thinking and creativity into a single dimension: critical and creative thinking (ACARA, 2010).

Peters (2009) contrasts two forms of creativity, 'personal anarcho-aesthetics' and 'the design principle' in order to interrogate the implications for education of recent developments in the creative economy and what he terms 'educational capitalism'. The 'personal' view of creativity outlined by Peters is firmly anchored in the Western romantic tradition, with concomitant concepts such as individualism, genius, emotion and feeling, mysticism, and aestheticism underpinning the view. He suggests that despite considerable critique of romantic views of creativity, this approach is still firmly embedded in current views of creative thought and practice. For example, Peters suggests that business development practices (and preparation for these in school settings) such as brainstorming', 'mind-mapping' and 'strategic planning', activities usually associated with notions of 'group creativity', are fundamentally 'romantic' in nature resting in a view of the individual tapping the unconscious albeit in the company of and in collaboration with others. As an aside, it should be noted that research has uncovered the unproductive nature of such processes (Simonton, 2000). Peters (2009) contrasts this with notions of creativity that are relational and social, where creative thought and practice are 'distributed' amongst individuals and artefacts, where 'collective intelligence' becomes the means by which creative processes and products are developed.

When we consider the *creative imaginary* of education as outlined above it is evident that there are a number of conflicting views of creativity and creative thought and practice that are held simultaneously. In responding to policy demands to educate for a life at work in the creative economy, education can find itself caught in a bind between the development of creative thought and activity as a general cognitive capacity to be put to work, as a means to shape a life (through the development of personal creativity), as a means to develop future creative workers in those domains of thought and activity that are culturally valued (such as music), as a means to raise questions within and through a domain of thought and activity that trouble the taken-for-granted ways of thinking and doing. Which of the above should be the focus of our activity? The answer is, I suggest, all of the above, and more.

13.8 Concluding thoughts

Ecological thinking understood as a striving for connectedness, for recognition of the relationship that holds between the self and the inter-connecting systems in which we live and work (cognitive, emotional, social, cultural, physical) has provided a means to 'trouble' the *creative imaginary*. My intent in this essay has not been to provide a definitive account of creative thought and practice in music or of the theory and practice of learning that supports the development of creative thought and practice in music. Rather, it has been to apply some of the practices of ecological thinking and recent uses of the concept of creative ecologies to some of the taken-for-granted assumptions that underpin the *creative imaginary* and to consider the implications of these for music and learning.

For those of us engaged in music education, consideration of our personal theories of creativity and the role of creativity in our learning and teaching is crucial. In troubling the *creative imaginary* we are engaged in a recursive and reflexive study of the pattern, context and meaning of our creative engagement as learners, teachers and musicians.

References

Australian Curriculum, Assessment and Reporting Authority (2009). *The shape of the Australian curriculum.* Canberra, ACT: Commonwealth of Australia.

Australian Curriculum, Assessment and Reporting Authority (2010). *The shape of the Australian curriculum: The Arts.* Canberra, ACT: Commonwealth of Australia.

Barone, T. (2001). Pragmatizing the imaginary: A response to a fictionalised case study of teaching. *Harvard Educational Review,* **71**(4), 734–41.

Barone, T. (2003). Challenging the educational imaginary: Issues of form, substance and quality in film-based research. *Qualitative Inquiry,* **9**(2), 202–17.

Barrett, M.S. (Ed.) (2010). *A cultural psychology of music education.* Oxford: Oxford University Press.

Bateson, G. (1972). *Steps to an ecology of mind: Collected studies in anthropology, psychiatry, evolution and epistemology.* New York: Ballantine Books.

Bindeman, S. (1998). Echoes of silence: A phenomenological study of the creative process. *Creativity Research Journal,* **11**(1), 69–77.

Boden, M.A. (2004). *The creative mind: Myths and mechanisms* (2nd edition). Abingdon, Oxon: Routledge.

Bronfenbrenner, U. (1979). *The ecology of human development: experiments by nature and design.* Cambridge, MA: Harvard University Press.

Bronfenbrenner, U. & Morris, P.A. (1998). The ecology of developmental processes. In W. Damon & R.M. Lerner (Eds.), *Handbook of child psychology, Volume 1.* New York: john Wiley & Sons, pp. 993–1028.

Capra, F. (1996). *The web of life: A new scientific understanding of living systems.* New York: HarperCollins.

Clarke, E.F. (2005). *Ways of listening: An ecological approach to the perception of musical meaning.* Oxford: Oxford University Press.

Code, L. (2006). *Ecological thinking: The politics of epistemic location.* Oxford: Oxford University Press.

Cole, M. (1996). *Cultural psychology: the once and future discipline.* Harvard, MA: The Bellknapp Press of Harvard University Press.

Craft, A. (2005). *Creativity in schools: Tensions and dilemmas.* Abingdon: Routledge.

Craft, A., Cremin, T., & Burnard, P. (2008). *Creative learning 3–11 and how we document it.* Stoke-on-Trent: Trentham Books.

Cresswell, T. (2002). Theorizing place. In G. Verstraete and T. Cresswell (Eds.) *Mobilizing place, placing mobility: The politics of representation in a globalized world.* Amsterdam: Rodopi, pp. 11–32.

Csikszentmihalyi, M. (1996). *Creativity: Flow and the psychology of discovery and invention.* New York: HarperCollins.

Cunningham, S. (2006). *What price a creative economy?* Strawberry Hills, NSW: Currency Press Inc.

Deliege, I. & Richelle, M. (2006). Prelude. The spectrum of musical creativity. In I. Deliege, & G.A. Wiggins (2006) (Eds.). *Music creativity: Multidisciplinary research in theory and practice.* Hove: Psychology Press, pp. 1–6.

Farrell, M.P. (2003). *Collaborative circles: Friendship, dynamics, and creative work.* Chicago, IL: The University of Chicago Press.

Feldman, D.H. (2003). The creation of multiple intelligences theory: A study in high level thinking. In R.K. Sawyer, V. John-Steiner, S. Moran, R.J. Sternberg, D.H. Feldman, J. Nakamura, & M. Csikszentmihalyi (Eds.) *Creativity and development.* New York, Oxford University Press, pp. 139–85.

Feldman, D.H. (2008). Foreward. In A. Craft, T. Cremin, & P. Burnard (Eds.) *Creative learning 3–11 and how we document it.* Stoke-on-Trent: Trentham Books, pp. xiii–xvii.

Finke, R.A. (1995). Creative realism. In S.M. Smith, T.B. Ward, & R.A. Finke (Eds.) *The creative cognition approach.* Cambridge, MA: MIT Press, pp. 301–26.

Flay, J.C. (1989). Places and places. In D.W. Black, D. Kunze, & J. Pickles (Eds.) *Commonplaces: On the nature of place.* Lanham, MD: University Press of America, pp. 1–9.

Florida, R. (2003). *The rise of the creative class.* Victoria: Pluto Press.

Florida, R. (2005). *The flight of the creative class.* New York: HarperBusiness.

Florida, R. (2008). *Who's your city?* New York: Basic Books.

Gardner, H. (1993a). *Creating minds.* New York: Basic Books.

Gardner, H. (1993b). Seven creators of the modern era. In J. Brockman (Ed.) *Creativity.* New York: Simon & Schuster, pp. 28–47.

Gardner, H. (1995). *Leading minds.* New York: Basic Books.

Gardner, H. (1997). *Extraordinary minds.* New York: Basic Books.

Graham, M.A. (2007). Art, ecology and art education: locating art education in a critical place-based pedagogy. *Studies in Art Education,* **48**(4), 375–91.

Gruenewald, D.A. (2003). The best of both worlds. A critical pedagogy of place. *Educational Researcher,* **32**(4), 3–12.

Guilford, J.P. (1950). Creativity. *American Psychologist,* **5**(9), 444–54.

Guilford, J.P. (1968). *Intelligence, creativity, and their educational implications.* San Diego, CA: Knapp.

Howkins, J. (2001). *The creative economy.* London: Penguin.

Howkins, J. (2009). *Creative ecologies: Where thinking is a proper job.* Brisbane: The University of Queensland Press.

Jeffrey, P. & Craft, A. (2004). Teaching creatively and teaching for creativity: Distinctions and relationships. *Educational Studies,* **30**(1), 77–87.

John-Steiner, V. (2000). *Creative collaboration.* New York: Oxford University Press.

Malpas, J.E. (1999). *Place and experience: A philosophical topology.* Cambridge: Cambridge University Press.

Marginson, S. (2009). Intellectual freedoms and creativity. In M.A. Peters, S. Marginson, & P. Murphy (Eds.) *Creativity and the global knowledge economy.* New York: Peter Lang, pp. 91–124.

Marginson, S. Murphy, P., & Peters, M.A. (2010). *Global creation: Space, mobility and synchrony in the age of the knowledge economy.* New York: Peter Lang.

Meusberger, P. (2009). Milieus of creativity: The role of places, environments, and spatial contexts. In P. Meusberger, J. Funke, & E. Wunder (Eds.) *Milieus of creativity: Knowledge and space 2.* Dordrecht: Springer Science + Business Media B.V., pp. 97–153.

Moran, S. & John-Steiner, V. (2003). Creativity in the making: Vygotsky's contemporary contribution to the dialectic of development and creativity. In R.K. Sawyer, V. John-Steiner, S. Moran, R.J. Sternberg, D.H. Feldman, J. Nakamura, & M. Csikszentmihalyi (Eds) *Creativity and development.* New York: Oxford University Press, pp. 61–90.

Moran, S. & John-Steiner, V. (2004). How collaboration in creative work impact identity and motivation. In D. Miell & K. Littleton (Eds.) *Collaborative creativity: Contemporary perspectives.* London: Free Association Books, pp. 11–25.

Morelock, M.J.F. & Feldman D.H. (1999). Prodigies. In M.A. Runco & S.R. Pritzker (Eds.) *Encyclopedia of creativity* (Vol 2). San Diego, CA: Academic Press, pp. 449–56.

Mumford, M.D., Reiter-Palmer, R., & Redmond, M.R. (1994). Problem construction and cognition: applying problem representations in ill-structured problems. In M.A. Runco (Ed.) *Problem finding, problem solving, and creativity.* Norwood, NJ: Ablex, pp. 91–122.

Murphy, P., Peters, M.A., & Marginson, S. (2010). *Imagination: Three models of the imagination in the knowledge economy.* New York: Peter Lang.

Osborne, T. (2003). Against 'creativity': a philistine rant. *Economy and society, 32*(4), 507–25.

Peters, M.A., Marginson, S., & Murphy, P. (Eds.) (2009). *Creativity and the global knowledge economy.* New York: Peter Lang.

Peters, M.A. (2009). Education, creativity and the economy of the passions. In M.A. Peters, S. Marginson, & P. Murphy, (Eds.) *Creativity and the global knowledge economy.* New York: Peter Lang, pp. 125–47.

Pickles, J. (1985). *Phenomenology, science, and geography.* Cambridge: Cambridge University Press.

TES Connect (2011). National curriculum in action – Creativity: Find it, promote it! Available at: http://www.tes.co.uk/teaching-resource/National-Curriculum-in-Action-Creativity-Find-it-promote-it-6000829/ (accessed August 25, 2011).

Reed, E.S. (1996). *Encountering the world: Towards an ecological psychology.* New York: Oxford University Press.

Rehn, A. & De Cock, C. (2009). Deconstructing creativity. In T. Rickards, M.A. Runco, & S. Moger (Eds.) *The Routledge companion to creativity.* Abingdon: Routledge, pp. 222–31.

Pratt, A.C. & Jeffcut, P. (2009). Creativity, innovation and the cultural economy: Snake oil for the twenty-first century. In A. C. Pratt & P. Jeffcutt (Eds.) *Creativity, innovation, and the cultural economy.* London: Routledge, pp. 3–19.

Richards, R. (Ed.) (2007). *Everyday creativity and new views of human nature: Psychological, social, and spiritual perspectives.* Washington, DC: American Psychological Association.

Robinson, K. (2001). *Out of our minds: Learning to be creative.* Chichester: Capstone Pub. Ltd.

Runco, M.A. (2004). Creativity. *Annual Review of Psychology, 55,* 657–87.

Runco, M.A. (2007a). *Creativity: theories and themes: Research, development, and practice.* Burlington, MA: Academic Press.

Runco, M.A. (2007b). To understand is to create: an epistemological perspective on human nature and personal creativity. In R. Richards (Ed.) *Everyday creativity: New views of human nature.* Washington, DC: American Psychological Association, pp. 91–108.

Sawyer, R.K. (2003a). *Group creativity: Music, theatre, collaboration.* Mahwah, NJ: Lawrence Erlbaum Associates, Publishers.

Sawyer, R.K. (2003b). *Improvised dialogues: Emergence and creativity in conversation.* Westport, CT: Greenwood.

Sawyer, R.K. (2006). *Explaining creativity: The science of human innovation.* Oxford: Oxford University Press.

Sawyer, R.K. (2008). *Group genius: The creative power of collaboration.* New York: Basic Books.

Simonton, D.K. (2000). Creativity: cognitive, developmental, personal, and social aspects. *American Psychologist, 55,* 151–8.

Sobel, D. (1996). *Beyond ecophobia: Reclaiming the heart in nature education.* Great Barrington, MA: The Orion Society and the Myrin Institute.

Stauffer, S.L. (2009). Placing curriculum in music. In T.A. Regelski & J.T. Gates (Eds.) *Music education for changing times.* Dordrecht: Springer Publications, pp. 175–86.

Sternberg, R.J. (1999) (Ed.) *The handbook of creativity.* Cambridge: Cambridge University Press.

Sternberg, R.J. (2003). The development of creativity as a decision-making process. In R.K. Sawyer, V. John-Steiner, S. Moran, R.J. Sternberg, D.H. Feldman, J. Nakamura, *et al.* (Eds) *Creativity and development*. New York: Oxford University Press, pp. 91–138.

Sternberg, R.J. & Lubart, T.I. (1991). An investment theory of creativity and its development. *Human Development*, **34**, 1–31.

Chapter 14

Organ improvisation: Edition, extemporization, expansion, and instant composition

Karin Johansson

Where do musical ideas come from? How do improvisers and composers think, feel, and act when they make music? Questions such as these are not always easy to answer, and artists' creative and interpretive processes in music-making are still often described as 'largely shrouded in mystery' (Juslin, 2001, p. 410). However, as demonstrated by a growing number of studies on artistic practice, these processes can be investigated fruitfully from the perspective of the 'insider'. Explorative, in-depth qualitative studies of musical experience, acting and thinking form an expanding field of research (Coessens, Crispin, & Douglas, 2009), in which artists and researchers explore aspects of musical expression and creative musicianship in combination with reflective and collaborative methods of analysis (Hultberg, 2005).

With examples from a recent study of such insider perspectives on musical practice (Johansson, 2008), this chapter will focus on the phenomenon of Western European organ improvisation.

14.1 Internalization, externalization, and expansive learning

In an overview of research on creativity research in music, visual art, theatre, and dance, Hickey (2002) points out the need for 'more contextual and confluence approaches to the study of creativity in the arts' (p. 408). Based in the Russian cultural-historical school of psychology, such contextual views on creativity had already been proposed in the 1930s by Vygotsky (2004), who also pointed out that creativity is a necessary part of human development and maturation and, simultaneously, is 'always based in lack of adaptation which gives rise to needs, motives and desires' (p. 29). Creative action is thus connected to history and to the present reality but also points towards the future: Why do we improvise? What is the object of making music? Where are we going? From this perspective, musical fantasy and imagination are seen as dynamic, social processes and the interplay between receptivity, creativity, and change might in Vygotsky's terms be expressed as a relationship between internalization, externalization, and transformation: 'Internalisation is related to reproduction of culture; externalisation as creation of new artefacts makes possible its transformation' (Engeström, Miettinen, & Punamäki, 1999, p. 10).

Transferred to the professional training of musicians, this means that the traditional focus on learning the craft, skill, rules and techniques of the trade corresponds to an emphasis on internalization (Vygotsky, 1978) while the production of yet unheard music—as in improvisation or composition—might be seen as exemplifying externalization. The practice of organ improvisation in itself holds a tension between reproductive and innovative aspects and may then be studied as a meeting point for internalization and externalization; between learning and creative processes. As argued by Yrjö Engeström in his descriptions of *expansive learning* (1987, 2005), theories of learning often presuppose the learning content to be stable, and as bringing about a change in the learner: they are consequently inadequate for describing and understanding transformative processes in which the learning content is not yet known or defined. Forms of activity that have to be 'learned as they are being created' (p. 66) also have the potential to connect private emotions with cultural, collective expression. Creativity and learning with a utopian and expansive quality can then be seen as another name for the individual's power to accomplish and take part in future social and cultural change.

The functions of internalization and externalization are connected to the reproduction and the transformation of culture, respectively (Engeström et al., 1999). A focus on the creative processes involved in contemporary musical practices such as interpretation, improvisation, and composition on professional levels presents the opportunity to study how internalization and externalization interact. Where does the music come from? How is it created?

A sociocultural perspective on improvisation means that individual and collective development are seen as inseparable (Rogoff, 2003) and that views of creativity as a personal asset, or ability, are insufficient for the study of artistic processes. Composers, interpreters, and improvisers alike never make music in isolation, even though they might be alone in a room. When playing and making music, we always relate to and improvise in and on the contexts of tradition and music history (Benson, 2003). The practising and performance of music thus do not occur in separate niches of the culture, but form parts of an ongoing sociocultural and musical dialogue—of discourse in music (Folkestad, 1996).

In the following, I will attempt to illustrate how:

- Organ improvisation has a historical background founded on a body of repertoire and liturgical practice.
- Contemporary musical practice comments on and develops the historical tradition through a close connection to written music.
- The epistemological and creative spaces offered to organists are shaped by the sociocultural performance contexts of the liturgy and the concert.
- Individual organists with this background are presented with a variety of creative choices.

14.2 **The historical background to organists' musical practice**

Organ playing has been described as the only area of art music in which improvisation has never ceased to exist (Bailey, 1992). In Europe, the art and craft of organists' improvisation represents an unbroken historical continuity, and this practice has played a crucial role in the formal and psychological development of Western music (Ferand, 1938). Historically, organists' improvisation was situated in the framework of the liturgy, where music was improvised in interaction with the immediate course of events. As pointed out by Butt (2002), the enormous amounts of immediate music that have always been expected from liturgical organists means that surviving written documents have to be seen as 'the notational tip of an enormous improvisational iceberg' (p. 113). The earliest surviving documents of liturgical organ playing date from around 1400 and reveal a performance practice in which organists elaborate on parts of the liturgical texts while other parts are sung by the choir (Higginbottom, 1998). Initially, the organist was probably one of the priests or monks selected to play the instrument, but with technical development and extended use of organ music in the service, the status of the organist as an independent musician rose (Wilson-Dickson, 1996).

In his systematic and still unsurpassed history of improvisational praxis in Europe, Ernest Ferand (1938) had already pointed out how the development of the organ as an instrument with manuals and pedals made 'true experimentation' (p. 333) in harmony, polyphony, and sound ('Klangraum') possible for one single person, and how this contributed to general musical development. For example, the 15th-century practice of playing preludes, or *intonazioni*, had the dual purpose of acquainting the musician with the tuning of the instrument(s) and of getting the audience into the right tune, or mood. This way of playing normally involved what Ferand calls musical experimentation, and is formally connected to the evolution of the toccata form, in practice as well as in composition. The close relationship between performance practice and written music has prevailed in organists' music-making, which is thus based on aural transmission as well as on relationships to scores in the classical tradition of composition.

Many forms that relate to written music were shared with other instrumentalists up until around 1850, such as the extemporizing of entire musical movements, ornamentation and embellishments of melodic lines, fantasies and elaborations on musical themes (Willstedt, 1996). From Conrad Paumann's Fundamentum (approx. 1452) through to contemporary performers (e.g. Hakim, 2001), organists have continually produced written music that exemplifies the living practice of the liturgy and its requirements for the musician (Silbiger, 2003). This tradition includes the practice of the French classical school where notable organists publish their own livre d'orgue (e.g. Couperin, 1690/1969; de Grigny, 1699/1967; Messiaen, 1951), Bach's collection of Protestant hymn preludes, Orgelbüchlein (1714/1999), Romanticism (Lemmens, 1862/1920), and modern classics (Dupré, 1962; Tournemire, 1936; Langlais, 1957).

The research field of organ improvisation is vast but largely unexplored when it comes to contemporary practice. Research has mainly studied organ building, interpretation, and historical practices (e.g. Jutten, 1999; Porter, 2006; Ruiter-Feenstra, 2006), or technical, cognitive, and musicological aspects (e.g. Nutting, 1989). A general impression is that research in this area, by its focus on the subject of improvisation as an isolated activity, contributes to the division of music-making into interpretation, improvisation, and composition. It thereby maintains the culturally established contrasts between, for example, creativity and reproduction, performance and playing, and interpretation and improvisation. The integration of artistic, theological, and pedagogical perspectives presented for example by Landgren (1997), Love (2003), and Tandberg (2008) appears to point in the direction of contextualizing and exploring present-day practices in dialogue with performers and listeners.

14.3 Organ improvisation and the expansive approach to written music

Organists' improvisation can be described as a range of musical options whose relationship to scores varies from close to non-existent. In a study of pianists, Hultberg (2000) has described a reproductive and an explorative approach to scores. With a *reproductive approach*, the musicians 'strive to play appropriately, corresponding to a specific interpretation represented through the explicit performance markings of the edition chosen' (p. 60), while the *explorative approach* corresponds to a search for 'the implicit musical meaning behind the very notes and the performance markings' (p. 61). With their differences concerning the individual musician's creative input, what both of these have in common is that they relate to the intentions of a known composer. As we will see, organists' music-making contains an approach to scores that does not fall into any of these categories.

The emic term 'koralinställningen' ('koral' in Swedish means 'hymn' and 'inställning' means 'approach') was used by one of the participants in my own study for describing the specific character of organists' relationship to scores. With a development of Hultberg's terminology, I called this an *expansive approach* towards written music. With this approach, scores represent a suggestion that is related to and realized according to the conditions of every specific situation. They may be used as starting points or means for inspiration as well as individual works of music. A consequence of this is that written music becomes subordinate to the requirements of the ritual, be it a concert or a liturgy. Organists' musical practice thereby bridges the usually separated concepts of interpretation and improvisation and deconstructs the opposition between them. It might be described on a continuum (see Figure 14.1).

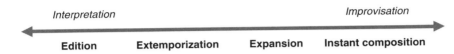

Fig. 14.1 Organists' music-making.

The positions on this continuum will be illustrated below by quotations from my study (Johansson, 2008). This project aimed to capture the complexity of speech and music in action at high artistic and musical levels. It was based on qualitative analyses of semi-structured, in-depth interviews, and observations of ten strategically selected players who perform publicly and can be seen as representatives of the contemporary society of professional organists. The in-depth interviews were made on instruments of the participants' choice, where they described their musical practice in words and playing. Observations were carried out at performances in which the organists improvised in public. Data consisted of 25 hours of filmed, recorded and transcribed material from interviews and performances and were analysed with the multi-media program Hyper Research. Verbal and musical statements were systematically coded and categorized, and the results suggested that the expansive approach is connected to the musical requirements of certain socially established situations rather than to individually based and chosen strategies.

14.3.1 **Improvisation as edition**

This relationship has its main background in the learning of, and daily occupation with, hymns in four-part harmony. Hymns are certainly notated, but are regarded as musical abstractions waiting to be arranged, edited and transformed into possible performances. One organist, Calle, expressed this as:

> I am really not dependent on scores, and in some services I don't play anything exactly as it is notated. That doesn't mean that I produce exciting new chords all the time, though. I might play in a style that corresponds to the hymnal, but then I find something that I think is better.

The score is referred to as a kind of blueprint that gives guidelines and directions for playing, while the final design has to be formulated and realized by the organist. Calle illustrated his habit of improvising a ritornello between each of the hymn verses when he changed the key. The reasons for this were that: 1) it is grounded in practice, and has been seen to improve congregational singing, and 2) it refers to the musical style. Firstly, the improvisation has a function, that is, to give breathing space in between verses, to musically create and comment upon the transition between keys, and to encourage singing. Secondly, the hymn was from the end of the 17th century, and it therefore was deemed suitable to use ritornellos instead of only dominant seventh chords when changing keys. Dominant seventh chords are common in popular music and might be used in hymns from, for example, the period of the religious revival in the 19th century, but they are not seen as part of the style—or musical discourse—of baroque music. The harmony is improvised in the sense that it is decided upon in the immediate moment of playing, and does not necessarily correspond to what is prescribed in the score. The score functions as a suggestion for realizing the given hymn into sounding music. By making decisions and shaping the hymn playing in ways that suit the occasion, the instrument and their personal inclinations, improvising organists act here as arrangers who make an immediate edition of their score.

14.3.2 Improvisation as extemporization

Historically, the extemporization of entire musical pieces which depart from basic melodic or harmonic structures has been an important part of organists' music-making. This background is evident in organists' practice, in which one type of liturgical improvisation involves the development of musical structures like melodies or harmonic progressions. Improvised hymn preludes such as the one described below demonstrate how complex musical processes may be built from relatively simple starting points. This is illustrated by a quotation from Erik's interview:

> I don't think there are any composed models for this, but I guess I have heard it as improvisations— you play the cantus firmus and a counterpoint part in the same hand on a solo registration, as a kind of extended cantus firmus, but instead of ornamenting the melody there's the extra part, which you play under the melody (plays the example). That can be quite expressive. There are pieces that resemble this, for example, Bach's variations on Von Himmel Hoch, with a strange kind of spontaneous and fluttering gestures in the solo part.

This type of structure has to be grounded in a concept of the harmonized hymn, which forms the basis for the melodic excursions of the contrasting part. A more common form is to embellish the melody with ornaments, but here it is allowed to appear in its simplicity while the solo part develops itself under the given melodic and harmonic conditions. Here, improvisation is defined as having a relationship to some kind of virtual score, and to traditional praxis, since in this case there is no written music present except for the melody of the hymn. Above all, the intention of the improvisation is to provide an inspiration for singing the hymn, which includes presenting the melody, and setting an atmosphere that suits its character. The historical connection to the time of its origin in the 16th century is emphasized through the choice of harmony and form. The style is related to pieces by Bach and clearly stands out as an example of the treatment of melody in a Protestant tradition.

14.3.3 Improvisation as expansion

Playing with a looser and more distant relationship to written music represents a form of improvisation that can be characterized as expanding on, or leaving, the score. Learning and playing repertoire pieces by heart is mentioned as a natural part in acquiring the technical ability and fluency necessary for improvising. Eva suggests that:

> It may seem like playing by heart and improvisation make for an impossible combination, but it is obvious that you benefit from it—you have to learn passages, and they have to be on an autopilot, technically, in all keys. You can learn such things, and they become mechanisms, instinctive mechanisms.

Written music then functions as a source that provides the language from which organists get their basic musical vocabulary. A thorough knowledge of compositional styles and forms is achieved through the playing of traditional repertoire, which might then be expanded upon. On the other hand, skills in improvisation are described as resulting in a deeper understanding of written music and as facilitating the analysis of compositions. With advanced skills in relating to written music and with the practical experience of instrumental idioms and conventions, the improviser can easily detect improvisatory techniques in notated music, as noted by Erik:

> For example, the music of Dupré is often quite hard to read, with many accidentals and a high degree of virtuosity . . . but if you look closer, the harmony is not systematic—rather, it's built on how you

take chords and how they suit your hands. This can be found with Buxtehude too, in the free sections that are based on dramatic effects more than on sophisticated musical processes; pauses, quick passages and sudden contrasts. Those are things that are easily invented in the moment if you're in the right mood. With Bach, however, everything is so thoroughly structured and organised that it's hard to repeat in improvisation, at least for mortal men.

In the process of becoming musically literate, the knowledge of how to improvise enhances and develops the ability to interpret written music, from whence the motivation and inspiration to improvise then also comes. In line with this, an important part of tuition in improvisation is described as focusing on the teaching of compositional styles and their characteristics. Before playing an improvisation, one of the organists asked 'and which composer do you think of when I play this?'. This kind of improvisation might be described as the fruit of a pedagogical process that involves analysing the musical parameters that give a certain piece its identity, and then transferring them for use in improvisations sounding like pieces that could have been made by the same composer. Improvisation in this category is thus to a great extent defined as resting on the learning, borrowing and integration of a musical language that is perceived as common. The knowledge acquired from scores is used as inspiration for expanding their scope or for further improvising.

14.3.4 Improvisation as instant composition

In the kind of instant composition that is sometimes described as 'free' improvisation, there is usually no intention or time to relate to scores, models, or musical memory on a conscious level. Instead, the important connection is the one to the stored musical knowledge that can be fetched from the unconscious when it is needed. Just like composed pieces, these improvisations are referred to as communicating important musical messages, with the difference that they are not as structured and are not planned in advance. The important thing is the will to tell a story, whose structure or final form is not known at the beginning, through instantaneous playing. The story that is to be told is a personal one, corresponding to an inner need for expression that can have no other outlet. Telling a story does not necessarily mean playing music that is completely unheard of, or breaking new ground in relation to music history; improvisation as an arena for the activity of 'having the courage to throw yourself out and fly' with a need for expression. Different genres and musical styles are referred to as backgrounds for improvisations that focus on the development of a personal style. In the field of 'free' improvisation, it is the individual improviser who constructs the framework and the criteria for what a good improvisation should be. Different genres and musical styles are referred to as backgrounds and musical tools. Dagmar makes this point:

> I think that the individual expression is made up of the unique mixture of tools—nobody shares the same kind of blend with me. Even if the tools are not unique, they create an impression that is only mine.

As suggested by these examples, organ improvisation is not only aurally transmitted but is characterized in all its aspects by relationships to scores, by intertextuality, and by being situated in the tradition of composition. The organists in the examples describe how they have become musically literate through extensive knowledge of major parts of the repertoire for the organ. From playing and interpreting a lot of composed music, they have gained a familiarity with various musical styles, obtained secure motor skills and formed personal relationships to musical history and performance traditions. Furthermore, they are influenced by various contemporary genres and contemporary musical developments. Internalized knowledge of the code of Western European music and the expansive approach to written music then function as psychological tools (Vygotsky, 1978;

Wells, 1999) for the individual organists and provide the means for creating expressions through the discourse in music. Their improvisations interact with the development of the existing body of written music, on which it in turn is dependent for inspiration and authorisation. This connects artistic and aesthetic dimensions with the development of compositional and instrumental techniques.

A parallel might be drawn at this point with jazz improvisation, in which similar relationships to existing musical material are common (Berliner, 1998). Benson (2003) compares jazz musicians' approaches to given melodies with classical musicians' embeddedness in performance practice, and suggests that music-making in both genres can be seen as 'interpretations of the entire tradition' (p. 145). Jazz musicians share a common grounding with organists in that their improvisations display varying degrees of closeness to the scores. Pressing (1988) discusses the distinction between using 'reproductive' approaches and 'internal images' (p. 145) when learning to improvise in jazz, which can be seen as describing a continuum similar to that in Figure 14.1, between edition, extemporization, expansion, and instant composition.

14.4 **Improvisation in the liturgy and in the concert: frames for imagination**

The musical character of improvisation, as well as the epistemological and creative space offered to organists (Kruger, 1998), is shaped by how improvisation is defined and enacted in the performance contexts of the liturgy and the concert. This illustrates organ improvisation as a function of the situations in which it occurs, and as situated in networks of musical and social relationships. The various European traditions for improvising on the organ have developed differently depending on national, religious, and liturgical cultures. The crucial matter seems to be the framing—the context—of making music. For example, the musical tasks of a Presbyterian organist usually differ a lot from what is expected of an organist in a Catholic church (Higginbottom, 1998). While learning to improvise as a Protestant organ scholar usually means practising hymn preludes, partitas, and fugues and other forms related to hymn melodies, for example, Catholic organists are taught to treat Gregorian chant and to create thème libre improvisations. The earlier and most influential schools of organ improvisation (e.g. Keller, 1939; Dupré, 1962) mirror this relationship, but reviews of later textbooks from other areas display an increasingly eclectic attitude, and attempts to cover major parts of the entire existing knowledge (e.g. Willstedt, 1996; Overduin, 1998).

Organ music in the church outside of the liturgy was an unknown phenomenon up until the Reformation, when the organ concert was invented as a paradoxical result of the ban on organ music in the services of the Dutch Reformed Church in the 17th century (Snyder, 2007). By then, the use of the organ was transferred to music performances that took place in the church in the evenings. This practice spread to the surrounding countries and, especially through Buxtehude's 'Abendmusik' in Lübeck, became widely known and expanded upon (Snyder, 2002). Along with the development of the concert form as a leisurely middle class activity with a paying audience (Chanan, 1994), organ concerts gradually came to attract large numbers of listeners, and to incorporate secular music in the repertoire. Notwithstanding the unifying factors of the organ and the physical and spiritual building of the church with its historical continuity, the practice of contemporary organ improvisation thus holds the two distinct and quite differing performance traditions of the liturgy and the concert.

Viewing improvisation as a discursive practice (Foucault, 2002) means studying it within the context of the musical, social, and historical rules and structures which determine its form. Seeing music as discursive implies: 1) that it plays a part in these contexts, regardless of whether it is conceived of as entertainment, fine art or a stabilizing factor in society, and 2) that it is possible to study how this is related to the shaping and appearance of improvised music. The socially established rituals of the liturgy and the concert both have stable frameworks for music-making. In the following it will be shown how both of these considerations set the conditions for improvising, and are connected to constructions of musical meaning and function through two differing discourses on music.

In the liturgy, the discourse *music as a means* describes the rules for a kind of music-making that does not relate to ideas of individual musical works or personal originality. Improvisation is defined as a means, for example, for illustrating the ritual events or creating collective feeling. The aim is to create a common musical experience corresponding to the moments of liturgical drama. The most important aspects of liturgical playing are seen as:

- Having a thorough knowledge of harmony and musical structure.
- Practising examples from musical history and tradition and using them as starting points when improvising.
- Relating to the surrounding contemporary musical landscape.

In improvisation, it is the aspects of music as a craft that are emphasized, with a focus on the familiarity with existing styles, where the individual musician acts as a carrier of traditional knowledge. Musical choices are made against the background of how they fit into the framework of the liturgy, with an awareness of how the parish at that certain moment will react to and experience the sounding music. Adapting to the given musical conditions is not described as a sacrifice of personal interests, but rather as liberating the musician from the demands of originality. Contrary to the Modernistic view that equates freedom with personal expression, individual uniqueness is here seen as a constraint. Freedom here thus means not having to be individually unique, and yet, this constantly results in music that has never been heard before.

In the concert, the discourse *music as an end in itself* defines improvising as relying on personal musical expressions that are formulated as unique musical messages. The improviser is a free artist without structural responsibilities, acting on the music market rather than in the establishment of the church. The musician produces original music, which is supposed to originate in the individual, on the spot. Musically, the orientation turns towards finding new and immediate expressions in the avoidance of traditional forms and patterns in individually conceived pieces of music. Individual musical expression is in focus, with the object of delivering a unique musical message to the audience. The main points in concert improvisation are described as:

- Refraining from using familiar musical styles and patterns.
- Practising a kind of spontaneous musical discourse, which is described as 'flying and throwing yourself out'.
- Inward listening, where the musical content is seen as emanating from an inner well with the aim of telling personal musical stories.

In the concert context, freedom is seen as diverging from constraining rules and supposedly restricting expectations. The aim is to open up for the music that is coming from the inside. Still, the resulting music often sounds familiar to the listener.

The two discourses might be illustrated with an extension as in Figure 14.2, which also illustrates how the epistemological and creative spaces of the liturgy and the concert differ. In the liturgy, it is important to learn about musical structure and harmony, while concert improvisers concentrate on knowing and keeping in contact with the expressive power and motivation that comes from inside the musician.

In the liturgy, improvisation mirrors the liturgical drama and establishes a common atmosphere. In the concert, improvisation is a creative language that develops musical content or expresses personal states of mind and feeling, with an intrinsic value for the individual musician.

Fig. 14.2 Improvisation in the liturgy and the concert.

While creative strategies in the liturgy use knowledge of and familiarity with musical history and notated music as tools, the organists playing in concerts depart from individual motivation and an expressive need.

14.5 **Creative copies and instant composition: organists' creative choices**

As described above, improvisation for organists is not a private or leisurely activity, but a practice in which individual musical actions in many respects are subordinate to the objects of the collective activity. Yet the gradual historical emergence of the concert might also be seen as an example of how individual expansion and creativity resulted in a greater variety of options for improvisation.

As individual musicians, professional organists are able to choose from the toolbox presented in Figure 14.1, and to make the most satisfactory choice in every specific situation. They are also orientated towards a common musical language, and relate to written or otherwise existing music that is supposed to be recognized and understood by its receivers. The use of techniques and musical expressions in improvisation are, so to speak, sanctioned by their existence in the literature, and at the same time perhaps comment upon and develop it. They have what I call a *discourse awareness*, which then includes differing options: 1) they may consciously refer to and use the common musical language, which in practice is regarded as everyone's property when they improvise, 2) they may also choose to refrain from a conscious use of the discourse in music, which might be compared to the phenomenological strategy of epoché.

Firstly, a conscious use of the common musical language presupposes having an overview of the discourses in a certain field, as well as the ability to use them, and not to be used by them. In the field of organ improvisation, musical styles and traditions can be said to rule and regulate the possible musical expressions and thereby represent the given structure, which in turn defines the creative space. Below, Adam, who has a Danish background, describes how he brings with him a certain way of playing as compared to French organists and composers. When meeting and becoming influenced by their musical style, he can consciously incorporate aspects of it that he likes and aspires to use:

> It often works well to combine a type of chorale prelude in Buxtehude's style with imitation, in a French way. Then you can create a nice counterpoint (plays). And what they often did in order to colour the counterpoint—especially Langlais—was to use fifths. By playing fifths in parallel, with the third in the middle you get a nice little improvisation that sounds very good (plays).

His way of playing is formed by accumulated knowledge and experiences, and he may also draw upon these intentionally, and form a style of his own choice. By relating his own actions to the existing canon of music, Adam has constant access to sources of inspiration through which he can extend his knowledge. In practice, this means staying in contact with music as a set of artefacts that 'crystallize subjective experience for others to experience' (Moran & John-Steiner, 2003: p. 26).

Secondly, a conscious bracketing of the knowledge and experience of the common musical language demands a focus on the present moment. Set models are described as inhibiting and as a hindrance to the improvisatory process. Music should flow freely, and established traditions of improvisation are seen as 'reproductive' because of their adherence to historical models and tonal systems where one constantly risks striking the wrong note.

Cecilie states that she produces improvisations by turning inwards and waiting for what she will hear while trying not to disturb the process by consciously thinking about it. While claiming that the music should be 'instant and just allowed to exist', she also points out that this is totally dependent on technical skills that have been acquired by playing the repertoire. This relationship is illustrated by her demonstration of what she is occupying herself with right now, which I personally strongly associate with Reger. Even though she likes his music and has played a lot of repertoire pieces, she does not explicitly mention a connection to Reger. She regards the imitation of styles as unnecessary and uninteresting in improvisation, in which the aim is to preserve her own expression. Cecilie does not make detailed preparations for improvisational performances, but relies on inner concentration and a sensibility to moods for getting the right inspiration at the right moment. The music she presents requires a lot of technical practice and structural thinking, but apparently this is something that takes place outside of the improvisatory situation. By consciously overlooking her earlier knowledge and experience when improvising she finds ways to produce viable musical expressions that give feedback and inspiration.

While these strategies both build on and presuppose a relationship with the common musical language, they differ in their approaches towards actual music-making. They vary from a kind of creative copying to instant composition, and can both be seen as creative. If creativity is not just associated with the production of 'new' and original products (Cropley, 2006), the copying and extension of existing musical artefacts might have the function of inspiring further musical exploration. As suggested by Tarling (2004), imitation can be used as 'a stimulus in order to attain the effectiveness of certain models, after which it passes into habit' (p. 18). With this kind of creative copying, the habits will become internalized and, in due time, a part of the intuition. In parallel, the instant composition of immediate and individual musical expression might be treated as a technique for feedback that displays the current intuitive content, and provides the player with suggestions of new ideas to pursue and explore.

These two approaches towards the act of improvisation can be seen as different ways of handling the problem of creative choice, as well as two aspects of intertextuality. The strategy for liturgical improvisation directs its attention to a collective level. With an extension of the concept a 'world of texts' (Fairclough, 2003, p. 40), it reaches towards a world of musical texts from which it also gains its inspiration in the deliberate, rational and active utilization of acquired knowledge. This knowledge is analysed, taken apart and scrutinized in order to reach its essence and content, which is then used as a model. The strategy for concert improvisation turns its focus towards the individual level of a personal universe of past and current experiences of music and musical texts, which Folkestad (Chapter 12 of this volume) calls the 'inner personal musical library'. For individual improvisers, this can be seen as having many departments.

14.6 **Coda**

Organists' music-making comes close to Benson's (2003) recommendations of a general improvisatory attitude, which, as he argues, challenges the hierarchy between the composer, the interpreter and the improviser: the Western European view of regarding musical history as consisting of a collection of individually conceived musical works is questioned by the sheer existence of improvisation when it is defined as, for example, edition or extemporization. With its free use of commonly known musical material, it challenges the notion of ownership and copyright. Any organist has the freedom to borrow the style or musical identity of any composer, and to continue in the same fashion. For example, many organists play Olivier Messiaen's music from notation, and it is possible to study his musical language and learn how to improvise in his style—as he also did himself. Thereby, any organist may create pieces that might very well have been composed by Messiaen, yet which are not. In other contexts, this would perhaps be described as forgery, but no organist would agree on that. Through improvisation, Messiaen's life and musical world can be prolonged, developed and perhaps even made everlasting. This places improvisers on an equal level with composers, as they have the licence to use whatever music they want with the pretext that it is an improvisation. It is not possible to establish where this music comes from and who owns it. Consequently, the professional roles of the improviser and the composer also come to overlap and deconstruct each other.

Improvisers apply the same learning procedures as composers by studying musical works and relating to existing styles, but then refrain from contributing with written works that develop the structure. With the pretext that it is an improvisation, they may both use existing compositional styles and choose from internalised musical conventions in performances. Excursions in different musical fields are facilitated by the expansive approach to written music. Their listeners share a common musical language, a discourse in music, which is commented upon and developed by momentary improvisations that last for a short time. Through this, music is simultaneously seen as perishable goods, and as forever in the hands of improvising craftsmen, belonging to the *musica practica* (Chanan, 1994).

References

Bach, J.S. (1999). *Orgelbüchlein* [Little organ book]. Kassel: Bärenreiter-Verlag.

Bailey, D. (1992). *Improvisation*. New York: Da Capo Press.

Benson, B.E. (2003). *The improvisation of musical dialogue*. Cambridge: Cambridge University Press.

Berliner, P. (1998). *Thinking in jazz: The infinite art of improvisation*. Chicago: University of Chicago Press.

Butt, J. (2002). *Playing with history*. Cambridge and New York: Cambridge University Press.

Chanan, M. (1994). *Musica practica. The social practice of Western music from Gregorian chant to postmodernism*. London and New York: Verso.

Coessens, K., Crispin, D., & Douglas, A. (2009). *The artistic turn. A manifesto*. Leuven: Leuven University Press.

Couperin, F. (1969). *Pieces d´orgue*. [Organ pieces]. Mainz: Schott.

Cropley, A. (2006). In praise of convergent thinking. *Creativity Research Journal*, **18**(3), 391–404.

Dupré, M. (1962). *Cours complet d`improvisation à l´orgue* [Complete course in organ improvisation]. Paris: Leduc.

Engeström, Y. (1987). *Learning by expanding*. Helsinki: Orienta-Konsultit Oy.

Engeström, Y. (2005). *Developmental work research: Expanding activity theory in practice*. Berlin: Lehmanns Media.

Engeström, Y., Miettinen, R., & Punamäki, R.L. (Eds.) (1999). *Perspectives on activity theory*. Cambridge: Cambridge University Press.

Fairclough, N. (2003). *Analysing discourse: Textual analysis for social research*. London: Routledge.

Ferand, E. (1938). *Die Improvisation in der Musik–eine entwicklungsgeschichtliche und psychologiche Untersuchung* [Musical improvisation-a study of its developmental history and psychology]. Zürich: Rhein-Verlag.

Folkestad, G. (1996). *Computer based creative music making. Young people's music in the digital age*. Göteborg Acta Universitatis Gothoburgensis.

Foucault, M. (2002). *Vetandets arkeologi* [The archaeology of knowledge]. Lund: Arkiv Förlag.

de Grigny, N. (1967). *Livre d´orgue* [Organ book]. Mainz: Schott.

Hakim, N. (2001). *Guide pratique d´improvisation* [A practical guide to improvisation]. Waltham Abbey: United Music Publishers Ltd.

Hickey, M. (2002). Creativity research in music, visual art, theatre, and dance. In R. Colwell and C. Richardson (Eds.) *The new handbook of research on music teaching and learning*. New York: Oxford University Press, pp. 398–415.

Higginbottom, E. (1998). The French classical organ school. In N. Thistlethwaite & G. Webber (Eds.), *The Cambridge companion to the organ*. Cambridge: Cambridge University Press, pp. 176–89.

Hultberg, C. (2000). *The printed score as a mediator of musical meaning*. Malmö: Malmö Academy of Music.

Hultberg, C. (2005). Practitioners and researchers in cooperation—method development for qualitative practice-related studies. *Music Education Research*, 7(2), 211–24.

Johansson, K. (2008). *Organ improvisation–activity, action and rhetorical practice*. Malmö: Malmö Academy of Music.

Juslin, P. (2001). Communicating emotion in music performance. In P. Juslin & J. Sloboda (Eds.), *Music and emotion*. Oxford: Oxford University Press, pp. 309–38.

Jutten, O. (1999). *L'enseignement de l'improvisation à la classe d'orgue du Conservatoire de Paris, 1819–1986, d'après la thèmatique de concours et* [The teaching of improvisation in the organ class at the Paris Conservatoire, 1819–1986, with specific reference to the themes set for examinations]. Paris: Université de Sorbonne.

Keller, H. (1939). *Schule der Choral-Improvisation für Orgel (mit 121 Notenbeispielen)* [Hymn improvisation for the organ]. Leipzig: Peters.

Kruger, T. (1998). *Teacher practice, pedagogical discourse and the construction of knowledge. Two case studies of teachers at work*. Bergen: Bergen University.

Landgren, J. (1997). *Music–moment–message: interpretive, improvisation, and ideological aspects of Petr Eben's organ works*. Gothenburg: Acta Universitatis Gothenburgensis.

Langlais, J. (1957). *Office pour la Sainte Trinité* [Organ pieces for the mass]. Leutkirch: Editions Pro Organo.

Lemmens, J.-N. (1920). *Ecole d'orgue* [Organ school]. Paris: Durand & Fils.

Love, A.C. (2003). *Musical improvisation, Heidegger, and the liturgy. A journey to the heart of hope*. Lampeter: The Edwin Meller Press.

Messiaen, O. (1951). *Livre d'orgue* [Organ book]. Paris: Leduc.

Moran, S. & John-Steiner, V. (2003). Creativity in the making: Vygotsky's contemporary contribution to the dialectic of creativity & development. In R.K. Sawyer (Ed.), *Creativity and development*. Oxford: Oxford University Press, pp. 61–90.

Nutting, R. (1989). A method of elementary improvisation for church organists. *Dissertation Abstracts International*, 50(2), 381A.

Overduin, J. (1998). *Improvisation for organists*. New York and Oxford: Oxford University Press.

Porter, W. (2006). Johann Arte prattica & poëtica: A Window into German Improvisational Practice. In *Orphei Organi Antiqui: Essays in honor of Harald Vogel*. Washington, WA: Westfield.

Pressing, J. (1988). Improvisation: methods and models. In J. Sloboda (Ed.) *Generative processes in music: The psychology of performance, improvisation and composition*. Oxford: Clarendon Press, pp. 129–78.

Rogoff, B. (2003). *The cultural nature of human development*. Oxford: Oxford University Press.

Ruiter-Feenstra, P. (2006). *Bach and improvisation*. Göteborg: GoArt Publications.

Silbiger, A. (2003). *Keyboard music before 1700*. London: Routledge.

Snyder, K.J. (Ed.). (2002). *The organ as a mirror of its time. North European reflections, 1610–2000*. Oxford: Oxford University Press.

Snyder, K.J. (2007). *Dietrich Buxtehude. Organist in Lübeck*. Rochester, NY: University of Rochester Press.

Tandberg, S.-E. (2008). *Imagination, form, movement and sound. Studies in musical improvisation*. Gothenburg: The Academy of Music and Drama.

Tarling, J. (2004). *The weapons of rhetoric. A guide for musicians and audiences*. St Albans: Corda Music Publications.

Tournemire, C. (1936). *Précis d'exécution, de registration et d'improvisation à l'Orgue* [Performance, registration and improvisation at the organ]. Paris: Editions Max Eschig.

Wells, G. (1999). *Dialogic inquiry. Towards a sociocultural practice and theory of education*. Cambridge: Cambridge University Press.

Willstedt, T. (1996). *Orgelimprovisation* [Organ improvisation]. Trelleborg: Trumph.

Wilson-Dickson, A. (1996). *Musik i kristen tradition* [Music in Christian tradition]. Stockholm: Verbum.

Vygotsky, L. (1978). *Mind in society*. Cambridge, MA: Harvard University Press.

Vygotsky, L. (2004). Imagination and creativity in childhood. *Journal of Russian and East European Psychology*, **42**(1), 7–97.

Chapter 15

Communication, collaboration, and creativity: How musicians negotiate a collective 'sound'

Karen Littleton and Neil Mercer

15.1 Introduction

Studies of collective rehearsal for musical performance are relatively scarce, reflecting both the paucity of interest within music education research in *creative* rather than *reproductive* musical activities and the enduring emphasis on composition as a solitary rather than a collective, community-based process (Young, 2008). Furthermore, as Sawyer and DeZutter (2009) have noted, even though there has been a wave of research that has recognized how creativity is embedded in social groups (e.g. Sawyer, 2006) and how creative products emerge from collaboration, we still have very little understanding of the processes whereby creative products emerge from groups:

> The most substantial studies of group creativity have been social psychological studies of brainstorming groups . . . but these studies have not analysed the interactional processes that occur within groups. This failure to analyse collaborative processes is a significant lacuna in creativity research because a wide range of empirical studies has revealed that significant creations are almost always the result of complex collaborations.

> (Sawyer & DeZutter, 2009: p. 81.)

One of our aims in this chapter is therefore to underscore the case that we should be studying these processes—both to advance our understanding of the nature of collaborative music-making and 'imagining' and collaborative creativity more generally.

A second aim is to suggest the suitability of sociocultural theory and discourse analysis as the basis for making such analyses, with the emphasis on the shared historical knowledge of communities (in this case, of musical genres and practices) and the importance of language and other communicative tools for pursuing and achieving common goals. To this end, in this chapter we will exemplify how sociocultural discourse analysis can shed light on: 1) the processes by which musicians negotiate musical common knowledge; 2) the significance of disputes and conflicts in the pursuit of common goals; 3) how influences are fused and connected to produce a distinctive and unique 'sound'; and 4) how language is used in conjunction with other modes to produce a persuasive 'discourse' in joint preparation for musical performance.

We will draw on audio-recorded material and field notes from observational studies of a series of rehearsals by three bands of musicians. All three bands were similar in that they were working to create new, distinctive performance repertoires. That is, they were not aiming to perform accurate representations of established musical arrangements, as would a classical ensemble or a popular 'covers' band. Rather they all wanted to offer a distinctive 'sound' in their performances (even if performing compositions created by others). The musical genres within which they were working also offered some opportunity for improvisation and renegotiation of arrangements through the rehearsal process. Moreover, all three were concerned with creating music which was not just instrumental, but was (at least in part) the accompaniment to a vocal performance. One is a rock band consisting of five members, four male and one female aged about 15 years (whose activities are discussed in more detail in Miell & Littleton, 2008). The second is a group of three male adult musicians (average age about 45) preparing to accompany the staging of a musical play. The third is a band of four members, three male and one female (average age about 52), who play country/roots music. Members of the first band were amateurs, while those of the two other bands were semi-professional. Transcripts from these case studies were specifically selected to explore the processes implicated in collaborative, creative music-making. Names in all transcripts are pseudonyms, and some other small details have been changed to ensure anonymity.

15.2 **Sociocultural research and discourse analysis**

The work being reported is framed within the sociocultural tradition (which sees creative processes as dynamic, fundamentally social, and necessarily collective and collaborative). The term 'sociocultural' has become associated with research which draws explicitly on the developmental psychology of Lev Vygotsky (1978; see also Wertsch, 1985a, b; Daniels, 2001). It represents an approach in which language is considered a 'cultural tool' implicated in the construction of understanding and the negotiation of meaning. Sociocultural research is not a unified field, but those within it recognize that the nature of human activity is that knowledge is shared and people jointly construct understandings of shared experience. Communicative events are shaped by cultural and historical factors, and thinking, learning, and development cannot be understood without taking account of the intrinsically social and communicative nature of human life. From a sociocultural perspective, then, humans are seen as creatures who have a unique capacity for communication and whose lives are normally led within groups, communities, and societies based on shared 'ways with words' ways of thinking, social practices, and tools for getting things done.

Many human activities involve not just the sharing of information and the coordination of social interaction, but also a joint, dynamic engagement with ideas amongst partners. When working together, we do not only interact, we 'interthink' (Mercer, 2000; Mercer & Littleton, 2007). Some sociocultural researchers have investigated how, in particular encounters or through a series of related encounters, two or more people use language to combine their intellectual resources in the pursuit of a common task. Good examples would include Middleton and Edwards' (1990) study of collective remembering, Elbers' (1994) research on children's play, and that of O'Connor and Michaels (1996) on the orchestration of classroom group discussions.

All conversations are, to varying extents, founded on the establishment of a base of common knowledge and necessarily involve the creation of more shared understanding. Conversational partners use language (and other modes of meaning-making) to travel together from the past into the future, mutually transforming the current state of their understanding of the topic(s) of their conversation. To do so, they need to build a contextual foundation for the progress of their talk; talk is also the prime means for building that contextual foundation. Gee and Green (1998) refer to this aspect of language use as 'reflexivity'. If one is interested in how talk is used to enable joint activity, one must be concerned with the ways that shared knowledge is both invoked and created in dialogue. It also requires a concern for how knowledge is developed as a joint resource over time—for example, through a series of rehearsals, or even through the whole 'life' of a performing band. For reasons of space, however, we are not able to pursue this temporal aspect of the nature of joint musical performance here.

Nevertheless, drawing on the methods of sociocultural discourse analysis (see Mercer, 2004 and Mercer & Littleton, 2007), and informed by multimodal analysis (Kress, 2010) we will offer an

Table 15.1 Talk and music as modes of communication for joint activity

Mode	Talk	Music
Affordances	Explicit presentation of ideas	Expression of tonal and temporal relations
	Flexible adaptability to specific contexts and to shared, specialized purposes of a community	Flexible adaptability to specific contexts (such as those of specific ensembles) and to shared, culturally-based aesthetic norms
Special functions (in band rehearsal settings)	Management of social relations	Demonstration of proposed musical features
	Invocation of past shared experiences	
	Direct instruction by one participant to others	Testing of musical ideas in practice
		Demonstration of problematic aspects and possible solutions
	Presentation of plans and arguments for change	
		Demonstrations of 'correct' performance by one participant to another
	Rhetorical efforts to pursue individual goals	
	Accountability for performance	

analysis of recordings of the talk and other forms of interaction in rehearsal sessions. This is a methodology we have developed through studies of the joint construction of 'common knowledge' in classrooms and similar settings (Edwards & Mercer, 1987; Mercer & Littleton, 2007). 'Sociocultural' discourse analysis differs from 'linguistic' discourse analysis in being less concerned with the organizational structure of spoken language, and more with its content, function, and the ways shared understanding is developed, in social context, over time. As with ethnography and conversation analysis, reports of such research are usually illustrated by selected extracts of transcribed talk, to which the analyst provides a commentary.

Of course, if we are to understand and characterize collaborative creativity in the context of musical practice, we need to examine not only the talk amongst band members but also the ways that other non-verbal means and cultural tools (including playing music) are used to constitute and sustain such activity. Language is part of a multimodal toolkit for thinking collectively, which is shaped by the practices of communities. The discourses of particular domains or communities of practice have distinctive forms, which have to be learned by novices. The playing of music may not only be the end-product of rehearsal, but also a mode of communication amongst band members which enables and sustains the rehearsal process. Human communication is commonly multimodal, so that conversation often involves the use of gestures, changes in voice pitch, the use of artefacts, and so on as well as word meanings. As Kress (2010) explains, different modes have *inherent affordances* and acquire (through historical shaping) *special functions*. Meanings in any mode are interwoven (in use) with those of others to produce a more global meaning. Modes are thus *networks of interrelated options for making signs*. We offer a brief comparison of the modes of spoken language and music in Table 15.1, with some illustrative affordances and functions of each (the lists are not claimed to be comprehensive). We will discuss aspects this in relation to our examples below.

15.3 **Analysis**

The aim of our analysis has been to reveal the communicative processes which enable band rehearsals to take place and achieve the desired outcomes. We will use selected transcripts of talk recorded in rehearsals (supplemented by observational notes) to illustrate our findings.

Our analyses revealed that the band members we studied rehearsing were highly engaged, repeatedly playing, replaying, and reworking songs, both new and old, in an attempt to reach collectively agreed versions and interpretations—which constitute a form of shared musical common knowledge. Such agreement was achieved through a complex transactional process in which the band members would continually evaluate their work, voicing their opinions on how particular pieces were working—offering ideas for improvement, modification, and change as they played through pieces or reworked specific phrases. Members would frequently build musically on each others' ideas, playing through and exploring alternative versions and subtle variations. But they also needed to resolve differences of view, in order to reach a consensus to underpin their joint performance. This can be seen in Extract 1 'Not sure about the E', which comes from a rehearsal session of the band preparing to accompany a musical play. At the point it begins, the band members Norm, Peter, and Kieran are reviewing a particular musical episode which would be played while characters interacted, at times without speaking or singing, during a scene which included much on-stage movement. Norm plays guitar, Peter is on keyboards, and Kieran is on bass. (There were other members of this ensemble, but they were not involved in this particular episode.) Part of the musical 'problem' they face is that the piece of music they are rehearsing has to function as an ambient accompaniment to an episode of dramatic interaction which has proved (in whole-cast rehearsals) to have an uncertain length. Their immediate concerns are how to segue from one section of the play to the next, and how to make sure the music can be sustained flexibly in conjunction with the dramatic action. The band therefore needs a contingency plan for how to respond to the circumstances flexibly. The ambient piece also has to provide a musical device for moving from the key of one song (G, sung before the piece) to the next (A, sung after the piece). This musical episode had evolved, rather than being first formally written, in the course of the play rehearsals. Aspects of it were thus still open to negotiation. At this point, it had been proposed that a transition through the chord of E major would help make the key shift, during the ambient phase: and it is this proposal which is in dispute in Extract 1.

15.3.1 Extract 1: Not sure about the E

Norm: We put the E in, it makes it slightly odd [sounding worried].
Peter: We've got to think in terms of words are concerned we only use, do that once at a time.
Norm: That's true.
Kieran: Yeh.
Peter: And then the, the long, the long A minors afterwards will simply be . . .
Norm: Yeh.
Kieran: Yeh, we can actually keep those cycling round as many times as we need to.
Norm: I'm not sure about the E [still sounds unconvinced].
Kieran: Right, OK.
Peter: I like it.
Norm: Yeh but except it's, because then you've got [demonstrates on guitar].
Peter: Yeh but hang on, I'm using G instead of E minor.
Norm: Yeh Yeh, all right. Perhaps it works.
Kieran: Let's try that, it goes straight to the F [they try it].
Kieran: Yeh I think it actually works on the same number of bars because we're holding the F and G twice as long.
Norm: Yeh.
Peter: That's right.

We see Norm first expressing his concern about a choice of chord—'E major' within the music. His reasons appear to be aesthetic—he doesn't like how it sounds in relation to the chords which precede or succeed it. His partners seem less concerned, with Peter seeming to argue for the relative unimportance of the issue in the context of the piece as a whole. Kieran joins in, but seems more concerned with the other issue of maintaining the music for a suitable time, rather than the problem chord. Norm and Peter then express strongly different views about the 'E'. Norm then supports his concerns with a musical demonstration of how he thinks the problem chord will sound in context. That is, Norm uses the music *rhetorically*, as an additional mode to support his spoken argument. He is thus using an affordance of musical demonstration as a mode of communication, to present a multimodal argument. This leads Peter to realize he had not been using the same chord as Norm to precede the 'E' ('G major' rather than 'E minor', each of which if played before E major creates a very different effect). Kieran suggests they try it, which they do; and as a result a happy consensus is achieved. As can be seen, the band often discussed, gave reasons for, and justified their particular preferences (in Norm's case, by using more than one communicative mode). However, sometimes it was the collective appeal of the sound that was critical, with relatively little explicit verbal appraisal accompanying the mutual recognition that something sounds 'right'. Music was thus not only the intended outcome of joint activity, but also a vital medium (used in conjunction with language to generate persuasive communications) through which the interdependent processes implicated in interpretation were constituted and negotiated. As we will go on to explain, our analyses suggest that this process of negotiating (using the modes of language, music and gesture) and establishing collectively agreed versions—shared musical common knowledge and understanding—could be a highly charged and deeply meaningful process for the band members. This is because the construction and negotiation of an agreed interpretation of a piece within their repertoire was inextricably interwoven with the negotiation of a distinctive band sound—a musical identity.

The next sequence, 'A hard fill', comes from a rehearsal of the country/roots band. Ivan is the main singer, and on guitar; Carl is also on guitar; Mac is on fiddle; Paula is on accordion; and Tom is on bass. As the extract begins, they have just been practising a song in which the accordion has to come in with a distinctive and precise run of notes (what is often called a 'fill' or 'riff') at a certain point in each verse.

15.3.2 **Extract 2: A hard fill**

[A song ends and people begin to talk.]
Mac: [to Paula] It's a hard bloody fill for you to do, that, isn't it?
I mean I wonder whether we . . .
Ivan: [interrupts] But it sounds . . .
Carl: [interrupts] When if works it's great.
Mac: I mean I would simplify it.
Tom: Yeah.
Mac: [to Paula] I mean I think we're asking an awful lot of you to do that [laughs] and I wonder if we shouldn't just do something simpler. You know, um.
Ivan: Well, for the first time out, trying in front of an audience, do something simple.
Mac: Yeah. Anyway, it's only an idea.
Paula: At the Canyon [referring to a music venue].
Ivan: . . . and then as we rehearse it more and more and get into it we increase the complexity . . .
Mac: I don't know what though, that's the point.
Ivan: . . . as you feel more comfortable.
Paula: It's only two weeks. What I need is a reminder. I'd forgotten about that one. Since I looked at it I haven't . . .
Ivan: Well how do you feel about it? Can you fit it in?
Paula: Um, I feel [long pause].

Mac: It's a tricky one, isn't it? To get it really sharp.

Paula: It's showing cos I haven't practised. This should ease up by the end of next week, I've got a, I've got a [inaudible].

Mac: [sings as plays notes of fill] doo doo doo doooh. How about at the end of it, right, do the whole thing, slowly.

Paula: [plays original version of fill].

Mac: You know [plays just some of the notes] If you could just do that.

Paula: If that fits in better [plays same notes as simplified version of fill].

Mac: [to whole band] Do it.

[Band plays whole section of song]

Carl: Hmm, it's [inaudible] [Some people still playing].

Paula: It's, it's the rhythm of doing it, to be honest.

Mac: I mean, just do something much simpler. I just really feel it's too hard to fit it in really sharply. I mean for me on the fiddle that is a doddle [plays it] cos it's all open strings, and you know.

Paula: What's wrong, am I getting the rhythm wrong?

Mac: No. Sometimes. It's just sometimes it sounds like its slowing us down slightly when, you know, you know it doesn't seem like its kind of just keeping up. And . . .

Paula: To be honest, I haven't tried it since last week and therefore . . .

Ivan: [interrupts] Could it just be three notes? [Sings an arpeggio, D, B, F].

Mac: I was just thinking that [plays] I mean the other, the simple thing to do could be to kind of, uh, the chords, the thirds [plays a sequence of pairs of notes which is less complex than the 'fill' in question]. You know.

[This issue is not resolved, and the band move on to rehearse another tune.]

In this extract we see a delicate issue being raised and discussed, of a type which is not uncommon in band rehearsals. It is whether, in the view one of the performers, another performer is playing their part in a way which is satisfactory. We see Mac raising the issue concerning one 'fill' with Paula, and then pursuing it somewhat relentlessly through this conversational extract. We might note that the essence of his position is that a less complex, 'simpler' series of notes might fill the slot in the arrangement better. Mac uses the terms 'simple/simpler/simplify' to repeatedly make this point. Ivan picks this up and uses 'simple' once, though Paula never does, though she does admit that the rhythm of the fill is posing problems. Her position, it seems, is that she just needs more practice with the arrangement as it is. As in Extract 1, musical demonstration is used by band members in a rhetorical way to support a multimodal argument. In this case, however, the argument is not carried by the demonstrations and the issue is not resolved. Nevertheless, this episode illustrates well the dynamic, multimodal, dialogical processes whereby issues of joint performance can be raised and pursued by members of an ensemble.

As we have already noted above, analysis of the interactions between band members often reveals that throughout their rehearsal time they are continually engaged in sustained joint evaluation and appraisal of their musical output and songs. Whilst such interactions between the band members are normally oriented towards achieving agreement and consensus concerning the 'sound' of particular songs, they may nevertheless be highly emotive and confrontational, with particular individuals sometimes being singled out for criticism. We can see a rather extreme example of this in Extract 3 below, from a rehearsal of the rock band. The evaluative language used in their rehearsals was frequently very direct and blunt, involving fierce critical commentary and frank assessment of the resultant 'vibe' or sound. Members sometimes engaged in what Storey and Joubert (2004: p. 46) have called 'lethal confrontations' in which they were intensely critical of each other's playing and creative contributions.

This confrontational dynamic can be seen in Extract 3, which comes from a rehearsal of the rock band. The band is working through a new piece and Dan is defending himself against Jack's accusatory comments that he is 'playing the wrong notes' and 'starting off on the wrong notes'.

15.3.3 Extract 3: Wrong notes

Dan: Did you say I was playing the wrong notes?

Jack: Well yeah, maybe it just didn't sound right.

Leah: Play it through just the two of you.

Jack: Let's just play it. . .

Dan: I'm sure I was playing what I was playing before. . .

Jack: . . . and I'll tell you if it sounds right.

Dan: No it's not the tuning, it must be the notes but I was playing what I was playing before. . .

Jack: . . . Well you can't have been man . . .

Dan: . . . Well I am . . .

Jack: . . . We would have heard man . . .

Dan: . . . I swear, I swear.

Jack: You start off with a wrong note

Dan: I'm not!

Jack: That's fucking . . . well it doesn't sound right does it!

Dan: Well that's what I was playing before.

Jack: Well we've got to do something new.

Dan: Play it right the way through.

Jack: It sounds shit man.

[The band try the same song again from beginning.]

What is notable is that despite the intensity, the collaboration between the band members did not break down in these moments of vehement intensity. Rather, these conflicts were the very sites or moments within which creative 'breakthroughs' seemed to happen, or which fuelled subsequent useful rounds of re-working and re-playing as was the case here. Such 'breakthrough moments' in their collaborative creativity seemed to arise after quite lengthy periods of musical experimentation—where alternative versions were tried repeatedly—interspersed by intense, often emotive, phases of debate and evaluation. That said, the collective sense of something 'working' was often hard won and could at times be fragile, becoming unevenly felt by the collaborators.

As noted earlier, all three of the bands studied were, to varying extents, working in an improvisational manner, rather than seeking to achieve canonical performances as is the case within the classical tradition (MacDonald, Hargreaves, & Miell, 2004). But the rock band, in particular, worked as 'freestylers' (Kjeldgaard, 2006) not looking for any one existing style to 'fit in to' but instead fusing, switching, and making connections between established musical genres, experimenting with and borrowing from them in order to forge and define their own distinctive sound (and musical identity) through negotiating their creative conflicts and tensions. This notion of a distinctive group vibe or sound was a crucial mediator of the groups' collaborative work and one that was explicitly discussed, as in Extract 4 below.

15.3.4 Extract 4: Bit too funky

Jack: That bit's just not sounding right . . . It's sounding a bit too, like, I don't know a bit too funky almost, in a way.

Matt: I don't know, it changes the vibe a bit.

Jack: Changes?

Matt: Just the mood of the band.

Jack: I know but that's not necessarily a good thing.

Matt: Yeah I know.

This musical (identity) work was at least partly resourced by their repeated experimentation and their acknowledgement of versions of a song or particular musical motifs as being provisional 'musical works in progress'—works that simultaneously embody the progress made and provide the focus for progressive and ongoing work as collaborators negotiate their desired sound. In Extract 4, sounds that change the vibe and the mood of the band are rejected as 'not right', even thought they might have some merit. This claiming of a distinctive sound was very important to this band. They were keen to acknowledge the key influences on their work, recognizing that their sound embodies a fusion of influences, but being careful not to appear derivative, as illustrated by Extract 5.

15.3.5 Extract 5: Refreshingly different

> Jack: If you take completely different bands like we do and you amalgamate something . . . then it completely changes it. So if I've got the bare bones of a song and let's say it's in a certain style like in the style of the band called Swans. Then we'll bring it and Dan will bring a certain influence like some sort of post-rock thing which he has been doing and Matt will bring a heavy kind of beat and Leah will bring sort of quirky weird things . . . and everything comes together.
> Matt: It's hard to label the sort of music. I mean I don't know, I haven't heard any bands that sound like us.
> Dan: It's refreshingly different I would say.

15.4 Discussion

We suggest that more needs to be understood about the interactional processes of creative collaboration, in music and other artistic spheres of activity. We also suggest that the potential of sociocultural theory and discourse analysis as a basis for the analyses of joint creative activity could usefully be explored further. The analytic work presented here has show how such collective creative activity is predicated on the shared historical knowledge of communities (in this case, of musical genres and practices) and the use of language as a cultural and psychological tool which is used with other communicative tools for pursuing and achieving both personal agendas and common goals. We have also seen how the processes of musical interpretation and musical identity construction are inextricably interwoven and mutually constitutive. What is lacking in our presentation here is an adequate recognition of how the cognitive and social resources for 'rehearsing together' are accumulated and refined over time through the very nature of the spiral of repeated rehearsal and performance, within which some process of reflective review will normally also take place. The cultural bases for musical practice, not only for professional musicians but for the amateurs and semi-professionals described here, are complex and important for understanding the processes involved. (See for example Finnegan's (2007) classic anthropological study of non-professional musicians in the same English town as two of the bands which feature in our study.) But if at least part of the nature of musical activity is accurately represented by our analysis, then it implies that such creative collaborations are of some significance and consequence to musicians, both established and aspiring. This in turn implies that the importance of such collaborative activity, and the communication skills which achieve it, need to be recognized not only in research on music making but also in music education.

References

Daniels, H. (2001). *Vygotsky and Pedagogy.* London: Routledge/Falmer.

Edwards, D. & Mercer, N. (1987). *Common knowledge: The development of understanding in the classroom.* London: Methuen/Routledge.

Elbers, E. (1994). Sociogenesis and children's pretend play: A variation on Vygotskian themes. In W. de Graaf & R. Maier (Eds.) *Sociogenesis re-examined.* New York: Springer, pp. 219–41.

Finnegan, R. (2007). *The hidden musicians: Music making in an English town.* Lebanon, NH: Weslyan University Press.

Gee, J.P. & Green, J. (1998). Discourse analysis, learning and social practice: A methodological study. *Review of Research in Education*, **23**, 119–69.

Kjeldgaard, D. (2006). The meaning of style? Style reflexivity among Danish high school youths. CD-ROM proceedings of *Child and Teen Consumption Conference*. Copenhagen: Copenhagen Business School.

Kress, G. (2010). *Multimodality: A social semiotic approach to contemporary communication*. London: Routledge.

MacDonald, R., Hargreaves, D.J. & Miell, D. (Eds.) (2002). *Musical identities*. Oxford: Oxford University Press.

Mercer, N. (2000). *Words and minds: How we use language to think together*. London: Routledge.

Mercer, N. (2004). Sociocultural discourse analysis: Analysing classroom talk as a social mode of thinking, *Journal of Applied Linguistics*, **1**(2), 137–68.

Mercer, N. & Littleton, K. (2007). *Dialogue and the development of children's thinking: A sociocultural approach*. London: Routledge.

Middleton, D. & Edwards, D. (1990). Conversational remembering: A social psychological approach. In D. Middleton & D. Edwards (Eds.) *Collective remembering*. London: Sage, pp. 23–45.

Miell, D. & Littleton, K. (2008). Musical collaboration outside school: processes of negotiation in band rehearsals. *International Journal of Educational Research*, **47**(1), 41–9.

O'Connor, C. & Michaels, S. (1996). Shifting participant frameworks: Orchestrating thinking practices in group discussion. In D. Hicks (Ed.) *Discourse, learning and schooling*. Cambridge: Cambridge University Press, pp. 63–103.

Sawyer, K. (2006). *Explaining creativity*. Oxford: Oxford University Press.

Sawyer, K. & DeZutter, S. (2009). Distributed creativity: How collective creations emerge from collaboration. *Psychology of Aesthetics, Creativity and the Arts*, **3**(2), 81–92.

Storey, H. & Joubert, M.M. (2004). The emotional dance of creative collaboration. In D. Miell & K. Littleton (Eds.) *Collaborative creativity: Contemporary perspectives*. London: Free Association Books, pp. 40–51.

Vygotsky, L.S. (1978). *Mind in society*. Cambridge MA: Harvard University Press.

Wertsch, J.V. (Ed.) (1985a). *Culture, communication and cognition: Vygotskian perspectives*. Cambridge: Cambridge University Press.

Wertsch, J.V. (1985b). Adult-child interaction as a source of self-regulation in children. In S.R. Yussen (Ed.) *The growth of reflection in children*. Orlando, FL: Academic Press, pp. 69–97.

Young, S. (2008). Collaboration between 3- and 4-year-olds in self-initiated play on instruments. *International Journal of Educational Research*, **47**, 3–10.

Chapter 16

Improvisation as a creative process within contemporary music

Raymond MacDonald, Graeme Wilson, and Dorothy Miell

> Improvisation enjoys the curious distinction of being the most widely practised of all musical activities and the least acknowledged and understood.
> *(Bailey, 1992 p. ix)*

Derek Bailey's now well-known claim undoubtedly highlights one of the fundamental paradoxes of improvised music. It is a universal and diverse form of musical expression, yet it retains a shadowy presence within the study of music from both a research and a performance perspective. This chapter focuses on the importance of improvisation as a particular site for creativity in music. We explore contemporary notions of improvisation in a broader than usual context (i.e. looking not just at jazz), draw out some important aspects of improvisation for furthering our understanding of musical creativity generally, and suggest that improvisation affords the opportunity to challenge musical and cultural hegemonies and develop new ways of collaborating and thinking creatively in music.

16.1 What is improvisation?

While there is no generally accepted single definition of improvisation, most accounts highlight the spontaneously generated nature of the musical material and the real-time negotiation of unfolding musical interactions (Nettl & Russell, 1998; Kenny & Gellrich, 2002; Berkowitz, 2010). It is perhaps most commonly discussed in relation to jazz, wherein musicians will deliver unrehearsed lines and rhythms and respond to each other's spontaneous contributions while (usually) maintaining a common tempo through repetitions of a harmonic framework (Sawyer, 1992). Successful jazz improvisation is held to depend on known social practices and a context of shared awareness among musicians with experiences in common (Sharron, 1985; Bastien & Hostager, 1988; Becker, 2000; MacDonald & Wilson, 2005; Wilson & MacDonald, 2005). Musicians must form expectations about what other players may do in any emergent musical situation, and be familiar with a wide repertory of tunes which can form the basis for elaborating new material.

It is often argued that expected musical and social norms should be adhered to in order for the improvisation to be viewed as 'authentic' jazz (Berliner, 2002) and there is considerable debate regarding what can be considered 'jazz music'. It may take years of study and practice to assimilate or improvise in the styles of jazz 'greats' such as Charlie Parker, John Coltrane, or Miles Davis. However, the view that this is an essential prerequisite to any successful jazz improvisation can be considered a musical hegemony that may inhibit people from engaging and experimenting with this way of making music (MacDonald & Wilson, 2006). This issue also has economic and social, as well as aesthetic, implications for those seeking to practise as jazz musicians since their livelihoods can depend upon working within the parameters of what is considered 'authentic' jazz (Fischlin & Heble, 2004).

However, improvisation takes place within an enormous range of musical contexts, not just jazz, and contemporary approaches to improvisation are diverse and wide-ranging. Examples can be found in contexts utilizing specialist computer technology such as that pioneered by groups like Evan Parker's Electroacoustic Ensemble, or minimalist improvisations sometimes termed 'lowercase', performed by Toshimara Nakamura or Mark Wastell. In such music, improvisations can take the form of incremental manipulations of an ongoing texture of non-referential sound (e.g. in the work of Keith Rowe), scattered and unpredictable interruptions of silence, or musicians responding to live electronically generated alterations of what they have just played. London-based pioneers of improvisation AMM have utilized many of these techniques in their recordings and performances for over 40 years (Prevost, 1995). Alternatively, musicians may seek out unfamiliar instruments or apparatus: Ornette Coleman playing violin is a good example of this approach. In this instance, Coleman was not only attempting to discover new elements in his own music-making by playing an instrument with which he was relatively unfamiliar, but in selecting the violin he was also challenging the hegemonic status of the violin as a signifier of music-making regulated and authorized by establishment powers (Wilson, 1994).

Deliberately avoiding conventional technique (e.g. Han Bennink screaming through a snare drum or Fred Frith rubbing the guitar body) can also be a means of generating original sounds. Loud, dissonant music using, for example, electronic feedback or randomly generated electronic signals with no recognizable reference to a shared tempo or harmonic structure may be argued not to be 'jazz' but nevertheless represents authentic improvisation (Hegarty, 2007). This approach, sometimes termed 'noise music', has roots stretching back to the work of Luigi Russolo at the beginning of the 20th century and influential contemporary artists such as Merzbow, Borbetomagus, and Nurse with Wound continue to explore improvisation within a noise music context. Other noise based improvisation developed out of rock, punk, and grunge traditions (e.g. Sonic Youth or Faust). A number of large ensembles such as the Glasgow Improvisers Orchestra or the London Improvisers Orchestra are committed to exploring innovative approaches to large ensemble improvisation including, for example, graphic scores, conduction techniques, conventional and non-conventional notation, musical interpretations of text and visual stimuli, etc.

While it is beyond the scope of this chapter to offer a full cross-cultural summary of improvisational practices, there are examples of improvisation taking place in many different cultural contexts, e.g. Javanese gamelan (Becker, 1980; Brinner, 2007), Indian and Iranian music (Nooshin & Widdess, 2006), traditional Chinese and Japanese music (Prevost, 1995), and in many other cross-cultural and intercultural situations. The observation that improvisation takes place in different contexts and in different cultures in no way suggests that, as a universal process, it functions in the same way across these situations. We suggest that understandings of 'authenticity' in improvisation are dependent on context, and that improvisation is present in many different forms of music, and is practised and experienced in ways shaped by these musical and cultural contexts.

While jazz improvisation is a construct built round the idea of a genre, genres can themselves be seen as somewhat fluid constructions. For instance, practising rock, jazz, and classical music improvisers asked to complete a questionnaire developed from the qualitative accounts of expert improvisers (The Improvisation Processes Questionnaire, Biasutti & Frezza, 2009), showed no significant differences across these different genres in scores representing key cognitive processes of their improvisation (such as anticipation, emotive communication, flow, feedback, and use of repertoire). Within the current musical landscape, genre distinctions are becoming increasingly ambiguous. Indeed, Lewis (2007) states that we are entering a period of post-genre music-making in which old genre distinctions become much more difficult to delineate.

Improvised music is central to this change since improvisation can be viewed not as a genre of music itself, or even a musical practice that defines certain genres, but rather as a process that can straddle all genres. As Bailey (1992) has claimed, it is non-idiomatic, and can be seen as a creative process that can exist without reference to any genre of music-making. The possibility of truly non-idiomatic improvisation remains a contentious issue and musicians such as Evan Parker have argued that, for any individual, all previous musical experience influences spontaneous music-making (Parker, 1992, 2007). Also, there is considerable discussion around the extent to which 'free' improvisations are ever 'free' in the sense that all improvisers must adhere to certain context-dependent expectations. However, recent decades have seen a blossoming of theories and texts around the wider cultural implications of different types of improvisational practices which move beyond purely musicological concerns, and help situate these debates within different yet related academic discourses. Some examples of these theories and texts are given below.

The writings of Prevost (1995), Lewis (2000), Oliveros (2005), and Stevens (2007) situate contemporary improvisational practices beyond jazz and within wider cultural, educational, and political contexts, viewing improvisation as a creative process that can facilitate group communication and personal growth. Both Stevens and Prevost describe improvisation as a process that can facilitate creative development and innovative collaboration through an egalitarian view of improvisational practices which prioritize freedom of expression above genre-based expectations of musical structure. Their approach can be viewed as a reaction to the more rule-based approach of mainstream jazz music, or other musics that have strict rules concerning what is permitted in terms of improvisation (e.g. classical Indian music). Borgo (2005) offers a new conceptual framework for understanding and analysing improvisation. Using theories from cultural and cognitive studies as well as from mainstream scientific approaches such as chaos theory, cybernetics, evolutionary theory, systems theory and cognitive science, he focuses on the dynamic moment-to-moment organic development of improvisations. Lewis' extensive writings highlight the psychological and social processes at the heart of improvisation and contextualize it within cultural and political contexts as a defining artistic movement of 20th century American culture (Lewis, 2007).

Oliveros (2005) has developed a unique approach to improvisation that prioritizes listening or what she terms *deep listening* as a primary activity within improvisation. Chapters 27 and 14 within this volume also underline the importance of a broad conception of improvisation. In particular, Wigram discusses the potential of clinical improvisation to facilitate positive therapeutic effects, while Johansson investigates improvisation within the context of classical organ performances. The crucial point emerging from this expanding and diverse field of theory is that improvisation is now conceptualized not only within a vast array of musical practices well beyond the realm of the jazz tradition, but also as a key driving force in the development of arts and culture in the modern and postmodern eras. As well as highlighting the universality of improvisation, these conceptual frameworks indicate the potential for improvisation to have beneficial effects upon, for example, health and well-being (Wigram, 2007), education (Hickey, 2009), and social cohesion (Lewis, 2008), and in particular as a means for achieving creativity (MacDonald, 2009).

16.2 **Educational issues**

The previous section has highlighted ways in which improvisation can be defined broadly. In this section we will use this broad definition of improvisation to demonstrate some educational opportunities in improvisation as a means of introducing creative musical practices to children and novices. A child's first experience of music is improvisatory. Think of how a young child first explores a piano or guitar: investigating the surface of the instrument, plucking strings, pushing keys, experiencing the sensual pleasure of sound and texture, and revelling in the newness of these explorations. Here, improvisation is an exploratory creative urge or a quest for newness and is uninhibited by notions of 'correct' or 'incorrect' musical practice and conventional judgements of aesthetic beauty. The improviser in this instance is not concerned with supposedly objective external judgements of quality; rather, the improvisation can be viewed as a creative exploratory process to facilitate the expansion of personal horizons. Even these solitary explorations of a child with a new instrument may be viewed as social given that they take place within a family or other social environment, which will influence if and when the child has access to an instrument, how s/he approaches and continues to explore and interact musically with instruments and with other people and/or instruments in the environment.

Within music education, such improvisatory exploration processes can be used as the basis of a very simple but provocative strategy that enables children to explore their creativity though music at the very start of their more formal educational introduction to music. For example, by using conduction techniques a facilitator can help young children explore their musicality through improvisation. In this instance the facilitator may use a variety of hand signals to children to enable improvisation within specific parameters (e.g. long notes, short notes, loud notes, quiet notes). Conduction is a type of structured free improvisation where one person directs and conducts an improvising ensemble with a series of hand and baton gestures. Lawrence D.'Butch' Morris is widely recognized as the principal theorist and practitioner in the evolution of conduction within this improvisatory context. Improvisation can also be utilized as a means of integrating very experienced musicians with individuals who have no experience of playing music, and it can also be used as an integrative process within situations that have both educational and therapeutic objectives (De Simone & MacDonald, 2009). Hickey (2009) presents further examples of the educational potential of improvisational practices and also discusses various ways in which improvisation technique can be taught.

Given the possible utility of improvisation as an educational tool, and the fact that it can be viewed as a fundamental aspect of musical creativity there is a paradox in the observation that many professional musicians claim not to be able to improvise. MacDonald, Byrne, and Carlton (2006) highlighted that many teachers, even after 20 years of conventional and in-depth musical training, report not being able to improvise and have anxieties about how to teach musical creativity in general, and improvisation in particular, in classroom contexts. Children taking part in a music workshop in primary school, for instance, may struggle to replicate or perform a specific piece of music, yet be easily able to make an improvised contribution to music as it is played. People trying to recall a song when singing to themselves or along with others will come up with a version of it that approximates to what they recall or 'fills in gaps'. Anyone has the potential to improvise music, yet we know comparatively little about how or why. Therefore, not only is the ability to perform and respond to music a universal quality that is now well evidenced, but the capacity to improvise is also universal and, within a musical context, these improvisational capacities can be utilized to help individuals develop musical skills and explore creative ideas in an empowering and rewarding way.

While there has been increased interest in improvisation since Bailey's observation over 20 years ago that opened this chapter, his comments are still relevant and support the notion that there remains an urgent need for investigation of the process and outcomes of improvisational activity particularly within an educational context (Lewis, 2000; Hickey, 2009; Sarath, 2009; Solis & Nettl, 2009). Biasutti and Frezza (2009), for instance, call for a curriculum for improvisation 'focused on processes, rather than on products' (p. 241) as an alternative to traditional approaches characterized by jazz training. Also, Borgo (2007) gives examples of how ecological psychology and the processes of improvisation can be utilized within educational contexts.

16.3 Distinct features of improvisation

In summary, we have so far outlined how improvisation can be seen as a fundamental aspect of music-making that cuts across genres and can be accessed by people without particular musical skills or knowledge. We have also highlighted a number of ways in which improvisation can be utilized and developed in educational contexts. A key point within this argument is that music is improvised in a wide range of settings, genres, and cultures and so it is important to outline key common features of this broad conception of improvised music that can be seen as central to all its manifestations.

16.3.1 Improvisation is creative

We would argue that the process is unquestionably creative in that improvising musicians produce novel music, within or beyond genre parameters, that may be similar to, but have substantive differences from, any previous musical performances. Audiences who appreciate improvised music have a strong expectation that they will hear in a concert either wholly new music, or novel versions of previous pieces that have been transformed in some way, and evaluate what they hear in those terms. Performers may, for example, keep a rhythmic, metrical, or harmonic framework in mind while varying the rhythms or pitches of a familiar melody; or may focus on features of a particular image while populating an emergent piece of music with impromptu musical utterances as they occur to them. The idea of not starting from a 'blank sheet of paper' but instead beginning with an existing piece of music, object, or idea and developing, elaborating on, or deconstructing this to arrive at something new is well recognized within creativity studies and more widely, as seen in a well known US legal ruling on an intellectual property claim:

> Nothing today, likely nothing since we tamed fire, is genuinely new: Culture, like science and technology, grows by accretion, each new creator building on the works of those who came before.
>
> (Kozinsky, 1993: White v. Samsung Electronics ruling.)

Improvising therefore generates new music, or new versions of music, in which musicians use their imaginations to develop and elaborate on their stock of knowledge of existing music forms.

16.3.2 Improvisation is spontaneous

Improvisation can be seen as spontaneous in that it is created *as it is being played*. Musicians create improvisations through moment-by-moment responses to immediate musical contexts, and do not seek to replicate exactly what they or others might have played at an earlier date, although they may be elaborating and modifying an earlier performance as mentioned above. If a recording of a performance is made, then that particular creative output can acquire ontological status, but what is created is otherwise ephemeral and located in the process rather than in a lasting musical product. Particular recorded improvisations have become viewed as 'classic', acquiring an iconic position within a particular field, such as 20th-century jazz in which Miles Davis' solo on *So What* or John Coltrane's solo on *Giant Steps* are two particular examples seen as lasting musical 'works'.

Bailey (1992) emphasizes the definition of improvisation as being 'in the moment' composition, rather than something seeking to replicate previous musical expressions. As he puts it, improvisation sets out 'to create something new in each performance, "composition in real time" as it is sometimes described' (p. 208). The possibly of creating 'something new' in each performance may in some sense seem utopian and somewhat romantic, particularly given the Kozinsky quote above. However, Bailey's definition does emphasize the importance of spontaneous musical and psychological processes that are central to improvisation. Specifically, while any given improviser may bring similar strategies (and some similar elements) to different improvisations, the goal of creating something new in an improvisation, while perhaps utopian, does serve to facilitate collaborative practices that emphasize spontaneous and real-time music-making.

16.3.3 Improvisation is social

Although cognitive models of musical improvisation have sought to map some of the processes taking place in unaccompanied solo performance (e.g. Pressing, 1988, 1998; Johnson-Laird, 2002) and some improvisatory practice is solo (e.g. Johansson, Chapter 14, this volume) the practice primarily takes place among a group of individuals involved in collaboration in order to produce a coherent piece of music spontaneously and simultaneously. Group improvisation involves the creation of music through the idiosyncratic contributions of two or more individuals, each interpreting and musically responding to the playing of the other(s). Any individual musical contribution is impromptu and is tailored to or dependent on the sounds, rhythms and tonalities heard from accompanying musicians (Bastien & Hostager, 1988; Mazzola & Cherlin, 2009). Since all have input into the overall sound—into what gets played and how—the creativity in improvisation can, we believe, best be seen as essentially social, rather than being attributable to or located within a single individual.

16.3.4 Improvisation is accessible

As stated earlier, improvisation is also something that everybody can engage in; we are all musical improvisers at some level. Not only is it a form of creative experimentation and a fundamental psychological process that underpins many aspects of daily life (e.g. conversations) but, from a musical perspective, improvisational forms are creative activities that can be undertaken by anyone, regardless of musical experience or technical proficiency. This facet of improvisation affords an egalitarian view of musical expression and communication, based upon exchange and negotiation of novel ideas and not necessarily upon the acquisition of advanced technical skills, and is another feature that gives improvisation particular utility across performance, educational and therapeutic contexts.

16.4 Theorizing about improvisation

Group improvisation in music is therefore an important psychological phenomenon: a form of creativity that is spontaneous and based on process rather than product, social rather than individual and a universal capacity, latent or otherwise. It shares some features with creative practices of stand-up comedy or theatre (Sawyer, 2007), but unlike these genres, it involves only non-verbal and essentially abstract output (even when singers improvise, they tend to avoid words) and performers play at the same time rather than waiting for each other to finish a contribution. These features taken together make group improvised music a unique and remarkable psychological phenomenon worthy of more psychological investigation than it receives. In particular they suggest a number of aspects of creativity that are mostly neglected when psychologists have attempted to theorize creativity more generally (Clarke, 2005).

16.5 Creativity as social activity

Creativity has primarily been treated within psychology as an individual difference or characteristic, yet the creativity of an ensemble improvising cannot be attributed to any one individual's input, or even to a sum of individual contributions, but to that particular configuration of musicians and their inter-relationships. The notion of individual genius in musical creativity is powerful, as Sawyer (2003) has argued; and although various authors have emphasized the need to consider creativity (e.g. Miell & Littleton, 2004) and indeed improvisation (Monson, 1996) as collaborative activities, this aspect is often overlooked when authors seek to account for, for example, Charlie Parker's improvisational prowess rather than the creativity of the various Charlie Parker quintets. Such an emphasis on collaborative creativity raises issues for mainstream psychological theories of creativity. Adopting instead a sociocultural approach to studying creativity highlights interesting features that occur as people work together in creative ways, and analysing groups composing, improvising or performing music together (and talking about these activities) provides a useful context for exploring these features.

In Sansom's (2007) study of creative processes in freely improvising duos, he asked each participant to comment on recordings of them improvising together and the interviews revealed how the social and interpersonal dynamics of the pair were, on many occasions, as important as, or indeed more so than, the musical factors influencing the nature of the resulting improvisation. The music seemed to flow from the social context of the relationship between performers.

These are features that are ignored, or less evident, in studies of individual creativity in which an individual's own imagination and personal emotional state are often proposed as the core features. However, such approaches do not help us to answer important questions such as 'how might coordinated inspiration or imagination emerge and develop simultaneously in a group of individuals?', or 'how should we understand music as being creatively shaped by the diverse or nuanced emotions of a group of players?' Other concepts that psychologists have related to individual creativity include personal motivation, passion (Bruner, 1962), persistence (Newell & Simon, 1972) and the drive for self-actualization (Rogers, 1954). The psychoanalytic approach suggests that creativity is a more socially acceptable outlet for inner tension and conflicts than other potential outlets. However, the processes singled out in such theories of *individual* creativity (motivations, passions, tension release, or persistence) may be features which would actually run counter to successful creativity within a collaborative process such as group improvisation. Individual ensemble members who let out their inner tension and conflicts, or express their own passions will not necessarily enhance, and may be detrimental to, what could be achieved by the ensemble.

While the process of (often iterative) evaluation of ideas and products is fundamental to most accounts of creativity provided by cognitive psychologists, how this evaluation is handled by a group involved in collaborative creative activities is regarded in sociocultural analysis as a key aspect of the interaction through which creativity is mediated. The need to establish and work within a common frame of reference and to have constructive means of handling conflict and disagreement are therefore seen as important in studies of collaborative creativity (Miell & Littleton, 2004) and a group improvisational setting is a useful setting for such studies.

16.6 **Process-based investigations**

Studies that consider musical creativity as an individual achievement often look to the outputs of great composers as exemplars of creativity (Sawyer, 2007). This approach undoubtedly individualizes the conception of musical creativity and is a by-product of Western approaches to music in which complex combinations of economic and artistic factors can be simplified by viewing creative endeavours as an individualistic pursuit. Yet to consider musical creativity from an individualistic perspective limits any definition of creativity to a small canon of achievements that have acquired value in feudal or capitalist societies and have been preserved. The vast majority of music that is produced in the world has been improvised and/or transmitted aurally and will never be heard again, or certainly not exactly as initially created. Creativity should not be measured only by the production of quantifiable cultural artefacts with objectively rateable indicators of creative quality, but should also be examined in the production of music in its more usual and immediate contexts. This suggestion has significant implications. For example, music education still focuses upon specific musical outputs produced by individuals (students). However, if creativity were to be viewed more collectively and from a more process-based standpoint, then perhaps assessment within music education could also adapt to this view. We might therefore ask whether historical accounts of creativity should be less focused upon individual 'greats' and take into consideration wider contextual issues.

Furthermore, when we listen to such recordings of group improvisations as exist, it is vital that these are understood as snapshots of a creative process in a social context: examining transcribed individual contributions to these recordings, for instance, does not facilitate understanding the performance as an interactive process of creation. Yet real-time processes that force on-the-spot responses at an almost instinctive level are, in many ways, more consistent with the association of creativity with a process of brainstorming or 'hypothesis creation' (Bruner, 1986), which leads to unique connections and unexpected solutions. On the other hand, the model of creativity seen in group improvisation, where it is viewed as a continuous and seamless process without intermediate reflection or use of language to evaluate and discuss the evolving product, is contrary to the importance laid on the evaluation of creative products by many theories of individual creativity.

16.7 **Normalizing creativity**

Spectacular improvising is intriguing and is where many expert musicians will look to develop their understanding and knowledge. Those keen to emulate, say, Charlie or Evan Parker must endeavour to figure out what such musicians do and how they do it. But for psychologists who may be interested in a creative non-verbal social process in which all of us have the potential to engage, it is surely important to consider creativity wherever it appears and not only where it is seen to be of the highest quality as judged by an elite. Creativity is a universal process, but from the point of view of the psychologist seeking to understand it, considerations of quality are secondary to that of the process itself. Indeed notions of quality are likely to be culturally shaped or defined and not universal.

In early psychological theorizing about creativity, Guilford (1950) proposed studying and measuring creativity as an intellectual human function and Torrance (1966) defined the processes that have been assumed since in the assessment of creativity: fluency (production of ideas), flexibility (production of different ideational categories), originality (production of unusual ideas), and elaboration (persistency of introducing new details to products). There has been a shift in emphasis in the last decade 'towards characterising, recognising complexity, focusing increasingly on the collective and collaborative, and increasingly recognising the situatedness of activity rather than seeing creativity as "universalised" in this way' (Craft, 2008: p. 241). Sociocultural analyses which adopt this different approach to understanding creativity define it as a situated and mediated human activity, arising 'from the interaction between the "intelligence" of individuals, the domain or areas of human endeavour, disciplines, crafts or pursuits, and the field, such as people, institutions, award mechanisms and "knowledgeable others"' (Loveless, 2002: p. 10).

Yet the features of creativity identified by Guilford and Torrance, all concepts that are hailed as important qualities of improvised music, might also be understood to be universal capacities, even if they are used with more success or frequency by some than others. A group of improvisers might play together flexibly and fluidly to some extent, with some originality and elaboration, and be judged 'high quality' by some 'knowledgeable others' but not by those with different 'knowledge'. The properties of creativity require explication as they appear in any group improvisation. A satisfactory theory of group improvisation as a universal creative process must account, for example, for children playing together and teenagers jamming as much as accomplished or famous musicianship; there is no reason to suppose that our understanding of group improvisation might be better served by looking at only the practices of a select and highly specialized few. Studies of the psychological processes of speech and language, for instance, would be sorely limited if they considered only great works of literature.

16.8 **Researching improvisation**

One way to investigate how the creativity of group improvisation operates is to ask those involved how they experience it. In a number of research studies we have asked jazz musicians, youths in rock bands, and an eclectic ensemble of free improvising musicians with backgrounds in different genres to describe what happens when they improvise together, and their accounts provide support for the version of creativity outlined above. A key point here is that we suggest that talking about music is an important part of the overall process of musical communication (MacDonald, Miell, & Wilson, 2005). Moreover, we suggest that talking about music influences how people hear music and how music is performed (MacDonald, Miell, & Hargreaves, 2008). For example, discussing the merits of a recording by Keith Jarrett, Prince, or Nusrat Fateh Ali Khan may influence how these recordings are heard and critiqued. Also, a conversation between two musicians about the important features of a Thelonius Monk piano solo may influence how those two musicians perform. The discussion may also demonstrate how musicians work within existing notions of improvisation, or reinforce established paradigms.

We have suggested above that contemporary approaches to free improvisation beyond genres constitute an area of musical practice in which the distinct properties of group improvisation are given greatest priority, and the practice of some of the free improvising musicians we interviewed corresponds most closely to the recent emergence of such improvising, with an explicit commitment to exploring non-idiomatic improvisation. For this part of the study reported below, 11 members of an ensemble of around 30 musicians were purposively sampled to maximize diversity in terms of instrumentation, musical background, and gender. Ten consented to individual in-depth interviews with a researcher who was also a member of the ensemble (co-author, GW), covering their musical practice and experience of improvising. The interviews were recorded, transcribed verbatim, and analysed using grounded theory and discursive psychological approaches. Another group's data, reported below, are drawn from a study of teenagers developing new music together in a band (Miell and Littleton, 2008). The young people (15–16 years old) who were members of the band were asked to keep a digital video diary of their group improvisation and development/rehearsal sessions over a 6-week period and analysis proceeded on the sections of the videos where they discussed their playing. Finally, we draw on analysis of interviews conducted with a sample of 16–17-year-olds about their experience of playing music collaboratively with various others both at home and at school.

As might be expected across such a diverse group of musicians, accounts of the music are not homogeneous. Nevertheless, musicians in these studies described improvising music as a creative practice involving social processes beyond their own individual endeavours; as something that takes place within an instantaneous or very short time frame, based on instinctive responses; and as something that did not necessarily require particular expertise. Examples are below.

16.8.1 Improvisation as a social process

Among the musicians from the large ensemble, having a large number of others improvise along-side you was treated as a significant influence on how music could be created:

> R: . . . so I found that quite hard, so it was very, it was (.) I suppose my initial feeling was (.) this [impro-vising in a large ensemble] just doesn't feel anything like playing with a a couple of people, it [yeah] it's not as rewarding, cause there isn't, there's not sort of immediate tangible results, [yeah] it was very much a big, it was fun, but it wasn't creatively as satisfying. [yeah] Initially, I mean that's definitely changed.

> I: How how do you think that's changed, or how has it become more satisfying?

> R: Um because I think you can, you start to sort of hear how you, you can be part of creating an overall coherence, and when I think there's an overall coherence, I mean even if you're not even playing, the fact that you're involved in creating this coherent sound in any way, is rewarding, cause of yes that works, that musically works; and that, you know I think there there were, there always have been musical moments, good moments, good sort of sort of occasions of beauty and everything, but the more, if that only happens very rarely it's kind of, there is this sort of element of frustration . . . (Interviewee 1)

Interviewee 1 constructs a creative experience when improvising with a large number of people that is qualitatively different to the experience of playing with a small number. He finds himself to be involved in creating an 'overall coherence' that can be 'beautiful' or 'rewarding', that 'musi-cally works', but is also 'frustrating' or less satisfying in that it is a creativity in which he has a partial role. He therefore recognizes a distinct creative practice when improvising with other musicians, moreover one which is experienced differently depending on the size of the group involved. This frustration also highlights the limitations of established musical systems where the individual is often foregrounded (and therefore regarded as the centre of creativity) at the expense of the collective.

This importance of mutual understanding and trust is often alluded to in sociocultural accounts of collaborative creativity, where the quality of the relationship between the members of the group is seen as an important factor in supporting the collaboration (Miell & Littleton, 2004). As a respondent reported in our interview study with young people,

> R: It's quite a big trust thing involved in making music . . . You have to say 'I like that', 'don't like that' and you have to be able to do that without people getting terribly stressed.

It is clearly not the case that group members have to *get on with* each other in order to be able to improvise collaboratively, but (perhaps particularly where the members are inexperienced musicians) an *understanding* of other members—their preferences and motivations—and an openness to sharing views with each other are likely to be important to allow them to take the necessary risks for creative leaps to be made (MacDonald, Miell, & Mitchell, 2002; Miell & MacDonald, 2000).

16.8.2 Improvisation as a real-time process

Music was also described as being created, generated, or developed within the time-frame of improvising together, rather than through prior individual or group choices:

> How do (.) it's purely by in (.) in here intuition though isn't it, is it not? You know for me I think you just react to what other, oh I mean well that's yeah, I guess that's what I'm doing reacting to what to what other people are doing and then, if once I feel comfortable with it and the, and the minute's right, I might just leap in and try and do my own thing, and see if anyone hooks onto that, or (.) you know so so it's er (.) it's a bit of a give and take, you know isn't it obviously. . . (Interviewee 6.)

Interviewee 6 from the study of a large mixed genre ensemble describes a process of creativity with other people through intuition, reaction, and feeling the minute to be 'right'. Processes of inspiration, invention reflection and evaluations separated out in other theories of creativity are here constructed as taking place within a simultaneous and social musical event as it unfolds.

In the interview study we conducted with 16–17-year-olds about their formal and informal experiences of music-making, interviewee Y stressed the importance of developing music in the process of playing together as he describes the improvisatory practices that he draws on as he and his band start to compose a new song:

> Y: I think the thing is that, you know, for a band to kind of sit down in a room and somebody will start playing something and the other two will pick up on it and then we'll write a song like that I think. I think that people, like in themselves, have to be really together.

He is emphasizing that as the group members improvise together they need to feel connected and 'in tune with' each other enough to readily pick up on and react to each other's contributions and musical offerings in order to effect creativity in their terms.

16.8.3 Resources that facilitate improvisation

We have indicated that some of our interviewees in the large ensemble of improvisers seek to create music beyond genres, and to this extent improvising might be seen as something whereby music can be created without necessarily requiring specialist knowledge, skills, or faculties. This was however a controversial issue within the large group of improvisers and we observed a range of discursive positioning in relation to the exclusivity of improvising:

> . . . when I've been doodling (.) either on the, on whichever instrument that I've been playing (.) that doesn't necessarily constitute improvising as I see it now. Where of course it is, but . . . (Interviewee 9.)

> Some people are very good at doing one thing, and they're they're, what they provide to the orchestra, in another sense isn't isn't isn't so um I don't know isn't, doesn't make as big a difference, it might make a difference, everything has it has it has its place . . . (Interviewee 8.)

Interviewee 9 above seeks to make a distinction between 'doodling' and 'proper' improvisation. Conversely, interviewee 8 suggests that being 'good at one thing' does not make a big difference to the creativity of the ensemble. Despite their antagonistic accounts, 8 and 9 do create improvised music together on a regular basis and we must regard their statements about what type of musician they are as positioning rather than reportage. These interviewees also knew the interviewer as a colleague in the same ensemble. Even though these are individual interviews, the discursive limitations on how colleagues can be talked about are apparent. Interviewee 9 has to attend to the possibility that his view might alienate colleagues who do not see their participation as requiring mastery of a genre or instrument ('Where of course it is. . .') while Interviewee 8 tries not to be seen as belittling 'experts', claiming 'everything has its place'. Thus, the capacity for individuals who are not necessarily specialists to contribute to the improvising of this ensemble, or to have a claim to identity as an improviser, is recognized in one way or another by both of these speakers.

In another of our studies, a video-diary based observational study of teenagers playing together in a band during their development of music/rehearsal periods and analysis of their talk together between periods of playing, revealed many examples of how they saw the process of developing a distinctive sound for their band. This sound was built up from each of them bringing very different stylistic elements and musical backgrounds to the improvisation process which was how they began the development of their songs:

> J: If you take completely different bands like we do and you amalgamate something . . . then it completely changes it. So if I've got the bare bones of a song and let's say it's in a certain style like in the style of the

band called Swans. Then we'll bring it and Dan will bring a certain influence like some sort of post-rock thing which he has been doing and Matt will bring a heavy kind of beat and Leah will bring sort of quirky weird things . . . and everything comes together.

M: It's hard to label the sort of music. I mean I don't know, I haven't heard any bands that sound like us.

D: It's refreshingly different I would say.

For this band, being able to define themselves as 'refreshingly different' from others was key to their playing. The music they created and which felt right to them flowed from and represented their particular relationships and was more than the sum of their individual range of influences and backgrounds.

16.9 **Conclusions**

It is our contention that improvisation is an important basis from which psychologists can understand more about creativity in music-making. By seeking to analyse improvisation practices in their broadest manifestations we can make progress in our growing understanding of musical creativity. Furthermore, at a time when all areas of music are facing extreme challenges (e.g. the shape of music education post global economic crisis, exploiting the opportunities which come with the technological revolution, the collapse in sales of music via CD) improvisation affords opportunities, since it is not rule-based and gives primacy to collaborative communication for new insights, new ways of collaborating and innovative exchanges of ideas.

Improvisation in music has been the subject of considerable musicological interest. Yet we have argued here that when musical improvising takes place between people in collaborative settings a unique creative process takes place for which psychology has not yet offered a satisfactory explanation, but should. Improvisation has been recognized as a central psychological process. Lewis (2007) discusses how philosopher and linguist Gilbert Ryle (1979) claimed that cognitive processing was a form of improvisation in itself, stating of any individual that 'if he is not at once improvising and improvising warily, he is not engaging his somewhat trained wits in some momentarily live issue, but perhaps acting from sheer unthinking habit' (Ryle, 1979). Music represents a uniquely social, interactive application of this human faculty for creative purposes and drawing on psychological and sociological theory to consider musical improvisation highlights how this can be an important site of creative exploration.

Improvisation is an approach to music whose time has come and these are exciting times to be involved in research focused upon its use within contemporary music-making. For example, considering the creativity of group improvisation opens up broad vistas for psychological investigation. There is a need, for example, to consider how individual creativity is qualified or constrained by participation in the social creativity of improvisation. Is the creativity that musicians experience when writing music or improvising on their own related to, or qualitatively distinct from, that which they experience in group improvisation? While we have argued that improvised music is ubiquitous, it is nevertheless extraordinarily diverse and theories about what features connect its various manifestations are in their infancy. This suggests there is considerable scope for the qualitative investigation of creativity in group improvisation as a means of building theory.

Furthermore, psychological theories that are associated with qualitative approaches might be considered most suitable to frame the phenomenon. This is a form of creativity through which music is constructed between individuals that is specific to the occasion and social context. In these terms, group improvisation might be considered readily explicable with reference to theories of social construction. For instance, exploring not just what musicians play, but what functions their individual contributions might have within the musical work and within the group of musicians, could allow us to explain better how the somewhat mystical process of improvisation takes place, in the same way that social constructionist explanations of dialogue have informed our understanding of the social practices and functions of conversation. This would in turn inform best practice for teaching people to enhance their improvisation beyond the constraints of genres and the requirements of professional practice.

Improvisation is rapidly expanding in numerous new directions. These developments not only afford numerous research possibilities and priorities but present exciting challenges to music education to embrace and utilize the creative possibilities produced by these advances. While improvisation is a ubiquitous musical practice, it is undoubtedly under-researched. Moreover, it is our contention that a multidisciplinary approach, incorporating psychological and musicological elements as a key foundation, will significantly enhance understanding of improvisation as a crucial creative process within the landscape of contemporary music.

References

Bailey, D. (1992). *Improvisation: Its nature and practice.* New York: Da Capo.

Becker J.C. (1980). *Traditional music in modern Java: Gamelan in a changing society.* Honolulu, HI; University of Hawaii Press.

Bastien, D.T. & Hostager, T.J. (1988) Jazz as a process of organizational innovation. *Communication Research,* 15(5), 582–602.

Becker, H.S. (2000). The etiquette of improvisation. *Mind, Culture, and Activity,* 7(3), 171–6.

Berkowitz, A.L. (2010). *The Improvising Mind: Cognition and Creativity in the Musical Moment.* Oxford: Oxford University Press.

Berliner, P. (2002). *Thinking in jazz: The infinite art of improvisation.* Chicago, IL: University of Chicago Press.

Biasutti, M. & Frezza, L. (2009). Dimensions of music improvisation. *Creativity Research Journal,* 21(2), 232–42.

Borgo, D. (2005). *Sync or swarm: Improvising music in a complex age.* New York: Continuum.

Borgo, D. (2007). Free jazz in the classroom: An ecological approach to music education. *Jazz Perspectives,* 1(1), 61–88.

Brinner, B. (2007). *Music in central Java: Experiencing music, expressing culture.* New York: Oxford University Press.

Bruner, J. (1962). Introduction. In L.S. Vygotsky *Thought and language.* Cambridge, MA: MIT Press.

Bruner, J. (1986). *Actual minds, possible worlds.* Cambridge, MA: Harvard University Press.

Clarke, E. (2005). Creativity in performance. *Musicae Scientiae,* 9, 157–82.

Craft, A. (2008). Studying collaborative creativity: Implications for education. *Thinking Skills and Creativity,* 3, 241–45.

De Simone, J. & MacDonald, R.A.R (2009). Thematic analysis of musical participation by individuals with mental health problems. *Paper presented at the 7th Triennial Conference of the European Society for the Cognitive Sciences of Music, Jyväskylä,* Finland, 11–16 August.

Fischlin, D. & Heble, A. (Eds.) (2004). *The other side of nowhere: Jazz improvisation and Communities in dialogue.* Middletown, CT: Wesleyan University Press.

Guilford, J.P. (1950). Creativity, American Psychologist, 5(9), 444–54.

Hegarty, P. (2007). *Noise music: A history.* Continuum: New York.

Hickey, M. (2009). Can improvisation be 'taught'? A call for free improvisation in our schools. *International Journal of Music Education,* 27(4), 285–99.

Johnson-Laird, P.N. (2002). How jazz musicians improvise. *Music Perception,* 19(3), 415–42.

Kenny, B.J. and Gellrich, M. (2002). Improvisation. In R. Parncutt & G.E. McPherson (Eds.) *The science & psychology of music performance: Creative strategies for teaching and learning.* Oxford: Oxford University Press, pp. 117–34.

Kozinsky, A. *White v. Samsung Electronics America, Inc.,* 989 F.2d 1512 (9th Cir. 1993) (Kozinski, J., dissenting in re court's refusal of en banc rehearing).

Lewis, G.E. (2000). Teaching improvised music: An ethnographic memoir. In J. Zorn, (Ed.) *Arcana: Musicians on music*. New York: Granary Books, pp. 78–109.

Lewis, G.E. (2007). Mobilitas animi: Improvising technologies, intending chance. *Parallax*, **13**(4), 108–22.

Lewis, G.E. (2008). *A power stronger than itself: The AACM and American experimental music*. Chicago, IL: University of Chicago Press.

Loveless, A. (2002). Literature review in creativity, new technologies and learning. Report 4: A report for NESTA Futurelab.

MacDonald, R.A.R (2009). Arts education and cultural communication: Music, learning and identity. In H. Ruismäki & I. Ruokonen (Eds.) *Arts: Points of contact between cultures*. Helsinki: University of Helsinki, pp.12–24.

MacDonald, R.A.R, Byrne, C., & Carlton, L. (2006). Creativity and flow in musical composition: An empirical investigation. *Psychology of Music*, **34**(3), 292–307.

MacDonald, R.A.R, Miell, D. & Wilson, G.B. (2005). Talking about music: a vehicle for identity development. In D. Miell, R.A.R MacDonald & D.J. Hargreaves (Eds.) *Musical communication*. Oxford: Oxford University Press, pp. 321–38.

MacDonald R.A.R, Miell D., & Hargreaves D.J. (Eds.) (2008). Musical identity. In S. Hallam, J. Sloboda & M. Thaut (Eds.) *The Oxford handbook of music psychology*. Oxford: Oxford University Press, pp. 462–70.

MacDonald R.A.R., Miell, D., & Mitchell, L (2002). An investigation of children's musical collaborations: the effect of friendship and age. *Psychology of Music*, **30**(2), 148–63.

MacDonald, R.A.R. & Wilson, G.B. (2005). Musical identities of professional jazz musicians: a focus group investigation. *Psychology of Music*, **33**(4), 395–417.

MacDonald, R.A.R. and Wilson, G.B. (2006). Constructions of jazz: how jazz musicians present their collaborative musical practice. *Musicae Scientiae*, **10**(1), 59–83.

Mazzola, G. & Cherlin, P.B. (2009). *Flow gesture and spaces in free jazz*. Heidelberg: Springer.

Miell, D. & Littleton, K. (Eds.) (2004). *Collaborative creativity: Contemporary perspectives*. London: Free Association Books.

Miell, D. & MacDonald, R.A.R. (2000). Children's creative collaborations: The importance of friendship when working together on a musical composition. *Social Development*, **9**(3), 348–69.

Miell, Dorothy D. & Littleton, K. (2008). Musical collaboration outside school: Processes of negotiation in band rehearsals. *International Journal of Educational Research*, **47**(1), 41–49.

Monson, I. (1996). *Saying something: Jazz improvisation and interaction*. Chicago, IL: University of Chicago Press.

Nettl, B. & Russell M. (Eds.) (1998). *In the course of performance: Studies in the world of musical improvisation*. Chicago, IL: University of Chicago Press.

Newell, A. & Simon, H.A. (1972) *Human problem solving*. Englewood Cliffs, NJ: Prentice-Hall.

Nooshin, L. & Widdess, R. (2006). Improvisation in Iranian and Indian Music. *Journal of the Indian Musicological Society* **36/37**: 104–19.

Oliveros, P. (2005). *Deep listening: A composer's sound practice*. New York: iUniverse.

Parker, E. (1992). Man and Machine 'De Motu' for Buschi Niebergall. Available at: http://www.efi.group. shef.ac.uk/fulltext/demotu.html (accessed 14 March 2011).

Parker, E. (2007). 211 Maxims and other thoughts from a life in improvised music. In J. Zorn (Ed.) *Arcana II: Musicians on music*. New York: Hips Road/Tazadik, pp. 156–78.

Pressing, J. (1988). Improvisation: methods and models. In J. Sloboda (Ed.) *Generative processes in music*. Oxford: Oxford University Press.

Pressing, J. (1998). Psychological constraints on improvisational expertise and communication. In B. Nettl & M. Russell (Eds.) *In the course of performance: Studies in the world of musical improvisation*. Chicago, IL: University of Chicago Press, pp. 47–67.

Prevost, E. (1995). *No sound is innocent*. London: Copula.

Rogers, C.R. (1954). Towards a theory of creativity. *ETC: A Review of General Semantics*, **11**, 249–60.

Ryle, G. (1979). *On thinking.* Oxford: Blackwell.

Sansom, M. (2007). Improvisation and identity: A qualitative study. *Critical Studies in Improvisation* **3**(1). Available at: http://www.criticalimprov.com/index.php/csieci/index.

Sarath, E. (2009). *Music theory through improvisation.* London: Routledge.

Sawyer, K. (1992). Improvisational creativity: An analysis of jazz performance. *Creativity Research Journal,* **5**(3), 253–63.

Sawyer, R.K. (2003). *Group creativity: Music, theater, collaboration.* Mahwah, NJ: Lawrence Erlbaum Associates.

Sawyer, R.K. (2007). *Group genius: The creative power of collaboration.* New York: Basic books.

Sharron, A. (1985). The mainstream of consciousness: An interactionist analysis of a phenomenological concept. *Symbolic Interaction,* **8**(1), 47–62.

Solis, G. & Nettl, B. (Eds.) (2009). *Music Improvisation: Art, Education and Society.* Chicago, IL: University of Illinois Press.

Stevens, J. (2007). *Search and reflect—A music workshop handbook.* London: Rock School Limited.

Torrance, E.P. (1966). *The Torrance tests of creative thinking.* Princeton, NJ: Personnel Press.

Viswanathan, T. & Cormack, J. (1998). Melodic improvisations in Karnatac music: the manifestations of raga. In B. Nettl & M. Russell (Eds.) *In the course of performance: Studies in the world of musical improvisation.* Chicago, IL: University of Chicago Press, pp. 219–37.

Wigram, T. (2007). *Improvisation: Methods and techniques for music therapy clinicians, educators and students.* London: Jessica Kingsley.

Wilson, G.B. & MacDonald R.A.R. (2005). The meaning of the blues: musical identities in talk about jazz. *Qualitative Research in Psychology,* **2**(4), 341–63.

Wilson, P.N. (1994). *Ornette Coleman: His life and music.* Albany, CA: Berkeley Hills Books.

Part 4

Perspectives from neuroscience

Chapter 17

Communicative musicality: The human impulse to create and share music

Colwyn Trevarthen

After the pleasures which arise from gratification of the bodily appetites, there seems to be none more natural to man than Music and Dancing. In the progress of art and improvement they are, perhaps, the first and earliest pleasures of his own invention. . . . Without any imitation, instrumental Music can produce very considerable effects . . . : by the sweetness of its sounds it awakens agreeably, and calls upon the attention; by their connection and affinity it naturally detains that attention, which follows easily a series of agreeable sounds, which have all a certain relation both to a common, fundamental, or leading note, called the key note; and to a certain succession or combination of notes, called the song or composition. . . . Time and measure are to instrumental Music what order and method are to discourse; they break it into proper parts and divisions, by which we are enabled both to remember better what has gone before, and frequently to forsee somewhat of what is to come after:. . . . the enjoyment of Music arises partly from memory and partly from foresight.

Of the nature of that imitation which takes place in what are called the imitative arts, Adam Smith (1777/1982)

17.1 The process and products of creation

Adam Smith wrote on 'the imitative arts' shortly after completing his most famous work 'The Wealth of Nations' (1776), on economic creativity by division of labour and mechanical industry, for sale in an open market place. It explains how wealth depends on human work, not just on trade. He had travelled on the continent and seen the prodigious development of industry and national politics in the mid 18th century.

After returning to Scotland in 1777 Smith began an essay on the imitative arts and lectured on the topic. The two works confront us with the dual meaning of the word 'creation'. Is it a verb, or a noun; a life 'process', *creating*, or the 'product' *created*? If the latter, does appreciation of the product require learning, or is the value of the act of creation sensed intuitively, by a kind of imitation of its making? Is there an important difference between hearing and feeling the inspiration of creation, alive in movement, and a more calculating seeing and touching the object that has been made?

Music, which Smith loved and knew well, was also being created in a more technical and literary way, with the aid of printing. Large works were composed as scores to direct future performances of disciplined choirs and orchestras. The church music of Bach and orchestral entertainments of Telemann and Handel, followed by the concertos and operas of Mozart and Beethoven were all products of complex cooperations between the composer and performers, mediated by interpretation of static, hand-made texts describing the sounds imagined in composition. The creative spaces between the composer, performer, and listener were becoming wider, the life of music being transmitted to seated and silent audiences, if they were not invited to sing or dance to it. This is a different process of creation from that of oral cultures, where music is with spontaneous exuberance in shared performance (Cross & Moreley, 2009; Dissanayake, 2009a; Merker, 2009b). 'In many, perhaps most, non-Western cultures, music requires overt action and active group engagement; the differentiation and specialization of the roles of performer and audience might almost be considered a minority practice.' (Cross & Morley, 2009: p. 66).

In writing about music as an 'imitative art' Smith is returning to an earlier concern with creation as the pleasurable 'process' of live human cooperation—and how imitation of actions brings life to a community. In his *Theory of Moral Sentiments* (1759) he saw society as a creation of *innate sympathy*. Music he perceives in a similar way, as a primitive generative activity of human minds and bodies—a more fundamental human creativity than the learned languages, customs, and beliefs that separate cultures and their histories. Music seems to be part of all humanity, and to gives rise to a pleasure essential for building relationships in community, as Darwin believed (Dissanayake, 2009b).

I will seek the source of the self-creative process that makes music by asking, how can a newborn baby, possessed of powerful means of soliciting the care of its life from a mother, also have the power to create or recognize music-like behaviour, and to share it (Trevarthen, 2011a) (Figure 17.1). It has been discovered recently that infants have a discriminating interest in both song and the sounds of musical instruments, and that they make an expressive response to assist in vocal improvisations with their parents. These abilities call for an enquiry into the evolutionary preconditions for musical creativity, in animal movement and vocal communication. Where do the essential parameters of music—its rhythms and its emotive, story-making melodies—come from?

17.2 The self-creation and cooperation of life in community

> There are . . . two sides to the machinery involved in the development of nature. On the one side there is a given environment with organisms adapting themselves to it . . . The other side of the evolutionary machinery, the neglected side, is expressed by the word creativeness. The organisms can create their own environment. For this purpose the single organism is almost helpless. The adequate forces require societies of cooperating organisms.
>
> (Whitehead, 1926: p. 138.)

Creativity and cooperation within and between live organisms, large and small, are complementary processes of survival, of self-regulation in response to stress, of development, and of evolution. They correspond, respectively, to the 'playful assimilation' and 'imitative accommodation' that Jean Piaget (1962) defined as the two sides of an individual child's adaptation for rational mastery of the physical world. The infant, using talents given by evolution, playfully 'asserts' its vitality in the environment, and imitatively 'apprehends' the opportunities for further activity and the benefits that may be gained.

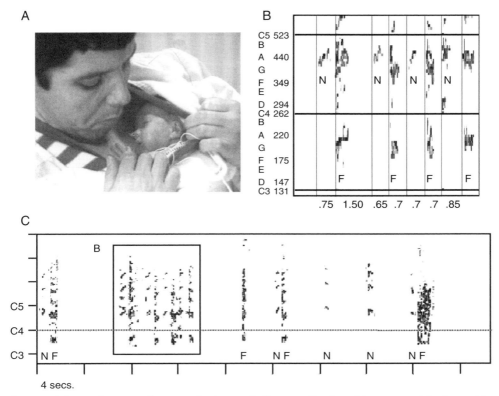

Fig. 17.1 Primary elements of communicative musicality: coordination of innate vocal rhythms with a premature infant. Nassira, born 3 months early, was filmed while she was 'kangarooing' inside her father's shirt when she was 2 months premature (A). A spectrograph (B) demonstrates that, in an exchange of short calls, the father (F) imitates the sounds of Nassira (N), which are pitched about 440 Hz. The timing is precise and regular with onsets of the sounds spaced at near 0.7 seconds, corresponding to *andante*. The group of sounds approximates to a spoken phrase of 8 syllables with one pause, and the last interval is longer at 0.85 seconds, showing the 'final lengthening' that normally signals the end of a spoken phrase. Just before this ending Nassira's last utterance is slightly higher in pitch and this appears to signal to her father that their co-created phrase is finishing. The 38-second extract below (C) shows that the rapid exchange (B) is situated in a context of sounds spaced several seconds apart, equivalent to phrases, or 'breath cycles'. Following B, the father calls, and after 4 seconds Nassira responds and is immediately acknowledged. Then the father is inattentive as Nassira calls at 4 second intervals, first faintly, then louder and a third time when the father respon ds by speaking to her. Filmed by Saskia van Rees in an intensive care unit in Amsterdam (van Rees & de Leeuw, 1993). © Saskia van Rees, 2011.

Most importantly, however, in ways not comprehended by Piagetian cognitive developmental psychology, motivation for creative human life and learning by the individual, their 'subjectivity', is complemented by *social creativity* requiring the transmission, by 'inter-subjective sympathy', of intentions and experiences in communication with companions and within a community. From rhythmic impulses of cooperation between human beings, adapted to imagine and remember an endless array of created plans and objects and sensitive to aesthetic and moral feelings transmitted in relationships, come the living forms of meaning—in culture, in language, in technology, in law and commerce, and in the arts, including music (Bruner, 1990; Wallin et al., 2000; Thompson, 2001; Zlatev et al., 2008; Bråten, 2009; Cross & Morley, 2009; Dissanayake, 2009b; Trevarthen, 1986, 2011b).

17.3 Biochronology: the rhythm of animal movement and human music

> The existence of biological clocks—clusters of rhythmically pulsing neurons that keep time for living organisms, regulate metabolism, procreation, movement, communication and even the temporal nature of human thought (Foster and Kreitzman 2004)—raises key questions about the relationship between the rhythm we experience in moving and that we easily share in music, our biology and neurobiology, and our culturally refined consciousness of time. . . . The spinal locomotor network even of a tadpole is modulated by a neurochemistry that amounts to the same emotional system as transforms skipping *allegro* to cautious *largo* (Sillar *et al.*, 1998).
>
> (Osborne, 2009a: p. 454.)

Life creates and measures time. All plants and animals possess intrinsic clocks or generators of rhythm that anticipate adaptive engagement with events in their worlds, from diurnal and seasonal changes in light and temperature, to the transforming present where response to circumstances and events requires moment by moment discrimination to fractions of a second. They generate a biochronology that gives a measured pace to the vitality of individuals, and to the habits of cooperation in communities and ecological systems.

The rhythmic movements of animals are created with fastidious efficiency by prospective 'motor images' of an imaginative time-keeping brain that directs the experience of action in the body-space of an integrated Self (Sherrington, 1906; Bernstein, 1967; Lee, 2005; Buzsaki, 2006). Animal societies grow and prosper by synchronizing movements of their members in a cooperative harmony of consciousness that is sustained by expressions of states of emotion, to which other selves with similar emotional constitution are immediately sensitive (Darwin, 1872; Panksepp, 1998; Panksepp & Trevarthen, 2009).

The power and versatility of an animal's body grows with the number of its separately mobile segments, and with the acquisition of new senses to detect the effects of moving in different bands of energy. Thus expanding consciousness, with its future-making temporal regulations, has evolved to conceive and regulate new prospects of mobility and to remember longer and richer periods of past experience. In proportion to the evolution of powers of movement, animal brains have evolved systems of 'proprio-ception' for the biomechanics of the body itself, and of 'exteroception' for conceiving the environmental media or objects towards which movements may be directed by intelligence (Sherrington, 1906; von Holst & von Saint-Paul, 1961; Clark, 1997; Damasio, 1999; Merker, 2005). They combine these with 'ex-proprio-ceptive' and 'visceroceptive' abilities which give them an awareness of their own creative mobility and emotional well-being in relation to the world that surrounds them. These latter functions have opened the way to intersubjective awareness or 'altero-centric participation' in one another's actions and feelings (Bråten & Trevarthen, 2007) enabling synchronization of purposes and pleasures in creative social cooperation and giving rise to the techniques and arts of cultural evolution.

Recognition of this driving life principle of a single consciously perceiving, imagining, and remembering *psyche* in each person, which is full of emotion and sensitive to its likeness in other persons, inspires a richer psychology of human nature, its sociability, and its cultural creativity (Bråten, 2009). Rhythmic semiosis, the communication of thoughts, intentions, and feelings between persons, cultivated in the metaphorical narrations of the temporal arts, is at the core of all meaning making in human communities, holding them to common rituals and beliefs and sustaining the creation and evaluation of great projects of practical work.

17.4 **The voice of emotion in song, and speech**

> The human voice, as it is always the best, so it would naturally be the first and earliest of all musical instruments.
>
> (Adam Smith, 1777/1982: Part II, pp. 187–8.)

Cooperative life in movement requires coordination of internal emotional states and emotional regulation of engagements between individuals with their different intentions. Voices of animals have evolved from visceral motor systems that sustain well-being of the body by controlling breathing, swallowing, and coughing. They are transformed to serve collaboration, expressing internal states of vitality and their changes so they may be coordinated in social engagements (Porges, 2003).

Emotions expressed in the timing and power of sound in the voice describe the coherence or organization of a person's intentions to move, and how their energy economy is to be regulated (Scherer, 1986; Zei Pollermann, 2007). The expressive and mimetic versatility of the human voice, cultivated in the sounds of song and imitated by movements of the hands in instrumental music evidently evolved before language, to serve communication of important life experiences and stories (Darwin, 1872; Donald, 2001; Cross & Morley, 2009; Dissanayake, 2009b). Human brains are shaped for life in a creative community of elaborated and highly vocal conscious awareness. They share intentions, imitate new ideas, and work together in the acquisition of skills by means of metaphorical and symbolic combinations of sounds that depend upon a sharing of feelings for which the human voice and human hearing are uniquely adapted. Already in the fetus the special organs of expression, especially eyes, oral and vocal system, and hands, have features adapted to this intersubjective life (Trevarthen, 2001a). We are made to laugh and cry in sympathy for one another's inner states of joy and sadness, to sing and dance together making musical narratives for celebration, as well as to learn how to speak with many words and to make elaborate artefacts with our hands to master the outer world of reality and to describe how its places and objects may be used in cooperative ways.

Music, with poetry and dance, creates dynamic events that hold communities in emotional fellowship, giving members a sense of identification with the distinctive creative style and meaning in a group and at a particular time, stimulating imagination of future inventions, and remembrance of valuable experiences shared—making a history of human-made sound in movement (Cross & Morley, 2009; Dissanayake, 2009a). From it, with the aid of the special human ability for inventing and imitating a host of discrete vocal sounds and their combination to make informative messages (Merker, 2009a, b), have been made spoken languages that have limitless capacity to represent experiences of other times and places. In technologically advanced cultures speaking is crafted into static forms of text incorporating formal rules of grammar and reference by which we may more effectively instruct one another about facts and procedures (Fonagy, 2001; Brandt, 2009; Kühl, 2007; Halliday, 2006).

17.5 **Can an infant make music?**

> The comparison of the natural genius of the child with the cultivated inventiveness of adult genius, especially at the highest levels, is justified by the fact that both ages are in search of *true metaphor[s]* which release the organizing powers of mind and nervous system into action and the making of meaning.
>
> (Cobb, 1977: p. 102.)

It may seem nonsense to imagine that an infant can create music. Surely music-making is a skill that requires years of intense practice under the guidance of a master teacher, by a mature rational intelligence with a fully mobile body? Is not all music a product of cultured imagination and diligent experience? Singing with strong and free vocal control and a sense of expressive melody, playing any musical instrument correctly with ease, improvising or composing music in forms that obey established cultural rules—all these skills of music-making are beyond all but a gifted and much trained minority of adults.

But in the natural world of music there is a paradox. Being musical is not only about *making* music. Without training for any kind of performance, we can, all of us, be *moved by* music (Figure 17.2), and we can be critical of the vitality, wit, and beauty of what we hear. Music touches deeply some faculty of experience and emotion in us all. Even the music of an alien culture, one that may not share our concept of music as an art distinct from dance and drama, is sensible to us as musical (Blacking, 1995; Fritz et al., 2009; Cross & Morley, 2009). We can appreciate elegant execution and be transported by a rhythmic pulse or the resonant harmonies that give activity and colour to a musico-poetic story (Gabrielsson & Juslin, 1996; Juslin, 2001). We feel emotion in any kind of music, even if the tonality and rhythm, or style, does not please us. We are all some kind of skilful *musical listener*, and may respond with eager approval or harsh disapproval to an artist's performance, however incapable of anything like it we ourselves may be.

Infants are moved by song or instrumental music, and may attempt to contribute vocal sounds that harmonize with the tones they hear (Papoušek & Papoušek, 1981; Malloch, 1999; Trevarthen, 1999; Trehub, 2006; Gratier & Trevarthen, 2008; Malloch & Trevarthen, 2009b). They may make gestures that synchronize to the beat, and body gyrations that imitate the surges of melody (Mazokopaki & Kugiumutzakis, 2009; Trevarthen, et al., 2011) (Figure 17.2). Toddlers, using new-found freedom of whole-body movement with strong vocal accompaniment, act as if they just have to be musical creators as well as imitators. Norwegian professor of musicology, Jon-Roar Bjørkvold (1992), believes they are just that, inventors of music among themselves, without adult teaching—making what he calls 'children's musical culture'. Young children happy in their surroundings may sing in inventive musical ways that do not simply imitate what they have heard.

> Music-making can be observed virtually anywhere children are present—in airports and subways, homes, synagogues and churches, playgrounds, restaurants, museums, concerts, birthday parties and even grocery stores. Children make music as 'soundtracks' to their experiences, and they respond musically to sounds in their environment.
>
> (Custodero, 2009: p. 518.)

When a loving mother speaks to a young infant, she addresses this discriminating listener attentively. Her voice becomes seductive, taking on a special melodious, singing quality called 'motherese' (or, more primly, 'infant-directed speech'). In this communication it is, of course, not the speech that matters—the meanings of words elude the infant completely. 'The melody is the message' (Fernald, 1989). Mothers instinctively 'attune' their sounds to imitate and elaborate the infant's utterances, or to mimic their gestures and face expressions, to reflect their emotion (Stern, 2000). This sympathetic maternal response encourages the highly pleasurable experience of shared and inventive imitation, which can be found even with a newborn baby (Trevarthen, 2011a) (see Figure 17.1).

The Papoušeks identified the 'musicality' of maternal expression as a carrier of cultural forms of expression that makes a bridge to the syllables and phrases of language, aiding the infant's mastery of the arbitrary articulated code (Papoušek & Papoušek, 1981). Previously, Mary Catherine Bateson (1979) had described the pattern of shared intention between a mother and a

Fig. 17.2 Infants enjoy the company of music, and are moved by it. These infants were amusing themselves alone at home in Crete when a recording of a cheerful children's song was played. Their rhythmic responses were recorded and analysed by Katerina Mazokopaki of the University of Crete. Top row) Georgos, 3.5 months, listens, responds with pleasure and gestures a performance to the sound of music. Katerina, 9 months, responds to music by looking, smiling and 'flying' into action. Bottom row) Nine-month-old Panos responding to music, looked surprised, smiled a greeting, then moved rhythmically, beating with his hand and 'singing'. Anna, 10 months, standing in her cot, was surprised by the music, then smiled and started dancing, swinging her hips and singing vigorously. All the infants behaved as if a musical friend had entered the room and invited them to dance and sing. (Mazokopaki and Kugiumutzakis, 2009.)

2-month-old as a 'proto-conversation', and she concluded this was the developmental source of language learning, and of 'ritual healing practices':

> The study of timing and sequencing showed that certainly the mother and probably the infant, in addition to conforming in general to a regular pattern, were acting to sustain it or to restore it when it faltered, waiting for the expected vocalization from the other and then after a pause resuming vocalization, as if to elicit a response that had not been forthcoming. These interactions were characterized by a sort of delighted, ritualized courtesy and more or less sustained attention and mutual gaze.

(Bateson, 1979: p. 65.)

Protoconversation with an infant about 2 months old has a pulse interval approximating to adagio (c. 0.9 s), and the infant's vocalizations are organized in syllables (0.2–0.5 s, with phrase-final lengthening), and phrases (3–5 s) (Lynch et al., 1995; Malloch, 1999; Trevarthen, 1999) (Figure 17.3). These motor times of mother-infant dialogue (Jasnow & Felstein, 1986) persist as cross-culturally optimal rhythmic units in poetry and music (Wittmann & Pöppel, 1999; Miall &

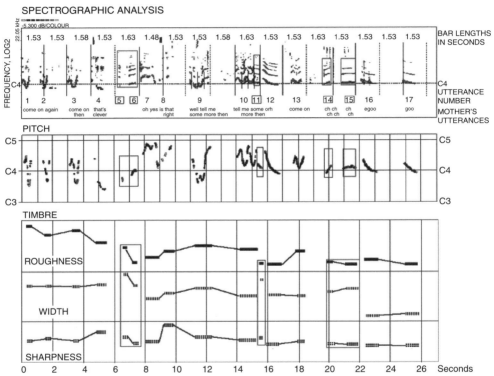

Fig. 17.3 Physical dimensions of a musical proto-conversation. Spectrograph, pitch and timbre plots of Laura, a 6-week-old infant, and her mother in dialogue. The vocalizations are represented on the spectrograph by fundamental frequency and overtones. The mother's utterances are written below the spectrograph, and each is numbered. The pitch C4 (261.63 Hz) is indicated by a horizontal line in the spectrograph, and C4 along with C3 and C5 are indicated on the pitch plot. A rectangle around an utterance number or vocalization on the graphs indicates an utterance by the baby. Numbers at the top of the spectrograph indicate the duration of the 'bars', which are determined by the occurrence of important acoustic events—vocalization onset or offset, top or bottom of a pitch 'bend', or word emphasis. A dashed bar-line indicates no vocal event marks its placement, which inferred from the duration of the surrounding bars. In the centre plot, pitch is indicated by dots, each representing 0.01 seconds of sound. Timbre is a multidimensional attribute of sound, here represented by three complementary measures. *Roughness* is a measure of the degree of 'beating' between acoustic partials. *Width* is a measure of how 'expansive' or 'narrow' a sound is heard to be. *Sharpness* is related to the relative position of a sound's loudness centroid within its spectrum. The timbre of the mother's voice changes after each of her infant's vocalizations. Immediately after all three infant vocalizations most of the timbre measures for the mother's voice drop. This may indicate the mother's wish to signal to her infant that she has heard her and make her voice more like her infant's. (Reproduced from S. Malloch, and C. Trevarthen, *Communicative Musicality: Exploring the Basis of Human Companionship*, 2009, with permission from Oxford University Press, adapted from Malloch 1999.)

Dissanayake, 2003). The baby is attracted to the whole constellation of maternal expressions; for example, fixating a mother's eyes more strongly when she vocalizes, or watching her lips to better discriminate her vocal sounds. The dialogue is co-created out of their playful intimacy of purpose, and the desire they share to transform the present experience of the actions they perform into a hopeful future of pleasures to come, and to store memories of forms of expression that will be recalled with enjoyment at a future time. They make together what Maya Gratier calls a 'proto-habitus' of performances, sharing agency to make a familiar way to be together in affection, and to make a 'common sense of moving' (Gratier, 2007; Gratier & Trevarthen, 2008).

These two aspects of creative art, the *purposeful* and the *social*, the *self-aware* and the *shared*, or *subjective* and *intersubjective*, were distinguished by the titles of two books in which John Macmurray reported his Gifford lectures on the *Field of the Personal*: *The Self as Agent* (1959) and *Persons in Relation* (1961). All of what Adam Smith called the 'imitative arts'—poetry, theatre, dance, music, and storytelling—have these two roots: self-motivated agency and seeking in imagination and memory for companionship. They are combined in a uniquely human way to build processes of invented meaning, to which an infinity of practical goals and names for actions and objects may be attached (Donald, 2001; Brandt, 2009). We are active in an imaginative, story-making way, and we constantly test one another's purposes and imaginations in playful negotiations that improvise or synthesise the memorizing of meaningful social forms of enactment.

17.6 Analysis of proto-musical dialogue with young infants

Stephen Malloch developed a sophisticated acoustic micro-analysis to detect expressive features of the voices of mothers and infants in communication (Malloch et al., 1997), and applied this to a proto-conversation between a 6-week-old girl and her mother. This produced spectrographs, pitch plots, and representations of the timbre or 'colour' of the vocal sounds (Malloch, 1999) (Figures 17.3 and 17.4). He discovered that this spontaneous and relaxed vocal dialogue lasting 27 seconds has musical features that are combined to create a melodic narrative in what he called 'communicative musicality' (Malloch & Trevarthen, 2009b). The sensitive participation of the infant in the duet showed she felt the rhythm of her mother's movements in her body, and that she sensed and strove to regulate the affective intensity or quality of the sounds she shared with her mother in musical time (Trevarthen, 1999). They were mutually aware in intense intersubjectivity (Newson, 1977; Trevarthen, 1998; Bråten, 2009). A remarkable example of how an infant feels a mother's song as movement in its body is shown later in this chapter in Figure 17.7, of a 5-month-old blind infant conducting the melody with her left hand.

Criteria were defined for dimensions of 'pulse', 'quality', and 'narrative' in intimate vocal performances of this kind (Malloch, 1999). *Pulse*, as measured, for example, on a spectrograph, is the regular succession of discrete behavioural steps—coos, syllables, the beat of utterances, and gestures. These are grouped in repeated 'bars' and phrases of a few seconds duration, and longer elements, all manifestations of the spectrum of the intrinsic motive pulse (IMP), a rhythmic time sense or 'future creating' process by which subjects may anticipate what might happen, and when, through different intervals of motor time in their interaction with the world or with one another (Trevarthen, 1999, 2009a; Osborne, 2009a). *Quality* consists of the melodic and timbral contours of expressive vocal and body gesture, demonstrating shapes of 'feeling' in movement. Variations in intensity, pitch and timbre of the voice and of the sounds of instruments being played mimic the transient 'vitality affects' generated within the human mind (Stern, 1999, 2010; Lee & Schögler, 2009).

In the *Narrative,* which Malloch (1999: p. 45) describes as 'the very essence of human companionship and communication', units of pulse and quality were linked together and shared as an

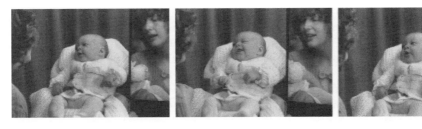

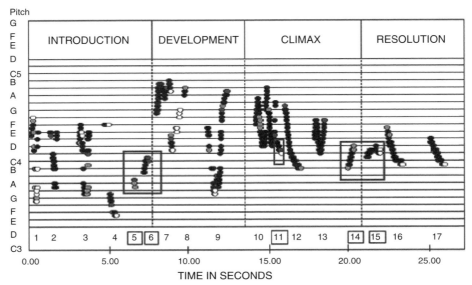

INTRODUCTION	DEVELOPMENT	CLIMAX	RESOLUTION

1 Come on
2 Again
3 Come on then
4 That's clever
5 INFANT
6 INFANT
	7 Oh yes!
	8 Is that right?
	9 Well tell me
	   some more then
		10 Tell me some
		   more then
		11 INFANT
		12 Ooorrh
		13 Come on
		14 Ch ch ch ch
		   With INFANT
			15 Ch ch
			   With INFANT
			16 Ahgoo
			17 Goo

Fig. 17.4 The melodic structure of the narrative in the proto-conversation analysed in Figure 17.3. Photos show the expressions of interest and enjoyment of Laura and her mother. The pitch plot of the vocal recording of their dialogue demonstrates the four parts of their musical story: *Introduction*, *Development*, *Climax*, and *Resolution*. The mother animates her voice rhythmically, exploring the octave above Middle C (C4). The infant's utterances, in boxes, have a much smaller range, but keep time with the mother. Utterance numbers, corresponding to those in Figure 17.3, appear immediately above the time axis and in the table. Vocalizations 5 and 6, fitting in a bar left vacant by the mother, form a rising utterance at the start of the *Development*; 11 precisely closes a bar with the mother in the *Climax*; and 14 and 15 exhibit a rise then a rise and fall which announces the *Resolution*. (Reproduced from S. Malloch, and C. Trevarthen, *Communicative Musicality: Exploring the Basis of Human Companionship*, 2009, with permission from Oxford University Press.)

affecting chain of expression, to make expectant 'emotional episodes' of a few tens of seconds (Trevarthen, 1993, 2001b; Trevarthen et al., 2011) (Figure 17.4), comparable to the 'proto-narrative envelopes' Stern had described in mother–infant play (Stern, 1995). Perception of musical companionship in the development of the melodic line supports anticipation of repeating harmonies, phrases and emotional forms in a performance that enables persons *to share a sense of passing time* (Malloch, 1999: p. 45). This sense of discrete elements combined in infinitely varied ways to represent a purposeful flow of meaning-recalling memories has been identified as a distinctive creative feature of human semiosis, essential for the development of the referential functions of linguistic discourse and rational thought (Brandt, 2009).

Malloch's account is in agreement with research proving that infants from early months are immediately receptive to the patterns and qualities of musical sounds (Trehub, 2006). Ellen Dissanayake (2000, 2009b) identifies this intimate and mutually supportive creation of 'proto-musical' communication between mother and infant as the source of art, most obviously musical, poetic and dramatic art, 'making special' dramatic stories of human interest. These stories become carriers of the conventional features and rituals of the mother's culture (Dissanayake, 2009a; Merker, 2009b).

That young infants anticipate concordant responses from a partner has been tested by asking a mother who has been enjoying a dialogue with her infant to stop moving and look at her baby with a 'still face' (Tronick et al., 1978; Murray & Trevarthen, 1985). The interruption of the mother's expressions of interest results in gaze avoidance by the baby and signs of confusion and distress. Further tests with 'double video replay' (Murray & Trevarthen, 1985; Nadel et al., 1999), in which transmission of behaviours by video link in real time is followed by a brief presentation to the attentive baby of the recorded actions of the mother when she was happily communicating a moment before, show that it is not just the immobile expressionless face and body that disturbs the infant, but the loss of the *contingent timing* of sympathetic response, behaviour that affirms the infant's feelings by the mother's 'interactional synchrony' with them (Condon & Sander, 1974; Feldman, 2007). With replay of the mother's communicative actions the baby becomes withdrawn and distressed. When, conversely, the baby's part is replayed to the mother, she senses that live contact has been broken and wonders what has gone wrong, sometimes blaming herself (Murray & Trevarthen, 1986). Nagy (2008) has shown that a newborn infant less than 2 days old is sensitive to the 'offence' of the 'still face' procedure. Such experimental tests confirm the essential dynamic intersubjective consciousness of human communication from its beginnings (Newson, 1977; Trevarthen, 1998).

A loving proto-conversation, or the intimate engagement of a happy mother or father with a newborn, is a kind of musical performance of reciprocal imitation in which adult and child cooperate, and from which they draw interest and pleasure, giving invitations and receiving responses and finding creativity in companionship (Kugiumutzakis, 1999; Nagy & Molnàr, 2004; Trevarthen, 2011a). The self-awareness of each is realized in the affectively intoned awareness of the other (Reddy, 2008). (Figure 17.5)

17.7 **Infant action songs: rituals of musical celebration**

[...] one of the most ubiquitous and powerful discourse forms in human communication is narrative. Narrative structure is even inherent in the praxis of social interaction before it achieves linguistic expression.

(Bruner, 1990: p. 77.)

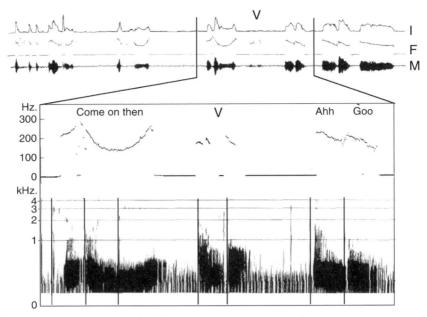

Fig. 17.5 An analysis of the prosody of the mother's expressions in the same proto-conversation as in Figure 17.3. The mother makes three 'invitations for response' with a U-shaped intonation. After the infant vocalizes a bi-syllable, V, the mother responds making three imitative utterances with a sympathetic or 'accepting' descending pitch. I = sound intensity; F = fundamental frequency; M = microphone signal. The sonogram and enlarged pitch plots below show the precise timing and inter-synchrony or coordinated timing of maternal and infant vocalizations (Trevarthen, 1984).

From the start, musical dialogues with infants have the potential to create vocal stories that can be learned and shared with a circle of companions. They give evidence that the convivial human mind is inherently 'literary' (Turner, 1996). We are born story-making, and story-sharing creatures. The phases distinguished in proto-conversation with a 2-month-old can be compared to the 'parabolic' form of an account of human events that holds attention through the evolution of a drama, with moods or episodes of 'introduction', 'development', 'climax', and 'resolution' or 'conclusion' (Malloch & Trevarthen, 2009b) (Figures 17.4 and 17.6). This dynamic form has the cohesion of a humanly motivated process that transmits emotional information about how the engagement is felt to be progressing, and what it affirms about the play of expressive impulses between mother and child, or any two or more persons—linking the phenomenal present to an expected future, and to a remembered past, as Adam Smith says music does (Smith, 1777/1982). It is the expression of impulsive behaviour that makes 'musical sense' (Kühl, 2007). It shows the motives for making meaning in discursive forms that are accepted to build a community (Bruner, 1990; Feldman, 2002; Gratier & Trevarthen, 2008).

After 3 or 4 months an infant becomes an attentive participant in the affecting rituals of baby songs and action games with preferred companions (Trevarthen, 1999, 2008). These have similar expressive poetic timing and melodic features across languages, being composed of repeating rhythms in phrases that are grouped in verses of stanzas with rhyming vowels that mark the primary divisions (Figure 17.6), but they are also are enormously 'plastic' or open to creative modification by imitation in social play, as is language (Merker, 2009a, b). The poetico-musical games

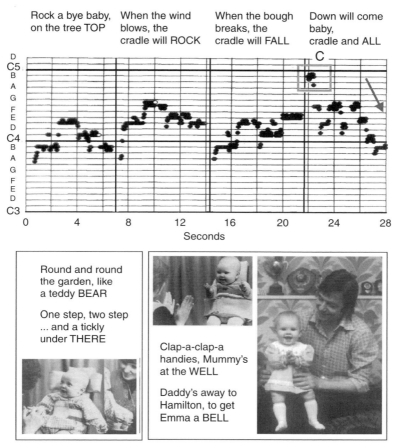

Fig. 17.6 The narrative structure of action songs for infants, and the expressions of pleasure they stimulate. Top) A trained female singer performs the lullaby, 'Rock-a-bye Baby'. The pitch plot demonstrates how the four stanzas of the song, each composed with four pulses, create a progressive story in three waves, rising to a climax (C), which is followed by a precipitous conclusion. First and second, and third and fourth stanzas have rhyming vowels at the conclusion, shown capitalized. Bottom, left) Leanne, 5 months, attends with pleasure as he mother recites 'Round and Round the Garden' with actions on the baby's hand and arm. Bottom, right) Emma, 6 months, learns 'Clapp-a, Clapp-a Handies' with her mother, and later at home on her father's knee demonstrates her skill when invited to do so, with a big smile of pride. Her father clearly admires her performance. These two last songs have rhyming vowels (capitalized) at the ends of the second and fourth lines.

thus become the habits or conventions of Maya Gratier's 'mini-culture' or 'proto-habitus' (Gratier & Trevarthen, 2008).

Improvised creations of meaning by parents and their children in play become treasured memories of their special relationships. Babies over 4 months old learn songs and action games quickly, and may move in rhythm to sounds of music, sometimes trying to sing (Mazokopaki & Kugiumutzakis, 2009; Powers & Trevarthen, 2009) (Figure 17.2). Their movements show instantaneous translations between modalities and forms of expression—between voice and visible

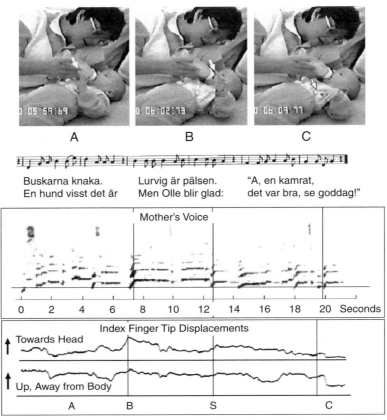

Fig. 17.7 Inter-modal equivalence of dancing gestures of the hand and the melody of a song. Maria, a 5-month-old born totally blind 'conducts', with flowing gestures, her mother's singing of a Swedish nursery song, 'Mors Lille Olle' by Alice Tegner, about a boy who meets a bear in the forest. Three bars of one verse are shown to illustrate how the movements of the infant's left hand 'describe' portions of the melody with flowing movements just like those of an orchestral conductor, occasionally with anticipation, 'leading' the mother. The photographs, at moments A, B, and C, show how the displacements of the infant's left index finger were plotted from the video. The graphs show movements in 'horizontal' and 'vertical' dimensions, corresponding to movements from the infants waist to her head, and forwards or back from her body, respectively. At B the hand moves 0.3 second before the mother's voice, and at C the infant closes the verse with a downward movement of her hand, again just before the mother ends the verse. At S the hand moves in synchrony with the mother's melody (Trevarthen, 1999).

gestures, both felt within the body as transforming pressures of expression (Figure 17.7). By 6 months a baby can be seductive performers of the specific actions to a shared song, and take pride in 'showing off' their skill, asserting a musical identity in the society of the family (Trevarthen, 1990, 2002) (Figure 17.6). They are developing the first signs of being autonomous music performers, using music to affirm shared being (Eckerdal & Merker, 2009).

This desire to perform with and for others can give rise to a theatrical event. Helena and Paulo Maria Rodrigues have created a theatre for groups of babies and parents which opens the way to a collective performance that brings joy and discovery, and they witness how even very young infants are naturally excited to perform on stage to a public in a lively crowd of actors (Rodrigues, Rodrigues,

& Correia, 2009). This theatre production, called *Bebé Babá* is intended to be educational and to stimulate the pleasure of shared creativity—to teach people how a performance can be made with infants supported by their parents, and how this strengthens a sense of community, as in a village celebration. The authors say, 'Our aim, we emphasize, was not to provide a ready-made show—not just to entertain . . . We provide the conditions, but the parents themselves have to be the artists for their own children' (p. 586). The same discovery of infant creative dramatics has been made in London by the Oily Cart company (http://www.oilycart.org.uk/early_years/), and in Edinburgh by Starcatchers (http://www.starcatchers.org.uk/).

17.8 Music education: sustaining creativity between learner and teacher

The vitality and very high quality of music-making among both pupils and teachers is testimony to the aim of providing a favourable environment for the blossoming of each young person. It is a broad aim which encompasses as much the musical expression as the technical base; the intuitive as much as the analytical process; the contemporary as much as the traditional; and the spontaneous as much as the studied and prepared.

(Yehudi Menuhin, 2010, on his School of Music in Surrey, England
http://www.yehudimenuhinschool.co.uk/index.)

A child who is asked to play a printed score must turn his attention from the primary experience of making music (spontaneous singing within the child culture, for example) to a kind of secondary music making in accordance with the notes on the page. For many children, the result is that their ability to make music in the primary sense withers and dies. . . . Their oral musical competence . . . can be irretrievably lost as a result of premature preoccupation with written music.

(Bjørkvold, 1992: p. 188.)

The spontaneous singing and dancing play of young children, like the most creative performances of mature artists in music or dance, are rich in metaphorical invention expressive of the ways human bodies regulate the energy and experience of their movements, making apparent how they imagine, think, feel, remember, and wish to communicate (Lakoff & Johnson, 1980; Varela, et al., 1991; Clark, 1997; Gallese & Lakoff, 2005; Custodero, 2009) (Figure 17.7). They show forms of vitality that communicate immediately, enabling actors to perform together in creative ways (Stern, 2010).

The Norwegian musicologist Jon-Roar Bjørkvold (1992) studied the musical games of children in Olso, Moscow, St Petersberg, and Los Angeles where educational practices differ. He asked, 'To what extent is there a common child culture irrespective of these enormous cultural, social and political differences?' In all three countries children showed spontaneous musicality, but in the larger nations of Russia and the USA training in music was given greater value than it was in Norway, and this had the effect of suppressing the spontaneous creativity of the playground. He insists, 'It is critically important for children to master spontaneous singing, for it is part of the common code of child culture that gives them a special key to expression and human growth' (Bjørkvold, 1992: p. 63). A comparable inhibitory effect of conventions of schooling has been recorded on the spontaneous expression of religious feelings and spirituality in the early years (Hay & Nye, 1998). These innate sources of human imagining have value for cultivation of advanced cultural ideas and skills.

Infants and young children use the voice with a singing kind of expression in progressively more 'symbolic' ways. *Fluid/Amorphous Songs* 'evolve in a completely natural way from the infant's babbling as part of its first playful experiments with voice and sound. This type of song, with its fanciful glissandi, micro-intervals, and free rhythms, is quite different from what we adults traditionally identify as song' (Bjørkvold, 1992: p. 65). *Song Formulas*, such as teasing songs, for example, assume symbolic forms are for communicating with other children. They emerge in action games with babies and flourish after the child begins to play with peers, typically at 2 or 3 years. Elements of musically more complex *Standard Songs* are picked up from play with adults and hearing them sing and soon are adapted to fit what the infant is doing, so they can appear surprisingly early. This progressive 'ritualization' of vocal creativity clarifies the adaptive motives for learning to sing, and how they express increasing narrative imagination for sharing ideas in arbitrary ways (Trevarthen & Gratier, 2005; Gratier & Trevarthen, 2008; Eckerdal & Merker, 2009).

Teachers of music at all levels, and senior students of music at an academy, may learn how best to do their work by deliberately invoking and supporting the impulses of such creative vitality (Flohr & Trevarthen, 2008). They can sense how to control their own art by watching infants and toddlers make imaginative play in affectionate friendships with parents or peers (Custodero, 2009). They can learn how to teach by helping relationships and invention of stories in groups of primary school children where occasions are provided for free instrumental play and dance performance (Fröhlich, 2009) A teacher in an academy can assist an advanced music student to master their instrument, as Jorge Correia does, by making their playing a dance to represent a narrative rich in expressed feelings (Rodrigues, Roedrigues, & Correia, 2009). Indeed a quality of 'teacher talk' that employs the musicality of the voice to represent events and to regulate discourse and joint attention in poetic/metaphorical ways is most effective for developing knowledge and ideas in all classroom work with young children (Erickson, 2009).

In all instances the motives of the learner, and how they may change with development of the body and experiences gained, and with more mature relationships, are of fundamental importance (Bannan & Woodward, 2009). The transmission of musical knowledge and skill is a two-way creative process of 'collaborative learning' (Bruner, 1996), in which the learner of cultural practices has to be active and interested as an apprentice who works in 'intent participation' with an expert (Rogoff, 2003). As with all education, the success of teaching depends on recognition of how children's 'zest for learning' (Whitehead, 1929) changes with age and the development of body and mind. And children belong to different places, where particular forms of music are cultivated for shared enjoyment in a living community of practices, myths, and values (Blacking, 1995; Cross & Morley, 2009)

Conversely, a strictly didactic form of music instruction according to an abstract, rationalized curriculum may stifle the zest for self-expression in receptive company, making the mastery of musical conventions, which necessarily requires dedicated attention and practice, slip out of the hands of the would-be learner (Bjørkvold, 1992; Bannan & Woodward, 2009). A young child's naturally singing voice may be lost as a school-age child learns they 'cannot sing in tune'. Luckily an adult who has become convinced they cannot sing can, perhaps with surprise and joy, discover that they sing beautifully as mother or father to an appreciative infant, or when sufficiently inebriated at a party. Performing in a group, as in a choir can perform the same miracle. Musical talent is released in live communication.

It has been demonstrated that the acquisition of high musical skill by an older child, over about 7 or 8 years, requires both many hours of practice and a close and sustained attachment to a responsive and appreciative teacher (Sloboda & Davidson, 1996). There is much evidence that the motivation, imagination, and memory of a child, and learning ability, are changing greatly after this age, a time when, in industrialised societies, formal schooling is beginning, or has already begun (Donaldson, 1992). As Yehudi Menuhin observes, high levels of musical performance are encouraged from this time of transition by a 'favourable environment' in a community dedicated to making, enjoying and perfecting music playing according to a living tradition.

In short, the way for a young child to learn how to read musical scores and master an approved artistic tradition of singing or playing is easier and learning more sure if the teacher strives to be a companion in the enjoyment of moving with the subtleties of children's musical invention and celebration (Hargreaves, 1996; Imberty, 1996; Papoušek, 1996; Sloboda & Davidson, 1996;

Trehub, 2006; Littleton, 2002; Custodero, 2002, 2009; Custodero & Johnson-Green, 2003; Flohr & Trevarthen, 2008).

17.9 Musical re-creation: the art of therapy with sound in shared movement

Musical structure in improvisation can provide a framework for creative development, and . . . more creative skills may well emerge given a structure than one might see from a purely free form of improvisation—where a lack of direction and model may leave the 'non-musician' client struggling to find out how they can 'create' music. . . . Creativity is a key process in improvisational music therapy, and demands substantial skill and flexibility in the therapists to nurture in clients for therapeutic benefit.

(Wigram, 2006.)

Like music education, improvised music therapy is a *creative partnership*, one that progresses with sensitive guidance of a skilled musician who has been trained in responsive therapy, to aid recovery of emotional self-confidence in communication. The anxious, confused, and self-absorbed client is given confidence and joy in company by carefully managed steps, the therapist using imitation and creative extension of any expression of discovery to build a turn-taking dialogue that leads to full participation in a flowing musical collaboration, with mutual affection (Nordoff & Robbins, 1977; Bruscia, 1987; Pavlicevic, 2000; Wigram, et al., 2002; Wigram, 2004; Oldfield, 2006; Zeedyk, 2008; Bond, 2009; Osborne, 2009b; Wigram & Elefant, 2009). The therapist assists the client to creative development by prompting recognition of a predictable structure or process to be discovered in the music, by using supportive repetition and teasing variation of rhythms, themes and contrasts in a 'playful' way, adjusting the 'framework' of creativity (Wigram, 2004).

The principles resemble those in jazz improvisation (Duranti & Burrell, 2004), which is based on reference themes and rules of variation in rhythm and harmony, predictability challenged with chance accidents and discoveries (Ansdell, 1995; Wigram, 2006; Gratier & Trevarthen, 2008). The creativity is the product of endless negotiation of a sensitive and sympathetic 'contract' between therapist and client in intimate communication.

Individual care that attempts to make creative contact with emotional responses as they occur is not easily assessed by standard medical trials designed to measure effects of limited treatments to populations with controls for chance effects, and this leads to uncomprehending denial of the 'validity' of claims that 'intersubjective' or 'psycho-social' therapies, including art therapies, may have beneficial effect (Trevarthen & Aitken, 2001; Trevarthen, 2009b). Experimental and non-experimental case studies using methods developed for the detailed analysis and interpretation of creative improvisation, as has been successful in research on communication with infants, confirm the therapeutic value of improvisational music therapy (e.g. Bruscia, 1987; Edgerton, 1994; Robarts, 1998; Holck, 2002; Nordoff & Robbins, 1977; Oldfield, 2006; Warwick, 1995; Wigram, 2000; Mukherjee, 2009). Stages of the process of music therapy can be measured by detailed analysis of the cooperative music-making in recorded sessions, demonstrating the gain in confidence and shared experience for individuals who have found communication and relationships difficult (Pavlicevic, 1995). Measures of responses to music therapy may also serve in diagnosis (Wigram, 2000).

Research on the difficulties children with autism have in sharing purposes and emotions and making the transition to cultural awareness and language has brought new understanding of the underlying developmental disturbance (Hobson, 2002). Children with autistic spectrum disorders (ASD) are helped to be sociable and learn by responsive music therapy, a form of communication that supports creativity and enjoyment in shared meaning at a basic level by 'attuning' to and synchronizing with the impulses of a child to move with curiosity and expression (Nordoff & Robbins, 1977; Edgerton, 1994; Robarts, 1998; Wigram, 2000, 2002, 2004; Holck, 2002; Oldfield, 2006; Jinah et al., 2009; Mukherjee, 2009; Wigram & Elefant, 2009).

There is a strong psychobiological theory or 'biopsychosocial paradigm' (Osborne, 2009b) for the creative and curative effects of intersubjective 'art' therapies that employ the vitality affects of regulated movement in live engagement to encourage communication and cooperation (Stern, 1999, 2004, 2010). The temporal arts—dance, music, drama, and poetry—entrain the vital regulations within the body and excite emotional states within the brain (Trevarthen & Malloch, 2000; Sacks, 2007; Haas & Brandes, 2009; Osborne, 2009b; Panksepp & Trevarthen, 2009; Robarts, 2009; Trevarthen, 2009b, c; Trevarthen et al., 2011; Wigram & Elefant, 2009). Interactive music therapy can support this autonomic/emotional regulatory system, modulating the impulses of a traumatized or avoidant psyche by way of sensitive hearing, coordinating heart beat, respiration and body movement, giving the self emotional harmony and promoting companionship in a 'psycho-biological loop' (Osborne, 2009b: p. 349).

> . . . the psychobiological concerns described above are connected, together with their associated symptoms, to psychological concerns, including cognition, memory, communication and hope, and related symptoms of trauma such as poor concentration, amnesia, avoidance, detachment and depression. These lead to psychosocial concerns involving identity, trust, self-belief and creativity, and associated symptoms such as depersonalization, lack of trust, self-confidence, motivation and anger. These are linked directly to both social and biosocial concerns such as socialization, social communication, attachment, social cohesion and synchronization.
>
> (Osborne, 2009b: p. 350.)

The practice of Community Music Therapy (Pavlicevic & Ansdell 2004), based on the theory of Culture-Centred Music Therapy (Stige 2002), makes use of the pleasure human beings have in collaborative music-making in groups where cultural practices flourish beyond the pleasures of intimate exchanges in dyads (Pavlicevic & Ansdell, 2009).

> For some music therapists, these changes within and without music therapy have led to a rethinking of the place and significance of communicative musicality in the rapidly developing interdisciplinary jigsaw of music in human life—of which we (among others) consider music therapy to be a small but important segment.
>
> (Pavlicevic & Ansdell, 2009: p.360.)

This approach to music therapy relates with developments in cultural musicology (Cross & Morley, 2009) and a cultural anthropology that attempts to understand the human experience of life in a creative world of traditional meanings and practices (Turner & Bruner, 1986).

17.10 Conclusion

There is, we must conclude, a natural creative process in the human mind, active from birth or before, for the receiving of music. It grows with the innocent pleasure of self-expression in play or reverie, to skill in ritual performance and the sophisticated appreciation of contrived forms of art. The *musicality* of communication with infants motivates parents to create stories of voice and gesture for their entertainment, stimulating their imagination and giving them productive memories, leading the child to language and other cultural tools, not just to music. Musical creativity is not a rare gift that prepares a young person for training to become skilled in a refined and difficult technique of performance. Making a work of art, of any magnitude, depends upon acceptance that its value will be judged by other human beings using talents that may be different from those that produced it. Its primary importance is the capacity of the creation to bring people together, to communicate its special human qualities. And these qualities may be used in 'ritual healing practices' of therapy.

References

Ansdell, G. (1995). *Music for Life.* London: Jessica Kingsley Publishers.

Bannan, N. & Woodward, S. (2009). Spontaneity in the musicality and music learning of children. In S. Malloch & C. Trevarthen (Eds.) *Communicative Musicality: Exploring the Basis of Human Companionship,* pp. 465–94. Oxford: Oxford University Press.

Bateson, M.C. (1979). The epigenesis of conversational interaction: A personal account of research development. In M. Bullowa (Ed.) *Before Speech: The Beginning of Human Communication,* pp. 63–77. London: Cambridge University Press.

Bernstein, N. (1967). *Coordination and Regulation of Movements.* New York: Pergamon.

Bjørkvold, J.-R. (1992). *The Muse Within: Creativity and Communication, Song and Play From Childhood Through Maturity.* New York: Harper Collins.

Blacking, J. (1995). *Music, Culture and Experience.* London: University of Chicago Press.

Bond, K. (2009). The human nature of dance: Towards a theory of aesthetic community. In S. Malloch & C. Trevarthen (Eds.) *Communicative Musicality: Exploring the Basis of Human Companionship,* pp. 401–22. Oxford: Oxford University Press.

Brandt, P.A. (2009). Music and how we became human—a view from cognitive semiotics: Exploring imaginative hypotheses. In S. Malloch & C. Trevarthen (Eds.) *Communicative Musicality: Exploring the Basis of Human Companionship,* pp. 31–44. Oxford: Oxford University Press.

Bråten, S. & Trevarthen, C. (2007). Prologue: From infant intersubjectivity and participant movements to simulations and conversations in cultural common sense. In S. Bråten (Ed.) *On Being Moved: From Mirror Neurons to Empathy,* pp. 21–34. Amsterdam/Philadelphia: John Benjamins.

Bråten, S. (2009). *The Intersubjective Mirror in Infant Learning and Evolution of Speech.* Amsterdam: John Benjamins.

Bruner, J.S. (1990). *Acts of Meaning.* Cambridge, MA: Harvard University Press.

Bruner, J.S. (1996). *The Culture of Education.* Cambridge, MA: Harvard University Press.

Bruscia, K.E. (1987). *Improvisational Models of Music Therapy.* Springville, IL: Charles C. Thomas/London Gollancz.

Buzsaki, G. (2006). *Rhythms of the Brain.* New York: Oxford University Press.

Clark, A. (1997). *Being There: Putting Brain, Body and World Together Again.* Cambridge MA: MIT Press.

Cobb, E. (1977). *The ecology of imagination in childhood.* New York: Columbia University Press.

Condon, W.S. & Sander, L.S. (1974). Neonate movement is synchronized with adult speech: Interactional participation and language acquisition. *Science,* **183**, 99–101.

Cross, I. & Morley, I. (2009). The evolution of music: Theories, definitions and the nature of the evidence. In S. Malloch & C. Trevarthen (Eds.) *Communicative Musicality: Exploring the Basis of Human Companionship,* pp. 61–81. Oxford: Oxford University Press.

Csikszentmihalyi, M. & Csikszentmihalyi, I.S. (Eds.). (1988). *Optimal Experience: Psychological Studies of Flow in Consciousness.* New York: Cambridge University Press.

Custodero, L.A. (2002). The musical lives of young children: Inviting, seeking, initiating. *Zero to Three,* **23**(1), 4–9.

Custodero, L.A. (2009). Intimacy and reciprocity in improvisatory musical performance: Pedagogical lessons from adult artists and young children. In S. Malloch & C. Trevarthen, (Eds.) *Communicative Musicality: Exploring the Basis of Human Companionship,* pp. 513–30. Oxford: Oxford University Press.

Custodero, L.A. & Johnson-Green, E.A. (2003). Passing the cultural torch: Musical experience and musical parenting of infants. *Journal of Research in Music Education,* **51**(2), 102–14.

Damasio, A.R. (1999). *The Feeling of What Happens: Body, Emotion and the Making of Consciousness*. London: Heinemann.

Darwin C. (1872). *The Expression of Emotion in Man and Animals*. London: Methuen.

Dissanayake, E. (2000) *Art and Intimacy: How the Arts Began*. Seattle, WA: University of Washington Press.

Dissanayake, E. (2009a). Bodies swayed to music: The temporal arts as integral to ceremonial ritual. In S. Malloch & C. Trevarthen (Eds.) *Communicative Musicality: Exploring the Basis of Human Companionship*, pp. 533–44. Oxford: Oxford University Press.

Dissanayake, E. (2009b). Root, leaf, blossom, or bole: Concerning the origin and adaptive function of music. In Malloch S. & Trevarthen, C. (Eds.) *Communicative Musicality: Exploring the Basis of Human Companionship*, pp.17–30. Oxford: Oxford University Press.

Donald, M. (2001). *A Mind So Rare: The Evolution of Human Consciousness*. New York: Norton.

Donaldson, M. (1992). *Human Minds: An Exploration*. London: Allen Lane/Penguin Books.

Duranti, A. & Burrell, K. (2004). Jazz improvisation: A search for hidden harmonies and a unique self. *Ricerche di Psicologia*, **3**, 71–101.

Eckerdal, P. & Merker, B. (2009). 'Music' and the 'action song' in infant development: An interpretation. In S. Malloch & C. Trevarthen (Eds.) *Communicative Musicality: Exploring the Basis of Human Companionship*, pp. 241–62. Oxford: Oxford University Press.

Edgerton, C.L. (1994). The effect of improvisational music therapy on the communicative behaviours of autistic children. *Journal of Music Therapy*, **31**(1), 31–62.

Erickson, F. (2009). Musicality in talk and listening: A key element in classroom discourse as an environment for learning. In S. Malloch & C. Trevarthen, (Eds.) *Communicative Musicality: Exploring the Basis of Human Companionship*, pp. 449–64. Oxford: Oxford University Press.

Feldman, C. (2002). The construction of mind and self in an interpretive community. In J. Brockheimer, M. Wang, & D. Olson (Eds.) *Literacy, Narrative, and Culture*, pp. 52–66. London: Curzon.

Feldman, R. (2007). Parent-infant synchrony and the construction of shared timing: physiological precursors, developmental outcomes, and risk conditions. *Journal of Child Psychology and Psychiatry*, **48**(3/4), 329–54.

Fernald, A. (1989). Intonation and communicative interest in mothers' speech to infants: Is the melody the message? *Child Development*, **60**, 1497–510.

Flohr, J. & Trevarthen, C. (2008). Music learning in childhood: early developments of a musical brain and body. In W. Gruhn & F. Rauscher (Eds.) *Neurosciences in Music Pedagogy*, pp. 53–100. New York: Nova Biomedical Books.

Fonagy, I. (2001). *Languages Within Language. An Evolutive Approach* (Foundations of Semiotics 13). Amsterdam/Philadelphia: John Benjamins.

Foster, R. G. & Kreitzman, L. (2004). *Rhythms of Life: The Biological Clocks That Control the Daily Lives of Every Living Thing*. London: Profile Books.

Fritz, T., Jentschke, S., Gosselin, N., Sammler, D., Peretz, I., Turner, R., *et al.* (2009). Universal recognition of three basic emotions in music. *Current Biology*, **19**(7), 573–6.

Fröhlich, C. (2009). Vitality in music and dance as basic existential experience: Applications in teaching music. In S. Malloch & C. Trevarthen (Eds.) *Communicative Musicality: Exploring the Basis of Human Companionship*, pp. 495–512, Oxford: Oxford University Press.

Gabrielsson, A, & Juslin, P.N. (1996). Emotional expression in music performance: Between the performer's intention and the listener's experience. *Psychology of Music*, **24**, 68–91.

Gallese, V. & Lakoff, G. (2005). The brain's concepts: The role of the sensory–motor system in reason and language. *Cognitive Neuropsychology*, **22**, 455–79.

Gratier, M. (2007). Musicalité, style et appartenance. In M. Imberty & M. Gratier (Eds.) *Geste, Temps et Musicalité*. Paris: L'Harmattan.

Gratier, M. & Trevarthen, C. (2008). Musical narrative and motives for culture in mother–infant vocal interaction. *Journal of Consciousness Studies*, **15/10–11**, 122–58.

Haas, R. & Brandes, V. (Eds.) (2009). *Music That Works: Contributions of Biology, Neurophysiology, Psychology, Sociology, Medicine and Musicology*. Vienna/New York: Springer.

Halliday M.A.K. (2006). *The Language of Science*. London/New York: Continuum International Publishing Group.

Hargreaves, D. (1996). The development of artistic and musical competence. In I. Deliège & J. Sloboda (Eds.) *Musical Beginnings: Origins and Development of Musical Competence*, pp. 145–70. Oxford: Oxford University Press.

Hay, D. & Nye, R. (1998). *The Spirit of the Child*. London: HarperCollins.

Hobson, P. (2002). *The Cradle of Thought: Exploring the Origins of Thinking*. London: Macmillan.

Holck, U. (2002). Music therapy for children with communication disorders. In T. Wigram, I.N. Pedersen, & L.O. Bonde (Eds.) *A Comprehensive Guide to Music Therapy: Theory, Clinical Practice, Research and Training*, pp. 183–7. London: Jessica Kingsley.

Imberty, M. (1996). Linguistic and musical development in preschool and school-age children. In I. Deliège & J. Sloboda (Eds.) *Musical beginnings: Origins and Development of Musical Competence*, pp. 191–213. Oxford: Oxford University Press.

Jasnow, M. & Feldstein, S. (1986). Adult-like temporal characteristics of mother-infant vocal interactions. *Child Developement*, **57**, 754–61.

Jinah, K., Wigram T., & Gold Christian, G. (2009). Emotional, motivational and interpersonal responsiveness of children with autism in improvisational music therapy. *Autism :The International Journal of Research and Practice*, **13**(4), 389–409.

Juslin P.N. (2001). Communicating emotion in music performance: A review and theoretical framework. In P.N. Juslin & J. Sloboda (Eds.) *Music and Emotion: Theory and Research*, pp. 309–37. Oxford: Oxford University Press.

Kugiumutzakis, G. (1999). Genesis and development of early infant mimesis to facial and vocal models. In J. Nadel & G. Butterworth (Eds.) *Imitation in Infancy*, pp. 127–85. Cambridge: Cambridge University Press.

Kühl, O. (2007). *Musical Semantics: European Semiotics: Language, Cognition and Culture 7*. Bern: Peter Lang.

Lakoff, G. & Johnson, M. (1980). *Metaphors We Live By*. Chicago, IL: University of Chicago Press.

Lee, D. & Schögler, B. (2009). Tau in musical expression. In S. Malloch & C. Trevarthen (Eds.) *Communicative Musicality: Exploring the Basis of Human Companionship*, pp. 83–104. Oxford: Oxford University Press.

Lee, D.N. (2005). Tau in action in development. In J.J. Rieser, J.J. Lockman, & C.A. Nelson (Eds.) *Action As an Organizer of Learning and Development*, pp. 3–49. Hillsdale, NJ: Erlbaum.

Littleton, D.F. (2002). Music in the time of toddlers. *Zero to Three*, **23**(1), 35–40.

Lynch, M.P., Oller, D.K., Steffens, M.L., & Buder, E.H. (1995). Phrasing in prelinguistic vocalisations. *Developmental Psychobiology*, **28**, 3–25.

Macmurray, J. (1959) *The Self as Agent* (Volume I of *The Form of the Personal*) London: Faber and Faber.

Macmurray, J. (1961). *Persons in Relation* (Volume II of *The Form of the Personal*) London: Faber and Faber.

Malloch, S. (1999). Mother and infants and communicative musicality. *Musicæ Scientiæ, Special issue, 1999–2000: Rhythm, musical narrative, and the origins of human communication* (I. Deliège, Ed.), pp. 29–57. Liège, Belgium: European Society for the Cognitive Sciences of Music.

Malloch, S. & Trevarthen, C. (2009b). Musicality: Communicating the vitality and interests of life. In S. Malloch & C. Trevarthen (Eds.) *Communicative Musicality: Exploring the Basis of Human Companionship*, pp. 1–11. Oxford: Oxford University Press.

Malloch, S. & Trevarthen, C. (Eds.) (2009a). *Communicative Musicality: Exploring the Basis of Human Companionship*. Oxford: Oxford University Press.

Malloch, S., Sharp, D., Campbell, D.M., Campbell, A.M., & Trevarthen, C. (1997). Measuring the human voice: Analysing pitch, timing, loudness and voice quality in mother/infant communication. *Proceedings of the Institute of Acoustics*, **19**(5), 495–500.

Mazokopaki, M. & Kugiumutzakis, G. (2009). Infant rhythms: Expressions of musical companionship. In S. Malloch & C. Trevarthen (Eds.) *Communicative Musicality: Exploring the Basis of Human Companionship*, pp. 185–208, Oxford: Oxford University Press.

Menuhin, Y. (2010). The Yehudi Menuhin School. Available at: http://www.yehudimenuhinschool.co.uk/index © Yehudi Menuhin School 2010.

Merker, B. (2005). The liabilities of mobility: A selection pressure for the transition to consciousness in animal evolution. *Consciousness and Cognition*, **14**, 89–114.

Merker, B. (2009a). Returning language to culture by way of biology. *Behavioral and Brain Sciences*, **32**, 460–1.

Merker, B. (2009b). Ritual foundations of human uniqueness. In S. Malloch & C. Trevarthen (Eds.) *Communicative Musicality: Exploring the Basis of Human Companionship*, pp. 45–60. Oxford: Oxford University Press.

Miall, D.S. & Dissanayake, E. (2003). The poetics of babytalk. *Human Nature*, **14**(4), 337–64.

Mukherjee, B.B. (2009). Nurturing musicality to enhance communication skills in children with autism- a study on musical interaction therapy. World Association for Psychosocial Rehabilitation, World Congress, 12–15 November, 2009, Bangalore, India.

Murray, L. & Trevarthen, C. (1985). Emotional regulation of interactions between two-month-olds and their mothers. In T.M. Field & N.A. Fox (Eds.) *Social Perception in Infants*, pp. 177–97. Norwood, NJ: Ablex.

Murray, L. & Trevarthen, C. (1986). The infant's role in mother-infant communication. *Journal of Child Language*, **13**, 15–29.

Nadel, J., Carchon, I., Kervella, C., Marcelli, D., Réserbat-Plantey, D., (1999). Expectancies for social contingency in 2-month-olds. *Developmental Science*, **2**, 164–73.

Nagy, E. (2008). Innate intersubjectivity: Newborns' sensitivity to communication disturbance. *Developmental Psychology*, **44**(6), 1779–84.

Nagy, E. & Molnár, P. (2004). *Homo imitans* or *Homo provocans*? Human imprinting model of neonatal imitation. *Infant Behaviour and Development*, **27**(1), 54–63.

Newson, J. (1977). An intersubjective approach to the systematic description of mother-infant interaction. In H.R. Schaffer (Ed.) *Studies in Mother-Infant Interaction: The Loch Lomond Symposium*, pp. 47–61. London: Academic Press.

Nordoff, P. & Robbins, C. (1977). *Creative Music Therapy*. New York: John Day.

Oldfield, A. (2006). *Interactive Music Therapy In Child and Family Psychiatry*. London: Jessica Kingsley.

Osborne, N. (2009a). Towards a chronobiology of musical rhythm. In S. Malloch & C. Trevarthen, (Eds.) *Communicative Musicality: Exploring the Basis of Human Companionship*, pp. 545–64. Oxford: Oxford University Press.

Osborne, N. (2009b). Music for children in zones of conflict and post-conflict: A psychobiological approach. In S. Malloch & C. Trevarthen (Eds.) *Communicative Musicality: Exploring the Basis of Human Companionship*, pp. 331–56. Oxford: Oxford University Press.

Panksepp, J. (1998). The periconscious substrates of consciousness: Affective states and the evolutionary origins of the self. *Journal of Consciousness Studies*, **5**, 566–82.

Panksepp, J. & Trevarthen, C. (2009). The neuroscience of emotion in music. In S. Malloch & C. Trevarthen (Eds.) *Communicative Musicality: Exploring the Basis of Human Companionship*, pp. 105–46. Oxford: Oxford University Press.

Papoušek, M. (1996). Intuitive parenting: A hidden source of musical stimulation in infancy. In I. Deliège & J. Sloboda (Eds.) *Musical Beginnings: Origins and Development of Musical Competence*, pp. 88–112. Oxford: Oxford University Press.

Papoušek, M. & Papoušek, H. (1981). Musical elements in the infant's vocalization: Their significance for communication, cognition, and creativity. In L.P. Lipsitt & C.K. Rovee-Collier (Eds.) *Advances in Infancy Research, 1*, pp. 163–224. Norwood, NJ: Ablex.

Pavlicevic, M. (1995). Interpersonal processes in clinical improvisation: Towards a subjectively objective systematic definition. In T. Wigram, B. Saperston, & R. West (Eds.) *The Art and Science of Music Therapy: A Handbook*, PP. 167–80. London: Harwood Academic.

Pavlicevic, M. (2000). Improvisation in music therapy: Human communication in sound. *Journal of Music Therapy*, **37**(4), 269–85.

Pavlicevic, M. & Ansdell, G. (2004). *Community Music Therapy*. London: Jessica Kingsley.

Pavlicevic, M. & Ansdell, G. (2009). Between communicative musicality and collaborative musicing: A perspective from community music therapy. In S. Malloch & C. Trevarthen (Eds.) *Communicative Musicality: Exploring the Basis of Human Companionship*, pp. 357–76. Oxford: Oxford University Press.

Piaget, J. (1962). *Play, Dreams and Imitation in Childhood*. London: Routledge and Kegan Paul.

Porges, S.W. (2003). The Polyvagal Theory: Phylogenetic contributions to social behavior. *Physiology and Behavior, 79*, 503–13.

Powers, N. & Trevarthen, C. (2009). Voices of shared emotion and meaning: Young infants and their mothers in Scotland and Japan. In S. Malloch & C. Trevarthen (Eds.) *Communicative Musicality: Exploring the Basis of Human Companionship*, pp. 209–40. Oxford: Oxford University Press.

Reddy, V. (2008). *How Infants Know Minds*. Cambridge MA: Harvard University Press.

Robarts, J.Z. (1998). Music therapy and children with autism. In C. Trevarthen, K. Aitken, D. Papoudi, & J. Robarts (Eds.) *Children with Autism: Diagnosis and Interventions to Meet their Needs*, pp. 172–202. London: Jessica Kingsley.

Robarts, J.Z. (2009). Supporting the development of mindfulness and meaning: Clinical pathways in music therapy with a sexually abused child. In S. Malloch & C. Trevarthen (Eds.) *Communicative Musicality: Exploring the Basis of Human Companionship*, pp. 377–400. Oxford: Oxford University Press.

Rodrigues, H.M., Rodrigues, P.M. & Correia, J.S. (2009). Communicative musicality as creative participation: From early childhood to advanced performance. In S. Malloch & C. Trevarthen (Eds.), *Communicative Musicality: Exploring the Basis of Human Companionship*, pp. 585–610. Oxford: Oxford University Press.

Rogoff, B. (2003). *The Cultural Nature of Human Development*. Oxford: Oxford University Press.

Sacks, O. (2007). *Musicophilia: Tales of Music and the Brain*. New York: Random House/London: Picador.

Scherer, K.R. (1986). Vocal affect expression: A review and a model for future research. *Psychological Bulletin*, **99**, 143–65.

Sherrington, C.S. (1906). *The Integrative Action of the Nervous System*. New Haven, CT: Yale University Press.

Sillar, K.T., Reith, C.A. & McDearmid, J.R. (1998). Development and aminergic neuromodulation of a spinal locomotor network controlling swimming in Xenopus larvae. *Annals of the New York Academy of Sciences*, **860**, 318–32.

Sloboda, J. & Davidson, J. (1996). The young performing musician. In I. Deliège & J. Sloboda (Eds.) *Musical Beginnings: Origins and Development of Musical Competence*, pp. 171–90. Oxford: Oxford University Press.

Smith, A. (1759). *Theory of Moral Sentiments*. Edinburgh.

Smith, A. (1776). *An Inquiry into the Nature and Causes of the Wealth of Nations*. Edinburgh.

Smith, A. (1777/1982). Of the nature of that imitation which takes place in what are called the imitative arts. In W.P.D. Wightman & J.C. Bryce (Eds.) *Essays on Philosophical Subjects*, pp. 176–213. Indianapolis, IN: Liberty Fund.

Sperry, R.W. (1952) Neurology and the mind-brain problem. *American Scientist*, **40**, 291–312.

Stern, D.N. (1995). *The Motherhood Constellation*. New York: Basic Books.

Stern, D.N. (1999). Vitality contours: The temporal contour of feelings as a basic unit for constructing the infant's social experience. In Rochat, P. (Ed.) *Early Social Cognition: Understanding Others In the First Months of Life*, pp. 67–90. Mahwah, NJ: Erlbaum.

Stern, D.N. (2000). *The Interpersonal World of the Infant: A View from Psychoanalysis and Development Psychology*, Second Edition. New York: Basic Books.

Stern, D.N. (2004). *The Present Moment: In Psychotherapy and Everyday Life*. New York: Norton.

Stern, D.N. (2010). *Forms of Vitality: Exploring Dynamic Experience in Psychology, the Arts, Psychotherapy and Development*. Oxford: Oxford University Press.

Stige, B. (2002). *Culture-Centered Music Therapy*. Gilsum, NH: Barcelona Publishers.

Thompson, E. (Ed.) (2001). *Between Ourselves: Second-Person Issues In the Study of Consciousness*. Charlottesville, VA/Thorverton, UK: Imprint Academic. [And *Journal of Consciousness Studies*, **8**, 5–7].

Trehub, S.E. (2006). Infants as musical connoisseurs. In G. McPherson (Ed.) *The Child as Musician*, pp. 33–49. Oxford: Oxford University Press.

Trevarthen, C. (1984). How control of movements develops. In H.T.A. Whiting (Ed.) *Human Motor Actions: Bernstein Reassessed*, pp. 223–61. Amsterdam: Elsevier.

Trevarthen, C. (1986). Development of intersubjective motor control in infants. In M.G. Wade & H.T.A. Whiting (Eds.) *Motor Development in Children: Aspects of Coordination and Control*, pp. 209–61. Dordrecht, Martinus Nijhof.

Trevarthen, C. (1990). Signs before speech. In T.A. Sebeok & J. Umiker-Sebeok (Eds.) *The Semiotic Web*, pp. 689–755. Berlin, New York, Amsterdam: Mouton de Gruyter.

Trevarthen, C. (1993). The function of emotions in early infant communication and development. In J. Nadel & L. Camaioni (Eds.) *New Perspectives in Early Communicative Development*, pp. 48–81. London: Routledge.

Trevarthen, C. (1998). The concept and foundations of infant intersubjectivity. In S. Bråten (Ed.) *Intersubjective Communication and Emotion in Early Ontogeny*, pp. 15–46. Cambridge: Cambridge University Press.

Trevarthen, C. (1999). Musicality and the intrinsic motive pulse: Evidence from human psychobiology and infant communication. *Musicæ Scientiæ, Special issue, 1999–2000: Rhythm, musical narrative, and the origins of human communication* (I. Deliège, Ed.), pp. 157–213. Liège, Belgium: European Society for the Cognitive Sciences of Music.

Trevarthen, C. (2001a). The neurobiology of early communication: intersubjective regulations in human brain development. In Kalverboer AF, Gramsbergen A (Eds.) *Handbook on Brain and Behavior in Human Development*, pp. 841–82. Dordrecht: Kluwer.

Trevarthen, C. (2001b). Intrinsic motives for companionship in understanding: Their origin, development and significance for infant mental health. *Infant Mental Health Journal*, **22**(1–2), 95–131.

Trevarthen, C. (2002). Origins of musical identity: evidence from infancy for musical social awareness. In R. MacDonald, D.J. Hargreaves & D. Miell (Eds.) *Musical Identities*, pp. 21–38. Oxford: Oxford University Press.

Trevarthen, C. (2008). The musical art of infant conversation: Narrating in the time of sympathetic experience, without rational interpretation, before words. *Musicae Scientiae, Special Issue, 2008*, 11–37.

Trevarthen, C. (2009a). Human biochronology: on the source and functions of 'musicality'. In R. Haas & V. Brandes (Eds.) *Music That Works: Contributions of Biology, Neurophysiology, Psychology, Sociology, Medicine and Musicology*, pp. 221–65. Vienna/New York: Springer.

Trevarthen, C. (2009b). The functions of emotion in infancy: The regulation and communication of rhythm, sympathy, and meaning in human development. In D. Fosha, D.J. Siegel, & M.F. Solomon (Eds.) *The Healing Power of Emotion: Affective Neuroscience, Development, and Clinical Practice*, pp. 55–85. New York: Norton.

Trevarthen, C. (2011a). What is it like to be a person who knows nothing? Defining the active intersubjective mind of a newborn human being. *Infant and Child Development*, **20**(1), 119–35.

Trevarthen, C. (2011b). Enactive human intersubjectivity: Acting imaginatively to create and share meaning. *Cognitive Semiotics.* (in press)

Trevarthen, C. & Aitken, K.J. (2001). Infant intersubjectivity: research, theory, and clinical applications. *Journal of Child Psychology and Psychiatry,* **42**(1), 3–48.

Trevarthen, C. & Gratier, M. (2005). Voix et musicalité: Nature, émotion, relations et culture. In M.-F. Castarède & G. Konopczynski (Eds.) *Au Commencement Était la Voix,* pp. 105–16. Ramonville Saint-Agne: Érès.

Trevarthen, C. & Malloch S. (2000). The dance of wellbeing: Defining the musical therapeutic effect. *The Nordic Journal of Music Therapy,* **9**(2), 3–17.

Trevarthen, C., Delafield-Butt, J., & Schögler, B. (2011). Psychobiology of musical gesture: Innate rhythm, harmony and melody in movements of narration. In A. Gritten & E. King (Eds.) *New Perspectives on Music and Gesture.* Aldershot: Ashgate, pp. 11–44.

Tronick, E.Z. (2005). Why is connection with others so critical? The formation of dyadic states of consciousness: coherence governed selection and the co-creation of meaning out of messy meaning making. In J. Nadel & D. Muir (Eds.) *Emotional Development,* pp. 293–315. Oxford: Oxford University Press.

Tronick, E.Z., Als, H., Adamson, L., Wise, S. & Brazelton, T.B. (1978). The infant's response to entrapment between contradictory messages in face-to-face interaction. *Journal of the American Academy of Child Psychiatry,* **17**, 1–13.

Turner, M. (1996). *The Literary Mind: The Origins of Thought and Language.* New York/Oxford: Oxford University Press.

Turner, V.W. & Bruner, E.M. (1986). *The Anthropology of Experience.* Chicago, IL: University of Illinois Press.

van Rees, S. & de Leeuw, R. (1993). *Born Too Early: The Kangaroo Method With Premature Babies.* Video by Stichting Lichaamstaal, Scheyvenhofweg 12, 6093 PR, Heythuysen, The Netherlands.

Varela, F., Thompson E., & Rosch, E. (1991). *The Embodied Mind.* Cambridge MA: MIT Press.

von Holst, E. & von Saint-Paul, U. (1961). On the functional organization of drives. *Animal Behavior,* **11**, 1–20.

Wallin, N.L., Merker, B., & Brown, S. (Eds.) (2000). *The Origins of Music.* Cambridge MA: MIT Press.

Warwick, A. (1995). Music therapy in the education service: research with autistic children and their mothers. In T. Wigram, B. Saperston, & R. West (Eds.) *The Art and Science of Music Therapy: A Handbook,* pp. 209–25. London: Harwood Academic.

Whitehead, A.N. (1926). *Science and the Modern World.* Lowell Lectures (1925). Cambridge: Cambridge University Press.

Whitehead, A.N. (1929). *The Aims of Education and Other Essays.* New York: Macmillan.

Wigram, A. (2000). Contact in music: The analysis of musical behaviour in children with communication disorder and pervasive developmental disability for differential diagnosis. In T. Wigram & J. De Backer (Eds.) *Clinical Applications in Developmental Disability, Paediatrics and Neurology,* pp. 69–92. London: Jessica Kingsley.

Wigram, T. (2002). Indications in music therapy: Evidence from assessment that can identify the expectations of music therapy as a treatment for autistic spectrum disorder (ASD): Meeting the challenge of evidence based practice. *British Journal of Music Therapy,* **16**(1), 11–28.

Wigram, T. (2004). *Improvisation: Methods and Techniques for Music Therapy Clinicians, Educators and Students.* London, Philadelphia: Jessica Kingsley.

Wigram, T. (2006). Musical creativity in children with cognitive and social impairment. In I. Deliège & G. Wiggins (Eds.) *Musical Creativity: Multidisciplinary Research in Theory and Practice.* London: Psychology Press, Taylor and Francis.

Wigram, T. & Elefant, C. (2009). Therapeutic dialogues in music: Nurturing musicality of communication in children with autistic spectrum disorder and Rett syndrome. In S. Malloch & C. Trevarthen (Eds.)

Communicative Musicality: Exploring the Basis of Human Companionship, pp. 423–45. Oxford: Oxford University Press.

Wigram, T., Pedersen, I.N. & Bonde, L.O. (Eds.) (2002). *A Comprehensive Guide to Music Therapy: Theory, Clinical Practice, Research and Training.* London: Jessica Kingsley.

Wittmann, M. & Pöppel, E. (1999). Temporal mechanisms of the brain as fundamentals of communication with special reference to music perception and performance. *Musicæ Scientiæ, Special Issue: Rhythm, Musical Narrative, and the Origins of Human Communication,* 13–28.

Zeedyk, S. (Ed.) (2008). *Promoting Social Interaction For Individuals With Communication Impairments.* London and Philadelphia: Jessica Kingsley.

Zei Pollermann, B. (2007). Voice and affect in speech communication. In K. Izdebski (Ed.) *Emotions in the Human Voice*, Volume 1, 215–32. Abingdon, UK/San Diego: Plural Publishing.

Zlatev, J., Racine, T.P., Sinha, C., & Itkonen, E. (Eds.) (2008). *The Shared Mind: Perspectives on Intersubjectivity.* Amsterdam: John Benjamins.

Chapter 18

Musicianship–how and where in the brain?

Mari Tervaniemi

Abstract

Musical expertise has its imprints both in brain function and structure. In this chapter, the evidence for this will be introduced. A special emphasis will be given to the most recent pioneering findings in which not only sensory-motor and cognitive but also more creative functions essential in musical behaviour and performance have been explored in the human brain. In parallel, the chapter will illuminate some methodological restrictions and some promising modern solutions to them.

18.1 Introduction

Musical expertise has its imprints in the neural architecture. Both brain function and structure can be shaped by the existence and even by the type of musical skills. These notions, despite their tacit characteristics, are a relatively recent outcome of the elaborated use of empirical methods of brain science to reveal the ways in which the human brain interacts with musical information. These findings parallel and extend the findings in other domains of cognitive neurosciences by highlighting the vast neuroplastic capacity of the brain to be adjusted by the environment and the demands set by it.

Empirical research in the neuroscience of musical expertise was started in two different modalities, namely in the auditory and somatosensory domains, more than 10 years ago. The pioneering works by Elbert et al. (1995) and Pantev et al. (1998) showed that in both modalities, the cortical areas receiving sound input (auditory cortex in the temporal lobe; Pantev et al., 1998), and those representing the fingertips (somatosensory cortex next to the precentral gyrus; Elbert et al., 1995), are expanded in musicians when compared to non-musicians (see Figure 18.1). Due to correlations between the age when active musical training started and the functional enhancement of the given cortical area (Pantev et al., 1998), it was concluded that the findings observed in the auditory cortex are due to training rather than to innate predisposition to music. Moreover, since the fingertips had unequally enlarged brain representations between the left and right hands in violin players (Elbert et al., 1995), attributed to different functional demands between the hands in their musical practising and performance, the findings in the somatosensory cortex were also considered to be more likely to be caused by musical training than by any pre-training factors.

In this chapter, some more recent findings will be introduced: first in the auditory modality, and thereafter in cross-modal functions. These pioneering findings will be followed by the most up-to-date pieces of evidence about the brain functions which might underlie the most creative forms of musical activities, namely, musical performance. Most findings introduced in the current chapter are chosen to illustrate the ways in which human brain function has been boosted by musical training (see also Kraus & Chandrasekaran, 2010). Structural evidence delineating the hard-wired changes in the brain anatomy, caused by musical training, has been reviewed elsewhere (Münte et al., 2002; Tervaniemi, 2009).

18.2 Sound perception and cognition–cornerstones of musicianship

Since the seminal findings of Pantev (see above), there has been a rapid expansion of findings emphasizing the capacity of the auditory cortex to be specifically tuned in musicians to process musical sounds.

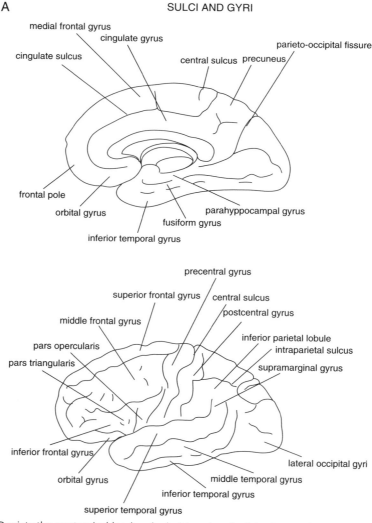

Fig. 18.1 A) Depicts the anatomical landmarks (sulci and gyri) of the human brain.

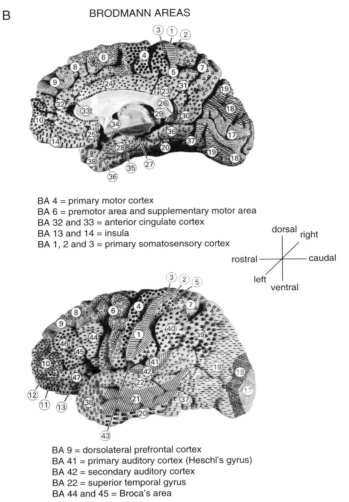

B BRODMANN AREAS

BA 4 = primary motor cortex
BA 6 = premotor area and supplementary motor area
BA 32 and 33 = anterior cingulate cortex
BA 13 and 14 = insula
BA 1, 2 and 3 = primary somatosensory cortex

BA 9 = dorsolateral prefrontal cortex
BA 41 = primary auditory cortex (Heschl's gyrus)
BA 42 = secondary auditory cortex
BA 22 = superior temporal gyrus
BA 44 and 45 = Broca's area

Fig. 18.1 (*continued*) B) Illustrates the Brodmann nomenclature to characterize cortical areas. Additionally, some functional areas of major importance in musical functions are listed at the bottom of the figure. Adapted from Brattico and Tervaniemi (2009). Reproduced from Bader Rolf, Neuhaus Christiane, Morgenstern Ulrich (eds.), Concepts, Experiments, and Fieldwork: Studies in Systematic Musicology and Ethnomusicology, Peter Lang, Copyright © 2010 http://www.peterlang.com/?58902.

In the first wave of studies on musical expertise and its neural architecture, it was shown that musicians, when compared to non-musicians without any formal training in music, are superior in reacting to sound stream presentation, especially when the sounds consist of timbres with which the musicians are most familiar (Pantev et al., 2001; Trainor et al., 2009). Musicians were also found to react more readily to small mistunings, especially in musically relevant sounds (Koelsch et al., 1999) and to relatively large pitch changes, especially in musical contexts (Brattico et al., 2001). In a similar manner, more efficient neural processing was seen in musicians when compared to non-musicians in response to rhythmic deviations (Rüsseler et al., 2001) and to deviations in relatively complex rules in grouping rules based on pitch information (van Zuijen et al., 2004). The importance of the left-hemispheric auditory areas (Heschl's gyrus) was highlighted by Schneider et al. (2002) using both anatomical and physiological indices.

These pioneering findings were largely obtained by comparing non-musicians with classically trained musicians who were either students in the conservatoires or professional musicians. More recently, again when contrasted to non-musicians, these results have been replicated in jazz musicians (Vuust et al., 2005) and in amateur band musicians (Tervaniemi et al., 2006). In these studies, the sound material which revealed musicians to have enhanced auditory processing incorporated acoustic parameters and musical features with which the musicians were most familiar: rhythmic patterns (jazz musicians; Vuust) as well as sound source and intensity (band musicians; Tervaniemi).

During the second wave of studies on musical expertise and its neural architecture, musicians with different training histories, in terms of musical instrument or musical genre, were compared. These comparisons included those between classical musicians with different instrumental training (conductors and pianists in the studies by Münte et al. (2001) and Nager et al. (2003); singers with and without instrumental training as well as instrumentalists (Nikjeh et al., 2008, 2009), as well as musicians with different strategies in practising (Tervaniemi et al. (2001) and Seppänen et al. (2007)).

Münte et al. (2001) and Nager et al. (2003) investigated whether conductors possess special accuracy in processing spatial sound information when compared with professional pianists and non-musicians. According to their hypothesis, the conductors were superior in processing spatial information as determined by brain responses to sounds delivered via six loudspeakers placed in front and on the right side of the subject. These brain mechanisms in conductors were enhanced during attentional listening and also during conditions in which they ignored the sounds, implying that the sound information is processed in a highly automatized manner in high-level experts.

Using brief melodic patterns transposed to 12 pitch levels, Tervaniemi et al. (2001) found that musicians who practise and perform with less emphasis on the musical score display facilitated neural processing when compared with more score-oriented musicians or with non-musicians. This finding was further elaborated by Seppänen et al. (2007), who showed that the neural discrimination of such transposed melodies with a change in the interval size (rather than in the melodic contour) was faster among the musicians using aural strategies—but only after they had listened to the melodies. No group differences were obtained with simple sound sequences or with melodies played before the attentive listening.

Most recently, Nikjeh et al. (2008, 2009) indicated how singers with or without instrumental training, instrumentalists, and non-musicians process sounds with different acoustical and thus informative content (pure tones, harmonically rich sounds, and speech syllables). Their data indicated, first of all, that even the most primitive auditory response termed P1 was modulated by the musical expertise and the sound type, being slower in musicians than in non-musicians with pure tones, but without such a group difference in musical harmonic sounds. Furthermore, the singers were most accurate in pitch discrimination with the smallest pitch change used in the paradigm. Moreover, brain processes reflecting involuntary activation of attentional systems were fastest in instrumental musicians, slower in singers, and slowest in non-musicians.

Finally, an elegant functional magnetic resonance imaging (fMRI) study recently compared violin players and flautists regarding their brain activation when listening to 12-second music excerpts performed by violin or by flute (Margulis et al., 2009). Despite the obvious acoustic similarity between the musical excerpts (all originating from Bach partitas, either for flute (Partita in A Minor) or for violin (Partita in D Minor), the brain areas activated by these excerpts differed between the musicians. Differences were found at various frontal, temporal, and parietal areas (right medial frontal gyrus, left inferior and medial frontal gyri, left inferior parietal lobule, left precentral gyrus, left globus pallidus, and left superior temporal gyrus). In addition to auditory functions, these areas are traditionally considered to be involved in syntactic processing, notions of self, and motor control, as well as in the mirror neuron network. This evidence thus illustrates well the multiple ways that brain functions can be adjusted by long-term musical training, even beyond pure perceptual processes. This viewpoint will be further elaborated in the next section, which looks at cross-modal functions in musicians.

18.3 Cross-modal brain functions in musicianship

Despite the emphasis in cognitive neuroscience on perceptual skills in musicians, musical training does not only consist of ear training—it is targeted to a train a multitude of independent skills in several modalities which also need to become integrated prior to performing a musical piece in an expressive manner. The brain basis for such cross- and multimodal integration has been of increasing interest in recent years.

The first evidence of the parallel activation in two modalities which is automatically formed in the brains of musicians was provided by Haueisen and Knösche (2001) between motor and auditory systems. They showed that in musicians, the motor areas in the brain were activated by merely listening to familiar piano pieces. Such co-activation did not occur in non-musicians. In a corresponding manner, it was subsequently shown that during score reading, even without sounds being present, musicians' brains reacted to mistakes in the score as if they heard the sounds (Gunter et al., 2003). Both findings have been repeated and extended more recently. For instance, there exists more elaborated multimodal processing of somatosensory stimulation of the mouth area in trumpet players than in non-musicians (Schulz et al., 2003), tighter coupling of the audio-motor areas (Bangert & Schlaug 2006; D'Ausilio et al., 2006), greater activation of the motor brain areas during visual observation of musical performance (Haslinger et al., 2005), and very early on, automatic brain activation caused by mistakes in the score material given to the musicians (Schön & Besson, 2005). For further evidence and an elegant model of the interactions between motor and auditory domains in music performance, see Zatorre et al. (2007).

Recently, it was shown in a longitudinal paradigm that, when compared to an instruction to listen and evaluate the musical material, the involvement of motor actions during perceptual learning dynamically enhanced auditory processing of sound deviations (Pantev et al., 2009). In another study, changes in the brain activity were followed in detail during a 5-day period while musically non-trained subjects learned a sound sequence by playing or merely by listening (Lahav et al., 2007). It was found that after the training phase, various cortical brain areas of the frontoparietal motor-related network (the premotor region, the intraparietal sulcus, and the inferior parietal region) were activated by listening to the melody they also learnt to play. However, this was not the case for an unknown melody or for the melody they only learnt by listening. It thus seems that even the most fundamental perceptual processes benefit from the involvement of other modalities during the learning phase (as suggested by Pantev et al.) and, moreover, that action-related learning also readily activates motor and action-observation areas (as suggested by Lahav et al.).

Highly relevant in the current context is the proposed involvement of mirror neuron networks in musical activities. Originally observed in animal models (Rizzolatti & Craighero, 2004), a corresponding system has also been postulated to exist in the premotor and parietal cortex in humans. These neurons react to visual input undifferentiated from the activation caused by an act by the observer him/herself (for a review, see Overy & Molnar-Szakacs, 2009). Enabling an individual to automatically adopt the intentions of another person, such a system might underlie emotional processes involved in music, and might also be highly important in musical training when students imitate the performance of their teachers and senior colleagues.

18.4 **Brain mechanisms underlying musical performance**

As in all motor actions, a complex sequence of brain activations is required to enable music performances. Activated areas include the cerebellum, basal ganglia, supplementary motor area (SMA), as well as the premotor and prefrontal cortices. Since the seminal paper by Sergent et al. (1992), the involvement of these cortical and subcortical areas in musical activities has been consistently reported (for a review, see Zatorre et al., 2007).

Yet, one should be aware of the fact that methodologically, these investigations are extremely challenging. This is caused by technical limitations of the brain research methods which, for example, prevent bringing any metal objects close to the measuring device (magnetoencephalography (MEG), magnetic resonance imaging (MRI), and fMRI). Additionally, in all of these methods, it is assumed that the participant stays in a relatively fixed position during the recordings, either sitting in a reclining chair (electroencephalography, EEG; MEG) or lying on a bed (MEG, (f)MRI, positron emission tomography (PET)). Such limitations are obviously more detrimental to investigations of performance than to those of perception of music and, consequently, have specifically delayed progress in this field of research. Luckily, however, there have been recent innovations in developing musical instruments suitable also for brain recordings (see below; for a recent review, see also Brattico & Tervaniemi, 2009).

Recently, a keyboard which also can be used during fMRI scanning experiments was designed (Berkowitz & Ansari, 2008). The authors describe the instrument as 'a five-note response box resembling a five-key piano keyboard'. During brain scanning, the musicians were asked to play a simple five-tone pattern from memory along with a metronome (both timing and pitch thus constant), to create a melody (timing constant, pitch freely chosen), and to create a melody without the metronome (both timing and pitch freely chosen). By these manipulations, the authors wished to isolate the brain structures and functions which are essential for creative forms of musical performance from those which are behind any motor act while playing.

When compared with playing from memory, pattern improvisation was associated with brain activity increase in several motoric areas (rostral cingulate zone, the anterior cingulate cortex, left ventral premotor cortex/inferior frontal gyrus, left dorsal premotor cortex, the right dorsal premotor cortex, and the left cerebellum). Most crucially, the areas overlapped to a great extent with those areas which were activated when the musicians were allowed to improvise in the rhythmic domain (instead of playing along with a metronome). Thus, when compared with direct recall of musical information from memory, online music generation seems to rely on those neural structures which are more generally involved in motor sequencing, voluntary actions, and movement coordination.

Using a corresponding paradigm, Limb and Braun (2008) manipulated the complexity of the musical material (jazz = complex; scale = simple) and mode of performance (repetition from memory; improvisation) used by professional jazz musicians using a 35-key keyboard. Their comparisons showed that various brain areas were specifically activated by the improvisation task, including the prefrontal, sensory (temporal and occipital), and motor (premotor cortex, cerebellum) areas as well as anterior cingulate cortex. Additionally, deactivation in the limbic structures (known to be involved in emotional processing) was observed during improvisation. However, due to the multiplicity of the activated areas, these findings should be treated as tentative ones. It seems likely that the neural network which is specifically activated by improvisation and other forms of creative performance is much more limited in its extent.

As the final example of musical creativity in the musician's brain, let's turn to the art of composition. As a mental act without necessary online outcome in auditory or visual format, it poses the utmost challenge to brain investigations which intrinsically need to have access to the participants' task and performance. Petsche (1996) solved this problem by comparing EEG recordings in three groups of subjects with different professional training. They were asked to mentally construct a short story (verbal task), draw a painting (visual task; painters), and compose a short musical piece (musical task; composers). EEG coherence increased during all these mental tasks between several brain regions, especially in the delta and theta frequency bands. In the verbal task, this was most pronounced in the left hemisphere. In the visual task, higher coherence between distant brain regions was observed, especially between occipital and frontal regions in all frequency bands. Finally, the composing task indicated increased coherence between several distant parts of the brain (between left frontal, temporal, parietal, and occipital regions, and the right frontal, paramedian, parietal, and occipital regions). This suggests that synergetic activation of several adjacent brain regions (largely outside primary and secondary auditory areas) is crucial for such a demanding task as composition.

18.5 Music-induced emotions in musicians

Even if perceptual, cognitive, and performance aspects of music activities are crucial for a successful musical experience, they are not necessarily sufficient when the ultimate motivation for musical activities is considered. According to several authors, we keep active in music listening and music making because of its affordances to our social and emotional lives—not because of its intellectual or motor challenges. Based on this, one might ask whether musicians and non-musicians differ in the brain determinants of their musical emotions. Once again, we need to acknowledge the short history of this research field which, in the special case of combined studies on music emotion and musical expertise, is in its infancy.

However, there are two recent studies which are likely to motivate the empirical efforts on this interesting interaction. First, James et al. (2008) constructed piano pieces which randomly had some incongruent chordal endings (IV or VI degree instead of the most congruent I degree). Behaviourally, these incongruent endings were readily detected by the professional pianists but not by the musically non-trained subjects. In electrical brain recordings, these endings elicited an early right-hemispherically dominant brain response in musicians. This response had generator sources in deep brain structures which belong to the cognitive and emotional networks of the brain (hippocampus, amygdala, and right insula). Based on this, one might assume that in highly trained musicians, it is not necessary or even possible to isolate cognitive and emotional processes from each other but that they rather form an integrated, automatically activated entity.

Second, Brattico et al. (2009) presented professional musicians and non-musicians with repetitive chord sequences, each consisting of major chords, intermixed in separate sequences either with minor, mistuned, or dissonant chords. During their MEG recordings, the participants were instructed to watch a silent movie without any particular intention to listen to the chords. When compared with non-musicians' responses, the results revealed musicians to have higher cortical sensitivity to mistuned and dissonant chords among major chords than to minor chords. This was interpreted to reflect more frequent exposure to such atypical (mistuned, dissonant) chords in musicians than in non-musicians.

On the basis of James et al. and Brattico et al.'s studies, one might speculate about the neural sensitivity of musicians vs. non-musicians with musical material (chords) generally judged to be unpleasant. Based on differential roles of dissonant intervals and passages in different musical genres, musicians might value such intervals differentially, and this might be reflected in their behavioural and neural response patterns.

18.6 General conclusions

In this chapter, the current state-of-the-art in neurosciences in music has been introduced, with the emphasis on the brain determinants of musical expertise and creativity. Apparently, in various modalities as well as in cross-modal functions, there is a good deal of evidence about the flexibility for music activities offered by the neuroplastic organization of the brain. In parallel, it is obvious that it is not yet possible to fully describe the brain architecture underlying musical expertise. Likewise, there is very little one can say about the brain basis of the most creative forms of music activities, e.g. improvisation or composition. However, bearing in mind that the current research orientation and methodology has existed for less than 20 years, the present achievements and results are noteworthy inside as well as outside the music-research community—music and musicians have offered a unique route to reveal the brain mechanisms of learning and memory within cognitive neuroscience. Most recently the investigations of music-induced and music-related emotions have broadened these avenues further. Studies of cognition and emotion have both benefited from the nature of music as a well-structured but also expressive domain of human behaviour.

When it comes to future empirical efforts in the field of musical expertise and its neural basis, one necessarily needs to encounter various demands which, luckily, are not too discrepant. The first of these is to increase the ecological validity of the musical material used in the investigations. In previous studies, stimulus material (called music or musical sounds) has been often repetitive and thus relatively distant from the ever-changing acoustic characteristics of real music. This has particularly been the case when electromagnetic brain responses have been of interest (EEG, MEG). This choice of the stimulation has been dictated by the intrinsic restrictions set by these methods: each experimental stimulus (e.g. sound) had to be repeated several tens of times in order to be able to differentiate stimulus-specific brain activity from background activity. During recent years, various creative ways to overcome this problem have been introduced, for instance, a constant sound sequence or a melody can be intermixed by several different sounds in parallel (see, e.g. Huotilainen et al., 2009), thus minimizing the repetitiveness. In brain mapping studies obtained with fMRI such limitations have never been overcome, however, since the acoustic scanner noise (up to 100 dB) has disrupted the sound scene during the investigations (see, e.g. Novitski et al., 2006). However, in recent years there has been rapid development both in acoustic sound attenuation and in developing the scanning sequences so as to interrupt auditory processing as little as possible, making music studies in fMRI scanners less problematic than some time ago.

The second demand is to increase the ecological validity of the listening environment. Until recently, all brain recordings were performed in laboratory settings, in small rooms with sound and electrical isolation. However, modern EEG amplifiers are also functional in more naturalistic environments. They are also very small in size. It is thus feasible to plan investigations to be performed in music academies or concert halls, instead of or in addition to traditional laboratory settings. Since the modern EEG devices also have integrated sensors for the biosignals caused by the autonomic nervous system (which, in turn, is activated by emotional experiences), we are getting close to measuring those phenomena which make music worth all the efforts that we, as listeners and performers, invest in it—in their original environment.

The third demand which one necessarily needs to encounter in the present context is the fundamental question in all training- and learning-related findings in cognitive neuroscience: the need to reveal the possible existence of functional and anatomical differences between two groups of participants which existed prior to the explicit training. In the field of music, this issue is of utmost importance—and also of the utmost complexity. The first source of that complexity originates from the fact that already in the fetus, the first stages of learning take place, thus affecting also the auditory neurocognition of newborns (see e.g. Tervaniemi & Huotilainen, 2003). The second source of complexity arises from the vast amount of implicit learning which is gained during passive exposure to daily sound environment (for reviews, see Bigand & Poulin-Charronnat, 2006; Hannon & Trainor, 2007). Thanks to careful correlational analyses between musical training (in particular the amount of practice and starting age) and neural indices, we can infer that most if not all functional and anatomical differences between adult musicians and non-musicians are caused by explicit training in music. Yet, the final answer to this complex and intriguing question can be given only after data from several longitudinal studies on children learning to play a musical instrument are available.

The final demand is that we need to encounter interindividual differences in various aspects of musical behaviour: it is quite likely that no two human beings experience music in a similar manner, who describe their experiences with similar verbal expressions, or who gained the same level of expertise on their instrument by using the same practising methods. By now, the majority of brain data have been analysed group-wise, due to the need to increase the signal-to-noise ratio and to be able then to use statistical methodologies in determining the reliability of the given signal or group difference. However, an increasing amount of effort is already being invested in finding ways to analyse individual brain signals. This, together with already existing methods such as correlation and regression models, will make it one day possible to know more about the individual brain architecture underlying subjective music experiences, emotions, and motivations.

References

D'Ausilio, A., Altenmüller, E., Olivetti Belardinelli, M., & Lotze, M. (2006). Cross-modal plasticity of the motor cortex while listening to a rehearsed musical piece. *European Journal of Neuroscience, 24*, 955–8.

Bangert, M. & Schlaug G. (2006). Specialization of the specialized in features of external human brain morphology. *European Journal of Neuroscience, 24*, 1832–4.

Berkowitz, A.L. & Ansari, D. (2008). Generation of novel motor sequences: the neural correlates of musical improvisation. *NeuroImage, 41*, 535–43.

Bigand, E. & Poulin-Charronnat, B. (2006). Are we 'experienced listeners'? A review of the musical capacities that do not depend on formal musical training. *Cognition, 100*, 100–30.

Brattico, E. & Tervaniemi, M. (2009). Creativity in musicians: Evidence from cognitive neuroscience. In R. Bader, U. Morgenstern & C. Neuhaus (Eds.) *Studies in Systematic Musicology—Festschrift in honor of Professor Albrecht Schneider.* Frankfurt: Peter Lang Verlag, pp. 233–44.

Brattico, E., Näätänen, R., & Tervaniemi, M. (2001). Context effects on pitch perception in musicians and non-musicians: evidence from ERP recordings. *Music Perception, 19*, 1–24.

Brattico, E., Pallesen, K.J., Varyagina, O. *et al.* (2009). Neural discrimination of nonprototypical chords in music experts and laymen: An MEG study. *Journal of Cognitive Neuroscience, 21*, 2230–44.

Elbert, T., Pantev, C., Wienbruch, C., Rockstroh, B., & Taub, E. (1995). Increased cortical representation of the fingers of the left hand in string players. *Science, 270*, 305–7.

Gunter, T.C., Schmidt, B.H., & Besson, M. (2003). Let's face the music: a behavioral and electrophysiological exploration of score reading. *Psychophysiology, 40*, 742–51.

Hannon, E.E. & Trainor L.J. (2007). Music acquisition: effects of enculturation and formal training on development. *Trends in Cognitive Sciences, 11*, 466–72.

Haueisen, J. & Knösche, T.R. (2001). Involuntary motor activity in pianists evoked by music perception. *Journal of Cognitive Neuroscience, 13*, 786–92.

Haslinger, B., Erhard, P., Altenmüller, E., Schroeder, U., Boecker, H. & Ceballos-Baumann, A.O. (2005). Transmodal sensorimotor networks during action observation in professional pianists. *Journal of Cognitive Neuroscience, 17*, 282–93.

Huotilainen, M., Putkinen, V., & Tervaniemi, M. (2009). Brain research reveals automatic musical memory functions in children. *Annals of the New York Academy of Sciences, 1169*, 178–81.

James, C.E., Britz, J., Vuilleumier, P., Hauert, C.A., & Michel, C.M. (2008). Early neuronal responses in right limbic structures mediate harmony incongruity processing in musical experts. *NeuroImage, 42*, 1597–608.

Koelsch, S., Schröger, E., & Tervaniemi, M. (1999). Superior pre-attentive auditory processing in musicians. *NeuroReport, 10*, 1309–13.

Kraus, N. & Chandrasekaran, B. (2010). Music training for the developement of auditory skills. *Nature Reviews Neuroscience*, **11**, 599–605.

Lahav, A., Saltzman, E., & Schlaug, G. (2007). Action representation of sound: Audiomotor recognition network while listening to newly acquired actions. *Journal of Neuroscience*, **27**, 308–14.

Limb, C.J. & Braun, A.R. (2008). Neural substrates of spontaneous musical performance: an FMRI study of jazz improvisation. *PLoS ONE*, **3**, e1679.

Margulis, E.H., Mlsna, L.M., Uppunda, A.K., Parrish, T.B., & Wong, P.C. (2009). Selective neurophysiologic responses to music in instrumentalists with different listening biographies. *Human Brain Mapping*, **30**, 267–75.

Münte, T.F., Nager, W., Kohlmetz, C., & Altenmüller, E. (2001). Superior auditory spatial tuning in conductors. *Nature*, **409**, 580.

Münte, T.F., Altenmüller, E., & Jäncke, L. (2002). The musician's brain as a model of neuroplasticity. *Nature Reviews Neuroscience*, **3**, 473–8.

Nager, W., Kohlmetz, C., Altenmüller, E., Rodriguez-Fornells, A., & Münte, T. (2003). The fate of sounds in conductor's brains: an ERP study. *Cognitive Brain Research*, **17**, 83–93.

Nikjeh, D.A., Lister, J.J., & Frisch, S.A. (2008). Hearing of note: An electrophysiologic and psychoacoustic comparison of pitch discrimination between vocal and instrumental musicians. *Psychophysiology*, **45**, 994–1007.

Nikjeh, D.A., Lister, J.J., & Frisch, S.A. (2009). Preattentive cortical-evoked responses to pure tones, harmonic tones, and speech: Influence of music training. *Ear & Hearing*, **30**, 432–46.

Novitski N., Maess B., & Tervaniemi M. (2006). Frequency specific impairment of automatic pitch change detection by fMRI acoustic noise: An MEG study. *Journal of Neuroscience Methods*, **155**, 149–59.

Overy K. & Molnar-Szakacs I. (2009). Being together in time: Musical experience and the mirror neuron system. *Music Perception*, **26**, 489–504.

Pantev, C., Oostenveld, R., Engelien, A., Ross, B., Roberts, L., & Hoke, M. (1998). Increased auditory cortical representation in musicians. *Nature*, **392**, 811–14.

Pantev, C., Roberts, L., Schulz, M., Engelien, A., & Ross, B. (2001). Timbre-specific enhancement of auditory cortical representations in musicians. *NeuroReport*, **12**, 169–74.

Pantev, C., Lappe, C., Herholz, S.C., & Trainor, L. (2009). Auditory-somatosensory integration and cortical plasticity in musical training. *Annals of the New York Academy of Sciences*, **1169**, 143–50.

Petsche, H. (1996). Approaches to verbal, visual and musical creativity by EEG coherence analysis. *International Journal of Psychophysiology*, **24**, 145–59.

Rizzolatti, G. & Craighero, L. (2004). The mirror-neuron system. *Annual Reviews in Neuroscience*, **27**, 169–92.

Rüsseler, J., Altenmüller, E., Nager, W., Kohlmetz, C., & Münte, T.F. (2001). Event-related brain potentials to sound omissions differ in musicians and non-musicians. *Neuroscience Letters*, **308**, 33–6.

Schneider, P., Scherg, M., Dosch, M., Specht H., Gutschalk, A., & Rupp, A. (2002). Morphology of Heschl's gyrus reflects enhanced activation in the auditory cortex of musicians. *Nature Neuroscience*, **5**, 688–94.

Schön. D. & Besson, M. (2005). Visually induced auditory expectancy in music reading: a behavioral and electrophysiological study. *Journal of Cognitive Neuroscience*, **17**, 694–705.

Schulz, M., Ross, B., & Pantev, C. (2003). Evidence for training-induced crossmodal reorganization of cortical functions in trumpet players. *NeuroReport*, **14**, 157–61.

Seppänen, M., Brattico, E., & Tervaniemi, M. (2007). Practice strategies of musicians modulate neural processing and the learning of sound-patterns. *Neurobiology of Learning and Memory*, **87**, 236–47.

Sergent, J., Zuck, E., Terriah, S., & MacDonald, B. (1992). Distributed neural network underlying musical sight-reading and keyboard performance. *Science*, **257**, 106–9.

Tervaniemi, M. (2009). Musicians–same or different? *Annals of the New York Academy of Sciences*, **1169**, 151–6.

Tervaniemi, M. & Huotilainen, M. (2003). The promises of change-related brain potentials in cognitive neuroscience of music. *Annals of the New York Academy of Sciences*, **999**, 29–39.

Tervaniemi, M., Rytkönen, M., Schröger, E., Ilmoniemi, R.J., & Näätänen, R. (2001). Superior formation of cortical memory traces for melodic patterns in musicians. *Learning & Memory*, **8**, 295–300.

Tervaniemi, M., Castaneda, A., Knoll, M., & Uther, M. (2006). Sound processing in amateur musicians and non-musicians: ERP and behavioral indices. *NeuroReport*, **17**, 1225–8.

Trainor, L.J., Shahin, A.J., & Roberts, L.E. (2009). Understanding the benefits of musical training: effects on oscillatory brain activity. *Annals of the New York Academy of Sciences*, **1169**, 133–42.

Vuust, P., Pallesen, K.J., Bailey, C., *et al.* (2005). To musicians, the message is in the meter. *NeuroImage*, **24**, 560–64.

Zatorre, R.J., Chen, J.L., & Penhune, V.B. (2007). When the brain plays music: auditory-motor interactions in music perception and production. *Nature Reviews Neuroscience*, **8**, 547–58.

van Zuijen, T., Sussman, E., Winkler, I., Näätänen, R., & Tervaniemi, M. (2004). Grouping of sequential sounds–an event-related potential study comparing musicians and nonmusicians. *Journal of Cognitive Neuroscience*, **16**, 331–8.

Chapter 19

Recreating speech through singing for stroke patients with non-fluent aphasia

Bradley W. Vines

19.1 Introduction

Recent advances in experimental techniques have enabled researchers to identify effects of music on the brain, body, and mind. Clinical scientists are beginning to explore the application of this knowledge to develop treatments aimed at activating particular areas of the brain and to elicit other physiological changes that promote healing. This chapter focuses on one example of this trend towards reconnecting music with medicine: using singing to promote speech recovery after stroke. The chapter includes an overview of basic research on the neuroscience of singing, how singing is related to the neuroscience of speech deficits, and a potential application of this knowledge in the form of a speech therapy for stroke patients with non-fluent aphasia: Melodic Intonation Therapy.

19.1.1 Music and medicine: a family reunion in progress

Through the ages, cultures around the globe have recognized the beneficial effects of music on the human mind and body (Kemper & Danhauer, 2005). Dating back to the Egyptian, Hebrew, and Grecian ancient civilizations, there are records that support a widespread recognition of the connection between music and medicine (Davison, 2006; During, 2008; Licht, 1946; Podolsky, 1945). To this day, traditional forms of medicine, such as Indian ayurveda, employ music as a healing tool (Sundar, 2007) and alternative forms of medicine in the West use music in support of medical treatments and for palliative care (Aldridge, 2005).

However, mainstream medicine has not found a place for music in standard practice. There is currently no mention of medical applications of music in the course catalogues and prospectuses of medical schools like those at Oxford University and Harvard. This may be due to the fact that music has eluded scientific inquiry of the sort that provides the foundation for medical advances. However, the potential now exists for this to change and for music to enter the mainstream of modern medical discourse.

Advances in behavioural, electrophysiological, and neuroimaging techniques are paving the way to understanding how music interacts with the human mind and nervous system. These new research tools, which have developed over the last several decades, make it possible to quantify how music affects brain structure, neural activity, hormone levels, blood pressure, heart function, mood states, and cognitive abilities (Boso et al., 2006; Krumhansl, 1997; Schlaug et al., 1995; Vines et al., 2005a, b, 2006a, 2011; West & Ironson, 2008). Much of this work has been basic in nature, that is, without a clear goal of advancing clinical techniques for treating patients. However, the body of knowledge amassed through basic research into music—driven by a fascination with the experience of music and a desire to understand it—has grown to the point where links with medicine are emerging. Now, medical researchers are beginning to study the healing powers of music in relation to specific disorders using the same scientific rigour and methods of research that they apply to any other technique in clinical practice. A prime example is the application of singing in medicine.

Singing is likely the oldest and most popular form of music, and the primary and most basic source of musical creativity (Besson et al., 1998). The voice is the instrument that all people possess, and which is the model for all other musical instruments (Khan, 1996). For this reason, singing is an ideal starting point for discussing research on the effects of music and the potential for music to contribute to medicine. Though there is research underway on the benefits of singing for several illnesses (e.g., Parkinson's disease; Haneishi, 2001; Satoh & Kuzuhara, 2008), perhaps the largest volume of research related to clinical practice has taken place in the context of speech recovery for stroke patients.

The neural underpinnings of singing may provide a key to language recovery for stroke victims. Singing holds particular relevance to people suffering from Broca's aphasia, or non-fluent aphasia, which is characterized by a deficit in the ability to speak. For stroke patients suffering from severe Broca's aphasia, singing may be a useful method for engaging areas of the brain that have the potential to support speech recovery.

19.2 The neural correlates of singing and speaking

Language and music are two highly complex and related communication systems of the human being. Both call on extensive cortical and subcortical resources in the brain (Patel, 2008). Singing with words involves a combination of language and music that activates brain centres involved in both forms of communication. Research has begun to explore the differences and similarities between singing and speaking language in terms of the underlying brain areas that support these two characteristically human behaviours.

Researchers have made efforts to determine whether language and music are associated with separate neural resources (Besson et al., 1998; Bonnel et al., 2001; Hebert et al., 2003; Peretz et al., 2004), or overlapping resources (Gaab et al., 2003; Koelsch, 2005; Koelsch et al., 2002, 2004; Maess et al., 2001; Patel, 2008; Patel et al., 2008; Price et al., 2005; Wong et al., 2007). The question of whether different processes underlie music and language is relevant to determining their respective evolutionary origins (Mithen, 2005). Evidence that separate neural modules support music and language largely comes from studies investigating the neuropsychology of brain damage. These studies describe individuals who have lost musical abilities but still have preserved language abilities, or who have lost language abilities but still have musical abilities (Peretz & Coltheart, 2003). In contrast, research with neuroimaging tools, such as electroencephalography, has revealed common brain activations for music- and language-related tasks (Patel, 2003). Given that there may be general-purpose brain centres for processing speech and non-speech sounds (Price et al., 2005), a particularly interesting question asks how spoken and sung languages differ in terms of their underlying neural correlates.

Relatively few neuroimaging studies have investigated singing, and fewer still have compared singing with speaking. The research to date provides evidence that singing and speaking draw on many of the same neural resources. Studies have consistently revealed that, like speaking, singing activates the following areas of the brain: segments of the primary motor cortex that control vocal muscles, the premotor cortex (which is important for auditory-motor associations), the anterior insula (a relay centre for producing complex, expressive vocal output, which is connected with auditory, somatosensory, premotor, and limbic regions), the cerebellum (a structure involved in fine-motor control of the voice), and the supplementary motor area (which is implicated in planning motor actions) (Jeffries et al., 2003; Ozdemir et al., 2006; Perry et al., 1999; Riecker et al., 2000).

Studies have also revealed differences between the brain activation patterns associated with singing and speaking. There appears to be some degree of lateralization differentiating the two. Findings suggest that speaking activates the left hemisphere to a greater extent than singing, particularly in the anterior insula (Jeffries et al., 2003; Riecker et al., 2000) and in peri-sylvian speech areas (Jeffries et al., 2003). In contrast, singing tends to engage the right hemisphere to a greater extent than speaking, particularly in the anterior temporal cortex (Jeffries et al., 2003), the anterior insula (Jeffries et al., 2003; Riecker et al., 2000), the superior temporal gyrus, and the inferior frontal gyrus (Ozdemir et al., 2006). One possible explanation for these asymmetries has to do with the fact that the rate of pronunciation is generally higher in speech than in singing. Neural processing for speech tends to be lateralized to the left hemisphere for higher rates of pronunciation (Schlaug et al., 2008a). This may be related to the finding that the left hemisphere is specialized for high-speed auditory processing, whereas the right hemisphere is specialized for spectral processing of pitch relations (Zatorre et al., 2002). Notably, Ozdemir and colleagues (2006) controlled for rate of pronunciation, which therefore was not a confounding variable in their study.

Neuroimaging studies have revealed areas of the brain that may be involved uniquely in singing as well, such as subcortical pleasure centres (Jeffries et al., 2003), and high-level auditory processing areas (Brown et al., 2004). Jeffries and colleagues (2003) found that only their singing condition activated the right ventral striatum, which is part of the basal ganglia and the cortico-lymbic circuit. Blood and Zatorre (2001) also found activity in this area during pleasurable experiences such as listening to emotionally evocative music. Jeffries and colleagues' (2003) findings, therefore, provide neuroimaging evidence that singing triggers activity in reward and pleasure centres of the brain.

Other research has found evidence that singing engages neural centres involved in imitation—an ability of fundamental importance to speech therapy. Brown and colleagues (2004) found that their singing tasks generated strong activity in areas of the brain related to imitation and self-monitoring, such as the inferior frontal gyrus. This brain region, in the area near Broca's area, is a neural correlate of the perception and production of sequences that unfold over time. Activity in this area is essential for perceiving and producing song and language, for example. The loss of the ability to interact socially is one of the most poignant deficits for patients suffering from Broca's aphasia. Brown and colleagues' study provides some evidence that singing may be an ideal activity in which to engage in order to activate areas of the brain involved in social interaction. Taken as a whole, these findings about the neuroscience of singing are relevant to therapies for language recovery, and recovery from Broca's aphasia in particular.

19.3 Singing as a technology for language learning

19.3.1 The neural correlates of Broca's aphasia

Aphasia is the loss of language function due to neural damage. Broca's aphasia, or non-fluent aphasia, is associated with a deficit in speech production. People with non-fluent aphasia are impaired in their ability to coordinate vocal actions that produce meaningful sequences of speech sounds. This form of aphasia occurs when there is damage to the inferior frontal lobe of the left hemisphere, including Brodmann areas 44 and 45. These brain centres make up Broca's area in the left inferior frontal gyrus (Luria, 1970). Broca's aphasia has a severe negative impact on quality of life, and the pathway to recovery remains unclear.

It is a matter of continuing debate whether the left or right hemisphere is most important for the recovery of language ability after stroke. A number of studies suggest that surviving neural tissue in the left-hemisphere takes over for the damaged tissue to promote recovery (Cappa & Vallar, 1992; Heiss et al., 1999). Other studies found evidence that the right hemisphere compensates for damaged language centres in the left hemisphere (Basso et al., 1989; Blasi et al., 2002; Cappa & Vallar, 1992; Cappa et al., 1997; Kinsbourne, 1998; Moore, 1989; Pizzamiglio et al., 2001; Thiel et al., 2001; Selnes, 1999; Weiller et al., 1995). It is possible that changes in brain activity in both hemispheres correlate with recovery (Heiss & Thiel, 2006; Mimura et al., 1998; Rosen et al., 2000; Saur et al., 2006; Winhuisen et al., 2005). In considering which hemisphere is important for language recovery after stroke, it is important to make the distinction between increases in brain activity that do sustain recovery and increases that do not (Price & Crinion, 2005). There is evidence that the projections across the corpus callosum connecting homologous areas of the brain in the two hemispheres are inhibitory in nature (Bloom & Hynd, 2005). A stroke that damages the language areas of the left hemisphere, therefore, will cause transcallosal disinhibition whereby the homologous areas of the right hemisphere will stop receiving as much inhibitory input from the left hemisphere, and will increase in activity as a result. Changes in brain activity like this, which usually occur soon after the stroke, do not necessarily relate to recovery. In contrast, increases in activity in the right hemisphere that are part of a compensatory strategy, to make up for the damaged left-hemisphere language centres, may be related to functional recovery (Price & Crinion, 2005). The debate over how the two hemispheres are involved in language recovery is relevant to Broca's aphasia in particular.

There appears to be a consensus for two neural pathways that lead to recovery from Broca's aphasia (Schlaug et al., 2008a, b). One pathway involves the re-activation of brain areas near the lesion in the left hemisphere; generally, this is only a possibility for patients who have smaller lesions that do not completely destroy Broca's area. The second pathway uses the right hemisphere to facilitate recovery and may be the only option for patients with large lesions in the left hemisphere. In the case of severe Broca's aphasia, brain centres in the right hemisphere, which have the capacity to support language, may compensate for the loss of 'eloquent' areas in the left-hemisphere.

19.3.2 If you can sing, you can talk

Broca's aphasia offers a particularly interesting neuropsychological model for studying language in speech and in music. Clinicians commonly observe that some people with Broca's aphasia can sing words and phrases, even if they are dramatically impaired in their ability to speak the same words (Gerstman, 1964; Geschwind, 1971; Goldstein, 1942; Hebert et al., 2003; Keith & Aronson, 1975; Kinsella et al., 1988). The traditional explanation for this phenomenon is that there are two routes for the production of words—one through the left hemisphere for speaking, and one through the right hemisphere for singing (Cadalbert et al., 1994). Along these lines, Samson and Zatorre (1991) theorized a dual-storage system for language and singing for which there is one purely verbal store and one store where language and melody are combined. This would explain why damage to the left hemisphere might affect speaking but spare the ability to sing words and phrases. But can this hypothesis and the corresponding clinical observations stand the test of a controlled scientific study?

Peretz and colleagues (Hebert et al., 2003; Peretz et al., 2004; Racette et al., 2006) sought to test the hypothesis that people with non-fluent aphasia can sing better than speak. In an initial experiment, they performed a case study with one non-fluent stroke patient who had a very unusual aphasic syndrome (Hebert et al., 2003). The patient, who was right-handed, suffered from non-fluent aphasia due to a lesion in the right hemisphere, which was presumably the patient's non-dominant hemisphere. The experiment was organized as follows. He pronounced sets of familiar and unfamiliar lyrics using three different manners: 1) singing the lyrics to the original melody, 2) singing the lyrics to a different but familiar melody, and 3) speaking the lyrics with natural speech prosody and no melody. The results showed that the patient performed equally well while singing and while speaking. There was no improvement in speech associated with singing (as measured by the number of words the patient pronounced correctly). Hebert and colleagues (2003) interpreted these results as showing that the same neural mechanisms supported verbal production whether it was spoken or sung, and that in general singing didn't facilitate word production in non-fluent aphasic patients. However, it was notable that the patient was able to pronounce the lyrics of familiar songs very well (100% accuracy for a number of songs), while he had much more difficulty with lyrics from novel songs (closer to 50% accuracy overall). The well-known song lyrics were accessible both while singing and while speaking, which suggested that the motor patterns for known lyrics were well preserved in the patient's brain, in spite of his severe speech deficit.

Peretz and colleagues (2004) replicated this result in a second case study. They investigated the singing and speaking abilities of a patient with primary progressive aphasia who had a severe speech deficit. Again, the patient's ability to sing lyrics was not significantly better than his ability to speak them. These two case reports left unanswered the question of whether there was something unique about familiar lyrics or if people with non-fluent aphasia retained the ability to pronounce any well-learned sequence of words.

Racette and colleagues (2006) included well-known prayers and proverbs in their study, in addition to song lyrics. They performed a series of experiments with eight stroke patients (three with Broca's aphasia, four with mixed aphasia and predominant expressive deficits, and one with anomia, which is a deficit in the ability to recall words or names). In one experiment, the participants pronounced familiar lyrics both by singing them with the familiar melody, and by speaking them without any melody. Additionally, they pronounced well-known phrases, such as prayers and proverbs, by singing them with a familiar melody that matched the number of syllables in the phrase, and by speaking them without any melody. Again, there was no advantage for singing over speaking, which Racette and colleagues (2006) interpreted as further evidence that singing would not facilitate speech production for patients with non-fluent aphasia. However, the participants pronounced far more correct words from the familiar lyrics than they did from the prayers and proverbs; this was the case both when the participants sang the words with a melody, and when they spoke the words without any melody. Therefore, the results of this experiment can be interpreted as providing evidence that singing encodes words in the brain in a unique way. It appears that patients with non-fluent aphasia are better able to pronounce words and phrases that they learned through singing, compared to words and phrases learned through other means.

In their series of studies, Racette and colleagues (2006) also investigated whether singing along with a recording might benefit speech production. Participants learned novel songs, and were tested while pronouncing the lyrics alone or along with a prerecorded voice. A remarkable finding of this experiment was that participants were significantly better at recalling lyrics while singing along with someone else, compared to speaking along or singing alone, even when controlling for the rate of pronunciation. Racette and colleagues suggested that choral singing (i.e., singing along with other people) could be an effective means to promote speech rehabilitation. They also suggested that choral singing might engage areas in the brain devoted to action-perception and imitation; neuroimaging findings would support their hypothesis (Brown et al., 2004; Ozdemir et al., 2006).

Not all studies have failed to find an advantage for singing compared to speaking. For example, Schlaug and colleagues (2008a) found that two patients with classic Broca's aphasia were able to pronounce more correct, meaningful words while singing familiar lyrics than while speaking them. Regardless, the work of Peretz and colleagues raises exciting questions about the privileged status of words learned through singing. For example, why does singing along with another person lead to better word recall, and why can patients with non-fluent aphasia sing and speak familiar song lyrics better than well-known proverbs and prayers? An important step towards answering these questions involves considering the effects of long-term training over multiple days and weeks.

Wilson and colleagues (2006) investigated whether training with singing might have a greater beneficial effect compared to training with speech. In their case study of a patient with non-fluent aphasia, they used novel phrases that the patient learned under two different conditions: 1) singing the phrase with a simple melody, while tapping the rhythm of the syllables, and 2) speaking the phrase with regular prosody while tapping the rhythm of the syllables. The patient underwent two practice sessions per week for 4 weeks (eight sessions in total) with a trained music therapist. The experimenters assessed the patient's ability to pronounce the phrases at baseline (prior to training), one week after the last training session, and 5 weeks after the last training session. As a control condition for the two training conditions, the assessment at each of the three testing points also included a test of the patient's ability to pronounce a set of phrases that he did not practise. At the first follow-up test, one week after the last training session, both the speaking and singing therapies had produced a significant improvement in speech output compared to the no-training condition. However, at the second follow-up test, 5 weeks after the last training session, the patient performed better on the set of phrases learned in the singing condition compared to those learned in the speaking condition. The difference in long-term maintenance was due to a decline in performance for the words learned in the speaking condition. Notably, the patient pronounced a greater number of complete utterances over the course of training during the singing therapy compared to the speaking therapy, and the patient used material from the sung phrases when making incorrect completions more often than material from the spoken phrases. These results highlight the benefits of using singing in speech-recovery training. The fact that the improvements in performance due to singing held for a longer period, compared to the non-singing therapy, suggests that singing encodes language in the brain more efficiently and effectively. The finding that error completions drew on material from the sung phrases also suggests that singing made phrases readily available to speech production.

The results of Wilson and colleagues (2006) study do not contradict those of previous studies, including those by Peretz and colleagues, which found no benefit of singing for verbal production at a particular snapshot in time. What Wilson and colleagues showed was that it may be training over multiple days or weeks with singing that can facilitate speech production. Their study also substantiated Peretz and colleagues' finding that phrases learned through singing were easier for non-fluent patients to produce, compared to other well-learned phrases.

Taken together, these studies support the value of using singing to promote speech recovery. Singing may be an ideal tool for promoting the recovery of language ability because it engages action-perception networks in the brain for imitation (Brown et al., 2004; Racette et al., 2006), which facilitates acquiring (or reacquiring) the movement-to-sound mappings involved in speaking. Singing also engages a network of brain areas in both hemispheres, including those involved in speech, which extends into language-capable areas in the right hemisphere (Jeffries et al., 2003; Ozdemir et al., 2006; Riecker et al., 2000). Furthermore, singing accesses pleasure centres in the brain, which makes it a naturally rewarding activity; this may encourage optimal effort and performance (Jeffries et al., 2003; Racette et al., 2006).

There is a Zimbabwean proverb that says *if you can talk, you can sing*. For patients suffering from non-fluent aphasia, the opposite may be equally true: *if you can sing, you can talk*. By utilizing the power of singing to engage the brain in the process of speech recovery, therapies may have the potential to lead stroke patients with non-fluent aphasia from singing to speaking again. There is a speech therapy that aims to do just that: namely, Melodic Intonation Therapy (MIT).

19.3 Melodic Intonation Therapy

MIT is an intonation-based speech therapy designed to emphasize melodic and rhythmic elements of speech. There is an established method for MIT, which involves a structured treatment schedule and three levels of training (Albert et al., 1973). During MIT training, patients learn to pronounce high-probability words and phrases by intoning them on two sung tones. The tones are separated by three semitones (a minor third) and each syllable in a phrase is pronounced on one of the two tones. Stressed syllables are sung with the higher pitch to exaggerate natural speech prosody. The therapist also moves the patient's left hand, tapping it on the table along with every syllable. MIT words and phrases increase in difficulty and length as the patient moves through three levels of the therapy. The words and phrases are associated with visual cues depicted on cards, which the therapist uses during the training sessions. Over the course of training, the patient progresses from pronouncing words and phrases with the intoned melody, to speaking with normal prosody. The goal of the programme is to facilitate conversational speech.

MIT uses an intensive training schedule involving sessions of about 1.5 hours per day for 5 days per week until the patient masters all three levels of the programme, which usually takes 75–80 sessions. Each of the three MIT levels involves a slightly different protocol (Norton et al., 2009). For example, during an elementary MIT session (level 1), the therapist interacts with the patient using the following prescribed sequence: 1) the therapist shows a visual cue and hums the target phrase, and then intones (sings) the phrase while tapping the patient's left hand with every syllable; 2) the therapist and patient intone the phrase together while the therapist taps the patient's left hand; 3) the therapist and patient again intone and tap out the phrase together, but the therapist fades out partway through the phrase while the patient and the hand tapping continue to the end; 4) the therapist intones and taps out the phrase again while the patient observes, and then the patient immediately repeats the phrase alone while the therapist taps with the patient's left hand to assist; 5) the therapist intones a question that cues the target phrase and the patient answers by intoning the phrase as the therapist does nothing more than assist with the tapping. MIT level 2 is very similar to level 1 except that there is no humming and there are delays of several seconds inserted before the patient intones the phrases alone. Level 3 adds 'Sprechgesang', which is a transition step from singing to normal speech in which the words are not sung but pronounced slowly with exaggerated stress on the accented syllables. Overall, the MIT training involves an interplay of observation, simultaneous performance, and imitation, all of which are capacities that singing engages (Brown et al., 2004; Racette et al., 2006).

Researchers using the MIT technique have found that it significantly improves speech production (Albert et al., 1973; Bonakdarpour et al., 2000; Laughlin et al., 1979; Schlaug et al., 2008a; Sparks et al., 1974; Wilson et al., 2006). This raises the question of what MIT might be doing to the brain to facilitate recovery.

Albert, Sparks, and colleagues hypothesized that MIT engages language-capable brain areas in the right hemisphere to compensate for damaged language centres in the left hemisphere (Albert et al., 1973; Sparks et al., 1974). Recent evidence from the neuroscience of singing supports this hypothesis. Because singing involves a bi-hemispheric neural network that is more inclusive than the network involved in speaking (Ozdemir et al., 2006), singing may utilize the potential of the right hemisphere to facilitate speech production. Alternatively, the melodic and rhythmic elements of MIT may engage both hemispheres in the process of speech recovery (Boucher et al., 2001; Cohen & Masse, 1993; Helm-Estabrooks & Albert, 1991; Sparks & Holland, 1976). To test these hypotheses, researchers have measured changes in brain function associated with MIT training.

The first neuroimaging study to investigate MIT found evidence contrary to the hypothesis that MIT engages the right hemisphere. Belin and colleagues (1996) used positron emission tomography (PET) to investigate brain function in nine patients. The patients had undergone a speech therapy similar to MIT. The experimenters assessed brain activity at only one time point—after the patients had received a variable duration of the therapy. In the scanner, the patients listened to words, and pronounced the words with intoned (i.e., singing) and non-intoned manners. When comparing the brain activity during the production of intoned words to the brain activity during the production of non-intoned words, Belin and colleagues found evidence for a significant difference in areas of the left hemisphere, including the left prefrontal cortex, anterior to Broca's area. However, a comparison between producing non-intoned words and hearing words revealed a significant change in activity in the right central operculum and in the right superior temporal gyrus. The following details of the study are useful for interpreting these surprising results: 1) only two of the patient participants had Broca's aphasia. The other seven had global aphasia, which involves a loss of language comprehension in addition to production; 2) the experimenters only collected neuroimaging data after the speech therapy, which made it impossible to determine what changes occurred in the brain due to the therapy; 3) they only analysed predefined regions of interest, without considering the entire brain. This neuroimaging study made an important first step towards investigating the effects of the MIT technique on brain function.

A more recent study by Schlaug and colleagues (2008a) sought to isolate the unique characteristics of MIT. They used a control treatment, Speech Repetition Therapy (SRT), which was identical to MIT except that it lacked intoned speech and rhythmic tapping. Two patients with comparable left-hemisphere lesions and severely non-fluent speech participated in the study. The study compared the effects of 40 sessions of MIT (1.5 hours per day, 5 days per week) on one patient with the effects of an equally intensive course of SRT on a second patient. In addition to measures of speech ability (based upon tasks for picture description, picture naming, and conversational interviews), Schlaug and colleagues collected functional magnetic resonance imaging (fMRI) neuroimaging data before and after the speech therapy. They found that both interventions improved speech production. However, MIT led to greater improvements on all the behavioural measures compared to SRT. For the patient who underwent MIT comparing the fMRI data for speaking with the data for the neuroimaging control condition (silence) revealed an increase in activity in areas of the right hemisphere, including the posterior middle premotor cortex, the inferior frontal gyrus, and the posterior superior temporal gyrus. For the patient who underwent SRT, there was an increase in activity in areas of the left hemisphere, including the pre- and post-central gyri, as well as an increase in activity in areas of both hemispheres (though stronger in the left hemisphere than in the right), such as the middle and posterior portions of the superior temporal gyrus and the superior temporal sulcus. This study showed that MIT engaged a network of brain areas that was mostly in the right hemisphere, whereas SRT enhanced activity in areas of the left hemisphere. Overall, the study supports both the efficacy of MIT and the original hypothesis that it works by engaging language-capable brain areas in the right hemisphere to support speech recovery. Other research has found evidence that MIT modifies brain structure in addition to brain function.

Schlaug and colleagues (2009) used diffusion tensor imaging (DTI) to investigate the effects of MIT on white-matter structure in the brain. DTI is a magnetic resonance imaging technique that measures the movement of water molecules to trace fibre tracts of bundled neuronal axons. These tracts connect different parts of the brain that communicate in support of brain function. For example, the arcuate fasciculus connects areas of the brain involved in language comprehension and production. In particular, the arcuate fasciculus links brain centres that are most likely involved in recovery from non-fluent aphasia, including the superior temporal lobe, the inferior frontal gyrus, and the primary motor cortex. Schlaug and colleagues measured the fibres making up the arcuate fasciculus in six patients with Broca's aphasia. They collected DTI and behavioural data before and after the patients underwent an intensive series of at least 75 MIT sessions. All six patient participants improved on the speech outcome measures, which were based upon tasks for spontaneous speech, picture description, and description of common procedures. The DTI analysis revealed a significant increase in the number of fibres in the right hemisphere and a significant increase in the volume of the right arcuate fasciculus due to the MIT training. This study provided evidence that MIT remodelled the structure of the brain in the right hemisphere in order to facilitate interactions between brain areas that supported the recovery of language function. The following question remains: By what mechanisms does MIT promote functional and structural changes in the brain to enable speech recovery for patients with Broca's aphasia?

The following are four unique characteristics of the MIT procedure that may be responsible for its efficacy as a speech therapy (Schlaug et al., 2008a): 1) *reduction of speed*: while singing, the pronunciation of words tends to be slower compared to the rate of normal speech. A slower rate of speech reduces the involvement of the left hemisphere, which is geared for temporal processing. It also activates the right hemisphere, which is involved in global processing such as melodic perception (Peretz, 1990; Schuppert et al., 2000). 2) *Syllable lengthening*: research has shown that syllable lengthening promotes speech fluency (Laughlin et al., 1979). This characteristic of singing, and of MIT in particular, provides an opportunity for patients to hear the speech sounds that make up words more clearly and to plan and produce those sounds. 3) *Syllable 'chunking'*: the contextual features of singing, such as pitch and rhythm, provide an elaborate framework for representing language in memory and for breaking a motor sequence into meaningful 'chunks' (Gobet et al., 2001). These chunks remain highly accessible to vocal production, which would account for the finding that phrases learned through singing are relatively easy to recall and produce for patients with non-fluent aphasia. 4) *Hand tapping*: when the patient taps the left hand with every syllable, with the aid of the therapist, it activates a sensorimotor network in the right hemisphere. The tap, therefore, may act as a stimulus for activating the vocal-motor programmes in speech. There is evidence that vocal and hand movements are controlled by some of the same neural centres, which would provide a mechanism for hand movement to trigger vocal action (Gentilucci et al., 2000; Meister et al., 2003; Tokimura et al., 1996; Uozumi et al., 2004). Together, these characteristics distinguish MIT from other speech therapies and may account for its potential to facilitate the recovery of expressive language skill.

Other more general processes that are inherent to MIT may also play an important role in facilitating speech recovery. Overy and Molnar-Szakacs (2009) developed the Shared Affective Motion Experiment (SAME) model to account for the depth and variety of emotional responses to music, as well as the value of music to communication, therapy, and education. The SAME model suggests that imitation, synchronization, and shared experience are important aspects of MIT, which are at the core of its efficacy. This interpretation of MIT based upon the SAME model is in accord with the involvement of imitation-related brain areas in singing (Brown et al., 2004), and research findings that suggest that singing along with another voice can improve speech output for patients with non-fluent aphasia (Racette et al., 2006). Furthermore, the SAME model proposes that the anterior insula acts as a conduit between the limbic system, which plays a central role in emotional response, and the mirror neuron system, which is the network of brain areas that may enable imitation and communication between individuals (Overy & Molnar-Szakacs, 2009); this could account for neuroimaging findings pointing to activity in the anterior insula during singing (Jeffries et al., 2003; Perry et al., 1999).

19.4 **Singing as a brain stimulation technique**

Researchers are developing methods to further enhance the beneficial effects of MIT based upon research on how MIT changes the brain. For example, Vines and colleagues (2008a, 2009, in press) investigated whether combining brain stimulation with MIT could generate greater improvements in speech ability. As mentioned above, neuroimaging research found that MIT increased activity in the inferior frontal gyrus of the right hemisphere. Vines and colleagues hypothesized that stimulating the right inferior frontal gyrus would further engage this brain area during MIT sessions and lead to greater improvements in speech ability for patients suffering from Broca's aphasia.

They used a safe, non-invasive brain stimulation technique, called transcranial direct current stimulation (tDCS). Research has shown that tDCS modulates neural excitability in the brain (Liebetanz et al., 2002; Nitsche & Paulus, 2001). tDCS is administered by placing two electrodes—an anode and a cathode—on a person's scalp, and running a low-level current from one electrode to the other; neural tissue completes the circuit. There is evidence that neural excitability increases in the brain area under the anode (i.e., the spontaneous firing rate of neurons increases), and decreases in the area under the cathode (i.e., the spontaneous firing rate of neurons decreases) (Nitsche & Paulus, 2000). To achieve these polarity-dependent changes in neural excitability, it appears that tDCS influences sodium and calcium ion channels as well as NMDA-receptor efficacy. Researchers have found that applying tDCS can significantly affect behaviour, cognitive performance, or mood, depending upon the brain area that is stimulated, the polarity of stimulation, and the task used to measure the effects of tDCS (Boggio et al., 2008; Vines et al., 2006b,c, 2008b,c). Because it is highly portable, inexpensive, and involves little discomfort, tDCS holds great potential as a therapeutic tool. It is also possible to apply this form of stimulation while a patient takes part in a behavioural therapy, such as MIT.

Vines and colleagues applied tDCS during MIT sessions and measured the effects on verbal fluency. Six patients with severe Broca's aphasia took part in the study. They each underwent two series of three tDCS+MIT sessions. During one series, they received anodal tDCS over the right inferior frontal gyrus, in the area homologous to Broca's area. The stimulation was applied for 20 minutes per session with an intensity of 1.2 mA (milliamperes) while the patient engaged in MIT with a trained therapist. Participants were tested on a combined measure of verbal fluency before and after each stimulation session. The tasks included automatic production of verbal sequences (e.g., counting from one to twenty-one, pronouncing the days of the week/months of the year, reciting the US pledge of allegiance, and describing flash-card scenes), as well as picture naming. During the other series of three sessions, the patients received sham (i.e., placebo) tDCS during MIT; the sessions were otherwise identical. Notably, sham tDCS has been found to be indistinguishable from active tDCS for naïve participants (Gandiga et al., 2006). The ordering for the two stimulation conditions (active tDCS and sham) was counterbalanced across patient participants such that half of them received sham first. The dependent variable for the analysis was the percentage of change in the sum duration of fluency measures from before the first of three stimulation sessions to after the last of three stimulation sessions. An improvement in fluency corresponded to a decrease in the sum duration of fluency measures, because a decrease meant that the participant was able to pronounce the same amount of verbal material in a shorter period of time, that is, with greater fluency. The results of the analysis revealed that three active tDCS+MIT sessions led to a significant improvement in speech fluency compared to the effects of three sham tDCS+MIT sesions. The tDCS may have further engaged a network of brain areas in the right hemisphere, including the homologue of Broca's area, in order to facilitate speech recovery. This study exemplifies the potential for combining MIT and other music-based therapies with complementary treatment techniques.

It could even be suggested that singing and tDCS are simply two different forms of brain stimulation. They both modulate brain activity in a predictable way. Based upon their known properties, it is possible that a clinician could apply these brain-stimulation tools to modify the brain in such a way as to promote recovery and health.

19.5 Lessons for recovery from Broca's aphasia from the neuroscience of singing

Studies on the neural correlates of singing are highly relevant to speech recovery after stroke. Research shows that singing engages a network of brain areas in both hemispheres. This network is involved in vocal production and largely overlaps with the network for speech. The tendency for singing to elicit more brain activity in the right hemisphere may be due to a number of factors, including a slower rate of verbal production, a rich array of structural features (e.g., melody and rhythm) which makes it possible to organize motor patterns into chunks, and the involvement of global processing for melody (Peretz, 1990; Schuppert et al., 2000). Singing, therefore, may be an ideal means for people with severe non-fluent aphasia to access preserved language-capable areas in both hemispheres of the brain.

There remains some debate as to whether patients with non-fluent aphasia are able to pronounce language better while singing than while speaking (Hebert et al., 2003; Peretz et al., 2004; Racette et al., 2006; Schlaug et al., 2008a). However, there is strong evidence that learning to pronounce words and phrases through singing has advantages over learning through regular speech (Racette et al., 2006; Schlaug et al., 2008a; Wilson et al., 2006). Furthermore, singing along with another person appears to improve speech production (Racette et al., 2006). This could explain why MIT works to facilitate verbal fluency. MIT is an intensive speech therapy programme, wherein a patient sings with, and in imitation of a therapist. It combines all aspects of singing that promote language recovery, namely training over multiple sessions, singing along with other people, and learning through singing. MIT also adds a rhythmic element in the form of hand tapping to engage a motor-output network in the brain. These unique features of MIT may be ideal for recruiting language-capable brain areas in both hemispheres, and especially in the right hemisphere. Neuroimaging research substantiates this hypothesis. Schlaug and colleagues (2008, 2009) found that improvements in speech due to MIT correlated with increases in brain activity and increases in white-matter connectivity in parts of the right-hemisphere, including areas that were homologous to language centres in the left-hemisphere. Though there needs to be much more research to substantiate the effectiveness of singing, and MIT in particular, for promoting speech recovery from Broca's aphasia and modifying brain structure and function, the research findings to date are very promising.

19.6 Conclusion

MIT is paradigmatic of the potential to apply music in clinical research and practice. Knowledge of the effects of singing on brain function opens the possibility for clinical scientists to employ singing as a tool for engaging areas of the brain in the process of recovering speech. This approach is representative of the growing involvement of music in medical research, though there may be some distance to cover before treatments based upon music are integrated into mainstream practice.

Basic research into the effects of music on everything from blood pressure to mood has revealed the diverse and substantial effects music can have on the body and mind. It is simply a creative application of this basic knowledge to develop clinical therapies involving music. In the future, it may be common practice to strategically incorporate music listening and various forms of musical performance and therapy into medical treatments. Clinical research is already moving in this direction. For example, researchers have found evidence that training on a musical instrument promotes motor recovery for stroke patients (Schneider et al., 2007), and that just listening to music in the first months after a stroke can lead to significant improvements in cognitive abilities and mood (Sarkamo et al., 2008).

A special feature of music-based therapies is the potential to involve creativity in the healing process. Creativity does not appear to have any one locus in the brain (Dietrich & Kanso, 2010). A stroke to the left hemisphere, such as might result in Broca's aphasia, for example, will not take away the potential for creativity. In fact, there is evidence that damage to the left hemisphere may actually release latent creative capacities in an individual (Seeley et al., 2008). These findings are in accord with a case study, which found that a music-based speech therapy involving improvisation and other forms of creative interaction led to clinically-significant improvements in language ability for a stroke patient suffering from aphasia (Jungblut et al., 2009). In addition to having the potential to enhance cognitive, speech, and motor function, engaging in music creatively also has the benefit of providing an opportunity for social engagement, which can have widespread positive effects on overall quality of life (Wigram et al., 2002).

Sometime in the future, doctors might regularly prescribe watching music videos, joining a chorus, learning a musical instrument, or taking dance lessons to treat various ailments and disorders. In short, we are at a crossroads that marks the re-emergence of music in medicine, and a return to the traditional relationship between these complementary practices.

Acknowledgements

I am much indebted to Gottfried Schlaug, without whose input this work would not have been possible. I am also grateful to Katie Overy for her comments on the chapter. Grants from the following sources supported this research: The National Institute of Neurological Disorders and Stroke (NS053326), the Grammy Foundation, and the Michael Smith Foundation for Health Research (ST-PDF-01729-(07-1)CLIN).

References

Albert, M.L., Sparks, R.W., & Helm, N.A. (1973). Melodic intonation therapy for aphasia. *Archives of Neurology*, **29**, 130–1.

Aldridge, D. (2005). *Music Therapy and Neurological Rehabilitation*. Philadelphia, PA: Jessica Kingsley Publishers.

Basso, A., Gardelli, M., Grassi, M.P., & Mairotti, M. (1989). The role of the right hemisphere in recovery from aphasia. Two case studies. *Cortex*, **25**, 555–66.

Belin, P., Van Eeckhout, P., Zilbovicius, M., Remy, P., François, C., Guillaume, S., *et al.* (1996). Recovery from nonfluent aphasia after melodic intonation therapy: A PET study. *Neurology*, **47**, 1504–11.

Besson, M., Faita, F., Peretz, I., Bonnel, A.M., & Requin, J. (1998). Singing in the brain: Independence of lyrics and tunes. *Psychological Science*, **9**(6), 494–8.

Blasi, V., Young, A.C., Tansy, A.P., Petersen, S.E., Snyder, A.Z., & Corbetta, M. (2002). Word retrieval learning modulates right frontal cortex in patients with left frontal damage. *Neuron*, **36**, 159–70.

Blood, A.J. & Zatorre, R.J. (2001). Intensely pleasurable responses to music correlate with activity in brain regions implicated in reward and emotion. *Proceedings of the National Academy of Sciences of the United States of America*, **98**(20), 11818–23.

Bloom, J.S. & Hynde, G.W. (2005). The role of the corpus callosum in interhemispheric transfer of information: excitation or inhibition? *Neuropsychology Review*, **15**, 59–71.

Boggio, P.S., Rigonatti, S.P., Ribeiro, R.B., Myczkowski, M.L., Nitsche, M.A., Pascual-Leone, A., *et al.* (2008). A randomized, double-blind clinical trial on the efficacy of cortical direct current stimulation for the treatment of major depression. *International Journal of Neuropsychopharmacology*, **11**(2), 249–54.

Bonakdarpour, B., Eftekharzadeh, A., & Ashayeri, H. (2000). Preliminary report on the effects of melodic intonation therapy in the rehabilitation of Persian aphasic patients. *Iranian Journal of Medical Sciences,* **25**, 156–60.

Bonnel, A.M., Faita, F., Peretz, I., & Besson, M. (2001). Divided attention between lyrics and tunes of operatic songs: Evidence for independent processing. *Perception and Psychophysics,* **63**(7), 1201–13.

Boso, M., Politi, P., Barale, F., & Emanuele, E. (2006). Neurophysiology and neurobiology of the musical experience. *Functional Neurology,* **21**(4), 187–91.

Boucher, V., Carrcia, L.J., Fleurant, J., & Paradis, J. (2001). Variable efficacy of rhythm and tone in melody-based interventions: implications for the assumption of a right-hemisphere facilitation in nonfluent aphasia. *Aphasiology,* **15**, 131–49.

Brown, S., Martinez, M.J., Hodges, D.A., Fox, P.T., & Parsons, L.M. (2004). The song system of the human brain. *Cognitive Brain Research,* **20**(3), 363–75.

Cadalbert, A., Landis, T., Regard, M., & Graves, R.E. (1994). Singing with and without words: hemispheric asymmetries in motor control. *Journal of Clinical and Experimental Neuropsychology,* **16**, 664–70.

Cappa, S. & Vallar, G. (1992). The role of left and right hemispheres in recovery from aphasia. *Aphasiology,* **6**, 356–72.

Cappa, S.F., Perani, D., Bressi, S., Alberoni, M., Franceschi, M., Bettinardi, V., *et al.* (1997). A PET follow-up study of recovery after stroke in acute aphasics. *Brain and Language,* **56**, 55–67.

Cohen, N.S. & Masse, R. (1993). The application of singing and rhythmic instruction as a therapeutic intervention for persons with neurogenic communication disorders. *Journal of Music Therapy,* **30**, 81–99.

Davison, K. (2006). Historical aspects of mood disorders. *Psychiatry,* **5**(4), 115–18.

Dietrich, A. & Kanso, R. (2010). A review of EEG, ERP, and neuroimaging studies of creativity and insight. *Psychological Bulletin,* **136**, 822–48.

During, J. (2008). Therapeutic dimensions of music in Islamic culture. In B.D. Koen (Ed.) *The Oxford Handbook of Medical Ethnomusicology.* New York: Oxford University Press, pp. 361–92.

Gaab, N., Gaser, C., Zaehle, T., Jancke, L., & Schlaug, G. (2003). Functional anatomy of pitch memory - an fMRI study with sparse temporal sampling. *Neuroimage,* **19**(4), 1417–26.

Gandiga, P.C., Hummel, F.C., & Cohen, L.G. (2006). Transcranial DC stimulation (tDCS): A tool for double-blind sham-controlled clinical studies in brain stimulation. *Clinical Neurophysiology,* **117**(4), 845–50.

Gentilucci, M., Benuzzi, F., Bertolani, L., Daprati, E., & Gangitano, M. (2000). Language and motor control. *Experimental Brain Research,* **133**, 468–90.

Gerstman, H.L. (1964). A case of aphasia. *Journal of Speech and Hearing Disorders,* **29**, 89–91.

Geschwind, N. (1971). Current concepts: aphasia. *New England Journal of Medicine,* **284**, 654–6.

Gobet, F., Lane, P.C.R., Croker, S., Cheng, P.C.H., Jones, G., Oliver, I., *et al.* (2001). Chunking mechanisms in human learning. *Trends in Cognitive Sciences,* **5**, 236–43.

Goldstein, K. (1942). *After effects of brain-injuries in war: Their evaluation and treatment.* New York: Grune & Stratton.

Haneishi, E. (2001). Effects of a music therapy voice protocol on speech intelligibility, vocal acoustic measures, and mood of individuals with Parkinson's disease. *Journal of Music Therapy,* **38**(4), 273–90.

Hebert, S., Racette, A., Gagnon, L., & Peretz, I. (2003). Revisiting the dissociation between singing and speaking in expressive aphasia. *Brain,* **126**, 1838–50.

Heiss, W.D. & Thiel, A. (2006). A proposed regional hierarchy in recovery of post-stroke aphasia. *Brain and Language,* **98**, 118–23.

Heiss, W.D., Kessler, J., Thiel, A., Ghaemi, M., & Karbe, H. (1999). Differential capacity of left and right hemispheric areas for compensation of poststroke aphasia. *Annals of Neurology,* **45**, 430–8.

Helm-Estabrooks, N. & Albert, M.L. (1991). *Manual of aphasia therapy.* Austin, TX: Pro-Ed.

Jeffries, K.J., Fritz, J.B., & Braun, A.R. (2003). Words in melody: an H-2 O-15 PET study of brain activation during singing and speaking. *NeuroReport,* **14**(5), 749–54.

Jungblut, M., Suchanek, M., & Gerhard, H. (2009). Long-term recovery from chronic global aphasia: A case report. *Music and Medicine*, **1**(1), 61–9.

Khan, H.I. (1996). *The mysticism of sound and music*. Boston, MA: Shambhala.

Keith, R.L. & Aronson, A.E. (1975). Singing as therapy for apraxia of speech and aphasia: report of a case. *Brain and Language*, **2**, 483–8.

Kemper, K.J. & Danhauer, S.C. (2005). Music as therapy. *Southern Medical Journal*, **98**(3), 282–8.

Kinsbourne, M. (1998). The right hemisphere and recovery from aphasia. In B. Stemmer & H.A.Whitaker (Ed.) *Handbook of Neurolinguistics*. New York: Academic Press, pp. 386–93.

Kinsella, G., Prior, M.R., & Murray, G. (1988). Singing ability after right and left sided brain damage. A research note. *Cortex*, **24**, 165–9.

Koelsch, S. (2005). Neural substrates of processing syntax and semantics in music. *Current Opinion in Neurobiology*, **15**(2), 207–12.

Koelsch, S., Gunter, T.C., von Cramon, D.Y., Zysset, S., Lohmann, G., & Friederici, A.D. (2002). Bach speaks: A cortical "language-network" serves the processing of music. *Neuroimage*, **17**(2), 956–66.

Koelsch, S., Kasper, E., Sammler, D., Schulze, K., Gunter, T., & Friederici, A.D. (2004). Music, language and meaning: brain signatures of semantic processing. *Nature Neuroscience*, **7**(3), 302–307.

Krumhansl, C.L. (1997). An exploratory study of musical emotions and psychophysiology. *Canadian Journal of Experimental Psychology*, **51**, 336–53.

Laughlin, S.A., Naeser, M.A., & Gordon, W.P. (1979). Effects of three syllable durations using the melodic intonation therapy technique. *Journal of Speech and Hearing Research*, **22**, 311–20.

Licht, S. (1946). *Music in Medicine*. Boston, MA: New England Conservatory of Music.

Liebetanz, D., Nitsche, M.A., Tergau, F., & Paulus, W. (2002). Pharmacological approach to the mechanisms of transcranial DC-stimulation-induced after-effects of human motor cortex excitability. *Brain*, **125**, 2238–47.

Luria, A.R. (1970). *The functional organization of the brain. Scientific American*, March.

Maess, B., Koelsch, S., Gunter, T.C., and Friederici, A.D. (2001). Musical syntax is processed in Broca's area: an MEG study. *Nature Neuroscience*, **4**(5), 540–5.

Meister, I.G., Boroojerdi, B., Foltys, H., Sparing, R., Huber, W., & Topper, R. (2003). Motor cortex hand area and speech: Implications for the development of language. *Neuropsychologia*, **41**, 401–6.

Mimura, M., Kato, M., Sano, Y., Kojima T., Naeser, M., and Kashima, H. (1998). Prospective and retrospective studies of recovery in aphasia—Changes in cerebral blood flow and language functions. *Brain*, **121**, 2083–94.

Mithen, S. (2005). *The singing Neanderthals: the origins of music, language, mind, and body*. London: Weidenfeld and Nicolson Ltd.

Moore, W.H. (1989). Language recovery in aphasia: A right hemisphere perspective. *Aphasiology*, **3**, 101–10.

Nitsche, M.A. & Paulus, W. (2000). Excitability changes induced in the human motor cortex by weak tDCS. *The Journal of Physiology*, **527**, 633–9.

Nitsche, M.A. & Paulus, W. (2001). Sustained excitability elevations induced by transcranial DC motor cortex stimulation in humans. *Neurology*, **57**, 1899–901.

Norton, A., Zipse, L., Marchina, S., & Schlaug, G. (2009). Melodic Intonation Therapy: Shared insights on how it is done and why it might help. *Annals of the New York Academy of Sciences*, **1169**, 431–6.

Overy, K. & Molnar-Szakacs, I. (2009). Being together in time: Musical experience and the mirror neuron system. *Music Perception*, **26**(5), 489–504.

Ozdemir, E., Norton, A., & Schlaug, G. (2006). Shared and distinct neural correlates of singing and speaking. *Neuroimage*, **33**(2), 628–35.

Patel, A.D. (2003). Language, music, syntax, and the brain. *Nature Neuroscience*, **6**, 674–81.

Patel, A.D. (2008). *Music, Language, and the Brain*. New York: Oxford University Press.

Patel, A.D., Wong, M., Foxton, J., Lochy, A., & Peretz, I. (2008). Speech intonation perception deficits in musical tone deafness (congenital amusia). *Music Perception*, **25**(4), 357–68.

Peretz, I. (1990). Processing of local and global musical information by unilateral brain-damaged patients. *Brain*, **113**, 1185–205.

Peretz, I. & Coltheart, M. (2003). Modularity of music processing. *Nature Neuroscience*, **6**, 688–91.

Peretz, I., Gagnon, L., Hebert, S., & Macoir, J. (2004). Singing in the brain: Insights from cognitive neuropsychology. *Music Perception*, **21**(3), 373–90.

Perry, D.W., Zatorre, R.J., Petrides, M., Alivisatos, B., Meyer, E., & Evans, A.C. (1999). Localization of cerebral activity during simple singing. *Neuroreport*, **10**(18), 3979–84.

Pizzamiglio, L., Galati, G., & Committeri, G. (2001). The contribution of functional neuroimaging to recovery after brain damage: A review. *Cortex*, **37**, 11–31.

Podolsky, E. (1945). *Music for Your Health*. New York: Bernard Ackerman, Inc.

Price, C.J. and Crinion, J. (2005). The latest on functional imaging studies of aphasic stroke. *Current Opinion in Neurology*, **18**(4), 429–34.

Price, C., Thierry, G., & Griffiths, T. (2005). Speech-specific auditory processing: where is it? *Trends in Cognitive Sciences*, **9**(6), 271–6.

Racette, A., Bard, C., & Peretz, I. (2006). Making non-fluent aphasics speak: sing along! *Brain*, **129**, 2571–84.

Riecker, A., Ackermann, H., Wildgruber, D., Dogil, G., & Grodd, W. (2000). Opposite hemispheric lateralization effects during speaking and singing at motor cortex, insula and cerebellum. *Neuroreport*, **11**(9), 1997–2000.

Rosen, H.J., Petersen, S.E., Linenweber, M.R., Snyder, A.Z., White, D.A., Chapman, L., *et al.* (2000). Neural correlates of recovery from aphasia after damage to left inferior frontal cortex. *Neurology*, **55**, 1883–94.

Samson, S. & Zatorre, R.J. (1991). Recognition memory for text and melody of songs after unilateral temporal lobe lesion: Evidence for dual encoding. *Journal of Experimental Psychology: Learning, Memory and Cognition*, **17**, 793–804.

Sarkamo, T., Tervaniemi, M., Laitinen, S., Forsblom, A., Soinila, S., Mikkonen, M., *et al.* (2008). Music listening enhances cognitive recovery and mood after middle cerebral artery stroke. *Brain*, **131**, 866–76.

Satoh, M. & Kuzuhara, S. (2008). Training in mental singing while walking improves gait disturbance in Parkinson's disease patients. *European Neurology*, **60**(5), 237–43.

Saur, D., Lange, R., Baumgaertner, A., Schraknepper, V., Willmes, K., Rijntjes, M., *et al.* (2006). Dynamics of language reorganization after stroke. *Brain*, **129**, 1371–84.

Schlaug, G., Jancke, L., Huang, Y., Staiger, J.F., & Steinmetz, H. (1995). Increased corpus callosum size in musicians. *Neuropsychologia*, **33**(8), 1047–55.

Schlaug, G., Marchina, S., & Norton, A. (2008a). From singing to speaking: Why singing may lead to recovery of expressive language function in patients with Broca's aphasia. *Music Perception*, **25**(4), 315–23.

Schlaug, G., Norton, A., & Marchina, S. (2008b). The role of the right hemisphere in post-stroke language recovery. *Stroke*, **39**(2), 542–3.

Schlaug, G., Marchina, S., & Norton, A. (2009). Evidence for plasticity in white-matter tracts of patients with chronic Broca's aphasia undergoing intense intonation-based speech therapy. *Annals of the New York Academy of Science*, **1169**, 385–94.

Schneider, S., Schonle, P.W., Altenmuller, E., & Munte, T.F. (2007). Using musical instruments to improve motor skill recovery following a stroke. *Journal of Neurology*, **254**(10), 1339–46.

Schuppert, M., Munte, T.F., Wieringa, B.M., & Altenmuller, E. (2000). Receptive amusia: Evidence for cross-hemispheric neural networks underlying music processing strategies. *Brain*, **123**, 546–59.

Seeley, W.W., Matthews, B.R., Crawford, R.K., Gorno-Tempini, M.L., Foti, D., Mackenzie, I.R., *et al.* (2008). Unraveling Bolero: progressive aphasia, transmodal creativity and the right posterior neocortex. *Brain*, **131**, 39–49.

Selnes, O.A. (1999). Recovery from aphasia: Activating the "right" hemisphere. *Annals of Neurology*, **45**, 419–20.

Sparks, R., Helm, N., & Albert, M. (1974). Aphasia rehabilitation resulting from melodic intonation therapy. *Cortex*, **10**, 303–16.

Sparks, R. & Holland, A. (1976). Method: Melodic intonation therapy for aphasia. *Journal of Speech and Hearing Disorders*, **41**, 287–97.

Sundar, S. (2007). Traditional healing systems and modern music therapy in India. *Music Therapy Today*, **8**(3). Available at: http://www.wfmt.info/Musictherapyworld/modules/mmmagazine/issues/200801080 93144/20080108100408/MTT8_3_Sundar.pdf.

Thiel, A., Herholz, K., Koyuncu, A., Ghaemi, M., Kracht, L.W., Habedank, B., *et al.* (2001). Plasticity of language networks in patients with brain tumors: A positron emission tomography activation study. *Annals of Neurology*, **50**, 620–9.

Tokimura, H., Tokimura, Y., Oliviero, A., Asakura, T., & Rothwell, J.C. (1996). Speech-induced changes in corticospinal excitability. *Annals of Neurology*, **40**, 628–34.

Uozumi, T., Tamagawa, A., Hashimoto, T., & Tsuji, S. (2004). Motor hand representation in cortical area 44. *Neurology*, **62**, 757–61.

Vines, B.W., Krumhansl, C.L., Wanderley, M.M., Dalca, I.M., & Levitin, D.J. (2005a). Dimensions of emotion in expressive musical performance. *Annals of the New York Academy of Sciences*, **1060**, 462–6.

Vines, B.W., Nuzzo, R.L., & Levitin, D.J. (2005b). Quantifying and analyzing musical dynamics: Differential calculus, physics and functional data techniques. *Music Perception*, **23**(2), 137–52.

Vines, B.W., Krumhansl, C.L., Wanderley, M.M., & Levitin, D.J. (2006a). Cross-Modal interactions in the perception of musical performance. *Cognition*, **101**(1), 80–103.

Vines, B.W., Schnider, N.M., & Schlaug, G. (2006b). Testing for causality with tDCS: Pitch memory and the left supramarginal gyrus. *NeuroReport*, **17**, 1047–50.

Vines, B.W., Nair, D.G., & Schlaug, G. (2006c). Contralateral and ipsilateral motor effects after tDCS. *NeuroReport*, **17**, 671–4.

Vines, B. W., Norton, A.N., & Schlaug, G. (2008a). Stimulating music: Combining singing with brain stimulation to help stroke victims recover speech. In K. Miyazaki, Y. Hiraga, M. Adachi, Y. Nakajima, & M. Tsuzaki (Eds.) *Proceedings of the 10th International Conference on Music Perception & Cognition, Sapporo, Japan, 2008*, pp. 15–19.

Vines, B.W., Cerruti, C., & Schlaug, G. (2008b). Dual-hemisphere tDCS facilitates greater improvements for healthy subjects' non-dominant hand compared to uni-hemisphere stimulation. *BMC Neuroscience*, **9**, 103.

Vines, B.W., Nair, D., & Schlaug, G. (2008c). Modulating activity in the motor cortex affects performance for the two hands differently depending upon which hemisphere is stimulated. *European Journal of Neuroscience*, **28**, 1667–73.

Vines, B. W., Norton, A.N., & Schlaug, G. (2009). Applying transcranial direct current stimulation in coordination with melodic intonation therapy to facilitate speech recovery after stroke. In S. Shioda, I. Homma & N. Kato (Eds.) *New Frontiers in Neuroscience: Transmitters/modulators in Health and Disease*. Tokyo: Springer Japan, pp. 103–14.

Vines, B.W., Krumhansl, C.L., Wanderley, M.M., Dalca, I.M., & Levitin, D.J. (2011). Music to my eyes: Cross-modal interactions in the perception of emotions in music. *Cognition*, **118**(2), 157–170.

Vines, B.W., Norton, A.C., & Schlaug, G. (in press). Non-invasive brain stimulation enhances the effects of melodic intonation therapy. *Frontiers in Auditory Cognitive Neuroscience*.

Weiller, C., Isensee, C., Rijntjes, M., Huber, W., Müller, S., Bier, D., *et al.* (1995). Recovery from Wernicke's aphasia: A positron emission tomographic study. *Annals of Neurology*, **37**, 723–2.

West, T. & Ironson, G. (2008). Effects of music on human health and wellness: Physiological measurements and research design. In B.D. Koen (Ed.), *The Oxford Handbook of Medical Ethnomusicology*. New York: Oxford University Press, pp. 410–43.

Wigram, T., Pedersen, I.N., & Bonde, L.O. (2002). *A Comprehensive Guide to Music Therapy: Theory, Clinical Practice, Research and Training*. London: Jessica Kingsley Publishers Ltd.

Wilson, S.J., Parsons, K., & Reutens, D.C. (2006). Preserved singing in aphasia: A case study of the efficacy of melodic intonation therapy. *Music Perception, 24*(1), 23–35.

Winhuisen, L., Thiel, A., Schumacher, B., Kessler, J., Rudolf, J., Haupt, W.F., *et al.* (2005). Role of the contralateral inferior frontal gyrus in recovery of language function in poststroke aphasia: A combined repetitive transcranial magnetic stimulation and positron emission tomography study. *Stroke, 36,* 1759–63.

Wong, P.C.M., Skoe, E., Russo, N.M., Dees, T., & Kraus, N. (2007). Musical experience shapes human brainstem encoding of linguistic pitch patterns. *Nature Neuroscience, 10*(4), 420–2.

Zatorre, R.J., Belin, P., & Penhune, V.B. (2002) Structure and function of auditory cortex: music and speech. *Trends in Cognitive Sciences, 6*(1), 37–46.

Chapter 20

Shared affective motion experience (SAME) and creative, interactive music therapy

Istvan Molnar-Szakacs, Vanya Green Assuied, and Katie Overy

20.1 Introduction

Humans are social animals, and have evolved in a subtle, ever-changing and complex social milieu. The typical healthy brain is endowed with neural systems that enable us to thrive in our surroundings and process the sophisticated (and often implicit) rules that govern our interactions with others with effortlessness. The last 20 years have seen enormous advances in our understanding of the human brain, and this has allowed us to begin to describe the neural foundations of our sociality. Acquisition of much of this new knowledge has been facilitated by developments in brain imaging technology including methods that: 1) measure neuronal firing patterns at the scalp (using electroencephalography; EEG); 2) measure the magnetic signal from neuronal firing patterns at the scalp (using magnetoencephalography; MEG); 3) measure the changing levels of de-oxygenated blood in response to neuronal firing patterns, throughout the whole brain (using functional magnetic resonance imaging; fMRI); and 4) measure motor evoked potentials caused by electromagnetic induction from a rapidly changing magnetic field that leads to depolarization in the neurons of the brain (using transcranial magnetic stimulation; TMS) (for a review of such methods, accessible to non-specialists, see Grahn, 2009).

The impact of such developments on our understanding of human musical behaviour is still in its early stages. Many of the first studies in music neuroscience were focused on the neural localization of specific aspects of musical processing, such as pitch, melody, or harmony (e.g. Zatorre et al., 1994). Further research focused on issues such as identifying differences in neural processing patterns between musicians and non-musicians, or between musical tasks and speech tasks (e.g. Besson et al., 1994; Stewart et al., 2001). More recent research has begun to explore questions such as the effects of musical training on the neural basis of other types of behaviour (e.g. language perception), the role of the motor system in music listening, and the complexities of imagined music (Meister et al., 2004; Wong et al 2007; Chen et al 2008). Such research has shown us that musical listening alone seems to involve more regions of the brain than any other activity yet identified, from the brainstem up to the frontal cortex, and in both cerebral hemispheres (for the proceedings of an international music neuroscience conference highlighting a range of research, see Dalla Bella et al., 2009).

For the authors of this chapter, one of the most exciting recent developments to emerge from cognitive neuroscience, with the potential to impact significantly both on our understanding of music *and* of the therapeutic uses of music, is the discovery of the so-called human mirror neuron system (MNS) (Rizzolatti & Sinigaglia, 2010). In essence, the MNS allows us to understand and predict the behaviour of others, by engaging the neural regions required to produce such behaviour ourselves. That is, when we see *another's hand* grasping an object, we activate the regions of *our brain* that control grasping; when we hear sounds associated with *someone else's action*, we activate the appropriate movement regions of *our brain*; and by extension, when we observe the *emotional states of others, we can feel the same emotion* in empathy (Carr et al., 2003; Gazzola et al., 2006; Molnar-Szakacs et al., 2006). It has thus been suggested, that 'mirror neurons are a kind of "neural wi-fi" that monitors what is happening in other people. This system tracks their emotions, what movements they're making, what they intend and it activates, in our brains, precisely the same brain areas as are active in the other person. This puts us on the same wavelength and it does it automatically, instantaneously and unconsciously' (Goleman, 2006).

The discovery of the MNS is leading to a significant conceptual shift in cognitive neuroscience research, since the brain can no longer be considered as an independent input–output, perception–action machine—it is deeply, intrinsically connected with our bodies, and most intriguingly, with our understanding of the actions of other individuals (Cattaneo et al., 2011). Such a conceptual shift offers a helpful new framework for our understanding of music, which of course almost always involves the body, and engagement with other humans. Two of the current authors have recently developed a working model of the potential role of the MNS in emotional, embodied responses to music, which we call Shared Affective Motion Experience—or SAME (Molnar-Szakacs & Overy, 2006; Overy & Molnar-Szakacs, 2009). The acronym 'SAME' aims to capture the sense of a shared communicative and emotional link created between and among individuals, and to signify that in fact the *same* neural networks can be activated in agent and observer during a musical interaction. According to the SAME model, musical sound is perceived not only in terms of the auditory signal, but also in terms of the intentional sequences of expressive motor acts behind the signal. Thus, even a simple musical listening experience carries within it the presence of human action and human agency, and can facilitate feelings of empathy and social bonding.

In this chapter, we elaborate upon and extend our argument in relation to creative, interactive music-therapy. We suggest that the situation of shared music-making is a sophisticated example of the potential of music to express emotion and stimulate empathetic understanding. We argue that, since physical and vocal gestures can express and convey basic emotional states, such gestures can be used in a musical context for self-expression, and interpreted by another individual in terms of their own repertoire of gestures and emotions—making possible empathy without the need for verbal explanation. Such non-verbal, socioemotional communication can serve as the foundation of creative, interactive music therapy, via processes such as mirroring, synchronization, improvisation, and shared musical experiences.

20.2 Creative, interactive music therapy—individual expression within a shared experience

Musical communication relies on sounds and actions rather than words alone to communicate, and as such can be an effective, non-verbal means of connecting and interacting. Unlike language, in which words refer symbolically to a certain emotion, music can be used to express the feeling of an emotion itself (Ansdell, 1995). 'We communicate with words to convey our meaning, whereas we improvise music to *find* something meaningful between us' (Ansdell, 1995: p. 26). In clinical music improvisation sessions, a therapist and client build a relationship together through spontaneous and purposeful expression (Aldridge, 2005), listening, and reflection: by responding to each other's emotional presence. In this process of establishing a connection, a therapist's intention to create an empathic experience with a client is embodied in the music, in a constantly unfolding musical dialogue. Music therapist Edith Boxill describes how such a therapeutic musical setting can provide an entree into what may otherwise be a 'hidden world' for individuals with limited awareness of themselves and their surroundings. In her 'Continuum of Awareness' model (adapted from Gestalt psychology), a relationship is cultivated through mirroring a client's actions or inaction: 'reflecting and coexperiencing what may be the person's only threads to "reality" can be a key to the person's center' (Boxill, 1985). 'Mirroring' a client's behaviour is considered to be critical in creating an empathic relationship in creative, interactive therapy. The movement of an individual, no matter how seemingly insignificant, once reflected in musical sound, can become the springboard to building a relationship based on empathetic understanding: 'Even if a client is unable or unwilling to play an instrument, I can improvise music to meet the timing of a rocking body or a pattern of breathing. There is always the possibility of some point of musical contact, however small and fleeting it may at first be' (Ansdell, 1995: p. 25). It is often the physical motion inherent in a musical signal that provides a locus for connection (Alvin & Warwick, 1991). In building rapport, a therapist may begin by 'mirroring' the musical gestures, patterns and qualities with which an individual plays, or narrating their movements through improvised music which may then lead to simple communication through 'call and response' interactions (the therapist responds to a musical phrase with a unique and relevant phrase), followed by a more complex, interactive musical 'dialogue' (in which the therapist facilitates creative expression within a structured format).

Musical experiences in a non-clinical setting can also be therapeutic—the salient differences between such music-making and music therapy relate to intention, progression and especially to the therapeutic relationship. The therapist's purpose is to assess current functioning in a client and then facilitate, support and encourage growth through musical interaction, from helping a client to communicate a simple preference to facilitating a genuinely cathartic experience. Several therapy methods using music (such as Melodic Intonation Therapy or Neurologic Music Therapy) outline highly specific clinical goals, with interventions designed to lead to direct achievement of these goals (Adamek et al., 2000; Thaut et al., 2009). Creative music therapy tends to defy rigorous methodological categorization, since its pioneers, educator Clive Robbins and composer Paul Nordoff, considered creativity to be central to the therapeutic process (Nordoff & Robbins, 1977; Robbins & Robbins, 1991; Aigen 2005).[1] Nordoff and Robbins' creative, flexible, improvisational approach emphasizes the importance of the therapist meditating on the client before a session and being in the 'creative now' during the session, leading to a fluid conception of therapeutic goals as 'frontiers on which one is working, freely and creatively' (Robbins, in Aigen, 1996: p. 11). In Nordoff–Robbins Music Therapy, sessions are recorded and later analysed in detail (Robbins & Robbins, 1991; Turry, 2009) in order to guide the therapist in understanding 'subtle or dramatic changes in the client's musical expression,' ultimately leading to a 'richer musical experience' (Aigen, 2005: p. 114).

A large body of literature regarding improvisational music therapy supports the idea that imitation, reflection and improvisation can lead to increased empathy. One of the seminal case studies of Nordoff–Robbins Music Therapy involved Nicole, who was born prematurely at 23 weeks weighing less than 2 pounds. By the time she left the neonatal intensive care unit at 14 months she had been diagnosed as blind and at 2 years of age she was diagnosed as autistic. Through consistent music therapy sessions with Clive and Carol Robbins over a period of 6 years, Nicole developed relationships through music and accomplished such milestones as vocalizing to the *Phantom*

---

[1] While trained music therapists from a diversity of backgrounds use creativity in their work with clients, Nordoff–Robbins Music Therapy requires significant training in the use of clinical improvisation. (NYU Steinhardt School of Culture, Education, and Human Development (2011) Nordoff–Robbins Center for Music Therapy.) For the purposes of this chapter, Nordoff–Robbins Music Therapy and 'Creative' Music Therapy refer to the specific practice, while the adjectival use of the word creative does not necessarily refer exclusively to this approach to music therapy.

of the Opera and saying the words 'momma' while touching her mother's face. While Robbins describes obstacles and challenges to engaging Nicole socially, it is clear that hearing her music reflected and built upon by others is central to bridging the gap between Nicole and the outside world. After significant effort, Nicole was even able to play at the piano bench alongside Carol Robbins: 'Rather than bypass rhythmic and melodic ideas Carol introduced, there was often "answering" from Nicole, sometimes in the form of imitation, sometimes with a new but complimentary melodic pattern' (Robbins, personal communication, March 2011).

'Vocal Holding' is another therapeutic approach using music in which the use of repeated and evolving melodic phrasing is described as significant in building a foundation for dialogue and trust (Austin, 2008). Improvisational music-making through 'Vocal Holding' can involve vocalizing in unison, mirroring (in which the therapist reflects what the client sings), and grounding (in which the therapist sings the root of the chords to support the client). Austin emphasizes the importance of listening, melodic interaction and gesture in building empathy: '[The client's] needs are met through the therapist's ability to attune to the uniqueness of each client and listen and respond empathically in the sounds, in the singing, in the words, through body language and physical contact' (Austin, 2008: pp. 197–8).

The role of physical gesture in creating empathy is further emphasized in other qualitative descriptions of music therapy sessions, for example Heimlich (1972) writes:

> As our instrumental dialogues develop, the child has occasion to imitate and identify with me. He sees how I use my body while employing the various expressive components of music. My hands, my arms, my shoulders, my head, my feet, all come into play and are an outgrowth of my instrumental expression. Simultaneously they often serve as an emphasis of the feelings I am expressing in the music. My facial expression changes, too, with the kinds of improvisation I am producing and the feeling I want to communicate: sadness, gaiety, exhilaration, tenderness. As I do this, I often see similar changes reflected in the child's bodily and facial expression.

Interestingly, evidence from music therapy literature indicates that linking a musical sound specifically to the agent or source of the sound can facilitate increased awareness of other individuals and external surroundings. Children on the autistic spectrum, for example, have been found to attend more to music when they are able to observe a musical partner playing an instrument, and to have improved motor skills when imitating and making music themselves (Alvin & Warwick, 1991). While working with children on the autistic spectrum, a therapist may employ a variety of musical interventions to engage them in developing a greater awareness—initially of themselves, then of the person with whom they are creating music, and then by extension, their external surroundings and other people.

An important aspect of such musical development and interaction is physical coordination in time, involving a developing awareness of the temporal linking of sounds with movements, as well as the potential for temporal synchronization between client and therapist. Such synchronization of shared actions, musical ideas and emotional expression can lead to strong feelings of togetherness, as well as improved motor coordination. In discussing the use of music therapy for individuals with neurological degeneration, David Aldridge suggests that a failure in synchronization leads to motor problems and that musical dialogue and gesture can be critical in the process of rehabilitation: 'While we can see and hear what others do, and this is important for understanding, it is precisely the elements necessary for gesturing that begin to fail in neurodegenerative diseases. Timing is lost and movements fail to be coordinated, so communication begins to fail. Music therapy has the potential to promote coordination such that communication is achieved' (Aldridge, 2000); 'we come together in mutual time; indeed mutuality is all about timing' (Aldridge, 2005). Aldridge suggests that the combination of listening and gesture in time, required for music-making within a music therapy context, can lead to improved levels of general functioning.

While moving to a fixed temporal pattern or rhythm may help to facilitate rehabilitation, it is important to note that music-making for therapeutic growth does not necessarily need to be locked into a strict beat (Aigen, 2005). In fact, a distinction can be made in music therapy between 'synchronization' and 'groove', the latter of the two relying on individual differences in rhythm, or participatory discrepancies (Aigen, 2005). Establishing a musical groove creates a certain gestalt wherein the music created is greater than the sum of the individual contributions and participants feel a sense of connectedness 'partly because we feel so alive in those moments . . . and partly because of the feelings of familiarity engendered by the experience' (Aigen, 2005).

Aigen (2005) presents Creative Music Therapy in stark contrast to more prescriptive approaches to music therapy and while he supports development of theoretical bases for music therapy practice, he eschews the value of looking to neuroscience to inform them. The present authors believe that evidence-based models with neurobiological foundations have the potential to offer 'bottom up' insights into the creative, interactive therapy approach. Creative improvisation, although context-dependent and constantly changing, is at its core a powerful empathic and social experience—and neuroscience is beginning to discover the neural scaffolding that supports these behaviours. It is through a fundamental understanding of the biological bases of these behaviours that we can further develop music therapy techniques and develop evidence-based models of their effectiveness.

20.3 Human empathy—a foundation for shared emotional experience

As discussed in the introduction, humans are very good at recognizing and understanding other people's actions. Additionally, we have a relatively highly developed capacity to deduce, on the basis of observed behaviour, the intentions and emotions of others. This information allows us to survive, learn and thrive in an incredibly complex social world by guiding our own intentions, actions, and feelings towards others and the environment. The concept of empathy—the capacity to share others' feelings and emotions—was, interestingly enough, introduced in aesthetics to indicate the attitude of an observer in front of an artist's work. Theodore Lipps in 1903 used the term 'Einfühlung'—an understanding, or sensitivity so intimate, that feelings of one person are readily understood by another—to describe the concept of empathy (Lipps, 1903). However, in this original definition the observer was described as having an aesthetic experience, rather than an interpersonal one. Music is of course also an aesthetic experience, and indeed has long been considered in such terms by philosophers and musicologists (e.g. Langer, 1954; Meyer, 1967). Music has the additional quality though, of requiring human performance for its realization, involving perfectly executed action in real-time. This multidimensional (temporal, physical, aesthetic) quality of musical experience brings additional layers to our empathic and emotional responses.

The notion that we possess a kind of immediate understanding of what others are doing or feeling is also rooted in philosophy. Adam Smith, in 1759, proposed the concept of sympathy, defining it as 'our fellow-feeling with any passion whatever' (p. 5), and according to him we are capable of feeling something similar to what others feel, by simply observing others' behaviour (Smith, 1759/1976). Smith continues by arguing that people feel pleasure from the presence of others with the *same* emotion as oneself, proposing that such mutual sympathy heightens the original emotion and 'disburdens' the person of sorrow, 'because the sweetness of his sympathy more than compensates the bitterness of that sorrow' (Smith, 1759/1976: p. 14). It is perhaps within this mutually created space of experience that music has qualities suited for enhancing the feeling of communal experience, providing a non-verbal pathway for empathic communication.

More recently, the nature of empathy has increasingly been considered in terms of the potential underlying sensory, cognitive, and physiological mechanisms. Current evolutionary evidence suggests that there are at least two main systems mediating empathy: a phylogenetically early emotional contagion system and a more advanced cognitive perspective-taking system (Preston & de Waal, 2002; de Waal, 2008). The basic emotional contagion system is thought to support our ability to empathize emotionally ('I feel what you feel'), and is of most immediate relevance to our current argument. Preston and de Waal (2002) formalized this notion in their Perception-Action Model (PAM), proposing that perception of another's behaviour automatically activates one's own representations for the behaviour, and output from this shared representation automatically proceeds to motor areas of the brain where responses are prepared and executed. This theory postulates that understanding actions and internal states of others can be achieved through an automatic process matching the sensory input with the internal motor knowledge of the observer—an inner imitation or mirroring of perceived behaviours. According to this view, internal motor representations play a crucial role, because they represent the personal knowledge through which every individual assigns meaning to the external world, guiding their actions and interactions. Emotional empathy may be considered a special case of a more general state-matching reaction that is fast, automatic and pre-cognitive—simulation. Simulation has been defined as the 'attempt to replicate, mimic or impersonate the mental life of the target' (Gallese & Goldman, 1998). Simulation can include representing the basic motor behaviours of others, but also the more complex emotional states of others, to understand and predict their behaviour (Adolphs, 2009). Thus, our ability to 're-present' through simulation, the emotional and motor behaviour of others within parts of our brain that are responsible for our own motor and emotional behaviour may serve as the foundation for our ability to learn and know about other minds (Gallese, 2007).

20.4 **Neural mechanisms of human empathy—the mirror neuron system**

During development and into adulthood, we acquire the basis of language and a multitude of motor skills, including how to play sports and musical instruments, through imitation, by reproducing observed behaviours. It is very likely that most of these functions have, at their bases, a simulation mechanism (Rizzolatti & Craighero, 2004; Pineda, 2008; Iacoboni, 2009). Simulation, or inner imitation refers to the fact that the same neural resources are recruited while one observes *and* while one executes an action, allowing the brain to link the perceptions of an observer to the actions of the agent at the neural level. Furthermore, the fact that the same neural networks are activated within the brains of individuals who participate in an interaction—the observer(s) *and* the agent(s)— allows for shared representations to be established among individuals, giving rise to a mutual understanding of the interaction. Thus, the capacity for emotional empathy—the inner mirroring of other's actions and emotions—allows us to co-create a shared, affective communicative experience, supported at the neural level by the human mirror neuron system (MNS).

Soon after the discovery of mirror neurons in the monkey brain using single-unit electrode recordings (di Pellegrino et al., 1992; Gallese et al., 1996; Rizzolatti et al., 1996a), non-invasive neuroimaging (Grafton et al., 1996; Rizzolatti et al., 1996b) and TMS studies (Fadiga et al., 1995) demonstrated a network with similar functional properties in the human brain. In addition to the early neuroimaging experiments cited above, a wealth of additional studies have shown that a simulation mechanism is involved in action perception and performance, meaning that overlapping neural systems are recruited during the observation and execution of actions (Fadiga et al., 1995; Grafton et al., 1996; Rizzolatti et al., 1996b; Binkofski et al., 1999; Iacoboni et al., 1999; Nishitani and Hari, 2000; Koski et al., 2002; Grezes et al., 2003; Johnson-Frey et al., 2003; Buccino et al., 2004; Iacoboni et al., 2005; Molnar-Szakacs et al., 2005; Oberman et al., 2005; Aziz-Zadeh et al., 2006). The presence of a MNS in the human brain is also corroborated by the fact that its main neuroanatomical nodes—inferior frontal gyrus (IFG) and premotor cortex (PMC) anteriorly and inferior parietal lobule (IPL) posteriorly—are considered homologous to the areas forming the MNS in the monkey (VonEconomo & Koskinas, 1925; VonBonin & Bailey, 1947; Petrides & Pandya, 1997; Amunts et al., 1999; Tomaiuolo et al., 1999; Mazziotta et al., 2001; Rizzolatti & Matelli, 2003) (Figure 20.1A). The evolutionary argument for the presence of mirror neurons in the human brain is that such a useful neural property would not be selected against, once it had evolved. In fact, it appears that the MNS may have further evolved to subserve more sophisticated functions in humans, that are only rudimentarily present or even completely absent in monkeys, such as imitation, recognition of intransitive and symbolic gestures, language, intention under-standing, self-representation, and of immediate interest to this chapter: musical behaviour and the representation and understanding of another's emotion.

Emotion understanding is at the core of empathy, and at the heart of most social bonds. As we discussed earlier, there are at least two main theories describing the mechanisms of understanding the feelings of others. One possibility, cognitive perspective-taking, implicates a top-down cognitive process, which supposes that emotion understanding occurs through inferential elaboration based on emotion-related sensory information. For example, recognizing a facial emotion requires matching the seen face to the known representation of the categories of human emotions into which expressions can be assigned—happiness, sadness, and so on. In contrast, the process of simulation which supports emotional empathy, allows us to understand emotions because emotion-related sensory information is directly mapped onto neural and bodily structures that, when active, create a similar emotional reaction in us, the observer. This type of emotion understanding relies on first person motor knowledge in the same way that has been proposed for the neural mechanism of action understanding, subserved by the human MNS. However, in processing emotion-laden information, another important neural structure is recruited in addition to the MNS, and that is the insular cortex, a structure involved in visceromotor output.

The anterior insula in particular, is critically involved in interoceptive processing, and the consolidation of bodily state information about oneself with contextual information from the environment to provide a neural substrate for the conscious experience of emotions (Craig, 2008). Anatomical data suggest that a sector of the insular lobe, the dysgranular field, is connected with posterior parietal, inferior frontal, and superior temporal cortices making up the human MNS, as well as to the limbic system (Augustine, 1996). The limbic system (a term often used to describe regions that constitute the 'emotional brain', including both cortical regions like the orbito-frontal cortex (OFC), the anterior cingulate cortex (ACC), the ventromedial prefrontal cortex (vmPFC) and the anterior insula, and subcortical structures including the amygdala, the nucleus accumbens (NA) and the hypothalamus) is critical for emotional behaviour and the representation of emotions, including pain (Pessoa, 2008). This limbic-insular-MNS connectivity pattern thus makes the insula an integral part of the neural network for empathy involved in representing and understanding the affective states of others (Pessoa, 2008; Iacoboni, 2009), see Figure 20.1A.

Brain imaging studies of empathic communication have begun to explore the activation patterns of such neural systems during different types of task. For example, in an fMRI study by Carr and colleagues, participants were asked to either observe or imitate emotional facial expressions. If simulation or inner imitation of the observed facial expression of others is truly a component of the empathic response, then the mere observation of emotional facial expressions should activate the human MNS. Thus, observation and imitation of emotional facial expressions should yield substantially similar patterns of activated brain areas. The results of the study confirmed this hypothesis, showing a similar network of activated areas (including the premotor face area, the

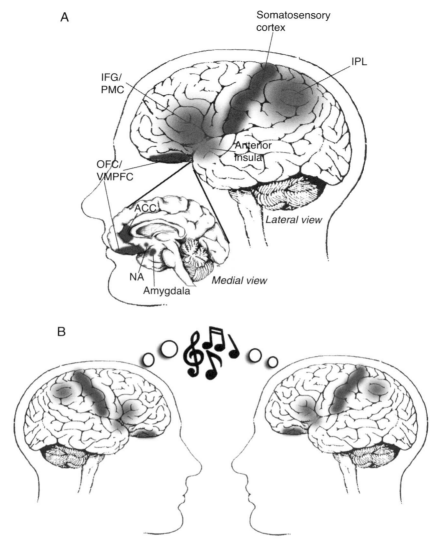

Fig. 20.1 (See also Plate 4) A) Schematic representation of the core neural systems implicated by the Shared Affective Motion Experience (SAME) model of emotional music perception. Regions of the limbic system (in blue) include both cortical regions like the orbito-frontal cortex (OFC), the anterior cingulate cortex (ACC), the ventromedial prefrontal cortex (VMPFC), and the anterior insula, and subcortical structures including the amygdala and the nucleus accumbens (NA). The main neuroanatomical nodes of the human mirror neuron system (MNS) are shown in red, including, the inferior frontal gyrus (IFG) and premotor cortex (PMC) anteriorly and inferior parietal lobule (IPL) posteriorly. The anterior insula (in green), is connected with posterior parietal, inferior frontal, and superior temporal cortices, linking the limbic system and the mirror neuron system. B) The fact that the same neural networks are activated within the brains of individuals who participate in an interaction—the observer *and* the agent—allows for shared representations to be established among individuals, giving rise to a mutual understanding of the interaction. From this basic understanding, a shared sense of experience between a performer and listener can be achieved, such that even simply listening alone to pre-recorded music will have the capacity to create a sense of shared experience.

posterior IFG, the superior temporal sulcus, the insula, and the amygdala) for both imitation and observation of emotional facial expressions (Carr et al., 2003). That is, it was shown that the observation of another person in a specific emotional state automatically activates a representation of that state in the observer, as was originally proposed by Lipps (1903). These data also provide support for the notion that empathy is a special form of simulation, or inner imitation. As predicted by the Perception-Action Model of emotional empathy (Preston & de Waal, 2002), seeing another person in a particular emotional state automatically activates neural structures subserving that state in the observer—leading to the sharing of emotional, physical and even neural states between individuals.

Similar brain imaging studies have investigated neural activity associated with empathic responses in the domains of touch, smell and pain. Results have revealed common neural responses elicited by the observation of pictures showing disgusted faces and smelling disgusting odours oneself (Wicker et al., 2003), by being touched and observing videos of someone else being touched (Keysers et al., 2004), and by feeling pain and watching a loved one feel pain (Singer et al., 2004). In the latter study, couples were recruited and brain activity was measured in the female partner while she had painful stimulation applied to her own hand and while she watched painful stimulation being applied to her partner's hand. When receiving pain, the imaging results showed neural activity in the primary and secondary somatosensory cortex. These areas are known to be involved in the processing of our pain experience—providing information about the location of the pain and its objective quality. In contrast, bilateral anterior insula, the rostral ACC, brainstem, and cerebellum were activated both when subjects received pain and while a loved one experienced pain. These areas are involved in the processing of the affective component of pain, that is, how unpleasant the subjectively felt pain is (Craig, 2002). Thus, both the experience of pain to oneself and the knowledge that a loved partner is experiencing pain activates similar affective pain circuits. Furthermore, individual participant's brain activity was correlated with scores on standard empathy questionnaires including the Empathic Concern subscale of the Interpersonal Reactivity Index (IRI; (Davis, 1980) and the Balanced Emotional Empathy Scale (BEES; Mehrabian & Epstein, 1972). The higher the subjects scored on these questionnaires, the higher was their activation in ACC and the insula. Such elucidative findings about the neural basis of human empathy suggest that our understanding of musical experience, and therein music therapy, might also be better understood by a consideration of the neural systems involved.

20.5 Shared affective motion experience—empathy through music

The powerful emotional effects of music have intrigued philosophers and theorists for centuries, while neuroimaging methods are beginning to reveal the direct involvement of the emotion networks of the brain during music processing (including the amygdala, hippocampus and limbic system) (Koelsch et al., 2005; Menon & Levitin, 2005; Koelsch et al., 2006). However, the question remains as to *how* music has such powerful effects. How is it that apparently abstract patterns of sound can make us want to physically move, dance, cry or laugh? The discovery of the human MNS provides a clue, as it suggests that music is unlikely to be interpreted by the brain as disembodied sound, as previously sometimes assumed. Rather, music is likely to be interpreted by the human brain in terms of the *action and the potential agent* that is implied by the sound. That is, music can be interpreted fundamentally as physical gestures emanating from another person—a person with emotions, moods and intentions—resulting in a shared affective motion experience (SAME) (Molnar-Szakacs & Overy, 2006; Overy & Molnar-Szakacs, 2009).

The SAME model proposes that the limbic–insular–MNS network described above is centrally involved in musical experience. An emotional response at the simulation level will include a sense of the motor gestures behind the signal, in relation to personal knowledge or experience of such gestures.

For musicians, this feeling could be quite specific, for example an oboist is likely to hear a familiar piece of oboe music in terms of the precise motor movements required. For non-musicians the feeling is likely to be more generalized, such as in terms of the vocal requirements of the melodic line, or an impression of the speed and intensity of movements (e.g. low pitched, slow, quiet music may convey low energy states such as calmness or sadness, while high pitched, fast, loud music may convey high energy states such as joy or anger). From this basic understanding, a shared sense of experience between a performer and listener can be achieved, such that even simply listening alone to pre-recorded music can have the capacity to create a sense of shared experience (Figure 20.1B).

On reflection then, the essence of human musical behaviour seems unlikely to lie in the perception of music, but rather in the *making* of the music itself: hitting things, blowing things, plucking things, and vibrating the vocal chords. Such performance usually involves interaction with other individuals, and often at times of shared social and emotional significance, such as at weddings, parties, funerals, community gatherings, during courtship, and as part of worship. Furthermore, music seems to play a strong role in the lives of infants and children, who are more attentive to 'musical' vocalizations (or 'motherese'), are soothed by lullabies and are highly entertained by nursery rhymes and action songs (Campbell, 1998; Trevarthen, 1999). The fact that musicality seems to be present at birth and to show an important role during development suggests that emotional and motor responses to music are probably innate, rather than culturally learned. Malloch and Trevarthen have proposed that musicality is in fact at the root of human communication, especially evident in the imitative, rhythmic, melodic interactions between infants and parents (Malloch & Trevarthen, 2009). A recent study exploring the potential evolutionary origins of music has even shown that 4-year-old children show more pro-social behaviour after a shared musical experience compared to a shared story-telling experience (Kirschner & Tomasello, 2009). Such evidence suggests that music is deeply linked with social behaviour.

Thus, we argue that emotional responses to music might be considered less in terms of the complex nature of the actual sound signal (rhythms, melodies, harmonies, structures), and more in terms of the physical, social, communicative, empathic and pro-social experiences involved; that is, as SAME. For instance, take an example from the end of the BBC Children in Need concert in 2009 at the Royal Albert Hall, when Sir Paul McCartney performed a rendition of 'Hey Jude'. By the last verse, all the performers of the evening had joined him on stage and the final chorus was repeated with the audience no less than 36 times, to a virtual crowd ecstasy. The behaviour of both performers and audience were similar—jumping, singing, smiling, laughing, and hugging *together*. Through the lens of the SAME model, some of the key elements of human musical behaviour are evident in this example—imitation, synchronization, and shared experience. We propose that it is these powerful, social elements of musical behaviour that might in fact be core to the pedagogical and therapeutic benefits of music.

Supporting evidence for the SAME model can be found in a number of recent studies of auditory–motor interactions and emotional responses to music. For example, several fMRI studies have found that trained pianists show significantly more pre-motor activation than non-musicians while listening to piano music, indicating a well-developed motor representation of the musical sound (Haueisen & Knosche, 2001; Haslinger et al., 2005; Bangert et al., 2006). The specificity of this motor understanding has been shown in a study by Lahav and colleagues, which involved training novices to play short melodies on the piano keyboard. Using fMRI, the researchers found that, after just five daily lessons on a collection of melodies, participants showed significantly stronger pre-motor activation while listening to the practiced melodies, compared to unfamiliar melodies involving the same notes (Lahav et al., 2007). The fact that only 5 days of training was required for this neural differentiation shows the plasticity of the system, and its potential role in musical learning.

Further studies have found that non-musicians activate vocal regions during music listening tasks. For example, an fMRI study by Koelsch and colleagues compared non-musicians while listening to 'pleasant' music and 'unpleasant' (distorted) music, and found that pre-motor regions in the vocal area were significantly more active during the pleasant music, suggesting some kind of sub-vocal engagement with the melodic line (Koelsch et al., 2006). An fMRI study by Brown and Martinez suggests that active, engaged listening might be important in order to show such pre-motor activation (Brown and Martinez, 2007): vocal pre-motor areas were activated significantly more during melody discrimination tasks than during passive listening tasks, suggesting that active, engaged listening was a key factor for such inner imitation or mirroring to take place.

Similar studies of vocal activation patterns have been conducted in speech research. One of the fundamental assumptions of The Motor Theory of Speech Perception is that the phonetic elements of speech are not sounds, but rather the articulatory gestures that generate those sounds (Studdert-Kennedy et al., 1970; Liberman & Mattingly, 1985; Browman & Goldstein, 1992; Liberman & Whalen, 2000). Thus, the theory suggests that the perception of speech is directly related to the experience of producing the precise motor gestures involved in syllable production. In an early fMRI study, the auditory cortex was activated during silent lip reading, suggesting that the observation of the motor components of speech influence the perception of speech (Calvert et al., 1997). A TMS study by Fadiga and colleagues showed a facilitation of motor-evoked potentials recorded from a subject's tongue muscles while they listened to words that strongly involved tongue movements. These data lend strong support to the theory of simulation and The Motor Theory of Speech Perception in turn, by showing that speech perception produces a phoneme specific activation of motor centres (Fadiga et al., 2002). Another TMS study found that linguistic perception, but not auditory or visuospatial processing activated the hand motor cortex, lending support to the idea that language evolved from an action-perception network able to represent communicative gestures, both perceived and performed (Floel et al., 2003). More recently, Wilson and colleagues used fMRI to show that perception *and* production of syllables recruit overlapping regions of the superior ventral premotor cortex, evidence that the motor system is indeed involved in speech perception—mapping auditory signals to an articulatory code (Wilson et al., 2004).

A recent fMRI study exploring the temporal dynamics of emotional responses to music has also found evidence in support of the SAME model (Chapin et al. 2010). The neural responses to an expressive performance of a Chopin Etude (Opus 10, no.3) were correlated with emotional valence ratings for the music and compared to those of a mechanical performance of the same piece of music, as a control condition. Results showed that several brain regions including those consistent with the MNS and the limbic system were activated most significantly during moments of strongest emotional valence, which were also the most expressive, temporally dynamic sections of the musical pieces. This result was particularly strong for the participants with musical experience, suggesting once again that prior experience has a significant effect on the perceptual/empathic response. In turn, this suggests that in order to fully understand the perception of musical emotion, we must turn to the neural basis of musical expression, and indeed to emotional expression in general.

20.6 **From emotion to motion: expressive communication**

Humans are known to be extremely skilled at expressing emotion non-verbally. Facial expressions have been particularly well studied and it is now clearly established that basic emotions (such as anger, fear, joy and surprise) are expressed in similar ways cross-culturally, and are universally recognized (Biehl et al., 1997). It has also been shown that vocal expressions of basic emotions (e.g. sighs, screams, gasps, laughs) show similarly universal recognition across cultures (Scherer et al., 2001). The universality of such forms of emotional expression highlights the fact that their production is rooted in human motor behaviour and thus human physiology: the possibilities and limitations of human facial muscles and vocal apparatus. That is, when we feel emotion we express it using the motor system available to us. Manfred Clynes has hypothesized that the human system for expressing emotion must be based on biologically fixed, universal, primary dynamic forms, and has shown that emotions conveyed by dynamic gestures of touch can be translated into sound and interpreted cross-culturally (Clynes, 1973). Further research has gone on to explore the potentially universal temporal dynamics of such physical, vocal and musical gestures, and their communicative potential within a range of different musical and non-musical contexts (Trevarthen et al., 2011).

Emotional expression is also affected by physiological arousal, for example a heightened emotional state (increased heart rate, increased breathing rate, and tense vocal chords) can have an impact on the quality of vocal expressions during that state (high pitched, fast vocalizations). Since the acoustic parameters of vocal expression are the same as to those of music—pitch, timbre, intensity, and duration—musical expression thus has the potential to approximate, imitate, and extend the natural qualities of emotional vocalizations to heightened pitch, dynamic, timbral, and temporal ranges. Singing can achieve this naturally, while musical instruments can expand the range still further, abstracted in terms of fixed timbres, pitches and scales. An early study by Scherer and Oshinsky showed that a variety of specific emotional states can be conveyed by certain characteristics of musical pitch sequences, for example sadness is conveyed most saliently by a slow tempo and low pitch level, while anger is conveyed most saliently by rising pitch sequences, and small pitch variation (Scherer & Oshinsky, 1977).

Of course, as well as universals, there are also cultural differences in emotional signals across vocal, musical, and physical gestures. Molnar-Szakacs and colleagues used TMS to explore neural representations of culturally specific manual gesture vocabularies, and found that neural activity was modulated by whether or not the actor and perceiver were from the same cultural group. In addition, it was found that, even when perceiving unfamiliar gestures from an unfamiliar cultural group, there was a stronger neural 'simulation' when the gestures had genuine meaning—that is, when the gesture itself was made in an intentional way (Molnar-Szakacs et al., 2007).

Thus, we suggest that it is the intentionality, and universality of musical expression that gives it exceptional power and utility in a non-verbal, therapeutic context. Without any reliance on language, an individual can express their emotional state through sound, and another individual can immediately comprehend and interpret this sound signal, based on their own motor, emotional, and musical experiences. The empathic communication between these individuals can lead to especially strong feelings of 'togetherness' as situations of imitation, synchronization and shared experience begin to arise, with the potential for powerful positive affect. Within a safe, therapeutic environment, musical imagination and creativity can then be explored together, in a growing, positive relationship between therapist and client.

20.7 Implications for creative music therapy

We know that music-making is a universal human behaviour, and that musical instruments are probably universal cultural artefacts, from primitive flutes dating back 30,000 years (Conard et al., 2009) to the current proliferation of the iPod (Cohen, 2007). Yet just as the existence of musical objects is not significant per se (but is made meaningful by the social function that music has and continues to have in cultures throughout the world), music therapy as a discipline depends chiefly upon the personal growth that can occur as a result of musical communication. Whether using the breathing rate of a neonate to dictate musical tempo or starting a musical improvisation based upon a client's foot tapping, music therapists are trained to use motor cues as a locus to initiating a musical dialogue—a dialogue which capitalizes on both the physical and emotional nature of music, and uses these as vehicles to build a therapeutic relationship. From heart-breaking ballads to sweat-inducing techno beats, it appears that listening to music has a unique ability to let us know that we are not alone, and to motivate us to move. The experience of creating music together in real-time—to hear our motion and emotions reflected and re-reflected in music—takes this power of music to another level. We surmise that creative music-making in a therapeutic setting, in which the client's needs are at the centre of the music, leads to empathic experiences of sharing that are even more powerful than during the music listening experiences found in every day life.

The SAME model arrives at a similar tenet, but from a neuroscience perspective, positing that both physical movement of a performer and dynamic motion of sound help to create the visceral recognition of another person's presence and action. Clinical evidence from music therapy indicates that engaged listening, reflection, improvisation, synchronization, and 'groove' are powerful tools with which to create a sense of shared experience. A description of the neurological processes underlying such creative, interactive behaviour has been lacking, but the SAME model can perhaps provide a basis for such clinical observations, indicating that music is at its core a way of organizing and connecting individuals emotionally, in an empathic way.

Thus, the SAME lens provides an evidence-based theoretical model to support the observation that music therapy techniques such as imitation, 'mirroring', call and response, and creative improvisation can increase empathy and communication between individuals. In the preceding sections, we have introduced the reader to the SAME model of emotional music perception through neuroscience research that was conducted primarily in neurotypical populations. However, it is evident from the case studies presented in the sections on the use of music in therapeutic settings that many of the same fundamental principles of communication and interaction also apply in clinical settings, where a shared experience is achieved through the use of music. Future studies in clinical populations, such as children with Autism Spectrum Disorders, are needed to elucidate the neural mechanisms of the beneficial effects of music, and to help further develop evidence-based musical interventions (Molnar-Szakacs et al., 2009). Music therapy as a field has developed a range of methodologies and theoretical bases, which at times appear to be at odds with one another. We posit that whereas biomedical perspectives on music therapy and concepts from neuroscience may generally have been applied to support more prescriptive models of practice (Standley, 2000; Thaut et al., 2009), developments in the neuroscience of emotional communication and empathy open the doorway to new ways of linking research and music therapy practice. The SAME model and the neural evidence supporting it suggest that creative, interactive music therapy may be particularly effective for increasing empathy and in turn improving outcomes and wellness across a wide range of populations. As improvisational music therapy extends its purview (Ansdell, 1995; Austin, 2008), this evidence-based support is increasingly vital. We are hopeful that the SAME model will inspire research, collaboration and a deeper understanding of the neurological basis for empathy in creative, interactive therapy.

20.8 Conclusions

This chapter began with the idea that humans are innately social animals—we have a need for affective contact with those around us for healthy social and emotional development, as well as for the acquisition of appropriate cultural knowledge. Advances in neuroimaging have allowed scientists to begin to elucidate the brain bases of this sociability. Notably, research on the human MNS has shown us that brain and body are deeply connected, and that neural systems of action perception and production intimately connect us to those around us. This neural system allows us to understand the intentions, emotions, and actions of others using the same networks that generate our own intentions, actions and emotions. Such internal imitation allows us to acquire knowledge and feel connected to others, and to communicate with others with facility even when verbal means are unavailable, or unnecessary. Such is the special case of music—a means of expression and communication that is at once personal and universal. In the SAME model of music perception, we propose that it is the ability of music to communicate social and affective information and to create the feeling of 'being together in time' that makes it so appealing to humans across all ages and cultures. In the case of pure music listening, the implication of the SAME model is that music provides not just a pleasant auditory signal, but a strong sense of an agent with intentions and emotions like our own. We hypothesize that within this capacity of music to create the sense of a shared experience, imitation, and synchronization are foundational components of successful therapeutic and educational music intervention activities. Creative improvisation provides the flexibility for a therapist, a musician, indeed for all of us, regardless of physical or developmental limitations, to respond and engage in a musical dialogue that is emotionally supportive and adventurous, both familiar and constantly changing.

Acknowledgements

The authors would like to thank the editors for the opportunity to contribute to this volume, an anonymous reviewer for insightful comments, Clive Robbins for his communication about Nordoff–Robbins Music Therapy and specifically the Nicole case study, and Nicolas Jean for creating the figures.

References

Adamek, M.S., Gervin, A.P., & Shiraishi, I.M. (2000). Music therapy and speech rehabilitation with brain-injured patients: Research, intervention models and assessment. In Association AMT (Ed.) *Effectiveness of music therapy procedures: Documentation of research and clinical practice.* Silver Spring, MD: American Music Therapy Association, PP. 112–34.

Adolphs, R. (2009). The social brain: neural basis of social knowledge. *Annual Review of Psychology*, **60**, 693–716.

Aigen, K. (1996). *Being in music: Foundations of Nordoff-Robbins music therapy.* St. Louis, MO: MMB Music.

Aigen, K. (2005). *Music-centered music therapy.* Gilsum, NH: Barcelona Publishers.

Aldridge, D. (Ed.) (2000) *Music therapy in dementia care.* London: Jessica Kingsley Publishers.

Aldridge, D. (Ed.) (2005) *Music therapy and neurological rehabilitation.* London: Jessica Kingsley.

Alvin, J. & Warwick, A. (1991) *Music therapy for the autistic child.* Oxford: Oxford University Press.

Amunts, K., Schleicher, A., Burgel, U., Mohlberg, H., Uylings, H.B., & Zilles, K. (1999). Broca's region revisited: cytoarchitecture and intersubject variability. *Journal of Comparative Neurology*, **412**, 319–41.

Ansdell, G. (1995) *Music for life: Aspects of creative music therapy with adult clients.* London: Jessica Kingsley Publishers.

Augustine, J.R. (1996) Circuitry and functional aspects of the insular lobe in primates including humans. *Brain Research Review*, **22**, 229–44.

Austin, D. (2008). *The theory and practice of vocal psychotherapy.* London: Jessica Kingsley Publishers.

Aziz-Zadeh, L., Koski, L., Zaidel, E., Mazziotta, J., & Iacoboni, M. (2006) Lateralization of the human mirror neuron system. *Journal of Neuroscience*, **26**, 2964–70.

Bangert, M., Peschel, T., Schlaug, G., Rotte, M., Drescher, D., Hinrichs, H., *et al.* (2006) Shared networks for auditory and motor processing in professional pianists: Evidence from fMRI conjunction. *Neuroimage*, **30**, 917–26.

Besson, M., Faita, F., & Requin, J. (1994) Brain waves associated with musical incongruities differ for musicians and non-musicians. *Neuroscience Letters*, **168**, 101–5.

Biehl, M., Matsumoto, D., Ekman, P., Hearn, V., Heider, K., Kudoh, T., *et al.* (1997) Matsumoto and Ekman's Japanese and caucasian facial expressions of emotion (JACFEE): Reliability data and cross-national differences. *Journal of Nonverbal Behaviour*, **21**, 3–21.

Binkofski, F., Buccino, G., Stephan, K.M., Rizzolatti, G., Seitz, R.J., & Freund, H.J. (1999). A parieto-premotor network for object manipulation: evidence from neuroimaging. *Experimental Brain Research*, **128**, 210–213.

Boxill, E.H. (1985). *Music therapy for the developmentally disabled*. Austin, TX: Pro-ed.

Browman C.P. & Goldstein L. (1992) Articulatory phonology: An overview. *Phonetica*, **49**, 155–80.

Brown, S. & Martinez, M.J. (2007). Activation of premotor vocal areas during musical discrimination. *Brain and Cognition*, **63**, 59–69.

Buccino, G., Lui, F., Canessa, N., Patteri, I., Lagravinese, G., Benuzzi, F., *et al.* (2004) Neural circuits involved in the recognition of actions performed by nonconspecifics: An fMRI study. *Journal of Cognitive Neuroscience*, **16**, 114–26.

Calvert, G.A., Bullmore, E.T., Brammer, M.J., Campbell, R., Williams, S.C., McGuire, P.K., *et al.* (1997). Activation of auditory cortex during silent lipreading. *Science*, **276**, 593–96.

Campbell, P.S. (1998). *Songs in their heads: Music and its meaning in children's lives*. Oxford: Oxford University Press.

Carr, L., Iacoboni, M., Dubeau, M.C., Mazziotta, J.C., & Lenzi, G.L. (2003) Neural mechanisms of empathy in humans: a relay from neural systems for imitation to limbic areas. *Proceedings of the National Academy of Sciences USA*, **100**, 5497–502.

Cattaneo, L., Barchiesi, G., Tabarelli, D., Arfeller, C., Sato, M., & Glenberg, A.M. (2011). One's motor performance predictably modulates the understanding of others' actions through adaptation of premotor visuo-motor neurons. *Social Cognitive and Affective Neuroscience*, **6**(3), 301–10.

Chapin, H., Jantzen, K., Kelso, J.A., Steinberg, F., & Large, E. (2010). Dynamic emotional and neural responses to music depend on performance expression and listener experience. *PLoS ONE* **5**, e13812.

Chen, J.L., Penhune, V.B., & Zatorre, R.J. (2008) Listening to Musical Rhythms Recruits Motor Regions of the Brain. *Cerebral Cortex*, **18**, 2844–54.

Clynes, M. (1973). Sentics: biocybernetics of emotion communication. *Annals of the New York Academy of Sciences*, **220**, 55–131.

Cohen, P. (2007) Apple: 100 million iPods sold, and counting. *Macworld*.

Conard, N.J., Malina, M., Munzel, S.C. (2009). New flutes document the earliest musical tradition in southwestern Germany. *Nature*, **460**, 737–40.

Craig, A.D. (2002) How do you feel? Interoception: the sense of the physiological condition of the body. *National Review of Neuroscience*, **3**, 655–66.

Craig, A.D. (2008). Interoception and emotion: A neuroanatomical perspective. In: M. Lewis & L. Feldman-Barrett (Eds.) *Handbook of emotions*, 3rd Edition. New York: Guilford, pp. 272–88.

Dalla Bella, S., Kraus, N., Overy, K., Pantev, C., Snyder, J.S., Tervaniemi, M., *et al.* (2009). The neurosciences and music III: Disorders and plasticity. *Annals of the New York Academy of Sciences*, **1169**, 1–569.

Davis, M.H. (1980). A multidimensional approach to individual differences in empathy. *JSAS Catalog of Selected Documents in Psychology*, **10**, 85.

de Waal, F.B.M. (2008). Putting the altruism back into altruism: The evolution of empathy. *Annual Review of Psychology*, **59**, 279–300.

di Pellegrino, G., Fadiga, L., Fogassi, L., Gallese, V., & Rizzolatti, G. (1992). Understanding motor events: A neurophysiological study. *Experimental Brain Research*, **91**, 176–80.

Fadiga, L., Fogassi, L., Pavesi, G., & Rizzolatti, G. (1995). Motor facilitation during action observation: A magnetic stimulation study. *Journal of Neurophysiology*, **73**, 2608–11.

Fadiga, L., Craighero, L., Buccino, G., & Rizzolatti, G. (2002). Speech listening specifically modulates the excitability of tongue muscles: a TMS study. *European Journal of Neuroscience*, **15**, 399–402.

Floel, A., Ellger, T., Breitenstein, C., & Knecht, S. (2003). Language perception activates the hand motor cortex: implications for motor theories of speech perception. *European Journal of Neuroscience*, **18**, 704–8.

Gallese, V. (2007). Before and below 'theory of mind': Embodied simulation and the neural correlates of social cognition. *Philosophical Transactions of the Royal Society of London—Series B: Biological Sciences*, **362**, 659–69.

Gallese, V. & Goldman, A. (1998). Mirror neurons and the simulation theory of mind-reading. *Trends in Cognitive Sciences*, **2**, 493–501.

Gallese, V., Fadiga, L., Fogassi, L., & Rizzolatti, G. (1996). Action recognition in the premotor cortex. *Brain*, **119**, 593–609.

Gazzola, V., Aziz-Zadeh, L., & Keysers, C. (2006). Empathy and the somatotopic auditory mirror system in humans. *Current Biology*, **16**, 1824–9.

Goleman D (2006). *Social intelligence: The new science of human relationships*. New York: Random House.

Grafton, S.T., Arbib, M.A., Fadiga, L., & Rizzolatti, G. (1996). Localization of grasp representations in humans by positron emission tomography. 2. Observation compared with imagination. *Experimental Brain Research*, **112**, 103–11.

Grahn, J.A. (2009) Neuroscientific investigations of musical rhythm: Recent advances and future challenges. *Contemporary Music Review*, **28**, 251–77.

Grezes, J., Armony, J.L., Rowe, J., & Passingham, R.E. (2003). Activations related to 'mirror' and 'canonical' neurones in the human brain: An fMRI study. *Neuroimage*, **18**, 928–37.

Haslinger, B., Erhard, P., Altenmuller, E., Schroeder, U., Boecker, H., & Ceballos-Baumann, A.O. (2005). Transmodal sensorimotor networks during action observation in professional pianists. *Journal of Cognitive Neuroscience*, **17**, 282–93.

Haueisen, J. & Knosche, T.R. (2001) Involuntary motor activity in pianists evoked by music perception. *Journal of Cognitive Neuroscience*, **13**, 786–92.

Heimlich, E. (1972). Paraverbal techniques in the therapy of childhood communication disorders. *International Journal of Child Psychotherapy*, **1**, 65–83.

Iacoboni, M. (2009). Imitation, empathy, and mirror neurons. *Annual Review of Psychology*, **60**, 653–70.

Iacoboni, M., Woods, R.P., Brass, M., Bekkering, H., Mazziotta, J.C., & Rizzolatti, G. (1999). Cortical mechanisms of human imitation. *Science*, **286**, 2526–8.

Iacoboni, M., Molnar-Szakacs, I., Gallese, V., Buccino, G., Mazziotta, J.C., & Rizzolatti, G. (2005). Grasping the intentions of others with one's own mirror neuron system. *PLoS Biol* **3**, e79.

Johnson-Frey, S.H., Maloof, F.R., Newman-Norlund, R., Farrer, C., Inati, S., & Grafton, S.T. (2003). Actions or hand-object interactions? Human inferior frontal cortex and action observation. *Neuron*, **39**, 1053–58.

Keysers, C., Wicker, B., Gazzola, V., Anton, J.L., Fogassi, L., & Gallese, V. (2004). A touching sight: SII/PV activation during the observation and experience of touch. *Neuron*, **42**, 335–46.

Kirschner, S. & Tomasello, M. (2009) Joint drumming: Social context facilitates synchronization in preschool children. *Journal of Experimental Child Psychology*, **102**, 299–314.

Koelsch, S., Fritz, T., Schulze, K., Alsop, D., & Schlaug, G. (2005) Adults and children processing music: An fMRI study. *Neuroimage*, **25**, 1068–76.

Koelsch, S., Fritz, T., Dye, V.C., Muller, K., & Friederici, A.D. (2006). Investigating emotion with music: An fMRI study. *Human Brain Mapping*, **27**, 239–50.

Koski, L., Wohlschlager, A., Bekkering, H., Woods, R.P., Dubeau, M.C., Mazziotta, J.C., *et al.* (2002). Modulation of motor and premotor activity during imitation of target-directed actions. *Cerebral Cortex*, **12**, 847–55.

Lahav, A., Saltzman, E., & Schlaug, G. (2007). Action representation of sound: Audiomotor recognition network while listening to newly acquired actions. *Journal of Neuroscience*, **27**, 308–14.

Langer, S.K. (1954). *Philosophy in a new key: A study in the symbolism of reason, rite, and art*, 6th ed. Cambridge: New American Library.

Liberman, A.M. & Mattingly, I.G. (1985). The motor theory of speech perception revised. *Cognition*, **21**, 1–36.

Liberman, A.M. & Whalen, D.H. (2000). On the relation of speech to language. *Trends in Cognitive Science*, **4**, 187–96.

Lipps, T. (1903). Einfuehlung, innere nachahmung und organenempfindung. *Archiv für die Ges. Psychologie*, **1**, Part 2. Leipzig: W. Engelmann.

Malloch, S. & Trevarthen, C. (2009). *Communicative musicality: Exploring the basis of human companionship*. Oxford: Oxford University Press.

Mazziotta, J., Toga, A., Evans, A., *et al.* (2001). A probabilistic atlas and reference system for the human brain: International Consortium for Brain Mapping (ICBM). *Philosophical Transactions of the Royal Society of London—Series B: Biological Sciences*, **356**, 1293–322.

Mehrabian, A. & Epstein, N. (1972). A measure of emotional empathy. *Journal of Personality*, **40**, 525–43.

Meister, I.G., Krings, T., Foltys, H., Boroojerdi, B., Muller, M., Topper, R., & Thron, A. (2004). Playing piano in the mind—an fMRI study on music imagery and performance in pianists. *Cognitive Brain Research*, **19**, 219–28.

Menon, V. & Levitin, D.J. (2005). The rewards of music listening: Response and physiological connectivity of the mesolimbic system. *Neuroimage*, **28**, 175–84.

Meyer, L.B. (1967). *Music, the arts, and ideas*. Chicago, IL: University of Chicago Press.

Molnar-Szakacs, I. & Overy, K. (2006). Music and mirror neurons: From motion to 'e'motion. *Social Cognitive and Affective Neuroscience*, **1**, 235–41.

Molnar-Szakacs, I., Iacoboni, M, Koski, L., & Mazziotta, J.C. (2005). Functional segregation within pars opercularis of the inferior frontal gyrus: Evidence from fMRI studies of imitation and action observation. *Cerebral Cortex*, **15**, 986–94.

Molnar-Szakacs, I., Kaplan, J., Greenfield, P.M., & Iacoboni, M. (2006). Observing complex action sequences: The role of the fronto-parietal mirror neuron system. *NeuroImage*, **33**, 923–35.

Molnar-Szakacs, I., Wu, A.D., Robles, F.J., & Iacoboni, M. (2007). Do you see what I mean? Corticospinal excitability during observation of culture-specific gestures. *PLoS ONE*, **2**, e626.

Molnar-Szakacs, I., Wang, M.J., Laugeson, E.A., Overy, K., Wu, W.L., & Piggot, J. (2009). Autism, emotion recognition and the mirror neuron system: The case of music. *McGill Journal of Medicine*, **12**, 87.

Nishitani, N. & Hari, R. (2000). Temporal dynamics of cortical representation for action. *Proceedings of the National Academy of Sciences USA*, **97**, 913–18.

Nordoff, P. & Robbins, C. (1977). *Creative music therapy: Individualized treatment for the handicapped child*. New York: John Day.

Oberman, L.M., Hubbard, E.M., McCleery, J.P., Altschuler, E.L., Ramachandran, V.S., & Pineda, J.A. (2005). EEG evidence for mirror neuron dysfunction in autism spectrum disorders. *Cognitive Brain Research*, **24**, 190–8.

Overy, K. & Molnar-Szakacs, I. (2009). Being together in time: Musical experience and the mirror neuron system. *Music Perception*, **26**, 489–504.

Pessoa, L. (2008). On the relationship between emotion and cognition. *Nature Reviews: Neuroscience*, **9**, 148–58.

Petrides, M. & Pandya, D. (1997). Comparative architectonic analysis of the human and the macaque frontal cortex. In: F. Boller & J. Grafman (Eds.) *Handbook of neuropsychology*. New York: Elsevier, pp 17–58.

Pineda, J.A. (2008). Sensorimotor cortex as a critical component of an 'extended' mirror neuron system: Does it solve the development, correspondence, and control problems in mirroring? *Behavioral and Brain Functions*, **4**, 47.

Preston, S.D., & de Waal, F.B. (2002). Empathy: Its ultimate and proximate bases. *Behavioral and Brain Sciences*, **25**, 1–20: discussion pp. 20–71.

Rizzolatti, G. & Matelli, M. (2003). Two different streams form the dorsal visual system: Anatomy and functions. *Experimental Brain Research*, **153**, 146–57.

Rizzolatti, G. & Craighero, L. (2004). The mirror-neuron system. *Annual Review of Neuroscience*, **27**, 169–92.

Rizzolatti, G. & Sinigaglia, C. (2010). The functional role of the parieto-frontal mirror circuit: Interpretations and misinterpretations. *Nature Reviews: Neuroscience*, **11**, 264–74.

Rizzolatti, G., Fadiga, L., Gallese, V., & Fogassi, L. (1996a). Premotor cortex and the recognition of motor actions. *Cognition and Brain Research*, **3**, 131–41.

Rizzolatti, G., Fadiga, L, Matelli, M., Bettinardi, V., Paulesu, E., Perani, D., & Fazio, F. (1996). Localization of grasp representations in humans by PET: 1. Observation versus execution. *Experimental Brain Research*, **111**, 246–52.

Robbins, C.E. & Robbins, C.M. (1991). Creative music therapy in bringing order, change and communicativeness to the life of a brain-injured adolescent. In K.E. Bruscia (Ed.) *Case studies in music therapy*. Gilsum, NH: Barcelona Publishers, pp. 231–49.

Scherer, K.R. & Oshinsky, J.S. (1977). Cue utilization in emotion attribution from auditory stimuli. *Motivation and Emotion*, **1**, 331–46.

Scherer, K.R., Banse, R., & Wallbott, H.G. (2001). Emotion inferences from vocal expression correlate across languages and cultures. *Journal of Cross-Cultural Psychology*, **32**, 76–92.

Singer, T., Seymour, B., O'Doherty, J., Kaube, H., Dolan, R.J., & Frith, C.D. (2004) Empathy for pain involves the affective but not sensory components of pain. *Science*, **303**, 1157–62.

Smith, A. (1759/1976). *The theory of moral sentiments*. Oxford: Oxford University Press.

Standley, J.M. (2000). Music research in medical treatments. In Association AMT (Ed.) *Effectiveness of music therapy procedures: Documentation of research and clinical practice*. Silver Spring, MD: American Music Therapy Association, pp. 1–64.

Stewart, L., Walsh, V., Frith, U., & Rothwell, J.C. (2001). Transcranial magnetic stimulation produces speech arrest but not song arrest. *Annals of the New York Academy of Sciences*, **930**, 433–5.

Studdert-Kennedy, M., Liberman, A., Harris, K., & Cooper, F. (1970). Motor theory of speech perception: A reply to Lane's critical review. *Psychological Review*, **77**, 234–49.

Thaut, M.H., Gardiner, J.C., Holmberg, D., Horwitz, J., Kent, L., Andrews, G., *et al.* (2009). Neurologic music therapy improves executive function and emotional adjustment in traumatic brain injury rehabilitation. *Annals of the New York Academy of Science*, **1169**, 406–16.

Tomaiuolo, F., MacDonald, J.D., Caramanos, Z., Posner, G., Chiavaras, M., Evans, A.C., & Petrides, M. (1999). Morphology, morphometry and probability mapping of the pars opercularis of the inferior frontal gyrus: An in vivo MRI analysis. *European Journal of Neuroscience*, **11**, 3033–46.

Trevarthen, C. (1999). Musicality and the intrinsic motive pulse: Evidence from human psychobiology and infant communication. In 'Rhythms, musical narrative, and the origins of human commuincation'. *Musicae Scientiae*, 1999–2000, 157–213.

Trevarthen, C., Delafield-Butt, J., & Schogler, B. (2011). Psychobiology of musical gesture: Innate rhythm, harmony and melody in movements of narration. In: A. Gritten & E. King (Eds.) *New Perspectives on Music and Gesture*. Aldershot: Ashgate, pp. 11–44.

Turry, A. (2009). Integrating musical and psychological thinking: The relationship between music and words in clinically improvised songs. *Music and Medicine*, **1**(2), 106–16.

VonBonin, G. & Bailey, P. (1947). *The neocortex of Macaca Mulatta*. Urbana, IL: University of Illinois Press.

VonEconomo, C. & Koskinas, G.N. (1925). *Die Cytoarchitektonik der Hirnrinde des erwasenen Menschen*. Berlin: Springer.

Wicker, B., Keysers C., Plailly, J., Royet, J.P., Gallese, V., & Rizzolatti, G. (2003). Both of us disgusted in My insula: The common neural basis of seeing and feeling disgust. *Neuron*, **40**, 655–64.

Wilson, S.M., Saygin, A.P., Sereno, M.I., & Iacoboni, M. (2004). Listening to speech activates motor areas involved in speech production. *Nature Neuroscience*, **7**, 701–2.

Wong, P.C.M., Skoel, E., Russo, N.M., Dees, T., & Kraus, N. (2007). Musical experience shapes human brainstem encoding of linguistic pitch patterns. *Nature Neuroscience*, **10**, 420–22.

Zatorre, R.J., Evans, A.C., & Meyer, E. (1994). Neural mechanisms underlying melodic perception and memory for pitch. *Journal of Neuroscience*, **14**, 1908–19.

Chapter 21

Enhancing imaginative expression in the performing arts with EEG-neurofeedback

John Gruzelier

21.1 Introduction

The application of electroencephalography (EEG)-neurofeedback to the performing arts in the UK began 10 years ago with our Leverhulme Trust funded project in collaboration with the Royal College of Music (RCM) with the aim of exploring the relevance for music performance of interventions from the field of sports psychology. This followed a BBC documentary called 'Losing It' in which Britain's Olympic gold medallists explained how on one occasion they won a medal while in similar competitions in close proximity they were less successful, yet they were at the same level of expertise and fitness. One popular explanation for the discrepancy was that they were in 'The Zone' when they won. The project was called 'Zoning In', and neurofeedback was contrasted with mental skills training and a programme of fitness training. The Zone is a popular term for a 'flow' state, which is a psychological construct (Csikszentmihalyi, 1996) describing that optimal experience when the performer is totally absorbed in performing and everything comes together, often associated with a 'high'. The resultant neurofeedback results have helped provide crucial evidence for validation of the largely forgotten field of EEG-biofeedback, and helped provide a stimulus for validation studies in optimal performance, educational, and clinical domains.

We have earlier (Gruzelier & Egner, 2004) acquainted a music readership with an introduction to neurofeedback in a chapter describing our RCM studies, the first two of the seven studies to be reviewed here, and readers are referred to that chapter. In brief, neurofeedback (earlier termed biofeedback) is a form of instrumental learning where through the feedback in real-time of the brain's electrical activity, participants learn to regulate it through reinforcers and the reinforcing consequences of mastering a skill, and so may transfer the learned state to the real world. The procedure was originally called biofeedback, a term now reserved for control of the peripheral nervous system, while neurofeedback refers to control of the central nervous system. There is a close association between the spectrum of EEG rhythms and arousal state, though alignment with arousal is merely a convenient simplification, and the precise cognitive and affective correlates of EEG activity are a central focus of cognitive neuroscience.

For didactic purposes, EEG spectral neurofeedback protocols may be divided into slow- versus fast-wave training, e.g. alpha/theta (A/T), and sensory-motor rhythm (SMR) training. The former, when conducted with eyes closed with auditory reinforcement, encourages states of deep relaxation, whereas fast wave training is conducted with eyes open while reinforcement is provided on a computer screen. Slow-wave neurofeedback aims to train the elevation of theta amplitude (5–8 Hz) to be higher than alpha amplitude (8–11 Hz), and is done by presenting pleasing sounds such as waves gently crashing on the beach or a babbling brook, contingent on the production of theta and alpha. The relative reward contingencies are gradually changed to maximize the theta-to-alpha ratio (see Egner and Gruzelier (2004b) for the temporal dynamics of the training protocol). With fast-wave training, operant contingencies determine the reward (i.e. points on a computer screen): these were contingent upon increments in either say SMR (12–15 Hz) or beta1 (15–18 Hz) without concurrent rises in frequencies lower and higher in the EEG spectrum.

Nowadays, neurofeedback training has enhanced attention, memory, learning, micro-surgical skills, mental rotation, intelligence, sleep, and well-being in healthy participants (Egner & Gruzelier, 2001, 2004a; Vernon et al., 2003; Barnea et al., 2005; Raymond et al., 2005a; Hanslmayer et al., 2005; Hoedlmoser et al., 2008; Ros et al., 2009; Keizer et al., 2010a, b; Zoefel et al., 2011), while in the clinic, controlled studies have shown efficacy inter alia for epilepsy (Rockstroh et al., 1993; Sterman, 2000), attention deficit hyperactivity disorder (ADHD: Arns et al., 2009; Gevensleben et al., 2009), autism (Mirjam et al., 2009), and insomnia (Cortoos et al., 2009). The slow-wave applications have included anxiety reduction, mood elevation, creativity, addiction, and post-traumatic stress syndrome, while fast-wave applications have included attention, perceptual-binding, learning, memory, mental-rotation, intelligence and skilled psychomotor performance, ADHD, autism, and insomnia. Studies of underlying mechanisms are beginning (Ros et al., 2010).

Of central relevance to musical imagination, A/T training has consistently enhanced interpretative imagination in the performing arts, and in fact the A/T protocol originated to enhance creativity (Green & Green, 1977), though this was lost sight of when pioneering attempts were unsuccessful (for review see Gruzelier, 2009). There had been extensive historical anecdotes that hypnagogia has facilitated creative associations in various cultural spheres (Koestler, 1964), while theta was considered to be an EEG marker of hypnagogia. Since then the production of theta with eyes closed has been shown to accompany states of deep relaxation close to sleep, meditation and hypnosis (Vaitl et al., 2005). As described by Schachter (1976), hypnagogia produces spontaneous visual, auditory, and kinaesthetic images, unusual thought processes and verbal constructions, and symbolic representations of ongoing mental and physiological processes.

21.2 **Zoning in: advanced music performance**

In the first of two studies (Egner & Gruzelier, 2003: Gruzelier & Egner, 2004), of the 36 students who participated, 22 were trained on two neurofeedback protocols (SMR and beta1) commonly used as tools for the enhancement of attention, followed by the deep relaxation A/T protocol. A random sub-sample of 12 of the neurofeedback group was additionally engaged in a 10-weekly regime of physical exercise as well as mental skills training derived from sports psychology. A third group of 14 consisted of scholastic grade- and age-matched no-training controls. The aim was to compare a mixed neurofeedback package with the same package with and without aerobic fitness and mental skills training.

In order to assess music performance, the mark scheme of the Associated Boards of the Royal Schools of Music (ABRSM; Harvey, 1994) was adapted, consisting of three main categories: technical competence, musicality, and communication, with ten further sub-categories (Thompson & Williamon, 2003). The 13 rating categories (see Table 21.1) were marked on a 1–10 scale which mapped directly onto the percentage scales frequently used in educational contexts. Pre-performance state-anxiety was assessed using an anxiety inventory (STAI; Spielberger et al., 1983). Before a panel of instrumental professors the participants gave recitals of up to 15 minutes. Video recordings were edited into a random order and sent to two external evaluators in the first study and three in the second. The same methodology is used in the subsequent performing arts studies in

Table 21.1 Music performance rating scales with correlations between changes in performance and alpha/theta learning

A/T learning	r	p
Overall quality	0.47	0.04
Perceived instrumental competence	0.50	0.03
Level of technical security	0.39	0.09
Rhythmic accuracy	0.65	0.00
Tonal quality and spectrum	0.39	0.14
Musicality/musical understanding	0.54	0.02
Stylistic accuracy	0.58	0.01
Interpretative imagination	0.48	0.04
Expressive range	0.53	0.02
Communication	0.55	0.01
Deportment	0.45	0.05
Communication of emotional commitment and conviction	0.51	0.02
Ability to cope with situational stress	0.44	0.05

the remainder of the chapter, with modifications as indicated. Readers should consult the empirical papers of the studies for methodological details.

The neurofeedback-only group was judged to have improved, while no improvements were found in the others (Figure 21.1). Improvement was found in all three domains: musicality, technique, and communication. The EEG in each protocol was correlated with changes in ratings in all 22 musicians receiving neurofeedback. Interestingly, an A/T training learning index correlated highly positively with improvements in each of the three domains: technique, musicality and communication (Figure 21.2). The full list of correlations is shown in Table 21.1 where it can be seen there were significant associations with A/T learning in virtually all subcategories. Neither the SMR

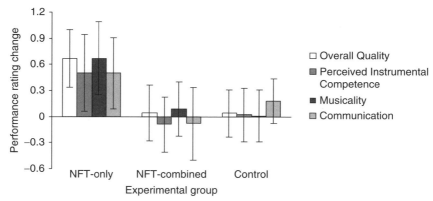

Fig. 21.1 Mean music performance rating change scores (± s.e.m.) on the main evaluation categories and overall quality for neurofeedback-only (NFT-only), neurofeedback and additional interventions (NFT-combined), and a no-training control group showing advantages for the neurofeedback-only group.

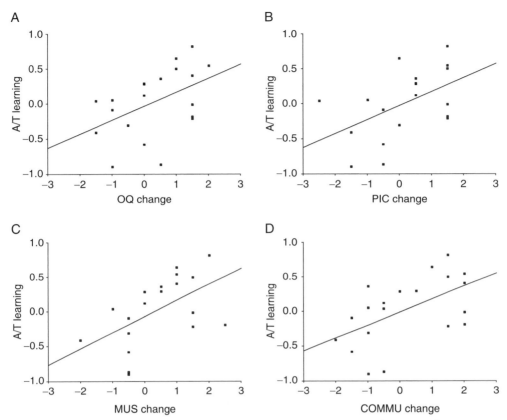

Fig. 21.2 Lines of best fit for bivariate correlations between A/T learning and music performance rating changes on the main evaluation categories of (A) Overall quality [OQ], (B) Perceived instrumental competence [PIC], (C) Musicality [MUS], and (D) Communication [COMMU].

nor the beta1 learning indices correlated with changes in music performance. Furthermore, differential improvement rates between the experimental groups were not related to pre-performance anxiety, which improved in all groups. The reduction in anxiety following fast-wave (SMR/beta1) training was supported by an interpretative phenomenological analysis (Edge & Lancaster, 2004). Fast-wave training was described as relaxing; as one said it 'lets my mind breathe'. However, these advantages did not carry over to performance ratings by the experts.

In a second investigation a constructive replication was undertaken with an independent-groups design (Gruzelier et al., 2002; Egner & Gruzelier, 2003; Gruzelier & Egner, 2004) involving a different cohort of 61 students who were randomly allocated to either A/T, SMR, or beta1 neurofeedback, physical exercise, mental skills, or the Alexander technique. The Alexander technique is widely used in performing arts conservatoires and involves a system of kinaesthetic education to avoid excessive postural tension.

In support of the first study, the A/T group displayed significant improvements. The beta1, SMR, Alexander, physical exercise, and mental skills training groups showed no post-training changes (Figure 21.3). A/T enhancing effects were replicable, particularly with respect to the parameters of musicality—stylistic accuracy and interpretative imagination—together with overall quality. As before, all groups tended to report less anxiety. Together, these results could be

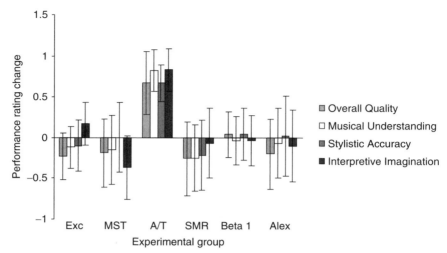

Fig. 21.3 Mean change scores (± s.e.m.) for the physical exercise (Exc), mental skills training (MST), alpha/theta (A/T), SMR (SMR), beta1 (Beta1), and Alexander Technique (Alex) groups on the main evaluation categories and overall quality showing advantages following A/T training.

interpreted as indicating that A/T training led to improvements, especially on attributes of artistic expression including interpretative imagination, which in turn improved performance overall. This was consistent with an impact on creativity. The increments in the ratings of the three experts represented average A/T group improvements of between 13.5% and 17%, with a mean improvement rate of 12% across all evaluation scales. This was equivalent to more that one class grade and was clearly of professional significance. In the year that followed the completion of the research neurofeedback training was offered as an option in the RCM curriculum.

In neither RCM study could the effects be accounted for by invoking practice, motivational, or generic neurofeedback factors. An explanation based simply on generic relaxation can also be discounted, on the grounds that in both studies A/T training was not associated with a greater decrease in pre-performance anxiety than was obtained in other groups. Additionally, a mental skills training group, which engaged in extensive relaxation training, showed no performance improvements. That the effects of A/T training may not necessarily be reflected in self-reported relaxation phenomenology was shown in a study in which appraisal, by medical students, of subjective arousal states with Activation-Deactivation scales (Thayer, 1967) did not differ between an accurate feedback and a mock feedback condition. Both were reported to be equally relaxing, even though significantly different EEG alpha/theta signatures were observed such that accurate feedback led to an increase in the theta/alpha ratio which was not observed with mock feedback (Egner, Stawson & Gruzelier, 2002).

21.3 **Novice versus advanced musical performance**

The promising outcome of neurofeedback training on music performance led to support from NESTA (the National Endowment for Science, Technology and the Arts in the UK), with the chosen over-riding goal of the impact on novice musical ability in both young adults and children. If successful, the pedagogic implications would be considerable and would not be limited to the very talented.

In adults, the strategy was adopted of examining novice singing ability in conservatoire instrumentalists in whom advanced instrumental performance was also rated. Given the impact on musical creativity, aside from examining musical ability with well-known pieces, improvisation was included with both voice and instrumental playing. Again we contrasted alpha/theta slow-wave training with fast-wave training but here focusing on SMR training, not beta1 training, for of the fast wave protocols, SMR training had the more generic benefits for laboratory measures of attention in the music students, as reviewed in the next section. We hypothesized firstly, that slow-wave training would enhance the three domains of music performance assessment; secondly, as SMR training had produced subjective reports of mental relaxation in musicians, and in other contexts had produced benefits in sustained concentration, working memory, learning, mental rotation and perceptual-motor skills, as referenced above, that SMR training should benefit music performance, which perhaps would be disclosed with novice abilities, here vocal performance.

Twenty-four music students from London universities were randomly assigned to one of three experimental groups: A/T, SMR or non-intervention controls. All were instrumentalists with a wide range of instrumental ability from advanced amateur to postgraduate, but with a singing ability at novice level and, indeed, a reluctance to sing. Music performances consisted of a choice of two unprepared Britten folk songs and self-selected prepared instrumental pieces. Vocal improvisation consisted of *Stripsody* (Berberian, 1966), in which notation was presented as a cartoon-strip on a stave with time and pitch axes, and performed 'as if by a radio sound man who must provide all the sound effects with his voice'. The aim was to facilitate highly expressive and imaginative performance, not requiring trained vocal ability. Instrumental improvisation involved the choice of one theme from a menu of topics. Evaluation was essentially as for the RCM studies, with additional scales for singing.

Neurofeedback successfully fulfilled the chief NESTA aim of a potential impact on novice musical ability. Both A/T and SMR neurofeedback protocols were found to enhance the novice singing ability of folk songs. A/T training had an impact on the musicality and communication categories, but not on technique. In contrast, SMR training for the first time disclosed suggestive evidence of enhancing music ability to some extent, and interestingly this was only with novice performance and was in the domain of technique, improving pitch and to some extent rhythmic accuracy and diction. Both protocols would therefore have a place in training musical ability, and in addition were seen to have complementary effects on novice performance—A/T having an impact on musicality and communication and SMR an impact on technique. Indeed, the impact of A/T on communication was observable to lay people as disclosed in their ratings of expressivity, confidence and stage presence.

As a secondary aim, improvisation was examined as a direct test of the impact of neurofeedback on creativity in performance. Vocal improvisation with *Stripsody* was enhanced following A/T in all domains, but most particularly regarding communication in performance. There was no advantage from SMR training with *Stripsody*. Instrumental improvisation was not influenced by neurofeedback, and was at a low level of ability (which may have been a function of our choice of material). Thirdly, we provided a further replication of the advantage of A/T training for higher level instrumental ability and this was found in all domains—musicality, communication, and technique, in replication of the first RCM study. Here as before there was no advantage for SMR training.

Thus, considering these various studies, A/T training showed consistent benefits for music performance in all three performance domains, in both advanced instrumental playing and novice singing. Interestingly, for the first time, SMR training was found to be beneficial, but only with technique in the low level novice singing ability measured with the Britten folk songs. This impact on novice ability, as will be seen below, chimes with the success of SMR training in children, but before considering the child studies ancillary studies on cognition and affect with musicians, university students and trainee doctors will briefly be outlined in view of the relevance for outcome in general but especially with children.

In conclusion, the NESTA aim of determining whether neurofeedback could have wide-ranging impact on musical education was vindicated through its efficacy with novice performance, aside from the demonstration of a further highly reliable impact of A/T on mature performance.

21.4 Attention, memory, perceptual-motor skills, and mood

In interpreting the benefits of A/T neurofeedback training with the RCM musicians it was noted that reduction in anxiety was an unlikely explanation, as was the case for improvements in attention per se. Germane to the latter, the students in both RCM studies had been examined for changes in laboratory measures of attention. It was the fast-wave training, the neurofeedback protocol which had not benefited music performance, which benefited attention, whereas effects of A/T training on attention were less clear.

One measure of attention was a widely used go/no-go continuous performance task (Greenberg & Kindschi, 1999) in which two types of errors can be incurred—errors of omission (failing to respond to a target stimulus), and errors of commission (erroneously responding to a non-target stimulus), which are held to reflect inattentiveness and impulsiveness respectively. A global attention index derived from signal detection theory (Green & Swets, 1966), termed 'd prime' (d') took into account both error types by expressing a ratio of hit rate to false alarm rate.

In the first RCM study we established that 10 sessions of beta1 and SMR neurofeedback led to highly significant improvements in commission error rates (Egner & Gruzelier, 2001). Learning indices of how well the students had learned to enhance the targeted EEG rhythms were correlated with changes in error rates in order to explore the linkage between the process of learned EEG self-regulation and reduction in impulsive mistakes. Considering here only the influence of SMR training, it was found that the relative success at enhancing the SMR was highly positively correlated with reduced commission errors, which in turn had an impact in elevating d'. The same attention task has been widely used to validate treatment outcomes in ADHD, disclosing following fast-wave neurofeedback improvements in d', commission and omission errors and reaction time variability (Monastra et al., 2005). It was therefore doubly relevant for our study with children.

SMR training has been found to enhance semantic working memory (Vernon et al. 2003), while SMR training of trainee eye surgeons performing a simulated cataract operation has resulted in a more efficient, modulated performance as indexed by both consultant surgeon subjective ratings of filmed performance and objective timed measures (Ros et al., 2009), and, importantly, has been shown most significantly with the more difficult perceptual-motor tasks. Attention, memory, and perceptual-motor abilities are all engaged in music performance, especially at a novice level. In the affective domain, we found that mood measured by the *Profile of Mood States* (McNair et al., 1992) was enhanced in socially withdrawn medical students (Raymond et al., 2005a). Students were randomized to either contingent or non-contingent (mock) A/T training, receiving 10 sessions in all. After A/T training participants rated themselves as significantly more compassionate, agreeable, elated, confident and energetic whereas controls were more compassionate but less energetic.

Both fast and slow-wave neurofeedback training therefore have an impact on cognitive and affective processes that theoretically might advance artistic performance. This is aside from the putative advantage of hypnagogia-induced creativity, the aim of A/T training—mechanisms for which will be elaborated in the final section.

21.5 **Neurofeedback training of musical ability in children**

The aims of the NESTA programme were to examine the effects of training on music performance in schoolchildren aged 11 years: on their application in the classroom as well as on well-being at school and at home, and above all the feasibility of neurofeedback within the school curriculum. Alongside rehearsed music performance we examined creative musical improvisation, while attention was examined with the sustained attention test, as for the RCM studies and the 'gold standard' measure of treatment outcome in the ADHD field for monitoring intervention success. The efficacy of neurofeedback in treating ADHD has now been the subject of sufficient studies to warrant a meta-analysis, confirming its efficacy across various neurofeedback protocols (Arns et al., 2009). As a subsidiary aim of our study it was of interest to determine the incidence of ADHD levels of inattention in the school and the efficacy of neurofeedback in moderating them.

The study was conducted at the ARK Evelyn Grace Academy, Brixton, London in the autumn term of 2009 (Gruzelier et al., 2011b) with 33 11-year-olds selected on three criteria: musical potential, behavioural issues, or a combination of the two. Music performances included either a vocal or instrumental solo piece of their choice as practised in class, and a vocal or instrumental improvisation on the theme of *the sea* pre-training or *a storm* post-training following 2 minutes of preparation. Performances were filmed, randomized for order and group and then rated by four teacher assessors in two joint rating sessions on items covering creativity, communication and technique.

Prepared vocal or instrumental performance showed improvement in technique following A/T training—consisting of vocal quality, clarity of diction and sense of pitch, and for instrumental playing control of the instrument. There were also benefits following A/T training with the communication category, consisting of ratings of confidence, posture, engagement with the audience, and enjoyment. Here there was no impact on creativity, nor any improvement in the other groups following SMR training, as was the case with controls. Creative improvisation did improve with both neurofeedback groups on a creativity subscale, whereas the control group declined, giving a highly significant advantage to neurofeedback training, and despite a relative advantage to the control children at baseline. Creativity included use of imagination, well structured performance, appropriateness to title, and expression (dynamics and articulation). The communication category scale showed an even more striking advantage to neurofeedback training for both A/T and SMR, whereas there was a significant decline in the controls. Communication was based on ratings of engagement with the audience and enjoyment in performance.

On the attention test there was a highly significant slowing in mean reaction times in the course of the study, attesting to the tiredness observable in all groups at the end of term; this was especially noticeable as the study began when children were fresh after the long summer vacation. The decline did not occur in reaction time variability, implying that it was unrelated to attention per se: this inference was supported by a highly significant improvement in the global attention index d', mainly reflecting a decrease in commission errors (impulsive responding). This improvement was found to follow neurofeedback training only, with a highly significant reduction in errors of commission following A/T, and a tendency towards improvement in the SMR group.

At the close of the study a structured questionnaire was administered; 19/22 children from the training groups felt improved well-being in the school context, and this could extend to the home. Impressions of a positive carry-over to the classroom situation were volunteered by eight children following fast-wave training and six following slow-wave training. Music performance aside, self-report impressions of a positive impact on academic subjects included science, maths, physical education, performing arts, and English.

In summary, rehearsed musical performance was enhanced by slow-wave training for the categories of technique and communication with subscales of confidence, posture, engagement, and enjoyment, as shown in our conservatoire studies. The category of creativity/musicality was not enhanced as it was in the adult studies, although creativity as indexed by musical improvisation was enhanced to a highly significant degree. Interestingly, in children this was achieved with both slow-wave and fast-wave training, as was the enjoyment in creative improvisation as communicated to the raters. Thus fast-wave training had an impact with children as it did with novice as distinct from advanced music performance in adults. This was despite the fact that reaction times were slower at the end of the study, validating the behavioural impression gained that the children were tired at the end of the school term, yet music performance following neurofeedback was buffered from the wear and tear of the school year. Similarly, improvements in attention were observed despite the fact that there was a high incidence (19/33) of children whose attention was within the ADHD range; evidence from the clinical ADHD field would recommend that more than double our ten training sessions would be necessary to fully improve attention for such a level of impairment. This indicates how valuable neurofeedback training would be as an integral part of the curriculum planning, quite aside from the benefits for music. The logistics of implementing the neurofeedback training proved eminently viable in the school setting, given the excellent collaboration from the staff and an expert timetabling schedule such that children did not miss the same subject too often. The ARK academies have expressed interest in embedding neurofeedback training in the curriculum in the future.

21.6 **Dance performance**

Two studies have examined advanced dance performance, the first with competitive university ballroom and Latin dancers at Imperial College London (N = 18; Raymond et al., 2005b), and the second with freshers at the Labin dance conservatoire (N = 64) (Gruzelier et al., 2011a). In both these studies A/T neurofeedback was compared with heart rate variability (HRV) biofeedback training. HRV aims to induce a coherent waveform as can be achieved with slow paced breathing.

Both neurofeedback interventions facilitated ballroom dancing in competitors who went on to win the UK championship. Dancers performed in male–female pairs but were evaluated individually by two qualified dance assessors with a scale used for national dance assessments with categories of technique, musicality, timing, partnering skill, performing flair, and overall execution. Both training groups improved more than the control group in overall execution, while on the subscales A/T training improved timing and HRV improved technique.

Contemporary dance was not improved. Here the 40 second dance phase, performed in groups of five, may not have been long enough to disclose benefits, and compliance with training was such that weekly sessions were missed, which we have shown may compromise the outcome (Ros et al., 2009). Notwithstanding, cognitive creativity assessed with the *Alternative Uses Test* (Guilford, 1967) was facilitated by A/T training, and HRV facilitated reduction in anxiety as measured with the *Depression, Anxiety and Stress Scale* (Lovibond & Lovibond, 1995).

21.7 **Acting performance**

With the support of the European Union's *Future and Emerging Technologies* initiative we revisited the effect of SMR training on creative performance with a technical innovation that gave the neurofeedback training context ecological relevance. Instead of the conventional screen which depicts brain wave changes by histograms moving up and down, or computer games unrelated to the training goals of enhancing performance, a theatre auditorium was rendered on the computer screen. This was an image of the Vanburgh Theatre, Royal Academy of Dramatic Art (RADA), as seen by the actor from the stage. Its ecological relevance would putatively allow for more effective transfer to the real world. We reasoned that the clear advantage with elite performance for A/T training over SMR training may lie in the fact that real world connections were made through imaginative visualization in the eyes-closed reverie. As one musician had expressed:

> During the training sessions I feel extremely relaxed, and as though my mind is able to freely glide with my creative ideas bringing a new kind of spontaneity and energy to my thought processes . . . this gives me the opportunity to explore other areas of creativity that were previously unavailable to me as I'm free from the physical act of playing the piano whilst mentally being in the state of a performance. It's an extremely satisfying state to be in as it's almost as though I've been introduced to thinking of nothing, which then takes me to a place where creative possibilities seem boundless.

(Gruzelier, 2009: p. 105.)

We also drew on theory from Visual Reality (VR) Presence research (Sanchez-Vives & Slater, 2005), which studies the illusion of being in a place facilitated by surrounding VR immersive images via CAVE-like and head-mounted displays (Cruz-Neira et al., 1993). The auditorium image was rendered in the ReaCTor (at University College London), where in a cave-like context, the actor was surrounded by the auditorium image and experienced it in three dimensions through glasses. We hypothesized that the more technically immersive ReaCTor would prove to be superior in transfer than the conventional computer screen approach to SMR training, although both media would be effective in enhancing creative performance.

Of further theoretical relevance for creative performance was the innovation of interfacing the learned control of brain rhythms with feedback which signified mastering the control of aspects of the performing space. Enhancement of SMR was represented by changes in the auditorium lighting, and inhibition of theta and high-beta by a reduction in intrusive audience noise. Mastery is central to creative performance, and the sense of control contributes to the subjective experience of flow. Flow is the psychological construct (Csikszentmihalyi, 1996) mentioned in the Introduction which describes that optimal experience when the performer is totally absorbed in performing, and for them everything comes together. The state is itself intrinsically motivating and does not rely on any product or extrinsic reward. It requires an optimal balance between skill, mastery, and challenge, with immediate feedback about accomplishment. It therefore involves intense concentration without self-consciousness, a feeling of satisfaction, and often the experience of a 'high'. Thus the learned control of brain rhythms was designed to be contingent on control of the computer rendered performing space, and the ensuing mastery was hypothesized to transfer to acting performance.

The performers' subjective flow state was examined with the *Flow State Scales* (FSS) of Jackson and Eklund (2004), which measure nine dimensions of flow: merging of action/awareness, clear goals, unambiguous feedback, concentration on the task at hand, sense of control, loss of self-consciousness, transformation of time, autotelic experience, and challenge–skill balance. In view of the relative brevity of the performances it was not anticipated that there would be evidence for unambiguous feedback or for transformation of time, the two scales which require a deep experience (Tenebaum et al., 1999).

All 15 members of a class of American drama sophomores on semester placement in London received neurofeedback or acted as controls (Gruzelier et al., 2010). Students were randomized to the two training groups—laptop screen (N = 6) or ReaCTor (N =5). Acting performances were rated from filmed studio monologues and *Hamlet* excerpts performed on the stage of Shakespeare's Globe Theatre by three experts from acting conservatoires blind to order and group. The *Acting Performance Scale* consisted of scales covering overall performance and categories of voice, movement, creativity and communication. The 11 scales were as follows: overall performance, vocal transformation, vocal expression, movement fluency, movement inhabitation, imaginative expression, imaginative conviction, imaginative characterization, seamlessly engaged, at-one with performance, and well-rounded performance.

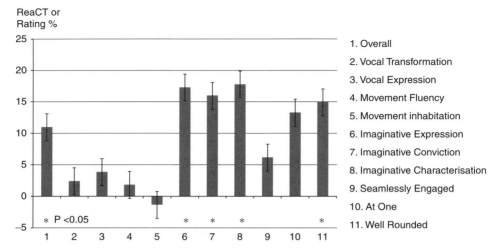

ReaCT or
Rating %

1. Overall
2. Vocal Transformation
3. Vocal Expression
4. Movement Fluency
5. Movement inhabitation
6. Imaginative Expression
7. Imaginative Conviction
8. Imaginative Characterisation
9. Seamlessly Engaged
10. At One
11. Well Rounded

* P <0.05

Fig. 21.4 Percentage improvement in acting advantage following training with the ReaCTor over the computer screen.

Learned control of brain activity was achieved with both training procedures. There was a slight advantage to the more immersive VR context in providing a learning curve asymptote of the SMR/theta ratio about a session earlier, coincidentally with identification of by the actor of 'At what stage did you recognize the mental state we were seeking in you?'. The VR procedure also had a greater impact on acting performance: the results are shown in Figure 21.4. It is noteworthy that of the various acting performance domains, improvements were found to be specific to creative acting performance—imaginative expression, conviction, and characterization—which carried over to ratings of acting performance overall and well-rounded performance.

Irrespective of training medium (laptop or ReaCTor) actors who had received neurofeedback experienced a higher flow state in performances on the Globe stage and studio than the controls, as shown in Figure 21.5. Advantages to neurofeedback were seen on flow ratings of sense of control, confidence or challenge-skill balance and there was a tendency with feeling-at-one with performance through the merging of action/awareness. Of importance for validation were the numerous positive correlations (see Table 21.2) between flow and the expert ratings of improvement or performance at the study end. The correlations involved all categories of acting performance and were found with five of the flow scales: sense of control, loss of self-consciousness, merging of action/awareness, challenge/skill balance, and autotelic experience.

In conclusion, in this exploratory study (N = 15) demonstrable benefits for acting performance were disclosed as the result of fast-wave SMR training in an ecologically valid training context, the theatre auditorium, hypothesized to facilitate transfer to creative performance. The immersive three-dimensional (3D) VR properties were superior to the two-dimensional (2D) properties, even though the same auditorium was depicted, as was also reflected in the speed of learning the self-control of brain rhythms, and as was seen in the expert rating of acting performance. This was especially true of the imaginative aspects of acting. Notwithstanding, the experience of flow in performance was superior in the actors trained with neurofeedback than in the untrained controls. Furthermore, enhancement in the subjective sense of flow state correlated comprehensively with ratings in all domains of acting performance by the experts. This was the first systematic examination of the subjective experience of the performer about their state during artistic performance as a result of neurofeedback training.

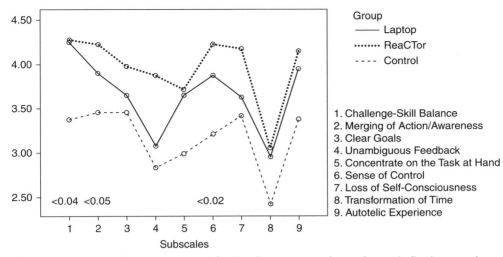

Fig. 21.5 Flow state self-ratings averaged for *Hamlet* excerpts and monologues indicating superior flow with neurofeedback training.

Table 21.2 Correlations between the actors' sense of flow post-training and experts' ratings of acting

Flow scale	Acting rating	*r*	*p*
Sense of control	Being-at-one with performance	0.62	0.03
	Vocal expression	0.52	0.07
	Well-rounded performance	0.53	0.07
	% improvement	0.58	0.05
Loss of self-consciousness	Creativity scales factor	0.69	0.03
	Conviction	0.66	0.04
	Movement fluency/inhabitation	0.64	0.05
	Mean of all acting ratings	0.62	0.06
Merging action & awareness	Being-at-one	0.56	0.06
	Vocal scales % improvement	0.60	0.04
	Vocal expression	0.55	0.06
	Imaginative expression	0.53	0.08
Challenge/skill balance	Being- at-one	0.56	0.06
	Well-rounded	0.52	0.08
	Vocal scales	0.53	0.07
Autotelic experience\enjoyment	Vocal scales	0.57	0.05

21.8 Synthesis: methodology and mechanisms

21.8.1 SMR neurofeedback

Through our studies of novice performance in young adults and children, and our study with actors in which the SMR training context was made relevant to performance, we may have resolved the initial puzzle that SMR training did not benefit music performance in the RCM studies even though the musicians acknowledged subjective benefits, and it improved their attention in laboratory assessments post-training (Egner & Gruzelier, 2001, 2004a), quite aside from its clear and germane cognitive benefits in other avenues of investigation (Vernon et al., 2003; Raymond et al., 2005a; Hanslmayer et al., 2006; Arns et al., 2009; Ros et al., 2009; Keizer et al., 2010a, b). The fact that lower level abilities and not higher level abilities were facilitated by SMR may indicate that its role in inducing a relaxed modulated attentional style has more impact in the novice than in the advanced performer; the latter has already through practice and experience mastered attentional requirements in rehearsed performance.

Notwithstanding, the acting study did demonstrate advantages from SMR training for adult advanced level artistic performance. Here the innovation of giving the neurofeedback training context ecological validity was the likely explanation for the striking relevance to artistic outcome.

This raises the important issue of the transfer of the learned control of brain rhythms to the real world. It does not necessarily mean transfer of the mental state achieved in neurofeedback training to performance; no one would perform incisively in a state of borderline sleep induced by A/T training, for example. Instead, with A/T training, it is proposed that the learning involves associations between the highly connected brain state achieved through hypnagogia with the world of performance (Gruzelier, 2009). Associations may be formed either unconsciously (since all our participants volunteered with the aim of improving their artistry), or through their creative visualisation in hypnogogia.

But in SMR training the transfer of the brain state that is achieved through training is more pertinent, for the outcome was successful in actors when there were direct links between training and outcome contexts, here achieved by the rendering of the theatre auditorium. Furthermore, the outcome was superior with the greater immersion allowed by the 3D CAVE-like environment compared with the 2D rendition. That the SMR training involved control of the acting space—auditorium lighting and intrusive audience noise—was putatively also salient. The success of this study on the outcomes of objective expert ratings and subjective flow state ratings, as well as the high degree of inter-relationship between objective and subjective ratings, is especially worthy of replication and extension to other participant domains. The fact that the impact was on the creativity category of performance ratings, extending to performance overall, is especially relevant to the theme of this book.

It was also the case that in actors all three dynamics of the SMR EEG protocol—the increase in SMR, and the decrease in both theta and high beta—were brought under learned control. Another potentially important issue concerns the relations of the three EEG bands to outcome. The reduction in high-beta activity reduction is of fundamental importance in SMR training. It indexes an activated state associated with over-arousal and anxiety, and indeed a reduction in fast beta band activity in frontal scalp regions was found to be the long-term outcome of A/T training in our original studies with musicians (Egner, Zech, & Gruzelier, 2003).

In our study with children, analysis of the EEG recordings disclosed that reduction in high beta was the main dynamic achieved in SMR training. However, the reduction in eyes-open theta is also important. It has not always been recognized that there are several kinds of theta, and that theta in eyes-closed and eyes-open states are different. The study of experienced meditators mediating to a blissful state exemplifies the positive hedonic tone associated with eyes-closed theta (Aftanas & Golocheikine, 2001). In contrast, eyes-open theta may be associated with negative affect, as disclosed in a recently conducted single-case study of treatment with psychotherapy and SMR and A/T training with a student suffering anhedonia, depression, cognitive confusion and psychological disintegration following long-term drug misuse. Treatment was effective. It is noteworthy that there were significant correlations between practitioner ratings of the mental state across the ten sessions and the eyes-open theta recorded during SMR training. These were in the direction of the *poorer* the mental state, the *higher* the eyes-open theta amplitude. Thus, training down eyes-open theta in SMR and training up eyes-closed theta have some complementary effects.

These findings suggest the way forwards with SMR training includes: 1) to give the training context ecological validity; 2) to harness the control of the brain state to the control of the performance arena—the theatre for performing artists and the schoolroom for school children; 3) to monitor learning curves of the enhancement of SMR amplitude and the reduction in adjacent slow and fast wave activity as an aid to ensuring that all three dynamics are being controlled.

21.8.2 Alpha/theta neurofeedback

Consistency has been the hallmark of the impact of A/T training on the domain of artistry in music and dance performance. In adults this encompassed musicality, stylistic accuracy, interpretative imagination and timing, and in children creative music improvisation including imagination (Egner & Gruzelier 2003; Raymond et al. 2005b; Gruzelier et al., 2011b). Outcome in music and dance also included affective and motivational variables which find expression in performance, as seen in the rating categories of communication and technique. These covered commitment, confidence, emotional expression, and enjoyment, which in turn had an impact on deportment, breathing, diction and stage presence.

The type of creativity traditionally associated with hypnagogia involves making new cognitive associations between items already stored in long-term memory. It has been demonstrated through learning and memory studies in animals that the slower rhythms alpha and theta carry information over long-distance distributed connections (von Stein & Sarntheim, 2000). Novel cognitive associations may require the integration of distributed neural networks and hence the value of hypnagogia in inducing slow wave activity and allowing for the long distance neural connections which underpin the creative associations to be made. Consistent with this, a study of creative thinking has confirmed an increase of anatomically widely distributed coherence of EEG oscillations, especially amongst the low end of the spectrum (Petsche, 1996). In meditation, theta power and low alpha power have been shown to dominate the EEG spectrum along with increased theta coherence between distal electrodes in the topographical EEG (Aftanas & Golocheikine, 2001). 'Accordingly, . . . it is hypothesised that creative cognitive associations arise from integration through the co-activation by slow wave activity of distributed neural networks, for which the relaxed hypnagogic state is especially conducive' (Gruzelier, 2009). This was further exemplified by the results with the test of cognitive creativity with the contemporary dancers following A/T training. Incidentally, while we refer to A/T 'training', this does not imply the need for higher centres to regulate lower centres to achieve the hypnagogic state, say through directed attention. In hypnagogia, as with hypnosis, there is an uncoupling of prefrontal processes, which in hypnosis accompanies the letting-go stage (Gruzelier, 1998, 2006; Egner et al., 2005; Oakley et al., 2007).

The breadth of impact of A/T training on performance comes as no surprise in view of the extensive theta correlates in animal and human studies. These include theta as a carrier of mnemonic processes which have pervasive influences on attention, effort and sensory-motor regulation, and with a role in the mediation of emotion, motivation, effort, and arousal circuits in limbic and cortico-reticular systems. Artistic performance requires integration and expression of past learning and expertise, imbuing this in performance, and communicating this to the audience with artistry. In putting their life experience into their creative performance, performing artists must draw on whole brain connections. Theta therefore is an ideal candidate for this integrating role. It is further proposed that these wide ranging influences of A/T training have a counterpart in theta's widely distributed neural connections, and would be in keeping with theta's role in mediating distributed circuitry in the brain giving rise to neural and psychological integration (Gruzelier, 2009).

21.9 Scientific and pedagogical implications

These validation studies have wide ranging scientific and pedagogical implications.

They have contributed to putting EEG-neurofeedback back on to the map of contemporary cognitive and affective neuroscience. The Society of Applied-Neuroscience (see http://www.applied-neuroscience.org) has been established for basic scientists and practitioners to achieve this aim, and to place neurofeedback within a broader scientific context. University-based research on neurofeedback and the adjunct field brain-computer interface is now widespread throughout Europe, and British universities include Bangor, Canterbury Christ Church, Goldsmiths, Greenwich, Imperial College London, The Open University, and University College London. University-based training and certification training courses are now an imperative, least the premature dismissal of this field that occurred in the 1970s, a classic case of 'throwing the baby out with the bathwater', is revisited due to the field being brought into disrepute through the spawning of practitioners with dubious qualifications.

While this chapter has focused on applications in the performing arts most activity in the field is clinical, and here the most widespread application is ADHD. Sufficient controlled studies have now been conducted in this field to warrant a meta-analysis, which has concluded firm evidence for an impact on inattention and impulsivity in children (Arns et al., 2009). The scale of grant funding has realized multicentre ADHD studies in Germany (Gevensleben et al., 2009). The most long-standing clinical validation concerns epilepsy (review by Sterman, 2000), to include recovery or reduction in anticonvulsant medication in chronic intractable patients (Rockstroh et al., 1993), but neurology has remained indifferent. Many other conditions have been treated beneficially and evidence is accumulating from controlled trials such as insomnia and autism (Cortoos et al., 2009; Mirjam et al., 2009).

Controlled evidence for optimal performance and educational applications is growing rapidly. Among young adults behavioural and electrophysiological evidence, including gamma rhythm feedback, of performance advantages have accrued from controlled studies of attention, memory, learning, sleep, feature binding and intelligence, mental rotation and emotion (Barnea et al., 2005, 2006; Egner & Gruzelier, 2001, 2004a; Hanslmayer et al., 2005; Hoedlmoser et al., 2008; Keizer et al., 2010a,b; Raymond et al., 2005a; Vernon et al., 2003; Zoefel et al., 2011). In educational settings we demonstrated that trainee eye surgeons achieved a more efficient and modulated performance in a simulated cataract operation (Ros et al., 2009). Our study with 11-year-olds (Gruzelier et al., 2011a, in preparation) aside from music performance, benefited sustained attention, and with subjective impressions by the children of carryover to classroom subjects, the school and family life. The academy school now seeks to embed neurofeedback training in the curriculum. The fact that so many of this mixed race and immigrant population were within the ADHD range in their attention itself discloses an important role for neurofeedback in facilitating academic performance. The University of Malta is also planning school studies in the light of these results.

Thus far the studies reported here are the only ones in the performing arts, although a large scale study with opera singers to include functional magnetic resonance imaging (fMRI) is under analysis in Germany (Kleber et al., 2008, 2010). Sporting applications lack controlled evidence, though there are anecdotal reports of successful teams in European football and the winter Olympics having been trained in neurofeedback, and a single case study has been reported (Pop-Jordanova & Demerdzieva, 2010). Neurofeedback capabilities have been demonstrated with fMRI (Rota et al., 2009; Scharnowski et al., 2004; Yoo & Jolesz, 2002; Yoo et al., 2004), while fMRI has been used both to elucidate the basic processes involved in EEG-neurofeedback (Ros et al., 2010) and to monitor training (Levesque et al., 2006).

Altogether, the pedagogical implications of the validation evidence speak for themselves. As evinced by the rapid acknowledgement from commentators (Stewart, 2002; Tilstone, 2003), and rapid access by the scientific readership for our neurofeedback article on microsurgery performance in trainee eye-surgeons (Ros et al., 2009), which received a highly accessed tag after publication and was in the top ten most viewed publications in its journal for a year after publication, while the A/T theoretical article (Gruzelier, 2009) was the most down-loaded article from its journal in 2009. The outcome on music performance was part of a 6-month neurobotics exhibition for the public at the Science Museum, South Kensington, London, 2007–2008. Although there are numerous scientific questions to address, the accumulating evidence base is already strong, and this is manifestly inspiring scientists and policy-makers to take up the challenge.

Acknowledgements

Appreciation is given to all my colleagues in undertaking these multifaceted studies which were extremely challenging to execute, and thanks too to all the participants for their commitment. Essential support was received from the European PRESENCCIA project (IST-027731), NESTA, ARK, the Leverhulme Trust, and Brainhealth London.

References

Aftanas, L.I., & Golocheikine, S.A. (2001). Human anterior and frontal midline theta and lower alpha reflect emotionally positive state and internalized attention: High-resolution EEG investigation of meditation. *Neuroscience Letters*, **310**, 57–60.

Arns, M., de Ridder, Strehl, U., Breteler, M., & Coenen, A. (2009). Effects of neurofeedback treatment on ADHD: the effect on inattention, impulsivity and hyperactivity: a meta-analysis. *Clinical EEG Neuroscience*, **40**, 180–9.

Barnea, A., Rassis, A., & Zaidel, E. (2005). Effect of neurofeedback on hemispheric word recognition. *Brain & Cognition*, **59**, 314–21.

Berberian, C. (1966). *Stripsody*. New York: C.F. Peters Corporation.

Berger, B. C. & Gevirtz, R. (2001). The treatment of panic disorder. A comparison between breathing retraining and cognitive behaviour therapy. *Applied Psychophysiology and Biofeedback*, **26**(3), 227–8.

Brown, T.A., Chorpita, B.F., Korotitsch, W., & Barlow, D,H. (1997). Psychometric properties of the Depression Anxiety Stress Scales (DASS) in clinical samples. *Behaviour Research &. Therapy*, **35**(1), 79–89.

Cortoos, A., De Valck, E., Arns, M., Breteler, M.H., & Cluydts, R. (2009). An exploratory study on the effects of tele-neurofeedback and tele-biofeedback on objective and subjective sleep in patients with primary insomnia. *Journal of Applied Psychophysiology & Biofeedback*, **30**(1), 1–10.

Cruz-Neira, C., Sandin, D.J., & DeFanti, T.A. (1993). Surround-screen projection-based virtual reality: the design and implementation of the CAVE. In *Proceedings of the 20th annual conference on computer graphics and interactive techniques*. ACM Press, pp. 135–42.

Csikszentmihalyi, M. (1996). *Creativity: Flow and the psychology of discovery and invention*. New York: HarperCollins.

Donchin, E., & Coles, M.G.H. (1988). Is the P300 component a manifestation of context updating? *Behavioral and Brain Sciences*, **11**, 357–74.

Edge, J. and Lancaster, L. (2004). Phenomenological analysis of superior musical performance facilitated by neurofeedback: Enhancing musical performance through neurofeedback: playing the tune of life. *Transpersonal Psychology Review*, **8**, 23–35.

Egner, T. & Gruzelier, J. H. (2001). Learned self-regulation of EEG frequency components affects attention and event-related brain potentials in humans. *NeuroReport*, **12**, 411–15.

Egner, T. & Gruzelier J.H. (2003). Ecological validity of neurofeedback: Modulation of slow wave EEG enhances musical performance. *NeuroReport*, **14**, 1225–8.

Egner, T. & Gruzelier, J.H. (2004a). EEG biofeedback of low beta band components: Frequency-specific effects on variables of attention and event-related brain potentials. *Clinical Neurophysiology*, **115**, 131–9.

Egner, T. & Gruzelier, J.H. (2004b). The temporal dynamics of electroencephalographic responses to alpha/theta neurofeedback training in healthy subjects. *Journal of Neurotherapy*, **8**, 43–57.

Egner, T., Strawson, E. & Gruzelier, J.H. (2002). EEG signature and phenomenology of alpha/theta neurofeedback training versus mock feedback. *Applied Psychophysiology and Biofeedback*, **27**, 261–70.

Egner, T., Zech, T.F., & Gruzelier, J.H. (2004). The effects of neurofeedback training on the spectral topography of the healthy electroencephalogram. *Clinical Neurophysiology*, **115**, 2452–60.

Egner, T., Jamieson, G., & Gruzelier, J.H. (2005). Hypnosis decouples cognitive control from conflict monitoring processes of the frontal lobe. *NeuroImage*, **27**, 969–78.

Green, D.M., & Swets, J.A. (1966). *Signal detection theory and psychophysics*. New York: Wiley.

Green E. & Green, A. (1977). *Beyond biofeedback*. New York: Delta.

Greenberg, L.M. & Kindschi, C.L. (1999). *Test of variables of attention: Clinical guide*. St Paul, MN: Universal Attention Disorders, Inc.

Gruzelier, J. (1998). A working model of the neurophysiology of hypnosis: A review of evidence. *Contemporary Hypnosis*, **15**, 5–23.

Gruzelier, J.H. (2006). Frontal functions, connectivity and neural efficiency underpinning hypnosis and hypnotic susceptibility. *Contemporary Hypnosis*, **23**, 15–32.

Gruzelier, J.H. (2009). A theory of alpha/theta neurofeedback, creative performance enhancement, long distance functional connectivity and psychological integration. *Cognitive Processing*, **10**, 101–10.

Gruzelier, J.H. & Egner, T. (2004) Physiological self-regulation: Biofeedback and neurofeedback. In A. Williamon (Ed.) *Musical Excellence*. Chichester: Wiley, pp. 197–219.

Gruzelier, J.H., Egner, T., Valentine, E., & Williamon, A. (2002). Comparing learned EEG self-regulation and the Alexander Technique as a means of enhancing musical performance. In C. Stevens, D. Burnham, G. McPherson, E. Schubert, & J. Renwick (Eds.) *Proceedings of the Seventh International Conference on Music Perception and Cognition*. Adelaide: Causal Productions, pp. 89–92.

Gruzelier, J.H, Inoue, A., Steed, A., Smart, R., & Steffert, T. (2010) Acting performance and flow state enhanced with sensory-motor rhythm neurofeedback comparing ecologically valid immersive VR and training screen scenarios. *Neuroscience Letters*, **480**(2), 112–16.

Gruzelier, J.H., Thompson, T., Redding, E., Brandt, R., & Steffert, T. (2011a). *Psychological predictors of dance performance in conservatoire freshers undergoing neurofeedback training: Presence-flow, personality and mood*. In preparation.

Gruzelier, J.H., Foks, M., Steffert, T., & Ros, T. (2011b) *Beneficial outcome from EEG-neurofeedback on music performance, attention and well-being in school children*. In preparation.

Guilford, J.P. (1967). *The nature of human intelligence*. New York: McGraw-Hill.

Hanslmayer, S., Sauseng, P. Doppelmayr, M., Schabus, M., Klimesch, W. (2006) Increasing individual upper alpha by neurofeedback improves cognitive performance in human subjects. *Journal of Applied Psychophysiology Biofeedback*, **30**, 1–10.

Harvey, J. (1994). *These music exams*. London: Associated Board of the Royal Schools of Music.

Hoedlmoser, K., Pecherstorfer, T., Gruber, G., Anderer, P., Doppelmayr, M., Klimesch, W., *et al.* (2008). Instrumental conditioning of human sensorimotor rhythm (12-15Hz) and its impact on sleep as well as declarative learning. *Sleep*, **31**, 1401–8.

Jackson, S.A, Eklund, R.C, (2004). *The flow scales manual*. Morgantown, WV: Fitness Information Technology.

Keizer, A.W., Verschoor, M., Verment, R.S., & Hommel, B. (2010a) The effect of gamma enhancing neurofeedback on the control of feature bindings and intelligence measures. *International Journal of Psychophysiology*, **75**, 25–32.

Keizer, A.W., Verment, R.S., & Hommel, B. (2010b). Enhancing cognitive control through neurofeeback: A role of gamma-band activity in managing episodic retrieval. *NeuroImage*, **49**, 3404–13.

Kleber, B., Gruzelier, J., Bensch, M., & Birbaumer, N. (2008). Effects of EEG-Biofeedback on professional singing performances. Society of Applied Neuroscience, second biennial meeting, Seville. *Revista Espanola de Neuropsicologia*, **10**, 77. 61.

Kleber, B., Veit, R., Birbaumer, N., Gruzelier, J., & Lotze, M. (2010). The brain of opera singers: experience-dependent changes in functional activation. *Cerebral Cortex*, **20**, 1144–52.

Koestler, A. (1964). *The act of creation*. London: Arkana.

Levesque, J., Beauregard, M., & Mensour, B. (2006). Effect of neurofeedback training on the neural substrates of selective attention in children with attention-deficit/hyperactivity disorder: A functional magnetic resonance imaging study. *Neuroscience Letters*, **394**, 216–21.

Lovibond, S.H., & Lovibond, P.F. (1995). *Manual for the depression anxiety stress scales*. Sydney: Psychology Foundation.

McNair, D.M., Lorr, D., & Droppleman, M.F. (1992). *Profile of mood states manual*. San Diego, CA: Educational and Industrial Testing Service.

Mirjam, E.J., Kouijzer, E.J., de Moor, J.M.H., Gerrits, B.J.L., Buitelaar, J.K., Hein, T., et al. (2009). Long-term effects of neurofeedback treatment in autism. *Research Autism Spectrum Disorders*, **3**, 496–501.

Monastra, V.J., Lynn, S., Linden, M., Lubar, J.F., Gruzelier, J., & LaVaque, T.J. (2005). Electroencephalograpic biofeedback in the treatment of attention-deficit/hyperactivity disorder. *Applied Psychophysiology & Biofeedback*, **30**(2), 95–114.

Oakley, D., Deeley, Q., & Halligan, P.W. (2007). Hypnotic depth and response to suggestion under standardised conditions and during fMRL scanning. *Journal of Clinical and Experimental Hypnosis*, **55**, 32–58.

Petsche, H. (1996). Approaches to verbal, visual and musical creativity by EEG coherence analysis. *International Journal of Psychophysiology*, **24**, 145–60.

Pop-Jordanova, N. & Demerdzieva, A. (2010). Biofeedback training for peak performance in sport-case study. *Macedonian Journal of Medical Science*, **3**, 113–18.

Raymond, J., Varney, C. & Gruzelier, J.H. (2005a). The effects of alpha/theta neurofeedback on personality and mood. *Cognitive Brain Research*, **23**, 287–92.

Raymond, J., Sajid, I., Parkinson, L.A. & Gruzelier, J.H. (2005b). Biofeedback and dance performance: A preliminary investigation. *Applied Psychophysiology and Biofeedback*, **30**, 65–73.

Rockstroh, B., Elbert, T., Birbaumer, N., Wolf, P., Duchting-Roth, A., Reker, M., *et al.* (1993). Cortical self-regulation in patients with epilepsies. *Epilepsy Research*, **14**, 63–72.

Ros, T., Moseley, M.J., Bloom, P.A., Benjamin, L. Parkinson, L.A., & Gruzelier, J.H. (2009). Optimizing microsurgical skills with EEG neurofeedback. *BMC Neuroscience*, **10**, 87.

Ros, T., Munneke, M.A.M., Ruge, D., Gruzelier, J.H., & Rothwell, J.C. (2010). Endogenous control of waking alpha rhythms induces neuroplasticity. *European Journal of Neuroscience*, **31**, 770–8.

Rota, G., Sitaram, R., Veit R., Erb, M., Weiskopf, N., Dogil, D., & Birbaumer, N. (2009). Self-regulation of regional cortical activity using real-time fMRI: The right inferior frontal gyrus and linguistic processing. *Human Brain Mapping*, **30**, 1605–14.

Sanchez-Vives, M.V. & Slater, M. (2005) From presence to consciousness through virtual reality. *Nature Reviews Neuroscience*, **6**, 332–9.

Schachter, D.L. (1976). The hypnagogic state: a critical review of the literature. *Psychological Bulletin*, **83**, 452–81.

Scharnowski, F., Veit, R., Goebel, R., Birbaumer, N., & Mathiak, K. (2004). Self-regulation of local brain activity using real-time functional magnetic resonance imaging (fMRI). *Journal of Physiology-Paris*, **98**, 357–73.

Spielberger, C.D., Gorsuch, R.L., Lushene, R., Vagg, P.R., & Jacobs, G.A. (1983). *Manual for the State-Trait Anxiety Inventory (Form Y1)*. Palo Alto, CA: Consulting Psychologists Press.

Sterman, M.B. (2000). Basic concepts and clinical findings in the treatment of seizure disorders with EEG operant conditioning. *Clinical Electroencephalography*, **31**, 35–45.

Stewart, L. (2002). Zoning in on music and the brain. *Trends in Cognitive Sciences*, **6**, 451.

Thayer, R.E. (1967). Measurement of activation through self-report. *Psychological Reports,* **20**, 663–78.

Tenebaum, G., Fogarty, G.J., & Jackson, S.A. (1999). The flow experience: A Rausch analysis of Jackson's Flow State Scale. *Journal of Outcome Measurement*, **13**, 278–94.

Thompson, S., & Williamon, A. (2003). Evaluating evaluation: Musical performance assessment as a research tool. *Music Perception*, **21**, 21–41.

Tilstone, C. (2003). Neurofeedback provides a better theta-rical performance. *The Lancet Neurology*, **2**, 655.

Vaitl, D., Birbaumer, N., Gruzelier, J., Jamieson, G., Kotchoubey, B., Kubler, A., *et al.* (2005). Psychobiology of altered states of consciousness. *Psychological Bulletin*, **131**, 98–127.

Vernon, D., Egner, T., Cooper, N., Compton, T., Neilands, C., Sheri, A., *et al.* (2003). The effect of training distinct neurofeedback protocols on aspects of cognitive performance. *International Journal of Psychophysiology*, **47**, 75–86.

Von Stein, A. & Sarntheim, J. (2000). Different frequencies for different scales of cortical integration: from local gamma to long range alpha/theta synchronisation. *International Journal of Psychophysiology*, **38**, 1–313.

Yoo, S-S. & Jolesz, F.A. (2002) Functional MRI for neurofeedback: Feasibility study on a hand motor task. *Neuro Report*, **13**, 1377–81.

Yoo, S-S., Fairneny, T., Chen, N-K., Choo, S-E., Panych, L.P., Park, H-W., *et al.* (2004) Brain-computer interface using fMRI: Spatial navigation by thoughts. *Neuro Report*, **15**, 1591–5.

Zoefel, B., Huster, R.J., & Hermann, C.S. (2011). Neurofeedback training of the upper alpha frequency band EEG improves cognitive performance. *Neuroimage*, **54**(2), 1427–31.

Chapter 22

Musical imagery and imagination: The function, measurement, and application of imagery skills for performance

Terry Clark, Aaron Williamon, and Aleksandar Aksentijevic

22.1 Introduction

Standing backstage, the familiar waves of nervous excitement race through the pianist's body. She takes a few deep breaths, shakes out her hands and arms, and readies herself. The hall lights are dimmed, a hush spreads through the audience and the stage manager tells her it is time to go on. She steps onto stage, taking in the sights and sounds of her surroundings. It is a packed house, yet she is feeling confident and in control. She bows, acknowledging the audience, and takes her seat at the piano, pausing for a moment to settle and feel comfortable, breathing deeply one more time. Gently, she raises her arms and plays. The sound of the first notes rings through the hall, she is pleased with this sound. As she progresses through the piece, she takes note of the physical sensations of performing. She comes to the last section—a demanding passage requiring both agility and precision. She feels her fingers dancing across the keyboard to the finish. As the sound fades away into the hall, she notices her heart rate and breathing, elevated through the physicality and excitement of what she has just done. The audience erupts into rapturous applause. The pianist stands, bows, and exits the stage, pleased with her performance. There is a knock on her dressing room door, it is time to go. The pianist opens her eyes having finished imagining her ideal performance, and heads toward the stage.

Musical imagery, or the deliberate use of imagination by musicians, has traditionally been viewed and considered as the ability to imagine sounds even when no audible sounds are present. However, imagery as used by musicians involves not only sounds but also the physical movements required to create sounds, a 'view' of the score or an instrument, and the emotions a musician wishes to express in performance. Early investigations into musical imagery explored the use of imagery to enhance musicians' physical practice. Current research is considering imagery use for functions including developing and enhancing expressivity during practice and performance, assisting with learning and memorizing music, pre-experiencing performance situations, and assisting in the prevention and treatment of playing-related injuries. A growing body of research employing functional magnetic resonance imaging (fMRI) suggests that functional equivalence exists between live and imagined performances within the auditory and motor systems involved in musical performance. This chapter explores the theories and findings this research has produced, together with the implications such findings have for performing musicians. Beyond understanding imagery at a functional level, the ways in which musicians engage with imagery are also of particular interest. While self-report measures addressing imagery vividness have seen widespread use, new methods involving naturalistic performance-based tasks, fMRI, and physiological responses are increasingly being employed to further our understanding of musical imagery. Finally, this chapter concludes with a summary of the current state of imagery research and the questions it poses.

22.2 Definitions of imagery

While often referred to as mental rehearsal by musicians, imagery is defined as:

> . . . an experience that mimics real experience. We can be aware of 'seeing' an image, feeling movements as an image, or experiencing an image of smells, tastes or sounds without actually experiencing the real thing. . . . It differs from dreams in that we are awake and conscious when we form an image.
>
> (White & Hardy 1998: p. 389.)

More in line with music performance, imagery can also be thought of as the:

> . . . cognitive or imaginary rehearsal of a physical skill without overt muscular movement. The basic idea is that the senses—predominantly aural, visual, and kinesthetic for the musician—should be used to create or recreate an experience that is similar to a given physical event.
>
> (Connolly & Williamon 2004: p. 224.)

Musical imagery has often been viewed and considered as the ability to hear or recreate sounds in the mind even when no audible sounds are present (Godøy & Jørgensen, 2001). However, imagery as used by musicians involves not only the melodic and temporal contours of music but also a sense of the physical movements required to perform the music, a 'view' of the score, instrument, or the space in which they are performing, and a 'feel' of the emotions and sensations a musician wishes to express in performance as well as those experienced during an actual performance.

Given these widespread functions, a number of terms have emerged to describe the imagery process as employed by musicians. Commonly used terms include mental rehearsal, mental practice, aural or internal representations, inner hearing, visualization, and finger practice (for further discussion, see Driskel et al., 1994). This broad variety of terms has no doubt contributed to some confusion in discussions of musicians' imagery use. Similar confusion has occurred within other domains, such as sport psychology. Morris, Spittle, and Watt (2005: p. 14) noted that there is a lack of consistency in the features that constitute the imagery process and that 'the focus of each definition seems to vary depending on the purpose for which the imagery description is used'.

22.3 How imagery works

A considerable body of research has found that use of imagery can enhance musical performance. But how does this happen? At the neurological level, musical performance and imagery function in a similar manner. Because of this, many of the benefits derived from physical practice can also be gained through imagery. Research employing fMRI and magnetoencephalography (MEG) has demonstrated the functional equivalence between live and imagined performances within the auditory and motor systems involved in musical performance (e.g. Mellet et al., 1998; Kosslyn et al., 2001). For instance, Halpern and Zatorre (1999; Zatorre, 1999) have explored the equivalence between a variety of perceived and imagined musical sounds and sound qualities. To do so, their participants completed tasks such as making similarity judgements about the timbre of heard or imagined instruments, listening to or imagining pitch intervals, and creating an image of raising a tone or chord stepwise. They found that musical perception and imagery do indeed engage similar regions within the auditory cortex.

Employing MEG, Herholz and colleagues (2008) investigated the ability of musicians and non-musicians to detect incorrect tones presented following imagery of a well-known piece of music.

The musicians elicited a right-lateralized early pre-attentive brain response in the secondary auditory cortex areas to unexpected incorrect notes placed alongside the imagined melodies, whereas the non-musicians did not. Zatorre, Evans, and Meyer (1994) also found that pitch processing during music perception and imagery is lateralized in the right hemisphere. These findings lend further support to the proposal that musical imagery and perception activate similar regions of the auditory cortex and that intensive musical training can strengthen these links.

When musicians imagine performing, activity has also been found in regions of the premotor and supplementary motor areas as well as the auditory cortices (Zatorre, 1999; Lotze et al., 2003; Zatorre & Halpern, 2005). Comparing physical and mental musical performances in pianists, Meister et al. (2004) found bilateral activation in the premotor areas, the precuneus, and the medial part of Brodmann Area 40 (Heschl's gyrus) during both forms of performance. Meanwhile, the contralateral primary motor cortex and posterior parietal cortex bilaterally were active during physical performance but not during the imagery condition. Meister et al. (2004) attributed these differences to the differing demands of the real and imagined performance and to the greater visuomotor integration required by the former.

When listening to musical rhythms, Chen, Penhune, and Zatorre (2008) found that activation occurred in the supplementary motor area, mid-premotor cortex, and the cerebellum. Lotze et al. (2003) found the premotor area to be active when hearing or singing a melody in one's head, which would closely resemble one of the main functions for which musicians employ imagery. It is possible that this is a general phenomenon related to 'silent' speech in which the motor activation could be associated with the preparatory motor activation aimed at the vocal apparatus. Inversely, Lotze et al. (2003) also observed that, when pianists rehearsed hand movements away from a piano, activity occurred in the right primary auditory cortex and the left auditory association cortex. To explain such phenomena, Bangert and Altenmüller (2003) have proposed a link between the auditory cortex and the primary motor cortex. Exploring the cortical activation patterns (DC-EEG potentials) induced by piano learning, they found that an audio-motor interface for the generation of a mental representation of the keyboard was located within the anterior regions of the right hemisphere. In addition to plastic changes in the music-related areas caused by many years of practice, Zatorre, Chen, and Penhune (2007) suggested that such interfaces may be a consequence of tight coupling between auditory cortex and portions of the supplementary motor area and premotor areas.

Beyond understanding imagery at a functional level, the ways in which musicians engage with imagery have also been of particular interest.

22.4 Research into imagery use

22.4.1 Imagery as practice: theory and use

The benefits of imagery for musicians' practice activities has been advocated for many years. In 1921, Jaques-Dalcroze wrote: 'Musical training should develop inner hearing—that is, the capacity for hearing music as distinctly mentally as physically. Every method of teaching should aim, before anything else, at awakening this capacity' (p. 98). Additionally, many famous musicians have stressed the importance of imagery, including Karl Leimer, Walter Gieseking, Pablo Casals, and Glenn Gould. Anton Rubinstein was known to practise on a paper keyboard in order to further develop his auditory representation of his music. Imagery and the formation of mental representations is no doubt of central importance to the creative process for composers and conductors as well.

Lehmann (1997: p. 143) made clear the importance of imagery to musical practice and performance by stating that 'the most important goal of performance is to match a highly vivid representation of the desired performance with the current execution'. In support of this statement,

Holmes (2003) found that, when practising, elite musicians form vivid representations of their music in their minds and then search for ways of translating those schemas/representations into reality. Expanding upon his claim, Lehmann (1997: p. 141) suggested that music performance requires three distinct types of mental representation:

1) A representation of the desired performance goal;

2) A representation that reflects the current performance; and

3) A representation of the music in terms of its production aspects.

The goal of practice and preparation is to strengthen these three types of representation as much as possible, ultimately striving to bring (1) and (2) in line with each other, using (3) as the means of doing so. In reviewing the literature, Lehmann (1997: p. 146) identified three different forms of mental representations a musician may employ, either in isolation or in combination, to create a more complete understanding of the music. The first is visualization, whereby the piece is memorized in terms of its compositional structure prior to practice. A visual representation of the music may also include an image of the actual, physical score in the mind's eye, which would allow the performer to 'read' the notes. The second type is audiation, or the ability to internally hear and comprehend music which is not physically present. Given the importance of strong aural abilities for the important aspects of musicianship such as intonation, timing, and communication, this may very well be the most crucial aspect. Indeed, many music teachers would insist that if a student cannot hear their music, they certainly will not be able to play it. The final type of representation that Lehmann identified is what he terms the photographic ear, whereby musicians claim to have voluntary access to individual notes within a memorized, or just heard, piece of music.

Interested in the occurrence and content of imagined music throughout a music student's typical week, Bailes (2006) asked music students to complete a questionnaire six times per day for 7 consecutive days. Her results indicated that during 44% of the episodes (those times when the participants were signalled by the researcher to complete the questionnaire), the participants were listening to music, during 32% they were imagining music, during 21% they were neither listening to nor imagining music, and during the remaining 3% of the episodes they were both listening to and imagining music simultaneously. Clearly, imagery seems to forms a significant part of musicians' daily activities.

Building upon her previous work (Holmes 2003) and investigating the links between imagery and memorization processes, Holmes (2005) employed semi-structured interviews with two elite solo musicians to explore how interpretation and different imagery processes influence learning and memorization. The interview questions addressed topics such as the cognitive processes and physical means involved in the transfer of an interpretative concept of the music into sound, imagery and its possible function within the memorization process, and further uses of mental rehearsal. From the interviews, three categories of imagery emerged. The first, as discussed previously, was mental rehearsal. Statements from the participants revealed that mental rehearsal could serve a number of functions: as a feedback channel, allowing them to think back through their performance without the need to attend to their playing, for reflective study of their current interpretation, to aid memory and reinforce a sense of security. Finally, mental rehearsal enabled deep concentration on the music without being physically tiring (Holmes, 2005: p. 226). This last point has interesting implications, as it suggests that mental rehearsal can serve as an effective alternative to physical practice when such practice may be prohibited due to various situational or health reasons.

The second category of imagery that emerged was auditory imagery, which pertains to the internal auditory impression of the music. Interestingly, the participants indicated a strong connection between auditory imagery and the third category, namely, motor imagery. A statement from one participant suggested that an auditory representation of the music could also translate into a physical or motor representation (Holmes, 2005: p. 225). In other words, a mental impression of what the music will sound like has the ability to generate a sensation of what it would feel like to play the music. This fascinating connection was well exemplified by the quote of one participant who stated (p. 227):

> . . . the other week when I was about to do that concerto, I listened to it on a recording the night before and I could imagine every single movement in my hands as I listened.

This also has great relevance to singers as their means of sound production is completely internalized. For a singer, each note, and indeed each way of delivering that note, will relate directly to the manner by which it is physically produced. Kalakoski (2001: p. 54) noted that 'mental imagery not only stands at the intersection of memory and perception, but also at the intersection of several sense modalities', which would seem apparent in the above quote. In summary, Holmes pointed out that while the use of imagery by musicians is not a new concept, the use of motor imagery, or imagining what a piece of music may physically feel like, is something that is not very well understood and, hence, is an area requiring further investigation.

22.4.2 Imagery as practice: empirical investigations into imagery's efficacy

Rubin-Rabson (1937) noted that imagery aided memorization by compelling the musician to focus on analysis when learning a piece of music. Comparing the effects of mental and physical practice on musicians' ability to memorize, Rubin-Rabson (1941) concluded that combining periods of mental rehearsal with physical practice was more effective than physical practice alone.

Ross (1985) compared the efficacy of five different methods of physical and mental practice with college trombone students. The practice methods included: 1) all physical practice; 2) all mental practice; 3) mental practice with simulated slide movement; 4) combined physical and mental practice; and 5) no practice. With the exception of the no-practice group, the participants were given three practice trials using their assigned method. Results indicated that the combined physical and mental practice group achieved the greatest amount of improvement, followed by the physical practice group, the mental practice with simulated slide movement group, the mental practice group, and lastly the no-practice group which achieved the least amount of improvement.

Coffman (1990) explored the effect of imagery on the ability of musicians whose principal instrument was not piano to learn a two-hand piano piece. The participants were divided into groups including physical practice, mental practice, alternating physical and mental practice, and a no-practice control group. Compared with the no-practice group, all three methods yielded significantly shorter performance times on the post-test trials, with physical practice and combined practice achieving better results than the mental practice alone method. However, no significant differences were demonstrated in regards to rhythm and pitch errors. Concluding, Coffman noted that, among other potentially confounding variables, a lack of familiarity with mental practice was identified by some of the participants, which could have rendered its use less effective.

Highben and Palmer (2004) investigated the effects of different forms of practice on pianists' ability to learn and memorize a novel piece of music. Four forms of practice were employed: normal practice, practice with no auditory feedback (sound turned off but still pressing the keys), practice with no motor feedback (not pressing the keys but hearing a recording of the piece), and mental practice with no auditory or motor feedback. The removal of auditory and motor feedback, independently and together, was found to be detrimental to learning and memory retention, with the normal practice method proving most effective. In addition, an assessment of the participants' aural skills indicated that those with strong aural skills were affected the least by the removal of auditory feedback during practice.

As demonstrated by these studies, investigations of this type have produced mixed results. In their meta-analysis of the mental practice literature, Driskell et al. (1994) concluded mental practice to be an effective means for enhancing performance but that mental practice alone was less effective than physical practice. In addition, while mental practice was found to be effective for both cognitive and physical tasks, it had stronger effects for more cognitive-based tasks. Further to this, their review also suggested that while experienced musicians benefited from mental practice regardless of whether the task was more cognitively or physically focused, less experienced musicians benefited more from mental practice on cognitive relative to physical tasks. Discussing the variety of results found in previous investigations, Gabrielsson (1999) highlighted the variability of the musical tasks used, participants' musical backgrounds, definitions of mental practice upon which the practice methods were developed, and the measures employed. Similar to conclusions by Driskell et al. (1994), Gabrielsson suggested that the less advanced the musician is on their instrument and the more difficult the music, the more important physical practice would be. Let us speculate on why this could be the case. A novice needs intensive motor practice in order to strengthen the cognitive schemas. This process occurs through the joint monitoring of movement and auditory and visual feedback. Once the mental schemas are strong enough, they will contain the combined (cross-modal) information. As such, they can then guide different sensory and motor functions. Physical practice becomes less important because the cognitive motor schemas are there already. All that is needed now is execution—the most important information has been internalized.

With a few exceptions (e.g. Pascual-Leone, 2001), one limitation with many of these studies is that imagery training or time to practise and become proficient with imagery was rarely provided. Rogers, Hall, and Buckolz (1991) noted that imagery ability, and subsequently imagery's effectiveness, can be increased through practising. Further to this, the potential role of imagery vividness, or clarity, as a moderator of imagery's usefulness, as found by Highben and Palmer (2004), has received strong support in the fields of applied psychology (e.g. Richardson, 1994), sports science (e.g. Gregg & Hall, 2006; Gregg et al., 2005) and recently in music (Gregg & Clark, 2007). A possible direction for future research into the role of imagery in musical practice could consist in providing participants with sufficient time to incorporate imagery into their training regimens. This would have a twofold effect of increasing the effectiveness of imagery-based rehearsal strategies as well as improving our understanding of the uses and efficacy of imagery in musical practice.

22.4.3 Broader functions

Beyond its efficacy as a practice method, a range of other functions for imagery have been identified. Based on their work with classical musicians, Connolly and Williamon (2004: p. 225) provided a list of functions for which imagery was deemed most beneficial. These included:

- Improving learning and memory.
- Making practice more efficient.
- Overcoming technical difficulties and developing skills.
- Heightening sensory awareness.
- Gaining more interest in the music itself.
- Refocusing attention during performance.
- Enhancing general confidence and resilience on stage.
- Achieving greater control over negative emotions.

◆ Achieving a greater connection and presence with the audience.

◆ Achieving peak experience.

So not only is imagery beneficial for learning and memorizing music, it is also of particular use for the development and communication of expressivity, for refining performance skills, and aiding in the successful delivery of those skills during performance. Further, it has been suggested that metaphorical imagery is particularly effective for helping develop appropriate emotion and rhythm in musical performance (e.g. Woody, 2002).

Extending work with athletes (Hall et al., 1998) and in order better to understand musicians' imagery use, Gregg, Clark, and Hall (2008) developed the Functions of Imagery in Music Questionnaire (FIMQ), which they administered to 159 university-level music students. Paivio (1985) theorized that imagery can subserve cognitive (i.e. learning and rehearsing particular skills, mentally rehearsing music, and developing and implementing various practice strategies) and motivational functions (i.e. goal setting, regulating arousal, and developing focus and concentration skills and confidence levels). In addition to these functions, results from this study indicated that musicians engage in imagery to assist with maintaining focus and recover from errors, to enhance mental toughness, display confidence, and manage mental and physical fatigue. Performance majors were found to engage in significantly more imagery relative to non-performance majors in order to enhance confidence, focus, and concentration. In addition, vocal majors reported employing imagery to enhance motivation more often than instrumental majors.

Investigating imagery use by dancers, Nordin and Cumming (2005) discovered a number of functions for imagery that are potentially relevant for musicians. The participants (14 professional dancers) described using imagery for healing and developing their artistry. Additionally, several participants reported using images that were metaphorical in nature and more indirect than those typically employed by athletes. An example provided involved imagining being a swan when dancing *Swan Lake*. One could see how such metaphorical images could be of use to musicians as well, for purposes such as achieving appropriate phrasing, the right kind of breath or note attack. Such imagery could be of great benefit for singers, who also have to attend to particular movements or represent a character when performing in an opera.

Interviewing 29 musicians, Clark, Lisboa, and Williamon (submitted) identified a number of imagery functions within performance preparation. Musicians spoke of imagining themselves on stage giving their performance, hearing how they would ideally like their performance to go, imagining the sound and physicality of performing their specific music, as well as performing their entire program in real time. Asked why they engaged in these activities, the musicians reported that they employed imagery to explore and enhance their expressivity during practice and performance and that imagery helped them to memorize, and strengthen their memory of, their music. The musicians also reported that employing imagery gave them a taste of what the performance would feel like. In a sense they were able to pre-experience the situation, together with all of its emotions and sensations. Employing imagery prior to a performance was also reported to enhance confidence and help control anxiety. Lastly, they also noted that imagery of ideal performances, much like the example at the beginning of the chapter, provided them with a concrete goal to aim for while on stage.

22.5 Assessing musicians' imagery abilities

Having the capacity to assess imagery abilities accurately is of particular benefit for researchers, musicians, and those involved in musicians' training. Given that music is a domain largely oriented towards sound, one would expect the ability to hear and recreate accurately a particular piece of music in the mind to be a central feature of musicians' ability to engage in imagery. This auditory imagery ability should include the ability to reproduce internally the melodic and temporal structure of the music, its expressive qualities, as well as to distinguish mentally the sound (timbre) of individual instruments and parts. However, musicians not only need to 'hear' or recreate each of these elements particular to the music they play but also need to 'see' the space in which they are performing and 'feel' the emotions and sensations experienced during an actual performance, as well as the physical movements required to sing or play their instrument. Additionally, rather than considering, and assessing, imagery as a single construct, it has been proposed that imagery has three distinct features that can be observed and measured (Denis, 1991; Moran, 1993). These include: 1) vividness, which refers to the clarity of an image; 2) controllability, which relates to the ease and accuracy with which a person can manipulate an image; and 3) accuracy of reference, or the extent to which the image accurately reflects the object it represents. While self-report measures addressing imagery vividness have seen widespread use, new methods involving naturalistic performance-based tasks and the measurement of physiological responses are increasingly being employed to further our understanding of musical imagery.

22.5.1 Questionnaires

One of the most common approaches to assessing imagery vividness has been the use of self-report questionnaires such as the shortened form of the *Betts' Questionnaire upon Mental Imagery* (Sheehan, 1967) and the *Vividness of Visual Imagery Questionnaire* (Marks, 1973). These questionnaires provide participants with a written stimulus or sensory experience, ask them to imagine or recreate that experience, and rate its vividness. However, questionnaires of this sort are currently rarely used with musicians as there are presently none that employ sensory experiences which bear much resemblance to the types of imagery in which musicians typically engage. In addition, the use of self-reported ratings can be problematic when aiming to compare scores between participants (Guillot & Collet, 2005). In response to this challenge, Guillot and Collet (2005) recommended incorporating a post-imagery manipulation check. This involves debriefing or interviewing the participant following their use of imagery to gain further insight into their particular experience with imagery.

22.5.2 Behavioural tasks

Beyond the use of questionnaires, a variety of music-specific tasks have been developed in order to provide a more contextual assessment of musicians' imagery abilities. Aleman et al. (2000) asked their participants to identify which of two preselected notes within a familiar song had a higher pitch, first by listening to the song and then by imagining the song. This permitted Aleman et al. to compare musicians' ability to discern pitch discrepancies both in the presence and absence of heard sounds. Doing so in the absence of heard sounds required the participants to form auditory representations of the songs accurate in terms of pitch. Fine and colleagues (Fine, 2002; Fine & Younger, 2004) explored singers' ability to sight-sing intervals or unfamiliar songs, investigating the influence that factors such as the presence of other singers or accompaniment and auditory representations have on this ability. Employing such a method provided an opportunity for Fine and colleagues to examine the extent to which singers' ability to sight-sing was dependent on external sources of auditory information (i.e. other singers or accompaniment) or whether the singers were capable of forming vivid enough auditory representations in the absence of these other sources of information to sight-sing accurately. Similar to this, Brodsky et al. (2003) employed a so-called 'notational imagery' technique. This approach required participants to identify a familiar melody embedded within a score of specially-composed music via silent sight reading. If the participants were not able to form and 'hear' accurate auditory representations of the specially-composed music, they would not have been able to elucidate the familiar melodies hidden within them. In general, these types of studies have led researchers to suggest that musicians are capable of producing musical images that contain precise information about pitch and tempo, as well as information concerning melodic and harmonic relationships.

22.5.3 Mental chronometry

The temporal aspects of musical imagery have also been investigated using a process referred to as mental chronometry, that is, comparisons of timing profiles from live and mental (or imagined) performances. These investigations have been concerned with whether or not beat-to-beat temporal fluctuations present in live performances are also present in mental performances. In two studies, Repp (1999a, b) investigated the effects of eliminating auditory and kinaesthetic feedback on expressive performance parameters by looking at the timing profiles of performances under different conditions. Repp posited that performances with no auditory or kinaesthetic feedback would allow insight into pianists' 'internal representations or mental images of the musical sound structure' (1999a: p. 412). To explore this, Repp (1999a, b) asked six pianists to perform the opening of a Chopin etude under three conditions: 1) normally; 2) with no sound (no auditory feedback); and 3) with no auditory or kinaesthetic feedback. When comparing the timing profiles of the performances from the first two conditions, he found that most of the pianists lengthened the final note in the condition with no auditory feedback, but otherwise the performances were similar between conditions. Comparing the first and third conditions, he found that the timing patterns were significantly positively correlated for four of the six pianists. This led him to conclude that during imagined performances temporal fluctuations do occur in a manner similar to live performances, just not to the same extent for all musicians.

Wöllner and Williamon (2007) recruited eight pianists and requested them to perform a piece of their choice within four different conditions: 1) normal performance; 2) no auditory feedback; 3) no auditory or visual feedback; and 4) tapping the beat of an imagined performance. For all eight participants, there were highly significant positive correlations for the timing profiles (inter-onset-intervals) between the normal performance and Conditions 2 and 3. With Condition 4, by contrast, only four out of eight participants achieved significant positive correlations. This led the authors to suggest that for some musicians, for reasons unknown, the removal of kinaesthetic feedback from a performance impairs their ability to produce consistent timing profiles than had previously been thought.

Building upon these previous mental chronometry investigations, Clark and Williamon (submitted) also explored how imagery use and vividness might relate to musicians' ability to maintain temporal consistency between live and mental performances. To do this, they asked 32 advanced musicians to give live and mental performances of a two-minute excerpt of their choice, as well as complete imagery use and vividness measures. As was found in the investigations by Repp (1999b) and Wöllner and Williamon (2007), variability emerged between the musicians in terms of their ability to maintain temporal consistency between performances within and between varying conditions. While significant positive correlations emerged for all participants between the timing profiles of their performances within the live condition, significant positive correlations emerged for less than 70% of the participants between the timing profiles of their performances within the mental condition and when comparing the two performance conditions. Relating these findings to the imagery use and vividness measures, significant correlations emerged between the imagery vividness measures and the normalized Z-scores from the live condition, while time employing imagery significantly correlated with the normalized Z-scores from the mental condition. An ability to provide multiple temporally consistent mental performances is dependent on the stability and controllability of the mental representations involved, implying that investigations of this type can shed light upon musicians' controllability of their imagery. Given this, together with the findings from this investigation, the authors concluded that chronometric comparisons could provide insight into the various features of musicians' imagery abilities. As the range of factors that may help or hinder musicians' ability to perform this type of chronometric task successfully is still somewhat unclear, the Clark and Williamon suggested that temporal comparisons should form part of a mixed-methods design for the assessment and further understanding of musicians' imagery abilities.

22.5.4 Physiological responses

Another line of inquiry into imagery ability is based on the view that imagery produces observable physiological responses. It has been proposed that movement planning and programming elicits responses in the autonomic nervous system (ANS) which anticipate and accompany behaviour (Collet et al., 1999). Additionally, it is presumed that ANS activation occurs pre-consciously and is beyond voluntary control (Jeannerod, 1994). The six types of commonly assessed ANS responses are grouped into the electro-dermal, thermo-vascular, and cardio-respiratory categories (Lacey & Lacey, 1958). These include skin resistance or conductance and skin potential, skin blood flow and skin temperature, and heart rate and respiration frequency. While ANS responses can be highly sensitive to individual differences, a number of studies have found ANS responses to be reliable as an indicator of motor imagery. Similar autonomic responses elicited by motor imagery and actual performance have been found in swimming (Beyer et al., 1990), speed skating (Oishi et al., 2000), and shooting (Decety, 1996). An excellent review of these methods and their findings has been provided by Guillot and Collet (2005). Experts have been found to possess greater imagery ability than non-experts (Barr & Hall, 1992; MacIntyre et al., 2002), and studies involving expert and non-expert athletes suggest that ANS responses can be used reliably to estimate motor imagery quality (Decety et al., 1991; Bolliet et al., 2005). It is important to note that some authors have cautioned that, while ANS responses do appear to provide an indication of motor imagery vividness, they do not offer evidence as to the controllability or temporal consistency of motor imagery and therefore should be used together with chronometric comparison methods to generate a more complete picture of imagery ability (Guillot & Collet, 2005; Hugdahl, 1996).

22.6 Implications for musicians and teachers

While the benefits for musicians of employing imagery are becoming increasingly obvious, imagery, like other musical skills, is one which must be practised in order to produce the desired effects. As well, while hearing one's music is a familiar concept for many musicians, musicians would further benefit from their imagery use by striving for a multisensory experience. For musicians, this would involve incorporating aural, visual, and kinaesthetic aspects of their music or performance experiences into their imagery. The objective of multisensory imagery is to create a vivid and realistic experience that closely resembles the actual activity.

Despite the presence of a number of anecdotal accounts of musicians' imagery use, as discussed above, few works provide suggestions as to how musicians might best develop their imagery abilities and incorporate imagery into their regular practice activities. Based on their work with musicians, Connolly and Williamon (2004) have offered the following suggestions:

◆ Practise regularly, especially in the morning, when concentration and focus levels are greatest.

◆ Given how mentally taxing imagery is, it is better to carry out short, regular mental rehearsal sessions than long, infrequent sessions.

◆ Start with relaxation exercises so that clear signals can be communicated between mind and body.

- Mentally rehearse specific skills or qualities you are working on in your technical training, close to or above your current level of performance.
- Keep your imagery positive; move toward what you want to focus on when developing and rehearsing mental representations and avoid ruminating on possible mistakes or errors.
- Use all of your senses, so that you believe that you are actually in the situation executing the skill.
- Notice how you visualize; whether you typically use, or prefer to use, an internal or external perspective of yourself performing.

Suggestions for effective imagery use have also been provided by Homes and Collins (2001) who recommend employing the PETTLEP approach. When engaging in imagery, this method advises that the following aspects be addressed:

- *Physical*: when imagining, strive for movements to occur as they would in physical performance. Within this, incorporate physical movements as necessary; this helps strengthen the memory trace produced by imagery and makes the experience more realistic to the brain.
- *Environmental*: ensure that imagery is location-specific. Imagine self-performing in actual hall for instance, and back up with pictures or videos if possible.
- *Task*: it is important to pay attention to the physical process of performing, not just the sound produced.
- *Timing*: attempt to imagine performing music in real time as this will produce the greatest amount of learning effects.
- *Learning*: as learning progresses, so too will the mental representation of a piece of music. As noted by Lehmann (1997), strive to maintain an image of the music that represents the current level of performance.
- *Emotion*: when imagining upcoming performances, incorporate the emotional aspects of performing as well. This will allow for the pre-experiencing of potentially negative emotions and assist with controlling and de-sensitizing them.
- *Perspective*: imagery can involve both internal and external perspectives which can serve different functions. While internal perspectives are useful for learning and memorizing music and pre-experiencing a performance, an external perspective can be useful for enhancing posture and stage presence.

Given these recommendations, it is important for each musician's imagery use to be personal and individualized, based upon their current situation and wants and needs. Support for the efficacy of the PETTLEP approach to imagery use has been found with hockey players (Smith et al., 2007); however, its efficacy with musicians has yet to be examined. A number of exercises useful for developing and enhancing imagery skills can be found in Connolly and Williamon (2004).

22.7 Directions for future research

The benefits for the creative process inherent in musicians' practice activities and performing that can be derived from imagery use have been well demonstrated, both through empirical investigations and qualitative feedback provided by elite musicians. However, the current state of research concerning musicians' imagery has generated a number of questions. Based upon investigations into the efficacy of imagery as a practice method, the potentially moderating effects of imagery vividness and controllability, the appropriate combination of mental and physical practice, the precise content of imagery, and how the use of various cognitively or motivationally-focused images might impact upon musicians' performance experiences require further exploration. In addition to this, the most efficacious methods for providing musicians with imagery training and enhancing their imagery abilities are still unknown. While valuable information as to how to provide such training may be gained from other domains (e.g. Vealey & Greenleaf, 2006), more research with musicians is necessary.

The notion of emotional imagery is of no doubt particular interest to musicians. There has been some exploration of emotional imagery in terms of the arousal-inducing effects of emotionally-laden imagery (e.g. Bachorowski & Braaten, 1994; Cumming et al., 2007; Damasio et al., 2000; Vianna et al., 2009; Vrana & Rollock, 2002), which might prove useful for helping musicians cope with or alleviate negative emotions connected with performing. However, there is still little understanding concerning how musicians might best make use of emotional imagery for developing emotional expressivity within their music and enhancing the projection of those expressive intentions during performance.

As well, there is evidence to suggest that imagery could also be employed by musicians to prevent the onset of injury (e.g. Holmes, 2005) and to assist with rehabilitation following the occurrence of an injury (Nordin & Cumming, 2005). Given the recent surge of interest into musicians' health and strategies for preventing the occurrence of career-interrupting (or even career-ending) injuries, the use of imagery for these ends will no doubt have great impact on musicians' careers.

References

Aleman, A., Nieuwenstein, M.R., Böcker, K.B.E., & de Haan, E.H.F. (2000). Music training and mental imagery ability. *Neuropsychologia*, **38**, 1664–8.

Bachorowski, J. & Braaten, E.B. (1994). Emotional intensity: Measurement and theoretical implications. *Personality and Individual Differences*, **17**, 191–9.

Bailes, F. (2006). The use of experience-sampling methods to monitor musical imagery in everyday life. *Musicae Scientiae*, **10**, 173–87.

Bangert, M. & Altenmüller, E.O. (2003). Mapping perception to action in piano practice: A longitudinal DC-EEG study. *BMC Neuroscience*, **4**, 26.

Barr, K. & Hall, C. (1992). The use of imagery by rowers. *International Journal of Sport Psychology*, **23**, 243–61.

Betts, G. (1909). *The Distribution and Functions of Mental Imagery*. New York: Teachers College, Columbia University.

Beyer, L., Weiss, T., Hansen, E., Wolf, A., & Seidel, A. (1990). Dynamics of central nervous activation during motor imagination. *International Journal of Psychophysiology*, **9**, 75–80.

Bolliet, O., Collet, C., & Dittmar, A. (2005). Autonomic nervous system activity during actual and mentally simulated preparation for movement. *Applied Psychophysiology and Biofeedback*, **30**, 11–20.

Brodksy, W., Henik, A., Rubinstein, B., & Zorman, M. (2003). Auditory imagery from musical notation in expert musicians. *Perception and Psychophysics*, **65**, 602–12.

Chen, J.L., Penhune, V.B., & Zatorre, R.J. (2008). Listening to musical rhythms recruits regions of the brain. *Cerebral Cortex*, **18**, 2844–54.

Clark, T., Lisboa, T., & Williamon, A. (submitted). The phenomenology of performance: The impact of experience on musicians' performance preparation, perceptions, and experiences. *Research Studies in Music Education*.

Clark, T. & Williamon, A. (submitted). Imagining the music: Methods for assessing musical imagery ability, *Psychology of Music*.

Coffman, D. (1990). Effects of mental practice, physical practice, and knowledge of results on piano performance. *Journal of Research in Music Education*, **38**, 187–96.

Collet, C., Dittmar, A., & Vernet-Maury, E. (1999). Programming or inhibiting action: autonomic nervous system control of anticipation. *International Journal of Psychophysiology*, **32**, 261–76.

Connolly, C. & Williamon, A. (2004). Mental skills training. In A. Williamon (Ed.), *Musical Excellence: Strategies and Techniques to Enhance Performance*. Oxford: Oxford University Press, pp. 221–45.

Cumming, J., Olphin, T., & Law, M. (2007). Self-reported physiological states and physiological responses to different types of motivational general imagery. *Journal of Sport and Exercise Psychology*, **29**, 629–44.

Damasio, A.R., Grabowski, T.J., Bechara, A., Damasio, H., Ponto, L.L.B., Parvizi, J., *et al.* (2000). Subcortical and cortical brain activity during the feeling of self-generated emotions. *Nature Neuroscience*, **3**, 1049–56.

Decety, J. (1996). Do imagined and executed actions share the same neural substrate? *Cognitive Brain Research*, **3**, 87–93.

Decety, J., Jeannerod, M., Germain, M., & Pastene, J. (1991). Vegetative response during imagined movement is proportional to mental effort. *Behavioural Brain Research*, **42**, 1–5.

Denis, M. (1991). *Image and Cognition.* New York: Harvester Wheatsheaf.

Driskell, J.E., Copper, C., & Moran, A. (1994). Does mental practice enhance music performance? *Journal of Applied Psychology*, **79**, 481–92.

Fine, P. (2002). Note-finding strategies in singing: An interview study on Schnittke's Bussvers XII. Presented at the 7th International Conference on Music Perception and Cognition, Sydney, Australia.

Fine, P. & Younger, H. (2004). Sight-singing performance and piano accompaniment. In S. Lipcomb, R. Ashley, R. Gjerdingen, & P. Webster (Eds.) *Proceedings of the 8th International Conference on Music Perception and Cognition, Evanston, IL, 2004.* Adelaide, Australia: Causal Productions, pp. 778–81.

Gabrielsson, A. (1999). The performance of music. In D. Deutsch (Ed.) *The Psychology of Music*, 2nd edition. San Diego, CA: Academic Press, pp. 501–602.

Godøy, R.I. & Jørgensen, H. (eds.) (2001). *Musical Imagery.* Lisse: Swets and Zeitlinger.

Gregg, M. & Clark, T. (2007). Theoretical and practical applications of mental imagery. In A. Williamon & D. Coimbra (Eds.) *Proceedings of the International Symposium on Performance Science 2007.* European Association of Conservatoires, pp. 295–300.

Gregg, M., Clark, T., & Hall, C. (2008). Seeing the sound: An exploration of the use of mental imagery by classical musicians. *Musicae Scientiae*, **12**, 231–47.

Gregg, M. & Hall, C. (2006). Measurement of motivational imagery abilities in sport. *Journal of Sport Sciences*, **24**, 961–71.

Gregg, M., Hall, C., & Nederhof, E. (2005). The imagery ability, imagery use, and performance relationship. *The Sport Psychologist*, **19**, 93–9.

Guillot, A. & Collet, C. (2005). Contribution from neurophysiological and psychological methods to the study of motor imagery. *Brain Research Reviews*, **50**, 387–97.

Hall, C., Mack, D., Paivio, A., & Hausenblas, H. (1998). Imagery use by athletes: Development of the sport imagery questionnaire. *International Journal of Sport Psychology*, **29**, 73–89.

Hall, C. & Martin, K. (1997). Measuring movement imagery abilities: A revision of the MIQ. *Journal of Mental Imagery*, **21**, 143–54.

Halpern, A.R. & Zatorre, R.J. (1999). When that tune runs through your head: A PET investigation of auditory imagery for familiar melodies. *Cerebral Cortex*, **9**, 697–704.

Herholz, S.C., Lappe, C., Knief, A., & Pantev, C. (2008). Neural basis of music imagery and the effect of musical expertise. *European Journal of Neuroscience*, **28**, 2352–60.

Highben, Z. & Palmer, C. (2004) Effects of auditory and motor mental practice in memorized piano performance. *Bulletin of the Council for Research in Music Education*, **159**, 58–68.

Holmes, P. (2003). How do they remember all those notes? A study of the integrated roles of emotion, imagery and technique during the learning and memorisation processes of two experienced solo instrumentalists. Unpublished MA Dissertation: University of Sheffield, UK.

Holmes, P. (2005). Imagination in practice: A study of the integrated roles of interpretation, imagery and technique in the learning and memorisation processes of two experienced solo performers. *British Journal of Music Education*, **22**, 217–35.

Holmes, P. & Collins, D. (2001). The PETTLEP approach to motor imagery: A functional equivalence model for sport psychologists. *Journal of Applied Sport Psychology*, **13**, 60–83.

Hugdahl, K. (1996). Cognitive influences on human autonomic nervous system function. *Current Opinion in Neurobiology*, **6**, 252–8.

Isaac, A., Marks, D., & Russell, E. (1986). An instrument for assessing imagery of movement: The vividness of movement imagery questionnaire (VMIQ). *Journal of Mental Imagery*, **10**, 23–30.

Jaques-Dalcroze, E. (1921). (Translated by Rubinstein, H.F. 1967). *Rhythm, Music and Education*. Woking: The Dalcroze Society Inc.

Jeannerod, M. (1994). The representing brain: neural correlates of motor intention and imagery. *Behavioral and Brain Sciences*, **17**, 187–245.

Kalakoski, V. (2001). Musical imagery and working memory. In R.I. Godøy and H. Jørgensen (Eds.) *Musical Imagery*. Lisse: Swets and Zeitlinger, pp. 43–56.

Kosslyn, S., Ganis, G., & Thompson, W. (2001). Neural foundations of imagery. *Neuroscience*, **2**, 635–42.

Lacey, J.L. & Lacey, B.C. (1958). Verification and extension of the principle of autonomic response-stereotypy. *American Journal of Physiology*, **71**, 50–73.

Lehmann, A. (1997). Acquired mental representations in music performance: Anecdotal and preliminary empirical evidence. In H. Jørgensen & A. Lehmann (Eds.) *Does Practice Make Perfect?* Oslo: Norges musikkhøskole, pp. 141–64.

Lotze, M., Scheler, G., Tan, H.R., Braun, C., & Birbaumer, N. (2003). The musician's brain: Functional imaging of amateurs and professionals during performance and imagery. *Neuroimage*, **20**, 1817–29.

MacIntyre, T., Moran, A., & Jennings, D. (2002). Is controllability of imagery related to canoe-slalom performance? *Perceptual and Motor Skills*, **94**, 1145–250.

Marks, D. (1973). Visual imagery differences in the recall of pictures. *British Journal of Psychology*, **64**, 17–24.

Martin, K., Moritz, S., & Hall, C. (1999). Imagery use in sport: A literature review and applied model. *The Sport Psychologist*, **13**, 245–68.

Meister, I.G., Krings, T., Foltys, H., Boroojerdi, B., Müller, M.,Töpper, R., *et al.* (2004). Playing piano in the mind: An fMRI study on music imagery and performance in pianists. *Cognitive Brain Research*, **19**, 219–28.

Mellet, E., Petit, L., Mazoyer, B., Denis, M., and Tzourio, N. (1998). Reopening the mental imagery debate: Lessons from functional anatomy. *Neuro-Image*, **8**, 129–39.

Milton, J., Solodkin, A., Hluštík, P., & Small, S.L. (2007). The mind of expert motor performance is cool and focused. *NeuroImage*, **35**, 804–13.

Moran, A. (1993). Conceptual and methodological issues in the measurement of mental imagery skills in athletes. *Journal of Sport Behavior*, **16**, 156–70.

Morris, T., Spittle, M., & Watt, A.P. (2005). *Imagery in sport*. Champaign, IL: Human Kinetics.

Nordin, S. & Cumming, J. (2005). Professional dancers describe their imagery: Where, when, what, why, and how. *The Sport Psychologist*, **19**, 395–416.

Oishi, K., Kasai, T., & Maeshima, T. (2000). Autonomic response specificity during motor imagery. *Journal of Physiological Anthropology and Applied Human Science*, **19**, 255–61.

Paivio, A. (1985). Cognitive and motivational functions of imagery in human performance. *Canadian Journal of Applied Sport Science*, **9**, 241–53.

Pascual-Leone, A. (2001). The brain that plays music and is changed by it. *Annals NY Acad Sci*, **930**, 315–29.

Repp, B.H. (1999a). Effects of auditory feedback deprivation on expressive piano performance. *Music Perception*, **16**, 409–38.

Repp, B.H. (1999b). Control of expressive and metronomic timing in pianists. *Journal of Motor Behavior*, **31**, 145–64.

Richardson, A. (1994). *Individual Differences in Imaging*. Amityville, NY: Baywood Publishing Company, Inc.

Rogers, W., Hall, C., & Buckolz, E. (1991). The effects of an imagery training program on imagery ability, imagery use, and figure skating performance. *Journal of Applied Sport Psychology*, **3**, 109–25.

Ross, S. (1985). The effectiveness of mental training practice on improving performance of college trombonists. *Journal of Research in Music Education*, **33**, 221–30.

Rubin-Rabson, G. (1937). The influence of pre-analytic study in memorising piano music. *Archives of Psychology*, **31**, 1–53.

Rubin-Rabson, G. (1941). Studies in the psychology of memorizing piano music: VI: A comparison of two forms of mental rehearsal and keyboard overlearning. *Journal of Educational Psychology*, **32**, 593–602.

Sheehan, P. (1967). A shortened form of Bett's questionnaire upon mental imagery. *Journal of Clinical Psychology*, **23**, 386–9.

Smith, D., Wright, C., Allsopp, A., & Westhead, H. (2007). It's all in the mind: PETTLEP-based imagery and sports performance. *Journal of Applied Sport Psychology*, **19**, 80–92.

Vealey, R.S. & Greenleaf, C.A. (2006). Seeing in believing: Understanding and using imagery in sport. In J.M. Williams (Ed.) *Applied Sport Psychology: Personal Growth to Peak Performance*, 5th edition. New York: McGraw-Hill, pp. 306–48.

Vianna, E.P.M., Naqvi, N., Bechara, A., & Tranel, D. (2009). Does vivid emotional imagery depend on body signals? *International Journal of Psychophysiology*, **72**, 46–50.

Vrana, S.R. & Rollock, D. (2002). The role of ethnicity, gender, emotional content, and contextual differences in physiological, expressive, and self-reported emotional responses to imagery. *Cognition and Emotion*, **16**, 165–92.

White, A., & Hardy, L. (1998). An in-depth analysis of the uses of imagery by high-level slalom canoeists and artistic gymnasts. *The Sport Psychologist*, **12**, 387–403.

Wöllner, C. & Williamon, A. (2007). An exploratory study of the role of performance feedback and musical imagery in piano playing. *Research Studies in Music Education*, **29**, 39–54.

Woody, R.H. (2002). Emotion, imagery and metaphor in the acquisition of musical performance skill. *Music Education Research*, **4**, 213–24.

Zatorre, R.J. (1999). Brain imaging studies of musical perception and musical imagery. *Journal of New Music Research*, **28**, 229–36.

Zatorre, R.J., Chen, J.L., & Penhume, V.B. (2007). When the brain plays music: Auditory-motor interactions in music perception and production. *Nature Reviews Neuroscience*, **8**, 547–58.

Zatorre, R.J., Evans, A.C. & Meyer, E. (1994). Neural mechanisms underlying melodic perception and memory for pitch. *Journal of Neuroscience*, **14**, 1908–19.

Zatorre, R. J., & Halpern, A. R. (2005). Mental concerts: Musical imagery and auditory cortex. *Neuron*, **47**, 9–12.

Part 5

Perspectives from education, psychiatry, and therapy

Chapter 23

The call to create: Flow experience in music learning and teaching

Lori A. Custodero

23.1 Introduction

I have learned much from observing young children engaged in music-making. Their keen sensitivity to the sonic environment suggests a convergence of self and music, witnessed in their spontaneous movement and vocalizations, often in imitation of sounds or people in their settings, as well as the transformation of their own and culturally familiar songs, chants, or articulated patterns. The compelling nature of musical materials—melodic contours, rhythmic vitality, phrase structures, and harmonic intensity—invites participation, and thereby offers opportunities for *creative action*. Such action might take the form of embodying the music performed by others or inventing one's own music as a vehicle for expression, communication, or regulation. Called to create, children attend and are responsive to what the music asks of them: 'Clap here!'; 'Sing higher' (or louder or slower); 'Change your movement to match the musical change!'. They also utilize the affordances of musical materials to comfort themselves (i.e. using familiar songs as transitional objects); to elaborate imaginative play scenes; to animate dialogue with peers; and to rhythmically structure a chaotic environment. Attuned to what the poet Tagore (1921) describes as the 'joy of life,' young children teach us how music can function as both road and home, as it 'leads us on yet gives us shelter' (p. 67).

In March, 2010, I participated in the 'Educating the Creative Mind' conference at Keane University in New Jersey, USA. One of my duties was to participate in a concert featuring young performers, interviewing them after they had played. I asked a 7-year-old to tell me about the most fun he's ever had with his violin, and without hesitation, he replied, 'Playing at Carnegie Hall'. When asked what made it fun, his response was 'because it was challenging'. Indeed, research into qualities of optimal experience has found that it occurs when people are engaged in activity for which they feel highly challenged and also feel highly capable (e.g. Csikszentmihalyi, 1975, 1990, 1997; Csikszentmihalyi & Csikszentmihalyi, 1988). These experiences have been described as rewarding and enjoyable, with each step along the road informing the next so that the progression of ideas and their manifestations flow with ease. Inasmuch as participants used the word 'flow' to describe their experience when involved in activity that often leads to invention and discovery, that term is used to represent a psychological state associated with creativity (Csikszentmihalyi, 1975, 1996). In this chapter, I address how observational studies of flow experience in music education settings have led to a framework in which learners are perceived as creative. Compelled by the accessible potential inherent in musical materials and social models, individual interpretations and transformations lead to insights, skill, and products newly constructed and experienced.

Consider the following childhood memory of an early career violinist-music educator:

My friend Ben and I would request that my mother put on a recording of Perlman playing Bazzini's 'Dance of the Goblins'. We would leap all over the living room—I recall thinking that the music could make me dance across the ceiling. The frenetic energy of the piece and of the performance filled me. It compelled me to move, to run around, to express that music.

Music calls forth imaginative thought and action through the multiple ways in which we conceptualize and engage with sound and movement. We respond to sensory impulses to move our bodies in correspondence to perceived corporeal relationships, and we interpret or convey emotions born of these associations. This convergence of self with music results in physical expression, and, although often more easily observable in children, it is also in the vocabulary of the expert musician. Arnold Steinhardt, first violinist with the Guarnari String Quartet, speaks of an excerpt from Beethoven's Op. 130:

> In bar 46 we find that special Beethoven notation: two notes of identical pitch and time value slurred together. . . . I try and make this double impulse heard and *felt* . . . One could call it a shudder or a cry. Even if he had written one note rather than two, I think one would know that something unusual is called for in the way of interpretation. You don't need a special notation; something has to speak to you from within to tell you what to do.
>
> (Blum, 1986: pp. 153–4.)

Both the child's embodied interpretation of frenzy in a leaping dance and the adult's carefully executed gesture guiding the bow across the string in an expression of despair reflect an active response to musical cues. Such actions, compelled by the clearly perceived feeling of music, reflect the call to create; the child's description that the 'music could make me dance', is an externalized version of the adult expert's more internalized listening to something 'speak to you from within to tell you what to do'.

In the following sections, I examine the role of creativity in learning and teaching through my research on how flow is experienced in music activity. Engagement in tasks whose challenges invite a person's best efforts generates flow. In order to sustain this optimal experience, skills must improve to meet new challenges, and in turn, challenges must improve to continue attracting enhanced skills, thus creating an ideal learning situation. This dynamic interaction, also known as emergent motivation (Csikszentmihalyi, 1978), is self-perpetuating: as an individual's skill level improves through practice, challenges must become increasingly complex. Such a framework draws on views of learning from research on childhood dealing with the importance of individually devised problem-solving and -finding strategies (e.g. Duckworth, 1996; Siegler, 2004). In essence, we learn through creating; we create as we accrue increasingly complex skill/knowledge through sustained inquiry. I adopt a model of creativity involving an individual's active construction of musical meaning through responsive interaction with [culturally understood] musical materials. I am interpreting music-making as creative action, a framework evolving from a focus on the function and pervasiveness of music in the lives of young children and the unfettered, honest quality of their interactions with music.

Given the wide disparity of characteristics denoting creativity in current scholarship, I begin by situating this work in the context of where, why, and how this notion of creativity is relevant to music education settings. Considering the intimate, embodied nature of musical knowing, the provocative genesis of creative action is reviewed and linked to characteristics of flow experience and learning. Activated by embodied knowledge, affirmed or resisted by extant shared cultural norms and values, musical responses take the form of created or re-created action in which the individual is agent. This self-initiated and directed character of response to the call to create advantages collective learning venues, as group members recognize and resource the actions of others.

Once introduced, these issues serve as a backdrop for understanding how children's learning processes can be considered creative, with evidence from my own studies of young children in which observable indicators of flow are identified and described. Looking at classrooms as sites of creative action, I draw from additional studies in which teachers involved in action research reflect upon the usefulness of flow indicators as ways to cultivate a pedagogical imagination and facilitate creative musical education.

23.2 Music as creative action

23.2.1 Creative convergence of music and self: embodied musicianship

Western music theorists have long used the human condition as metaphor: themes *develop*, melodies *rise and fall*, tempo *accelerates*, harmonies *pull and rest*. Music has a *pulse*, multiple musical lines are referred to as *voices*, tonic is 'home'. Our vocabulary for music is anthropomorphic—descriptions of music reveal a conception rooted to human physicality. In the violinists' experiences described in the introduction, actors are responding to human correspondences in perceived musical cues. The child's legs are animated by what is heard in Perlman's tempo, and the corresponding behaviour is one best described as a joining with the music. Similarly, the asynchronous 'planned chaos' in the Beethoven quartet is created by thwarted attempts by the first violinist to join the music, resulting in a sense of exhaustion, and leading the expert musician to move his arm to convey the 'shuddering' desolation in a twice articulated pitch. Through the experience of these emotional correspondences between music and self, the distance between sound and its interpreter is reduced. Sound becomes embodied by the individual who interprets, and the body becomes the site of a new and intimate context for knowing.

In her analyses of literary authors' accounts of their own childhoods, Cobb (1977) refers to Bernard Berenson's (1949) appreciation of such depth as he remarked that he has 'never enjoyed to the utmost a work of any kind, whether verbal, musical, or visual, never enjoyed a landscape without sinking myself deeply into that work of art, without becoming it . . .' (p. 20). Sinking into music becomes a sensory experience, drawing upon the human correspondences mentioned above—to feel the accelerated tempo moving you more quickly through time, or to feel a sense of resolution and gratification at the final cadence. For children, this comes much easier because they are less encumbered by the weight of years spent regulating emotional and physical responses; for adults it requires risk-taking and oftentimes, emotional vulnerability due to this intimate nature of artistic knowing (Dissanayake, 2000). Led by the call to create, this idea of 'becoming' is very different from 'losing oneself' in the artistic experience; vulnerability in this sense provides openness to a more informed sense of reality rather than an escape from reality (Csikszentmihalyi, 1993).

In flow experience, deep involvement is a key descriptor, described psychically as a merging of action and awareness. Such convergence of knowing and doing is especially significant in musical experience, which occurs across time and requires a 'reflective immediacy' to the resources and needs of the moment joined with the collective wisdom of past experience. Noted by Dewey (1934/1980) in his discussion of children's play, this merging is paramount to learning, which he describes as when 'idea and act are completely fused' (p. 278). Cobb (1977) echoes these sentiments, and articulates this condition vis-à-vis the affective component, writing of the 'delighted awareness that knowing and being are in some way coincident . . .' (p. 32). Considering music as creative action, we note the convergence of self and source to create a depth of understanding.

23.2.2 Creative belonging: movement, self, and other

The idea of 'becoming' in order to truly know, as well as the relatedness of that state to feeling, is noted by Blacking (1987), who is mindful of how new knowledge is constructed both from the body as a vehicle for change, and from interactions with others. In making an argument for the evolutionary primacy of song and dance over speech and walking, he describes his ethnomusicological observations on the value of celebrations and rituals:

> . . . periods of intense social interaction are most deeply experienced and most likely to generate conceptual thought when inner feelings are publicly shared through a counterpoint of body movement. . . . ideas may come from movement. . . . I suggest that we strive to be moved to think, to *be* thought. It is sometimes called inspiration, insight, genius, creativity and so on. But essentially it is a form of unconscious celebration that is most evident in artistic creation: it is the movement of the body. We are moved to creative and reflective thinking as a result of greater intensity of feeling.
>
> (Blacking, 1987: pp. 63–4.)

Blacking reflects on embodiment as linked to a depth of feeling which moves us, both literally and conceptually. Similarly, Dissanayake (2000) writes of the importance of body movement and emotions as key to the effectiveness of ceremonial rituals. Creativity then needs a milieu to invoke influence; the convergence of self and source is meaningful when it finds resonance in community. The intimate relationship between self and music is intensified when shared—this shared experience contributes to the empowerment of creative action and to learning as we see the conceptual mirrored in others. From the musicality present in cross-cultural studies of mothers' infant-directed speech (Papousek, 1996), to more culturally differentiated daily musical practices and elaborated ceremonies, music-making is a social experience.

Experience mediates our ability to know deeply—our cultural associations with sound are learned very early as a reflection of social connections and shared goals. This means that musical idioms and constructs like 'in tune' and 'steady beat' may be understood and valued differently (if at all) in various musical communities, cultures, and genres. Our experiences of music are shaped by virtue of our understanding of what music is, defined apart from noise by a recognizable framing of meaningful patterns. In music built on Western scalar and rhythmic orientations, for example, this may include periodic phrase structure and harmonic tension and resolution defined by tonic-dominant function; there is evidence we respond to these orientations in infancy (e.g. Trehub & Trainor, 1993).

These cultural understandings are crucial to music learning, as they are the foundation on which we make musical judgements; they provide definitive boundaries and direct typical responses which provide the background for appreciating innovation and personal style. Dewey (1934/1980) speaks of the significance of purpose as an impulse translated into a plan of action, giving direction. Having clear goals is a characteristic of flow experience, and research on flow has indicated their importance in learning (e.g. Rathunde, 1988). However, the relationship between creativity and goals is complex, as demonstrated in Csikszentmihalyi's early work with Getzels, focusing on visual artists. A longitudinal study of art students rated discovery orientation, that is, the ways in which artists approached a particular project, in this case, a collage. The participants who allowed the materials to direct them to new ideas resulting in new goals were identified as having high discovery orientation; 10 years later these artists were found to have more professional success than those who had followed their pre-determined plan for the artwork, and were less disposed to change their conception in the process (Getzels & Csikszentmihalyi, 1976).

Clear feedback is crucial to flow experience; it is also based in culturally idiomatic features and reflective of cultural values. The multisensory characteristics of musical interactions provide multiple opportunities for feedback. We can receive music through our auditory system, perceive representations of music visually in musical scores and in responsive human movement, feel music in our bodies as we sing or play an instrument or in the physical vibrations of sound through a conduit like a wooden floor, and in the physical empathic responses such as accelerated heartbeat alluded to in the discussion on embodiment above. Because music happens in time, the feedback is simultaneous with experience, contributing the immediacy necessary for flow experience.

'Being with' both the music and others provides resources for constructing meaning through creative activity (Custodero, 2005). Creative dispositions are valued based on cultural interpretations of music; as in the convergence of self and source, there is a convergence of self with others that defines creative activity as alternative activity, whether it innovates or transgresses established practices. The Centennial Exhibition of the Nobel Prize in 2001 used creativity as a theme, as it was common feature of all the recipients' work, yet was manifest in a variety of ways through their achievements. The accompanying publication states 'Creative processes are encouraged by diversity and variation rather than by homogeneity and similarity' (Larsson, 2002, p. 163).

23.2.3 Creative construction: discovery, invention, and development

Valuing creativity means valuing alternative ways of doing, thinking, being—it is honouring the unexpected and suggests a commitment to an embodied depth of knowing within a social milieu. Being creative gives meaning to action; it is the ultimate act of agency and has been singled out as the attribute which makes us human by scholars such as Dissanayake (2000), who has written of the need to 'make special,' by elaborating the everyday activities through the adornment of ritual and decoration.

In flow experience, individuals must sense personal control, that what they do matters. This feeling of consequential action requires sensitivity to the artistic materials and the social resources as well as the cultural memes which define the practice in which they are engaged. In order to heed the call to create, culturally relevant feedback must occur, so that the creative freedom of 'listening to the materials' and provides direction, creating expectations for what might follow.

Developmental theorists have linked creativity to the processes by which children typically accrue knowledge about the world. Piaget's (1962, 1969/2000) theory of cognitive development offers a constructivist perspective, one that acknowledges children's roles in creating their own understanding through interaction with their environment. His concept of equilibration suggests that children monitor their own learning processes: through mental reflection and action they either interpret physical truth unconventionally in order to explore its functions within their existing schemas (assimilation), or change their perceptions to accommodate the new information.

In a discussion of these manipulative strategies, Feldman (1994) refers to Piaget's work as 'the first distinctly psychological theory of intellectual change' (p. 149). He delineates between Piaget's two categories of change, assimilation and accommodation, which move *toward* stabilized knowledge, and what he terms the 'transformational imperative,' which moves *away from* stability. When considered in the context of domain-specific understanding, this developmental urge to change the given is what is meant by the call to create. The child's experience is similar to that of the creative artist or scientist—the materials (words, objects, people, movements) call the individual to act—to transform, to repeat, to represent. In music, creativity and learning come from listening and responding to the potentials inherent in music such as beat, melody, or rhythmic patterns. When they are attuned and aware that they can make consequential changes, and that the changes suggest further action, flow experience is sustained.

One example of this is the 'Peek-a-boo' song I've used in early childhood music classes. Adapted from the common game used by parents to teach turn—taking and variations on expectation (Bruner & Sherwood, 1976), the musical component provides a timing structure that can be manipulated by children in creative ways:

> We are playing the Peek-a-Boo game with scarves and each child in the Infant Room has chosen their preferred color. We wait for the children to either put the scarves over their own heads or indicate that

they'd like their caregiver to do so, and then we begin singing 'Where is John? Wish I knew! Pull down the scarf and say 'Peek-a-Boo'!' John (7 months old) is smiling at the end of the song—he has played with expectation: About half way through the song he pulled slightly down on his scarf to reveal his eyes, then lifted it to cover them again, and finished the song by dramatically removing the scarf from his head at the cue 'Peek-a-Boo!'.

Here the affordances (Gibson, 1977) available in the environment facilitated John's spontaneous transformation of the ritual. In addition to the scarf and song, the presence and actions of others were key components to the experience. Rather than place the scarves on the infants, we waited for them to initiate, and that sense of personal control engendered creative action, even in these very young children,

Csikszentmihalyi (1993: pp. 1–2) wrote about children's natural proclivity for flow:

> Children—provided they are healthy and not too severely abused—seem to be in flow constantly; they enjoy 'unfolding their being' as they learn to touch, throw, walk, read, and grow up. Unfortunately they soon have to stop 'unfolding' as school starts to force their growth into patterns over which they have no control. When that occurs, flow begins to become rarer, and many young people end up experiencing it only in games, sports, and other leisure activities with peers.

Given the salience of children's music-making during childhood (e.g. Campbell, 1991; Malloch & Trevarthen, 2009) one might ask if music education settings might be school-based contexts where more flow-oriented experiences might occur. Viewing music learning as creative action means viewing students as agents of change. Using flow experience as a basis for assessing music education requires attending to the transformational potential of musical materials in the context of music instruction. How do learners demonstrate what and how they know musically and, from an educational perspective, what they next need to know in order to follow the call to create? In the following section, operationalizations of flow experience are reported and their implications for teaching and learning discussed.

23.3 Creative children: The call to learn

> Four-year-old Samuel picks up two small maracas and begins vigorously playing along with the recording of the samba performance, his motions reflecting the musical rhythms. A nearby mirror catches his attention and he shakes his maracas in time while exploring the myriad possibilities of facial contortions. He then is drawn to the group of 8 other children who are also moving and playing along with the recording and he negotiates space, weaving through his peers, moving to the beat of the music as he continues shaking the maracas. In the 4.5 minute duration of the recording, Sam tries out several moves, interacting with the music and his cohorts, plays the instruments on his stomach; returns to the mirror and places the maracas near his two ears. His final effort is perhaps the most novel—he reaches to the back legs of his pants and places one maraca in each pocket, proceeding to shake his legs and backside in beat with the music.
>
> (Custodero, 2005, p. 48.)

It was in the microanalyses of children's imaginative use of musical materials that I began to note their actions as creative. As I spent time repeatedly looking at video images of children engaging in music-making, I became more aware of their abilities for devising unique strategies to sustain their engagement, as exemplified in Sam's use of the maracas above. My curiosity found a framework for investigation in Csikszentmihalyi's (1975, 1996, 1997a) work on optimal, rewarding, and enjoyable activity. Using his Experience Sampling Methodology (ESM) as a guideline for observing children's behaviours, I videotaped lessons of 4–5-year-olds and looked for examples of children feeling highly skilled and highly challenged. The videotape was event-sampled, that is, it framed experience parsed into particular activities such as singing a song, playing a piece on the keyboard, or doing an ear training game. The 12 children in the class were randomly sampled for each recorded event so that the videographer would focus on a single group of children for the event, and then choose another group for the next event. There were between 15–20 events for each of eight 1-hour lessons. There were 441 units of analysis representing each child visible on tape for each event in each class.

In the initial study, the experience sampling methods developed by flow researchers (Csikszentmihalyi & Csikszentmihalyi, 1988) were followed as closely as was possible, making the necessary adaptations for examining the experience of young children rather than adolescents and adults. Conditions required participants be observed and interviewed rather than be responsive to questions in written form, and were limited to events sampled in a single setting, a music classroom, rather than random samples of daily activity. Modelled on the Experience Sampling Form (ESF) (Csikszentmihalyi & Csikszentmihalyi, 1988), the Flow Indicators in Musical Activity (FIMA) form was used to code the videotaped experiences of the students (see Figure 23.1). The affective indicators represented by semantic differential scales were taken directly from ESF: the behavioural indicators were represented by Likert items and based on key questions from the ESF and grounded theoretical applications of observable behaviours of preschool-aged children (and subsequently, older and younger children, see Custodero, 2005b) in the music education setting. A global rating of flow was based on the following description, in which one can see the active nature of the learning process:

> The child is focused and absorbed in the present event. Gaze is usually attentive on the facilitating person or object. However, when physical manipulation is not a task-defining element, a less focused gaze may reflect an internal 'working out'—a personalizing or 'taking ownership' of the less tangible event. Affect is often positive and sometimes neutral, within varying levels of intensity usually reflective of individual personality differences. It is never negative. At the completion of the event there is usually a heightened observable affect due to awareness of success. There may be a desire to share that awareness with a nearby significant other. There is a level of obliviousness to one's physical condition. Physical movement toward the facilitating person or materials is common.

(Custodero, 1997, p. 68.)

Factor analyses were run on the affective items, resulting in three meaningful dimensions matching previous studies on flow, which contributed to content validity of the adaptation. Factor analyses of the behavioural items resulted in three additional dimensions. Using the flow ratings as the dependent variable, regression analyses were then run to see which of the dimensions predicted flow experience.

Viewing and coding the videotapes provided a means of reflective observation; I was stunned by the degree to which students made the effort to remain engaged, demonstrating musical response and invention that typically went unnoticed. These were displays of children being called to create—embodying musical characteristics, striving to belong to the classroom musical culture, and proactively defining challenges and meeting them, imagining what could be, and taking action. Two findings in this original investigation are specifically relevant to the relationship between children's music learning and creativity: the function of imitation and the observed pervasiveness of inventive transformations.

23.3.1 Imitation as a precursor to creativity and flow

Intensity of imitation was included as a possible indicator of flow because of its representation of task absorption and its role in generating activity from which one can then read feedback. This variable was coded through observing imitative facial expression and body movement, as well as

FLOW INDICATORS in MUSICAL ACTIVITIES FORM

Specific activity:_____ Length of activity:_____ Date:_____

Familiarity with activity: _____   Child: _____

v=very, q=quite, s=somewhat, n=neither

	V	Q	S	N	S	Q	V	
Happy	O	o	.	—	.	o	O	Sad
Cheerful	O	o	.	—	.	o	O	Irritable
Involved	O	o	.	—	.	o	O	Distracted
Alert	O	o	.	—	.	o	O	Drowsy
Active	O	o	.	—	.	o	O	Passive
Excited	O	o	.	—	.	o	O	Bored
Satisfied	O	o	.	—	.	o	O	Frustrated
Successful	O	o	.	—	.	o	O	Failure
Comfortable[a]	O	o	.	—	.	o	O	Uncomfortable

	not at all			somewhat			quite		very	
How difficult was the perceived challenge?[b]	0	1	2	3	4	5	6	7	8	9
Was child aware of adult approval?	0	1	2	3	4	5	6	7	8	9
Was child aware of peers?	0	1	2	3	4	5	6	7	8	9
Did child anticipate activity?	0	1	2	3	4	5	6	7	8	9
Did child expand activity?	0	1	2	3	4	5	6	7	8	9
Did child extend activity?	0	1	2	3	4	5	6	7	8	9
Imitation intensity	0	1	2	3	4	5	6	7	8	9
Performance accuracy	0	1	2	3	4	5	6	7	8	9
Was child in flow?	0	1	2	3	4	5	6	7	8	9

Comments:

Fig. 23.1 Flow in Musical Activities (FIMA) form (Custodero, 1997) Notes: a) this item was dropped due to low variability; b) in later studies this was separated into 3 individual indicators: Self-initiation, Self-correction, and Deliberate gesture.

pantomimed or actual replication of speech or singing, that mimicked another who was in the participant's line of vision. Imitation is a conventional instructional technique used in most children's music education settings, (e.g. Campbell, 1991; Haston, 2007) and figures prominently in the general developmental literature (e.g. Piaget, 1962; Vygotsky, 1978) and in current investigations (e.g. Thompson & Russell, 2004). Because of these links to engagement and learning, the assumption was that imitation was a characteristic of flow. However, the relationship as revealed in this study was not direct, yet functionally important and analytically complex. Considering the role of imitation in both flow experience and creativity provides insight to its use and misuse in music educational settings.

The first surprise about imitation was who the students were imitating. In an educative setting, it was assumed they were imitating the teacher: however, factor analyses indicated that imitation was aligned with peer awareness and not adult awareness. Awareness of others was rated by inter-actions that involve prolonged gaze, head turning, or physical movement toward another person, as well as attempts to engage another person physically or verbally. This has implications about how and why we provide models and what young students might expect from peers vs. adults, whose suggested role in this study was linked to children's perceptions of challenge and the affirmation of success. The second surprise was that the factor including peer awareness and imitation was not predicative of flow. Imitation seemed to be an adaptive strategy that students used relative to the perceived challenge—it was a vehicle to get into flow, but not an indicator of being in flow. Intently utilizing other people in the environment as models appeared to provide feedback and either confirm performance or initiate self-correction to direct paths to meaningful activity.

This function of imitation was clear when examining learning over time. In comparing degrees of familiarity, measured by the number of weeks spent on an activity, imitation was inversely related to flow. For the first week in which an activity was introduced, dimensions predicting flow were low and imitation was high; all the predictors of flow were highest at the 3–4-week level, with perceived challenge significantly so, and imitation was at its lowest. This U-curve for imitation signals its complexity and usefulness, as it seems functional in helping students understand what is being taught when first introduced to an activity, and later, to help sustain an interest in activity in which skills are already mastered, by providing a resource for creative adaptation.

23.3.2 Transformations of musical materials as creative action

When children looked to be in flow, they were actively engaged with the materials of music. Much like the discovery orientation of Getzels' visual artists, they manipulated these materials—'listening' to the capacities and potentials of sound in time and investigating how it moved, how it felt. Three time-linked transformational behaviours were consistently observable. They loaded onto the discrete factor which also contained 'skill,' suggesting that these behaviours were observed to be manifestations of learning.

The first of these, Anticipation, was demonstrated by verbal interjections or physical gestures which reflected understanding of 'what comes next' in the teacher-guided activity; children exhibiting this indicator were compelled by a clear sense of instructional direction, and were accelerating their experience of time through this merging of action and awareness. Students were following the unfolding of the *lesson* intently and with a sense of urgency. This meant there was no longer a sense of following the *teacher*, but of collaborating with her, eventually leading to the learner's becoming the constructing agent. Anticipatory behaviours, such as extemporaneous verbal interjections during 'teacher talk', may be related to the embodiment/imitation conundrum, namely that the students are engaged through imitation of teacher's interest, and are moved into the embodied state guided by the music.

Indeed, flow scholars' views on pedagogical practice involve the teacher's own passion for a topic (Csikszentmihalyi, 1978; Nakamura & Csikszentmihalyi, 2005). Teachers' ability to sustain an evolving interest provides a model for students to likewise seek surprising insights with which to imagine and create. In her study on the work of professors in a variety of disciplines, Neumann (2009) speaks of their 'passionate thought'. She noted that when considering their work as creative, participants described their experiences as involving 'peak emotion, personal absorption in the work, physical sensation of and interrelation with a subject of study, and intensified awareness of the subject studied and the process of the study' (p. 61). Sharing this with students was gratifying and helpful in the progress of scholarly work. A study by Bakker and colleagues (2005) found that flow experience in music teachers was relatively high, and that there was a high contagion factor between teacher and students, a mutual sharing of passionate thought.

Expansion, like Anticipation, also occurred during the periods of instruction, yet was less reliant on teacher interactions and more on the potential of the musical materials. This indicator seems most obviously linked to creativity, as it involved the transformations of the 'given'—the teacher-offered musical materials. Students drew upon their awareness of what the musical activity could be, based on their awareness of what the materials could do, invoking a 'what if?' attitude that sustained their interest and supported learning. One of the most pervasive ways in which children expanded the presented musical material was to embody the beat, tempo, or rhythmic patterns of music made by someone else, re-creating what was heard into expression of what was felt. Other examples included playing 'air piano' when singing pitches in imitation of the teacher—simply imitating was not challenging enough. As the space of experience is broadened through realizations of these potentials, time seems to stand still, as opposed to seemingly be pushing forward, as in Anticipation.

Observations of Expansion provide evidence for Feldman's 'transformational imperative'; the potential in musical materials called these students to create newly born renditions of tunes by speeding them up, exaggerating words, or adding body movement. Their transformations of the task were ways to raise the challenge levels for themselves, such as proclaiming 'I can play this song with my eyes closed!'. Often these expansions are quickly dismissed by teachers as 'off-task behaviour' rather than creative actions because they weren't included in teachers' predicted outcomes. It may be that teachers open to the possibility of unexpected interpretations may discover new dimensions of their subject of study as well as new insights on how best to share their own knowledge as they make note of students' expansions of their ideas.

How we might choose to respond to the potentials in musical materials reveals much about our enculturation with music. Meyer (1973) writes of expectations set up by idiomatic practices of various musical styles, and of our experiences being characterized by realization of those expectations or by surprise. When teachers teach to flow experience, they are looking for expansions as feedback from which to generate meaningful teaching. Rather than viewing the students' actions as demonstrations of deficit understanding, unrealized expectations may generate reconsideration of what skills and concepts are indeed being learned. Such an approach is a call to create new teaching strategies based on what Tagore (1926/1997) referred to as 'surprise achievements' (p. 256) of students. In the beginning of the section, the episode of Sam's use of the maracas went beyond keeping the beat—his discovery of multiple ways to do so might be deemed a surprise achievement—it was definitely unexpected, and required a wider sense of the possible for teachers to feel comfortable allowing such exploration.

The third indicator, Extension, occurred outside the specific instructional context and was observed as a continuation to engage in the activity, even though the teacher and class had moved on to something else. This is often difficult to document, as it also might happen outside the classroom contexts, where children returned to the activity, bringing it in to new contexts, similar to Piaget's concept of delayed imitation. Here, the call to create with the components of an activity extended past instruction and were implemented by students-as-agents, often in private places or places in which adults are not necessarily invited. Because of the intimacy of music's convergence with self, surveillance of children's private music-making can curb creative action. Learners find ways to extend what is introduced in classrooms in different environments, free from adult supervision, in playgrounds, in garages and attics, and on the Internet.

23.3.3 Learning observations

What is the relationship of imitation to creativity in educational settings? Looking through the lens of flow experience, in which the role of others has always been context specific (Csikszentmihalyi, 1997), raises important issues around *who* students imitate and *why* they imitate. Additionally, the pervasive transformations of teacher-given materials bring into question the definition of tasks and expectation of outcomes for students whose music learning seems often to be emergent and unpredictable.

Learners embody conceptual information and imitate others' embodiment of conceptual information. The indirect relationship between flow and imitation suggests a lack of intimacy with the conceptual focus—the student's attention is drawn to how others are interpreting rather than to the subject of interpretation itself, here musical activity. Yet, another interpretation may point to the importance of community, a theme in St John's (2006) research on flow experience and music as well as the work on communicative musicality as discussed in this volume by Colwyn Trevarthen (see Chapter 17). The human need to belong, and to use music as a way to know another, has interdisciplinary significance.

The importance of others as resources in learning is also supported in neuroscience, specifically in research on mirror neurons, which suggests a co-representation and sharing of experiences such as embodied responses to music is imprinted on the brain (Overy, 2009). It may be that we embody the conceptual, in this case, music, and imitate another's embodiment, drawn to the other because of the social rewards of musical belonging. In this way imitation may be conceived as a trying on of possible sense-making: a resource that, when applied to former knowledge, may lead to perceptions of compelling challenges and worthy contributions in the particular musical activity with which one is engaged.

With multiple peers as embodied resources to imitate, creative action may be generated through the spiralling of imitation into a newly embodied conceptual understanding. As Blacking pointed out, experiences together with others create opportunities for conceptualization, and I would add, creative action, adding personal meaning to the newly accrued skill sets by attending to the social feedback in the environment. Studies of children's musical creativity have found this relationship between personal and social knowledge construction to be critical in children's musical development, and as can be seen in the analyses of children's compositions by Swanwick and Tillman (1986).

Learners are drawn to imitation as agents in their own learning. In flow experience, having a sense of personal control is paramount, and in imitating peers, students were making choices on their own to imitate—it was not part of the teacher-defined task. In the informal contexts of popular music learning, young musicians listen and imitate, yet, like the students looking to imitate peers in order to be in flow in the activity, they are motivated by wanting to know, by the call to create.

The call to create may be problematic in current educational settings, which favour imitation over transformation. The expansions and extensions, and even anticipations exhibited by students are often unwelcome in a classroom or studio whose sustenance is dictated by outside review, based on global standards and limited indicators of successful learning. This issue raises questions about whether or not it is possible or even desirable to teach to flow, to facilitate creative renderings in school. In the following section, perspectives of teachers as researchers are offered to address this issue.

23.4 Creative music education: teaching to the call

Many teachers respond to the call to create as an invitation to envision the world as it could be, to facilitate and support the active imagination in efforts to express, innovate, and invent. Often these efforts are resisted by the institutional expectations of conformity; however, it seems that teaching to flow may be the way in which teachers can retain their own sense of enjoyment and sustain an attitude of inquiry about subject matter they have seemingly mastered. In my own work with several groups of teachers in systematic studies, it seems clear that there is more to be learned about musical learning by watching the students respond to and transform the materials of musical instruction. The research design included a questionnaire for teachers to assess their own strengths, weaknesses, and positionality in the classroom; introduction of the flow indicators; informal observations of the indicators during their teaching; design and assessment of a teaching plan to facilitate flow experience; and reflection. These were carried out in the USA (unpublished data), Greece (Custodero & Stamou, 2006; Stamou & Custodero, 2007a, 2007b), and Korea (Bae, 2010). Findings from these studies are used to further elucidate the roles of embodiment, culture, and agency in music educational contexts. The ability to observe indicators of flow, and to value and teach music as creative action offers many challenges in terms of trusting students as agents, addressing individuals' pedagogical needs and cultural dispositions within a group framework, and feeling comfortable with the intimate nature of music learning as an emotional, embodied experience.

23.4.1 Bodies in creative musical action

Participants were asked about their own experiences with flow indicators and if they had observed them in students. One teacher's description of observed Extension in her own students involved embodied learning, seemingly out of the vision of their teacher:

> After teaching the 5th graders I often accompany them as they wait for their parents to pick them up. I remember one afternoon out of the corner of my eye, I saw a group of girls continuing to practise the song I taught them working on the choreography waiting for their parents.

Another participant similarly described observing Extension in a peer group circumstance as well as a more private moment, both of which also reflect the agency of imaginative creative action:

> While conducting our 'Peter and the Wolf' program . . . I was able to witness several examples of Extension. During the beginning of the program, the children were required [sic.] to move like the characters in the story. Later on, while working on the visual arts aspect of the activity, many children continued to extend upon the movement activity. As they exited the room following the conclusion of the program, many imitated the character's movements. As I exited the building to return home, I was able to observe one child, already a block away from the school, was still acting out the movement of the little bird.

These two examples show how teachers were reading students by recognizing the behaviours they exhibited as related to what had been 'taught'. The embodiment of musical ideas is so readily observable in children, yet it is more difficult as older children learn how to resist the inclination to express themselves in their bodies and to 'use their words'. Teachers also noted their own embodiment of the conceptual and pedagogical lenses that were introduced:

> We had anticipation, a special kind of anticipation, which we would characterize as anticipation for understanding and strengthening of our students' skills through teacher's comments/observations . . . the student hurries to show in her own way that she understood the teacher's sayings before the teacher finishes her sentence/explanations. We'd say that she is craving, anticipating with enthusiasm and even nervousness the internalization/accumulation of the new information/data.

23.4.2 Juxtaposition of perceived expectations and responsive practice

One of the most interesting findings was revealed in two specific items in the questionnaire, completed on the first day: the first asking what they would like to improve on as a teacher and the second, a narrative description of a memorable teaching moment. This response was typical for the first mentioned question:

> I would like to be more organized, to be more strong/imposing and not to get disappointed that often.

Yet, when describing the memorable moment, the same teacher was less strong and imposing and more vulnerable:

> In a tough classroom with many disputes between the students, I thought of bringing my guitar (even though I am a beginner) and singing a love song. I feel I succeeded because I wasn't afraid to play the guitar, an instrument I do not know very well, and sing a love song in front of the class. The result was unbelievable. The students were attentive and quiet through the whole song; they formed a circle around me holding each other. There was a beautiful sense of peace and harmony that made a real impact on me.

Such differences were common, especially with the Greek teachers, who seemed to have one idea of societal expectations, which was not evidenced in what they felt were memorable moment of teaching. This experience of sharing one's passion for music is what Neumann discussed as the core to meaningful work, and what Nakamura and Csikszentmihalyi (2005) meant when discussing engagement in a profession.

23.4.3 Critically constructing and re-constructing

Several teachers wrote about their own experiences with Extension, and how they were compelled to create a product or, as in the first example, create a synthesis of understanding. In both cases (USA) the effort is self-initiated:

> Just last Monday my English Methods teacher introduced Allen Ginsberg's poem, 'America'. I was thoroughly fascinated by his poetry and his bohemian lifestyle. After class, I spent the entire night looking up his biography and reading every single poem he has ever written. It was such a thrilling experience because I felt like some sort of detective trying to put his life and his art together.

> During one of Dr. B.'s classes I wanted to keep playing a certain piece, but I had to stop so I wouldn't be disruptive. After the class finished I went into my practice room and continued working on that piece for some time. I felt like if I did not work on it I will forget what musical ideas I wanted to include in it.

This agency was not only recognized in their own experience as learners, but also in their teaching. This Greek music teacher's response to the question 'What, if anything, surprised you about the study?' illuminates the importance of teachers as flow-seekers; considering context as different for each class session, each child bringing different experiences on difference days, and how engaging teaching can be when one is awakened to the richness and challenge of noting and understanding student responses:

> The thing that surprised me the most in this study is that I thought of things . . . I didn't apply something I got from someone else, in other words 'the magic pill', which I gave to my students and worked . . . I sat down and thought, I organized ideas I had in my head for a long time now and were floating around and I managed to make them happen . . . and I actually dealt with different situations in a critical way, I was thinking more . . . for example, I did not say: oh, today I was not in a good mood and that's why the lesson wasn't successful or my student is not so focused today so what can you do? Let it be . . . I was judging all the time the situation and the result was of a conscious effort and not an accidental/random result, which however good it is, it is a lot better to design and challenge a result in that way.

23.5 **Closing**

In summary, the call to create in music teaching and learning is a call to reciprocal influence and mutual rewards. We are drawn to music because of its direct correspondences with body motion and vocal expression; its dynamism replicated in our experience of being moved *by* sound and being moved *to* create musical sounds ourselves. The reciprocal influences of our bodies as both why we know and how we know can support and/or inhibit perceptions of high skill and challenge as we engage in musical action. Likewise, our sense of belonging is shaped by creative action, and individual agency is supported and resisted by the collective.

This chapter began with examples from novice and expert musicians whose experiences reflected the call to create. I end with two more descriptions of learning which were written several generations removed, yet bear startling similarities as regards the dynamism of learning and teaching experience. The first is a return to Dewey (1934/1980: p. 36), and it contains allusions to embodiment vs. imitation, the pervasiveness of culture, and the power of diversity to direct action:

> In such [real] experiences, every successive part flows freely, without seam and without unfilled blanks, into what ensues. At the same time there is no sacrifice of the self-identity of the parts. A river, as distinct from a pond, flows. But its flow gives a definiteness and interest to its successive portions greater than exist in the homogeneous portions of the pond. In an experience flow is from something to something. As one part leads into another and as one part carries on what went before, each gains distinctness in itself. The enduring whole is diversified by successive phases that are emphases of its varied colors.

The second reference is from a music teacher-participant in a study on action research and flow experience in Greece (Custodero & Stamou, 2006; Stamou & Custodero, 2007b). It is her reflection on a drawing she made on the first day of a 3-week study to represent herself in a teaching context. This reflection is in response to a question asked the final day: 'Would you change anything about your drawing?':

> There was a river, big and blue, and there were trees around it. Neither do I remember nor can I imagine why I drew this or what I wanted to express. The truth is that I really love blue and water. Finally, though, I think that this drawing really reflects me as a teacher. A big blue river, in the middle of the forest, that gives birth to affluent, smaller rivers, offers dew and life to the little trees and its existence becomes meaningful through them. I would like this picture, at some point in the future, to have a small river, big and many affluent rivers and many big trees.

It seems as though this teacher sees her work as creative and as reciprocally influencing and being influenced by her students. The river spreads in different directions, the tributaries taking form through its origins and their newly constructed paths, and the new growth of the trees signalling changes in the environment—the creative action having ramifications beyond the immediate into the ecological realm of greater mutual influence.

References

Bakker, A.B. (2005). Flow among music teachers and their students: The crossover of peak experiences. *Journal of Vocational Behavior*, **66**, 26–44.

Bae, S.Y. (2010). Designing constructivist piano instruction: Collaborative action ressearch with teachers in Korea. Unpublished doctoral dissertation, Teachers College, Columbia University, New York.

Berenson, B. (1949). *Sketch for a self-portrait*. Toronto, ON: Pantheon.

Blacking, J. (1987). '*A common-sense view of all music*': *Reflections on Percy Grainger's contribution to ethnomusicology and music education*. Cambridge: Cambridge University Press.

Blum, D. (1986). *The art of quartet playing: The Guarneri quartet in conversation with David Blum*. Ithaca, NY: Cornell University Press.

Bruner, J.S. & Sherwood, V. (1976). Peekaboo and the learning of rule structures. In J.S. Bruner, A. Jolly, & K. Sylva (Eds.) *Play—its role in development and evolution.* New York: Basic Books, pp. 277–85.

Campbell, P.S. (1991). *Lessons from the world: A cross-cultural guide to music teaching and learning.* New York: Schirmer Books.

Cobb, E. (1977). *The ecology of imagination in childhood.* New York: Columbia University Press.

Csikszentmihalyi, M. (1975). *Beyond boredom and anxiety.* San Francisco, CA: Jossey-Bass.

Csikszentmihalyi, M. (1978). Intrinsic rewards and emergent motivation. In M.R. Lepper & D. Greene (Eds.) *The hidden costs of reward: New perspectives on the psychology of human motivation.* Hillsdale, NJ: Lawrence Erlbaum Associates, pp. 205–16.

Csikszentmihalyi, M. (1993). *The evolving self.* New York: Harper Collins.

Csikszentmihalyi, M. (1996). *Creativity: Flow and the psychology of discovery and invention.* New York: Harper Collins.

Csikszentmihalyi, M. (1997a). *Finding flow: The psychology of engagement in everyday life.* New York: Basic Books.

Csikszentmihalyi, M. (1997b). Intrinsic motivation and effective teaching: A flow analysis. In J. L. Bess (Ed.) *Teaching well and liking it: Motivating faculty to teach effectively* (pp. 72–89). Baltimore, MD: John Hopkins University Press.

Csikszentmihalyi, M. & Csikszentmihalyi, I.S. (1988). *Optimal experience: Psychological studies of flow in consciousness.* New York: Cambridge University Press.

Custodero, L. (1997). *An observational study of flow experience in young children's music learning.* Unpublished doctoral dissertation, University of Southern California, Los Angeles.

Custodero, L.A. (1998). Observing flow in young children's music learning. *General Music Today*, **12**(1), 21–7.

Custodero, L. (2002). Seeking challenge, finding skill: Flow experience and music education. *Arts Education Policy Review*, **103**(3), 3–9.

Custodero, L.A. (2003). Perspectives of challenge: A longitudinal investigation of challenge in children's music learning. *Arts and Learning*, **19**, 25–53.

Custodero, L.A. (2005a). Being with: The resonant legacy of childhood's creative aesthetic. *Journal of Aesthetic Education*, **39**(2), 36–57.

Custodero, L.A. (2005b). Observable indicators of flow experience: A developmental perspective of musical engagement in young children from infancy to school age. *Music Education Research*, **7**(2), 185–209.

Custodero, L.A. & Stamou, L. (2006). Engaging classrooms: Flow indicators as tools for pedagogical transformation. *Proceedings of the 9th International Conference on Music Perception and Cognition.* Bologna: Bononia University Press.

Dewey, J. (1934/1980). *Art as experience.* New York: Berkley Publishing Group.

Dissanayake, E. (2000). *Art and intimacy: How the arts began.* Seattle, WA: University of Washington Press.

Duckworth, E. (1996). *The having of wonderful ideas and other essays on teaching and learning* (2nd edition). New York: Teachers College Press.

Feldman, D.H. (1994). *Beyond universals in cognitive development* (2nd edition). Norwood, NJ: Ablex.

Feldman, D.H., et al. (2003). Key issues on creativity and development. In K. Sawyer (Ed.) *Creativity and development.* New York: Oxford University Press, pp. 217–42.

Getzels, J.W. & Csikszentmihalyi, M. (1976). *The creative vision: A longitudinal study of problem finding in art.* New York: Wiley.

Gibson, J.J. (1977). The theory of affordances. In R. Shaw & J. Bransford (Eds.), *Perceiving, acting, knowing: Toward an ecological psychology.* Hillsdale, NJ: Erlbaum, pp. 67–82.

Haston, W. (2007). Teacher modeling as an effective teaching strategy. *Music Educators Journal*, **93**(4), 26–30.

Larsson, L. (Ed.) (2002). *Cultures of creativity: The centennial exhibition of the Nobel Prize* (Revised edn.). Canton, MA: Science History Publications.

Malloch, S. & Trevarthen, C. (2009). Musicality: Communicating the vitality and interest of life. In S. Malloch & C. Trevarthen (Eds.) *Communicative musicality: Exploring the basis of human companionship*. London: Oxford University Press, pp. 1–12.

Meyer, L.B. (1973). Explaining music: Essays and explorations. Berkeley: University of California, Press.

Nakamura, J. & Csikszentmihalyi, M. (2005). Engagement in a profession: the case of undergraduate teaching. *Daedalus*, **134**(3), 60–7.

Neumann, A. (2009). *Professing to learn: Creating tenured lives and careers in the American research university*. Baltimore, MD: John Hopkins Press.

Overy, K. (2009). Being together in time: Musical experience and the mirror neuron system. *Music Perception*, **26**(5), 489–504.

Papousek, M. (1996). Intuitive parenting: A hidden source of musical stimulation in infancy. In I. Deliège & J. Sloboda (Eds.) *Musical beginnings: Origins and development of musical competence*. New York: Oxford University Press, pp. 88–112.

Piaget, J. (1962). *Play, dreams, and imitation in childhood*. New York: Norton.

Piaget, J. (1969/2000). *The psychology of the child*. New York: Basic Books.

Rathunde, K. (1988). Optimal experience in the family context. In M. Csikszentmihalyi & I. Csikszentmihalyi (Eds.) *Optimal experience: Psychological studies of flow in consciousness*. New York: Cambridge University Press, pp. 342–63.

Sawyer, K. (1999). Improvised conversations: Music, collaboration, and development. *Psychology of Music*, **27**, 192–216.

Sawyer, K. (Ed.) (2003). *Creativity and development*. New York: Oxford University Press.

Siegler, R.S. & Alibali, M.W. (2004). *Children's thinking*. Mahwah, NJ: Prentice-Hall.

St. John, P.A. (2006). Finding and making meaning: Young children as musical collaborators. *Psychology of Music*, **34**(2), 238–61.

Stamou, L. & Custodero, L.A. (2007a). Flow experience seminars as catalyst for discovery: Greek music teacher identity and pedagogical change. Invited symposium, 5th conference of the Greek Society for Music Education, June, Thessaloniki, Greece.

Stamou, L. & Custodero, L.A. (2007b). Searching for a 'different' music lesson: The study of flow experience in Greece. Paper presented at the conference for the Greek Society of Primary Music Teachers, April, Athens, Greece.

Swanwick, K. & Tillman, J. (1986). The sequence of musical development: A study of children's composition. *British Journal of Music Education*, **3**(3), 305–39.

Tagore, R. (1921). *Thought relics*. New York: Macmillan.

Tagore, R. (1926/1997). A poet's school. In K. Dutta & A. Robinson (Eds.) *Rabindranath Tagore: an anthology*. London: Macmillan, pp. 248–61.

Thompson, D.E. & Russell, J. (2004). The ghost condition: Imitation verses emulation in young children's observational learning. *Developmental Psychology*, **40**(5), 882–9.

Trehub, S.E. & Trainor, L.J. (1993). Listening strategies in infancy: the roots of music and language development. In S. McAdams & E. Bigand (Eds.) *Thinking in sound: The cognitive psychology of human audition*. New York: Oxford University Press, pp. 278–327.

Vygotsky, L. (1978). *Mind in society: The development of higher psychological processes*. Cambridge, MA: Harvard University Press.

Chapter 24

Musical creativity, biography, genre, and learning

Graham F. Welch

24.1 Introduction

A Taiwanese piano graduate from a London conservatoire estimated that she had spent between 16 and 56 hours a week in piano practice from the age of 4 years. By the time that she was 23, this amounted to approximately 27,000 hours practising the piano. By any normal definition of the term, she was an expert pianist.

> Therefore, one could understand the level of frustration that I experienced when I found out that I could not obtain a job in London after graduating from [named London conservatoire] because I had limited transferable improvisatory keyboard skills, such as improvising for a dance company, or becoming a music therapist, improvising for a musical theatre or even jamming in a traditional English pub.
>
> (Hsieh, 2009: p. 25.)

The musical expertise that she had gained embraced the knowledge, skills, and understanding required for a professional standard performance of classical piano music within the Western canon. Yet she was unable to use this knowledge to create music at the piano without recourse to a musical score. Indeed, when she subsequently began a personal research study of how she might develop piano improvisatory skills, she found that she had to learn the piece from musical notation first in order to commit this to memory and then to attempt improvisation. Within this sequence, memorization strategies had to be worked out consciously, drawing on her previous experience of memorizing for concert performance, and included slow practice, 'chunking' (learning small sections), playing through, repeating, separate hand practice, and spreading chords practice. When she then sought to apply these strategies to her initial attempts to engage with improvisation of a jazz piece for the first time, she noted that her learning strategies became more elaborate because the novel style of the music presented greater memorization difficulties.

Her reflections on how to engage with the process of improvisation as a novice echo those reported by Berliner (1994). He distinguishes between improvisation as a 'noun', i.e., improvisations as artistic products that suggest a relationship between the product and its original model, and improvisation as a 'verb', as a dynamic process, a form of real-time composition, which also includes 'precomposed ideas'.

> At one moment, soloists may play radical, precomposed variations on a composition's melody as rehearsed and memorised before the event. The very next moment, they may spontaneously be embellishing the melody's shape, or inventing a new melodic phrase. There is a perpetual cycle between improvised and precomposed components of the artist's knowledge as it pertains to the entire body of construction materials on any and every level of solo invention.
>
> (Berliner, 1994: p. 222.)

It would seem that the Western classical pianist's musical biography had enabled her to gain mastery of a specific group of musical skills that focused on the re-creation and (to a limited extent) interpretation of music from a score within a particular genre, yet—at the same time—had also precluded her from other forms of musical development (such as in how to improvise).

24.2 **Musical creativity and biography**

Musical behaviours do not occur in a vacuum. They are the product of a complex interaction between biological, developmental, and environmental factors over time. Furthermore, the nature of this interaction is not uniform across the species because of relative differences and biases in the ways that our basic neuropsychobiological design and maturational processes interface with, and are shaped by, experience and sociocultural imperatives (Altenmüller, 2004; McPherson, 2006; Welch, 2011). One outcome of this interaction is that *particular* musical behaviours may be more or less developed. Consequently, we are likely to exhibit a musical profile that is both relatively *unique* and peculiar to us as individuals, whilst having some *commonality* with others of a similar sociocultural background, age and experience (Welch, 2000).

The underlying reasons for a particular pattern of musical development in an individual relate to the ways that the human mind makes sense of its sonic world from the moment that hearing is functional from late pre-birth onwards (Lecanuet, 1996; Welch, 2005; Woodward, 2005; Parncutt, 2006). In general terms, Bruner (1996: p. 155 *et seq*), drawing on earlier work with colleagues at Harvard, has suggested that there are three ways by which the world comes to be represented in the human mind: through 1) enaction—a form of knowing from the process of doing, related closely to motor behaviour; 2) imagery—episodic experiences that can serve as prototypes, then archetypes for classes of events as instances of categorical perception; and 3) symbolic representation—constructing and using symbols to represent experience. Similarly, Eraut (2004), drawing on the work of Sternberg et al. (2000) in his research on informal workplace learning, offers a very complementary account to explain how tacit knowledge (knowledge that is not readily articulated) can draw on: 1) episodic memory—specific, personally experience events; 2) semantic memory—explicit verbally-based knowledge that transcends episodes and which can be acquired either through formal teaching, private study, or personal reflection on episodic experience; and 3) procedural memory—specific context-sensitive action-based memory that link personal experience and received knowledge. Eraut suggests that intuitive understanding also has a temporal dimension in which people may assess situations almost instantly through pattern recognition, less rapidly by drawing on their intuitive understanding of the situation, or more deliberately by using reflection and analysis.

Both Bruner's and Eraut's accounts (linking enaction/procedural memory, imagery/episodic memory, symbolic representation/semantic memory) offer complementary perspectives of how the process of creative musical behaviour (such as improvisation) is inextricably interwoven with an individual's musical biography and their resultant musical identity—of how individuals see themselves in relation to musics (plural) as art forms within the culture. Within the field of early childhood music education research, there is now a considerable body of evidence to illustrate how these different forms of representation are evidenced in young children's behaviours and also of how creative children can be in response to their immediate soundscapes. For example, Tafuri (2009) provides longitudinal evidence of enactive representations in how babies between the ages of 2 to 8 months explore pitch and rhythm in their developing mastery of vocal sound, with descending pitches emerging as predominant. De Vries (2005) recounts how his 2-year-old son's vocal improvisations and song acquisition were extended ('scaffolded') through their father–son call-and-response play. By the age of 31 months, the young infant favoured opening his improvisations with a pitch interval of a 5th, which was seen as evidence of his imaginative borrowings from the opening phrases of his two favourite songs 'Twinkle, Twinkle, Little Star' and 'Baa Baa Black Sheep'. Similarly, a variety of self-initiated musical behaviours have been observed in children and young people with profound and multiple learning difficulties (PMLD)—often perceived to be the most developmentally restricted group within the special educational needs disability spectrum—as well as musical behaviours prompted through interaction with others (Welch et al., 2009). In contrast, Pramling (2009) reports how two 5-year-olds were able to represent their musical experience in the form of a series of different-shaped wooden building blocks, with the 'architecture' of an improvised melody using three different sounds that were symbolized by the constructed physical pattern of the blocks. He also noted that his participant children used onomatopoeia to mimic vocally the qualities of sounds that they had heard previously from instruments when singing their improvised melodies. These examples, drawn from Italy, Australia, England, and Sweden respectively, are indicative of how playful exploration in music is a common characteristic of childhood.

This early, natural propensity for musical creativity—related to both of Berliner's conceptualizations of improvisation as a noun and a verb—continues to be shaped by experiences in the home, school, and wider community (such as with peers) towards particular musical behaviours that have cultural value and that tend to predominate within these sociocultural settings. For example, the relative informality of peer-led adolescent music-making, such as encapsulated by the 'garage band' scene of the 1970s and 1980s in which groups of young people got together to make and rehearse music, sometimes creating new styles out of their experimentation that were taken up by other young people (cf. McLucas, 2010), is evidence of young people 'at play' in their music-making rather than 'at work' (cf. Green, 2008: p. 170)—in the sense of being engaged in a musical activity that allows them to explore, try out ideas, and solve musical problems in a collegial and 'fun' context. Indeed, it has been argued that the digitalization and digital distribution of music has significantly increased young people's opportunities for musical creativity and 'mixed up the roles of the artist-producer and the audience-consumer' (Väkevä, 2010: p. 61).

24.3 Opportunities and limitations for musical creativity in school

However, such learner-centred activity may be in stark contrast to the very limited *opportunities* for musical creation found in the same adolescents' secondary schools. The Office for Standards in Education (Ofsted)—the statutory body responsible for overseeing the quality of education in English schools—continues, for example, to express concern about the lack of opportunities for pupils to foster their musical imagination, to 'hear' and create music in their heads (Ofsted, 2009):

> Generally, the schools missed opportunities to develop pupils' creativity in performing activities and in extracurricular ensembles through, for example, improvising and considering questions of interpretation.

(Ofsted, 2009: p. 44.)

This is despite 'creativity' being one of five key concepts that explicitly frame the design of the statutory English National Curriculum for music for children and young people up to the age of 14 (QCA, 2007). Although the evidence is that the propensity to be creative is part of our human design, it would seem that some formal educational settings find the enabling of this core capability difficult to support.

Yet music is a central feature of many people's leisure activities (e.g. Tarrant, et al., 2002; ONS, 2004). For example, the British Music Rights Survey (2008) surveyed the musical experiences and behaviour of 773 young people aged 14–25+ years. They found that music 'is an absolutely integral part of young people's lives', with 14–17-year-olds listening to music over 6 hours per day, either in the background or as the main focus of their attention. Ninety-two per cent of respondents in this age group had their own MP3 player. When asked what three items they would take with them to a desert island, music was selected most often by all age groups. Their personal music collection was reported to be 'their most treasured possession' (British Music Rights Survey, 2008: p. 9). Young people have an enormous repertoire of musical experience on which to draw for the creation of music if the opportunity allows. However, in England, in contrast to their engagement with music outside school settings, customarily only 7–8% (on average) of young people over the past 10 years have continued to study music formally within the secondary school curriculum beyond the age of 14 years when the subject becomes optional rather than compulsory, in part at least because of a mismatch for the majority between what is being offered in school music and their own musical identities and priorities (Saunders, 2008), such as their ability to create music.

24.4 Biases in teachers' musical biography and creativity

The relative paucity of creative opportunities in some schools is likely to be closely linked to the musical biographies of the music teachers, who predominantly have a Western classical music background. A study of beginning secondary school music teachers in England, for example, found that relatively few had experience of jazz, popular, traditional or non-Western musics (Hargreaves & Welch, 2003; Welch et al., 2011). Similarly, a related study of final year music undergraduates found that only 11% had experience of performing in jazz ensembles or big bands and only 6% had been members of pop, rock, or soul groups (Purves et al., 2005). These undergraduate and postgraduate experiences in Western classical music will have been biased towards activities that focused on the re-creation of notated scores for performance (unless they were organists, guitarist or composers), rather than activities that were more explicitly creative, such as are characteristic in jazz improvisation, or the many opportunities for popular music creation that arise when young people are in informal group settings.

When these various trends in contemporary music education and musical engagement are set alongside each other, a picture emerges of an English education system in which the types of music with which young people identify (both as musical genres and in relation to their inherently creative musical practices) are often under-represented. Arguably, this is likely to be a key reason why relatively few young people opt to study music formally when it becomes non-compulsory at age fourteen, fewer study music in school at advanced level (ages 16–18) and even fewer take music degrees on leaving school (Welch et al., 2011). Overall, certain kinds of music and associated music practices tend to dominate the formal music education landscape in a cyclical fashion (as portrayed in Figure 24.1).

There is also a general bias in the UK towards Higher Education (HE) study and awards that are focused on Western classical (high art) music (Welch, 2008). This is in marked contrast to the evidence that the vast majority of performing musicians (87%) find employment in other musics, such as pop, rock, country, folk, jazz, and world (Rogers/Youth Music, 2002: p. 8), although with a caveat that such employment is still likely to be biased, at least initially, towards the use of a nota-tion-based musical skill set for those with a solely Western classical music background. A similar bias is evident with regard to leisure interests and music: a 2005/06 national UK Government survey reported that people were three times more likely to attend a live musical event of popular

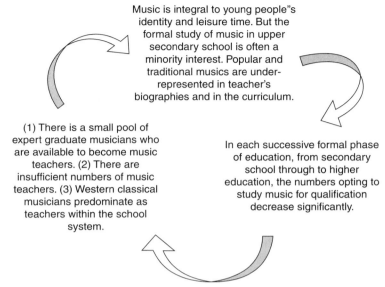

Music is integral to young people"s identity and leisure time. But the formal study of music in upper secondary school is often a minority interest. Popular and traditional musics are under-represented in teacher's biographies and in the curriculum.

(1) There is a small pool of expert graduate musicians who are available to become music teachers. (2) There are insufficient numbers of music teachers. (3) Western classical musicians predominate as teachers within the school system.

In each successive formal phase of education, from secondary school through to higher education, the numbers opting to study music for qualification decrease significantly.

Fig. 24.1 The cycle of music education in England that is characterized by the persistence of a relative insufficiency in the supply of appropriately qualified music teachers and a relative over-representation of Western classical educated musicians in schools within those recruited. Reproduced from Welch, G.F. (2008). Teaching and Learning Music in Higher Education: A Discussion Paper. Proceedings. ESRC TLRP International Symposium on Teaching, Learning and Assessment, Invited speaker, Hong Kong Institute of Education, Hong Kong, China. 22-24 April. With permission from the TLRP.

music or jazz compared to classical music or opera performances (ONS, 2008).[1] Younger respondents (aged 16–24 years) tended to avoid classical and opera events, whereas these types of music were more popular by a factor of 3 or 4:1 with older respondents (aged 45 years and older).

It is not surprising, therefore, that a dominant experiential bias towards re-creative musical practices in the biographies of secondary school music teachers is reflected in their views on pupils' musical creativity. Research suggests that teachers with more experience of different musical styles and composing activities are likely to be more aware of the different ways that students can approach a creative task in the curriculum, such as a composition assignment (Odena & Welch, 2009). Those with limited experience tend to have a more limited view of what is possible.

24.5 Differences between musical genres in the biography of creativity

Theories of expertise and expert performance across diverse learning domains—such as those of Sosniak (1990), Manturzewska (1990), and Ericsson and Smith (1991)—offer useful insights into the development of the professional musician. The research suggests that extended expertise is the result of deliberate, goal-directed practice and allied monitoring skills (Ericsson, 2006), embracing

[1] The survey for the Department of Culture, Media and Sport 'Taking Part: the National Survey of Culture, Leisure and Sport' reported that 24% of respondents aged 16 years plus had attended a live popular music event and 6% a live jazz event, compared to 8% attending classical music and 4% opera.

aural, cognitive, technical, musicianship, performance, learning, and life skills (e.g. Hallam, 2005), often in the context of extrinsic motivation by others (cf. 'in the shadow' of experts—Gruber et al., 2008: p. 254).

Nevertheless, much of this evidence has arisen from studies concerning the development of individual Western classical musicians. Less has been reported in the social science literature about the musical expertise development of popular musicians, not least because musical cultures that are other-than-classical have received less attention in the music psychology literature (Sloboda, 2000). However, the recent establishment of a number of innovative undergraduate degrees in the UK that specialize in other-than-classical genres such as jazz, popular, and traditional music are seen to pose new challenges for formal HE music education where Western classical music has predominated (e.g. Lebler, 2007).

Within the few existing studies in the learning literature comparing musical genres prior to the past 5 years, classical musicians are reported to focus more on solitary practice, mastery of technical requirements, and acquiring new pieces. In contrast, jazz musicians are seen as likely to try to improve their performance through communal as well as solitary practice, observation of jam sessions, and active listening of other musicians (Gruber et al., 2004). A Norwegian study, for example, found that 85% of jazz/rock/pop students, but only 36% of Western classical students, practised with other students in a group each week (Jørgensen, 1998). In terms of their musical biographies, Degner et al. (2003) reported that jazz guitarists usually started their instrumental training relatively late compared to their Western classical music peers and frequently lacked some form of institutional support at the beginning of their studies.

Recently, the comparison of music learning in different musical genres was the focus for the *Investigating Musical Performance (IMP): Comparative Studies in Advanced Musical Learning* research project (2006–2008). The project was devised to investigate how aspiring and established professional musicians deepen and develop their learning about performance in undergraduate, postgraduate and wider music community contexts. Funded by the UK Government as part of the Economic and Social Research Council's Teaching and Learning Research Programme (TLRP),[2] the IMP project grew out of another TLRP project *Learning to Perform*, a longitudinal study of undergraduate musicians at the Royal College of Music (e.g. Mills & Burt, 2006). IMP sought to provide comparative insights into aspects of higher (and post-higher) education teaching and learning in music across four musical genres (Western classical, jazz, popular, and Scottish traditional music).

An overview of some of the main IMP research findings indicates that learning and teaching in HE music (and beyond) are subject to many of the tensions outlined earlier in this chapter. For example, the musical biographies of IMP participants (n=244, aged 18–62 years, mean 25 years 9 months) revealed distinctive genre differences in the developmental profiles between classical and other-than-classical musicians (jazz, popular, Scottish traditional).[3] Western classical performers

---

[2] The *Investigating Musical Performance (IMP): Comparative Studies in Advanced Music Learning* research project was funded by the UK Government's Economic and Social Research Council as part of its Teaching and Learning Research Programme under award RES-139-25-0101. The award holders were Welch, Duffy, Potter, and Whyton, with data gathering based in London, Glasgow, York and Leeds. The 2-year research project (2006–2008) commenced in April 2006 and was completed in July 2008. See http://www.tlrp.org/proj/Welch.html.

[3] Detailed statistical analyses of participants' questionnaire responses revealed that these three 'other-than-classical' genres could be treated as having similar characteristics in their responses in contrast to their Western classical peers. Hence the discussion above that focuses on these two main groupings, Western classical and other-than-classical.

began their first study instrument earlier (mean age 9.2 years) and were more influenced musically by parents, instrumental or vocal teachers and membership of formal groups, such as county orchestral ensembles. In contrast, other-than-classical musicians tended to begin their engagement with instrumental learning several years later (approaching adolescence at the age of 12 years), often through an encounter (real or virtual) with the music of a well-known performer (Creech et al., 2008). Other-than-classical musicians were also influenced by peers and by membership of informal music groups in their choice of musical instrument and subsequent development. For example, when asked to explain early formative influences, a jazz drummer replied:

> I've sort of jumped from person to person; I've jumped from styles of music. Basically, I've learned the drums off a friend who was better than me, so I just watched him. So that, at the time, was probably my biggest influence. Now, obviously, there are more big named people that I look up to, just by listening to their records. But that's changed, because at first I wanted to play pop and rock music. I still like that music, but now, as a player, I want to play jazz music.

Although the other-than-classical musicians tended to begin their instrumental studies at a significantly later age, nevertheless there is a sense that they undergo an accelerated form of musical development, related to their strong emotional commitment to their instrument and its music. An adult jazz saxophonist recounted the strength of his youthful motivation:

> ... when I was an adolescent, I remember having some very difficult conversations with my father who really thought I'd had my chance [because] I had piano lessons when I was younger [and gave up] and he ... yeah, I remember when I wanted to buy a saxophone, he said 'Well, if you want to buy a saxophone, you have to do that yourself, because you know, you've had your chance of playing music'. And I distinctly remember taking a job in a garage ... so I'd serve petrol at the garage for a pound an hour with a view to buy one saxophone after like a year or so.

This motivation to learn is reflected in other-than-classical musicians gaining sufficient performance expertise to be accepted for entry for undergraduate music studies alongside their Western classical music peers by the age of 18, despite having had a shorter time on average to gain this level of performance proficiency.

Genre group membership factors were also evidenced in the different ways that musicians used their time each week across different types of musical activities. The other-than-classical musicians spent much more time across the week in listening to their own music, playing for fun, either alone or with others, using mental rehearsal as a learning technique, and acquiring general musical knowledge. They also enjoyed networking and particularly valued musical memorization and improvisation. They regarded the ability to 'sight read' (playing from musical notation at first sight) as unimportant (Papageorgi et al., 2010). This is not surprising if we compare the conventions of Western classical music with those of popular, jazz, and folk music. A Scottish traditional singer makes this point in an interview about her musical upbringing:

> Well I think, people like [names artist], they've been brought up and had these songs passed down generations and generations; they've been brought up, so that's all, that's what they know. But it would be different for a classical musician rather than a traditional musician. We don't have training as such, you know, obviously we get taught how to play the actual instrument, but we don't get taught how to play an actual tune or how to sing a song. I don't know, it's just your interpretation of how to do it.

Other-than-classical musicians rely more heavily on skills such as improvisation, memorization and playing 'by ear', whilst classical music performance is more associated with the reading of notation and mastering the Western musical canon. Classical musicians reported that it was particularly important to practise alone and favoured notation-based music-making, although some recognized that their musical biography might need some broadening if the possibility arose. For example, when asked to describe himself compared to his 'ideal' musician, a trumpeter brought up in the Western classical tradition said:

> I'm not rounded enough, I would say . . . I've only had classical in my experience before I came here, so you know, now I'm branching out that now I'm here I do big band, wind band, and things like that, I play in brass bands now. I've only started broadening out since I arrived here, whereas up to now it would just have been all youth orchestras, youth wind bands, no brass bands, no jazz, although you kind of start to improve those aspects, I think I'm still lacking still in those. Everything except classical I'm still lacking.

Furthermore, an examination of the data on enjoyment and self-regulation in music learning indicated that popular, jazz, and Scottish folk musicians reported experiencing more pleasure in musical activities than their classical counterparts. This finding resonates with comments from Green's (2001) study in which she contrasts the 'fun' and 'enjoyment' described by her informants in their accounts of learning popular music with the 'alienation' that many experienced when receiving classical music tuition (pp. 134–5). This may be a key reason why many popular, jazz, and folk musicians continued to pursue their own musical interests in a more autonomous fashion outside of the constraints of scheduled educational timetables (de Bézenac & Swindells, 2009).

Whilst all musicians, irrespective of genre, tended to listen to music outside their preferred performance field, Western classical musicians spent much less time than their other-than-classical peers in listening to music of their own performance genre. This could be interpreted as evidence of a lack of prioritization by the former towards listening as a means of acquiring competence in instrumental playing skills within their notation-bound field of Western classical music. In contrast, within-genre listening is interwoven in the predominantly oral/aural traditions of popular, jazz and traditional folk music (as exampled by the Scottish traditional singer's quote above) in order to ensure that their 'entire body of construction materials' (Berliner, 1994: p. 222) is firmly grounded in appropriate stylistic content and processes.

Furthermore, when individual Western classical musicians discussed the playing of established artists, their comments tended to focus on particular technical features of the individual's performance behaviours. Other-than-classical musicians were more likely to compare themselves with peers or with the complete individual style of a 'great' performer—a category of reference that was not mentioned by any Western classical participant. This personalized, holistic view may explain why other-than-classical undergraduate musicians tended to have comparatively lower musical self-efficacy ratings and lower perceived levels of expertise, i.e., they focused on a perceived 'gap' between their own current abilities and those of their peers or known 'great' performers, whose perceived artistry is demonstrated within genres for which creativity is seen as central to the musical act (Welch et al., 2008).

Neurological studies indicate that creativity is likely to function best in an absence of threat, i.e., the neural basis of creativity is believed to be associated with frontal lobe function linked to the limbic system—such as activity within the hippocampal system (Pribram, 1999) and raised levels of dopamine (Flaherty, 2005). High negative stress, therefore, is inimical to creativity. However, performance anxiety is unevenly distributed across musical genres and practices and can interfere with creative behaviour. Western classical musicians, for example, report higher performance anxiety levels than their other-than-musical peers. This is related to the formers' sense of striving for technical excellence, as well as the high importance that they give to solo performance (Papageorgi, 2008). Nevertheless, for all musicians, performance anxiety is perceived to be less when playing in a group—a common performance context for other-than-classical musicians.

Concerning the learning environment and its support for creative practices, different spaces of learning were reported to exist within the observed higher education music environment, particularly pedagogical, and informal space. With *pedagogical* spaces, the teaching style of the teacher was observed to have a large part to play in students' individual learning-scapes. If a tutor allowed the student to develop according to their needs and desires, there were fewer perceived boundaries or restrictions placed on the learning map. Concerning *informal* spaces, within the course design there was potential for extant and predominant methods of learning other-than-classical music by ear and in differing social situations, such as through group work. Students stated that this allowed them the most chance to listen to their fellow students playing, to be creative in arranging music and playing as a group. Students were also part of informal learning networks that took place outside of the institution, such as for concerts, and in learning from media (Morton et al., submitted).

With regards their own experiences of teaching, irrespective of genre, undergraduate music students engaged with teaching in ways that were creative and thoughtful, and they clearly derived pleasure and personal benefit from their own teaching opportunities. Echoing Eraut's (2004) model, they were able to bring together episodic, semantic, and procedural memories as the basis for their own teaching. They tended to rely on the memories of their own learning and on models of previous or current teachers to inform their teaching, but were unaware of training opportunities and recent pedagogical literature. They saw themselves as developing primarily through increased experience. Modelling and motivation were mentioned as important aspects of teaching; although in some cases students found it difficult to separate the needs of the pupil from their own. In general, students found that teaching had increased their confidence and given them other benefits, including improved understanding of their playing or singing, greater awareness of what was happening in their own lessons, and an increased ability to cope with the demands of rehearsal and performance (Haddon, 2009).

24.6 **Conclusions**

A pattern begins to emerge from this research evidence: certain types of music (exampled here by jazz, popular, and traditional) are more likely to be practised and performed within a group, where performance anxiety levels are lower, perceived enjoyment is higher and, in particular, creativity (such as exploration, working out, improvisation, adaptation) is a core component and interwoven in the expected performance practices of the particular musical genres. Overall, the IMP and related findings suggest that the type of music being studied, practised, and performed has an effect on learning and the development of creativity. This perspective is in accordance with findings from other higher education research outside the field of music. The contextual specificity of learning (Entwistle, 2007) is related to the 'ways of thinking and practising' within a subject area (McCune & Hounsell, 2005). Each subject (in this case, each musical genre) has an inner logic that relates to its pedagogy and the ways of thinking and practising in that area (also referred to as 'signature pedagogies'—see Shulman, 2005). Although there are supra-genre and cross-institutional similarities in the development of skilled musicians that transcend the particular and the local—such as a deep commitment to music, sustained instrumental or vocal practice, and the overall importance of music in individual self-identity—creativity is not equally nurtured. This is because, within each genre, teaching and learning are commonly focused on the communal maintenance of particular practices and understandings that are regarded as important and central to that particular musical community. Only where creativity is explicitly part of the genre culture will it be regarded as important, nurtured, and sustained.

Beyond undergraduate studies, for example, the work of portfolio career musicians continues to interweave personal and professional experiences with the cultural expectations inherent in the practices of their chosen musical genre (in line with Eraut's (2004) research on workplace learning). Similarly, these career experiences (and expectations) are coded into the music curricula content of educational institutions. The specific coding for 'creativity' depends on the degree to which the informal learning practices of the wider musical genre community (such as reported by Scottish traditional, jazz, and popular music participants) are seen as requiring pedagogical space within the timetable. This, in turn, often relates to the professional biographies of the individual HE tutors who, themselves, represent a genre-specific community of practice, with membership fostered since they first began to engage with their chosen instrument.

In terms of opportunities for the development of creativity in their core musical behaviours, other-than-classical musics are very much rooted in a sense of the collective, with frequent structured and unstructured opportunities for blurring the boundaries between formal and informal learning. Although all music undergraduates have solo tuition and opportunities to perform as soloists as part of their studies, the nature of the other-than-classical musics reported above (jazz, Scottish traditional, popular) also prioritize group activity, with the small ensemble being a central characteristic of the ways that such music is practised and performed, much more so than for Western classical musicians (Figure 24.2). This group bias feeds through to the students' weekly timetable where opportunities for small group practice and rehearsal are also important and part of the formal expectation of the informal use of time—whilst also being welcomed by the students themselves.

Although there is evidence of key differences in the teaching and learning cultures between musical genres and also that 'difference' is a comparative characteristic of particular group identity and related musical practices, this does not necessarily imply that education should accept and

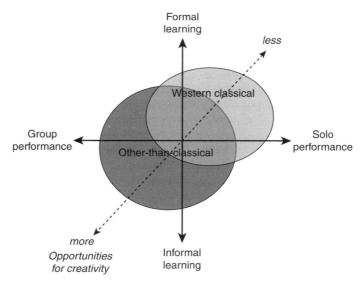

Fig. 24.2 Mapping the musical genre-biased opportunities for the development of creativity in relation to two continua: formal/informal musical learning and the relative bias towards group/solo practice and performance.

reify these, especially if this means that opportunities for creative musical behaviours continue to be unevenly available. It is necessary to explore how music curricula can both engage with, yet also transcend, any genre-specific concerns and issues.

This chapter began with a report of a classical pianist who regarded her many thousands of hours of sustained musical experience as inadequate preparation for any subsequent activity that required an ability to improvise, to be 'at play' with her music rather than 'at work' (cf. Green, 2008). Nevertheless, as a result of reflecting on her experiences and subsequent research, she discovered that improvisation could be seen as part of a core creative skill set for all student musicians (undergraduate and postgraduate), not just for some, such as those studying jazz (Hsieh, 2009). The recent research rehearsed above indicates that, customarily, improvisation skills are often most likely to be learned and developed successfully within group settings, through a process of exploration, imitation, and play, by seeking shared 'solutions' to musical 'problems' and as part of a collective with a common goal. Unfortunately, this pianist's biography was characteristically biased towards solo performance learning of the Western canon and embraced few opportunities to take a more exploratory and creative role to the music being studied. It was also a solitary existence. Yet this need not be the case because the practice of creativity in music is socially constructed, a cultural artefact and—as such—open to change and transformation if those who have and take responsibility for the music education of others are open to an alternative view.

In summary, although 'creativity can be viewed as a fundamental behavioural trait that is grounded in the basic biology of the brain' (Greenberg, 2004: p. 310), the research suggests that there continues to be insufficient opportunity within our educational systems for this aspect of our musical birthright to be fostered and celebrated for everyone. Opportunities for creation as well as re-creation should have equal places in the lives of all musicians, irrespective of their 'home' genre. Arguably, through such a holistic musical education they will be better placed to fulfil their individual potential, to lead more successful musical lives and to enrich and extend the musical cultures of which they are part.

References

Altenmüller, E.O. (2004). Music in your head. *Scientific American,* **14**(1), 24–31.

Berliner, P.F. (1994). *Thinking in Jazz*. Chicago, IL: University of Chicago Press.

British Music Rights Survey (2008). *Music Experience and Behaviour in Young People*. Hatfield: University of Hertfordshire.

Bruner, J. (1996). *The culture of education*. Cambridge, MA: Harvard University Press.

Creech, A., Papageorgi, I., Duffy, C., Morton, F., Haddon, L., Potter, J., *et al.* (2008). Investigating musical performance: commonality and diversity among classical and non-classical musicians. *Music Education Research*, **10**(2), 215–34.

De Bézenac, C., & Swindells, R. (2009). No pain, no gain? Motivation and self-regulation in music learning. *International Journal of Education and the Arts*, **10**(16). Available at: http://www.ijea.org/v10n16/ (accessed 7 March 2010).

Degner, S., Lehmann, A.C., & Gruber, H. (2003). Expert learning in the domain of jazz guitar music. In R. Kopiez, A.C. Lehmann, I. Wolther, & C. Wolf (Eds.), *Proceedings of the 5th Triennial ESCOM Conference*. Hannover: University of Music and Drama, pp. 384–8.

De Vries, P. (2005). Lessons from home: Scaffolding vocal improvisation and song acquisition with a 2-year-old. *Early Childhood Education Journal*, **32**(5), 307–12.

Entwistle, N. (2007). Research into student learning and university teaching. In: N.J. Entwistle (Ed). *Student learning and university teaching* (British Journal of Educational Psychology Monograph Series II: Psychological Aspects of Education – Current Trends). Leicester: British Psychological Society, pp. 1–18.

Eraut, M. (2004). Transfer of knowledge between education and workplace settings. In H. Rainbird, A. Fuller, & H. Munro (Eds.), *Workplace learning in context*. London: Routledge, pp. 201–21.

Ericsson, K.A. (2006). The influence of experience and deliberate practice on the development of superior expert performance. In K.A. Ericsson, N. Charness, P.J. Feltovitch, & R.R. Hoffman (Eds.), *The Cambridge Handbook of Expertise and Expert Performance*. Cambridge: Cambridge University Press, pp. 683–703.

Ericsson, K.A., & Smith, J. (1991). *Toward a general theory of expertise*. New York: Cambridge University Press.

Flaherty, A.W. (2005). Frontotemporal and dopaminergic control of idea generation and creative drive. *Journal of Comparative Neurology*, **493**(1), 147–53.

Green, L. (2001). *How Popular Musicians Learn*. Farnham: Ashgate Press.

Green, L. (2008). *Music, Informal Learning and the School: A New Classroom Pedagogy*. Farnham: Ashgate Press.

Greenberg, N. (2004). The Beast at Play: The Neuroethology of Creativity. In R.L. Clements & L. Fiorentino (Eds.) *The Child's Right to Play: A Global Approach*. Westpost, CT: Praeger Publishers, pp. 309–27.

Gruber, H., Degner, S., & Lehmann, A.C. (2004). Why do some commit themselves in deliberate practice for many years—and so many do not? Understanding the development of professionalism in music. In M. Radovan, & N. Dordevi (Eds.), *Current issues in adult learning and motivation*. Ljubljana: Slovenian Institute for Adult Education, pp. 222–35.

Gruber, H., Lehtinen, E., Palonen, T., & Degner, S. (2008). Persons in the shadow: Assessing the social context of high abilities. *Psychology Science Quarterly*, **50**, 237–58.

Haddon, E. (2009). Instrumental and vocal teaching: how do music students learn to teach? *British Journal of Music Education*, **26**(1), 57–70.

Hallam, S. (2005). *Enhancing motivation and learning throughout the lifespan*. London: Institute of Education.

Hargreaves, D.J. & Welch, G.F. (2003). *Effective teaching in secondary school music: teacher and pupil identities*. ESRC End of Award Report, Award R000223751.

Hsieh, S.C. (2009). Cognition and Musical Improvisation in Individual and Group Contexts. Unpublished PhD Thesis. London: Institute of Education.

Jørgensen, H. (1998). *Tid til øving? Studentenes bruk av tid til øving ved Norges musikkhøgskole. 2. Del.* [Time for practising? Students' use of time for instrumental practising at the Norwegian State Academy of Music. 2. Part]. Oslo: Norges musikkhøgskole, NMH-publikasjoner [cited in Jørgensen, H. (2009). *Research into Higher Music Education*. Oslo: Novus.]

Lebler, D. (2007). Student-as-master? Reflections on a learning innovation in popular music pedagogy. *International Journal of Music Education*, **25**(3), 205–21.

Lecanuet, J.-P. (1996). Prenatal auditory experience. In I. Deliège & J.A. Sloboda (Eds.) *Musical beginnings*. New York: Oxford University Press, pp. 3–34.

Manturzewska, M. (1990). A biographical study of the life-span development of professional musicians. *Psychology of Music*, **18**(2), 112–39.

McCune, V. & Hounsell, D.J. (2005). The development of students' ways of thinking and practising in three final-year biology courses. *Higher Education*, **49**, 255–89.

McLucas, A.D. (2010). *The Musical Ear: Oral Tradition in the USA*. Farnham: Ashgate Press.

McPherson, G. (Ed.) (2006). *The Child as Musician*. New York: Oxford University Press.

Mills, J. & Burt, R. (2006). Taking the plunge: the hopes and fears of students as they begin music college. *British Journal of Music Education*, **23** (1), 51–73. See also: http://www.tlrp.org/proj/phase111/L2P.htm.

Morton, F., Duffy, F., Haddon, E., Potter, J., De Bézenac, C., Bates, A., *et al.* (submitted). Spaces of learning and the place of the conservatoire in Scottish music: a case study of the Royal Scottish Academy of Music and Drama.

Odena, O. & Welch, G.F. (2009). A generative model of teachers' thinking on musical creativity. *Psychology of Music*, **37**(4), 416–42.

Office for Standards in Education [Ofsted]. (2009). *Making more of music*. London: Ofsted.

ONS [Office for National Statistics]. (2004). *Social Trends. 34*. Cardiff: Office for National Statistics.

ONS [Office for National Statistics] (2008). *Social Trends. 38*. Basingstoke, UK: Palgrave Macmillan.

Papageorgi, I. (2008). Investigating musical performance: Performance anxiety across musical genres. *TLRP: Teaching and Learning Research Briefing* **57**.

Papageorgi, I., Creech, A., Haddon, E., Morton, F., De Bézenac, C., Himonides, E., *et al.* (2010). Perceptions and predictions of expertise in advanced musical learners. *Psychology of Music*, **38**, 31–66.

Parncutt, R. (2006). Prenatal development. In G. McPherson (Ed.) *The child as musician* (pp. 1–31). New York: Oxford University Press.

Pramling, N. (2009). External representation and the architecture of music: Children inventing and speaking about notations. *British Journal of Music Education*, **26**(3), 273–91.

Pribram, K. (1999). Brain and the creative act. In M.A. Runco, & S.R. Pritzker (Eds.) *Encyclopedia of Creativity*. New York: Academic Press, pp. 213–17.

Purves, R., Marshall, N.A., Hargreaves, D.J., & Welch, G.F. (2005). Teaching as a career? Perspectives from undergraduate musicians in England. *Bulletin of the Council for Research in Music Education*, **163**, 35–42.

Qualifications and Curriculum Authority [QCA]. (2007). *Music. Programme of study for key stage 3 and attainment target*. London: QCA.

Rogers, R./Youth Music (2002). *Creating a land with music*. London: Youth Music.

Saunders, J. (2008). Pupils and their engagement in secondary school music. Unpublished PhD Thesis, Institute of Education, London.

Shulman, L.S. (2005). Signature pedagogies in the professions. *Daedalus*, **134**(3), 52–9.

Sloboda, J.A. (2000). Individual differences in music performance. *Trends in Cognitive Sciences*, **4**(10), 397–403.

Sosniak, L.A. (1990). The tortoise and the hare and the development of talent. In M.J.A. Howe (Ed.), *Encouraging the development of exceptional skills and talents*. Leicester: British Psychological Society, pp. 149–64.

Sternberg, R.J., Forsyth, G.B., Hedlund, J., Horvath, J.A., Wagner, R.K., Williams, W.M., *et al.* (2000). *Practical Intelligence in Everyday Life*. New York: Cambridge University Press.

Tafuri, J. (2009). *Infant Musicality*. Farnham: Ashgate Press.

Tarrant, M., North, A.C., & Hargreaves, D.J. (2002). Youth identity and music. In A.R. MacDonald, D.J. Hargreaves, & D. Miell, (Eds.), *Musical Identities*. New York: Oxford University Press, pp. 134–50.

Väkevä, L. (2010). Garage band or GarageBand®? Remixing musical futures. *British Journal of Music Education*, **27**(1), 59–70.

Welch, G.F. (2000). The ontogenesis of musical behaviour: A sociological perspective. *Research Studies in Music Education*, **14**, 1–13.

Welch, G.F. (2005). Singing as communication. In D. Miell, R. MacDonald & D. Hargreaves (Eds.), *Musical Communication*. New York: Oxford University Press, pp. 239–59.

Welch, G.F. (2008). *Teaching and Learning Music in Higher Education: A Discussion Paper. Proceedings. ESRC TLRP International Symposium on Teaching, Learning and Assessment*, Invited speaker, Hong Kong Institute of Education, Hong Kong, China. 22–24 April.

Welch, G.F. (2011). Culture and gender in a cathedral music context: An activity theory exploration. In M. Barrett (Ed.), *A Cultural Psychology of Music Education*. New York: Oxford University Press, (pp. 225-258).

Welch, G.F., Papageorgi, I., Haddon, E., Creech, A., Morton, F., de Bézenac, C., *et al.* (2008). Musical genre and gender as factors in Higher Education learning in music. *Research Papers in Education*, **23**(2), 203–17.

Welch, G.F., Ockelford, A., Carter, F-C., Zimmermann, S-A., & Himonides, E. (2009). 'Sounds of Intent': mapping musical behaviour and development in children and young people with complex needs. *Psychology of Music*, **37**(3), 348–70.

Welch, G.F., Purves, R., Hargreaves, D., & Marshall, N. (2011). Early career challenges in secondary school music teaching. *British Educational Research Journal*, **37**(2), 285–315.

Woodward, S.C. (2005). Critical matters in early childhood music education. In D. J. Elliott (Ed.), *Praxial Music Education*. New York: Oxford University Press, pp. 249–66.

Chapter 25

Music, music therapy, and schizophrenia

Denise Grocke and David J. Castle

This chapter looks at the association between music and schizophrenia, interrogating the phenomenon of musical hallucinations ('hearing' music when there is no music to be heard); investigating links between schizophrenia and musical creativity; and finally outlining how music and music therapy in particular might assist people with schizophrenia deal more effectively with their psychotic symptoms and enhance their socialization. But first, we provide a brief description of what schizophrenia is: the interested reader is referred to Castle and Buckley (2008) for further details.

25.1 The nature of schizophrenia

Schizophrenia is a complex disease which is still ill-understood in terms of aetiology, with genetic and various environmental factors playing a part. It manifests with certain symptoms and behaviours which are outlined below. The illness shows a variable longitudinal course, but is all too often associated with restriction of social and vocational functioning. The core symptoms and behaviours are generally considered to be:

(a) Positive symptoms: these include delusions and hallucinations. *Delusions* are fixed false beliefs held by the individual with unshakeable tenacity, and which may be very distressing for the individual. The content may include persecution, grandiosity, and referential ideas such that normal events are interpreted with reference to the individual (e.g. obtaining special meaning from conversations, songs on the radio, or television programmes). Delusional content can also be quite bizarre, such as believing that one's thoughts are being removed from one's mind by an intergalactic machine, or that one's actions are being controlled by some external force, leaving one feeling like a robot or a puppet. *Hallucinations* are abnormal perceptions that can affect any of the sensory modalities, but which are mostly auditory ('hearing things') or visual ('seeing things'). Auditory hallucinations are often of derogatory voices criticizing individuals or commenting on their actions. Musical hallucinations are relatively rare in schizophrenia (see below).

(b) Negative symptoms are characterized by apathetic social withdrawal, avolition, lack of engagement with others, paucity of thought (manifested by reduced spontaneous speech and short unembellished answers to direct questioning), and restriction of affect (affect being the external expression of internal emotion: severely restricted affect is sometimes referred to as 'blunted'). Negative symptoms have a profound impact on the individual's ability to socialize and integrate into society. Cognitive dysfunction, notably in some critical abilities such as verbal fluency, is also impaired in many people with schizophrenia, and adds to the burden they carry.

(c) Finally, many people with schizophrenia suffer from disorganization symptoms, which affect both speech (muddled, disjointed thinking patterns which can be difficult to for the listener to follow, and which can include the use of made-up words called neologisms) and actions (evidenced by an inability effectively to sequence tasks, making difficult even simple day-to-day activities such as making a cup of tea) (Castle & Buckley, 2008).

Schizophrenia is ubiquitous around the world, irrespective of country or culture, afflicting around 0.5% of the population. It usually onsets in the later teens or early 20s in males and slightly later in females; however, a significant minority of cases only manifest in later life. There is significant associated disability and a general lack of engagement with society. Modern antipsychotic medications have improved the ability to control positive psychotic symptoms, but negative and cognitive symptoms are much less amenable to pharmacological interventions, and these are the symptoms that carry most of the disability (Castle & Buckley, 2008).

In the days before de-institutionalization, many people with severe chronic schizophrenia were housed in long-stay psychiatric hospitals. The locus of care of modern mental health services is the community, and many countries have abandoned the old asylums in favour of community living with ambulant care delivered in clinics or though home outreach by mental health professionals. Unfortunately many people with schizophrenia, though physically located in the community, remain socially excluded due to a combination of illness factors, social disadvantage, and societal stigma.

25.2 Musical hallucinations

Although hallucinations, and auditory hallucinations in particular, are among the most common features of schizophrenia, they have no specificity for that illness, being found also in certain organic states such as temporal lobe epilepsy, or in association with external factors such as imbibing dopaminergic drugs such as amphetamines. They can also occur in the setting or mania or severe depression.

Of particular relevance to this chapter are musical hallucinations, in which an individual actually 'hears' music when there is no music actually being played. It is a phenomenon quite distinct from merely the experience of having a musical tune going round in one's head: people with musical hallucinations 'hear' the music through their ears, just as if they were at a concert or listening to a song on the radio. Musical hallucinations are rare, and again have no diagnostic specificity. In a Japanese study in a general psychiatric hospital setting with a wide array of psychiatric disorders (including schizophrenia, bipolar disorder, depression, somatoform disorders, and dementia), Fukunishi and colleagues (1998) reported an overall rate of 0.16%, representing only six of 3678 cases. Of these six, five were female, three elderly, and three used hearing aids. The authors suggested that in three cases the musical hallucinations occurred as part of other psychiatric symptomatology, and in the other three as a distinct phenomenon. Unfortunately they do not report which diagnostic groups experienced the hallucinations.

Berrios (1990) has reviewed the historical literature on musical hallucinations along with ten of his own cases. Overall, amongst the 46 cases included in the review, he found strong associations with being elderly (mean age 60 (SD 19) years), being female (80%) and having a hearing deficit (67%). Only 12 of the 46 (26%) had a demonstrable psychiatric disorder (mostly depression: no cases were reported to have schizophrenia). In contrast, 39% had organic brain disease, including brain tumours, epileptic foci, and strokes. There was an excess of lesions in the non-dominant cerebral hemisphere. Berrios points out that clinical reports of musical hallucinations confine themselves to people hearing tunes or melodies, excluding parameters such as harmonics, rhythms, and timbres. He also conjectures that the experience of musical hallucinosis might in part at least be explained in terms of the hearer's musical training. In any event, these are rare symptoms, and exceedingly rare in schizophrenia despite the overall high rate of auditory hallucinations amongst people with that disorder.

25.3 **Musical creativity and schizophrenia**

The notion that creativity and madness are associated with each other has general currency. However, the vast majority of the literature linking artistic creativity and mental illness is in the domain of the mood disorders (depression and bipolar disorder) and alcohol abuse (which may be associated in part at least through its independent link with mood disorders). There is indeed but scant evidence of any robust association between schizophrenia and artistic creativity, and most notably this is the case for creativity in musical composition. For example, Nancy Andreasen's (2005) book *The creating brain: The neuroscience of genius* records high rates of bipolar disorder and depression (43% and 37%, respectively) amongst creative writers, but has no references to schizophrenia amongst prominent musicians. In her celebrated review of creativity and mental illness, Kay Jamison (1995) confines herself exclusively to the mood disorders in her overview of creativity and 'madness': here musicians such as Robert Schumann and Charlie Mingus do feature. Andreasen (2005: p. 98) states:

> The evidence supporting an association between artistic creativity and mood disorder is quite solid, as is the absence of an association with schizophrenia. The nature of artistic creativity . . . is probably not compatible with the presence of an illness like schizophrenia, which causes many of its victims to be socially withdrawn and cognitively disorganized.

Published reviews of mental illness in creative persons support Andreasen's conclusion, and underscore the rarity of successful musicians with schizophrenia. For example, Post (1994) reviewed the biographies of 291 famous men from the arts, sciences and politics. Fifty-two were composers. Of these 52, nearly 50% were assessed as having 'severe psychopathology', compared with 88% of writers and 57% of painters and sculptors. Again, the most prominent diagnoses were of mood disorders and alcoholism, along with unusual personalities, some of which might be considered schizoid or schizotypal. But only 1.7% had a definite history of a psychotic illness (all were writers), and none were considered to have schizophrenia. In our own unsystematic review, we found at least three famous musicians (one from the classical, one from the jazz and one from the rock fields) who possibly had schizophrenia; their stories are shown in Box 25.1.

According to Post (1994), and compatible with our unsystematic review, the rate of schizophrenia amongst musicians, if anything, is reduced relative to the general population. It is likely that this is related in part to the negative symptoms of schizophrenia that would preclude 'engagement' with music, though as discussed later in this chapter, they can respond to music being played and can benefit from 'guided' composition as part of a music therapy intervention. Perhaps more of a barrier to composition is the symptom of disorganization experienced by many people with schizophrenia, which would impair the ability to spend the requisite time organizing music into a composition. Added to these inherent problems of the disease process, is the social exclusion of people with schizophrenia, and the concomitant lack of opportunity in terms of musical creativity. Our three case examples of prominent musicians who might have had schizophrenia (Alexander Scriabin, Bud Powell, and Brian Wilson—see Box 25.1) are all people with a relatively late onset of illness, and in whom the majority of completed compositions were achieved before the illness took hold fully.

25.4 **Music therapy and creativity in schizophrenia**

Having explored the links between schizophrenia and music as seen in respected musicians, the question arises whether people with schizophrenia can engage with music, particularly if they are musically naïve, and whether engagement in music can affect any of the symptoms of the illness.

Box 25.1 Famous musicians with possible schizophrenia

Alexander Scriabin: Scriabin (1872–1915) was a composer of five symphonies, ten piano sonatas, and numerous other works. He brought an idiosyncratic atonal style to his compositions, and developed a musical notation based on colours (though whether he actually experienced synaesthesia is doubted). Towards the end of his life (he died of septicaemia at the age of 47) he appears to have become increasingly odd, saying he was God and that he could walk on water. He also embraced Theosophy, and his final (unfinished) composition was to be a massive work (the Mysterium) that he wanted played over the course of 7 days in the Himalayan Mountains, whereafter he stated Earth would disintegrate. A definitive psychiatric diagnosis is difficult, but bipolar mania and schizophrenia are both possible; a compromise diagnosis or schizoaffective disorder—with features of both schizophrenia and bipolar disorder—may be most readily defended.

Bud Powell (1924—1966) was an American jazz pianist who, along with Thelonious Monk, is credited with being one of the major influences on the evolution of bop. He was a creative pianist who used his left hand for 'comping' with single bass notes, liberating his right hand for 'continuous linear exploration'. In 1947 he spent a year in a psychiatric hospital, being treated with electroconvulsive therapy and antipsychotic medication. He continued to have psychiatric problems throughout his life, and was noted to be 'odd' and to behave strangely at times; his playing prowess showed a gradual decline. He had a number of further psychiatric hospitalizations, and moved to Paris in 1959 where he contracted tuberculosis. He returned to New York in 1963 and in the years leading to his death he was increasingly erratic in his behaviour, neglected his self care, and was unable to perform musically. The long-term general psychosocial decline suggests a diagnosis of schizophrenia (Wills, 2003).

Brian Wilson (born 1942), lead member of the band The Beach Boys, is considered one of the most creative musicians of his day, and was inducted into the Rock and Roll Hall of Fame in 1988, along with The Beatles and Bob Dylan. His early songs boast unique vocal harmonies and an unusual lyric style. After the success of The Beach Boys' early singles and albums (notably 'Pet Sounds', still considered one of the best rock albums of all time), Wilson stopped touring with the band and became increasing obsessional in his composition and production of songs, running vastly over time and budget. Whilst recording the album *Smile*, and at the time of the birth of his first son, he experienced a mental breakdown compounded by cocaine use which left him essentially bedbound for some 3 years: his only compositions during this time were of fragments of old songs tacked together. By the 1970s he had come under the influence of the controversial therapist Eugene Landy, who oversaw almost every aspect of his life and medicated him with antipsychotic drugs. It was only when he had freed himself of Landy, had regular antipsychotics, and kicked his cocaine habit that he was able to return to complete the unfinished *Smile* album, eventually released in 2004. Wilson has been labelled as having schizophrenia, but the impact of illicit substances clouds the clinical picture and again bipolar disorder or schizoaffective disorder are supportable diagnoses.

Since World War II, music therapists have facilitated music experiences for people who have severe mental illnesses, and the research literature suggests there are distinct benefits. Indeed the beginnings of music therapy in the USA were founded in Veteran's hospitals, for soldiers suffering shell shock (psychosis; Davis, Gfeller, & Thaut, 1992). Over many decades music therapists have engaged with mentally ill patients in individual therapy and in groups. However, with the de-commissioning of psychiatric hospitals throughout the world, new models of music therapy have developed to focus on community-based therapy (Ansdell, 2002; Pavlicevic & Ansdell, 2004) within a resource-oriented philosophy (Rolvsjord, 2004), building on skills and coping strategies for people living with severe mental illness. Resource-oriented music therapy is closely aligned to the recovery model of psychiatric care in that it emphasizes 'strengths and resources' (Rolvsjord, 2004) and promotes music as playful, and a form of non-verbal communication that is mutually engaging for therapist and patient. Within the resource-oriented approach respect for the patients' wishes is seen as the best means to achieve meaningful engagement, and to promote a sense of empowerment for the client (Gold et al, 2005b).

Different philosophical approaches and methods in music therapy and schizophrenia are evident across the world. Improvisation (Wigram, Pedersen, & Bonde, 2002) is predominantly practised in psychiatry in Europe, often within institutional practice in psychiatric hospitals. In the US, cognitive-behavioural programs are the main focus of music therapy practice (Cassity & Cassity, 1996; Silverman, 2003; Silverman & Marcionetti, 2004), whereas in Australia a more eclectic based music therapy approach is adopted, including songwriting (Grocke, Bloch, & Castle, 2009).

Research on the effect of music therapy for people with mental illness has generated only a few studies of rigorous standard. In a recent Cochrane review (Gold et al., 2005a) 34 potential studies were found, and of those only four met the rigorous Cochrane standards. The studies showed differing interventions, dosage and duration. All investigated music therapy with inpatients who had psychoses (lasting for 2–26 years), and interventions included active music making (improvisation), listening to music with discussion, and group singing. The number of therapy sessions ranged between 7–78, over 1–3 months. The meta-analysis concluded that music therapy compared with 'standard care' improved mental state and social functioning.

Apart from the Cochrane review, other controlled studies have added important insights into the role of music and schizophrenia. One study investigating music improvisation (Pavlicevic, Trevarthan, & Duncan, 1994) measured the effect of individual improvisation sessions with 21 patients diagnosed with chronic schizophrenia, and a matched control group. Scores on a standardized psychometric rating scale improved significantly for those in the music therapy condition who received weekly session over 10 weeks, compared with those of the control group, who received improvisation at week 1 and week 10 only. In addition, music interaction was measured for length of time involved in improvisation, and these scores increased over time in the music therapy group compared with controls. The authors cautiously suggest improvisation may be effective in developing capacity for communication.

The above-mentioned studies were conducted with hospitalized patients, and few efforts have been made to measure the effects of music therapy within a community model. In a study of patients with chronic mental illness attending a day program, de l'Etoile (2002) found interesting results—six of nine symptom dimensions improved from test 1 (baseline) to test 2 (mid-point), including those symptoms linked to anxiety. However, the changes were not sustained from the mid-point to the end-point of the study, indicating that the changes were not enduring. In addition the sample size was small (n=8), and the improvement from week 1 to week 4 (mid-point) may have been influenced by the novelty factor.

25.5 Song-writing study

One of the greatest challenges for people living with severe mental illness (particularly schizophrenia) is to maintain social networks, and group music therapy provides an essential opportunity to develop appropriate social and communicative skill. Music therapy brings people together in a shared experience that encourages verbal and musical interaction, which in turn assists in building relationships (Storr, 1972).

We have recently completed a feasibility study (Grocke, Bloch, & Castle, 2009) to determine whether group music therapy increases quality of life and decreases social anxiety, in participants with severe mental illness living in the community. The most common music therapy methods outlined in the literature as effective for people with severe mental illness are song singing and improvisation: we were interested, however, in trialling a method that would lead to a tangible outcome. Writing original songs that are subsequently recorded is now an established music therapy method that enables a person who is musically naïve to compose original lyrics (often on topics that relate to his/her life situation), and with the guidance of a music therapist compose the musical structure and form, choosing the genre, melodic, rhythmic, and harmonic features. This process is acknowledged as a strengths-based approach to therapy; it builds resourcefulness and resilience and in the case of people with long-standing mental illness, provides an opportunity for participants to access untapped creativity.

In our study, participants were people with severe, long-standing mental illness (mostly schizophrenia) who were resident in the community. We recruited through community mental health centres, and after 18 months five groups comprising four to six participants had completed the song-writing programme. An experienced music therapist conducted weekly sessions over 8 weeks. Each session included song singing, song writing and improvisation. Participants first decided on a theme for the song, then brainstormed statements that formed the lyrical content of the song. Over a period of weeks the song took shape, including several verses and chorus. The music therapist guided the music writing which also developed over several weeks, by asking the group members to decide on the genre, style, melodic shape, chord sequence, tempo, and dynamics. Towards the end of the programme (weeks 6 and 7) the song was rehearsed and instrumental accompaniment added (e.g. guitars, drums, tambours, and wind-chimes).

Three of the five groups wrote only one song over the 8 weeks, indicating the amount of time needed to complete the creative process. Two groups wrote two songs. Each group recorded the original song/s in a professional recording studio, and copies of the CD were then presented to the participants. Quality of life (QoL) and social anxiety were measured pre- and post-study and a statistically significant improvement was detected on six items of the World Health Organization (WHO) Qol BREF (Hawthorne et. al., 1999) scale, and one item on the social anxiety scale (Mattick & Clarke, 1998), an improvement on 'making eye contact with others'.

We also conducted focus groups with the participants in order to gather qualitative data about their experience of being in a group, what they gained, if anything, from the song-writing experience, and anything that should be changed about the programme. The focus group interviews were transcribed verbatim and a thematic analysis of the interview transcriptions was undertaken. We used an adapted phenomenological analysis (Forinash & Grocke, 2005) for each of the five interview protocols, involving four steps: 1) one researcher read through all five transcripts to obtain an overall sense of the groups' experiences and then identified key statements in each group; 2) these statements were grouped as 'units of meaning' and each category assigned a title that captured its essence; 3) statements common to all the groups were synthesized to create global themes; 4) verification was completed by another researcher, who read the transcripts and derived meaning units, and confirmed the themes of the interviews. An additional theme was created after verification.

The global themes were that: 1) group music therapy gave pleasure and joy and was relaxing; 2) working in a team was beneficial; 3) participants were surprised that the team produced a creative product; and 4) there was pride in the group song—members referred to it as 'our' song; 5) group members were surprised that even though they were not musically gifted or trained, they could write an original song; and finally 6) a sense of achievement in rehearsing the song, and recording it to a standard that could be shared with family and friends. Another theme indicated that the group members felt 1 hour was not long enough to work on a song, and that 8 weeks did not allow sufficient time to put the finishing touches to the song. This last theme is particularly interesting given that patients with mental illness have difficulty with concentration, and maintaining motivation for a task. Attendance at the sessions was also high (on average, 80% of sessions were attended), indicating that for these participants, group song writing provided motivation and stimulation for them to attend each week. Given that one of the most debilitating negative symptoms of schizophrenia is avolition, the attendance rate was particularly encouraging.

We also conducted a systematic analysis of the song lyrics, again adopting a phenomenological process involving four steps: 1) the researcher identified the key phrases of the first song and placed them within provisional categories; 2) key phrases were identified in the other songs, and phrases with similar meaning placed under the provisional categories created in step 1. New categories were established as required; 3) after all seven songs had been analysed, categories were reviewed and confirmed; 4) the music therapist who lead the groups verified these themes.

The lyric analysis of the groups' original songs found six common themes: 1) a concern for the world and environment; 2) coping with mental illness was difficult; 3) coping with mental illness requires strength; 4) religion and spirituality (such as being close to nature) were sources of support; 5) living in the present is healing; and 6) working in a team is enjoyable. We were impressed by the positive themes that emerged from both the focus groups and the lyric analysis of the songs. Few lyrics described the difficulty of living with mental illness: there was far greater emphasis on caring for nature and each other, and drawing on strengths for comfort.

In order to analyse the musical structure of the seven songs written by the five groups in the study, the Structural Model of Music Analysis (SMMA) (Grocke, 1999) was used. The SMMA was designed to analyse music elements in recorded pre-composed music. It functions as a checklist whereby several selections of music can be compared for common and distinguishing features. In Grocke's (1999) study of pivotal moments in Guided Imagery and Music (GIM) therapy, the SMMA allowed a comparison of four selections of music to determine the characteristics of music selections that underpinned challenging imagery. The SMMA is divided into 15 features, with sub-descriptors in each. The features are: 1) style and form, 2) texture, 3) time, 4) rhythm, 5) tempo, 6) tonality, 7) melody, 8) embellishments, ornamentation and articulation, 9) harmony, 10) timbre and quality of instrumentation, 11) volume, 12) intensity, 13) mood, 14) symbolic/associational features, and 15) performance.

A comparison of the musical characteristics of the seven songs composed by the five groups in our study (see Table 25.1) indicated that all songs were simple in structure, repetitive, and mostly verse/s and chorus. Rhythmic aspects were consistent throughout the song with little variance in tempo. The melodic structure of the songs indicated a narrow range of 5–7 notes for all songs, indicating that the group composed the song to suit vocal ranges that were on the whole untrained. The harmonic structure was predictable. Six of the seven songs depicted positive feelings and were sung with bright vocal tone. Only one song depicted a depressed and negative mood, in both lyrics and tone of voice.

Our pilot study demonstrates that music therapy positively affects the quality of life of people living with severe mental illness. Given the severity of the illness, and the perpetual assault on the person's state of well-being, any form of therapy that improves the quality of daily life has to be important. The themes emanating from the focus group interviews indicated that these participants with severe and enduring mental illness were concerned for the world and for each other, and the lyrics of the songs indicated a sense of spirituality in connection with nature and healing. These themes stand in contrast to the earlier literature in the chapter indicating that the impact of symptoms of schizophrenia, particularly lack of cognitive organization, renders composition virtually impossible. Furthermore, the participants in our study were musically naïve, as the basic

Table 25.1 Structural model of music analysis (SMMA) (Grocke, 1999)

	Song 1	Song 2	Song 3	Song 4	Song 5	Song 6	Song 7
	Ballad of better world	Lonely Nomad	Heart and Control	Pop song	Too long ago	Gospel Song	The Present
1. Style and form							
1.1 Period of composition	n/a	n/a	n/a	n/a	n/a	n/a	n/a
1.2 Form	3 verses + chorus	2 verses + chorus	4 verses + chorus + rap	4 verses + chorus	4 verses + chorus + spoken introduction	5 verses	2 verses + chorus, + middle section
2. Texture							
2.1 Texture: thick/thin	Thick chords, thin unison sung line	Thin vocal line	Thick	Thin	Thin	Thin	Thin
2.2 Mono/homo/polyphonic	Monophonic	Monophonic	Monophonic	Monophonic	Monophonic	Monophonic	Monophonic
3. Time							
3.1 Metre	4/4	4/4	4/4	4/4	4/4	4/4	4/4
3.2 Complexity/variability	No variation	No variation	No variation	No variation	No variation	No variation	Variation in middle section
3.3 Silences /rests/ pauses	Ritardando at end	None	None	None	None	None	Middle section much slower with pauses
4. Rhythmic features							
4.1 Underlying *pulse*	Duple	Duple	Duple	Duple	Duple	Duple	Duple
4.2 Important rhythmic motifs	None	None	None	None	None	None	None
4.3 Repetition in motifs	None	None	None	None	None	None	None

4.4 Variability in rhythm—predictable/unpredictable	No variation	No variation	Rap in chorus	No variation	Change of rhythm between verse & chorus	No variation	Rhythm suspended in middle section
4.5 Syncopation	None	In melodic line	None	None	In melodic line and guitar accompaniment	None	In melodic line
5. Tempo							
5.1 Fast/slow/moderato	Moderato	Moderato	Moderato	Slow	Moderato	Slow	Slow
5.2 Alterations in tempo	Tempo alters with spoken word at end of song	No alteration	No alteration	No alteration	No alteration	No alteration	Tempo alters within middle section—one part intoned.
6. Tonal features							
6.1 Key in which work is written	A min (chorus) E min (verse)	G maj	A maj	D maj	E min/G maj	C maj	Bb maj
6.2 Key diatonic; modal	Diatonic	Diatonic	Diatonic	Diatonic	Diatonic	Diatonic	Middle section is modal & intoned
6.3 Major/min alternate	Min thru'out	Maj thru'out	Maj thr'out	Maj thru'out	Minor in verse/major in chorus	Maj thru'out	Major (verses), minor in chorus, modal in middle section
6.4 Chromaticism	None	None	None	None	None	None	In middle section. Rich modulation by semi-tone
6.5 Modulation points	At start of chorus	None	None	None	At start of chorus	None	Modulates from Bb to Db (minor 3rd)

(continued)

Table 25.1 (continued)

	Song 1	Song 2	Song 3	Song 4	Song 5	Song 6	Song 7
	Ballad of better world	Lonely Nomad	Heart and Control	Pop song	Too long ago	Gospel Song	The Present
7. Melody							
7.1 Main themes	N/a	N/a	N/a	N/a	N/a	N/a	N/a
7.2 Significant melodic fragment	None	None	None	None	None	Falling leap of 5th	none
7.3 Structure of the melody	Repetitive AAA + chorus	AAA + chorus	AA– chorus: BB	Repetitive: AAAA/BB/CC	AABB AABB CC	Repetitive: AAAB	AAAA BBBC Upward movement by one tone
7.4 Significant intervals	Upward leap of 5th	Oscillates between 6th and 5th note of scale (descending)	Step-wise movement ascending of melody line	None	Falling 3rd in melody line	5th	Modulation to chorus (guitar chord) by semi-tone
7.5 Shape of melody	Ascends, drops 5th	Flat, inverse	Propinquity in verse, ascending line in chorus	Descending line in verse, ascending in chorus	Ascending	Flat	Varies: ascending in verse, descending in chorus, chant in middle section
7.6 Length of phrases	2 bar	4 bar	1 bar	2 bar	2 bar	1 bar	1 bar
7.7 Pitch range of melody	Narrow: 5 notes	Narrow: 7 notes	Narrow: 7 notes	Narrow: 6 notes	Narrow: 7 notes	Narrow: 5 notes	Narrow: 6 notes
8. Embellishments, ornamentation, and articulation							
8.1 Embellishments	None	None	None	None	None	None	None

8.2 Trills/appoggiaturas	None	None	None	None	None	None	None
8.3 Marcato, accents	None	None	None	None	None	None	None
8.4 Pizzicato/Legato	Legato	Legato	Legato/ rap at end	Legato	Legato	Legato	Legato
8.5 Use of mute	n/a	n/a	n/a	n/a	n/a	n/a	n/a
9. Harmony							
9.1 Consonant/dissonant	Consonant	Consonant	Consonant	Consonant	Consonant	Consonant	Consonant
9.2 Consonance/dissonance	n/a	n/a	n/a	n/a	n/a	n/a	n/a
9.3 Significant harmonic progressions	I-IV-V	I-11-V-1	1-1V-V-1	1-V6		I-1V-V	
9.4 Rich harmonies	None	None	None	None	None	None	Yes
9.5 Predictable harmonies	Predictable	Predictable	Predictable	Predictable	Predictable	Predictable	Unpredictable in middle section
9.6 Unpredictable harmonies	None	None	None	None	None	None	In middle section
9.7 Cadence points	Each 2 bars	Each 2 bars	Each 2 bars	Avoided	Each 2 bars	Each 2 bars	
10. Timbre and quality of instrumentation							
10.1 Solo instr; instr; vocal	Spoken line at end; vocal group	Solo voice for verse, vocal group for chorus	Vocal group; solo voice rap	Vocal group	Voice predominates, group quieter	Vocal group	Vocal group
10.2 Accompaniment	Guitar	Guitar	Guitar	Guitar and wind chimes	Guitar	Guitar	Guitar
10.3 Small groupings	Vocal	Vocal	Vocal	Vocal	Vocal	Vocal	Vocal

(continued)

Table 25.1 (continued)

	Song 1 Ballad of better world	Song 2 Lonely Nomad	Song 3 Heart and Control	Song 4 Pop song	Song 5 Too long ago	Song 6 Gospel Song	Song 7 The Present
10.4 Instrument groups	Vocal	Vocal	Vocal	Vocal	Vocal	Vocal	Vocal
10.5 Interplay btwn instr.	n/a	n/a	n/a	n/a	n/a	n/a	n/a
10.6 Layering	n/a	n/a	n/a	n/a	n/a	n/a	n/a
11. Volume							
11.1 Predominantly loud or soft	Soft	Soft	mf	Soft	mf	mf	Soft
11.2 Special effects in volume	n/a	n/a	n/a	n/a	n/a	n/a	n/a
12. Intensity							
12.1 Tension/release	None	Tension in melody line oscillating between 6th note of scale resolving down to 5th thru'out	None	None	None	None	At modulation point middle section
12.2 Crescendi building to peak, and resolution	None	None	In chorus	None	None	None	None
12.3 Tension in harmony, texture and resolution	None	None	None	None	None	None	At modulation point in middle section
12.4 Delayed resolution	None	Yes, in melody line	None	None	None	None	None

12.5 Ambiguity resolved	None	None	None	None	None	None	None
13. Mood							
13.1 Predominant mood, depicted by melody, harmony, & predominant instrument	Bright mood	Monotone, flat, depressed	Ascending melody line suggests positive mood	Flat melody line, flat dynamics	Bright enthusiastic	Joyful	Mellow, spiritual, & reflective
13.2 Feelings represented	Concern for the world	Depressed	Bright-happy in chorus	Flat—brighter in chorus	Fun	Praising the Lord	Spiritual & reflective
14. Symbolic/ associational							
14.1 Cultural associations	None	None	None	None	None	None	None
14.2 Metaphoric associations	None	None	None	Wind chimes used to depict sun rising	None	None	None
15. Performance							
15.1 Quality of the performance	Sung in tune Words enunciated clearly	Solo voice out of tune. Recording enhanced—re-verb noticeable	Vocal group out of tune	A solo voice in tune predominates, but group is out of tune	Some singers out of tune	Voice in tune predominates, group is out of tune	In tune, sensitively sung
15.3 Stylistic interpretation—artistic merit	Well rehearsed	Chorus notes not secure	Rap introduced toward end of song	Imbalance between leading voice and group	Some singers out of tune	Imbalance between leading voice and group	Well balanced, sung sensitively
15.4 Articulation of feelings and emotion	Hopeful feelings expressed	Depressed voice, quiet	Love song—positive	Joyful	Positive	Joyful	Reflective

tenet of music therapy is that all people are eligible to receive music interventions, irrespective of musical ability. Indeed the recordings of the songs indicate some members of the groups could not sing in tune, and could not sustain a note once intoned. Yet, the participants were proud of their songs, and felt an ownership of them. Group song writing, then, is an effective intervention to adopt for people with severe and enduring mental illness, who are living in the community, and for whom socialization remains one of the major challenges. Music engagement fulfils the need for social interaction, and has the potential for a group reward in the form of a composed song. Encouraged by the results of our pilot study, we are now embarking on a larger study, adopting the same methodology, but designed as a randomized controlled trial to add rigour to the study.

25.6 **Conclusion**

There is a demonstrated need for further rigorous research that provides evidence of the effectiveness of different treatments, and while music therapy has made some advances in the research arena, greater activity is required. 'Mental illness' covers a diverse range of illnesses, including severe psychoses such as schizophrenia, but also mood disorders, such as bipolar disorder and depression. Other mental illnesses include personality problems such as borderline personality disorder, dissociative disorders, and post-traumatic disorder, and each of these illnesses has an idiosyncratic trajectory, requiring different therapeutic interventions. There is no shortage of research projects to be done. In particular, music therapy research needs to address which intervention is more effective with different types of illness, and the amount (dosage) and frequency of sessions, and the length of therapy in order to achieve significant results.

References

Andreasen, N.C. (2005). *The creating brain: The neuroscience of genius.* New York: Dana Press.

Ansdell, G. (2002). Community music therapy and the winds of change—A discussion paper. In C. Kenny & B. Stige (Eds.) *Contemporary voices in music therapy.* Oslo: Unipub Forlag, pp. 109–43.

Berrios, G. (1990). Musical hallucinations. A historical and clinical study. *British Journal of Psychiatry,* **196**, 188–94.

Cassity, M. & Cassity, J. (1996). *Multimodal psychiatric music therapy for adults, adolescents and children: A clinical manual.* Saint Louis, MO. MMB.

Castle, D. & Buckley, P.F. (2008). *Schizophrenia.* Oxford: Oxford University Press.

Davis, W., Gfeller, K., & Thaut, M. (1992). *An introduction to music therapy: Theory and practice.* 2nd edition. Boston, MA: McGraw-Hill.

De l'Etoile, S. (2002). The effectiveness of music therapy in group psychotherapy for adults with mental illness. *The Arts in Psychotherapy,* **29**, 69–78.

Forinash, M. & Grocke, D. (2005). Phenomenological inquiry. In B. Wheeler (Ed.) *Music therapy research.* 2nd edition. Gilsum, NH: Barcelona publishers, pp. 321–34.

Fukunishi, I., Horikawa, N., & Onai, H. (1998). Prevalence rate of musical hallucinations in a general hospital setting. *Psychosomatics,* **39**, 175.

Gold, C., Heldal, T.O., Dahle, T., & Wigram, T. (2005a). Music therapy for schizophrenia or schizophrenia-like illness (Review). *The Cochrane Library,* issue 2.

Gold, C., Rolvsjord, R., Aaro, L.E., Aarre, T., Tjemsland, L., & Stige, B. (2005b). Resource-oriented music therapy or psychiatric patients with low therapy motivation: Protocol for a randomised controlled trial. *BMC Psychiatry,* **5**(39), 1–8.

Grocke, D. (1999). A phenomenological study of pivotal moments in guided imagery and music (GIM) therapy. Unpublished PhD dissertation, University of Melbourne.

Grocke, D., Bloch, S., & Castle, D. (2009). The effect of group music therapy on quality of life of participants with severe mental illness. *Journal of Music Therapy*, **46**(2), 94–104.

Hawthorne, G., Richardson J., & Osborne, R. (1999). The assessment of quality of life (AQoL) instrument: Psychometric measure of health related quality of life. *Quality of Life Research*, **8**, 209–24.

Jamison, K. (1995). Manic-depressive illness and creativity. *Scientific American*, February, 62–7.

Mattick, R.P. & Clarke, J.C. (1998). Development and validation of measures of social phobia, scrutiny, fear and social interaction anxiety. *Behaviour Research and Therapy*, **36**, 455–70.

Pavlicevic, M. & Ansdell, G. (Eds.) (2004). *Community music therapy*. London: Jessica Kingsley.

Pavlicevic, M., Trevarthen, C., & Duncan, J. (1994). Improvisational music therapy and the rehabilitation of persons suffering from chronic schizophrenia. *Journal of Music Therapy*, **31**, 86–104.

Post, F. (1994). Creativity and psychopathology. A study of 291 world-famous men. *British Journal of Psychiatry*, **165**, 22–34.

Rolvsjord, R. (2004). Therapy as empowerment. *Nordic Journal of Music Therapy*, **13**, 99–111.

Silverman, M. & Marcionetti, M. (2004). Immediate effects of a single music therapy intervention with personal who are severely mentally ill. *Arts in Psychotherapy*, **31**(5), 291–301.

Silverman, M. (2003). The influence of music on the symptoms of psychosis: A meta-analysis. *Journal of Music Therapy*, **XL** (1), 27–40.

Storr, A. (1972). *The dynamics of creation*. London: Penguin.

Wigram, T., Pedersen, I., & Bonde, L.-O. (2002). *A comprehensive guide to music therapy: Theory, clinical practice, research and training*. London: Jessica Kingsley Publishers.

Wills, G. (2003). Forty lives in the bebop business: Mental health in a group of eminent jazz musicians. *British Journal of Psychiatry*, **183**, 255–9.

Chapter 26

Creativity in improvisational, psychodynamic music therapy

Jaakko Erkkilä, Esa Ala-Ruona, Marko Punkanen, and Jörg Fachner

26.1 Introduction

In this chapter, music therapy is considered in a psychiatric context. To be exact, the focus is on improvisational psychodynamic music therapy (IPMT). The main influences of IPMT come from the theory and concepts of psychoanalysis, although the numerous reforms to the original theory, as well as the many unique qualities of IPMT, have shaped it in many ways over the decades. The concept *psychodynamic* has been developed for describing those models of therapy, which more or less deviate from classical psychoanalysis and its theoretical standpoints. In his book on music psychotherapy, Kenneth Bruscia (1998) defines music psychotherapy as the 'use of music experiences in addition to or in lieu of the traditional types of verbal discourse . . . in short, music psychotherapy is the use of music experiences to facilitate the interpersonal process of therapist and client as well as the therapeutic change process itself'. In music therapy within the context of psychiatry, the psychodynamic approach is the most common. Perhaps the biggest effort in early years in connecting the theory of psychoanalysis and music was by Pinchas Noy, who in the 1960s wrote his famous series of articles in the *Journal of Music Therapy* (Noy, 1966, 1967a, b, c, d).

26.2 Musicality and creativity in IPMT

A fundamental basis of music therapy is that it is not restricted to those people with musical training or talent. Active music therapy, in which clients are supposed to play or improvise music, is based on the idea that every human being has a natural propensity to create and respond to sounds expressively and aesthetically (Bruscia, 1998). Even when talking about free improvising, making music in music therapy is still connected to the idiomatic nature of one's musical, social, and cultural history (Metzner, 1999). That is, although clients in music therapy may have diverse connections to and capacities in music, there is always some kind of common root or core, which helps them engage in music-making.

In IPMT, free improvisation can be seen as a means of self-projection and free association (Hadley, 2003). Bruscia (1998) defines improvising in music psychotherapy as 'playing around with sounds until they form whatever patterns, shapes, or textures one wants them to have, or until they mean whatever one wants them to mean' (p. 5). In IPMT, the therapist's role (not only the client's) as an expressive and creative actor is one of the unique characteristics of music therapy. While this aspect of music therapy is no doubt challenging and not always easy to manage, many clinicians see this feature as being beneficial, for instance, when creating the working alliance with the client.

If a music therapy client does not have to be musically trained or talented, what is the situation with regard to creativity? If a therapy, such as music therapy, is based on the exploitation of a form of art, doesn't it require a special creative competence? It is true that creativity is often associated with the extraordinary capacity of a person who may be a recognized painter like Picasso, or an excellent scholar such as Einstein, and that intelligence and creativity are often thought of as being interrelated. However, research on creativity suggests that the relationship between intelligence and creativity is rather weak, with various relationships possible (Barron & Harrington, 1981; Simonton, 1994; Sternberg, 1997; Torrance, 1975). Similarly, it can be concluded that there are many layers of creative functioning from simple, everyday insights to seminal breakthroughs in art or science. One of the starting points of music therapy is a human being's 'propensity to create', the idea of which obviously assumes that that every human being *can* create.

In music therapy, it is the client who is the focus of the work. Thus, it is the client's willingness, capacity, and competence to express himself/herself musically or to be creative that defines the pace and the profoundness of the therapeutic work. Whatever the client's starting point in music therapy—due to their personal and illness-related factors—it is the clinician's task to adapt to it, as well as to communicate on the basis of the client's moment-to-moment expressive, interactive, and creative potential.

26.3 **Some client groups with limited ability to create**

Some psychiatric problems narrow the client's emotional, social, and cognitive life, causing withdrawn-like behaviour, and even limit or hinder the function of symbolic processes. These kinds of shortcomings inevitably affect one's creative ability and mental work in general. In psychosis, for instance, the client's ability to symbolize can be provisionally hindered. According to Schaverien (1997), psychosis can be characterized as the absence of symbolic forms and the impossibility of communal understanding. Basch-Kahre (1985) stresses that borderline patients are also not normally able to use nor understand symbols, but they tend to split the symbols as well as the emotional sensorimotor configurations into meaningless fragments. Because the symbols are out of context they tend to be used in an aggressive and destructive way.

Music therapy clinicians who have worked with people with psychosis have noticed how their inability to symbolize shows up in improvisational work. One of the most profound analyses and descriptions of improvisational music therapy with psychotic clients has been made by De Backer (2004; De Backer & Van Camp, 2003). He has specified different phases in psychotic clients' improvisational music therapy, from non-communicative and non-symbolic play (sensorial play) to communicative and symbolic play (musical form)—a journey which is often long and hard. Interesting here is the finding that even though there is no sign of symbolic processes, interaction, or creativity in the first place (in sensorial play), it is nonetheless an important preparatory phase for the latter, more dynamic phases, and for the process of recovery.

Mood disorders such as depression and anxiety may also affect symbolic processes and creative functioning. It is known that depression and anxiety induce social and interpersonal withdrawal behaviour and negative emotional states in daily life.

Withdrawal from novel and unfamiliar stimuli is associated with frontal brain asymmetry, as correlated in electroencephalography (EEG) studies of depressed patients (Tomarken & Keener, 1998). According to Tomarken and Keener (1998), depressed individuals are characterized by a bias in favour of a negative valence withdrawal system to a positive valence approach system. Withdrawal motivation is strongly influenced by a negative event or expectations (Elliot, 1999), diminishing interest toward activities, and causes a loss of energy, indecisiveness, and lack of concentration, which, in terms of searching for social connection, enrichment, and solutions for their problems, will decrease their creative behaviour.

Craig (2005) explains that emotional asymmetries in the left and right forebrain are mediated via an autonomous para-/sympathetically innervated energy expenditure/maintenance system connected to the limbic insula and cingulate activations. Depressed clients' dominant right frontal withdrawal activation prevents energy expenditure on relationships and approach behaviour in the social world. Thus, depressed clients are mostly absorbed inwardly, spending their energy on introspection and rumination while being highly sympathetically aroused.

26.4 **Theory and practice of IPMT in a nutshell**

Psychoanalytic theory has had a strong influence on psychiatric music therapy since the early years of professional music therapy. Musical meanings and experiences have qualities that have much in common with the core ideas and concepts of psychoanalytical theory, which is probably one of the reasons for this 'alliance'. For instance, unconscious feelings, or the contents/functions of pre-conscious level (see Figure 26.1) such as emotions, metaphors, associations, and images are also core elements of musical experiences (Erkkilä, 1997a, b ; Wigram et al., 2002). When considering clinical improvisation from a psychoanalytic perspective, its role is to activate the symbolic process, and let the improviser act creatively in the domain of non-verbal experiences, i.e. at the pre-conscious level, and thus bring out primary process orientated material to be dealt with verbally.

The primary process consists of qualities that are often associated with creativity as well. After Rapaport (1950), the primary process is seen to regulate unconscious wishes, needs, and affect, is able to tolerate and master warded-off affect, and in addition allows the mobility of ideas, i.e. memories and experiences are fluently interchangeable. No wonder, then, that in the analytical music therapy tradition (Priestley, 1975, 1976, 1983) clinical improvisation is seen as representing the domain of primary process functions (Bruscia, 1987, 1998; Erkkilä, 1997a, b). The secondary process is a conceptual organization of memory, responsible for logical, practical, and realistic behaviour and thinking. It also controls and restricts affect (Rapaport, 1950). In improvisational music therapy, secondary process functions are present, for instance, when verbally dealing with the experiences triggered by improvisation. Usually this happens after improvising, and tends to concretize and make logical what has been experienced while improvising.

Many music therapy clinicians have found Winnicott's ideas about *potential space* and importance of play highly relevant to improvisational music therapy. He writes that 'psychotherapy has to do with two people playing together. The corollary of this is that where playing is not possible

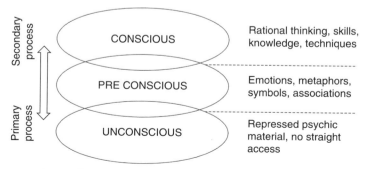

Fig. 26.1 Primary and secondary processes associated with the functions of the different layers of consciousness.

then the work done by the therapist is directed toward bringing the patient from a state of not being able to play into a state of being able to play' (Winnicott, 1968). Bringing the patient into that state presupposes creating a specific, holding environment between the therapist and client, and this environment is called a potential space. In his essay on Winnicott's concept, Ogden (1985) describes the potential space as an area of experiencing that lies between fantasy and reality, including, for instance, the play space, the area of cultural experience, and the area of creativity. These definitions characterize nicely the ideal setting of improvisation in music therapy. When Winnicott talks about play, he of course means playing like in children's play. However, music is also 'played', and there is much in common between these two forms of play.

Some music therapy theorists (De Backer, 2004; Metzner, 1999) describe the clients' experiences in improvisation as proto-symbolic. They refer to Winnicott's ideas about transitional space and transitional object when interpreting certain musical phenomena—such as appearance of melody in improvisation—as not yet being a symbol as such, but a symbol in a pre-state. Thus, a melody in a client's improvisation may be a 'signifier' but not an 'open signifier' (De Backer, 2004), and can thus be seen as the first marker of awakening symbolization. This kind of possibility of operating in the proto-symbolic field of experiencing enables work with clients with limited symbolic capacity, such as psychotic clients or borderline clients.

26.5 **Role of music in IPMT**

Numerous case studies and clinical reports have demonstrated how communication via music has been possible with clients with severe mental retardation. These findings have led music therapy scholars to seek answers from theories of early interaction, in particular in finding out the role of sounds as such (e.g. sound communication between the mother and child), separately from music. There is something of a consensus that the origin of music arises from the earliest non-verbal human communication, and thus came before speech. In particular, Daniel Stern's (1985) theories have had a strong influence on recent definitions of the meaning of music in music therapy.

A newborn baby is said to perceive music as being meaningful, not as music as a form of art, but as part of her innate capacity to recognize various dynamic forms in the music due to their affective meaning, no matter whether they represent auditory, visual, or tactile domains (Erkkilä, 1997a; Pavlicevic, 1997; Lehtonen, 2007). Thus, beyond the music-specific rules and theories there is a world of universal meanings embedded in music, which is accessible to nearly everyone. In IPMT, the most relevant musical meanings are perhaps more often based on emotionally loaded dynamic forms than music-specific phrases and patterns with certain musical logic. Furthermore, when removing the 'meanings' from their 'musical mask', it is easier to make connections between primary process functions and meanings embedded in the improvisation. In summary, how we understand music in IPMT differs substantially from traditional definitions of, and meaning formation in, music. In addition, music in IPMT is often understood as representing primitive and early forms of communication, thus having a specific potential for reaching warded-off experiences (passing the defences) as well as acting on the areas—such as proto-symbolic expression—not easily accessible in the verbal domain.

The ideas presented above are not dissimilar to concepts of verbal psychotherapy. De Alvarez De Toledo (1996) describes somewhat similar ideas in the psychoanalytic process when she describes the difference between the content of speech and unconscious impulses behind it. She points out that sometimes the client's unconscious impulses are manifested in the analyst's emotions and experiences, and that the content of the client's speech is not necessarily connected to these emotions and experiences. She continues that sometimes those emotional experiences with most direct connections to unconscious fantasies are not at all comprehensible based on the content of the speech. In IPMT, improvisation can be seen as a natural, non-verbal medium for such emotional experiences.

26.6 A model of the recovery process in IPMT—creativity perspective

The model to be represented next was developed and revised into its final form during the training of research therapists who worked in our depression study (Erkkilä et al., 2008). For this article, we have refined the model by focusing more on creativity aspects. The therapeutic approach to the study of music therapy for depression is based on the ideas and principles presented in the previous chapters of this article.

The goal of the training was to achieve a shared understanding of theoretic-clinical issues, and to develop appropriate and suitable interventions to meet the needs of the target group. A particular emphasis was placed on process handling—how to build up and maintain a therapeutic relationship, how to achieve balance between verbal and musical processing, and how the therapeutic process is conducted in this particular setting and frame of therapy (Erkkilä, 2007; Erkkilä et al., 2008).

It is interesting that the meaning of creativity has not only been a matter for art therapies. After Benau (2009), psychopathology can be understood to represent an incomplete or interrupted creative process, and psychotherapy as a collaboration between patient and therapist with the aim of liberating the patient's innate, creative potential. Benau argues that there is a long history of trying to delineate the conceptual and practical connections between the creative process and the procss and techniques of psychotherapy. The isomorphism between creativity and psychotherapy probably originates from the findings that many great artists have struggled with mental problems, in particular with depression, and that the symbol formation and creative process in general can be seen as an attempt to articulate a personal problem via the symbolic product (Rothenberg, 1979; Heilman et al., 2003).

In the definitions there are determinants of creativity such as *novelty* and *originality* (Heilman et al., 2003; May, 1975; Soukhanov, 1988), *passion* and *commitment* (May, 1975), different stages such as *preparation, incubation, illumination*—or 'Aha!' experience (Heilman et al., 2003)—and *verification* (Wallas, 1926), and *finding unity* in what appears to be diversity (Bronowski, 1972). When investigating creativity in the context of working life, for instance in the design industry, determinants such as *appropriateness* (Sternberg & Lubart, 1992) and *producing* (Naiman, 2006; Soukhanov, 1988) are employed.

These determinants of creativity can be related to the process of creativity in IPMT. For instance, when improvising music there are numerous possibilities to create novel sound patterns and sound combinations with a special meaning. However, without certain commitment or passion it is not likely that this will happen. It is also typical in IPMT, in particular at the beginning of the process, that the meaning of improvisation is more or less unclear. The improvisation may sound like a collection of divergent notes with no sense of unity. What often happens, however, is that after a while, the client becomes increasingly engaged in improvising, and becomes gradually able to make connections between the sound patterns and their symbolic meanings—i.e. to see the unity. This phase can be compared with the concepts of *incubation* and *illumination*. Before these, the preparatory phase is, of course, necessary. Finally, a very important aspect of IPMT is its goal orientation. Creativity is harnessed for recovery, which means that the creative insights should serve the client in finding solutions for her problems, and in putting them into action.

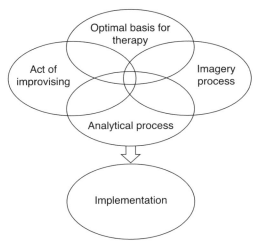

Fig. 26.2 A model of the recovery process in IPMT. Some of the model elements overlap each other.

In the next section, a model consisting of five progressing stages of creativity in IPMT will be presented (see Figure 26.2). These are: 1) *optimal basis for therapy*, 2) *act of improvising*, 3) *imagery process*, 4) *analytical process*, and 5) *implementation*. These stages can be seen within a single therapy session (micro level) but also during the whole course of a therapy process (macro level). The focus of the examination here is on creativity, but it is interesting to see the many connections between the two concepts, creativity and recovery.

26.6.1 **Optimal basis for therapy**

Regardless of the form of therapy, there are certain commonalities and contents that have a crucial effect on the successful clinical process (i.e. Wampold, 2001). According to Grencavage and Norcross (1990), the common factors of psychotherapy are client characteristics, therapist qualities, change processes, treatment structures, and relationship elements. To mention some of the contents of these factors, the success of therapy (partly) depends on the client's motivation and expectations, the therapist's emphatic competence and encouragement, how therapeutic change processes are enabled and present in the work, how coherently and faithfully the clinical approach is carried out, and how good a relationship and working alliance there is between therapist and client. In IPMT these factors are important as well.

26.6.2 **Act of improvising**

Improvisation can be a creative process, but this is not always the case. If there is not an optimal basis (Stage 1) for therapeutic work, or the client's ability to symbolize is deficient due to illness or other reasons, improvising is not much more than action. When improvising is in a therapeutic sense productive, it is linked to *potential space* (Winnicott, 1968), and presupposes certain commitment, passion, and motivation. Only then can improvising lead to a new kind of thinking, or diverse thinking (Heilman et al., 2003), which is one of the determinants of creativity.

26.6.3 **Imagery process**

When clinical improvisation has creative potential it triggers images, emotions, symbols, memories, and associations—all very important for therapeutic work, being a kind of window to one's unconscious (Erkkilä, 1997a, 2004). These experiences can occur simultaneously with the improvisation (non-verbal), but often they are brought out verbally when listening to the improvisation, and when discussing it with the therapist. The imagery process is primary process orientated, and includes processes typically associated with right hemisphere functions such as primary emotion, emotional communication, and global attentional perspective (Barret et al., 1998; Heilman et al., 2000; Robertson et al., 1988). When the imagery process is activated by the improvisation, creativity is involved.

26.6.4 Analytical process

Because IPMT is goal-orientated work, creativity as such, without appropriate connections to the issues of recovery, is not sufficient as a goal. If the product of a creative act—improvisation—is an image with emotional loading, shedding light on the mental problems and their solutions, there is still a need for analytical and more cognitive integration of experiences. Gaining new kind of understanding and relating the creative insights to the client's everyday life can be associated with secondary process thinking, and with left hemisphere functions such as focused attention and analytical and logical thinking (Barret et al., 1998; Heilman et al., 2000; Robertson et al., 1988). When the analytical process is linked to the imagery process in an appropriate way, by serving the goals of therapy, it may result in solutions (or changes) that are ready to be put into action.

26.6.5 Implementation

Naiman (2006) defines creativity as the act of turning new and imaginative ideas into reality. This is exactly what the client has to do with the creative innovations and solutions born in therapy. In psychotherapy terminology the 'action plan' is often called a change, which can be whatever change from pathological behaviour, functioning, feeling, or thinking to non-pathological. Implementation is successful if the client feels better and has a better quality of life, and at least to some extent gets rid of the illness.

26.7 Clinical examples of a creative process

The cases presented in this chapter are based on a study in which we investigated the effect of active music therapy in the treatment of depression. That study was a randomized controlled trial (RCT) with a two-arm design (33 clients in intervention, 46 clients in control group). The amount of individual music therapy offered was 20 biweekly sessions, each lasting 60 minutes. The selection of instruments was confined to mallet midi instruments, electronic hand drums, and Djembe-drums. This setting enabled musical interplay and expression in both a rhythmic and melodic-harmonic way, but was easy enough for everyone to employ. All music produced in the sessions was recorded to computer, and it was possible to listen to these during the same session or afterwards for further processing and discussion regarding emerging themes. No other listening to music was used as a method (Erkkilä et al., 2008).

The basic principle in the sessions was to encourage and engage a client in expressive musical interaction based on a free starting-point, or certain idea. The aim was to establish a shared creative space for providing favourable conditions for the therapeutic change. The therapeutic process was based on mutual construction of meaning of emerging thoughts, images, emotions, and expressive qualities. Musical expression and verbal discussion took turns, and this was individually modified depending on the personal needs and conditions of a client. Because of the special setting and frame of research therapy, some supportive and resource-orientated elements were added to the approach (Erkkilä et al., 2008).

26.7.1 **The case of Erik**

Erik, a young male adult, started his music therapy clearly motivated. Having suffered from anxiety and depression for years, and having also had problems with insomnia, he ended up suffering from exhaustion. He received antidepressant medication, and some remedy for his sleeping problems, too. During the last year before music therapy he had not been able to take care of his work. The motivation for therapeutic work rose from his experience that he 'knows' his problems, but had not found any relief or change to come true in real life. Something was missing.

Optimal basis for therapy (stage 1): the first phase of the process was building up safe enough conditions and the basis of a working alliance. Erik adopted the therapeutic approach quickly, and musical interaction started relatively easily. Musical interplay also revealed an evident analogy between characteristics of his musical interaction and his script in social situations. He recognized his problems in losing personal integrity and pleasing others (also the therapist), in particular, feeling anger was threatening, and he had to force these feelings back. But when beating a drum he was able to discharge his inner tensions, and he named an extremely powerful improvisation in session 4 as 'the story of me'. He felt safe enough to be able to express his real emotions, and started to explore them.

Act of improvising (stage 2) and Imagery process (stage 3): the act of improvising offered a new perspective on his previous life history and negative experiences. Erik explored his inner feelings and reactions in a very sensitive way by using musical interaction or playing alone. The emerging themes and emotions were further examined both verbally and musically. His curiosity was awakened, and Erik started to find new ways to experience and see himself. Occasionally, there were also moments when Erik felt guilt and shame, hopelessness, and despair. In some of these situations Erik got stuck with his expression and he did not find his way out. However, he used the therapeutic support very elegantly by inviting the therapist into the interplay and having the needed emotional experience of unconditional acceptance. The emotional bond was deep, and Erik experienced this mutual presence as a significant reconstructive moment. Musical interplay became synchronized and emotionally congruent.

Analytical process (stage 4): analytical processing progressed hand in hand with the imagery process. Erik's emerging curiosity, creativity, and willingness to react in the here-and-now situation led the process to another level. He was aiming to experience happiness, joy, and feeling free. Erik accepted his rights for taking care of his own needs and to nurture his own well-being. Erik gained lot of new insights into his personal history with its emotional loads. The interrelatedness between the past, the present, and future started to look understandable and meaningful. The emotional spectrum extended, and he was encouraged to show his feelings and talk about his real thoughts in social situations. He was reaching for his independence.

Implementation (stage 5): during the last phase of the therapy process, Erik was able to go back to work. He also took up some hobbies, and he trained his 'new potentials' in different social situations.

Table 26.1 Psychiatric test scores of Erik before and after music therapy

	Erik (pre)	Erik (post)
MADRS	26	9
HADS-A	10	5
GAF	61	71
RAND-36	65	81
TAS-20	70	48

With the help of his physician, his antidepressive medication was reduced. Erik described his therapy process afterwards by writing:

> Connection with the therapist was established quickly. Therapy sessions became to be kind of an asylum, a place where it felt good to be in. One of the finest experiences in the therapy was when I realized how much new possibilities music and playing brings to the processing of depression. If I was in trouble, the grounding rhythm by the therapist enabled me to explore new ways and let the creativity flow. Also when we played together by giving the space and taking it, was a fine experience of mutual sharing.

It is obvious that what was missing in the beginning was found during the process, and the desired change was realized.

26.7.2 The case of Kati

Kati was a 40-year-old married woman with three children. She had been depressed for many years and she also had anxiety disorder, and took medication for both. She felt that she couldn't express her feelings in her relationship and that her husband didn't understand her emotional needs. She felt that she was alone with her feelings of frustration, depression, and anxiety. She also noticed her attempts to reach perfection in her activities and difficulties in setting boundaries, which easily led her to a state of fatigue.

Optimal basis for therapy (stage 1): Kati was curious about participating in IPMT, but at the same time she was very scared that she would fail. She thought that improvisational music-making would be some kind of performance where she could fail and embarrass herself. We used the first five sessions to build and create enough safety and trust for creative acts to happen. That meant gradual, safely-limited mutual experiments with instruments and a lot of empathic support and encouragement from the therapist to help Kati feel safe enough.

Act of improvising (stage 2): at the beginning of the therapy process Kati's improvisations had very clear structure, which indicated her insecurity and need to control the situation. Gradually she was able to liberate herself from this strict structure and she started to play around, trying to find new ways to express different emotions through the instrument. That made her smile, and she felt more calm than usual. Symbolism also appeared more and more in her playing. Gradually she started to play about her relationships and get more in touch with her real feelings, like anger and sadness. She could express those feelings in her playing, and afterwards when we listened to the improvisations she could also reflect and verbalize it.

Imagery process (stage 3) and Analytical process (stage 4): session 12 was a clear turning point in Kati's therapy process. It was also very meaningful when evaluating the development of her symbolic process through improvisation. In initial discussions, Kati said that she had felt very anxious during the day and tried to regulate that through different activities. She said that she really needed something new in her life. The starting point for our improvisation was to express

Table 26.2 Psychiatric test scores of Kati before and after music therapy

	Kati (pre)	Kati (post)
MADRS	31	15
HADS-A	14	2
GAF	51	68
RAND-36	35	62
TAS-20	42	34

her present feelings through sounds. What followed was a 30-minute long improvisation. The main difference between this improvisation and her earlier improvisations was the great use of dissonance and chaos in her playing. There were no longer strict limits or restrictions in Kati's musical expression, and for the first time she also used drums by her own choice. This demonstrated a remarkable progression and change in her recovery because drums symbolized for her most clearly feelings of aggression and hate, which had been forbidden and frightening emotions to her for many years. When she reflected upon her emotional state after the improvisation she said that she felt relieved and much calmer than before the improvisation. After some hesitation, she also told me that she 'committed suicide' in that improvisation.

Implementation (stage 5): this was clearly a symbolic and creative act to express and share something that she had held inside of her for many years. Now she was able to express her anger outwardly, and experience that another person can tolerate and share her emotions. After this improvisation Kati's recovery process developed very nicely. She was able to participate in and enjoy activities that she used to love but which had been impossible for her during her period of severe depression and anxiety.

26.8 Measuring recovery in IPMT

26.8.1 Results of psychiatric tests

Before music therapy Erik met the criteria for moderate depression (MADRS scores 20–29), for mild anxiety (HADS-A scores 8–10), and for alexithymia (inability to recognize and verbalize emotions, TAS-20 scores ≥61). After the music therapy he was no longer depressed, anxious, and alexithymic, and his social, occupational, and psychological functioning (GAF) and quality of life (RAND-36) had increased (see Table 26.1).

Kati was severely depressed (MADRS scores >29), and moderately anxious (HADS-A scores 11–14) before music therapy. After the music therapy there was only mild depression (MADRS scores 11–19) and no anxiety. Also her social, occupational and psychological functioning (GAF) and quality of life (RAND-36) had increased markedly (see Table 26.2).

26.8.2 Electroencephalography and creativity in IPMT

EEG measures the actual state and working mode of brain processing, and when compared to an EEG database of normal processing z-scores may indicate possible abnormalities or subtle developments. Frontal alpha asymmetry measures the degree of lateralization of approach and withdrawal behaviour in depression. Looking at their changes in the rest EEG (as a default state of brain activity) tells us about general changes due to interventions (Niedermeyer & Lopes de Silva, 1993).

26.8.3 Frontotemporal and parietal change in potential space

Erik had been under high emotional tension, and was also angry and fearful of being neglected in social relationships. This high tension was reflected in his pre-test theta z-scores that were above normal. Comparing his brain activations in rest before and after therapy, theta indicates more left frontotemporal amplitude increases and a strong decrease of left parietal alpha. Both topographic changes in the post MT rest EEG may reflect the change in the scores and indicate a change of attentional processing, sensory integration, and possibly a more distinct and rational differentiation of his emotional processes.

In Kati's case, comparing pre- and post-rest EEG power, a parietal change on theta and in high alpha frequencies as well as an increase of frontal midline theta was revealed. High alpha reflects changes in long-term-memory retrieval (Klimesch, 1996) and differentiation during music listening (Krause et al., 1999; Petsche et al., 1997). As parietal cortex is concerned with attention, spatial cognition, and sensory integration (Kolb & Whishaw, 2009), parietal increases in theta and alpha may reflect an increased awareness and shift of attention towards her new experienced degrees of freedom and recognition of own emotions and space needed for herself.

26.8.4 Anxiety, theta changes, and relaxation in 'therapy asylum'

The increases of frontal midline theta may reflect reduced anxiety. Does music therapy act like an anxiolytic or is it offering a way to relaxation and positive imagery in action? Anxiolytics are also found to increase frontal midline theta power; theta increases have been reported in meditative concentration, reduced anxiety and sympathetic autonomic activation, in task demands in virtual spatial navigation, focussed and sustained attention, working and recognition memory (Mitchell et al., 2008; Gruzelier, 2009). In a music listening study, frontal midline theta increased significantly when comparing EEGs before and after 22 seconds of listening to the music with content rated before as pleasant (Sammler et al., 2007). This research correlated the process of getting into a state of relaxed focused attention on perceiving the flow of music. When training musicians for optimal performance, those who received theta biofeedback prior to their performance were judged by independent raters as significantly better then those who received no such feedback (Egner & Gruzelier, 2003).

When individuals are in a 'playspace' they can produce a positive image of themselves acting and train their brain to make new connections in order to be prepared for real-life situations. Heilmann et al. (2003) suggest that a low-arousal and relaxed state promotes novelty and creativity in terms of illumination processes and memory retrieval by connecting different brain areas than those normally used for problem solving. Getting relaxed in a 'therapy asylum', and interactive play within a potential space of perceiving and acting during improvisation and imagery processes, is a prominent part of IPMT. Thus, creativity in music therapy offers a framework for utilizing divergent brain connectivity and new approaches towards former habituated behaviour patterns to be explored.

26.8.5 Right frontal hemisphere processes and perception-action system in music therapy

After therapy, Erik displayed lower scores on depression and anxiety scales, but in both cases alpha activity measured at electrode sites F7 and F8 in the frontotemporal cortex shifted to the right. This shift may indicate that the emotional process targeted in music therapy helped the clients on a prosodic level to express and differentiate the underlying emotional tension, anger and anxiousness of their withdrawal. Koelsch has stressed the close connection of semantic and syntactic functions in music and speech processing (Koelsch et al., 2004). Processing of melody is connected to pre-motor speech process activation at larynx level, as music listening initiates pre-motoric level movement processes such as dance, and facilitates hand–eye coordination (Aldridge, 1996). The music therapy process focuses on the performance and expression of emotions musically on pre-verbal and symbolical level in a space of play. Thus, music therapy structures and integrates the auditory perception and the motor action system (also discussed as the mirror neurone system: Koelsch, 2009), which mediates and organizes learning and recognizing where and when to act, as done in the temporal flow of improvisation with symbolic content. This process seems to transfer from pre-conscious to consciousness and motivates acting and performing verbal interaction in the social domain.

26.9 **Conclusion**

Improvisation plays an important role in non-verbal expression and interaction in music therapy. Psychotherapists in the verbal domain have also dealt with the psychotherapeutically relevant meaning of non-verbal expression and experiences. However, what usually separates verbal psychotherapy and IPMT is that the music therapist has a more active role as a creative, expressive actor. This may make IPMT sometimes difficult to control and manage for a therapist, but it also opens new channels of information flow and experience to the client's world.

In this chapter we have defined creativity as the competence of everyone, and as the quality, which we all need, when finding solutions in challenging situations, no matter whether they are in the emotional, social, or cognitive domain. In music therapy, restoring the previously lost ability of creativity may be a specific focus of the therapeutic work. This is true in particular with some pathological states such as psychosis, with clients with borderline diagnosis, or sometimes with clients with depression or anxiety diagnosis.

The concepts of recovery and creativity seem to be strongly inter-related in psychotherapeutic work. It is interesting that the inter-relatedness of the two concepts have been quite often made outside art therapies. In particular, psychoanalytic and psychodynamic psychotherapy traditions seem to stress the connection between creativity and recovery.

As IPMT music therapists we have often seen how creativity and recovery go hand in hand in an appropriate way. Rather often the clients adopt a method of working (clinical improvisation) quickly—during the first two to four sessions of the therapy process—even though the method may at first glance appear rather extraordinary for them. When the method has been adopted in its full sense, the various psychic contents that are linked to the clients' illness become both a motivating force and a target of the creative process of recovery. Flinging oneself into the creative process of IPMT, and into the symbolic and emotional working that follows, often leads to the development of new insights into one's illness, while at the same time guiding the client towards the necessary process of change.

A big challenge for all forms of therapy in Western healthcare are the issues of effectiveness and evidence. In our RCT we administered an exhaustive battery of psychiatric measures, and used brain imaging methods, when evaluating the effect of IPMT. The two client cases of this paper, both being examples of clients who according to the outcome measures did clearly benefit from the therapy, fitted well to the progressive model of recovery/creativity as well. Thus, emerging creativity during therapy, as it was described in our model, may act as an indicator of the process of recovery in general. Adopting methodology and techniques of brain research seem promising from psychotherapy research point of view as well. Freud's initial psychotherapy concept was based on neurologists' ideas communicated to Wundt in 1895. Recently, his ideas have been reconsidered in terms of brain plasticity and when looking at two cases from the stance of rest EEG we were able to describe changes that were linked to the process of recovery in IPMT, displaying decreases in psychometrics and, accordingly, different activations and connections of brain areas.

References

Aldridge, D. (1996). *Music therapy and research in medicine - from out of the silence*, London: Jessica Kingsley Publishers.

Barret, A.M., Beversdorf, D.Q., Crucian, G.P., & Heilman, K.M. (1998). Neglect after right hemisphere stroke: A smaller floodlight for distributed attention. *Neurology*, **51**, 972–8.

Barron, F. & Harrington, D. (1981). Creativity, intelligence and personality. *Annual Review of Psychology*, **32**, 439–76.

Basch-Kahre, E. (1985). Patterns of thinking. *International Journal of Psycho-Analysis*, **66**, 455–69.

Benau, K.S. (2009). Contrasts, symbol formation and creative transformation in art and life. *The Psychoanalytic Review*, **96**, 83–112.

Bronowski, J. (1972). *Science and human values*, New York: Harper and Row.

Bruscia, K.E. (1987). *Improvisational models of music therapy*, Springfield, IL: C.C. Thomas.

Bruscia, K.E. (1998). *The dynamics of music psychotherapy*, Gilsum, NH: Barcelona Publishers.

Craig, A.D. (2005). Forebrain emotional asymmetry: a neuroanatomical basis? *Trends in Cognitive Sciences*, **9**, 566–71.

de Alvarez de Toledo, L. (1996). The analysis of 'associating', 'interpreting', and 'words': Use of this analysis to bring unconscious fantasies into the present and to achieve greater ego integration. *The International Journal of Psychoanalysis*, **77**, 291–317.

de Backer, J. (2004). *Music and psychosis*. Aalborg: Institute of Music and Music Therapy, University of Aalborg.

de Backer, J. & Van Camp, J. (2003). The case of Marianne: Repetition and musical form in psychosis. In S. Hadley (Ed.) *Psychodynamic music therapy: Case studies*. Gilsum, NH: Barcelona Publishers.

Egner, T. & Gruzelier, J. H. (2003). Ecological validity of neurofeedback: modulation of slow wave EEG enhances musical performance. *Neuroreport*, **14**, 1221–4.

Elliot, A. (1999). Approach and avoidance motivation and achievement goals. *Educational Psychologist*, **34**, 169–89.

Erkkilä, J. (1997a). Musical improvisation and drawings as tools in the music therapy of children. *Nordic Journal of Music Therapy*, **6**, 112–20.

Erkkilä, J. (1997b). *Musiikin merkitystasot musiikkiterapian teorian ja kliinisen käytännön näkökulmista*. Jyväskylä: Department of Music, University of Jyväskylä.

Erkkilä, J. (2004). From signs to symbols, from symbols to words–About the relationship between music and language. *Music Therapy and Psychotherapy. Voices*, **4**.

Erkkilä, J. (2007). Improvisaatiopainotteisen musiikkipsykoterapiakoulutuksen kokemuspohjaisia sisältöjä. *Musiikkiterapia*, **22**, 76–88.

Erkkilä, J., Gold, C., Fachner, J., Ala-Ruona, E., Punkanen, M., & Vanhala, M. (2008). The effect of improvisational music therapy on the treatment of depression: Protocol for a randomised controlled trial (ISRCTN: 84185937). *BMC Psychiatry*, **8**.

Grencavage, L.M. & Norcross, J. (1990). Where are the commonalities among the therapeutic common factors? *Professional Psychology Research and Practice*, **21**, 374–76.

Gruzelier, J. (2009). A theory of alpha/theta neurofeedback, creative performance enhancement, long distance functional connectivity and psychological integration. *Cognitive Process*, **10**(Suppl 1), S101–9.

Hadley, S. (2003). Psychodynamic music therapy: An overview. In S. Hadley (Ed.) *Psychodynamic music therapy: Case studies*. Gilsum, NH: Barcelona Publishers.

Heilman, K.M., Blonder, L.X., Bowers, D., & Crucian, G.P. (2000). Neurobiological disorders and emotional dysfunction. In J.C. Borod (Ed.) *The neuropsychology of emotion*. New York: Oxford University Press, pp. 367–412.

Heilman, K.M., Nadeau, S.E., & Beversdorf, D.O. (2003). Creative innovation: possible brain mechanisms. *Neurocase*, **9**, 369–79.

Jausovec, N. & Jausovec, K. (2005). Differences in induced gamma and upper alpha oscillations in the human brain related to verbal/performance and emotional intelligence. *International Journal of Psychophysiology*, **56**, 223–35.

Klimesch, W. (1996). Memory processes, brain oscillations and EEG synchronization. *International Journal of Psychophysiology*, **24**, 61–100.

Koelsch, S. (2009). A neuroscientific perspective on music therapy. *Annals of the New York Academy of Science*, **1169**, 374–84.

Koelsch, S., Kasper, E., Sammler, D., Schulze, K., Gunter, T., & Friederici, A.D. (2004). Music, language and meaning: brain signatures of semantic processing. *Nature Neuroscience*, **7**, 302–7.

Kolb, B. & Whishaw, I.Q. (2009). *Fundamentals of human neuropsychology*, New York: Worth Publishers.

Krause, C.M., Porn, B., Lang, A.H., & Laine, M. (1999). Relative alpha desynchronization and synchronization during perception of music. *Scandinavian Journal of Psychology*, **40**, 209–215.

Lehtonen, K. (2007). *Musiikin symboliset ulottuvuudet*. Jyväskylä: Suomen musiikkiterapiayhdistys r.y.

May, R. (1975). *The courage to create*. New York, London: W.W. Norton & Company, Inc.

Metzner, S. (1999). Psychoanalytically informed music therapy in psychiatry. In T. Wigram, & J. de Backer (Eds.) *Clinical applications of music therapy in psychiatry*. London: Jessica Kingsley Publishers.

Mitchell, D.J., McNaughton, N., Flanagan, D., & Kirk, I.J. (2008). Frontal-midline theta from the perspective of hippocampal 'theta'. *Progress in Neurobiology*, **86**, 156–85.

Naiman, L. (2006). *What is creativity?* Vancouver, BC: Linda Naiman & Associates Inc.

Niedermeyer, E. & Lopes de Silva, F. (1993). *Electroencephalogralography*, Baltimore, MD: Williams and Wilkins.

Noy, P. (1966). The psychodynamic meaning of music—Part I. *Journal of Music Therapy*, **3**, 126–35.

Noy, P. (1967a). The psychodynamic meaning of music—Part II. *Journal of Music Therapy*, **4**, 7–23.

Noy, P. (1967b). The psychodynamic meaning of music—Part III. *Journal of Music Therapy*, **4**, 45–51.

Noy, P. (1967c). The psychodynamic meaning of music—Part IV. *Journal of Music Therapy*, **4**, 81–94.

Noy, P. (1967d). The psychodynamic meaning of music—Part V. *Journal of Music Therapy*, **4**, 117–25.

Ogden, T. (1985). On potential space. *International Journal of Psycho-Analysis*, **66**, 129–41.

Pavlicevic, M. (1997). *Music therapy in context: Music, meaning and relationship*. London: Jessica Kingsley Publishers.

Petsche, H., Kaplan, S., Vonstein, A., & Filz, O. (1997). The possible meaning of the upper and lower alpha frequency ranges for cognitive and creative tasks. *International Journal of Psychophysiology*, **26**, 77–97.

Priestley, M. (1975). *Music therapy in action*. New York: St. Martin's Press.

Priestley, M. (1976). Music, Freud and the port of entry. *Nursing Times*, **72**, 1940–1.

Priestley, M. (1983). *Analytische Musiktherapie*, Stuttgart: Klett-Cotta.

Rapaport, D. (1950). On the psychoanalytic theory of thinking. *International Journal of Psycho-Analysis*, **31**, 161–70.

Robertson, L.-C., Lamb, M.R., & Knight, R.-T. (1988). Effects of lesions of temporal-parietal junction on perceptual and attentional processing in humans. *Journal of Neuroscience*, **8**, 3757–69.

Rothenberg, A. (1979). *The emerging goddess: The creative process in art, science and other fields*, Chicago, IL: University of Chicago Press.

Sammler, D., Grigutsch, M., Fritz, T., & Koelsch, S. (2007). Music and emotion: electrophysiological correlates of the processing of pleasant and unpleasant music. *Psychophysiology*, **44**, 293–304.

Schaverien, J. (1997). Transference and transactional objects in the treatment of psychosis in Killick, K. & Schaverien, J. (Eds.) *Art, psychotherapy and psychosis*. London: Routledge.

Simonton, D. (1994). *Greatness: Who makes history and why?* New York, Guilford Press.

Soukhanov, A. (1988). Creativity. *Webster's II, New Riverside University Dictionary*. Boston, MA: The Riverside Publishing Company.

Stern, D. (1985). *The interpersonal world of the infant: A view from psychoanalysis and developmental psychology*. New York: Basic Books.

Sternberg, R. (1997). The concept of intelligence and its role in lifelong learning and success. *American Psychologist*, **52**, 1030–7.

Sternberg, R. & Lubart, T. (1992). *Defying the crowd: Cultivating creativity in a culture of conformity*, New York: Free Press.

Tomarken, A.J. & Keener, A.D. (1998). Frontal brain asymmetry and depression: A self-regulatory perspective. *Cognition and Emotion*, **12**, 387–420.

Torrance, E. (1975). Creativity research in education: Still alive. In Taylor, I. & Getzels, J. (Eds.) *Perspectives in creativity*. Chicago, IL: Aldine, pp. 278–95.

Wallas, G. (1926). *The art of thought,* New York: Harcourt Brace.

Wampold, B.E. (2001). *The great psychotherapy debate–Models, methods, and findings.* Mahwah, NJ: Lawrence Erlbaum Associates.

Wigram, T., Nygaard Pedersen, I., & Bonde, L.O. (2002). *A comprehensive guide to music therapy,* London: Jessica Kingsley Publishers.

Winnicott, D.W. (1968). Playing: Its theoretical status in the clinical situation. *International Journal of Psycho-Analysis,* **49**, 591–99.

Chapter 27

Developing creative improvisation skills in music therapy: The tools for imaginative music-making

Anthony Wigram

Applied improvisation in clinical work relies on the development of a range of musical techniques combined and integrated with therapeutic methods. Creative skill in improvisation is developed through the learning and practice of a wide range of musical techniques which can be spontaneously and intuitively drawn on to construct a flow of music. Improvisation has been described as a spontaneous creation of sounds and silence constructed within a framework of beginning and ending. The degree to which this production creates structured or unstructured music will be discussed, as well as which musical frameworks and styles can be incorporated. The differences between improvisation and extemporization, and between free and structured improvisation will be addressed, as well as the dynamics of the music and how they influence its character and mood. Examples from clinical cases will demonstrate the potential for inter-musical social engagement, musical and emotional synchronicity, and communicative musicality through improvisation.

27.1 Introduction

Improvisation is a creative process both for the player and the listener, and imagination plays a central role in that process. In music therapy, imagination finds its place in the creative development of improvised music, and this chapter will explore both the technical aspects of improvisation as a creative force as well as the potential for themes, images, stories, and pictures to provide the imaginative fuel to drive the improvisation experience. There is something about improvisation that fascinates some and terrifies others. We know it can be the most creative experience in the world, but it can also be the most frustrating and challenging. The art of composition is inextricably linked to improvisation, and the spontaneous creation of music in all societies is centred around cultural styles of improvisation. It has attained some of its most complex expression in the free jazz culture emerging throughout the 20th century, and the skills of jazz improvisers fascinate and hypnotize their audiences of aficionados. However, it is still considered almost a magical skill by many—a gift granted to the chosen few, while the rest are left with pieces of paper covered in black dots as their 'inspiration'.

This chapter discusses the acquisition of improvisation skills, different styles of improvisation, and how such a flexible and creative form of music-making can be applied in therapeutic work. Finally, the results from a research study where improvisational music therapy was applied to achieve measurable benefits for young children with autism will be described. The first steps for learning how to improvise may happen early in life, while for some musicians improvisation may never be either taught by instrumental teachers or studied and acquired as a skill. Yet all musicians at some stage 'doodle' and spontaneously make up melodies, rhythmic patterns, and accompaniments—the building blocks of improvisation skills. The intention in this chapter is to describe more specifically some of the musical techniques and therapeutic methods learned when studying the applied use of improvisation in music therapy. Three case vignettes from the fields of autism, learning disability, and dementia then illustrate these techniques. The chapter ends with a research study that looks closely at the impact of improvisational music therapy when compared with free play activities on shared attention and social behaviour in autistic children.

The subject of improvisation as a clinical tool in music therapy is very well covered and explored in a variety of different books and articles, both from the field of music and also from the field of music therapy, and the music therapy literature is full of explanations, well-documented theories, and arguments about the development and value of improvisation in clinical work (Bonde et al., 2001; Bruscia, 1987; Milano, 1984; Nordoff & Robbins, 1977; Pavlicevic, 1997; Pressing, 1988; Priestley, 1994; Robbins and Robbins, 1998; Schwartz, 1998; Wigram & De Backer, 1999a, b; Wigram et al., 1995, 2002). In the more general field of music performance, a comprehensive text (Nettl and Russell, 1998) covers a wide range of improvisational media with many perspectives on cultural diversity, training skills, and facets of improvisation in individual artists from the worlds of jazz, classical, and Eastern traditions.

Improvisational techniques are used in song-writing approaches for people living with mental illness (Grocke et al., 2009), in structured work with children with attention deficit hyperactivity disorder (Rickson, 2006), with those dealing with grief in childhood and adolescence (Hilliard, 2007; McFerran & Wigram, 2004), and for the assessment of parenting competencies for children at risk of being taken into care (Jacobsen & Wigram, 2007). Hilliard (2007) reported the use of and instruction in clinical improvisation in music therapy education in the USA. Cobbett (2006) reported on the value of improvisation and music when working with children in a school for the emotionally and behaviourally disturbed. He described play and imagination dramas involving music-making with this population. The emotional value of music-making is also well articulated in an article on the use of humour in improvisational music therapy in child psychiatry (Haire and Oldfield, 2009). Lee (1995) draws on methods of musicological analysis to look closely at the structure of musical improvisation with clients, and Ansdell (1997) explores the relationship between music therapy and new musicology. Songwriting also employs improvisational techniques (Baker & Wigram, 2005), and has addressed specific emotional needs in the fields of oncology and palliative care (Aasgaard, 2005; Dileo & Magill, 2005; O'Brien, 2005).

Many of these articles and studies report the use of clinical improvisation. Music therapy theoreticians were concerned to differentiate between musical improvisation and clinical improvisation so as to prevent a perception of music therapy being simply an artistic/creative musical process. The definition of musical improvisation proposed by the Association of Professional Music Therapists in the United Kingdom is: 'Musical improvisation: Any combination of sounds and sounds created in a framework of beginning and ending'.

This allowed all sorts of noises to be included and defined as musical improvisation, and originated from Alvin's concepts of atonal improvisation emerging from the radically new musical composition styles, including those of Stravinsky and Schoenberg, in the late 19th and early 20th century. Utilizing the definition of musical improvisation, a clearer perspective of clinical improvisation established therapeutic purposes for the process, and thus was defined in the following way: 'Clinical improvisation: The use of musical improvisation in an environment of trust and support established to meet the needs of clients'.

The critical part of this definition is '. . . to meet the needs of the clients', which should be placed at the centre of any musical process that has an underlying therapeutic purpose.

27.2 **Playing by heart—the first stage**

When children start to learn to play instruments, particularly perhaps the piano, the first priority is almost always to learn to read music. Then they learn to 'interpret' the music, incorporating all the marks of expression that composers write into their scores, and create feeling and style in their playing. Finally, teachers demand that students learn the music well enough to play without having to look at the score—'playing by heart', as it is sometimes quaintly called in the English language—or playing from memory. Students are still reproducing another's composition, staying (within the frame of their own interpretation) true to how they think the composer intended the music to sound.

27.3 **Playing by ear—the key to improvisation**

Playing (or singing) 'by ear' is a technique that can function at a very simple, or very complex level—depending how well developed the understanding and ability to use harmonic, melodic, and rhythmic structure is. The process involves listening to some music—a solo melody, song with harmony, ostinato rhythm, symphony—and then working out how to 'reproduce' the music on piano, voice, or another instrument without ever seeing the music as a notated score. It is not easy to explain how this skill is acquired, but practice and developed memory are key factors. Moog (1976) studied the acquisition of melodic and rhythmic patterns in infants and young children. The melodies are frequently phrases in popular songs, and the rhythmic patterns are likewise linked to the music around them. This skill is derived from developing memory and an increasing understanding of and ability to reproduce musical structure. Sloboda and Parker (1985) reported that people with quite limited musical training are able to reproduce characteristic melodic and rhythmic patterns with correct metrical structure and harmonic sequences.

While these skills can be acquired by normally developed children and adults, there are also some notable cases of autistic 'savants', with remarkable musical abilities, who can hear and accurately reproduce music without ever learning to read a score (or indeed to read words or numbers). This skill is certainly enhanced by the acquisition of musical knowledge, but also appears to be honed by considerable practice, and an ability to hear when the reproduction sounds 'right' and is the most accurate reproduction of the original. The main reason it helps prepare for the development of improvisation skills is that one becomes quite at home with picking up an instrument and creating music, without relying on the notes in a score. Of course, it is most developed in everyday singing, in which humming tunes that one picks up is characteristic in every culture. These perspectives on playing by heart and by ear are mainly offered from the author's own experience, and there is an extensive literature on how musical skills develop in children. McPherson (2006) reports a variety of aspects relating to the development of musical skills, including the development of vocal and instrumental skills.

27.4 **Pastiche improvisation—using a framework or genre as a structure for improvisation**

Playing 'in the style of . . .' is different from playing by ear. Here, one gains enough experience and practice in a style of music to be able to improvise in that style. The word pastiche is more applied to this process in composition, where one actually writes music in the style of a composer—and is more typically applied to classical music, which is sometimes taught by teaching how to write Bach chorales and fugues, or string quartets 'in the style of' Mozart. Some enthusiastic composers continue to write pastiche music—preferring to reproduce a much loved and understandable style than to try and develop a new style. In the 1960s and 1970s there was a quiz programme on British television called 'Face the Music' presented by the incomparable Joseph Cooper, in which a team of three celebrities tested their knowledge of classical music through musical 'games' that included such gems as the 'dummy keyboard' on which Cooper played, and the team had to try to work out what he was playing by watching his fingers. Another game was the 'hidden melody', in which Cooper took a well-known melody and disguised it in the style of more than one composer—sometimes up to four different styles—in a prepared example. This 'hidden melody' was pastiche—or 'playing in the style of' at its best—and it was fascinating to watch Cooper subtly adapt well-known melodies such as 'It's a Long Way to Tipperary' or 'Auld Lang Syne' into the style Debussy, Brahms, or Bach.

27.5 **Flexibility in free improvisation**

Improvisation is a much freer and more flexible way of creating music than either playing by ear or playing 'in the style of'. It can be both more simple and more complex, and also essentially original and idiosyncratic. Learning to improvise is a valuable skill for children learning music. An important and interesting perspective on the art of improvisation, with a particular focus on some of the processes involved in teaching this difficult subject, was documented by Schwartz (1998). Schwartz explored the whole process of learning improvisation as a student and teaching improvisation as an educator by undertaking qualitative interviews with students and teachers of improvisation.

Learning to improvise can be challenging because you are spontaneously creating music which is your own, and this impromptu composition can attract the same subjective and objective criticism that any composition attracts—'too repetitive, too loud, too dull, not a good structure, no nice melodies, poor harmonic modulations, limited, confusing, no direction etc., etc.'. Those who begin to improvise, especially as a performance for others, are creating music that is essentially drawn from their own technical and musical resources, and creative impulse. As one of the most significant pioneers in music therapy in Europe during the middle of the 20th century, Juliette Alvin (1975) once described, 'music is a creation of man—and that is why we can see man in his music'.

Schwartz (1998) captured the defensiveness and insecurities of people embarking on developing their improvisation skills, and comments he noted as typical included:

> 'You're no good at improvisation.'
> 'You can't do this! You're not free enough.'
> 'This is a waste of time.'
> 'OK, enough!'

Musicians can quickly become very dissatisfied with how they play and what they play when improvising, as compared to being able to play a pre-composed song (even their own), or a Beethoven piano sonata, and the problem is frequently due a lack of technique.

27.6 **Improvisation involves the development of a range of techniques and skills**

Teaching improvisation is, in itself, a skill that has to be learnt, developed, and honed into the ability to tease out and nurture the creative, flexible musicality and technical skills in a student. It's not magic, and improvisation doesn't come like a gift, except to a very few. Even those for whom it appears to be an inborn skill will experience limitations in their potential unless they find a way to develop their talent. Most of us work hard at it, building up our skills and abilities, remembering to take into consideration many different aspects while we're playing and incorporating them as we develop more and more complex styles of improvisation. Nevertheless, it can be quite soul-destroying when practising alone, if everything goes wrong and the creative juices don't flow! Particularly when trying to improvise in tonal frameworks, people confront their difficulties in creating spontaneous melody with a sense of line and direction, managing harmonic structure, and achieving a sense of form in the music. When this doesn't work, they can resort to atonal music to avoid such challenges in the hope they will be free of musical rules, conventions and demands. This may result in even greater disillusionment as atonal music that lacks form or creativity can also become limited and directionless.

In music therapy, atonal improvisation is generally regarded as the medium by which the clients who are referred for therapy can most authentically reveal inner states, unconscious conflicts and repressed expression (Priestley, 1994; Wigram et al., 2002). While no musical skill is supposed to be necessary in the clients, therapists have the responsibility to model and evoke musical creativity in the clients in order for them to access this medium. Just as therapists have achieved their own improvisational skills, so their skill is also to equip the clients with the confidence and ability to enter into musical improvisation as a therapeutic process. It has to be recognized that while music therapists undergo extensive training to be able to improvise, the clients do not, and may even be overwhelmed by the therapist's improvisational strategies. But the argument for the accessibility of music therapy as a therapeutic medium is that everyone has musical resources, if accessed sensitively, to play and create.

Learning to improvise is a tremendously exciting and satisfying experience. One is not exactly becoming a composer of music, as unless one has the equipment for recording and reproducing the improvisation, it will probably never be heard again. Improvisation is spontaneous and can frequently never be repeated in the same way. So while it is not composed music, it is personal and individual music which, as Juliette Alvin says, represents various aspects of the person. To be clearer, those 'aspects' of a person can and do include various different influences and elements, because the production they make on any occasion will contain include the past and the present:

The past:

◆ Musical culture from which they come.

◆ Musical skills they have acquired.

◆ Musical taste and preferences.

◆ Influences in the way they have been taught, or learnt, music.

◆ Associations to the past, and past life events.

The present:

◆ Current musical 'fad' or interest.

◆ Life events that influence them currently.

◆ Mood or emotional state at the time.

◆ Personality, character as it is developed at the time.

The variability of dynamics often affects the quality and creativity of improvisation, and subsequently the impact of improvisational techniques as therapeutic tools designed to promote expressions and communication. Developing these skills is a process, and acquiring a range of simple to complex techniques is the first step in the process that then moves on to incorporating into those 'techniques' those musical parameters that can vary the quality and style of the playing. Having achieved these steps, and becoming consciously aware all the time to sustain either variability or stability in the music, one then develops into a process of simultaneously integrating and diversifying one's improvisation skills.

Bruscia (1987) documented a lengthy list of improvisational techniques that are appropriate in therapy, to which this author has extended existing methods and added new methods and concepts (Wigram, 2004). In his foreword to Wigram's (2004) text, Bruscia comments that 'It is the first book to extricate improvisation training from specific clinical models of music therapy. It is the first book geared toward musicians who may be beginning pianists. It is the first book that includes improvisation on different instruments. And it is the first book to integrate musical and clinical techniques of improvisation for both individual and group sessions' (p. 15). This chapter will refer to many of the important methods explained in this book, which has become a core text for improvisation in several countries. Many people, musicians and non-musicians, recognize the creativity and potential of improvising, and not in music alone. Theories abound to explain the characteristics and infinite possibilities generated through improvisation, but I centre my work on explaining methods and techniques and devising teaching strategies for developing improvisational skills which often need to be concretely taught. As Bruscia comments, 'This is not a book that theorizes about improvisation, it is a book that actually teaches someone how to go about the musical task of building one's own improvisatory repertoire of skills, written by someone who knows what the problems are' (p. 16).

27.7 The language of musical expression

Music is often described as a language. Well, for it truly to be a language, it would have to have a much clearer structure of recognizable symbols, and a more developed syntax and semantic framework. Melody, for example, has many of the components of spoken language, with its inflexions and its phrasing. Meaning in improvised music is usually specific to the person who is creating it, however, and the empathic level of sharing that goes on is not precise—although it can be authentic in reflecting moods, emotions, and attitudes. There is an extensive literature on the relationship between music and language in music psychology. Sloboda (1985), in describing the cognitive psychology of music, makes pertinent comparisons between music and language in relation to phonology, syntax, and semantics.

Musical elements play a tremendously important role, and the core elements of music—pitch/frequency, tempo/pulse, rhythm, intensity/volume, duration, melody, and harmony—determine the style and quality of what one hears. Hallam et al. (2008) recently published a comprehensive handbook of music psychology that defines musical elements in relation to human perception and development. The balance of melody against harmony, the use of pulse and phrasing, the structure of the harmonic frame and the influence of harmonic change or modulation, often characterize the aesthetic qualities and 'beauty' of music, which is complemented by the more 'primitive' elements of tempo and rhythm which can influence dynamic quality and the level of energy. The variability and flexibility with which an improviser can employ and integrate all of these elements is what characterises improvisational skill.

The imagination expressed within any musical production involves changes in expression and dynamics, which can either be subtle or dramatic, to convert what is initially a combination of frequencies played with different timbres into an expressive and communicative experience. If the improviser takes away some of these elements, reducing the number that can be employed, the result often enhances the communicative potential. For example, given a drum or tambour, two individuals, or a group, can play around with rhythms, tempo, metre, and accents, and put aside harmony and melody. 'Drum talk', used in group improvisation, can be a more exciting and communicative medium of expression than when potentially more complex and expressive instruments such as metallophones, guitars, and pianos are the tools of the experience.

27.8 Improvisation training begins with musical techniques

Individuals who create improvised music deploy their own musical techniques and styles, and the music they create will be influenced by their own technical skill, cultural background and musical preferences. In music therapy, a wide range of musical styles, idioms, and techniques is needed in order to meet the idiosyncratic preferences of all of our clients in order to establish a good enough musical relationship with them. However, an important caveat in musical improvisation with people with serious mental, physical, or emotional problems is the need for some form or structure, and the therapist's ability to utilize improvisation is most effective and creative when a simple idea is repeated, varied, extended, and creatively expanded. People's first attempts at improvisation are often characterized by running from one musical idea to another, frequently changing the music in order to meet an imagined ideal that the music needs to continuously change and develop.

To achieve flexibility and variability in improvising, skills need to include how to establish a pulse, lose a pulse, how to establish a metre or change a metre and lose a metre, how to develop a 'recitative' style of playing and then move into a pulse, and how to develop simple harmonic accompaniments from which one can improvise freely. Many of these techniques are extremely useful and applicable in therapeutic work. Musical techniques also need to include varying volume, tempo, timbre, rhythm, duration, and pitch. The potential for an improvisation to be colourful, imaginative, creative, developing, and dynamic depends on the variability of these elements. It is not uncommon for the creative process to be hindered and blocked by becoming stuck in tempo, mezzoforte playing and a lack of accents, rhythmic variability and undirected or rigid melody and harmony. Considering the classical examples of thematic improvisation found in the works of Bach (e.g. C minor Passacaglia for organ), Mozart (e.g. D Major Sonata, variations) or Beethoven (e.g. 5th Symphony, 1st movement), many are strongly characterized by an underlying pulse and metre. The pulse provides the driving force of the improvisation, and the metre gives it structure. In present day improvising, beginning from the creation of completely new music, not only do we often still need to ground our improvised music in a stable pulse—with or without changes in tempo, but there is also frequently the presence of a sense of metre in the rhythm and tempo of the music. Metre can act as a valuable 'anchor' in defining the structure of the music, but it can also function as a musical 'prison', because the presence of strong beats confirmed by regular accentuation establishes a fixed pattern.

The common metres such as 4/4, 3/4, and 2/4 provide clear accents in the music. Compound time, with metres such as 6/8, 9/8 or 6/4, offer different possibilities for strong beats, and then irregular metres such as 5/4 or 7/8 give us a sense of structure with either a syncopated or cross rhythmic effect. One of the other great values of providing an established metre is that it allows the development of syncopated playing with unexpected and irregular accents. It is also possible to alter the metre flexibly, using the pulse as a pivot to move from 3/4 to 4/4, or from 6/8 to 7/8. Figure 27.1 provides an example of a tonal melody developing into a chordal 1st inversion and second inversion improvisation over octaves with flexible metres.

The piece begins in 2/4, shifts into 3/4 without changing tempo, and then continues to change metre. At bar 17, an irregular 5/8 metre begins, followed in bar 22 by letting go of any sense of metre in the music. The music continues moving in and out of metre to demonstrate the importance of allowing flexibility in musical tempo and metre, avoiding getting 'stuck' in an unchanging 4/4 or 3/4/pattern.

27.9 Therapeutic methods

The musical techniques are then utilized in discrete but connected therapeutic methods, such as matching, reflecting, accompanying, dialoguing, extemporizing and frameworking: these terms are defined below, as well as in Wigram (2004). Musical techniques and therapeutic methods are areas of knowledge and skill that complement each other, and while one cannot use a therapeutic method without the musical technique, the musical techniques on their own, without a focus for

Fig. 27.1 Metre and lack of metre in a piano improvisation using 6ths and 3rds over an octave bass. Reproduced by kind permission of Jessica Kingsley Publishers from Wigram, T. (2004) *Improvisation: Methods and Techniques for Music Therapy Clinicians, Educators and Students*. London: Jessica Kingsley Publications.

therapeutic intervention, lack purpose. Addressing all of these methods is beyond the scope of this chapter, but perhaps the most relevant one from the perspective of imaginative play is the use of musical and therapeutic dialogues. Recitatives and duets in opera and oratorio give us a strong foundation for the potential of dialogue through music. Words are involved, and the dialogue in these styles of composition become musical conversations. But a conversation can equally be

Fig. 27.1 (*Continued*)

non-verbal, and can be either a turn-taking dialogue such as the cat duet (Duetto buffo di due gatti: Rossini, 1816), or heard as a continuous exchange of musical themes and ideas, as found in the opening movement of the Concerto for two violins by Bach. Many of Bach's contrapuntal compositions for solo or several instruments can be heard as musical dialogues, as can the quartet from Verdi's *Rigoletto* or the Octet in the last scene from Mozart's *Don Giovanni*. So in improvisational music therapy, the role of music-making as a vehicle for a creative and imaginative 'duet' is one of the most important and potentially unique mediums for communication—particularly with those who are functioning at a pre-verbal or non-verbal level. Music can contain a gentle chat, exciting discussion or dynamic argument. Dialogues as used in music therapy are defined as follows:

'Turn-taking' dialogues: making music together where the therapist or client(s) can cue each other to take turns in a variety of ways, musical or gestural. This 'turn-taking' style of dialogue requires one or other to pause in their playing and give space to the other.

Continuous 'free-floating' dialogues: making music in a continuous musical dialogical exchange— a free-floating dialogue. Here participants (therapist(s) and client(s)) play more or less continuously and simultaneously. In their playing musical ideas and dynamics are heard and responded to, but without pause in the musical process' (Wigram 2004, p. 98).

27.9.1 **Case vignette**

Joel was a 7-year-old boy with suspected autism spectrum disorder. From the beginning of a diagnostic assessment session, he demonstrated a high level of interest in music-making, as well as a style of playing that reflected his pathology in the presence of repetitive patterns in the way he played, and some preoccupation with the mechanical structure of the instruments he was using. This case was previously reported in some depth (Wigram, 2002). In a turn-taking imaginative game, Joel accompanies himself on the piano and develops vocal turn-taking with the therapist. The therapist alternates a microphone that can amplify between Joel and himself, switching it every two bars within a 4/4 structure. Joel plays randomly on the piano, a steady pulse, while improvising in the style of a children's song. More and more spontaneous language emerges, as when Joel takes his turn to sing into the microphone he makes up short melodic fragments. This is later transferred into the next improvisation, in which Joel has taken over the microphone himself and is singing spontaneously with the therapist, providing a tonal, jazzy supportive framework. Joel then reverses the situation, and every four bars he points the microphone at the therapist to 'give him his break'. It is an example of turn taking that then develops into a simultaneous dialogue.

27.10 **The need for structure—extemporizing and frameworking**

Whereas improvising could be described as the process by which one spontaneously creates 'new' music, and the musical material does not rely on a pre-defined set of criteria or structures from music that is already composed, published or recorded, extemporizing employs quite a different model. Extemporization is the ability to improvise on some existing composed musical material, or in a known style. When applicants are interviewed for the 5-year education in music therapy at Aalborg University, Denmark, they are given a short 2 to 4-bar melody fragment in a specific style and they are asked to '. . . continue to make up (improvise) a melody in the same style as the fragment. . . .'.

This is very much what extemporizing is about, and is why it is such a useful technique, both as a musical exercise and skill, and also as a technique in music therapy. One works with situations and clients in which the use of free improvisation or atonal improvisation might be inappropriate (or perhaps even contraindicated), and the clients might find it quite difficult to deal with freely developed and spontaneously created sounds for various different reasons. For example, it has often been said that elderly clients with senile dementia or Alzheimer's disease find atonal or free improvisation a difficult medium in music therapy, and are much more attracted to working with structure and with songs that they know. Consequently, the ability to extemporize in a certain style, giving a starting point, is a very useful skill and technique for music therapists. It also offers the possibility of developing or making a transition from a song or a piece of music into something more improvised, and perhaps more personally expressive. At the same time, when one develops the extemporization, because one is working within a style of a piece of music, it enables one to return to the original composition or song at moments when the client demonstrates some insecurity, confusion, or resistance. My own definition of extemporization (Wigram, 2004) is as follows:

27.10.1 **Extemporize/extemporization**

'Improvising on some given musical material, or as a pastiche of a style of composition, maintaining the musical and dynamic characteristics of the style.'

This requires an ability to develop a musical structure that is related to, and congruent with, an existing musical style given in a song, piece, or musical example. The extemporized music is an extension of some music in which one is improvising 'in the style of' that music, using the same musical elements and staying close to the original material. In guiding this approach, there are some methods to develop these skills:

◆ Notice carefully the harmonic and rhythmic structures of the music, and use them in the extended material.
◆ Choose the moment in the music where the extemporization can begin—for example avoiding a perfect or a plagal cadence at the end of a 'verse', 'section', interrupting the cadence and starting the extemporization.
◆ If the music is centred around the tonic, dominant and sub-dominant and mediant (minor) types of harmonies, use these structures in the extemporization while varying the melodic style.
◆ Incorporate slowing down, speeding up, getting softer and louder into the extemporization, as well as some pauses in the music.
◆ Use some of the principles of thematic improvisation to pick out parts of the musical material in the original music to make some specific developments, e.g. melodic phrases or rhythmic patterns.
◆ Develop an ability to slip back into the original music, sometimes when it's a song going back in at a chorus section or half way through.

(Wigram, 2004: pp. 114–15.)

Extemporizing can be quite simple, but can also be quite complex and skilful. When using more tonal music, the practitioner needs to have quite a good understanding and facility with using modulation and transposition, and an understanding of choral structure and tonal sequences. The cycle of fifths is commonly used in many compositions, and can be employed in extemporization as well. It is equally important to remember that the skill of extemporizing is to use the existing material, staying true to the existing musical ideas and components, but also to develop the creative 'improvising' process in the music. Therefore, many musicians and practitioners may find extemporizing a greater challenge to their musical (and therapeutic) skills than improvising—in which one retains the freedom to invent and create music. However, the objective (and value), clinically, is to stay close to the material with which the client feels most comfortable, while introducing the potential for the music to become more individually expressive and representative of the client's own feelings and ideas. Simply playing a song that clients request from beginning to end, and then stopping, does not allow them to represent their own feelings to the extent they may need to in the music, as they are confined by the performance and style of the song. Extemporization is a very good alternative to playing or using an existing piece of music, or freely improvising.

27.10.2 Case vignette

Joan (now deceased) was a 64-year-old lady with learning disabilities and dementia. Using free improvisation with Joan, especially atonal improvisation without a clear rhythmic structure or tempo, left her confused and unable to play or sing. For Joan, music-making involved singing her most favourite songs, usually songs from the war years such as 'It's a Long Way to Tipperary' and 'Underneath the Arches'. She was also very familiar with all the songs from the shows, and while she could not recall what she had for breakfast, would demonstrate complete recall of words when singing 'Surrey with the Fringe on Top' or 'Oh what a Beautiful Morning'. While this satisfied her very much, and provoked nostalgia and sadness as well as humour, therapy sessions began to lack creativity and imaginative potential. Joan liked to play a drum or metallophone when singing, just to accompany herself.

The structure of a song such as 'Oh what a Beautiful Morning' is clear and simple, and at the end of the chorus, instead of ending with a perfect cadence (G major 7 to C major), completing the song, I interrupted the cadence (G major 7 to A minor), modulated into D minor, and developed a new section to the song in the minor, colouring the music with softer dynamics, then a staccato section (still maintaining the waltz style and the tempo) and expanding into a recapitulation of the theme. Joan stopped singing when the music deviated from the melody of the song, but continued playing. As new ideas came into the musical extemporization, including the staccato section, soft playing, Joan adapted her playing, and began to demonstrate creative engagement with the therapist's music, following ideas within this style, and becoming more expressive. For Joan, extemporizing provided her with a familiar extension to the style of music-making she could engage with, while allowing her to explore a creative way of increasing and extending her capacity for expression.

27.11 The use of a musical framework for creativity and imagination

If extemporizing is a method of extending in the same style a musical improvisation, then creating a musical framework has the function of 'Providing a clear musical framework for the improvised material of a client, or group of clients, in order to create or develop a specific type of musical structure' (Wigram 2004: p.118). Bruscia describes a process called 'Experimenting'—and explains that it involves 'providing a structure or idea to guide the client's improvising, and having the client explore the possibilities therein' (Bruscia 1987: p. 536).

This technique emerged from the author's lengthy period of clinical practice in a large institution for people with mild to profound intellectual and developmental disability. Such clients often have very limited ability at first when playing, and may be restricted to single and occasional bangs on a drum, or perhaps a continuous slow pulse. When matching this empathically, the resulting music from therapist and client can remain as a limited and repetitive series of meaningless sounds. Providing a musical framework utilizing a style or genre from classical, popular, ethnic, or folk music can inspire and stimulate their response. The consequence is that their response does become more excited, more engaged with the music of the therapist, and quite often more complex. Frameworks can be simple (a structured melody, harmony, or rhythm) or complex (involving all three within in a musical form). One essential element for a framework to be understandable and usable by the client is a degree of predictability and structure. So if a jazz framework is used, it will need to contain a sure enough bass structure such as a walking bass, chords that follow a predictable pattern—tonal or dissonant, and melodic style that also contains repetitive figures. There needs to be some direction and familiarity in the musical material. As well as jazz frameworks, one can work equally well with well-known songs or pieces interspersed with improvised or extemporized sections.

27.11.1 Case vignette

Jamie was a 5-year-old child with odd communicative behaviour attending for diagnostic assessment. He failed to recognize or engage in conventional social exchange, and while he was friendly, he also appeared not to follow or understand social behaviour. He was assessed by a variety of professionals from disciplines including psychology, speech and language therapy, and music therapy to reach a diagnostic opinion. Jamie engaged very quickly with music-making, and the best example of frameworking was in a piano duet. Jamie was playing in the upper half of the piano with the therapist (the author) in the bass. Turn-taking started the playing, followed by a simple melody with a harmonic structure using the cycle of fifths. Jamie began to play randomly but in time using both hands—the left to copy chords and the right (mostly on one note) to match melody. The therapist's music got faster, and Jamie followed the tempo. The genre of the music changed, with the therapist offering a 1920s Charleston style structure, at which Jamie laughed with delight and excitement and he tried to follow the melody idea on the piano. The therapist then softened the style, slowed the tempo, and as the assessment was being undertaken near to Christmas, used first 'I'm Dreaming of a White Christmas' followed by 'Jingle Bells' as frameworks. Jamie continued to play, but also began to sing with both songs. It was clear that he did not know White Christmas well, and just 'la la'd along to it. But he was more accurate with 'Jingle Bells'. While Jamie was ultimately diagnosed as a boy with autism spectrum disorder (ASD), in this improvisation, he demonstrated both a close response to the ideas of the therapist, an ability to play imaginatively and creatively, and demonstrably good inter-subjective behaviour and referencing. The framework offered the structure he needed to understand how to play together with another, one of the biggest pathological difficulties for those with ASD.

27.12 **Research on improvisational music therapy**

There is an extensive literature which documents a variety of research studies with many populations using clinical (musical) improvisation as the primary therapeutic intervention to address their clinical needs, including patients with psychotic disorders (De Backer, 2008), those with severe intellectual and developmental disability (Holck, 2004), with schizophrenia (Pavlicevic, 1995), with young hearing-impaired populations with cochlear implants (Kerem, 2008), and children and adolescents with autism (Di Franco, 1999; Edgerton, 1994; Wigram & Gold, 2006). Trondalen (2003) studied the process of self-listening in a young woman suffering from anorexia nervosa.

To illustrate the significance of improvisation as a therapeutic tool, one particular study will be described in this chapter. Kim (2006) undertook a doctoral investigation at Aalborg University to measure the effects of improvisational music therapy on the development of joint attention behaviours in children with ASD. Members of this population are known to experience disturbances in the development of their joint attention skills as part of social deficits such as impairments in social interaction and social communication, and rigid patterns of behaviour.

In the improvisational music therapy literature, some qualitative studies and many clinical reports demonstrate that 'the controlled use of musical attunement' (Wigram & Elefant, 2008), directed by the therapist towards the child's musical and non-musical expression and state, promotes the child's capacity for self-expression, emotional communication, and social interaction (Alvin & Warwick, 1991; Brown, 1999; Edgerton, 1994; Holck, 2004, 2007; Kerem, 2008; Wigram, 1999a, b, 2002). Without the capacity for joint attention, communication and social interaction becomes disordered and impaired, and the learning ability of a child is significantly affected. Kim's (2006) main hypothesis was that: 'Finely tuned, sensitive and attentive use of improvised music (musical attunement) towards the developmental needs and state of the child with ASD will open and maintain the communicative channel with the child. The child's ability in joint attention will increase positively over time, and musical attunement will play a significant role in improving joint attention behaviour of the child with ASD' (p. 54). In the context of the improvisational music therapy approach used in this study, joint attention involved finding 'an interactive state of joint engagement that involves the self (the child), another (the therapist), and objects in musical form (instrumental, or vocal joint engagement), or in play (toys)' (p. 288).

A randomized clinically controlled study was designed using a repeated measures, within-subjects comparison, in which ten children aged from 3–6 years recruited for the therapy sessions had 12 individual free play sessions with toys as a control condition to compare with 12 individual improvisational music therapy sessions. Duration and approach were matched in the two conditions.

In addition, to explore arguments for or against more directed or less directed approaches, each session began with 15 minutes of child-led music or play activity, followed by 15 minutes of therapist-led activity. The range of instruments used in the study always included a piano, large drum, standing cymbal, alto xylophone (diatonic), and chroma harp, and also available on the shelves in the room were horns and whistles (a pair of Nordoff–Robbins pitched horns, bird whistles, pair of kazoos), smaller instruments such as egg shakers, tone bars, hand bells in different colours, and Guiro and Remo (brand name) paddle drums.

Target behaviours (dependent measures) that were clear indicators of joint attention (and social behaviour) included frequency and duration of eye contact, events of joy, turn-taking, emotional synchronicity, musical synchronicity, and frequency of initiation of engagement by the child and by the therapist, and events where the child imitated the therapist. These behaviours were measured by detailed video analysis of samples (two 4-minute extracts) from sessions 1, 4, 8, and 12. Interobserver agreement was measured by intraclass correlation coefficients, and on all target behaviours except imitation (0.69), correlations were between 0.86 and 0.98.

The results from both the standardized and non-standardized measurements were generally that music therapy was more effective than free play, and that these measures indicated improvements in the joint attention behaviours of children over time. Kim found that the process of music therapy facilitated the simultaneous coordination of 'listening', 'looking at the therapist', and 'responding' and 'engaging', and the results suggested that improvisational music therapy facilitated social learning of children with ASD. Increased motivation was an important outcome, and was noticeable in the musical interactions in which improvisational music therapy produced 'joy' and 'emotional synchronicity': these events were more frequent and of a longer duration than free play episodes, and so clearly influenced the degree of spontaneous 'initiation of engagement' behaviours in children (Kim, 2006).

Improvised music-making in music therapy often allows flexibility in following and leading behaviour, and the balance between these continues to be important for people with ASD. When two or more people improvise together, a process of intuitive give and take, spontaneous musical dialogue and freedom of autonomy are necessary to develop a sharing in the music-making. An important outcome from this study was thus the finding that there were markedly more 'joy', 'emotional synchronicity', and 'initiation of engagement' events in the first (non-directed or child-led) 15 minutes of the sessions than in the second (more therapist-directed) 15 minutes, suggesting that these children were happier, more able to express their emotions and to share their affects with the therapist: they also displayed more initiatives when they were leading and controlling the musical interaction with the therapist. Figure 27.2 illustrates the difference between the two conditions when the frequency and duration of events of emotional synchronicity are greater in the music therapy sessions than the free play sessions ($p < 0.0001$), but also demonstrates that in the undirected half of the session, the frequency ($p = 0.0006$) and the duration ($p = 0.0079$) of emotional events is greater. There is an improvement over time in the music therapy sessions in frequency ($p < 0.0001$) and duration ($p = 0.0012$), when compared with free play. An analysis of the salient musical elements in events that were categorized as musical synchronicity found rhythm and dynamics to be the key parameters that facilitated this, with much less influence from vocalization and melody.

While this may be connected to the pathology of autism spectrum disorder, in which there is a need for control, and for play to be 'on the child's terms', the social events noted in the musical improvisational play are nevertheless particularly important for engaging in a healthy and friendly social relationship (Wigram, 2002; Wigram & Elefant, 2008). These children displayed more co-operative and interactive behaviours in music therapy. Kim (2006) reported that her study supported the long-lived claims of improvisational music therapy as an intervention that promotes

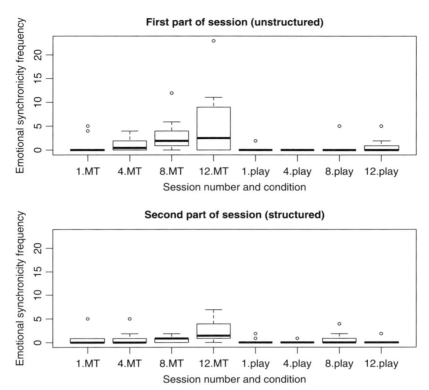

Fig. 27.2 Frequency of emotional synchronicity events when comparing music therapy with play in both the undirected and directed parts of the sessions over eight pre-chosen samples from sessions 1, 4, 8 and 12. From Kim, J., Wigram, T., & Gold, C. (2009). Emotional, motivational and interpersonal responsiveness of children with autism in improvisational music therapy, *Autism*, **13**(4), 389–409. Copyright © 2009 by Sage publications. Reprinted by permission of SAGE.

'self expression, emotional communication and social interaction' (p. 290). A similar pattern was found when analyzing the data for the frequency of events in initiation of engagement (Figure 27.3). Kim's study demonstrated the applied use of improvisation techniques to achieve joint attention and social engagement, and, together with the author, adopts an approach to engaging children that is grounded both in the improvisational techniques described in this chapter, and in the phenomena of affect attunement and intersubjectivity described by Stern (2010). In a recent keynote presentation delivered to the Nordic Conference of Music Therapy, Stern said that:

> If I take something like Tony Wigram's concept of 'matching'—when he talks about matching in music therapy as (as he puts it) one of the most valuable techniques or modalities that music therapists have, he is talking about taking some kind of musical event and keeping some aspects of it the same in response—let's say the key, or the dynamic texture, or the tempo etc.—but you change something. So it's not an imitation, but a matching. Now this is absolutely fascinating, because in all of our developmental research and a lot of our adult psychotherapy research we find that this kind of inter-subjective matching which we call affect attunement is at the base of so much of the relationship and the transmission and communication between therapist and client.

Improvisational approaches to children with ASD, as demonstrated in Kim's study, achieve the effect they do through these modalities and methods.

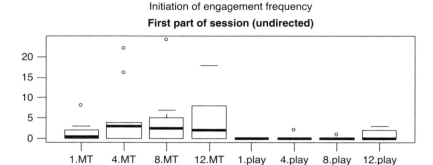

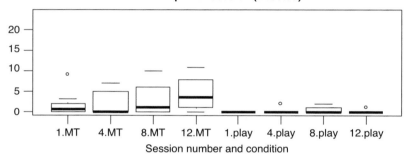

Fig. 27.3 Frequency of initiation of engagement events when comparing music therapy with play in both the undirected and directed parts of the sessions over eight pre-chosen samples from sessions 1, 4, 8 and 12. From Kim, J., Wigram, T., & Gold, C. (2009). Emotional, motivational and interpersonal responsiveness of children with autism in improvisational music therapy, *Autism*, **13**(4), 389–409. Copyright © 2009 by Sage Publications. Reprinted by permission of SAGE.

27.13 Conclusion

This chapter has explored the extensive and complex field of improvisational music therapy to describe some of its techniques, and to illustrate its use in clinical practice and research. Music provides a very flexible and wide-ranging tool for expressive and imaginative creative play, and improvisation is a medium which is increasingly valued. While conventional composition in all genres of music up to the beginning of the 20th century often involved a degree of improvisation, the performance aspect relied on the musicians following the written score of the composer. Composers were nevertheless frequently gifted improvisers, and that emerged in all styles. In the field of music therapy, improvisation is a skill that is widely taught, and offers the necessary flexibility, structure and lack of structure for a client to be able to access music-making as a medium for therapeutic change, whether or not they have previous musical training or skills.

Bibliography

Aasgaard, T. (2005). Assisting children with malignant blood disease—to create and perform their own songs. In F. Baker, & T. Wigram (Eds.). *Songwriting: Method, techniques & clinical applications for music therapy clinicians, educators and students*. London: Jessica Kingsley Publications, pp. 206–25.

Alvin, J. (1975). *Music therapy (revised edition)*. London: Claire Books.

Alvin, J. & Warwick, A. (1991). *Music therapy for the autistic child* (Second Edition). Oxford: Oxford University Press.

Ansdell, G. (1997). Musical elaborations: What has the 'new musicology' to say to music therapy? *British Journal of Music Therapy*, **11**, 2.

Baker, F. & Wigram, T. (2005). *Songwriting: Method, techniques & clinical applications for music therapy clinicians, educators and students*. London: Jessica Kingsley Publications.

Bonde, L., Nygaard Pedersen, I., & Wigram, T. (2001). *Når ord ikke slår til: En håndbog i musikterapiens teori og praksis i Danmark* [Music Therapy: When words are not enough. A handbook of music therapy theory and practice in Denmark]. Aarhus: KLIM.

Brown, S. (1999). The music, the meaning, and the therapist's dilemma. In T. Wigram & J. De Backer (Eds.) *Clinical applications of music therapy in developmental disability, paediatrics and neurology*. London & Philadelphia: Jessica Kingsley Publishers, pp. 183–97.

Bruscia, K. (1987). *Improvisational models of music therapy*. Springfield, IL: Charles C. Thomas Publications.

Cobbett, S. (2006). Music therapy for excluded adolescents with challenging behaviour: Finding the right language. Conference of the British Society for Music Therapy and the Association of Professional Music Therapists: 'The Sound of Music'. Personal communication.

De Backer, J. (2008). Music and psychosis: A research report detailing the transition from sensorial play to musical form by psychotic patients. *Nordic Journal of Music Therapy*, **17**(2), 89–104.

Di Franco, G. (1999). Music and autism. Vocal improvisation as containment of stereotypes. In T. Wigram & J. De Backer (Eds.) *Music therapy applications in developmental disability, paediatrics and neurology*. London: Jessica Kingsley Publishers, pp. 93–118.

Dileo, C. & Magill, L. (2005). Songwriting with oncology and hospice adult patients from a multicultural perspective. In F. Baker & T. Wigram (Eds.) *Songwriting: Method, techniques & clinical applications for music therapy clinicians, educators and students*. London: Jessica Kingsley Publications, pp. 226–45.

Edgerton, C. (1994). The effect of improvisational music therapy on the communicative behaviours of autistic children. *Journal of Music Therapy*, **31**(1), 31–62.

Grocke, D., Bloch, S., & Castle, D. (2009). The effect of group music therapy on quality of life for participants living with a severe and enduring mental illness. *Journal of Music Therapy*, **46**(2), 90–104.

Hallam, S., Cross, I., & Thaut, M. (Eds.) (2008) *The Oxford handbook of music psychology*. Oxford: Oxford University Press.

Haire, N. & Oldfield, A. (2009). Adding humour to the music therapist's tool-kit: reflections on its role in child psychiatry. *British Journal of Music Therapy*, **23**, 127–34.

Hilliard, R.E. (2007). The effects of Orff-based music therapy and social work groups on childhood grief symptoms and behaviors. *Journal of Music Therapy*, **44**(2), 90–112.

Holck, U. (2004). Interaction themes in music therapy—definition and delimitation. *Nordic Journal of Music Therapy*, **13**(1), 3–9.

Holck, U. (2007). An ethnographic descriptive approach to video microanalysis. In T. Wosch & T. Wigram (Eds.) *Microanalysis in music therapy. Methods, techniques and applications for clinicians, researchers, educators and students*. London: Jessica Kingsley Publishers, pp. 29–40.

Kerem, D. (2008). The effect of music therapy on spontaneous communicative interactions of young children with cochlea implants. Unpublished doctoral thesis, Aalborg University, Denmark.

Kim, J. (2006). The effects of improvisational music therapy on joint attention behaviours in children with autism spectrum disorder. Unpublished doctoral thesis, Aalborg University, Denmark.

Kim, J., Wigram, T. & Gold, C. (2009). Emotional, motivational and interpersonal responsiveness of children with autism in improvisational music therapy. *Autism*, **13**(4), 389–409.

Jacobsen, S. & Wigram, T. (2007). Music therapy for the assessment of parental competencies for children in need of care. *Nordic Journal of Music Therapy*, **16**(2), 129–43.

Lee, C. (1995). Transcription of an improvisation from a session with a client living with HIV Aids. In C. Lee (Ed.) *Lonely waters*. Oxford: Sobell Publications.

McFerran, K. & Wigram, T. (2004). Articulating the dynamics of music therapy group improvisations: An empirical study. *Nordic Journal of Music Therapy*, **14**(2), 33–46.

McPherson, G. (Ed.) (2006). *The child as musician: A handbook of musical development*. Oxford: Oxford University Press.

Milano, D. (1984). Jazz pianist and psychiatrist Denny Zeitlin on the psychology of improvisation. *Keyboard*, **25**, 30–5.

Moog, H. (1976). *The musical experience of the pre-school child* (C. Clarke, Trans.). London: Schott.

Nettl, B. & Russell, M. (1998). *In the course of performance: Studies in the world of musical improvisation*. Chicago, IL: University of Chicago Press.

Nordoff, P. & Robbins, C. (1977). *Creative music therapy*. New York: Harper and Row.

O'Brien, E. (2005). Songwriting with adult patients in oncology and clinical haematology wards. In F. Baker & T. Wigram (Eds.) *Songwriting: Method, techniques & clinical applications for music therapy clinicians, educators and students*. London: Jessica Kingsley Publications, pp. 185–205.

Pavlicevic, M. (1995). Interpersonal processes in clinical improvisation: Towards a subjectively objective systematic definition. In T. Wigram, B. Saperston & R. West (Eds.) *The art and science of music therapy: A handbook*. London: Harwood Academic Publishers, pp.167–80.

Pavlicevic, M. (1997). *Music therapy in context: Music, meaning and relationship*. London: Jessica Kingsley Publishers.

Pressing, J. (1988). Improvisation: Methods and models. In J.A. Sloboda (Ed.) *Generative Processes in Music*. Oxford: Clarendon Press, pp. 129–78.

Priestley, M. (1994). *Essays of analytical music therapy*. Gilsum, NH: Barcelona Publishers.

Rickson, D.J. (2006). Instructional and improvisational models of music therapy with adolescents who have attention deficit hyperactivity disorder (ADHD): A comparison of the effects on motor impulsivity. *Journal of Music Therapy*, **43**(1), 39–62.

Robbins, C. & Robbins, C. (Eds.) (1998). *Healing heritage: Paul Nordoff exploring the tonal language of music*. Gilsum, NH: Barcelona Publishers.

Schwartz, D. (1998). The search for magic: Teaching music improvisation. Unpublished master's thesis: University of East Anglia, UK.

Sloboda, J.A. (1985). *The musical mind: The cognitive psychology of music*. Oxford: Clarendon Press.

Sloboda, J.A. & Parker, D.H.H. (1985). Immediate recall of melodies. In P. Howell, I. Cross, & R. West (Eds.), *Musical structure and cognition*. London: Academic Press, pp. 143–67.

Stern, D. (2010). The issue of vitality. Keynote address to the Nordic Conference of Music Therapy. *Nordic Journal of Music Therapy*, **19**(2), 88–102.

Trondalen, G. (2003). "Self-listening" in music therapy with a young woman suffering from anorexia nervosa. *Nordic Journal of Music Therapy*, **12** (1), 3–17.

Wigram, T. (1999a). Assessment methods in music therapy: A humanistic or natural science framework? *Nordic Journal of Music Therapy*, **8** (1), 7–25.

Wigram, T. (1999b). Variability and autonomy in music therapy interaction: Evidence for diagnosis and therapeutic intervention for children with autism and Asperger's syndrome. In R. Pratt & D. Grocke (Eds.) *MusicMedicine 3: MusicMedicine and music therapy: Expanding horizons*. Melbourne: Faculty of Music, University of Melbourne.

Wigram, T. (2002). Indications in music therapy: Evidence from assessment that can identify the expectations of music therapy as a treatment for autistic spectrum disorder (ASD): Meeting the challenge of evidence-based practice. *British Journal of Music Therapy*, **16**(1), 11–28.

Wigram, T. (2004). *Improvisation: Methods and techniques for music therapy clinicians, educators and students*. London: Jessica Kingsley Publications.

Wigram, T. & De Backer, J. (1999a). *Clinical applications of music therapy in developmental disability, paediatrics and neurology*. London: Jessica Kingsley Publishers.

Wigram, T. & De Backer, J. (1999b). *Clinical applications of music therapy in psychiatry.* London: Jessica Kingsley Publishers.

Wigram, T. & Elefant, C. (2008). Therapeutic dialogues in music: Nurturing musicality of communication in children with autistic spectrum disorder and Rett syndrome. In C. Trevarthen and S. Malloch (Eds.) *Communicative musicality.* Oxford: Oxford University Press, pp. 423–45.

Wigram, T. & Gold, C. (2006). Research evidence and clinical applicability of music therapy for autism spectrum disorder. *Child Care: Health and Development,* **32**(5), 535–42.

Wigram, T., Saperston, B., & West, R. (1995). *The art and science of music therapy: A handbook.* London, Toronto: Harwood Academic Publications.

Wigram, T., Nygaard Pedersen, I., & Bonde, L.O. (2002). *A comprehensive guide to music therapy. Theory, clinical practice, research and training.* London: Jessica Kingsley Publications.

Part 6

Afterword

Chapter 28

Beyond creativity?

Nicholas Cook

28.1 A sociocultural approach

Both musicology and psychology have from the beginning been motivated by the desire to uncover the hidden, to penetrate the mysterious, and a fascination with the questions posed by the act of creation is deeply built into both disciplines. Traditionally answers were sought through a focus on the individual genius. Approaches were premised on the assumption that creativity is a rare gift, that the function of art is to address the individual subject, that in music the highest expression of this art is composition, and that art stands at a remove from the world. In contrast, creativity emerges from this book as having exactly the opposite characteristics: it is a fundamental attribute of humanity, it revolves round social interaction, it is most strongly expressed in performances (for Mari Tervaniemi 'the most creative forms of musical activities'), it is embedded and embodied in the practices of everyday life. According to Juniper Hill, 'over emphasis on individuality . . . obfuscates the collective nature of musical creativity', and the contributions to this book make a strong claim that the same can be said about other aspects of traditional approaches to musical creativity.

Where traditional models of creativity were oriented towards enduring products, such as musical works, this book focuses rather on creativity as something you do, something that not only generates social or aesthetic meaning but is also inherently pleasurable. (The pleasure of creation is rarely thematized in this book, though Emery Schubert's discussion of dissociation furnishes an exception, but it is everywhere implied.) In Ian Sutherland's and Tia DeNora's words, creativity 'affords a space for thinking about the world around us', a resource for acting within it. They are talking about Paul Hindemith, who was forced by the circumstances of interwar Germany to refashion his professional identity, and whose creative work reflects the processes through which he did so. Another such resource is what Göran Folkestad calls the 'personal inner musical library', the virtual playlist we all carry around in our heads, which serves to define who we are both in our own eyes (and ears) and in those of the other people in our lives. All identities are relational—we define ourselves in relation to others—and so the inner musical library is not the purely subjective construction as which it may appear: it is oriented towards the other, just as Hindemith's refashioning of the self was not a purely private process but was translated into explicit social action and interaction through such initiatives as the *Plöner Musiktag*. There is, then, a continuity between the apparently private 'space for thinking about the world around us' to which Sutherland and DeNora refer, and the 'potential' and 'play' spaces which Jakko Erkillä and his co-authors describe in relation to that most intensely interpersonal of situations, the musical therapy session. Creativity is enacted in the transformation of the self with respect to the other, and music has a special role in the delineation of creativity as a medium that combines heightened sociality, instantaneous feedback, and transparency: as Lori Custodero says, quoting the words of John Blacking, through music 'inner feelings are publicly shared'.

This book, then, locates the core of musical creativity in social interaction, and accordingly—as Eric Clarke observes—grounded in the larger social and institutional systems of which it is, in a sense, a product. Such a sociocultural approach, as the editors term it, draws in part on the concept of distributed cognition: as embodied in Edwin Hutchins's (1995) famous study of the operation of a naval ship, this involves not only the distribution of knowledge across different individuals, but also negotiations of knowledge between them. Karen Littleton and Neil Mercer coin the term 'interthinking' to describe this relational process, and both their chapter and that of Raymond MacDonald and his co-authors illustrate how, in music, knowledge is not only shared but transformed in the course of rehearsal. This is not simply a matter of interpretation, in the narrow sense in which performance practice studies use that term, but one of negotiating personal and group identity: in Littleton and Mercer's words, 'this process of negotiating . . . could be a highly charged and deeply meaningful process for the band members', one which was 'inextricably interwoven with the negotiation of a distinctive band sound'. But there is a further crucial feature of the multilateral interactions that make up ensemble performance, whether in rehearsal or concert. As Keith Sawyer has argued with particular reference to jazz improvisation, each player's interpretive choice at each moment impacts on all the other players' choices, and the result is what he terms a 'combinatorial explosion' of potential interactions: 'this wide range of possible trajectories', Sawyer (2003: p. 91) continues, 'results in unpredictable emergence'. In other words, the act of real-time performance generates meanings, whether interpretive, acoustic, or interpersonal, that are emergent in the sense that they could not have been predicted by any of the performers, or on the basis of the various inputs to the performance event. Sawyer's argument becomes the more powerful when that event is construed (as it is in this volume by Folkestad and by David Hargreaves and his co-authors) as an extended network that encompasses all its participants, audience included, and if there is one feature that underlies the sociocultural concept of creativity as it is developed in this book, it is perhaps this quality of emergence.

When creativity is understood as subsisting in social interaction, the kind of individualistic creation that formed the focus of traditional, genius-oriented creativity research becomes a special case. MacDonald and his co-authors argue that even the 'solitary explorations of a child with a new instrument may be viewed as social given that they take place within a family or other social environment', while Folkestad claims that making music is 'always a collective activity, regardless of whether it is done individually or in a group'. The apparent paradox is resolved if we think of solo performance as involving an internalization of the processes of interaction that characterize collective performance. A straightforward example is provided by a study of a contemporary piano work in rehearsal and performance (Cook, 2005). Although the score of the work in question, Bryn Harrison's être-temps, looks like a highly prescriptive specification of the performer's interpretation, the pianist, Philip Thomas, treated it much more like a real-time interlocutor. In interview he described one passage notated by means of nested irrational rhythms as 'a classic kind of notational device to prompt the performer to respond in ways which will always keep it floating and never rooted in anything, always keep it changing'; in conversation with the composer he said how he practised the music, 'and then you get used to it, and it gets compromised again, so I've got to keep kicking myself in the arse to kind of take it apart again, I think that's the problem, I've got to keep unravelling it'. Interaction of another kind is illustrated in the present volume by Karin Johansson, who locates the spectrum of organists' performance practices from interpretation to improvisation within a universe defined by multiple texts: 'organ improvisation', she writes, 'is not only aurally transmitted but is characterized in all its aspects by relationships to scores, by intertextuality, and by being situated in the tradition of composition'. This rich contextualization of the self in relation to the others who collectively make up the tradition of organ performance might be seen as corresponding to the interactive networks of collective performance, although the element of emergence is less strongly present. But then, if creativity is seen as grounded in social interaction, it follows that it is not so much enacted as represented in solo performance.

28.2 **Does creativity exist?**

Juniper Hill, who complains about the overemphasis of individual creativity, also points out that 'an overemphasis on collective composition by earlier generations of folk music scholars ran the danger of mystifying creative processes into myth and making invisible the creative contributions of individuals'. Might it then be argued that an exclusively sociocultural approach to creativity represents an over-reaction against older, more individualist approaches, and risks diluting the concept of creativity through excessive breadth? As with John Cage's maxim on composers, if we are all creative, what does being creative actually amount to?

In their contributions to this volume, Simon Frith and Margaret Barrett observe that it is generally taken for granted that creativity is inherently good, despite its obvious potential for being used to evil ends. (The same might be said of music, except that its usefulness for evil ends is more limited.) Creativity is associated, for instance, with the carer/child interactions described by Colwyn Trevarthen, and with Daniel Stern's 'vitality affects'; it is embodied in what Tony Wigram calls the 'affect attunement' and 'emotional synchronicity' of improvisation-based music therapy, one of the basic of tenets of which (as Denise Grocke and David Castle say) is its accessibility to all regardless of training. Again, Istvan Molnar-Szakacs and his co-authors see it as inherent in the construction and communication of empathy. The prominence in this volume of studies based in therapy reflects the extent to which this has become a paradigmatic model of music's socially transformative potential in general, but it goes further than that: the definition of creativity as a social good is evident in Trevarthen's very vocabulary when he attributes it to the faculties 'enabling synchronization of purposes and pleasures in creative social participation and giving rise to the techniques and arts of cultural evolution'. The question that arises is how far it is always possible to identify exactly what is meant by creativity over and above social good: Bradley Vines's contribution, for instance, is not obviously about creativity in any direct sense, but rather about the undoubtedly beneficial potential of music for the treatment of stroke patients with non-fluent aphasia.

But the charge of excessive breadth is not restricted to the sociocultural approach to creativity embodied in this book. Schubert's 'mechanical' (one might say quasi-neural) model of creativity defines creativity in terms of the generation of a new pathway between 'two unrelated concepts', an approach which echoes Arthur Koestler's once influential theory of bisociation. That in itself was a variant of metaphor theory, since Koestler's time developed (by George Lakoff and Mark Johnson, and thereafter by Gilles Fauconnier and Mark Turner) into a general model of conceptualization. In other words, the concept of emergence on which Fauconnier and Turner's conceptual blending approach is based has been transformed from the context of elite creativity with which Koestler was concerned to a ubiquitous, even universal feature of human thought and communication: creativity becomes the norm, something we become aware of only when, exceptionally, it is absent (for example, in the case of those therapeutic clients with whom music functions as a means of eliciting social interaction). Perhaps then, creativity might be thought of in much the same way that the American Standards Association defines timbre: not as a unified phenomenon definable in its own right, but rather as what is left over once you have accounted for the various categories of rational thought (logical, mathematical, and so on). Folkestad stresses the situated nature of all creative practice, and for this reason prefers to replace the reifying noun 'creativity' by the verb 'to create'; outside this book, Pam Burnard (forthcoming) also avoids the term 'creativity' and speaks instead of 'creativities'.

Margaret Barrett's overview in this volume of creativity research, brief as it is, makes Burnard's point. Indeed several of the contributions provide illustrations. Shira Lee Katz and Howard Gardner describe quite distinct approaches to creation (distinct creativities?) among contemporary composers. Eric Clarke shows how the approaches to jazz improvisation of Philip Johnson-Laird and David Sudnow respectively reflect its cognitive and embodied dimensions: should we think of these as different dimensions of a single creative practice, or as complementary modes of creativity? More generally, it is hard to see any particularly convincing reason for believing that Boden's and Csikszentmihalyi's approaches to creativity deal with different sides of one phenomenon rather than distinct, if sometimes co-occurring, phenomena. It may, in short, be futile to attempt an overall definition of creativity that is more specific than that it feels good, does good, and leaves traces which may prompt future acts of feeling or doing good; that it involves some quality of emergence; and that it doesn't fit into categories of rational discourse. It is noticeable that most attempts to define 'creativity' in this book are either similarly broad (for example, Erkkilä), or conflations of a number of previous definitions (for example, Hill or Katz and Gardner). While I shall continue in this afterword to speak of 'creativity', then, I mean the term to refer to an indefinite number of related concepts or behaviours.

In any individual instance, however, the invocation of creativity is likely to mean something more specific than this might suggest. The polemical thrust of Konečni's contribution to the present volume, which ascribes emotivist approaches to creativity to 'the contemporary anti-narrative and anti-intellectual social relativism', offers one illustration, but the general point can be illustrated through a more everyday example: the sense of jarring that arises when questions relating to individual creativity (intention, expression, and so on) are posed in relation to folk crafts or vernacular architecture. The jarring arises through a mismatch of aesthetic and ideological premises, and—rather as in the case of Hill's complaints about individualism and collectivity—it could equally be argued that individualistic conceptions drawn from high art are being inappropriately imposed on vernacular crafts, or that attention is being drawn to unthinkingly stereotyped assumptions about the nature of communal practice. My point is simply that any real-world invocation of creativity comes with a range of connotations, that these connotations are intrinsic to the ascription of creativity, and that to this extent creativity cannot be comprehensively or exclusively evaluated on the basis of material artefacts. It is a bit like art dealing, where you may be able to prove that a supposedly 17th-century painting is a fake through physical analysis (for instance, if it contains synthetic pigments), but proving that it is original will almost certainly require a provenance, in other words information external to the object. In the same way, aesthetic originality depends not just on the artefact in which it is embodied, but (as Clarke puts it in a passage to which I have already referred) on the larger 'social systems making judgments about individuals' products'.

Any such principle of the social production of creativity is bound to create problems for psychological approaches that 'place creativity firmly inside the heads of its creators', as Clarke continues, and in particular neuropsychological approaches that seek to ground experiences and behaviours in biological processes. Although Schubert is careful to distinguish his 'mechanical' model of creativity from a neural one ('These nodes and links are analogous to biological neurons and synapses respectively, but are generally not intermingled to avoid an implied assertion that they necessarily the same thing'), his contribution provides a striking illustration of the problem: he cites, as if it were authentic, a famous statement about Mozart's compositional process that was long attributed to the composer but—as Maynard Solomon (1980) has conclusively shown—was actually written in 1815 by Johann Friedrich Rochlitz, who edited the *Allgemeine musikalische Zeitung*, in which it was first published. (Vladimir Konečni, in his contribution, cites a barely more reliable source, not in fact a letter by Beethoven but a report published more than 50 years after the composer's death by his acquaintance Louis Schlösser, which contains rather too many echoes of Rochlitz's fabrication for comfort.) Of course such statements are good historical evidence, but they are evidence of aesthetic ideology and mythologization rather than of the actual practices of musical composition, evidence in other words of the sociocultural web within which creativity is produced—and the same might indeed be said of many statements that really were made by composers.

There is, in short, an irresolvable tension between two approaches which both feature strongly in this book: on the one hand the sociocultural and ecological approaches that understand creativity to be socially produced, with Rochlitz's and Schlösser's claims being part of that process of social production, and on the other hand those physical and biological approaches which, in Tervaniemi's words, locate 'musical creativity in the musician's brain'. In saying this I do not intend to denigrate neuropsychological approaches to musical creativity. It is probably fair to say that musicology and other disciplines of music study are at the present time net exporters of knowledge to neuropsychology: some of the work Tervaniemi reports provides confirmation of processes or abilities that are so musically self-evident that failure to confirm them might cast doubt upon the principles of brain localization or the techniques used to detect it. But that is of course exactly how one makes progress in an area of extremely complex research which, as Tervaniemi makes clear, is still in its early stages. The balance of trade between musical and neuropsychological knowledge may well change in the future. But even then, to demonstrate a neural correlate of a musical phenomenon is not necessarily to explain it in a culturally useful sense, any more than you can explain the qualities of Shakespeare's plays through a chemical analysis of the first folio, and for this reason there is little cause to believe that cultural approaches to creativity will be rendered obsolete through the advance of neuropsychological ones. Returning then to the irresolvable tension to which I referred, the appropriate response is not to attempt to resolve it, but rather to acknowledge that any approach to complex cultural phenomena must be partial and complementary to other approaches, that it is indeed likely to be most informative when deployed in relation to other approaches, and that the more such an approach delimits the scope of creativity (as in the case of Schubert's definition of it in terms of spreading activation theory), the more it should probably be seen as representing one out of an indefinite number of creativities.

For some of the contributors to this volume, recognition of the social embeddedness of creativity prompts analysis of what might be done to foster it, particularly in the context of politicians' prioritization of the 'creative economy'. Barrett cites John Howkins's argument that creativity depends on 'a rich mix of ecological factors, primarily diversity, change, learning, and adaptation. It exists only where the ecology permits'. And that is in effect the starting point for Hill's contribution, which offers a cross-cultural comparison of creative ecologies, focusing on the beliefs, aesthetic ideologies, and institutional structures that promote or inhibit creativity. Other contributors, however, develop the argument about the social constructedness of creativity in a more radical direction, reflecting long-standing sociological suspicion of the way in which discourses of creativity not only obfuscate processes of cultural production but also mask underlying agendas. A classic example of this is Tia DeNora's (1995) study of the sociocultural factors underlying the construction of Beethoven's genius, but in the present volume this argument is presented most strongly by Frith. 'Music', he says, 'is the result of institutional practices in which some musicians have authority over others; creativity is both an explanation and justification of that authority'. He analyses these institutional practices and their ideological underpinnings, focusing in particular on the New Labour and the 'creative economy', and on constructions of authenticity in rock: to identify creativity with freedom and claim that all humans are creative, he argues, is to overlook the way in which creativity is socially produced, for 'in capitalist societies musicians are *constrained* to be creative, both culturally and as a matter of political economy'. All this, Frith continues, means that 'the concept of "musical creativity" is more of a hindrance than a help in understanding music-making practice', and so he concludes, 'we should cease to use the term altogether'.

Even the editors of this book seem to have taken this critique to heart: the term 'creativity' has been demoted to the subtitle, being replaced in the main title by 'imaginations'—a term which they see as more inclusive in its scope, and which at the same time serves to distance the book from more traditional approaches to the subject. It has to be said, though, that most of the contributors write as if the main topic of the book is musical creativity, whatever that may be, and I am no exception.

28.3 Creativity everywhere

Given that creativity proves to be such a slippery topic, we should probably be mistrustful of any binary oppositions that depend on it, of which there are many. The ubiquitous concept of 'creative practice', which embraces making music, visual practice, and creative writing, is an example: it is used in academic management contexts in order to draw a distinction with academic writing, in other words uncreative practice, though that term is not in common currency. The problem is obvious. The distinction between fictional and non-fictional writing lies hardly at all in processes of origination or qualities of emergence; it lies to only a limited degree in criteria of truth and value, but is rather grounded in the historical, institutional, and ideological contexts of cultural production. But whereas this particular binary looks implausible as soon as it is spelled out, many others are in common currency, including in this book: examples include creation versus reproduction, improvisation versus performance, and interpretation versus imitation. In each case the ascription of creativity to the first term devalues the second. I wish to argue that all of these represent continua rather than categorical distinctions, that in each case the behaviour designated by the second term is more complex and indeed creative than it is generally given credit for, and that it is particularly undesirable to map such oppositions onto different musical genres.

The concept of imitation allows me to make the point on the basis of contributions to this book. Adam Ockelford's study of memorization, focusing on the playing of the savant Derek Paravicini, echoes and extends the findings of Sloboda and Parker's (1985) classic study: musical imitation involves breaking down stimuli into intelligible units and reconstructing them in accordance with available cognitive schemata. In other words, it is intrinsically interpretive. What Ockelford shows particularly clearly is how, as memory demands increase, use is made of precisely those techniques of 'borrowing, transforming, and recombining materials' which, in the more prestigious contexts of jazz improvisation and classical composition, are regarded as emblematic of creative practice. (The moral seems to be: when all else fails, be creative.) A parallel might be drawn between the interweaving in Paravicini's playing of relatively literal and more overtly interpretive imitation and the way in which organists, responsive to the demands of unfolding liturgical events, interweave composed and improvised elements in their playing: Johansson speaks of 'a kind of creative copying' through which existing style elements are internalized. Imitation of quite a different sort is a fundamental dimension of collective performance, ranging from realization of the imitative textures composed into baroque chamber music to dialoguing in jazz improvisation, and two contributions to this volume explore this in different contexts. Molnar-Szakacs and his co-authors stress the links between imitation and empathy: 'the inner mirroring of other's actions and emotions', they write, 'allows us to co-create a shared, affective communicative experience'. Finally Custodero speaks of the intensity with which children imitate one another when making music together as 'a possible indicator of flow', in other words as an index of creativity, and speaks more generally of its 'complexity and usefulness'. When one considers the role of imitation in historical and non-Western cultural practices (think of Wagner writing out the full score of

Beethoven's Ninth Symphony, or the close copying through which traditional Chinese painting is taught), it may well appear that an unreflective focus on a poorly defined 'creativity' has militated against appreciation of the complexity and value of imitation, not only as a vehicle for teaching and learning but also as a fundamental feature of human interaction.

An opposition that perhaps bears more directly on the concerns of this book, however, is that between improvisation and the performance of composed music. Graham Welch's contribution turns on the contrast between a classical tradition oriented towards the reproduction of pre-existing texts within a predominantly solo context, and what he terms 'other-than-classical' traditions (including popular, jazz, and folk) that are oriented towards real-time creation in contexts of group performance: his basic argument is that the former is greatly over-emphasized in music education relative to the latter. At one level the contrast is self-evident, but at another it warrants scrutiny. An obvious point is that playing from notation is not restricted to classical music, and improvising is not restricted to other-than-classical music: MacDonald and his co-authors report a questionnaire study of rock, jazz, and classical improvisers which showed that 'key cognitive processes of their improvisation (such as anticipation, emotive communication, flow, feedback, and use of repertoire)' were consistent across these different genres. Again, Johansson graphically demonstrates how there is a continuum of practices between the extremes of near-literal reproduction and near-free improvisation, and how these are routinely intertwined with one another, in the classical sub-genre of liturgical organ performance. But the point is really a much more general one. Performers of, for example, a classical string quartet are not simply executing the instructions in the composer's score. They are constantly adjusting their timing, their intonation, their dynamics, and their tone production to those of the other players: the nominal values in the score (where every crotchet is exactly twice as long as a quaver) form a framework within which actual values are negotiated in real time, giving rise to the same kind of combinatorial explosion that Sawyer theorizes in relation to jazz improvisation. In this sense the quartet players are improvising within the framework of the score, and it is because this entails constant interaction with the other players—because improvisation subsists in openness to the other—that Ingrid Monson's (1996: p. 84) observation that, in jazz, 'To say that a player "doesn't listen" . . . is a grave insult', applies with equal force to classical musicians. The same applies to Monson's (1996: p. 186) observation that music has 'as one of its central functions the construction of social context'.[1]

Custodero's observations about imitation emerge from what she calls the 'microanalysis' of interactions between children making music together, and this echoes Eve Harwood's work on African American girls' singing games: Harwood (1998: p. 123) concludes what might be termed a series of microanalytical case studies with the comment that 'The improvisations may be on a miniature scale but they are significant within this community, where informants are sensitive to and highly critical of even slight deviations from the prescribed texts, tunes, and methods for play of their standard repertoire'. This in turn resonates with Ockelford's observation that classical composers exercised their creativity within tight stylistic constraints, and he adds that 'the degree of novelty required to create an original piece of music is surprisingly small' (he even provides the figures to back this up). In the same way, the improvisation inherent in classical performance is exercised within tight compositional constraints, but is significant within a musical community whose participants—listeners as much as performers—are highly sensitive to nuance, to the meaningful, negotiated shaping of the notes: it is, after all, in such shaping that the art of classical performance lies, given that, in some classical repertories at least, deviating from the prescribed notes may be highly criticized. It is, perhaps, the long tradition of ocularcentrism in Western

---

[1] I have explored these issues in greater detail in Cook (forthcoming).

culture—the idea that things are only really there if you can see them—that leads people to draw a categorical distinction between improvisation that generates new notes and can therefore be transcribed, as in the case of jazz, and improvisation that shapes existing notes and therefore falls between traditional notational categories. But if creativity is to be defined in sociocultural terms, the key point is that both forms of improvisation, or performance, involve real-time interaction and hence combinatorial emergence. Hill's definition of musical creativity in terms of 'the creation of a sound product that does not conform to an entirely predetermined model', then, must clearly embrace classical as well as other-than-classical performance, while the quality of emergence is captured in Clarke's suggestion—following Chaffin and his co-workers, and specifically referring to classical performance—that 'this kind of creativity is unintended, inevitable, and yet meaningful'.

Of course, none of this changes Welch's key point, which is that old-fashioned ideas of cultural improvement and entrenched patterns in teacher education have resulted in a still largely intact imbalance between the interests and skills of students on the one hand, and the music on which curricula are built on the other. (If it is a basic educational principle that one builds on what students can do towards what they can't, then teenagers' extreme sensitivity to the innumerable sub-genres of popular music and to the sound qualities of studio production represent a colossal wasted resource for music teaching.) Positive discrimination, which is in effect what Welch advocates, may be indispensable if change is to be effected, but it always creates the danger of further entrenching existing prejudices. I would suggest that the real target for an educational agenda aimed at promoting creativity should be not be one genre of music or another, but rather the ways of thinking, talking, and writing about music that we have inherited from the 19th and 20th centuries. As long as we think that things are only really there if we can see them, and that musical meaning and value are consequently inscribed into scores, we will treat music as if it existed only in the past tense, something that has always already been created, and will accordingly undervalue the acts of making and listening to music together that this book understands to be the core of musical creativity. It is in essence the concept of musical creativity as something rare and valuable, exercised by a solitary individual and embodied in an enduring product, that lies behind such unedifying episodes as George Martin slagging off his session musicians, and John Lennon in turn slagging off Martin (both mentioned by Frith). It also lies behind the reservations concerning current music education that are most explicitly voiced by Welch but to a greater or lesser degree shared by other contributors to this collection. Better practices of teaching, in short, depend on better models of creativity.

But of course the most extreme collisions between today's practices of music and entrenched modes of conceptualization are to be found in copyright law, which is unambiguously based on the assumptions this book sets out to question. The whole idea of intellectual property is predicated on the assumption that creativity is something rare and hence valuable, in the manner of scarce mineral resources. It equally depends on the assumption that creativity is embodied in a tangible artefact of some description (copyright protects not an idea but the expression of that idea). And although the law accepts the idea of joint creation and hence joint ownership, it does so only grudgingly and inelegantly. Its most perverse premise, however, is one that has been formulated by Boden in a passage which Hill quotes: 'If we take seriously the dictionary-definition of creativity, "to bring into being or form out of nothing", creativity seems to be not only unintelligible but strictly impossible'. (One might wonder whether the field of creativity studies would ever have come into being had it not been for the way in which such thinking turned creativity into a problem.) Certainly such a view is incompatible with musical creativity as it emerges from this book. Johansson observes that organists' 'free use of commonly known musical material . . . challenges the notion of ownership and copyright'. And Hill cites a variety of non-Western cultures in which creativity subsists in the recycling of what might be termed shareware musical materials, ranging from Yugoslavian or Korean epic recitation to the Conimeña festival music of Peru and Finnish folk music.

It would be possible, and true as far as it goes, to argue that copyright law attempts to impose first-world ideologies throughout the globe, as if they were somehow self-evident and universal. (Referring specifically to music, Eric Lewis (2007: p. 182) has criticized copyright law for attempting 'to hide its exclusionary nature behind a metaphysics of the musical work which purports to be objective and universal, but in fact is not'.) This does not, however, go far enough. The idea of creation *ex nihilo* is hardly more applicable to canonic Western musics, from jazz improvisation (often analysed on the same basis as epic recitation, in terms of the recombination and adaptation of pre-existing formulae) to the works of classical composers: Mozart's music, for example, is mainly made up of anonymous stylistic material ranging from Alberti basses to the stereotyped referential types known as topics, together with authored materials such as operatic tunes of the day, use of which under such circumstances would nowadays be clearly illegal. It is not, then, simply a matter of the collision between what Lawrence Lessig (2008) characterizes as traditional 'Read Only' culture, in which the public passively consumes the works of musical and other authors, and the new 'Read/Write' culture of remixes and mashups, in which pre-existing artefacts are digitally appropriated—remixed—in order to generate new meanings. Lessig sees it as part of his mission to promote remix culture, but there is a sense in which there has never been anything else. Given the degree of investment in the legal status quo and the extent to which it protects powerful interests, copyright law—in effect the reverse side of traditional creativity theory—may prove the biggest impediment to the more realistic and enlightened views promulgated in this book.

References

Burnard. P. (forthcoming). *Music's creativities in real world contexts*. Oxford: Oxford University Press.

Cook, N. (2005). Prompting performance: Text, script, and analysis in Bryn Harrison's *être-temps*. *Music Theory Online* **11/1** (March 2005). Available at: http://mto.societymusictheory.org/issues/mto.05.11.1/mto.05.11.1.cook_frames.html.

Cook, N. (forthcoming). Scripting social interaction: Improvisation, performance, and Western 'art' music. In G. Born, E. Lewis, & W. Straw (Eds.), *Improvisation and social aesthetics*. Hanover, NH: Wesleyan University Press.

DeNora, T. (1995). *Beethoven and the construction of genius: Musical politics in Vienna, 1792–1803*. Berkeley, CA: University of California Press.

Harwood, E. (1998). Go on, girl! Improvisation in African-American girls' singing games. In B. Nettl with M. Russell (Eds.), *In the course of performance: Studies in the world of musical improvisation*. Chicago, IL: University of Chicago Press, pp. 113–25.

Hutchins, E. (1995). *Cognition in the wild*. Cambridge, MA: MIT Press.

Lessig, L. (2008). *Remix: Making art and commerce thrive in the hybrid economy*. New York: Penguin Press.

Lewis, E. (2007). Ontology, originality and the musical work: Copyright law and the status of samples. In Faculty of Law, McGill University (Ed.), *Meredith lectures 2006: Intellectual property at the edge: New approaches to ip in a transsystemic world*. Montréal: Editions Yvon Blais, pp. 169–206.

Monson, I. (1996). *Saying something: Jazz improvisation and interaction*. Chicago, IL: Chicago University Press.

Sawyer, K. (2003). *Group creativity: Music, theater, collaboration*. Mahwah, NJ: Lawrence Erlbaum.

Sloboda, J.A. & Parker, D. (1985). Immediate recall of melodies. In P. Howell, I. Cross, & R. West (Eds.), *Musical structure and cognition*. London: Academic Press, pp. 143–68.

Solomon, M. (1980). On Beethoven's creative process: A two-part invention. *Music and Letters*, **61**, 272–83.

Author index

Subject index

Note: 'n.' after a page reference indicates the number of a note on that page.